THE
BRITISH
WITCH

The Biography

P. G. MAXWELL-STUART

AMBERLEY

ABOUT THE AUTHOR

P. G. Maxwell-Stuart is Reader in History at the University of St Andrews. He lives in St Andrews.

PRAISE FOR P. G. MAXWELL STUART

Satan
'Devilish' Professor James Sharpe, *TLS*

Ghosts
'Scholarly and well-written ... a wide-ranging account' *THES*

Witchcraft
'Combines scholarly rigour with literary flair' *Independent on Sunday*

Witch Hunters
'Still makes for shocking reading today' *The Daily Mail*

Wizards
'A fascinating, well-researched and lucid book' *The English Historical Review*

First published 2014
This edition published 2016

Amberley Publishing
The Hill, Stroud
Gloucestershire, GL5 4EP

www.amberley-books.com

British Library Cataloguing in Publication Data.
A catalogue record for this book is available from the British Library.

ISBN 978 1 4456 5543 7 (paperback)
ISBN 978 1 4456 2218 7 (ebook)

Typesetting and Origination by Amberley Publishing.
Printed in the UK.

CONTENTS

For Michael Thompson
Amicitia donum Dei

I warn all you of these superstitious witchcrafts and charms that be much used and done to deceive many persons that, for the unlawful love unto the health [they have] of their bodies or of their children or beasts or other goods lost or stolen, will go to seek wise men or wise women (for so they call the Devil's proctors that do use such witchcrafts and charms): then do they seek, I say, and put themselves subject unto the false god, the Devil, and his ceremonies, to get health unlawfully by the means of those witchcrafts forbidden by the Church.

> Richard Whitford, *A Work for Householders or for Them that have the Guiding or Governance of any Company* (1531)

Whoever wants to discuss, persecute, and judge sorcery must also be able to entertain the notion, and be so disposed as to comprehend, that he is not dealing with physical and visible creatures alone. He needs to know this and pay attention to God's word as well as his own experiences, all of which tell him that the earth, water, and air are full of devils and evil invisible ghosts which envy the human race, are full of hatred towards it, and view it as their enemy.

> Hermann Wilken, *Christliche Bedencken und Erinnerung von Zauberei* (1597)

To deny the possibility, nay, the actual existence of witchcraft and sorcery is at once flatly to contradict the revealed word of God in various passages both of the Old and New Testament, and the thing itself is a truth to which every nation in the world hath, in its turn, born testimony by either example seemingly well attested or by prohibitory laws, which at least suppose the possibility of a commerce with evil spirits.

> Sir William Blackstone, *Commentaries on the Laws of England* (1766–1770)

PREFACE

Discussing magic, of which witchcraft is simply one manifestation, can be a treacherous business. Ever since the mid-seventeenth century we have developed and embraced the mental habit of imposing a structure on history, regardless of the fact that what happened in the past, just as what is happening in the present, is messy, fragmentary, and highly localised. We also have the tendency to be seduced into judging the past in terms of present givens, assumptions, and expectations, and our practice of compartmentalising knowledge means that we can find it difficult to envisage what we regard as separate and incompatible bodies of thought – astronomy and astrology, for example, or magic and medicine – not only as coexisting, but as embracing each other in such a way as essentially to form a single field of knowledge or expertise. When, therefore, we say that people in the past believed in magic, witches, demons, and so forth, what do we mean by 'believe', and do we actually understand what magic, witches, and demons meant to them in practice?

It may be best to be clear right from the start that while 'magic' has been interpreted somewhat differently at different times, the concept of 'witchcraft' has been much less flexible, even though in practice the boundaries between it and other forms of magic have been more blurred than theory would have them. Witchcraft, in effect, has been regarded as a vilified subdivision of magic, which, in turn, has been regarded as a vilified subdivision of religion, by which one means Christianity. For, although pre-Christian cultures recognised the existence of a system of words and actions operating and operated outwith the established forms of religious worship, it was Christianity that specifically tied the performance of those words and actions to pagan idolatry and demon worship, and so opened a route which led to that particular set of associations called 'witchcraft' by state and ecclesiastical authorities. The term 'witch' is thus inappropriate for magical operators outwith the Christian tradition. Accompanying the official Christian view of this kind of Otherness was the long-standing assumption that things can act on one another at a distance because of hidden sympathies existing between them, as well as because such action and reaction might receive assistance from sources of power other than human. Hence magic could broadly be divided, for the purposes of intellectual and theological discussion, into three types: theurgical, natural, and demonic.

The first, which sought to evoke supernatural or preternatural presences with a view to the magician's gaining superior wisdom for his own and perhaps society's betterment – John Dee's experiments with scrying are the obvious example – tended to restrict itself to an élite, clerical or lay, since it required of its practitioners time, effort, expenditure, and a degree of learning. The second studied nature with the intention of discovering her secret connections and their powers. Giovanni Pico della Mirandola described it in 1486 as 'embracing the most profound contemplation of things which are very secret' and 'knowledge of the whole of nature', an activity which 'calls forth, so to speak, from their hiding places into the light powers broadcast by God's kindness and planted in the world'.[1] However, in a world view positing the existence of other planes of being, apart from the created and material, such activity was always open to the accusation of dangerous irresponsibility, since it invited contamination of both procedure and operator by spirits hostile towards humans, and evil in their intent. So, however much 'natural magic' might appear to be harmless intellectual curiosity, it never managed to shake off its critics' accusation that it was essentially demonic on the one hand or, if actually harmless, still tainted by obscurantism and irrationality, a charge which was exploited from the seventeenth century onwards by those eager to seize investigation of nature for themselves. Demonic magic, by definition, took active co-operation between humans and evil spirits for granted. However, as its opponents tended to lump together disparate activities such as divination, enchantment, necromancy, and the practices of cunning folk, along with those of any woman or man seeking to manipulate a situation for good or ill by the use of words and gestures regarded, for whatever reason, as 'powerful', the concept 'witchcraft' was never one easily definable in secular or canon law. Essential to people's understanding of it, however, was the assumption that the witch, male or female, had entered into a pact with Satan or one of his demons, that this was the source of whatever power she or he was thought to have, and that, because he or she had exercised free will in entering into that contract, witches were not innocent victims of the Devil, but his active accomplices and instruments. Hence Jean Bodin's simple definition: 'A witch is someone who knowingly tries hard to accomplish something by diabolic means', which meant that each magical action such a person performed, whether with beneficent or maleficent intent, constituted a crime, and the witch could therefore be held legally and criminally accountable.[2]

However, these definitions and understandings are those of intellectuals, today's or yesterday's, and while they may help us to grasp what the authorities thought they were faced with, and why they tried to deal with the problem in the various ways they did, they do not explain what the majority of people thought they were doing when they worked magic themselves, consulted a magical practitioner for assistance beyond their own abilities, or witnessed the results of magical practice in their own communities. Gossip was (as it still is) the lifeblood of reputation, and a person's reputation in her or his community both created and kept on recreating that person's relationships with both neighbours and acquaintances, which, in turn, helped fix that person's standing within the community. The name of 'witch', once gained, even in the past by a relative no longer living, was impossible to shake off, and it was not difficult for someone to arouse suspicion that he or she was a witch. People lived cheek by jowl in both countryside and city in a way the Western world has largely forgotten, conscious of the every movement of family and neighbours. People noted not only what others did but what they did not do, what they said, how they said it, and what they passed over in silence, along with who was lucky and who was not. In these conditions, envy flourished, and envy, as Francis Bacon opined in his essay on the subject, was one of the strongest emotions that led to witchcraft and the suspicion of witchcraft, here characterised particularly as casting the evil eye.

There be none of the affections which have been noted to fascinate [*cast the evil eye*] or bewitch, but love and envy. They both have vehement wishes, they frame themselves readily into imaginations and suggestions, and they come easily into the eye, especially upon the present of objects, which are the points that conduce to fascination, if any such thing there be. We see likewise, the scripture calleth envy an evil eye, and the astrologers call the evil influences of the stars evil aspects, so that still there seemeth to be acknowledged, in the act of envy, an ejaculation or irradiation of the eye. Nay, some have been so curious as to note that the times when the stroke or percussion of an envious eye doth most hurt are when the party envied is beheld in glory or triumph, for that sets an edge upon envy: and besides, at such times the spirits of the person envied do come forth most into the outward parts, and so meet the blow.[3]

Unusual behaviour, or an exchange of heated or ill-intentioned words followed by some misfortune, was enough to draw that particular condemnation to a person. Adam Ashforth remarked of his experience in Soweto at the beginning of the twenty-first century,

We know what we know about [the witch's] witchcraft, just as we know we all know it – and we know she knows that we know – through gossip. And though her neighbours may laugh at her as a witch, they are careful nonetheless. For hers is the name that comes to mind when suspicions of malefaction arise or when a healer specifies an unnamed 'neighbour' as the source of illness or misfortune. She is the embodiment of her neighbours' generalised fears of evil forces at work in the world.[4]

Ashforth also includes the telling observation about a particular witch, that 'no one has ever openly accused that old lady of being a witch, certainly not in the decade or so that I have known her'. This silence may suggest why it was common for the witches of an earlier period to be able to operate for years in their communities without being denounced to anyone. It was partly because the witch was difficult to pin down. South African experience is again suggestive because of its parallels with early modern Europe.

By day witches were ordinary people who might even appear to be sociable, friendly, kind, and hospitable. However, at night, when everyone else slept, witches committed malicious deeds. Even then witches were thought to be invisible as they moved about, or to assume the shape of their familiars.[5]

On the other hand, what witches were thought capable of doing was also useful – harming, curing, procuring, discovering, foretelling – and denunciation would probably deprive people of those services.

The power through which these things were done was also a cause for caution. Magic, to be sure, might be a specialised ability, which is why one approached a witch or charmer (think of our going to a doctor or chemist, for example), but in simple form it was also a way of exercising preternatural power in a manner open to everyone (think of our taking an aspirin or disinfecting a cut; no specialist needed). That the practice of magic was not necessarily restricted meant that it was not only the witch who was a potential, if obvious, source of extra-human events. If anyone can do magic, even in simple form, then everyone must come under suspicion if things take an odd or unhappy turn, and this underlying mutual suspicion breeds silence. Hence, as Jeanne Favret-Saada found in mid-twentieth-century Normandy, silence can be both potent and complicated, because speaking is an admission that one is in a less powerful position than the witch, an admission one's amour propre may not wish to make, and talking immediately involves one in the process of magic, as a bystander or observer, as a participant, or as a victim.[6] It therefore takes a crisis to precipitate an action intended to release an individual from this silence, such as openly confronting the witch either in person or with the morale-boosting presence of others, fighting her or his magical attack with counter-magic, or complaining to the authorities and so setting in train a sequence of events which will immediately pass beyond one's personal control. Witches' immunity from complaint over a long period of time is thus to be expected rather than wondered at.

When it comes to 'belief' in witchcraft, we should try to sidestep the word 'belief', which, in this context, tends to imply trust in the validity of some kind of system, and posit instead an expectation that ritual language and gesture, or indeed ritual language alone, perform the specific tasks required of them. (One does not 'believe' in electricity as a concept when one presses a light-switch. One performs an action and the light goes on or off.) 'Ritual language', observed Ariel Glucklich, 'is affective in a biological, almost genetic, sense ... This language is not true or false – as science claims to be – by reference of "objective" facts; it is felicitous or infelicitous, depending on how well it transforms the awareness of the ritual participants.'[7] Glucklich is talking about magic in modern India, but his remarks illustrate the way earlier European magic was probably seen by practitioners and non-practitioners alike – as an 'active experience in' rather than a 'passive acceptance of'. For people of earlier times (as for many in the modern world), neither witchcraft and magic nor any of their associated practices were in the least unusual or irrational. To have any hope of coming to terms with these aspects of history, we are therefore obliged to put aside both preconceptions and modern intellectual clichés, and look, or at least try to look, at our forebears through their eyes and not through ours. Only by making this effort can we manage to have some kind of intelligible conversation with them. Otherwise our historical dialogue will amount to little more than talking to ourselves in the midst of exotic scenery, as though we were theatregoers who have strayed on to a pantomime set. 'When we ignore the awkward realities and contradictions of ... any period,' warns Erik Midelfort,

> We shortchange the past. We shortchange ourselves as well. If we choose to remember only the 'progressive' parts of history, the ones that readily 'make sense' to us, we oversimplify the past and our own lives. We cultivate an artificially naïve view of the world.[8]

INTRODUCTION

Some time between 30 and 26 BC, the Roman poet Tibullus addressed lines to his mistress, a married woman he calls 'Delia'. He has made use of a cunning woman, he says, who will enable them to make love without her husband's realising what they are doing.

> Your husband won't believe it, Delia, as an honest cunning woman has promised me with her magical ministration. I have seen her drawing stars down from the sky. She turns the course of a rapidly-flowing stream with an incantation. With her chanting spells, she splits open the ground and draws the spirits of the dead out of their tombs, and calls down the bones from a pyre which is still warm. At one time she holds crowds [of spirits] from the underworld in her power by means of her magical hissing; at others, she sprinkles them with milk and tells them to go back. When she wants to, she drives away the clouds from a gloomy sky. When she wants to, she summons snow from the summer firmament. She alone, it is said, has Medea's herbs in her possession. She alone, [it is said], has thoroughly tamed the wild dogs of Hekate. She has devised incantations for me, with which you may be able to deceive [your husband]. Chant them three times, and when you have done so, spit three times. He will not be able to believe anything anyone [says] about us – not even his own eyes, should he see us in our pleasant bed. (1.3.43–58)

This reads like a portrait. Some of the details appear to be believable; others, while obviously exaggerated, might be explained as stemming from the cunning woman's own convictions about the extent of her powers. The scenario itself is perfectly credible, and so we may find ourselves tempted to take the account with full seriousness, and opine that this is the kind of thing Roman cunning women did and believed they could do, and the sort of service their clients paid for in the belief that the women's powers were genuine, at least in the part which concerned them most. Unfortunately, however, there are difficulties in the way of using this text as a source of reliable information about Roman magic. To begin with, the text is a poem. This does not immediately render it untrustworthy, of course, but it does mean we have to examine it first as a work of art rather than as a piece of forensic evidence. Some of Tibullus's details, for example, come from a literary tradition: wicked women exercising illegitimate power, illicit love magically pursued, inversion of the natural order of the world, spirits of the dead summoned, baleful sacrifice. All these can be paralleled from the work of other poets, and are included in their work for similar reasons, namely, to comment upon a contemporary preoccupation by the Roman state with the behaviour of its leading women. In other words, these and other portraits of women transgressing official and current expectations of what should be lawful and proper conduct are part of a politically inspired moral discourse which may or may not have roots in actuality. Now of course there would be no point in Tibullus's drawing attention to the cunning woman and her powers if cunning women did not exist in Roman society, and if some people at least did not take those powers seriously. Nevertheless, it is worth noting that while the claims to upset nature cannot be accepted at face value, and the observation about sprinkling milk to dismiss the ghostly spirits is mistaken – milk was used to attract, not banish – the smaller details such as the hissing, the prescribed incantations, and the spitting three times, not to mention the scenario of consulting a cunning woman with a view to her aiding adultery, are entirely believable, and can, in fact, be supported by evidence from elsewhere, such as magical papyri intended to provide practical instruction in this and other forms of preternatural manipulation.[1]

Faced by historical records of magic and the practice of magic, therefore, we are obliged to tread very carefully. Context is of paramount importance, and by 'context' one means the context of the period in question, not a psychohistorical context, which views the details of any given case *sub specie aeternitatis*, and tries to remove the incident in question from its own immediate ambience and treat it as though it belonged to what Robert Davidoff has called 'a timeless context of universal applicability'.[2] A world in which God exists but takes an active role in directing, subverting, or assisting the most ordinary and seemingly trivial incidents of a person's life; a world which is merely one visible part of a concatenation of planes of existence, most of them invisible to the human eye unless it please God to reveal them or the entities belonging to them; a world in which the relationships between things – whether people, animals, or inanimate objects – are not compartmentalised after the modern fashion, but are allowed to flow into and out of each other as amorphous functions upon the created continuum; such a world demands and gets a psychology quite different from our own, and any exploration of it is thus pregnant with potential misunderstandings, assumptions both crude and sophisticated, and simple blindness to its different operations of cause and effect. Pursuing the elusive figure of the witch who has over time been delineated in surprisingly consistent lines of black and white, with little or no shading, relief, or subtle colouring, is therefore a hazardous enterprise, dependent not only on sources which may often be dubious in content and intention, but also on our own preconceptions, prejudices, or presurmises, which too frequently turn out to be *ignes fatui*, misleading in the directions they will us to take, and unhappy in their conclusions.

Let us begin, then, with a Britain which was far from being in unity and whose inhabitants, along with those of much of the rest of northern Europe, were coming piecemeal to Christianity. When St Augustine arrived in England in 596, for example, he discovered a motley collection of peoples, with a preponderance of Saxons lording it over the collapse of Christian Celtic kingdoms while largely retaining their own pagan beliefs and practices: hence Adomnan's *Life of Columba* was able to lament that the whole country was 'darkened by the shadow of heathendom and ignorance', an exaggeration, but an understandable one. Gradually, however, through the baptism of their chieftains and the subsequent seemingly ineluctable tide of conversions, each region, from Ireland to Kent, developed what Peter Brown has called 'its own distinctive micro-Christendom',[3] meaning that a strict uniformity of creed, liturgy, and sacramental practice was far from being established. Roman Christianity, which came to be dominant over its Celtic sister, was therefore a varied and variable experience, and its responses to the natural world and the problems, accidents, and catastrophes arising in that world from time to time, if not every day, were conditioned to some extent by local practice and circumstance. Secular clergy, monks and nuns did not live in isolated towers, cut off from the people they served and from whom they had sprung in the first place. Let us take language. For the most part their grasp of Latin was tenuous, limited, by and large, to the practicalities of celebrating Mass and reciting the Divine Office, and their usual mode of communication was the vernacular, the language in which they had been brought up and through which they passed on to the laity the basic prayers and formulae of the Faith. So, should the forces of nature prove awkward or hostile, as they often did, the clergy and other religious people tended to face down that apparent enmity, account for it, and cure or banish it with a mixture of Latin and the vernacular, the one being the tongue they used to speak to God and the latter that they used to teach, instruct, and comfort their people. For when it came to dealing with unseen forces, people were conscious that there existed two competing systems of power: on the one hand Christianity, which preferred to express itself mainly in Latin, and then the Other – perhaps a remnant paganism or simply a tradition of practical magic handed down alongside the 'new' religion. So people were able to turn in their difficulties from Christianity to magic, from magic to Christianity, or to rituals – charms, incantations, curses, or entreaties – which combined the two, in accordance with which arrangement belief or experience had taught them was the more effective.[4] Hence, sometimes it is difficult to know whether a rite was entirely Christian or magical, or a combination of both. We may therefore not be surprised to find clergy themselves crossing boundaries. One ritual from the early eleventh century, for example, intended to improve the quality of one's land and protect it from 'all and any enemies', requires, among other things, that specially prepared turfs be lifted from the field and taken to church, where the priest will sing Mass over them four times. Another spell from about the year 1000 gives instructions for making a herbal salve and, again, involves a priest who is to bless the butter and herbs that will make up the salve by saying the following prayer:

> Holy Lord, Almighty Father, eternal God, by the laying on of my hands let the hostile devil flee from the hair, from the head, from the eyes, from the nostrils, from the lips, from the tongue, from beneath the tongue, from the neck, from the chest, from the feet, from the heels, from all the joints of his limbs, so that the devil may not have power, either over his speaking or his silence, his sleeping or his rising, by day or by night, in sleep or in motion, over his seeing or his smiling, his touching or his reading: but [let him be safe] in the name of the Lord Jesus Christ who redeemed us with His holy blood, [and] who lives and reigns with God the Father for ever and ever, Amen.

From about the same time, too, comes a charm against some kind of illness, which implies the co-operation of one's parish priest.

> Against a dwarf [*or perhaps fever*] one must take seven small wafers such as are used in worship, and write these names on each wafer: Maximian, Malchus, John, Martimian, Dionysius, Constantine, Serafion. Then again one must sing the charm which is quoted below, first in the left ear, then in the right, then over the top of the person's head. Let a virgin hang it round his neck, and let this be done for three days. The patient will soon be better.[5]

It is interesting that a priest may have been involved here (unless we assume the unconsecrated Hosts were stolen), and that the magic requires physical objects used in Christian worship. That the power of the charm is to be directed against a *dweorh*, which may mean 'dwarf' or some kind of illness, however, presents us with a problem of interpretation. If *dweorh* actually does refer here to a dwarf, it appears to suggest that a non-human creature could have been thought of as the originator or cause of the illness. On the other hand, the second half of the charm (not quoted here) refers to a spider riding the patient as though he or she were its horse, and Matthew Lewis has argued that, since *dweorh* may be related linguistically to *dverg* ('spider'), there are reasons to think that this charm may be connected to the crushing or paralysing symptoms often attendant upon nightmares.[6] Difficulties in understanding the text, then, sometimes add to the problems one encounters in trying to catch the drift, the tone, and the meaning of these magical relics.

This mixture of Christian with pagan words and phrases can be seen from the early days of Christianity, when the names of Jesus Christ and the saints[7] appeared in many magical charms and incantations, along with some of God's titles in Hebrew, and both traditions rubbed shoulders with Greek or Coptic or pseudo Names of Power. So the question is bound to arise, does the appearance of Christian names, terms and phrases, or supplications in clearly magical texts from the first century onwards indicate a continuation of non-Christian adaptive practice, or are we to understand, however tentatively, that at any rate some of these texts represent attempts to counter their pagan elements by including names of genuine power from the Christian faith? The former would represent a continuous, if changing, tradition, the latter, a conscious endeavour to manipulate existing beliefs and practices for specific, non-magical ends, more or less in the manner recommended to Christian missionaries by Pope Gregory, and we must always be prepared for the possibility that tradition may shape the way succeeding magic is conceived, devised, or reported. So when some people made use of these charms, spells and incantations, did they think they were actually performing a religious act, and that what they were doing was somehow compatible with orthodox religion because their charms, spells and incantations included phrases or sentences lifted from the Gospels or the liturgy, or took the form of prayers which, outwith their magical context, could easily have been addressed to God or the saints with the Church's open approval? Indeed, can we argue that paganism continued to flourish side by side with an immigrant Christianity, or that one religious system permeated the other somewhat after the fashion of, let us say, Santería which represents a merging of aspects of Yoruba religion with aspects of Catholicism in some South

American countries during the early modern period?[8] Not really. What happened in Britain (and elsewhere in Europe) cannot properly be likened to this adaptive process, if only because both the Yoruba religion and Catholicism were fully developed faiths with theologies and rituals peculiar to themselves, something which cannot be said of British-European paganism because their 'paganism' was not a coherent or consistent religious system. Indeed, 'paganism' is merely a useful label to stick on a very large number of different theogonies, beliefs, and practices which certainly varied from country to country, and might well show regional variations within those countries. Paganism as an '-ism', then, does not really exist, and so when we use the word, usually as an antonym of 'Christianity', whose beliefs may have been more or less uniform, but whose rites – even those of the Mass – and sacramental practices were undoubtedly different in each country and each region, we should avoid picturing an institution similar to that of the Church, with a theology capable of being defined, explained, and debated, and should instead be prepared to visualise a kind of spiritual jumble whose constituent parts dipped into and out of local Christian practice on the one hand and similarly localised 'pagan' or traditional (the two words are not synonymous) beliefs and practices on the other.

Still, it is true to say that even when Christianity became firmly established in a country, the ancient deities might easily continue to appear in magical texts, and not always transformed into demons. So, for example, a charm found in the margin of an eleventh-century manuscript from Canterbury invokes the power of Thor against a spirit which causes illness. 'Gyril, wound-causer, go now! You are found. May Thor bless you, lord of ogres! Gyril, wound-causer. Against blood-vessel pus.'[9] Magical behaviour, then, and expectations of what magic might be able to achieve for the individual practitioner continued to be part of everyone's mindset even while the Christian era rolled forwards and while, at varying periods, both Church and state took an official stance against magical practice. Manuals of penance written for the guidance of parish priests are constant in their condemnation of a wide range of magical behaviours, and the continuing necessity for such condemnations over several centuries suggests that those behaviours were not easily uprooted or, indeed, modified. Thus, the penitential attributed to Theodore of Tarsus, Archbishop of Canterbury between 668 and 690, lays down that 'a person who sacrifices to demons for trivial reasons must do penance for one year, but the person who [does this] with serious intentions must do penance for ten years'. The anonymous *Burgundian Penitential* (early eighth century) deals with poisonous magic (*veneficium*) and love magic, saying that if the person who performs the latter is a deacon, he will have to do penance for three years, but if he is a priest, for five years. The ninth-century Penitential of Silos from Spain condemns Christian clients of diviners, enchanters, and fortune tellers, and the Corrector of Burchard of Worms's *Decretum* (early eleventh century) provided questions to be asked of a penitent: has he or she consulted magicians or diviners? Has he or she worshipped the stars and planets as pagans do? Has he or she made magical knots or incantations (these last while weaving or gathering medicinal herbs), or cast lots with the help of small objects or by using books such as the Gospels and the psalter, or helped magicians to raise storms? Does she or he believe there are women who can work magic, or who ride with others in a part-human, part-demonic wild hunt?[10] All these, with the possible exception of the last two questions, are directed primarily against what people did rather than what people believed, and this is partly because what people believed could be extraordinarily fluid, and partly because there was in any case a recurrent debate between Christian theologians about whether the effects allegedly belonging to magic were real or illusory.

Christian scholars, for example, sometimes scoffed at pagan worship, or at those who continued to observe pagan customs in spite of belonging to a Christian society. 'Some people are so blinded,' wrote Aelfric in his *Lives of the Saints*,

> that they bring their offerings to a stone fixed fast in the ground, and even to trees and well-springs, just as cunning women (*wiccan*) instruct, and will not understand how foolishly they are behaving, or how the lifeless stone or voiceless tree can help them or give them health since they [*the stones*] are fixed fast in the ground.[11]

Still, we need to bear in mind that Mediaeval modes of thinking did not always feel the need to differentiate in the same way ours do between events and experiences whose origins could be attributed to the workings of nature and those which stemmed from preternatural or supernatural causes. Did someone die after drinking an enchanted herbal mixture because the physical ingredients were poisonous, or because the enchantment turned out to be hostile? Did a fighting man wearing an amulet survive a battle because of his skill with a weapon, through luck, because God and the saints had preserved him, or because the protective magic had worked? To the Mediaeval mind these were not stark choices – either/or – but a range of equally possible explanations, the spiritual, preternatural, and supernatural claiming an even-handed consideration with appeals to the natural, and the final choice of interpretations resting upon which of these possibilities best answered the immediate circumstances. So with these reservations and caveats in mind, let us now look further at magical practice during this early period and see, among much else, whether the figure we claim to recognise as a witch had yet made her or his appearance in society.

Magic may have been a special type of 'doing', and its techniques easily passed from one generation or from one person to another, but the power which enabled the words and actions to become effective came from sources other than human, and these sources took a range of different forms and were granted a number of different abilities. We start, as is proper, with God, who communicated with people not only through the channels provided by the Church but also through His own creation in the form of portents, omens, signs, and auguries. St Isidore of Seville made this clear in his book on the etymology of words:

> Portents are also called signs, omens, and prodigies because they are seen to portend and display, indicate and predict future events ... God sometimes wants to indicate what is to come through some defects in the newly-born, just as through dreams and oracles, by which He may foreshadow and indicate future calamity for certain peoples or individuals, as is indeed proved by abundant experience.

Nature, in fact, was a kind of book – as Bernard Silvestris (first half of the twelfth century) said overtly: 'The sky ... which is like a book with its pages spread out in plain view ... and contains the future in secret letters' – and it could be read in several different ways. One was to take it at face value and describe in simple terms what was presented to the five senses; another was to treat it as a text to be moralised. Hildegard of Bingen noted this in her *Scivias* (1151 or 1152): 'God who has established everything by His will, created it to make His name known and honoured; and in addition, He manifests in everything not only the things which are visible and temporal, but also those which are invisible and eternal.'[12] This, then, was a cast of mind which, while being open to Biblical accounts of meaningful omens and apocalyptic expectations on the one hand,[13] was by no means without sophistication, for it was neither satisfied with the mere appearance or surface of things and wished to delve beneath that superficies to find out what, if anything, might lie beneath, nor content with the assumption that everything must necessarily have some hidden meaning. Phenomena could simply have their origins in nature and be attributable to nothing more than natural forces.

Some events, then, were recorded without further comment or interpretation, such as the earthquake at Oxenhale in 1179, during which 'the earth raised itself up on high as though it were a tall tower and stayed there without moving from nine o'clock until evening when it fell down with such a dreadful roar that it terrified everyone near it'; or a rain of blood on the Isle of Wight in June 1177, which fell for nearly two hours and soaked linen cloths which had been spread out on hedges to dry. Such observation, made out of what one may call disinterested curiosity, was common enough and, indeed, an increasingly frequent practice, especially from the twelfth century onwards, as curiosity about the natural world in some writers began to take a turn away from symbolic interpretation to explanation which rested upon the physical rather than the preternatural relationships between things.[14] Other occasions, other phenomena, however, could be and were still seen as calling for more than mere recording. 'Comets,' said Bede, 'are stars with long hair made of flames. They come into existence suddenly and foretell change in a kingdom or disease or wars or winds or tides,' and the simplest occurrence might also be interpreted as something more meaningful. When the English king Henry II stepped ashore in Ireland in October 1171 on a mission of conquest, 'a white hare jumped up out of some bramble-bushes and was immediately captured and given to him *as a sign of victory*'.[15] So nature's component parts did not invariably require further interpretation, otherwise the implication would be that God was constrained to make everything everywhere on every occasion mean something in addition to itself, an implication which would be self-evident nonsense. Nevertheless, God was perfectly capable of conveying some message or warning to people via any one of His myriad created things, and so it behoved people to be alert to such possibilities and not to fail to notice them if they were there. Nevertheless, context, of course, was important, which is why John of Sacrobosco, for example, noted that the eclipse which happened during the crucifixion was not natural but miraculous and therefore contrary to nature.[16]

Thunder, lights in the sky, unexpected storms, multiple births or births of deformed young, even the flight of birds, were all pregnant with possible meaning and, again according to context, might require interpretation. 'Have you believed what some people are accustomed to believe?' asked one of the penitentials.

When they make any journey, if a crow croaks from their left side to their right, they hope on this account to have a prosperous journey. When they are worried about a lodging place, if then that bird which is called the mouse-catcher (because it catches mice and is named from what it feeds on) flies in front of them, across the road on which they are going, they put more trust in this augury and omen than they do in God. If you have done or believed these things, you should do penance for five days on bread and water.[17]

Such beliefs and incidents were not only common currency but also held in common across all ranks of society, thus forming a cultural bond uniting literate and illiterate, rich and poor alike, and this general preparedness to accept that, while certain beliefs might be condemned by the Church as superstitious, merely because these were possibly false or invalidly founded did not imply that all similar manifestations in nature were equally foolish or untrue. Indeed, the widespread assumption that God might be speaking through nature, or that a natural event might have an unnatural side to it, could be and was used by the Church to underline certain important messages. Histories, for example, which were usually written by clerics, might incorporate supernatural or preternatural events in their narrative. Thus, Roger of Howden recorded that when Thomas Becket returned to the abbey at Sens after meeting Henry II in October 1173, he heard a voice from the sky, saying to him, 'Get up quickly and go to your own diocese, and you will glorify my Church with your blood and be glorified in me.'[18] Such an anecdote will be useless if its audience is not willing to allow that God may indeed speak to humans in such a way. Of course there was Biblical precedent for such a thing, for when Jesus was baptised by John, 'a voice from heaven said, This is my son, the beloved, in whom I am well pleased' (Matthew 3.17).

Likewise, a story about a pregnant woman's meeting the Devil could be employed to make what appears to be a personal political point. She had run away from home because she was afraid of her parents' reaction to her pregnancy, and was caught in a storm. When she prayed for help and appeared to receive no answer from God, she called on the Devil, who immediately appeared in the shape of a young man with bare feet, took her to a sheepcote where he lit a fire and went off to fetch bread and water. However, two men had noticed the firelight and came to investigate. Hearing from the woman that it was the Devil who had lit the fire, they urged her to have faith in God and the Blessed Virgin, and then went to the nearby village where they told everyone what they had seen and heard. Meanwhile, the Devil returned and the woman gave birth to a son. The local priest, however, alerted to the situation, came and drove the Devil away with holy water, much to the woman's apparent relief: 'Now I really do know that the Lord has snatched me from the hand of the enemy.' She then revealed that the Devil had told her nothing caused so much grief and distress in Hell as someone's taking the cross as a crusader, although she also said that the crusaders would turn out to be so sinful that 'God will remove them from the book of life'.[19] Roger of Howden, the author, had been on the third crusade and was therefore in a position to know how some of the crusaders could behave, a knowledge he seems to have transferred to 1185, the ostensible year of this incident. What interests us, however, is not the sardonic comment, but the appearance of the Devil. Again, there was no point in his being included in an historical narrative unless the readers were prepared to acknowledge, first, that the Devil exists, secondly, that he exists as a personal entity and not merely as an abstract conception, and thirdly, that he can and does appear in the material world, and interacts with human beings.

Now, the description of him here is interesting because it seems to be derived from a popular tradition which envisaged his appearance as human-like, non-threatening, and almost ordinary, as opposed to a clerically inspired tradition of image-making and theatrical presentation, in which he was depicted either as a terrifying non-human hybrid or as an ostensibly amusing imp, capable of raising smiles and uneasy laughter.[20] In Roger's anecdote there is nothing to distinguish the Devil as the Devil, except for the woman's telling the two men it was the Devil who had lit the fire, and his disappearance as soon as the priest sprinkled holy water at him. Otherwise he is merely 'a young man with bare feet, dressed as a traveller', who acts in an entirely human way by bringing the distressed woman to shelter, lighting a fire, making her a seat from fresh straw, going away to look for bread and water, then helping her to give birth and holding the baby in the crook of his arm. This, as we shall see later, is entirely consistent with accounts of his appearances to other women who subsequently became witches. Even the detail about his bare feet is significant, for the Devil was usually depicted with cloven or animal- or bird-like feet, and here there is no indication that the young man's feet were in any way abnormal. The woman thinks he is the Devil because he appeared 'immediately' (*statim*), as if in answer to her blasphemous prayer: 'If you, o God, despise my supplication, may the Devil come to my aid.' Even the woman's tranquil acceptance of (or resignation to) his presence and help is paralleled in the reports of later such encounters, so everything which could distract the reader from the principal message of the anecdote is omitted. Should we regard this as a deliberate narrative device, or can we accept that this was generally the way the actors in these real-life dramas reported their experiences to others who eventually committed the reports to writing? Both are possible, of course, although later witchcraft narratives incline one to believe that the second has the greater weight behind it.

However, if the Devil could make appearances in the world and thereby interact with human beings, so too could a host of other beings. Angels, for example, acted as God's messengers, a simple truth well known to everyone from both the Old and the New Testaments, and they could be seen in painted and sculpted images both on and in churches everywhere. As early as the fifth century, they are shown as flying figures in long white robes, with wings and haloes; and, while later artists depicted them in robes of different colours, they were never without their wings and haloes – essential marks of identification, of course, in static art, which cannot use verbal expressions or physical movement to furnish a clue to their real identity.[21] Like the grotesque, animalistic images of Satan which appeared in the same places, however, these depictions of angels belong to one tradition, while meetings between angels and humans were reported according to another. In his biography of St Cuthbert, for example, Bede describes one such.

Early one morning he left the inner monastery buildings for the guesthouse and found a young man sitting inside. Thinking he was a human being, he thereupon greeted him in his usual kindly way and gave him water so that he could wash his hands. He himself washed his feet, dried them with a piece of linen, and humbly put them in the fold [of his habit next to his chest] so that he could warm them up with his hands. He asked [the young man] to wait until the third hour of the day so that he could be refreshed with food, because if he were to leave with an empty stomach, he would faint from hunger as well as the winter cold. [*The youth took a lot of persuading, but St Cuthbert made him stay by invoking the name of God, and as soon as Terce was over, he came back and gave the young man some food*.] 'Please refresh yourself, brother,' he said, 'while I go and bring you a warm loaf, because I expect they are baked by now'. [*When he came back with the loaf, however, the young man had gone, leaving no trace in the freshly fallen snow. However, as St Cuthbert replaced the table in the storeroom, he noticed a wonderful fragrance in the air and found three freshly baked loaves* 'of unusual whiteness and excellence.'] Struck with fear, he said to himself, 'I see it was an angel of God I received, who came to feed, not to be fed'.[22]

Again we see that the preternatural visitor looks like, and is taken to be, a human being. St Cuthbert – who is here portrayed as Christlike: one thinks of Christ's washing the feet of His disciples (John 13.3–10) – treats him as simply another traveller, and it is not until he notices the youth has left no footprints that he begins to suspect something is unusual. Even so, it is the fragrant smell and the unexpected discovery of the three warm loaves that finally open his eyes to the identity of his visitor.

However, even if we take Bede's account of the incident (which he seems to have borrowed from an earlier anonymous *Life of St Cuthbert* where the author states clearly from the start that the visitor was an angel) to have been inspired by St Paul's injunction, 'Do not neglect to show hospitality to strangers, for by doing that some have entertained angels without knowing it' (Hebrews 13.2), it is still true that the intended audience was presumed to believe that angels, too, existed, that they were able to enter the world of matter, and that they were able to communicate comprehensibly with human beings. These are big assumptions. Theologians had difficulties in explaining how such appearances and exchanges were possible, but outwith learned circles it seems clear there was enough uncomplicated acceptance of these possibilities to make stories about visitant angels merely another fact of everyday existence.[23]

Both Satan and angels, then, could appear to anyone at any time, but not necessarily in the guise people regularly saw them wear in pictures and statues, and the same can be said for demons. Now, according to Geoffrey of Monmouth, God assigned special places in creation for angels, demons, and other spirits. Angels inhabit 'the ethereal heaven', that is to say an upper plane of pure air; other spirits live in an aerial plane, that is the lower atmosphere where the air is not so pure. These spirits 'sympathise or rejoice with us as things go well or ill, [and] are accustomed to carry humans' prayers through the air and to beseech God to have mercy on them, and to bring back intimations of God's will, either in dreams or by voice or by other signs'. Then there is another space, beneath the moon, which 'abounds in evil demons who are skilled in cheating, and deceive and tempt us. Often they assume a body made out of air and appear to us'.[24] This tripartite division of spirits in a system of multiple heavens is a picture that would have been readily acknowledged as both possible and probable by theologians and natural philosophers of the twelfth century in particular, for this was a century which saw an increasing interest in the location and composition of celestial and natural hierarchies.[25] However, if there was heightened awareness of such spirits among the literate, there was no less recognition among the rest of society that, because of their proximity to earth, demons were the most likely of the spirits to be those with whom humans had contact. As long ago as the fourth century, Prudentius had made this clear in his poem on the origin of sin:

> We are fighting with spirits of darkness by night and by day, and this damp, heavy air submits to their tyranny with its sluggish clouds. That is to say, this middle [region], which stretches between the sky and the lowest part of the earth and suspends the clouds in its empty, gaping space, submits to the bridle of various Powers and shudders at the hostile [beings] who, under the command of Belial, are driving it.[26]

Demons in particular, then, are humankind's closest spirit companions, and while Biblical precedent suggested that angels were likely to appear as humans among human beings, experience, especially that of clerical writers, said that, while demons were perfectly capable of appearing much as they were depicted by artists and sculptors, they preferred to take human or animal shape in order to lure their intended victims into some kind of false tranquillity. Their plan, however, tended to be unsuccessful, since something about their appearance usually alerted the object of their malice to the truth of their nature. Thus, the *Life* of St Robert of Molesmes tells us that a human figure almost immediately betrayed itself as demonic.

> One night, the holy man saw something malign lingering at the entrance to the choir. It made frequent attempts to enter, but was unable to do so. It looked like someone wearing peasant dress. Its shanks were long and bare. It was carrying a little basket on its back and a piece of wood bound with rope at its chest. Well now, it began to circle the choir, its neck thrust forward, intently casting its eyes upon the brethren to see whether it could discern any mark of favour to itself in anyone. But the man of God [*St Robert*] prayed vehemently, rousing the brethren from their torpor, and the insolent spy lingered expectantly for a long time in vain. Since it saw it was making no headway, it took itself off, full of indignation, to the lay brothers' choir. There it stared attentively at everyone, and if any of them was nodding off, it cackled loudly and made a scornful gesture ... If anyone was engrossed in wicked thoughts, it applauded ... At last, it found a young man among the novices, whose mind was wandering off to forbidden subjects, present only in body and actually thinking about running away in secret. Noting, therefore, that it and the young man were two of a kind, the malignant creature picked him up with a little trident, thrust him into its little basket, and quickly rushed away.

Likewise, the Dominican, Étienne de Bourbon, gives an exemplum in which a knight, keeping a vigil of penance in a church during the hours of darkness, sees, by means of light provided by the Devil, men and women entering the church, followed later by two more demons, one of whom looked like his wife and the other like his son; and then, still later, came more demons in the form of the local bishop and his clerics actually saying words of benediction. None of this, however, distracted the knight from his prayers, and when he made the sign of the cross on his breast, 'the demons were thrown into confusion, turned themselves into dreadful shapes, and began to beat the knight to death and subject him to exquisite tortures'. Guibert de Nogent, a Benedictine, records the visit of several demons appearing to a novice of the Order while he was asleep – the demons were 'wearing sporrans slung round their hips in Scottish fashion' – followed by another visit of two demons to a monk belonging to his own house. They came at night and perched on a bench near his bed. However, although they looked like monks, one had red hair, which was very suspicious, as red hair was commonly associated with the Devil, and the other kept his face concealed under a black hood. Indeed, so acute was this belief that demons could transform themselves into any shape they wanted, it did not take much for a demon to be seen or even just felt almost anywhere at any time. Guibert de Nogent tells us that 'no one should be surprised in our day by the power these maleficent spirits have, whether it be to trick or hurt people', and he goes on to give one example of nobles from the Vexin who thought they had captured a badger, but it turned out to be a demon.[27] One is reminded of later English witches' familiars who took the form of various animals, birds, or insects.

Richalm von Schöntal heard demons speaking to one another. These, he maintained, were not voices in his own head but voices external to himself. 'Do you hear demons speaking with the voice of a physical human being [*corporaliter*]?' he was asked once. 'I certainly do,' he replied. 'In fact, as things stand, I think there is no way they are able, or are accustomed to speak except with the voice of a physical human being'; he notes elsewhere that 'an old man heard, in human voices outwith himself, a demon bewailing a brother who was wasting away'. Sometimes, an apparently inexplicable incident is blamed on the action of a demon, as Guibert de Nogent illustrates by means of an anecdote about a peasant who, tired out after a hard day's work, sat down on the bank of a stream and removed his socks and shoes so that he could wash his feet.

Suddenly from the bottom of the water in which his legs were soaking a devil came out and grabbed his feet. Feeling himself trapped, the peasant cried to his neighbours for help. They carried him back to his own home where, in their typical gruff manner, they tried by every means to free his feet. They struggled for a long time in this useless round of efforts, but all their attempts to free the man were in vain. Spiritual things can be counteracted only by spiritual things. Finally, after they had gone round in circles for a long time, a pilgrim joined them, who pounced on the man's fettered feet while [the other people] looked on, and freed them within seconds. After this he vanished before anyone could even ask who he was.[28]

Demons, then, were everywhere and might not only plague people from outside, but enter a person's body and occupy him or her until dislodged by exorcism. Hence, presumably, the instruction contained in the monastic *Rule of the Céli Dé* (perhaps ninth century), which said that, because the Devil lives in the urinals and toilets, anyone who entered those parts of the monastery building should bless it and then himself before doing anything else; for the same reason, a monk was forbidden to pray in such places.[29] Afflicting from the outside ('obsession') or from within ('possession') was done by demons either out of personal malice or because they had been deliberately sent to possess the unfortunate individual. One such was a girl called Francesca, who had had a demon inflicted upon her by magic. A priest who had lusted after her conjured him up and sent him to make her life a misery, from which she was rescued only after a great deal of prayer and effort by St Giovanni Gualbert. Even so, the moment she was released from the demon she contracted an illness that covered her body with sores, and caused her to discharge blood from every orifice, an affliction which lasted, apparently, for several years.[30] It was not only the religious, however, who were liable to be attacked or possessed by demons, although it required the religious means of exorcism to free them, often involving an enormous amount of hard work mixed with intensive spiritual concentration. The thirteenth-century Cistercian hagiographer Caesarius of Heisterbach recorded the difficulties attending the exorcism of a male demoniac who was taken to his local monastery in hope of a cure. Neither saints' relics nor prayers nor holy pictures appeared to make any difference to his condition until the abbot put a psalter over the demoniac's head and waited patiently until, after an hour of screaming and frothing at the mouth, the man calmed down and said he had been liberated from the Devil.

However, people could also be subject to demonic or diabolic affliction without necessarily being possessed or obsessed. Richalm von Schöntal makes this point clearly when he says,

> There are certain demons which are accustomed to cause people distress, not in their spirit but in their flesh. They prick the flesh the way fleas usually do, and appear to the person in the form of a wasp, and call themselves 'wasps'. People are often disturbed by them and believe they are being attacked by fleas or other vermin [*literally* 'worms']; and since people are taught to keep the various parts of their body still in front of others, [the demons] often cause people to keep on endlessly rubbing themselves.[31]

The simplest discomfort as well as the most dramatic mental disturbance might therefore be attributed to demonic interference. One stresses 'might', because people were not foolish and were perfectly well aware that events of whatever kind, large or small, could have a natural rather than a preternatural origin. A particular and specialised problem for clerics in particular was how to distinguish between natural and preternatural causes and, in the case of visions or visitations, how to tell whether the visitant was a good or an evil spirit, since the latter might easily disguise itself as the former. For St Paul had warned long ago, 'Even Satan disguises himself as an angel of light' (2 Corinthians 11.12), and St John had advised, 'Test the spirits to see whether they are of God' (1 John 4.1).

Now, it is true, of course, that most of this information about demons comes from clerics who were writing with a purpose – to illustrate various moral points for the benefit of their clerical readers and, through them and the sermons they preached, the general populace. However, if clerics seized upon such anecdotes as suitable vehicles for their specific purposes, we should remember that this was not exploitation of popular beliefs for confessional purposes – although even if it had been, its success would still have depended on those beliefs' being genuinely held by a majority of listeners – but use of a culture which they and their congregations had in common. The appeal to belief in the reality of angels and demons was thus not only valid but effective, since even if the listeners' immediate experience had not yet included visions or visitations, or major or minor afflictions from malignant spirits, there was always the chance it might, because such things were inherently possible, and the existence of that possibility in people's mindset, coupled with reports, rumours, anecdotes, and illustrations of one kind and another, rendered that possibility not just 'possible' but probable, if not today, then at any time in the future.

However, angels and demons, while frequent companions, visible or invisible, of humanity, were not the only visitants from other planes of being. Christian Europe shared with its pagan past a lively awareness of the dead, who were apt to appear to the living for a variety of reasons: to beg for help, to ask for settlement of a debt or promise left unfulfilled at the time of their death, to warn, to curse, and, in a number of cases, to answer questions. This last involved magic, the deliberate evocation of a ghost by necromancy for the purpose of interrogating him or her about the afterlife. That apart, however, the relationship between the living and the dead was one which much concerned the living. There was no question of turning one's back on them – the process disguised as 'moving on' or 'obtaining closure' in that unhappiest of modern jargons – but rather of redefining the relationship so as to accommodate the dead, now potentially more powerful than they had been in life, and to reintegrate them into that human community of which they were still an important, if altered, part. Failure to accommodate them satisfactorily – which in practice meant to *their* satisfaction – would probably result in haunting, and that would require action additional to that which may have taken place already at the funeral, burial, or cremation.[32]

The dead might appear as ghosts or revenants, that is, as William of Newburgh explained, 'corpses [which], animated by some evil spirit, come out of their graves and wander around'. Thomas of Cantimpré tells the story of a young woman who was praying in church early one morning and did not realise that a dead body had been brought in during the night. The Devil wanted to disturb her, so he entered the corpse, which began to move about and then rose from its coffin and shouted at her. Terrified, the young woman seized a staff which had a cross on top of it, and smashed it against the corpse's head, laying it low and expelling the Devil from it. Mediaeval European literature is full of such anecdotes, and so it is clear that in this we have evidence of a widespread and common belief that the dead could walk among the living, not merely as wraiths but also in physical form. These animated corpses were frequently violent. The body of an excommunicate monk came back to life and settled upon the roof of people's homes or storehouses, violently resisting all attempts to dislodge him thence, and finally coming into a house and battering the inmates with blows and missiles;

and a dead man was said to have returned to his widow's bed, lain heavily upon her, and then brought terror to the rest of the family and its neighbours. These are but two examples out of many. A common way of dealing with such revenants was to dig up the corpse and burn it, at which time it was often found that, while the body was hugely swollen, it gushed blood when struck. Although this may remind us of vampire stories from central and Eastern Europe, it should be noted that in Britain, at any rate, this practice of opening graves and destroying undecayed bodies did not really last as a way of laying such animated dead much beyond the twelfth or thirteenth century. Even when the dead person manifested as a spirit rather than as a corpse, however, physical violence was still possible. Thietmar of Merseburg tells us of a priest who saw and heard dead people in his church, and was ordered by his bishop to spend the night there. He did so, but the dead threw him out bodily, and when he went back the next night, armed with relics and holy water, the dead lifted him on to the altar and killed him. Likewise, Gervase of Tilbury says that a woman who had remarried in spite of a pledge to her first husband on his deathbed was killed by his ghost.

On the other hand, the ghost might keep his or her distance and simply ask for prayers or issue a warning to the living to repent an evil life. Peter the Venerable wrote of the ghost of a landowner, Bernard le Gros, who appeared to his former steward, and asked him to implore the Abbot of Cluny to take pity on his soul and help release him from Purgatory; William of Malmesbury relates the return of a dead soul from Hell to warn his friend in life to change profoundly, otherwise he too would end by suffering eternal torment.[34] The dead also moved in numbers as well as individually, and stories were told of their appearing in groups, in crowds, and in whole armies. Rudolf Glaber, for example, noted one such gathering in around 1048, as did, perhaps most famously, the Benedictine Orderic Vitalis, who reported a priest's experience of the ghostly army known as 'Hellequin's Hunt'.

(a) One Sunday evening [a priest] walked across to his window before dinner to pass the time and, on looking out, saw a huge number of riders drawn up as though in a battle line, moving steadily from north to west. After watching them closely for some time, he became alarmed and called out to a member of his household to come and see them, but as soon as he had called out, the figures dissolved and disappeared.

(b) [*The priest Walchelin was called out to attend a sick man and heard what he thought was the onset of a large army.*] First of all a large crowd on foot appeared, bearing on their shoulders and draped round their necks the animals, clothes, furniture, and household possessions that make up the plunder of every raiding army. However, they all complained bitterly and chivvied each other onwards. Walchelin saw among them many of his fellow-villagers who had died recently, and heard them lamenting the fact that they were in torment because of their sins. Next came a group of bearers ... supporting the weight of some five hundred biers, with two men carrying each bier. On these biers were seated dwarfs with huge barrel-shaped heads. One gigantic beam was carried by two Ethiopians, and a hapless man was tightly lashed to this beam, undergoing severe torture and screaming aloud in his pain. A terrible demon sitting astride this beam was digging into his back and thighs with red-hot spurs so that the blood flowed freely ... Next came a group of women who seemed to the priest to be innumerable, riding side-saddle in the fashionable manner, but with their saddles studded with red-hot nails ... The next group to come along was an assembly of clerics and monks, and he could see their leaders, bishops and abbots, carrying their pastoral staffs. The clerics and their bishops wore black caps; the monks and abbots were dressed in black cowls. They moaned and complained, and some of them even hailed Walchelin and besought him to pray for them for old times' sake ... Next to come along was a great troop of knights, with no colours except that of darkness and flickering flame. All the knights rode enormous horses, all of them were armed as if they were charging into battle and all of them bore pennants of deepest black. Among this troop were Richard and Baldwin, the sons of Count Gilbert, who had recently died.[35]

It may be imagined, then, that the dead were never far away, and indeed Jacques Fournier, Bishop of Pamiers, observed, 'People who move their arms and hands away from their sides when they walk about do much harm ... [for] by moving their arms about in such a way, they knock many of the souls of the dead to the ground.'[36] Ghosts and revenants, however, did not complete the number of non-human entities that could be encountered by humans during the course of their everyday lives. Neither exactly spirit nor human, both living within the physical world and yet apparently in some dimension of it not normally penetrated by human beings, a host of preternatural creatures – fairies, elves, goblins, trolls, and so forth – existed side by side with human society, and might have to be placated, wooed, avoided, or used according to circumstance. The etymology of the word 'fairy' is disputable. The creatures themselves seem to be connected with the notion of 'fate', even if their name is not necessarily derived from Latin *fatum*: Scottish 'fey taikin', for example, means to have a presentiment of impending death.[37] However, Scottish Gaelic *sìth* ('fairy') is certainly connected with *sìth* ('hill'), and so reminds us that fairies, however developed by later folklore, were much like the Latin *genius loci*, 'spirit of a place', and thus rooted in the landscape. According to Robert Kirk's version of them, recorded in 1691, the *sìthean* had bodies made from congealed air, 'somewhat of the nature of a condensed cloud and best seen in twilight'. They could be heard going about their daily tasks, changed habitation frequently, and attended human funerals.[38] These propositions link them with a plane of being parallel to that of humans, which to some extent mirrored the human world, and these, along with *sìthean*'s connections with the dead, seem to be consistent beliefs in various European societies.

So, too, is the notion that humans, whether babies or adults, were sometimes kidnapped by fairies who might or might not choose to leave a substitute in their place. Ralph of Coggeshall in the thirteenth century tells the story of Malekin, who claimed to be a changeling held captive for fourteen years, at the end of which (she said) she would be allowed to exchange her present form, that of a tiny child, for her appropriate human shape. 'Lancelot of the Lake' was also stolen, according to a thirteenth-century prose romance, *Lanzlet*, and held as a fairy's plaything.

Now the story says that the Damsel that carried Lancelot into the lake was a fay. In those days all maidens who knew enchantments or charms were called 'fays', and there were many of them at this time, and more in Great Britain than in other lands.

They knew, as the story says, the virtue of herbs and of stones and of charms, whereby
they might be kept in plenty and in the great wealth they possessed … The Lady who
nourished him dwelled only in woods and in forests which were vast and dense, and
the lake into which she sprang with the child was naught but enchantment, and it was
in the plain at the foot of a hill that was lower than that on which King Ban had died.
In the part where the lake seemed widest and deepest the Lady had many fair and noble
dwellings, and in the plain below there flowed a little stream which abounded in fish.
Her abode was so hidden that none might find it, for the semblance of the lake covered
it so that it might not be seen.[39]

This episode, of course, reminds us that fairies played a large part in Mediaeval
romantic literature, in which the figure of 'the Lady' sometimes slips into that of a
character closely resembling a witch. Thus, Marie de France's *Lanval* depicts a
fairy-woman who seduces a knight of King Arthur's court; Melusine is half-fairy, half-
snake, and marries a human being, who loses her when he breaks an important tabu;
and a more sinister 'Dame d'Amour' deliberately keeps the hero Lybeaus from his
wife by enchanting his eyes with glamours.[40] However, while these tales were aimed
at a courtly audience, everyday folk were obliged to cope with such entities on a far
more mundane level. Brownies, pixies, goblins, gnomes, boggarts, trolls – by whatever
name they were known – were usually conceived as small, and were often thought
of as human in general shape, although sometimes that shape was grotesque; they
either helped or interfered with people's daily activities. Echoes of this can be found in
modern times. Scottish Highlanders would leave out food and drink for the brownies
who would work for them in return; Savoyards did the same as late as 1900; in the
Hautes-Pyrénées, a good meal was set out for visiting fairies on New Year's Eve in the
hope that the next year's harvest would be good and the flocks would multiply; and in
south-western France, fairies and spirits of the dead had to be propitiated with food
while black puddings were being cooked, otherwise the puddings would be spoiled.
In the district of Arles, too, women used to invoke a fairy called Esterelle in the hope
of becoming pregnant. However, all this placatory behaviour might easily come to
nothing if the fairies, whose nature was fickle and mischievous, decided to make life
difficult, as Ben Jonson made clear:

> This is Mab, the mistress fairy
> That doth nightly rob the dairy,
> And can hurt or help the churning,
> (As she please) without discerning.
>
> You will anon take warning,
> She, that pinches country wenches
> If they rub not clean their benches,
> And with sharper nails remembers
> When they take not up their embers;
> But if so they chance to feast her,
> In a shoe she drops a tester …

> This is she that empties cradles,
> Takes out children, puts in ladles:
> Trains forth midwives in their slumber,
> With a sieve the holes to number,
> And then leads them, from her burrows,
> Home through ponds and water furrows.[41]

These early modern and modern instances cannot, of course, be taken as entirely mirror images of Mediaeval belief, but we can see similarities in some Mediaeval texts, sufficient to let us think that the modern anecdotes are part of a long-standing tradition rather than peculiarities of their own particular period. In the nineteenth book of his *Decretum*, for example, the eleventh-century Burchard of Worms has the confessor ask,

> Have you made little boys'-size shoes and thrown them into your storeroom or barn so that satyrs or goblins can play with them, [in the hope that] they will bring you other people's belongings and so make you richer? If you have, you shall do penance for ten days on bread and water.

This was repeated in the twelfth-century penitential of Bartholomew Iscanus, which says, 'Anyone who throws into a granary or storehouse a bow, or any such thing, for the devils they call "fauns" to play with, [in the hope of persuading them] to bring more grain, shall do penance for fifteen days.' In the early fourteenth century, too, there was still clerical concern about such beliefs, for the Dominican Bernard Gui instructed inquisitors to ask (among other things) what penitents knew about 'the female spirits whom they call *Good People* who, according to what they say, move about in the night', 'Good Deeds' being a euphemism after the same fashion as *Eumenides*, 'Kindly Ones', applied to the Erinyes, the fearsome Greek spirits of blood-vengeance. We should also bear in mind the fairy tree at Domrémy, which St Jeanne d'Arc used to decorate with garlands of herbs and flowers when she was very young, a behaviour not in the least peculiar to her but one common and traditional to the area; for, although the villagers tried to distance themselves from this tradition when they were questioned by clerics, it is clear that, as Karen Sullivan says,

> like Joan, the villagers treated the fairy ladies as a third category of supernatural beings, neither angelic nor demonic, neither inside nor outside Christianity, neither to be venerated as one venerates God and His saints, nor to be abhorred as one abhorred the Devil and his minions, but to be accepted as one accepted the tree and the spring themselves, as part of the landscape.[42]

Elves, who, other than fairies, were the preternatural creatures most frequently encountered, like fairies, lived in small hills and natural mounds, and were left offerings of food and drink. They also manifested roughly the same kind of ambivalence of character as their fairy counterparts, although the likelihood was that they would do more harm than good, and in the eleventh-century *Utrecht Psalter* they are depicted as tiny winged assailants who have just shot arrows into a human, an emblem of the belief that they were responsible for a wide range of ailments, including heartburn and measles. Chaucer's elf, for example, was, in the words of Alaric Hall, 'an incubus, an active, violent, and demonic being', and this seems to be borne out by a large amount of available evidence, although, as Hall points out, there is an argument to be made that these elf illnesses were often inflicted in answer to or as a warning anent some failing or transgression in the human beings. Not surprisingly, therefore, we find that Scottish Highlanders used to fix nails to the front of the bed in which a woman was due to give birth, in order to ward off the elves.[43]

The potential for encountering non-human entities, however, was by no means exhausted by angels, demons, fairies, elves, and the like. The uncultivated landscape was full of unknowns, especially at night, and monstrous 'somethings' could appear without warning and frighten the unwary intruder. Caesarius of Heisterbach tells the story of a parish priest in charge of two churches, who was hurrying from one to the other one day as night was drawing in, and feeling extremely nervous – so much so that he kept his sword unsheathed.

> When he came to a certain wood, so great a fear and terror seized him that all his hair stood on end ... As soon as he turned his eyes towards the wood, he saw a hideous-looking man standing near a tall tree and, as he looked, this man grew suddenly so vast in size that his height was equal to that of the tree. Around him all the trees were crashing [to the ground] and there were fearful blasts of wind. Terrified beyond measure, the priest fled and was pursued by the devil with a whirlwind until he came to the town of Rode.[44]

It is easy and possibly tempting for us to try to rationalise this incident and others like it as not much more than an over-imaginative response to a particular type of geography encountered at a sensitive time of day. Large tracts of scarcely inhabited forest were the norm rather than the exception, and such territory could well provide lairs for dangerous animals, outlaws, robbers, and other undesirables. The perils of travelling alone in or near forestland at night were therefore real enough, and if one adds to these physical hazards the equally real risk of meeting and perhaps being attacked by some kind of preternatural creature, the nature of the response of Caesarius's priest cannot be so easily dismissed. If demons and fairies are real, there is no reason to suppose that monsters, amorphous or physical, may not be real as well, even if sophisticated theologians seek to explain them as merely deceitful illusions created by the Devil.[45] Certainly it was not difficult for anyone to see pictures of monstrous beings of one kind and another, for they were illustrated in picture and statue in many Mediaeval churches. Frescoes in Raby church in Denmark depicted some of the monstrosities which had been described centuries earlier by Pliny the Elder; scenes showing Hell's mouth and the Last Days greeted worshippers on the doorway of the twelfth-century church of St Mary and St David in Kilpeck, not far from Hereford; and even God was sometimes represented as a three-headed oddity, disturbingly parallel with depictions of a three-headed Satan. Clerics, of course, could find other representations in the manuscripts they read, studied, and used, and for this reason if no other are likely to have been somewhat more aware of the monstrous 'Other' than many layfolk.[46] St Isidore of Seville described them under the heading of 'portents', which he said were unnatural beings either very large or very small. They were not, he added, 'created according to nature, but contrary to what is known in nature' – an important distinction – and their purpose was to foreshadow future events or act as a warning. The Anglo-Saxon epic *Beowulf* lumped them together with demons:

> Grendel ... had dwelt with a monster race awhile since the Creator had condemned him. Almighty God had requited the act of him who slew Abel on Cain's kindred. Nor did Cain rejoice in that battle. God for that crime banished him far from mankind. From him were born all monsters, giants and elves, and hell demons, as well as the giants who strove with God a long while.[47]

However, even if this was so, it was clear they inhabited a world quite different from that of demons – the wildness which encroached upon human habitation and which seemed to be full of possibilities, both imagined and unimaginable.

The Church was not happy about this mindset, which was prepared to see Otherness everywhere, and did her best to condemn it as superstitious or mistaken. In around 800, an Irish cleric, while copying an epic about the ancestors, filled with references to their other-worldliness, decided to add a note to his text, expressing reservations about much of the story.

> But I who have written out this history, or rather this fable, give no credence to the various incidents related in it. For some things in it are the deceptions of demons, others are flights of poetic fancy. Some are probable, others improbable, and others are intended for the amusement of foolish people.[48]

Notice he does not dismiss everything as fantasy, and includes alongside his doubts his acceptance of the implicit reality of demons who use their powers to deceive. A similar line was taken in the fourteenth century by an anonymous compiler of model sermons.

> But I ask, what shall we say of those superstitious wretches who claim that at night they see the most beautiful queens and other girls dancing in the ring with Lady Diana, the goddess of the heathens, who in our native tongue are called 'elves'? And they believe that these can change both men and women into other beings and carry them with them to *elvenland* where there are already, as they say, those strong champions such as Onewynn and Wade and others. All this is nothing but phantoms shown them by a mischievous spirit.[49]

Churchmen, in other words, were trying to combat what was evidently a widespread and more or less intractable set of beliefs and behaviours which engaged the minds of learned and unlearned alike, and their evidence, while illustrating their own limited scepticism and anxiety for the spiritual welfare of their flocks, also bears witness to the size and depth of the problem they perceived in contemporary society.[50] There was a problem in trying to warn the public, of course, for if the priest went into too much detail, especially during his sermons, he might run the risk of making these beliefs and practices even more attractive, or of actually teaching his parishioners something they did not know before. Preachers and pastors therefore trod a difficult path. Speaking about the other world was undoubtedly a duty they owed to their flocks, but how exactly were they to represent it in their monitions: as a matter for concern, as a curiosity which should be condemned but also dismissed as a piece of mere foolishness, as an illusion which should not be taken seriously, or as a reality which ought to be resisted and combated?

Now, the contacts between worlds we have been discussing so far have been, apart from the special case of necromancy, involuntary experiences from the humans' point of view. When people had seen and heard and been touched by angels or demons or the rest, the reports of those incidents suggest that it was the non-human entities who were the active participants in the relationship, and the humans who were passive. However, this passivity was merely one side of a coin, the other being the deliberate attempt by human beings to contact the other world and hence its inhabitants. This attempt is known generally as 'magic', and magic provides a set of techniques for making this kind of contact and for making use of the additional powers and possibilities which are envisaged to flow along the channels so opened. One difficulty in the Church's suggestion that connections between this and another world were – if not in every case, at least frequently – delusions is not simply that under those circumstances it becomes difficult to tell which other-worldly experience is real and which is not, but that contacts between the physical world and other planes of existence seemed, to those who chose to employ them, clearly to result in real and desirable physical effects. In other words, magic worked, and if it did not work every time, it worked often enough to make it an appealing and valid recourse in time of trouble. One common contact could be found in the amulet, a protective device meant to ensure the safety of the individual who wore it from preternatural attack. Amulets had been worn or carried since earliest times, of course, and almost anything portable could fulfil this defensive office, including plants of various kinds, which were dried and carried about the person. Betony, it was said, for example, 'keeps both the souls and bodies of men. It is effectual against both night-walkings and harmful places and difficult sleeps.' This ancient recommendation was repeated in the fourteenth century: 'Whoso has travail in his sleep, or fantasies, let him hang betony about his neck and it shall do them away, for it is a powerful herb.' Mugwort, too, was useful, but for a different purpose, and *Bald's Leechbook* (ninth century) suggests,

For a long journey over land, lest he tire, let him take mugwort in his hand or put it in his shoe lest he weary; and when he wishes to pick it, before sunrise, let him say these words first: *tollam te, artemisia, nisi lassus sum in via* ('Let me pick you, Mugwort, so that I may not be weary on the way'). Sign it with the sign of the cross when you pull it up.[51]

It is these ritual words and this ritual action, together with the intention of the user, that make an amulet of the plant, although the effective channel of power could be inscribed on suitable material rather than merely spoken over it – which is not to say, of course, that the inscription was not read aloud either during the carving or on some subsequent occasion. There are hundreds of amulets with runic inscriptions, for example, some of which consist of only a word or two, others of whole sentences. One of these last was engraved on a twelfth-century bronze amulet, and sought to protect the wearer against several spirits – the walking one, the riding, the running, the sitting, the travelling, the flying – which spread disease, and threatened them with death. Another amulet seeks to cure a horse which has been [elf-]shot.

> Take then the knife whose handle is made of the fallow horn of an ox and on which there are three bronze nails. Cut Christ's mark on the forehead of the horse so that it bleeds. Then cut Christ's mark on the back and on each of the limbs you can reach. Then take the left ear and pierce it, keeping silent. This you must do. Take a stick, strike [the horse] on the back, and then the horse will be healthy. Write on the knife-horn these words: *Benedicite omnia opera Domini domin[or]um*. Be the elf whatever it may, this will be a remedy for it.[52]

These Christian amulets frequently included Latin as the language of the key words or phrases, probably because Latin was the language of the liturgy, and the liturgy was the most effective source and descent of power known to their users. However, it was not only objects created specifically to bear these magical formulae (such as rune-sticks or lead rolls and tablets, which are often big enough to provide room for quite extensive inscriptions), but everyday objects – a brooch, a comb, a wooden spatula – and ecclesiastical adjuncts such as bells, which bore warnings, petitions, or simply Biblical references. Ringing the church bells, itself a possibly magical act in as much as the sound was meant to ward off evil spirits or prevent a thunderstorm, activated the power inherent in their inscription, and translated it into effective sound. One such inscription, dating from 1228, manages to combine an invocation of the Blessed Virgin and St Dionysius with the essentially magical formula AGLA (*Ata Gabor Leolam Adonai*, 'Thou art mighty for ever, o Lord'). Other objects, however, depend not on any inscription, uttered or not, for their effectiveness, but on some innate power they were supposed to have. Thus, we find that amber was worn, especially in necklaces, a practice condemned by Caesarius of Arles as early as the sixth century AD; the 'gagate' could be used for somewhat intrusive magical purposes – 'to make a woman say what you ask her, take a stone which is called a *gagate* and lay it on her left breast, without her knowing it, while she is asleep, and if the stone be good, everything you ask her she will tell you, whatever she has done'. Various animal parts were used as well.

> Take [a badger's] liver, divide it, and bury it at the corners of your land-boundaries and of the foundations of your fortifications, and hide the heart at the gates of your fortress. Then you and yours will be free to go and to return home; all disease will be removed; and what was done earlier will not harm anything; and there will be little danger from

fire. It is also known that his hide is useful to put on dogs and all four-footed beasts against the pain of disease. Have pieces of the hide in your shoes; you will not feel any pain in your feet ... For headache, take a fox's genitals, wrap them around the head; the headache will quickly be driven away. For intercourse with a woman, the tip of a fox's tail hung on the arm.[53]

A quite remarkable range of objects, then, was capable of providing the basic material for magical *instrumenta*, and it is not altogether clear whether knowledge of which inscriptions to use under which circumstances was part of a long-standing tradition, or whether each inscriber improvised each time according to what he or his client wanted. Charms, however, were somewhat different, for these did not necessarily involve techniques such as carving or engraving, and needed no more than memory to have them at hand and ready for use. Charms may consist of words accompanied by a ritual act or actions, or words without such actions, although the former is by far the more common. Thus, to stop a nosebleed one is supposed to say,

Christ went to the Jordan to be baptised by John. John stood still and was amazed. Just so let the drops of blood which are falling from this person N's nostrils be amazed. I adjure you in the name of Christ: may the blood stop + may the blood stop + may the blood stop.[54]

Largely words, this charm still requires the operator to make two signs of the cross at the key moment, and these, while not magical in themselves, are nevertheless meaningful actions, deliberate in their intent. Meaningful to whom? one may ask. To the participants, operator and client, who are reminded of Christ's presence and authority and can take comfort and confidence therefrom, but also to the blood itself, or to the demon/elf/spirit which may be the cause of the client's distress and is hereby reminded that there is a power greater than his, which cannot be disobeyed. Who is the operator? Since the charm is recorded in Latin, he may have been a priest or at least someone in holy orders; but the original of the charm may not have been Latin at all, in which case any lay person would have been entitled to work it, and indeed even if the original had been Latin, there is no telling whether a lay person could not have learned it by rote and applied it as required. A simple example of a charm using a short Latin sentence is one which seeks to cure a pain in the stomach.

When you see a dung beetle digging in the earth, take it with two hands along with what it has dug up. Wave it about a great deal with your hands and say, *Remedium facio ad ventris dolorem.* ('I make a remedy for stomach pain'). Then throw the beetle away over your shoulder. Take care you do not watch after it. When someone's stomach or abdomen hurts, hold it with your hand. The person will be better immediately.[55]

Appeals to Biblical, specifically New Testament, precedent are extremely common. One set of charms to cure eye disease, for example, imitates the actions of Jesus in John 9.6. 'At this point touch the ground and make mud from the dust and the saliva, and with this make a cross on top of [his or her] eyes'; 'At this point touch the ground and then the eyes in the form of a cross'. Malicious magic, however, as well as curative could make use of Biblical precedent, even if the connections were slight. Thus, a charm to cause fever involves indirect reference to instruments of the crucifixion.

> In order to make someone suffer from a fever, have three nails made, like those of our Lord Jesus Christ. Go to the tree which is called *Ispm* and stick these nails [in it], saying, 'Just as this tree has trembled, so may he and she tremble and suffer from fever as long as these nails are fixed in the tree.'[56]

Charms such as these could be carried out by anyone. Others, much more elaborate, required the co-operation of the parish priest. One of these dates from at least the early eleventh century, and is recorded in a mixture of Anglo-Saxon and Latin. It is intended to free fields from the effects of hostile magic directed against them, and involves removing four turfs, one from each corner of the field, before dawn, and dripping holy water three times on their undersides, saying, 'Grow and multiply and fill up the earth,' followed by the Lord's Prayer recited three times. Then the turfs are to be taken to the church, where the priest sings three Masses over them. The implication of the text is that they are placed on the altar itself, and that the Masses are celebrated on top of them, green side uppermost, after which, according to the instructions, they are turned over so that the green side rests upon the altar. Why this last was done is not explained. Were they meant to absorb whatever emanations might be coming from the relics enclosed in the altar-stone itself? This done, they are returned to their respective places in the field before sunset. Further elaborations follow, involving the practitioner's saying the Lord's Prayer, the Litany, the Sanctus, the Benedicite, and the Magnificat.[57] Were these recited in Latin or the vernacular? Since, as we have seen earlier, Latin seems to have been prescribed for the prayers and invocations contained in these various charms, and since, like the Hebrew and Greek which frequently appear in magical formulae, it has the status, through its use in the liturgy, of a language of power, the greater likelihood is that the prayers were recited in Latin. Now, there is no indication in the rubrics that the practitioner had to be a priest or a cleric – indeed, the instruction, 'Let the Mass-priest sing four Masses over the turfs,' suggests he was not – so we are bound to entertain the notion that the person in question knew quite a number of Latin prayers by heart, and was able to recall and recite them when required. Parts of the liturgy, then, appear to have impressed themselves on people's memory, largely no doubt through years of hearing them day in, day out, and so were available for magical as well as devotional use.

However, magic of any kind posed a problem for the Church. For if liberating one's field from the effects of harmful magic was one thing, endeavouring to afflict someone else with fever was quite another, and pastors were clearly nervous of any kind of practice which sought to contact and make use of power beyond the normal range of human, even if that power was nominally the power of God. Surrounded as everyone was by a multiplicity of non-human powers, the ever-present danger was that demons or other undesirables would see an opportunity even in 'harmless' magical working to slip into the operation and subvert it from within, thereby deceiving the human practitioner as to the real cause of any success he or she might have, and encouraging him or her to dabble further in potentially dangerous practices. 'In almost every region everywhere on earth,' wrote Thomas of Cobham in the early thirteenth century, 'certain idolatries hold sway, and preachers and priests should be armed against them. For there are many men and women who are given to acts of poisonous magic [*veneficiis*] and divination [*sortilegiis*] and do not believe they are idolatry.'[58] To churchmen, superstition was a great enemy. By 'superstition' they meant 'perversion of religion', and we can see from the land ceremony discussed above why their suspicions might easily be aroused by certain practices. By the end of the twelfth and beginning of the thirteenth century, however, suspicion was intensifying and hardening, and so we find the Fourth Lateran Council (1215) establishing Papal legates with special commissions to investigate heresy, and making confession mandatory for all Christians at least once a year. In consequence, pastoral care took a further and closer interest in what people were thinking and doing as Christians, and became if anything even more alert to beliefs and practices it regarded as suspect. A further question, lurking in the background, also raised itself: was demonic influence actually increasing as time went on? The closer the Church's examination of the problem, the greater that problem seemed to grow, and the Church's condemnation therefore grew stronger with it.

> [The parish priest] should instruct his parishioners that they should not practise the magical arts, incantations, or sorcery, since these things have no power to cure either human or beast and besides are utterly worthless and unlawful. Moreover clerics who do these things shall be degraded and lay people shall be excommunicated.[59]

'Sorcery' was *sortilegium*, but the principal meaning of the word is actually 'divination', and this particular practice, as much as any magic, was equally open to the kind of dangers which concerned the clergy. 'Interpreters of lots [*sortilegi*] are those who profess the knowledge of divination under the name of a false religion,' wrote St Isidore, and a series of penitentials agreed, calling the practice 'sacrilege' and 'a demonic thing' in turn. Thus, the *Burgundian Penitential* (eighth century) prescribed three years' penance for anyone who took auguries 'by birds or by whatever evil device', and five years for soothsayers, 'those whom they call diviners', because this too was a demonic practice; and things did not improve, because 450 years later Bartholomew Iscanus had to condemn anyone 'who practises divinations from the funeral of any dead person or from his body or from his clothing' in case the dead should be offended and decide to take vengeance. Once again, however, the clergy was not immune to the curiosity about the future which impelled people to divine themselves or ask others to do it for them. Guibert de Nogent noted that, on the very day and hour of his installation as Abbot of Nogent, 'one of the monks who knew his scripture and was also curious, I suspect, about the future course of my life, opened the text of the Gospel *which had been placed for this purpose on the altar*, [intending] to take as an omen the first passage that caught his eye'. Just as bad as this misuse of the Bible and altar were the provisions laid down in the late eleventh-century *Lots of the Twelve Patriarchs*.

When you want to find out the future by casting lots, pray and fast for two days, keep vigil and make humble entreaty for the whole of the previous night, and have a candle of double weight. Then, after Mass has been said and you have been sprinkled with holy water, don't forget [to say] 'Our Father' and the Creed, and don't fail to make the sign of the cross over the place nearest the altar. Then genuflect three times and, in that place, cast two lots; and while this is happening, make sure that twice six indigent people are being fed. In this way, the trustworthy lot, once thrown, tells you whatever you want to know.[60]

Here, misuse of both liturgical and sacred space must have required at least the tacit consent of the priest, or his turning a blind eye to what was going on, and one can see why the Church decided to rein in such practices, and at least attempt to banish them from her own premises and punish those clerics who aided or encouraged people in these dubious pursuits. However, clerics, of course, were not the only individuals to whom people could have recourse for magical or semi-magical answers to their problems. Diviners, magicians, cunning folk, and witches provided just such services on the grounds that they had the necessary expertise, either through their knowledge of relatively simple charms and incantations, or because they were, in effect, professional augurers and workers of magic who had built up a reputation for competence and perhaps possessed a book of instructions, a grimoire, whose genre the Bishop of Paris condemned in 1277 for 'containing necromancy or experiments of sorcery, invocations of demons, or conjurations hazardous for souls'.[61]

Diviners and magical workers of almost every kind seem to have been common in all ranks of society. Gerald of Wales talks about Welsh visionaries who went into ecstatic trances and uttered apparent nonsense which later turned out to be true or valuable, a behaviour similar in its fashion to that of the ancient Pythia at Delphi. Sheep farmers in the south of Wales were able to say what was happening in far-off places by reading the surfaces of rams' shoulder blades. Astrologers plied their increasingly sophisticated craft for those who could afford them, although astrology was regarded with suspicion by the Church, partly on the grounds that seeking to know the future trespassed upon God's omniscience, which should of right belong to Him alone, and partly because of the fear that demons might take the opportunity to interfere with the process in some way. Necromancers, too, seem to have been common, although 'necromancy' was often used as a pejorative term for ritual magic in general, and did not necessarily involve summoning up the souls and bodies of the dead, as its name implies. Necromancy, however, tended to be largely in the hands of the clergy, since its elaborate procedures required a degree of learning in the practitioner. Nevertheless, resuscitation of the dead, it was maintained, could be done by others, even if writers were divided on whether these attempts would be successful or not. Aelfric denied it. 'Witches still go to crossroads and heathen burials with their delusive magic,' he said, 'and call to the Devil; and he comes to them in the likeness of the man who is buried there, as if he is arising from death. But she cannot bring it about that the dead arise through her magic.' Gerbert de Montreuil, on the other hand (admittedly in the context of an epic poem), tells us that the knight Perceval sees a hideous old woman carrying two small barrels which contain magic ointments she uses to raise dead bodies and heal them of their wounds.[62]

Necromancy and the more elaborate forms of magical practice apart, the practitioners one was most likely to find in one's own village, or in another village probably not too far away, operated charms – for curing disease in humans or animals, for creating or dispelling love, for consecrating amulets, for ensuring protection against adverse weather or the malicious magic of some other party, for doing harm to another, for exorcising demons regarded as responsible for unwanted conditions such as illness – and relied on a knowledge of words and actions calculated in some way to effect the desired change in circumstance which would otherwise be beyond normal human power.[63] 'In some way' may be taken to reflect the uncertainty about how or why those words and actions worked. The Church suspected the assistance of demons, even if the desired end was beneficent and intended to be helpful; the individual practitioner may have agreed, while deliberately conjuring a demon to assist the process. For the most part, however, our reports and records do not mention any such deliberate conjuration, but either tacitly assume that a demon has worked the magic, or ask no questions at all and simply take the operation and its effect or non-effect for granted; and in this it is likely they reflect the psychology of those involved, who probably asked for the magic and did the magic without any particular debate, internal or external, about the morality or the mechanics which might be involved therein. Witch, cunning man or woman, magician – to all intents and purposes these were the same person. Some might specialise in love or curative magic; some might be able to do only one thing, such as cure or tame a horse, because that was the only charm they knew; some might be prepared to range over the continuum of magic and do harm as well as good; some might possess a modicum of learning, even a book, which would give them a reputation – an advantage in ordinary circumstances, a potential disadvantage in others.

What we need to keep constantly in mind is that our modern compartmentalisation of religion, magic, and science had not yet taken place in earlier periods. Consequently people were happy to slip from one to the other in seeking practical answers to their problems, as though the three were all one, differing from each other only to a very limited extent. Scholars, certainly, were capable of drawing some kind of distinction between them, but that was principally a theoretical exercise and did not materially come into question when a practical problem of a certain kind called for a practical solution of a certain kind; for churchmen, as we have seen, were as likely as anyone else to practise magic alongside their theology on the one hand and their natural philosophy ('science') on the other. What we also need to remember is that those who practised magic were not behaving irrationally. On the contrary, given their interpenetrating universes, which allowed humans and non-human entities of all kinds to interact, it was entirely rational to argue that techniques, from prayer to unorthodox ritual actions which facilitated that interaction and caused or allowed it to happen for people's greater benefit or satisfaction, were entirely legitimate and rational modes of behaviour. In their contexts, therefore, the cunning person, the witch, and the magician were neither more bizarre nor more exotic in themselves than modern physicists, doctors, or theoretical mathematicians are in theirs; and since we are dealing here specifically with the witch – who could be male as well as female, and the possessor of some kind of knowledge as well as being a possible summoner of demons – it is important that we keep a balanced view of this individual.[64]

The historical portrait we have of her (principally a 'her') is heavily coloured by the Church's suspicions, which are transmitted in so much of the literature that gives us our information, and by the requirements of fiction, verse and prose, which both like and need a villain. If context helps us to define the witch, it is worth recalling that her usual context was clearly that of wife, daughter, sister, neighbour, living exactly the same kind of life as the rest of her community. The one thing that made her stand out from her neighbours was what she 'knew' – the words and actions of her charm or invocation – and, since her special knowledge could be put to good use as well as harmful, she was, for the most part and until alteration in circumstances dictated otherwise, a useful member of her society. This, then, is her context, rather than that of the Church's unease or the poets' or chroniclers' fantasy of evil, and is the one we should try to keep hold of as we follow her changeable history.

1

POLITICAL CRIMES, DIVINATION, AND DEMONS: 1222–1390

It is easy, perhaps too easy, to allude to the Church in connection with the changing reputation and treatment of the witch during the thirteenth and fourteenth centuries. While her caution in approaching people's frequent recourse to magic in their everyday lives is entirely understandable, and her desire to free religious belief and practice from superstitious accretions scarcely surprising, it must not be forgotten that the secular state had an interest, and often a very close interest, in the activities of its citizens, especially those with some degree of pretension to social status and influence. Investigating the future through forms of divination could be seen as a political act, as ancient Rome had well understood, for it expelled astrologers and other diviners on various occasions during the first two centuries BC and in the first AD under Augustus and Tiberius, while the Theodosian Code of the fourth century condemned astrologers and magicians alike.

> No one shall consult a haruspex [*someone who prognosticates from the internal organs of sacrificed animals*], or an astrologer or soothsayer. The depraved trade of augurs and seers is to stop. Chaldaeans and magicians and others, whom the general populace calls 'workers of harmful magic' (*malefici*) because of the magnitude of their crimes, shall stop doing anything of that sort. Curiosity to read the future shall cease. Anyone who fails to obey these commands will suffer capital punishment by the sword.[1]

Subsequent European governments understood perfectly. In England, for example, King Edgar and the witan and King Aethelred (tenth century) forbade magic and divination, with the witan calling for their practitioners' expulsion from the community, a provision repeated by the fourth secular law of King Cnut.[2] Inquisitiveness might lead someone to ask when the ruler would die and who was likely to be his or her successor; or to find out whether such and such an uprising, rebellion, or war stood a chance of being successful; or to discover a person's career prospects in royal or imperial service. Should the individual's prospects look favourable or grim, they could always be assisted by magic. So, too, a rebellion or the succession to the throne. Consequently both divination and magic could be seen as fraught with danger to the authority and stability of the state, a challenge the state could hardly be expected to ignore.

It follows, of course, that charges of divination or practice of harmful magic could be levied against important or influential people in the hope of affecting their status

and significance. One obvious example is that of Adam de Stratton, one of the most
important moneylenders and financial administrators of Edward I's reign. He was
in holy orders and made his way through royal service to accumulate a number of
posts and benefices which, in addition to his extensive moneylending, enabled him to
become a remarkably rich man. Never one to avoid forging a document or escaping
from a tight hole by bribing the right people, Stratton finally fell temporary victim
to his enemies' complaints and the king's sudden interest in corruption among
royal officials, after his long absence in Gascony. Gascony had been expensive, and
Edward could not afford to have people diverting monies from his use to theirs;
hence a number of individuals (about a thousand) found themselves facing a royal
commission of investigation. The purge included Stratton, who had been in trouble
ten years previously over a forged document, and had acquired a certain notoriety
along with the enemies which accompanied it. However, notoriety was not his only
acquisition. We are given an account of his downfall in 1289 by a monk from the
cathedral church of Norwich, Bartholomew de Cotton, who includes the details in his
Historia Anglicana, written not long after the events he describes.

> Immediately afterwards, Adam de Stratton, Clerk of the Royal Exchequer, who had
> appeared before the King accused of murder, sedition, and various other outrages,
> was assigned to the King's custody in the Tower of London, and all his goods were
> confiscated. Among his belongings were found £10,000 in old money and £20,000
> in new, and 60 lbs of gold. Two gold crowns were also found, and a number of other
> precious objects. A silken box[3] was found in his belongings in which he had kept human
> nail-clippings, women's pubic hair, toads' feet and moles' feet, and other devilish things.
> Now, the said box had had a seal attached to it by the King's Justice, and because
> [Stratton] removed the seal and threw the said box into a latrine, everyone considered
> him to be a traitor to the King, and he was accused of belonging to that group of people
> called *sortilegi* ('sorcerers').[4]

We need not assume or suppose that these magical impedimenta had necessarily been
planted to incriminate Stratton further, or that Bartholomew was being credulous
in recording the story. As we have seen earlier, clerics as well as lay people practised
magic, and the kind of material found in Stratton's receptacle was not in the least
unusual – it suggests love magic on the one hand and curative magic on the other
– and the epithet *diabolica*, which Bartholomew uses to describe the contents, is quite
in keeping with a monk's reaction to them. That Stratton should try to get rid of
them is not surprising, either. To be accused of murder, sedition, and 'various other
outrages' – in other words, peculation on a grand scale – was bad enough to ensure
his execution if he were found guilty. So there would have been no need to plant extra
evidence to make certain of an adverse verdict; and given the prevalence of magic
among churchmen and the ordinariness of the contents of Stratton's little box, we
may venture to accept this aspect of his case as accurate reporting on Bartholomew's
part. The impedimenta would have served only to make Stratton's position worse, of
course, and indeed it seems to have done so, for Bartholomew goes on to tell us that

Adam de Stratton had been condemned to death. But because he was a cleric, his lands, possessions, and other belongings, to the value of £50,000, were paid to the Tax Office and he retired from the royal Court with every mark of shame. He retained his Church revenues, however, which amounted to £1,000.

But even after this, Stratton failed to amend his ways, and within a few months was found guilty of forging the seal to a document which made it look as though the Prior of Bermondsey had left him a manor house in his will. For this, Stratton was sentenced to perpetual imprisonment, and his various benefices were confiscated. Thus, Bartholomew, who adds as a final sentence to his account: 'The moon was seen to be full and [appeared] black, golden-yellow, and varied in hue.'[5] Why mention this? Its position in the narrative suggests that Bartholomew meant it to be significant: nature's (that is, ultimately, God's) comment upon the episode.

Stratton, however, was not the only high-ranking individual to fall victim to charges of undesirable magic, for only ten years later we find another churchman accused for what appears to be a mixture of political and personal reasons. Walter Langton had begun his serious climb to royal favour in 1290 when he was appointed Keeper of the Wardrobe, a post he held for five years before becoming Treasurer of the Exchequer. In 1296 he was consecrated Bishop of Coventry and Lichfield, a position he both used and exploited to add to his burgeoning wealth. Like Stratton, Langton was a notable pluralist, and he quickly became unpopular for his exactions and personal greed, so it was not long before his enemies struck. These included the Archbishop of Canterbury, who demanded his resignation as Treasurer in 1301, and a knight, John Lovetot, whose father was Langton's close friend. Sir John alleged that his own stepmother had become Langton's mistress and that together she and Langton had strangled his father; that Langton had bought and sold ecclesiastical offices and was guilty of pluralism – these two allegations undoubtedly true – and that he had done homage to the Devil (or a devil, the Latin is ambiguous), had kissed his backside, and spoken to him many times. This accusation, that he was in effect a demon worshipper, reached the Papal Court, which referred it to the Archbishop of Canterbury, who, in spite of their mutual enmity, came to the conclusion that the charge was baseless, a verdict ratified (but not until two years later) by Boniface VIII. It is a noteworthy allegation because, while Lovetot's motive in making it was probably stimulated by personal animus – it is quite possible, for example, that his stepmother had indeed been Langton's mistress – the suggestion that Langton worshipped the Devil makes one wonder who thought of it and persuaded Lovetot to level it because, as Elliot Rose remarks, 'However false the story, something must have suggested it. Lovetot is not likely to have invented this detail of infernal etiquette.'[6]

Now, although allegations of demon worship had a long history going back to those times when Christianity was making advances against paganism, but had not yet reduced the older religious rites to negligible (and illegal) practice, the dualist heresy of Catharism had been seen as a particular threat to orthodox belief, especially in the late twelfth and early thirteenth centuries. With its contention that the Prince of Darkness was a power sufficient to challenge that of God in this world, Catharism was easy to identify with demon worship, and charges of demon worship were still being made against practitioners of magic at this same period, as is evidenced by a letter from the Cardinal of Santa Sabina to the Inquisitor of Carcassonne in 1320.

> Our most holy father and lord, by God's providence, Pope [John] XXII, fervently wishing to drive away from the middle of God's house workers of harmful magic, who are infecting the Lord's flock, wishes and ordains that you undertake, with his authority, [to move] against those: (i) who sacrifice to demons, or worship them, or do homage to them by giving them a signed written document or anything else, or who make pacts with them which [they consider] legally binding; (ii) who make or get someone else to make some image or anything else to bind a demon to them, or invoke demons to get them to perpetrate some act of harmful magic; (iii) who, in an abuse of the sacrament of baptism, baptise or get someone else to baptise an image made from wax or anything else, or, in other circumstances, invoke demons in some fashion to make [such an image] or get someone else to make it, or knowingly repeat baptism ordination, or confirmation.[7]

Kissing the Devil's backside had long been believed to form an integral part of a certain kind of demon worship, one associated with witches when they attended mass meetings known as 'Sabbats' to do homage to their infernal master, report their evil doings, and receive further instruction in wickedness from him or his representative. The 'shameful kiss' (*osculum infame*) was thus a well-known feature of these assemblies. Alain de Lille and the Welshman Walter Map had both drawn attention to it during the twelfth century, and in the thirteenth it was mentioned by the Franciscan, David of Augsburg, and most famously, perhaps, by Pope Gregory IX in his Bull, *Vox in Rama*, promulgated on 13 June 1233. According to what His Holiness had been told by the inquisitor Konrad of Marburg,

> when any novice is received in this assembly and enters it for the first time, there appears to him or her a kind of frog which some people have been accustomed to call a 'toad'. Certain people kiss it on its backside ... Next, while the novice is making his or her way forward, he or she is met by a human who is extraordinarily pale, has black eyes, and is extremely thin and emaciated. The novice kisses him and feels that the man is cold, like ice ... Through [the legs of] a statue which they usually have in this individual's assemblies, a cat the size of an ordinary dog, comes down backwards with its tail drawn back. First the novice, then the man in charge, then each person in turn kisses it.[8]

Only six years after Langton was accused of this offence, the downfall of the Templar order brought allegations that Templars were accustomed to worship a demon image and to kiss one another on the backside, a combination of heretical and sexual misbehaviour which seems to have had a particular place in contemporary public consciousness, for we find that in 1292 no fewer than three Parisians had acquired, for whatever reason, the nickname 'Kiss-the-Devil'.[9] So when we come to the accusation against Langton, it is worth our bearing in mind that there was a fairly widespread notion, in learned circles at least, that some heretics worshipped demons and kissed the

Devil's arse; that the association of heretics and magical practice was not uncommon; and that many of the clergy practised magic of one kind or another. To lay a charge of demon-worshipping and arse-kissing against a churchman was, therefore, neither bizarre nor exotic, and however much our own incredulity in the matter may tempt us to suggest that such a charge must have been false – as, indeed, the archbishop's investigation later decided – contemporaries would have found it perfectly possible. Indeed, had they not done so, there would have been little sense in levelling it only to have it dismissed at once as a piece of nonsense. Moreover, the inherent believability of the charge in its contemporary context must also suggest that, while both the Archbishop of Canterbury and the Pope seem to have been satisfied there was no basis to it in this instance, Langton could have been guilty in part. That is to say, had he indeed practised magic of some sort, as so many clergy did, this could have been taken as a starting point and the charge further developed into one of demon worship and therefore heresy. A finding that Langton was not guilty of the latter charge did not necessarily mean he could not have been guilty of the former.[10]

Why was it that charges of magic, often allied to 'sodomy' (a word of much wider range of meaning then than now), could be brought against notable persons, especially clerics, in the expectation they would be believed? The answer is partly that such things were in the air. Pope Boniface himself had to face charges that in his younger days he had been a magician and had had an evil spirit at his beck and call (a charge which went back to 1277–1280); that he committed 'sodomy' with boys and women; and that he had murdered his papal predecessor, Celestine V, charges levelled against him at the instance of the French king, Philippe IV, in 1303.[10] Here was a trend which continued as the fourteenth century got under way. John Tanner (alias Canne) was hanged in 1314 or 1315 after claiming to be a son of Edward I and endeavouring to lay hands on the crown with the aid of the Devil, whom he had worshipped for the past three years. In France, the Bishop of Troyes, who had had a dazzling career up to 1301, fell victim to a series of accusations, first of corruption, then of employing a Jewish magician to evoke a demon who would force the French queen to drop her enmity towards him, and then in 1308 of having practised harmful magic in company with a witch from his diocese, his design being to cause the death of the queen. The bishop was eventually found not guilty, but not until 1311, and he did not regain his full liberty for another three years, by which time the Templars, whose trials had been scandalising France and the rest of Europe, had been destroyed, and the aims of King Philippe achieved.[11] Indeed, France appears to have been alive at this time with similar accusations as high-ranking officials and their associates were charged with magical plots to kill the reigning monarch, first Louis X and then his brother, Charles V,[12] and so it comes as little surprise to find that in 1325 individuals were also put on trial in England, accused of making magical attempts on the life of Edward II and members of his court. It started in Coventry when John of Nottingham, a local magician, was approached by a number of people who wanted him to kill the Prior of Coventry, against whom they had a grudge, along with the king, the Earl of Winchester, Sir Hugh le Despenser, and others. John was to be assisted by his lodger, Robert Marshall (who later turned King's evidence), and the method would be a standard one – making a wax image of each intended victim and enchanting it with a view to causing his death. Both John and Robert accepted the commission (which was very well paid), and began a remarkably protracted process on 7 December. One says 'protracted' because they were still occupied with it in May the following year. One victim, Richard of Sowe, succumbed to the magic. A sharpened pin made of lead had been thrust deep into the forehead of his image, and when Robert called on him the next day to ascertain his condition, he found him screaming and unable to recognise anyone. He was left in this state, however, for over three weeks, until at last John withdrew the pin from the image's forehead and drove it into its heart, whereupon the man died four days later.[13]

If politically motivated accusations of hostile magic were common at this time, dualist heresy in the form of Catharism was also at its most influential, and had to be suppressed by both military and evangelical aggression, the latter principally through the efforts of the Dominican order, founded specifically to preach the Faith and confront and confute heresy. Satan loomed large in Catharist beliefs. The majority of men and women, they said, lived in Satan's domain, and he kept them subject to him by means of their sexuality, which he himself had created. In one version of this creed, Satan was a fallen angel who had made the material world and peopled it with bodies, which served as receptacles for his companion fallen angels. In another, there existed an evil as well as a good God, and the former had invaded Heaven and carried off a number of good angels whom he then imprisoned in the material world and the bodies he had created for them.[14] These notions, accurately absorbed or distorted by exaggeration and misunderstanding, would not have escaped the notice of high-ranking clerics and lay people from any of the states which made up the island of Britain. There was constant toing and froing between Britain and the rest of Europe – England, indeed, was at war with France between 1290 and 1390 – so no one of any political or religious standing could have remained immune to the contemporary zeitgeist. We may say, then, that, while linking heresy with magic through charges of demon worship was a fairly obvious connection to make and one which might be difficult for an accused to refute completely, the peculiarity of the religious and political climate at the turn of the fourteenth century meant that it would be a particularly damaging accusation to bring, not only against clerics but against lay folk.

Now, up to this point I have tried not to use the word 'witch' in connection with these incidents of politicised magic. This is because the majority of our records are in Latin, and Latin uses a wide variety of terms for magical practitioners, terms which tend to suggest the special talent or magical focus either belonging or attributed to the individual concerned, a diversity obscured by the single term 'witch'. Thus, *malefica* = 'female worker of harmful magic'; *sortilega* = 'female diviner'; *lamia* = 'child eater'; *strix* = 'vampire-like person'; *venefica* = 'worker of poisonous magic'; *sortiaria* = 'female diviner' (a variant of *sortilega*). All these terms except *lamia* have their male counterpart, and so 'witch' can be misleading as a translation, especially as it tends to suggest a female as opposed to a male practitioner and emphasises the harmful character of the magician's practices at the expense of the curative or divinatory.[15]

Some of the variety of magical behaviour can be gauged from instances brought before the authorities at this period. In 1222, a Jewish necromancer was accused of wrapping a boy in a dead man's skin so that, via this contact, the dead man could speak through the boy and answer questions about the future. (Was this merely a piece of anti-Jewish propaganda? It is always possible, of course, but it is also possible that the charge was essentially true. Not every accusation of necromancy and divination laid against someone, Jewish or not, was necessarily false.) In 1279, jurors at an assize in Northumberland acquitted John de Kerneslawe of unlawfully killing an unknown woman who had entered his house at the time of Vespers and attacked him. John, suspecting, for whatever reason, that the intruder was a witch, made the sign of the cross and felled her with a piece of firewood.[16] The record calls her a *sortilega*, and, since John did not know her, she may have been a traveller of some kind, hoping perhaps to earn a little money by offering to tell people's fortunes. If so, she need not have been a 'witch' or a 'sorceress', as modern interpretations assume. The local clergy ordered her body to be burned. Was that a recognition that she was a witch? Not necessarily. Cremation was most unusual and had nothing to do with any such suspicion. Witches in England were hanged, not burned, and so burning the body probably did not express clerical conjecture about who or what she was. The clergy's instructions smack rather of a fear that the dead woman might rise from her grave and take revenge on the living, and cremation would be an obvious solution to prevent this from happening, as can be seen from an incident related by William of Newburgh. A man's corpse, he said, started to wander round his district at night, causing fear and attacking anyone it met. At last, after it had killed a number of folk, the locals lost their terror, went to the grave, dug up the man's corpse, tore out his heart, and then burned the whole body on a hastily constructed pyre, after which there was no more trouble.[17]

The thirteenth century, in fact, seems to have found itself faced by lay and clerical intransigence when it came to magic of all kinds, for synodal statutes had to be issued and reissued again and again, forbidding the practice of magic and divination. Nor was there any sign of any relaxation as the fourteenth century began, for in 1311 the Bishop of London felt obliged to instruct his archdeacon to initiate legal proceedings against anyone using magic to recover lost or stolen goods, foretell the future, evoke evil spirits, or divine by means of stones or mirrors.[18] It is in this general context, then, that we should see the case of Alice Kyteler from Kilkenny in 1324.[19] She and eleven others, men and women, were charged with a variety of offences, including (apart from heresy) *sortilegium*, demon worship, love magic, and attempted murder by harmful magic. All these offences, as we have seen, were common, and we have plenty of evidence from Britain and elsewhere to suggest they were real enough, in the sense that people did indeed carry out rituals, small and more elaborate, in pursuit of occult power and the effects that power might allow them to achieve. There is therefore no point in our looking at Alice's list of alleged offences and dismissing them out of hand as false and impossible, even though it may be admitted that the personalities and motives of those involved in the case seem to have been complex and not easy to understand.

The outline of events, based largely on a contemporary narrative, probably written by one of the principals in the case, Bishop Ledrede or one of his supporters, is as follows. Alice Kyteler lived in Kilkenny, an important town situated between Leinster and Munster in the south-east of Ireland. Justice eyres and parliaments were held there from time to time, and one-third of it belonged to Hugh Despenser, an English magnate, with the other two-thirds belonging to the English king. In 1324, Edward II's reign was beginning to fall apart, and these English stirs made themselves felt in Kilkenny, with local quarrels and disturbances always threatening to take on an English dimension.[20] The situation was not helped by the appointment of Richard Ledrede, an English Franciscan, to the see of Ossory in 1317, the bishopric having its seat in St Canice's Cathedral in Kilkenny. In 1324, therefore, Kilkenny was more or less ready for a conflict of some kind.

Alice Kyteler belonged to a distinguished Anglo-Norman family which had settled in Kilkenny after the Norman conquest of Ireland in 1169 and had made itself rich through moneylending and trade with Flanders. She married four times. Her first husband, William Utlagh (or Outlaw), came from a prominent merchant family in the town, and together they had a son, also named William, who later became a banker and moneylender, like his father. William senior was elected mayor of Kilkenny in around 1301, but not long afterwards died, and not unnaturally Alice was married again, to another local banker and merchant called Adam le Blond. In 1301 or 1302 he and Alice entrusted £3,000 to William Utlagh junior for safekeeping, and he buried this large sum of cash beneath his house – a common enough practice at a time when banks in our sense did not exist, and money chests might be thought too conspicuous. Knowledge of the money and its whereabouts, however, leaked out, and one of Alice's relatives, William Kyteler, who was sheriff of Kilkenny at the time, together with one Fulk, his seneschal, broke into the house, dug up the money and carried it off, along with £100 of William's own money. Charged with theft and trespass, William and Fulk retorted that, because they had had to dig up the money, it constituted a treasure trove, and countercharged that Adam and Alice were guilty of homicide, a nonsensical claim which was quickly brushed aside, but not before Alice, Adam, and a Roesa Utlagh – perhaps Alice's daughter or stepdaughter – had been thrown into prison for a while. This experience was followed by two possibly related incidents. In 1307 Adam decided to grant effective control of all his possessions to his stepson, William Utlugh, and then either in that year or the next he died, leaving Alice free to remarry for a third time in around 1310.

Husband number three was Richard de Valle, and once again Alice had married well, for Richard's family, originally from Pembrokeshire, held land in Tipperary. However, something obviously went wrong in the relationship between Alice and Richard's immediate family, because, when he died in 1316, Alice was obliged to take his son to court to ensure her due payment, as Richard's widow, of a third of his possessions.[21] Women, it is clear, were not only able to be active participants in business, but could also increase their personal fortunes by judicious marriage or, as in Alice's case, a sequence of marriages. So the fact of her remarrying often was not in itself particularly unusual or suspicious. Nevertheless, she, her husbands, and her son William Utlagh had undoubtedly made enemies, not only among the people of Kilkenny because of their moneylending, especially William to whom many of the principal men of the district were heavily in debt, but also among the children of her second and third marriages. So when Alice married for a fourth time in around 1320

– another man of wealth and social importance, Sir John le Poer – the stage was set, and a melodrama about to begin. By around 1324, Sir John's health had declined considerably. The *Narrative*, which is the principal record of these events, tells us that 'his whole body was emaciated, his nails torn out, and all hair removed from his body', a deterioration he seems to have found suspicious, because, with the help of a servant, he wrested Alice's keys from her and opened her household boxes, in one of which he discovered a sack full of 'vile and horrible ingredients'. What these ingredients were is not specified at this point, but one of the accusations later levelled against her and her associates was that they would use dead people's nails, buttock-hairs, and the clothes of children who had died before they could be baptised, as some of the constituents in the manufacture of powders, ointments, lotions, and candles which they would then employ for magical purposes, principally maleficent. No wonder, therefore, that Sir John called in two priests – *Narrative* calls them calls them *religiosi*, which means they were devout, and so presumably could be trusted not to practise magic themselves – and told them to take the sack and its contents to Bishop Ledrede. No more will have been needed to stimulate the enmities of some of Alice's stepchildren, for we are told that they appealed to the Bishop for remedy and assistance.

> Openly and in front of people, they alleged that she had used sorceries of this kind [*i.e.* maleficia, '*acts of harmful magic*'] to murder some of their fathers and to infatuate others, reducing their senses to such stupidity that they gave all their possessions to her and her own son, thus impoverishing for ever their sons and heirs.[22]

Bishop Ledrede immediately instituted an investigation, as he was clearly bound to do in view of the seriousness of the allegations, and was assisted by five knights and a number of other men of high social standing. Their inquiries elicited the disturbing revelation that for a long time in Kilkenny a good many heretical *sortilegae* had been practising magic and flouting their religious duties. For a month or a year at a time they would deny the Faith, refuse to go to Mass, and would not receive the Eucharist, all with a view to putting themselves in the right frame of mind to work some kind of magical ceremony. This is an interesting observation which is not generally made explicit elsewhere and suggests a certain level of sophistication. Witches, as we know from many later records, frequently used the opportunity afforded them by Holy Communion to secrete the Host under their tongue, which they then removed in the privacy of their own homes and used as a magical ingredient in their workings. In Kilkenny, the psychology seems to have been entirely different, and does indeed suggest genuine apostasy rather than the more usual sacrilege. So, heretical these women certainly were. (One says 'women' because *sortilegae* is a feminine noun. Their practices, *sortilegia*, go well beyond simple divination and so it looks as though *sortilegae* may well refer here to witches and *sortilegia* to sorceries or acts of witchcraft.)

Next, it was claimed these women would cut living animals into pieces and scatter them round crossroads as a sacrifice to demons, and to one demon in particular who called himself 'the son of the art, belonging to the more servile [inhabitants] of Hell', and would seek advice from these demons and answers to questions. Demon worship, as we have seen, had been a continuing practice, which worried the Church and caused her to issue condemnations of it and injunctions against it at fairly frequent intervals. However, the detail about scattering fresh, bleeding lumps of meat as though the demons were a species of wild animal to be tempted and trapped by such means is unusual. In 1320 and again in 1326, Pope John XXII forbade sacrificing to demons, worshipping them, and seeking responses from them, and fifty years later Nicolau Eymeric wrote about sacrificing animals and birds to demons, and catching their blood to use as a curative agents. 'Sacrificing', however, suggests something other than cutting up animals' bodies and leaving them at crossroads as bait. So it may be that we have here – if we accept the accusation as true – record of a practice peculiar either to these individuals or to the neighbourhood, similar in some respects to what the Church was condemning, but not in others.[23]

Further to these accusations, it was alleged that the *sortilegae* would also meet at night and behave as though they were priests, performing an act of excommunication against specific individuals, including their own husbands. They held lighted candles, named each part of the person's body 'from the soles of his or her feet to the top of the head', and then blew out their candles with the exclamation 'Fi, fi, fi, Amen!'[24] Now, according to Gratian, the ritual of excommunication involved twelve priests who 'must stand round the bishop in a circle holding burning candles in their hands, which at the conclusion of the anathema or excommunication they must fling to the ground and extinguish with their feet'.[25] (The number of thirteen persons involved here should not be misunderstood. These represent Christ and His apostles, and thirteen has nothing to do with any supposed coven, that number being a fantasy of Margaret Murray in the twentieth century.) If we allow for differences in ritual practice from place to place and time to time, and if we compare the form of excommunication issued by Bishop Ledrede himself in 1317 against various offenders including sacrilegious persons, *sortilegos* (note that this includes men as well as women), and public heretics, we still do not mirror the reference to named parts of the body from sole to crown. Where we do find very frequent reference to such comprehensive inclusion in a ritual or ritualised context, however, is in later confessions, which tell us that a novice witch gave herself to the Devil 'from the soles of her feet to the crown of her head', and so one is tempted to ask whether Ledrede may not have misunderstood or misinterpreted terms he did not understand from some kind of ritual reception of a candidate into the company of these *sortilegae*. This depends, of course, upon one's acceptance of the truth, part or whole, of this particular accusation. However, if a group of heretics did indeed exist in Kilkenny, they may have been obliged to receive newcomers during the hours of darkness – patterns of sleep at this time meant that people were often up and about in the middle of the night, so there is nothing inherently odd or suspicious about this detail of nocturnal meetings – but we are in the hands, so to speak, of a partisan record, and therefore need to exercise caution anent every aspect of its case.[26]

In addition to these accusations, it was said that the personal demon called 'son of the art' or 'Robin' acted as Alice's incubus, that he sometimes appeared to her as a cat or a shaggy black dog, and that sometimes he took the shape of a black man (*Aithiops*), on which occasions he was accompanied by two demons bigger and taller than himself, one of them carrying an iron rod. It was to 'the son of the art', said the allegation, that Alice owed her wealth and all her possessions. Now, the notion that demons could and did have sex with human beings had been current since the days of St Augustine – 'Certain incubi are often said to have appeared to reprobate women and to have assaulted them and had rough sex with them' – and St Thomas Aquinas had recorded that, while demons could have sex with humans, any children produced from that act could not have been engendered by the demons themselves but must have come from human semen used by the demons for that purpose: an opinion not universally accepted.[27] Here, however, there is no suggestion that any of Alice's children were the offspring of her demon – some of them were, after all, her accusers – merely that she herself 'submitted to him carnally'.

His choice of shape-changing was by no means unusual. Norman Cohn notes that in the fifteenth century a demon called 'Mermet' appeared to his human invoker first as a cat, then as a black man with horns on his feet; another called 'Brunet' materialised as a black dog and then as a black man; and other demons would first appear as cats or crows before changing their form into that of a black man.[28] 'Aithiopians' were well known to Mediaeval Europe as one of the 'monstrous' races from sub-Egyptian Africa. They were black, barbarian, and exotic. 'Anyone who saw them in another country would say they were devils,' wrote Marco Polo, and maps showed them as descendants of Noah's cursed son, Ham. Aithiopia was also astrologically dominated by Saturn, whose malign influence was clearly believed to affect its inhabitants.[29] Church paintings, too, regularly depicted demons as both humanoid and black – one thinks of Duccio di Buoninsegna's *Temptation on the Mount* (1308–11), for example, or Giotto's *Last Judgement* (1304–13) in the Arena chapel in Padua. One is mindful, too, of their representation in theatrical performances:

> We, that were angels so fair
> and sat so high above the air,
> now are we waxen black as any coal.
>
> (*Towneley Cycle: Creation*, 134–136)

So it was quite natural for Alice's demon to be described as *Aithiops*. What is not quite so straightforward to interpret is the iron rod carried by one of his frequent attendants. The Latin is *virga ferrea*, 'virga' meaning a 'switch, rod, wand, staff' and thus suggesting an implement of punishment or a symbol of office. (*Virga episcopalis*, for example, is a bishop's crosier.) Jeffrey Russell suggests that it may have been 'the sceptre of power sometimes borne in the fifteenth century by the Devil',[30] but I wonder whether there is not a connection between this rod and the later assertion that, if witches attending a Sabbat failed to please the presiding demon, they were beaten. The observation that the rod was made of iron takes us to the Bible: 'You will break them with a rod of iron' (Psalms 2.9; cf. Apocalypse 2.27), and 'From his mouth comes a sharp sword with which to strike down the nations, and he will rule them with a rod of iron' (Apocalypse 19.15). So I am inclined to think that this demon's rod was an instrument of control and potential punishment.

Of the seven charges arising from Bishop Ledrede's initial investigation, then, one related to apostasy and the other six to demons and the practice of harmful magic

– one of which involved the murder of Alice's first three husbands and the attempted murder of her fourth. So far, except for relatively minor and probably local details, none of the accusations makes Alice's case stand out as unusual in comparison with later cases or, indeed, contemporary cases elsewhere in Europe. What does single it out is its date, for it appears to be one of the earliest to link *organised* heresy with demonic magic. Now, Bishop Ledrede's reaction to these findings needs to be seen not only in the context of his realising he had a major problem of apostasy in his diocese, but also in the light of both Irish and papal politics; that Ireland was suffering badly in the 1320s from the effects of severe famine and the recent Scottish invasion; that the rule of law was weak, fragile at the centre and almost powerless at the margins; and that the English were menacing and the Pope distracted by problems of his own. These problems included recurrent upsurges of magic among both laity and clergy, some of it directed against him personally. Thus:

1317, Hugues Géraud, Bishop of Cahors, was arrested for trying to kill the Pope by poison and harmful magic.

1318, Robert Mauvoisin, Archbishop of Aix, was charged with employing a Jew to practise divination, specifically 'the art of astrology which has been condemned and forbidden by law', in order to find out his future and to ascertain how long the Pope would live.

1318, the Pope directed the Bishop of Fréjus to investigate widespread use of magic at the Papal Court, then in Avignon, including necromancy, geomancy, and rituals intended to summon demons, with a view to harming or killing others.

1319, a Franciscan, Bernard Délicieux, was condemned to life imprisonment for possessing a grimoire, a seemingly harsh sentence until one remembers he had also been charged with poisoning Pope Benedict XI. Although he had been acquitted of that particular allegation, mud certainly tends to stick.

1319, the Bishop of Pamiers was instructed by the Pope to proceed against three people – a priest, a Carmelite, and a woman – for practising magic and consulting demons.

1320, the Visconti family in Milan was said to have tried to kill the Pope by magical means.

1320, eight noblemen from Recanati were accused of worshipping the statue of a demon, who advised them in everything they did.

1323, the Inquisitor of Paris tried the Abbot of Sarcelles and various other people because the abbot had employed a magician to discover who had stolen some valuables and where those valuables were now.[31]

All this is relevant to Bishop Ledrede because he had been at the Papal Court in Avignon, 'nurtured, educated, and promoted [there]', as he himself put it in the *Narrative*, and had acquired a sufficient reputation for scholarship to make him a suitable candidate for consecration as Bishop of Ossory.[32] He had therefore had plenty of time to absorb the Church's growing hostility towards magic and magicians, a hostility fuelled by the notorious suppression of the Templars in 1312 and the death of their Grand Master with three of his officers in March 1314. Since the charges against them had included apostasy, demon worship, and the belief that they owed their wealth to the goodwill of their idol Baphomet,[33] one can see how easy it might have been for Ledrede to draw mental parallels between these allegations and those lodged against Alice Kyteler and, with his likely awareness of at least some of the magical scandals of Pope John's reign so far, why he should have been determined to snuff out any organised heresy and magical practice in his own diocese. The prevailing disorderly secular situation, too, meant that Ledrede represented a more stable centre of authority, and since he was an Englishman who had never been in Ireland before, he was not bound by personal ties to any particular faction or party and therefore could not be accused of partisanship in his exercise of governance and discipline.

He set about heresy the moment he arrived in Kilkenny and made it clear he would tolerate no interference from any secular source in Church matters or privileges. His specific references to lay people's taking away ecclesiastical possessions, violently removing anyone seeking sanctuary, or plundering goods left in churches and cloisters for safekeeping suggests the degree of social disturbance then prevalent in his diocese.[34] That he was determined to bring order to his section of the Irish Church is clear both from his *Constitutions* and from his relentless pursuit of heretics wherever they were to be found, and he was quite prepared to antagonise both the Archbishop of Dublin and the Chancellor of Ireland by accusing them of aiding and fostering heretics. Now, the Chancellor was Roger Utlagh, a relative (perhaps a brother) of Alice's first husband and hence a relative (perhaps an uncle) of her son William, and so when Alice was charged, the bishop immediately had a powerful enemy. However, Utlagh was not the only one. The Seneschal of Kilkenny, Arnold le Poer, was probably related to Alice's fourth husband, and certainly disliked Ledrede intensely, describing him as 'a meddlesome foreigner, intent on slandering the religious heritage of the Irish and introducing oppressive alien customs'.[35] So of course Le Poer, too, felt bound to come to Alice's aid, and thus Ledrede found himself embroiled not only with two powerful secular figures but also, they being royal officials, with a network of their supporters, stretching from the south of Ireland to the English court in London.

Investigation of the charges laid against Alice led to the bishop's writing to Roger Utlagh in his capacity as Chancellor of Ireland asking for a warrant to have her arrested along with eleven other named individuals implicated in her alleged crimes.[36] However, the moment Alice's son learned of this, 'he went round the royal officials and other nobles of the land, using his ill-gotten gains to win their friendship', as the *Narrative* explains it. Needless to say, Arnold le Poer joined forces with Roger Utlagh in opposing the bishop's action, to which Ledrede retorted that it was a matter involving the Faith, and in consequence he would neither drop his action nor adjourn it. 'Heretics must be handled differently from other excommunicates', he said, 'because otherwise once they know the Church intends to proceed against them, they can immediately run away to another district and so cause a great scandal which damages the Faith.'[37] The royal warrant for which he had applied to Utlagh, however, was not granted, and so Ledrede, on his own authority as bishop, summoned Alice to appear in his ecclesiastical court; but she anticipated this move and fled instead to Dublin. The bishop then excommunicated her, charged her son with heresy and shielding heretics, and summoned him to attend his court. (The plural 'heretics' is interesting, since it implies that William had tried to extend his protection to persons other than his mother. The eleven accused along with her included Petronilla of Meath, Alice's maidservant, and Petronilla's daughter, so it is quite possible that these two women, if not the others, may have taken refuge with their mistress in William's house. If so, Ledrede's second accusation against William makes good sense.)

The tension between ecclesiastical and secular authority now broke into action, for Le Poer issued a warrant for the bishop's arrest, a dangerous thing to do, because the Second Lateran Council of 1139 had forbidden anyone to offer violence to a cleric. However, Le Poer probably calculated this would remove Ledrede from the scene at least until the date given in the bishop's citation of William to appear in his court had passed. Ledrede astutely made no resistance to his arrest and submitted to his imprisonment with apparent grace, but meanwhile he placed his diocese under interdict, thereby ensuring that all sacramental life there ceased. He also skilfully used the support of the clerics and laypeople who came to the gaol in large numbers, 'as pilgrims flock round a place of pilgrimage', to wrong-foot Le Poer and Utlagh. After seventeen days, he was released and immediately restarted proceedings against Alice and the others; but Alice had been using her time in Dublin to good effect for, as the *Narrative* records,

> the said lady, a diviner [*sortilega*], heretic, and magician [*maga*] was freely allowed to consort in the town with the faithful [*cum fidelibus*], often in the company of William Doucemanne from the town of Dublin [*Douce was actually Mayor of Dublin at the time*], and many other clerics and laymen; and she was usually placed with the great men and leaders of the land in public assemblies.

(Davidson and Ward translate *cum fidelibus* as 'with her comrades', which is a perfectly possible way of putting it, since *fidelis* may mean 'trusted person, confidant'. If this is correct, it implies that Alice was enjoying the company of other heretics and *sortilegi/sortilegae*. If, on the other hand, *fidelibus* here refers to orthodox Catholics, the implication is that this heretic witch was allowed to consort with the faithful and thus radiate a dangerous influence. Either of these is likely to have sown Ledrede's long-lasting conviction that the Archbishop of Dublin was, as he put it, 'a notorious fosterer of heretics'.)[38] It was now late April 1324. Ledrede had issued a citation to Alice and William to appear before him. Roger Utlagh countered by summoning Ledrede to appear before the justiciar's court in Dublin to explain why he had put Ossory under interdict, and to answer legal points anent his citation of Alice and William. Ledrede refused to go on the grounds that it would be too dangerous for him to travel through lands under Le Poer control, but he did turn up at the seneschal's court in Kilkenny, and a confrontation between himself and the seneschal degenerated into a shouting match which, fortunately, ended before actual violence broke out.

Now events moved even more quickly. Alice had accused Ledrede of defaming her and of excommunicating her without due legal process. Summoned to Dublin to answer these charges, Ledrede agreed to go, but took a circuitous route, and on his arrival found Dublin largely hostile to him. Nevertheless, he faced down an audience dominated by Le Poer and the inimical archbishop, and explained that far from tarring all the Irish with a single dismissive brush, as his opponent had alleged, he readily acknowledged that the presence of one rotten apple in a basket did not mean that all the rest were equally contaminated. However,

> in our diocese, in the midst of many law-abiding people, we have found a nest of devils [*nidum diabolicum*] more foul than any that has ever been found in the kingdom or dominion of the King of England. When we proceeded to purge this nest, as we are bound to do under the duties of our office, we endured no little opposition, unheard of in modern times.

Ledrede thus countered the charge of being an interfering, slanderous foreigner, and warned his audience that he would not be deterred from doing his episcopal duty.[39] Both parties then made an insincere rapprochement – Le Poer apologising for having had Ledrede imprisoned, Ledrede saying he forgave him, provided he did not protect and harbour heretics – and the way was open for the bishop to make formal application for Alice's arrest. The authorities' insincerity at least was borne out by their continuing to frustrate this legal process, which allowed Alice to escape to England, where she remained. Her associates, however, were not so blessed with influential friends and were 'one by one openly censured and disgraced', following which they were arrested and imprisoned. Ledrede then hastened back to Kilkenny, went to the various prisons with a large number of clerics, monks, and notables from the city, and examined the prisoners who, perhaps not unsurprisingly, given the circumstances, 'immediately owned up in their presence to all the charges ... and publicly confessed to being guilty of these and many other abominable crimes'.[40]

Now, these individuals are referred to in the *Narrative* as Alice's 'six associate *sortilegi/sortilegae*' and cannot be the same as the eleven named people we have met before, because it was only after the six's arrest and interrogation that Bishop Ledrede wrote to Roger Utlagh, the chancellor, and to Walter de Islip, an official charged with administering the district of Kilkenny, on 6 June 1324, asking them to authorise the arrest of a number of people[41], and here their names are given. Who the six were we do not know, but their testimonies, if we believe them, imply that Ledrede was right in thinking that heresy and magic were rife within his diocese. Yet still some of the authorities in Dublin and Kilkenny prevaricated and sought to deny the bishop his warrant, even though one had been signed and issued by the Justiciar of Ireland, who also agreed to turn up in Kilkenny himself to see its provisions carried out. Encouraged by this, Ledrede summoned William Utlagh to answer charges of heresy, usury, perjury, adultery, and clericide, and when the justiciar finally arrived, the bishop took the opportunity to condemn Alice as a diviner (*sortilega*), magician (*maga*), heretic, and someone who had fallen away from the Faith (*relapsa*),[42] who was to have her goods confiscated and be handed over to the secular arm for due punishment. This implies burning, the ultimate punishment for heresy. (Her activities as diviner and magician exacerbated this greater offence but would not have caused her to be burned had she been caught. The distinction is important.)

William Utlagh, who had been entertaining the Dublin officials in his own house – an example of the factionalism which divided Ireland at this time – eventually presented himself at the bishop's court, where he was accused and convicted of helping heretics and of being a heretic, too. For this he was put in prison. Under pressure, Ledrede agreed to commute this sentence to hearing three Masses a day for a year, giving food to the poor, and restoring the cathedral's roof at his own expense. William, however, failed to abide by this lighter punishment and so was sent back to prison, and this left the bishop free to turn his attention to Alice's confederates who must have been under guard by this time. Of the eleven named individuals, we are told only about Petronilla of Meath, Alice's maid. She had been arrested on the grounds that she was a heretic (*deprehensa quod esset haeretica*)[43], and beaten on six successive occasions with a heavy stick by the bishop on account of her *sortilegia* (*fuit per episcopum fustigata pro sortilegiis*). Davidson and Ward interpret *per episcopum fustigata* as 'whipped on the order of the Bishop', and understand 'whipping' to be the same as torture. Self-evidently, however, they are not, and a *fustis* was not a whip but a cudgel. So, while there can be no doubt that Petronilla was subjected to brutal treatment, that treatment was actually behaviour permitted in law to husbands disciplining their wives, and thus, by extension, to men punishing recalcitrant women for acts of defiance. Gratian's *Decretum* is clear on the point. 'A man may chastise his wife and beat her for her own correction ... The husband is bound to chastise his wife in moderation ... unless he is a cleric, in which case he may chastise her more severely'.[44] Clerical celibacy had been the rule since 1139, but here Ledrede seems to have been acting very much in the spirit of Gratian's decree, and the fact that he did so on six separate occasions suggests that Petronilla was being defiant and refusing to answer his questions.

Eventually, however, she gave in and began to confess a number of crimes, largely of demon worship, divination, and harmful magic, although she started by acknowledging that she had denied the faith of Christ and of the Church in its entirety. This, then, was a confession of apostasy and would have been enough in itself to cause her to be burned as a heretic. It forms part of what was probably the formal text of her confession, read aloud at her execution, for we are told that she confessed 'in the presence of all the [assembled] clerics and laity'. After this principal acknowledgement of apostasy, details of magic followed, with frequent reference to Alice as controller and instigator of the various acts. On three occasions, she said, she had sacrificed on Alice's behalf to demons, and on each occasion dedicated three cockerels at the crossroads outwith Kilkenny to 'Robert, the son of the art' by pouring out their blood and dividing their bodies into pieces. Under Alice's instructions she used these birds' intestines, along with spiders and other black scorpion-like 'worms' (*vermibus*), the herb milfoil, other herbs, and hateful 'worms', the brain of a child who had died before being baptised, and scraps of its clothing, to make a large number of concoctions, *pixides* (thick black liquids similar to pitch), and powders, mixing them together in the skull of a thief who had had his head cut off. These preparations, she said, 'were to cause injuries to the bodies of the faithful, to rouse loves and hatreds, and also, when certain incantations had been added, to make the faces of certain women appear in front of certain people as though they had horns, like those of she-goats'.

Here are four separate magical operations: (i) harming people physically; (ii) stirring up love; (iii) stirring up hatred; (iv) creating an illusion. This suggests that the list of ingredients does not refer to a single occasion, but to several, with different functions in spite of their being lumped together. This may be a deliberate attempt on the part of the recording clerk to make the preparation sound much worse, or is merely the result of the recorder's memory which had latched on to the ingredients but forgotten they were constituents of separate potions and powders. Thus, spiders and pseudo-scorpions suggest poison and so doing physical harm; but milfoil (*Achillea millefolium*) was part of the Mediaeval pharmacopoeia, and was used to staunch blood and help eliminate toxins – not, therefore, a suitable companion for pounded spiders and cockerels' intestines. In spite of its being grammatically linked with 'hateful worms', then, it looks like part of a recipe for curative magic. Body-parts, however, were certainly used in magic intended to manipulate the emotions. *A Summary of the Duty of the Inquisition* in around 1270 said that accused idolaters and workers of harmful magic should be asked 'if they have made anything from the head of a person living or dead, or from their clothes or hair [to achieve] hatred or love'; and in around 1450 a treatise on the Sabbat, *Errores Gazariorum*, noted that witches manufacture an ointment 'from children's fat ... mixed with very poisonous creatures such as snakes, toads, lizards, and spiders', and that 'they make powders with which to kill people. These powders are made from children's guts mixed with the poisonous creatures mentioned above.'[45] As for the faces of women appearing to those who saw them to have horns, we may suggest that some of the 'other herbs' mentioned in the list perhaps had hallucinogenic properties, although in what form these herbs could have been administered we cannot tell. Nor should we confine ourselves to the possibility of hallucinogens, because the Middle Ages were well acquainted with what we should call 'conjuring tricks' and 'illusions', and something of the kind could have been involved here. We lack the information to make any firmly based hypothesis, and should not leap upon the notion of hallucinogenic herbs simply because it appeals to our modern preference for materialist explanations.

Having elicited from Petronilla her account of these ingredients, Ledrede then burned them on a large fire in the centre of Kilkenny. The magical operations for which they were intended were not, apart from the vision of the horned women's heads, unusual. Nor, on the whole, was the remainder of Petronilla's confession. On many occasions, she said, at Alice's urgent insistence she had consulted demons and received answers to her questions, presumably meaning questions put by Alice, and the fact that Alice had to goad Petronilla into doing this suggests some reluctance on Petronilla's part. Sometimes Alice was present, sometimes not. However, the two women had come to an agreement (*ex pacto convenisse*) that Petronilla would act as a go-between (*mediatrix*) when she contacted the demon Robert, Alice's *amicus*. This word means 'friend', but may also mean 'protector, patron', and such is probably the sense which best applies here. 'In public' – that is to say, in front of the clerics and laypeople who had come to hear her make her confession – she said she had seen Robert with her own eyes, a demon with three aspects, namely three black men (*Aithiopes*), each carrying an iron rod.[46] This, of course, is odd. The official charge sheet, if one may call it that, said that Robert appeared on more than one occasion, sometimes as a cat, sometimes as a dog, sometimes as a black man with two companions. The details as recorded in the later part of the *Narrative*, however, lead us to believe he appeared only once – *vidit ubi daemon apparuit*: both verbs are in the perfect tense, implying a single occasion only – although Petronilla may mean this was the only occasion she actually saw him and her mistress having sex. It happened during the daytime, an important point, since it clearly implies that both women were wide awake and that Petronilla was not dreaming or having a half-asleep hallucination. Still, seeing Robert under three aspects, each identical, suggests a distinctive visionary experience, but one which is impossible to explain, because we lack the information necessary to do so.

Having seen the demon have sex with Alice, an action the *Narrative* designates a *tantum scelus*, 'such a great enormity', Petronilla wiped 'the place of foul shamefulness' with a canvas sheet from her own bed. Vision the demon may have seemed to be, but the results appear to have been physical enough or, if not actually physical, sufficiently real to Petronilla to require physical action on her part. The canvas sheet is an odd detail, not because the sheet was made of canvas – this was common enough material for undersheets on Mediaeval beds – but because *kanevicium lecti sui* must refer to a whole sheet and not just a scrap of cloth. Why did Petronilla use a whole sheet to clean up semen stains (since this is clearly what the text is referring to)? Were there no towels or kerchiefs or other small pieces of cloth in the room? It is a detail for which we do not appear to have a reasonable explanation.

Thus far her confessions about demon worship, evocation, and consultation. The *Narrative* then turns to the charge of excommunicating Petronilla's husband[47] 'by lighting wax candles and spitting at various points as their ritual required'. Who is 'their'? The Latin is *eorum*, a plural which may include both men and women, but does not refer to women alone, and, had 'their' referred to Alice and Petronilla, a different word would have been used. So 'their' refers to other people, and one must presume that 'they' were the individuals who made use of this form of what Ledrede calls 'excommunication'. It does look, therefore, as though both Alice and Petronilla belonged to some kind of organisation that had a formal way of excluding from itself named persons who, for whatever reason, had incurred that organisation's displeasure. This 'their', however, can be contrasted with another. Immediately after the details about 'their' ritual of excommunication, the *Narrative* goes on to say that 'although [Petronilla] was an appointed instructress in their cursed trade, she said she was nothing in comparison with her mistress, from whom she had learned all these things and many others'. The words 'their accursed trade', *in arte earum maledicta*, now imply something slightly different. *Earum* refers exclusively to women, so do we understand this to be a scribal mistake for *eorum*, in which case the implied group is the same as that of 'their ritual'; or should the previous *eorum* have been *earum*, in which case the implied group would consist entirely of women; or are two groups involved, one of men and women, the other of women alone? Since both men and women were arrested along with Petronilla, and later suffered a variety of punishments or fates, it is perhaps more plausible to suggest that *earum* is an error, and that therefore a single mixed group is involved here. However, the difficulty does show the problems attendant upon our trying to interpret documents, especially when, as in this case, we have only one extant manuscript, and lack the relevant details prevailing in the contemporary context. Still, if we accept the existence of some kind of organisation to which Petronilla and the others belonged, the next piece of information makes better sense, even though once again the Latin text presents us with a slight problem. Petronilla's designation, 'appointed instructress' (*solennis magistra*), may also be translated as 'instructress of the ceremony'. It depends on whether one takes *solennis* as an adjective or a noun. *Magistra*, too, is a little ambiguous since, although it may mean 'a woman in charge', its most usual meaning refers to a woman who instructs other people in how to do something. One is reminded of a common title given to Satan or the presiding demon at a Sabbat: *magister*, 'teacher' or 'director'. While Satan is clearly in charge of proceedings, records tell us that he actually instructed the attending witches in techniques of further evildoing, and sometimes gave them the means – ointments, powders – to carry these evils into effect. So it seems reasonable to envisage Petronilla as someone who knew how the rituals of magic should be performed and taught others how to do them; and this in turn, with the adjective 'appointed', suggests that she belonged to an organisation with its own hierarchy and complex ways of performing ceremonies and carrying out certain acts.[48]

Petronilla, truthfully or not, continued to put blame on her absent mistress; if she herself was a teacher, she had been taught by Alice. Here the Latin text uses the phrase *quin potius*. This acts as a kind of break in the flow of a narrative, as though someone had asked a question, querying the truth or probability of what had just been said. So we can envisage Ledrede, for example, saying, 'Do you really mean to tell us that your mistress, a wealthy woman of high social standing, taught you these heretical (or magical) procedures?' To which, or to something like it, Petronilla replied that there was no one with greater expertise (*peritior*) in the whole of the King of England's domain, and that it was her opinion that Alice had no equal in the world when it came to her skill (*in arte sua*). Her confession made, execution by burning duly followed. James Grace, a native of Kilkenny who may have had access to extra information, recorded in his *Annales Hiberniae*, written over 200 years after the event, that at the stake Petronilla declared that William Utlagh 'deserved death as much as she did, because for a year and a day he had worn round his naked body the Devil's girdle' (or 'the belt of a devil'). The *Annales Hiberniae* of John Clyn, a contemporary of the events he describes, however, makes no mention of this, which is not to say that Grace simply fabricated it. Curiously enough, one of the accusations laid against the Templars was that they wore next to their skin a belt which had touched the head of their idol, Baphomet. Templars did indeed wear such a belt, which was actually to remind them of their vow of chastity,[49] but one can see how rumour may have picked up the accusation and spread it, in which case, if William had worn some kind of a cord for religious reasons, it would have been easy to misinterpret it in the light of Templar gossip, for the trials were only twelve years old, and knowledge of them, however distorted, could easily have been current.[50] Grace also adds that Alice's goods contained a Host with the name of the Devil (or a devil) written on it, and a small box containing an ointment which she would smear on a coulter and so be transported wherever she wanted. This, of course, was written when stories were well known about how witches would mount broomsticks and fly to a Sabbat, so we may discount the flying-ointment, although it is quite possible that, if she had indeed been a witch, Alice may have retained a consecrated Host for use in magic, as this was by no means uncommon during the fourteenth century. Even later, in 1577, Raphael Holinshed published *Chronicles of England, Scotland, and Ireland* which added further details to the story: that Alice used to sacrifice nine red cockerels and nine peacocks' eyes to her demon Robert, and that 'she swept' – either once or habitually is not made clear – 'the streets of Kilkenny between Compline and twilight, raking all the filth towards the doors of her son William Outlaw [Utlagh], murmuring secretly with herself these words, "To the house of William my son/Hie all the wealth of Kilkenny town".' This may be an interesting illustration of the popular saying, 'Where there's muck, there's brass', but such self-evident twaddle does nothing to illuminate the actual historical case, and, if we are not careful, muddies the water by implying that all the charges laid against Alice and the others were equally silly.

The others suffered various fates. Some were burned, some publicly abjured their heresy, some were beaten as a punishment in the town and marketplace, some were exiled, and some were excommunicated in their absence because they had run away and had not yet been found at the time of the *Narrative*'s being written.[51] It sounds very much as though we are dealing with more than eleven people, unless by 'some' the text means 'one' or 'two'. All, however, are described as heretics and *sortilegi/sortilegae* 'of the well-known disease-bearing fellowship of Robin, son of the art'. *Societas*, 'fellowship, association, community, league, alliance, confederacy', suggests some kind of organisation, however loose, and this underlines Ledrede's conviction that he was dealing with much more than a few individual heretics who also practised magic. The charges against them were serious, much more serious than accusations of occasional fortune-telling, manufacturing love spells or carrying out acts of malefice. That those charges should not be easily dismissed is therefore, I hope, reasonably clear: were they actually melodramatic or incredible? Bernadette Williams has suggested that the description of Sir John le Poer's deteriorating physical condition might owe something to poisoning by substances such as thallium or selenium, which were available in the Middle Ages: 'poisonous magic [*veneficium*] was sometimes difficult to distinguish from deliberate poisoning;'[52] the accusations of demon worship, consultation of demons, love magic, and harmful magic involved nothing people had not been accused of for many a long century; and the charge of heresy, more particularly apostasy, was, as we shall see later, one which could have been, and was, levelled at many of the Irish during this period. Waldensians and Cathars, to name only two of the more prominent heresies of the time, were causing great stir in the Church, which sometimes identified them as, in effect, worshippers of Satan. So Ledrede was not unjustified in fearing heretic groups, and while actual Satan-worshipping groups many not have existed, heresy and organised heretical associations and networks certainly did.[53]

So the charge of heresy which was laid against Alice, Petronilla, and William Utlagh may not have been untrue. Denying the Faith as taught by the Church, and refusing to go to church or take Communion were undoubtedly marks of a heretic, as was Petronilla's refusal of the sacrament of penance at her execution. Since she had already made a public confession of her apostasy and trafficking with a demon, her refusal to make a private or semi-private confession to a priest when death stared her in the face does not make sense, unless she refused for reasons of religious conviction – that is, reasons which obviously did not come within the Church's teaching on the subject. Notice, too, that neither Alice nor Petronilla was condemned as a heretic *because* she practised magic. They were condemned as heretics *and* they practised magic, a somewhat different situation; and although it may seem that John Clyn lays stress on the *sortilegium* when he records that she was burned for this and for offering sacrifice to demons, he goes straight on to say that 'before her, even in olden days, it was neither seen nor heard of that anyone suffered the penalty of death *for heresy*'.[54] Much of this, of course, depends on how much faith one is willing to put in the validity of the confessions and the record of the whole episode. The *Narrative* was written either by Ledrede or by one of his supporters, and is therefore a partisan document. Nevertheless, unless one is going to take the radical and unwarranted step of dismissing it as an entire fiction, one is obliged to read it, however cautiously, as an account of genuine events and genuine opinions. The accusations made therein would be meaningless, of course, if people in general did not believe that magic was an activity based upon access to real greater-than-human power, that individuals were capable not only of accessing that power but of using it successfully, and that the people against whom such practices were alleged were indeed capable of being guilty. Malice, to be sure, might well play a part – motives for making these accusations were rarely simple – and even a hundred years or so later, the Archbishop of Armagh was complaining that it was all too easy to harm someone of importance by accusing him of practising magic, the charges being 'the subtle malice and malicious suits of certain persons slandering a man of rank … ruining or destroying any man by sorcery or necromancy'.[55] Perfectly true. We have seen examples earlier of accusations of attempts to use magic for political purposes, and the English court itself continued to use them, for in 1330 the younger brother of the late King Edward II was executed for political reasons intentionally made worse by the accusation that he had consulted a friar who had conjured a demon for him so that he could find out whether King Edward was really dead or not.[56]

Whatever the motives in our Irish case, then – and as far as Alice is concerned there can be no doubt that financial envy may have given rise to familial and social enmity – fear of the magician was a genuine emotion to be tapped and raised against the accused, perhaps cynically, but more likely (in view of the prevalence of magic among all social classes) not. We should also bear in mind that if people had wanted to destroy Alice, proven accusations of apostasy and heresy would have been enough to do it. If she had been a genuine apostate, as it seems Petronilla was, she would have been broken socially and therefore financially, which would have been her accusers' aim. Allegations of demon worship, divination, and practising magic merely made things worse. They would almost certainly not have brought her to the stake or financial ruin by themselves, for under English legal usage, which was the system prevalent in Ireland at the time, witchcraft, as Davidson and Ward remark, 'was a commonplace accusation and was usually treated as a petty offence'.[57] Ledrede, too, it is clear was motivated by hatred of heresy rather than magic.[58] Indeed, he made himself a positive nuisance by seeing heresy everywhere. Yet in around 1331 the Justiciar and Council of Ireland, on behalf of the Dean and Chapter of Dublin Cathedral, wrote to Pope John XXII, asking for his immediate support, because Ireland was awash with heresy and sacrilege of the most violent sort; and even if the justiciar and council exaggerated somewhat – but again, they may not have done – Ledrede manifestly cannot be charged with personal oversensitivity to the local situation.[59]

The importance of Alice Kyteler's case in the history of witchcraft, then, rests, if John Clyn is correct in his *Annales Hiberniae*, partly on the fact that Petronilla's execution for heresy was the first of its kind in the country; partly upon the implicit link between heresy and magic, a link which had not yet grown sufficiently elsewhere to form the basis for the developed theory of diabolical witchcraft; partly upon the possible revelation, dark and obscure, that there may have been some kind of heretical group in Dublin to which she and several others, including her son, belonged; and partly that she engaged at least once in sex with a demon, whom she also used as a source of information, the sexual allegation once again not yet being common in cases of this kind. So what this case provides is an Irish illustration of the problems that were troubling Pope John XXII, partly in the relatively new link being made between heresy and magic, and partly in the further link between these and the invocation of demons, to all of which the Holy Father drew attention in 1318 and again in 1320, culminating in his Bull of 1326.[60] However, conjuring demons, as Petronilla's case makes clear, was not a piece of magic restricted to the clergy, and many others appear to have practised it, not always with Petronilla's apparent success. In 1337, a manor court at Hatfield in Yorkshire heard the case of two local men who, like Alice and Petronilla, seem to have had a contract.

> Robert de Roderham and John de Ithen for that he had not kept the agreement made between them, and therefore complains that on a certain day and year, at Thorne, there was an agreement between the aforesaid Robert and John whereby the said John sold to the said Robert, the Devil, bound in a certain bond, for three pence halfpenny, and thereupon the said Robert delivered to the said John, one halfpenny, as arles, by which the property of the said Devil rested in the person of the said Robert, to have livery of the said Devil on the fourth day next following; at which day the said Robert came to the forenamed John, and asked delivery of the said Devil according to the agreement between them made. But the said John refused to deliver the said Devil, nor has he yet done it, etc., to the great damage of the said Robert to the amount of lx shillings, and he has therefore brought his suit, etc. The said John came, etc., and did not deny the said agreement; and because it appeared to the court that such a suit ought not to subsist among Christians, the aforesaid parties are therefore adjourned to the infernal regions, there to hear their judgement.[61]

The court's humour seems to suggest it did not take the men seriously, but this may well be because it knew the two men well and understood the circumstances of the situation, vital parts of the context missing to us. More grave was the case of a carpenter who was said to have been the Devil's servant (or a devil's servant) for fifteen years, in return for excelling any other carpenter in his craft. Having foreknowledge of his own death (which sounds rather as though he had made what would later be called a diabolical pact destined to run for a fixed term only), he asked his fellow workmen not to let him do anything that would hurt any of them. They said they would do everything they could, and put him in an empty room to get some sleep. However, not long afterwards they came back, roused by his shouting, and when they entered the room they found him with his guts hanging out of his stomach. Pushing them back in, the men sent for his neighbours and a priest, and he was able to make his confession and receive Communion before he died.[62] If true, his story reminds us of later individuals, some of them witches, who thought the Devil was urging them to kill themselves: as, for example, Agnes Cairns from Kirkcudbright, who met Satan when she was still a child, and later became his servant. Arrested and imprisoned with other witches, she told the examining magistrates that 'Satan came to her while she was in prison, held in a room just above Helen Hare, on the night Helen committed suicide, and told her he had just strangled Helen and would do the same for her, if she wished'.[63]

The source of the anecdote anent the carpenter, John of Reading, was particularly keen to record wonders of every kind. 'His pages are besprinkled,' writes his editor, 'with marvels and portents, eclipses and northern lights, blood-coloured crosses in the sky, airy visions of phantom armies locked in combat, second crops of roses, duels of eagles, and battles of sparrows.' The Devil (or a devil), too, appeared at or in the monastery of Reading in the form of a misshapen man – hardly surprising, says John, because of the frivolity of the English in running after foreign fashions.[64] In this, however, John was little different from other clerical writers – he himself seems to have been a monk of Westminster – and had good excuse to be depressed at the state of the country and the world, since he was living through and writing not long after the Black Death of 1348. His story rings true in at least some of its details. The man's seppuku may be an unusual way for a Westerner to commit suicide, but if he had a knife and no rope, and was in a highly disturbed mental state – as clearly he was – hanging was not available as a means of death. We have no idea why he was so disturbed, unless we accept that he had indeed been occupied in ritual magic for many years, and that the occupation of evoking spirits had gradually unsettled his mental and emotional equilibrium. He was certainly not the only working man to have tried his hand at this type of magic, for in 1371 a man was tried by the Court of King's Bench for possessing a grimoire and a skull, but was released on his promise to pay the expenses of having these items burned, and not to practise magic in future.[65]

Concern over the connection between magic and demons, however, had not yet become an overriding preoccupation of the authorities, and we find that a majority of cases in the second half of the fourteenth century involved simpler techniques and far less sinister means. The most notorious involved Alice Perrers, the king's mistress. According to the writer of the *Chronicon Angliae*, a cleric violently hostile to her, she had formed an alliance with a Dominican friar, described as a *magus* ('magician'), and controlled the king as absolutely as she did because the friar had made two waxen images – one of the king, the other of herself – which he empowered by means of incantations and the juices of powerful herbs, and two rings 'of forgetfulness and memory' for the king, which caused him to forget his wife (dead since 1369) and remember only Alice. However, in 1376, a year when the state's accumulated dissatisfaction with Edward's governance burst out in Parliament, the friar was arrested. Two knights from the shires went to him in disguise and asked him where they could find someone to cure illnesses. They had brought urine samples with them, and at the sight of the bottles the friar thought there was money to be made. So he told the knights he was the physician they were looking for, and promised to provide them with a remedy. He must have said or done something else, because the knights then arrested him. The whole episode was obviously a sting, but physicians regularly looked at urine as part of their standard diagnosis, so the knights' bottles alone cannot have been enough to cause him to be arrested on charges of illicit magic. While they were leading him away, a female servant asked him sarcastically why he had not seen it coming, since he made a habit of foretelling the future for other people, after which he was taken and interrogated by the Duke of Lancaster and other magnates. He wasted their time throughout the day, however, by giving silly answers to their questions, and so many of the committee wanted to have him burned. From this he was rescued, with difficulty, by the Archbishop of Canterbury, who was patron of the Dominican order in England, and almost certainly did not want to see a cleric subjected to any rough or prejudiced justice. So he handed the man over to the custody of his brethren and they kept him in close confinement, for how long we do not know.[66]

Equally lenient in their fashion were the mayor and aldermen of London, who heard a number of cases involving magical thief-detection in 1382. In March that year, Henry Pot, a German, pleaded guilty to deceiving Simon Gardiner, who had recently lost a valuable cup. Henry came to him – an interesting observation, as it suggests he had caught rumour of the loss and decided to get a little business for himself – and promised to discover who had stolen it. To do this, he made thirty-two balls of white clay and enchanted them (presumably by incantation of some kind), after which he was able to say that Christina, wife of Nicholas Freeman, was the thief. Taken to court for slander, Henry admitted his guilt and acknowledged 'that he had many times before practised divers sorceries, both within the city and without, through which various persons had undeservedly suffered injury in their character and good name'. The court therefore sentenced him to stand in the pillory for one daylight hour. Its grounds are interesting: not simply that Henry was a slanderer, but that 'sorcery or the magical art manifestly redounds against the doctrine of Sacred Writ'. This, then, was more important than his slander. Notice, too, that the deceit and falsehood of the case lie in Henry's accusing the wrong person – in other words, his incompetence in magic – not in the magic he is employing. This is made clear partly because of similar cases heard by that same court in October 1382 and March 1390, for in the latter year the council of the Duke of York approached one John Berkyng and asked him to discover who had stolen two of the duke's silver dishes and where they were now. Once again the wrong person was accused and the magician duly punished, but notice that individuals with a reputation for this kind of magic were approached by high persons as well as those low in society, and asked to exercise their skill.

Confidence in the validity of those skills, therefore, appears to have been undiminished by cases where their employment was unsuccessful, or even by the occasional self-evident fraud, as in a case from December 1382. Alice, wife of Andrew Trig, had recently had a headscarf stolen from her house, and another Alice, wife of John Byntham, was accused. Mrs Byntham then went to William Northampton, a cobbler, asked him to exonerate her, and told him certain private information which would convince Mrs Trig that he had special (that is, magical) powers of perception. This information is described as consisting of *condiciones* and *intersigna*, somewhat vague terms which seem to refer to certain circumstances and some kind of tokens (marks on the body usually unseen by strangers?) peculiar to Mrs Trig. William duly went to Mrs Trig, impressed her with his 'knowledge', and then told her that Mrs Byntham was innocent of the theft. For good measure he also added 'that she herself would be drowned within a month from that time', a revelation she believed, 'seeing that he had told her divers secret matters as to her own private affairs, [and so] she fell into such extreme melancholy that she had nearly died of grief'. This over-egging of his mission probably led to a complaint about his behaviour and hence to his downfall. Nevertheless, the incident shows that it was possible for someone simply to pretend to be a magician and be taken seriously.[67]

Magic, in a word, was everywhere, even upon the scaffold, for in 1388 Sir Robert Tresilian, executed for treason in February that year, when stripped naked by the executioner was found to be wearing amulets consisting of *experimenta* and *signa*, that is to say strips of parchment bearing words and drawings, some astrological (*ad modum caracterum celi*), some demonic (*unum caput demonis*, and *plura nomina demonum*).[68] Where in all this, one may ask, is the witch? The answer is partly that during this period witches were as likely to be men as women, and partly that the concept 'witch', as understood by later centuries, had not yet been formulated. Many of the practitioners we have been discussing were men, magic in the thirteenth and fourteenth centuries was frequently in the hands of clerics, and, when laypeople were involved, a majority of those who found themselves in court were men and therefore appeared in the historical record. Even so, women did appear in court every so often, having been slandered as witches. Dionysia Baldwin, the municipal court of Exeter was informed in 1302, used to entertain John of Wormhill, Agnes his wife, and Joan the Cornish woman from Teignmouth, 'who are witches and enchanters'; and in the same year before the same court Reginald Kene complained that John Mody

on Wednesday in the feast of St Peter-ad-Vincula [*1 August*] attacked him and his wife Juliana, calling her a wicked witch and thief, and charging her with having surreptitiously taken the thread of the women and good men of the city, and sold it, and of gaining a living in this manner,

in addition to which Kene accused both John and Juliana of other 'enormities'.[69] In real life, this tended to be the extent of legal complaints against women in connection with the practice of magic, although it is true that it was women who tended to be accused of making men impotent through magic. In literature, on the other hand, we deal with queens, wicked stepmothers, and fairies, such as the various incarnations of

Morgan le Fay, or Dame Ragnell, in the *Wedding of Sir Gawain and Dame Ragnell*, who complained, 'I was shaped by necromancy with my stepmother,' or Queen Braunden in *William of Palerne*, of whom the author says:

> But certainly that lady in youth had learned much shame,
> For all the work of witchcraft well enough she knew,
> Nor had she more of necromancy to learn,
> Of cunning of witchcraft well enough she knew.[70]

These creations specialise in shape-changing, such as turning a man into a werewolf, which is what Queen Braunden does to the hero of her romance, before being forced to use her magic to change him back again. However, her powers, and those of her literary compeers, have nothing to do with denial or perversion of the Faith, and in the real world, as in that of theological speculation, the full-blown female heretic worker of harmful magic, in spite of Alice Kyteler and Petronilla, was yet to emerge, even though she might be lurking in the wings. The Church, however, found herself in something of a quandary. She hesitated to acknowledge that the witch had genuine powers of any kind, of course, because the consequences would be dire, but while she firmly dismissed magical beliefs and practices as mere superstitions, as though they were childish and silly, she also threatened believers and practitioners with excommunication, a forcible penalty reserved for grave offences. This swithering one can glimpse in the anonymous preaching manual, *Fasciculus Morum*.

> What a deplorable thing it is these days that men as well as women attack the Faith and set themselves against it, while the Devil spurs them on, and, against God's ordinance and that of the Church, attribute to created things what most properly belongs to God, the creator of everything: namely, how to know and predict future events, and how to lay on and remove health and sickness by means of dissembling incantations. To this kind belong enchanters [incantatores], in English 'tilsters',[71] who carry out their trade with words and promise health with their chanted spells and other irksome things. For example, when someone's stomach is weighed down and made ill with too much food and drink, they say, 'His mother's fallen down', and then they have to fetch some wretched elderly woman who has been trained in this kind of practice, so that she can rub his stomach and sides. Often this does more harm than good, especially in the spiritual sense, because techniques of this kind are forbidden, and consequently in such cases one has to consider whether or not the outcomes of this kind of thing appear to have a natural cause – because if they don't, it follows they belong to a skill demonic [in origin] ... All this is false, delusive, and superstitious ... According to every Catholic scholar, these things and every single one of this kind of thing are cursed by God and His holy Church four times a year.[72]

Obviously, although the preacher does not say so – perhaps because he had no need – the woman coming to cure the bloated stomach must have done more than merely rub the person's belly and sides, otherwise there would have been nothing for the preacher to condemn, or for his audience to be wary of. Some kind of accompanying whispered or silent charm was clearly taken for granted. Why is the woman picked out as 'elderly'? Because when one asks for magical treatment, an experienced performer rather than a novice is preferable. The congregation who heard these sentiments, then, would certainly have gathered that the Church disapproved of those hundred and one little words and actions with which people sought to resolve a problem or smooth away thorns; but they may have been somewhat puzzled by the frequent presence of clergymen among those who offended in this fashion and found themselves in court. For if all magic, no matter how trivial, was wrong, why would a priest or a monk or a friar be so often arrested and tried by the bishop for helping his flock in ways they both approved and understood?

2

'SORCERY' AND TREASON:
1401–1499

In 1406 Henry IV was sufficiently disturbed by reports that Lincolnshire was rife with undesirable practitioners of magic to order the Bishop of Lincoln to root them out. 'We are given to understand', he wrote,

> that there are in your diocese a good many *sortilegi*, magicians [*magici*], chanters of spells [*incantatores*] necromancers [*nigromantici*], diviners [*divinatores*], demon worshippers [*arioli*], and fortune-tellers [*phitones*] who carry out all kinds of dreadful and hateful things every day, and cause a large number of our people within the said diocese to be destroyed and slandered by means of their wicked practices.[1]

This list of occult workers gives us an idea of the variety of such people operating in what is likely to have been more or less every parish in the country, for there is no reason to suppose that Lincolnshire was uniquely endowed with them. *Arioli* were originally classed as diviners, since their name is connected with the Greek word for entrails, and their association with pagan sacrifice, which one finds in St Isidore (*Etymologies* 8.9.16), accounts for the link between them and demon worship. *Phitones* were a little different, but still associated with demons. While St Paul and Silas were going to pray in Philippi, they met 'a girl who had a spirit of divination [*spiritum pythonem*] and brought her owner a great deal of money by telling fortunes [*divinando*]'.[2] In other words, she had control of a spirit, or allowed herself to be taken over temporarily by a spirit, which enabled her to answer questions about the future, rather like the so-called 'witch of Endor', called *mulier pythonem habens* ('a woman having a spirit for divination') in 1 Kings 28.8 (Vulgate), who was able to command this spirit to take on the likeness of the dead prophet Samuel in response to King Saul's command.

While demons were never far away from the minds of those who used these various Latin terms, the writers were also aware that the words could not simply be lumped together as though they were a bran tub of synonyms from which one could pick out an expression or two at random. It will have been noticed that so far I have tended to be sparing in my use of the words 'witchcraft' and 'witch', and that I have preferred to reproduce the Latin words *sortilegium*, *sortilegi*, and *sortilegae* instead. The reason is that, until our sources start appearing in the vernacular instead of in Latin, we are dependent on a variety of Latin terms to describe magical workers who, as we have seen, practised a wide range of occult activities. Latin takes this diversity into account with its vocabulary; English, with 'witch, sorcerer, sorceress' does not. Language, of course, especially spoken language and the records of the spoken language, is changeable, and one cannot expect Latin terminology for workers of magic to remain entirely static. Nevertheless, given that most magical workers were prepared to undertake several different kinds of magic – divination, evocation of demons, spells of love, hatred, or cure, acts of maleficent intention, image magic, control of the weather – and given that Latin can provide a separate word for each of these, it is not surprising to find that, when an author writing in Latin uses one term rather than another for the person whose activities he is describing, he may well have a distinct meaning in mind, or if not narrowly distinct, a meaning at least related to the Latin root that produced the word. I have already pointed out, for example, that *sortilegium*, which is sometimes translated as 'sorcery', refers principally to the process of foretelling the future by casting lots [*sortes*], and indeed 'sorcery' itself is derived from the Latin *sortiarius* meaning 'someone who casts lots with a view to predicting future events'. The linguistic situation is complicated, however, by early English usage. Galfridus's dictionary for children, the earliest English–Latin dictionary we have, produced in around 1440, translates *wycch* as 'magus', sortelegus (masc.), 'sortilaga' (fem.), and *wycch-crafte* as 'sortilegium', 'fascinum'.[3] Still, this serves to show that English subsumed the variety of Latin under a couple of related terms. It does not mean that the various Latin words were synonymous, nor does it give us licence to translate them all by 'witch' or 'witchcraft'. These days especially, 'witch' and 'witchcraft' have connotations the earlier English words did not, and in any case, those who used Latin to record events and actions, and employed it in their own professional lives, were bound to be at least partly alive to the differences between the Latin terms they were using. Translating them now, therefore, poses difficulties, and suggests that we too should be aware of their possible implications.

So in 1417, we have John Smith, a *sortilegus*, being tried before the episcopal court in Sleaford. He was uncovered during inquiries into the activities of heretics and their supporters in the diocese of Lincoln, and the record makes his particular offences clear.

He, against and contrary to the written testimony of the Old and New Testament and the correct decision of holy Mother Church, in and within the diocese of Lincoln, both in public and in private had practised the art of necromancy, divination [*sortilegium*], illicit and prohibited conjurations, and the invocation of wicked spirits along with pieces of bread prepared for this purpose; and especially when the parish church of Buckworth in the said diocese had been plundered in predatory fashion by certain degenerate sons of the most holy church, this same John exercised his criminal skill and publicly slandered one Roger Butcher from Buckworth in respect of this predatory plundering, alleging that the said Roger had plundered and despoiled the said church. In consequence of this allegation, Roger was arrested, put in prison, and reduced practically to nothing.

This, however, was not the full extent of John's culpability, for the notification of this incident, sent to the Archbishop of Canterbury, gives further detail.

In addition, this same John has said within the diocese, and both publicly and privately asserted and maintained that it is lawful to make use of conjurations and divination [*sortilegium*] because St Peter and St Paul did so.

As a result of his public notoriety and the information laid against him, John was brought in front of the bishop's court, where he acknowledged what he had done.

He confessed that he performed conjurations and divination [*sortilegium*] of this kind in the foresaid manner, but only on the occasion of the plundering and spoliation of the said Buckworth church; and he further confessed and publicly acknowledged that after he had performed his conjurations and divination [*sortilegium*], he found quite clearly through the conjurations and divination [*sortilegium*] he performed that the said Roger Butcher plundered and despoiled the said Buckworth church.

Asked whether he had said publicly that such conjurations and divination were licit, he answered he had, because he had been told so by one William Fyllyman from Alconbury. Now, however, being better informed, he acknowledged his faults and wrongdoing and so had his sentence of excommunication lifted from him. Nevertheless, he was told he would be kept in prison until the next convocation in Canterbury.[4]

Necromancy, *sortilegium*, conjurations, and invocation of spirits, then, provide a list of John's activities, all of which he said he believed were acceptable. Since his object was simply to uncover the identity of a thief, one may suspect that the record was perhaps listing the various possible ways in which this could be done, rather than telling us that John had actually tried them all for this single purpose. Ritual summoning of the dead does seem an unlikely recourse in these circumstances, but conjuring and invoking spirits by means of specially prepared bread sounds rather like a practice condemned by the Bishop of London in 1311.

We have been given to understand that in order to recover things which have been lost, and to inquire more fully into the hidden things of the future and the past, people make use of conjurations and divinations [*divinationibus*], some of them via combination of the practice of magic and a knowledge of incantations, some of them because they are simple-minded, excessively credulous, empty-headed and self-indulgent. They hold meetings in secret, construct circles as though for the invocation of demons, and invoke them by means of pieces of bread [*panes*] and spinning knives [*cultellos volubiles*].[5]

Where, then, does this leave the *sortilegium*? The record links 'conjurations' and *sortilegium* several times as a self-contained phrase, so we should probably understand the *sortilegium* as referring to the divinatory part of the ritual, reading which way the handles of the knives stuck in the bread were pointing, as an indication either of where the thief was to be found or, if names were uttered, of the identity of said thief, at whose name the knives stopped moving. A similar instance occurred in August 1426 when a commission was issued to the authorities in Somerset because Ralph Botreaux, a knight, and William Langkelly, a yeoman, along with 'other malefactors of their coven [*group of associates*] and assent' had hired John Alwood, Hugh Bowett, a chaplain, and John Newport, 'who are said to practise soothsaying, necromancy, and the art of magic', to cause William Botreaux to fall ill and die: apparently a family dispute in which the son tried to kill his father, or a brother his brother, by magical means. Once again, 'soothsaying' – looking into the future – is separated from the other two forms of magic, and one is therefore inclined to treat it as a distinct operation, not merely a superfluous synonym of both or either. It is also reasonable to suppose that the three arts mentioned represent the range of the trio's magical activities. (The coincidence of there being three occult arts and three named practitioners does not imply the men each had only one speciality. Had that been so, the record would have been worded differently.)[6] Looking into the future at the beginning of the fifteenth century, however, was not a simple or harmless act, for it could easily be regarded as a political offence; and since practitioners of magic were not merely *sortilegi* or *sortilegae*, but persons liable to practise other forms of magic as well, including those which did or were intended to do harm, a 'soothsayer' might find him- or herself subjected to arrest and investigation by nervous authorities. Something of the kind surely accounts for the arrest and imprisonment in the Tower of London of John Kyme, described in the record as a soothsayer, and apprehended and jailed on the orders of Richard II himself. The record of Kyme's release is dated 15 October 1401, but as King Richard had been deposed in 1399 and murdered in 1400, it means Kyme had suffered a lengthier internment than he might have done had political upheavals in the capital not been so dramatic during the intervening year or so.[7]

'Necromancy' is another term whose meaning is not altogether easy to pin down. Originating in the Greek *nekros* and *manteia*, 'corpse prediction', necromancy involved summoning up the spirit or reanimated body of a dead person with a view to receiving answers to questions about the afterlife and the future, and this was still the meaning recognised by St Isidore of Seville in his *Etymologies* (8.9.11). However, Christian theology was not happy with the notion that the dead might be brought back to life by human intervention (even though the concept of the *vrycolax*, the animated corpse causing havoc in the locality of its previous life, was well known and widespread during the Middle Ages), and so the theory of demonic deception grew, to account for apparent successes by magicians of this sort. Even St Isidore included this idea in his definition. 'The blood of a corpse is applied for the interrogation, for demons are said to love blood; and for this reason, whenever necromancy is practised, gore is mixed with water so that they are called more easily by the gore of the blood' (8.9.11). Hence 'necromancy' came to imply the deliberate invocation of demonic agencies, and while this was principally the specialisation of clerics because of the elaborate ritual frequently used in summoning the spirits, it was not confined to them, and hence anyone might find himself – overwhelmingly these magicians were men – accused of necromancy along with other forms of occult or magical practice.[8] Benedek Láng perceives three possible uses of the word: (i) 'a rhetorical designation of something illicit, harmful, and rejected'; (ii) a 'demonic subtype of ritual magic, or even certain demonic practices of image magic'; (iii) 'the science dealing with all the things that are hidden from the senses or from the intellect, the functioning of which most people do not understand'.[9] As Láng points out, however, this third definition is based upon a passage in *Picatrix*, a manual of image magic translated into Latin during the thirteenth century. So for all practical purposes 'necromancy' should be taken either as an emotive term implying forbidden and therefore presumably demonically assisted magic, or a form of ritually elaborate divination which calls upon the dead, or demons in the form of the dead.[10]

We can see these definitions at work in episodes involving the highest authorities. On 25 September 1419, for example, the Archbishop of Canterbury, who had received the report on John Smith two years previously, wrote to all English bishops that the life of Henry V was being threatened *superstitiosis necromanticorum operationibus* ('by the heathenish rituals of necromancers'), and ordered that prayers be said and processions (of the Blessed Sacrament) held every Wednesday and Saturday to counter these rituals.

> The clergy and people should pour out their prayers to God especially for him, so that in response to their devout prayers the Father, dispenser of mercies and every goodness and grace, aroused [thereby] in His very great mercy, may deign to preserve, watch over, and protect him from all the abominable, malicious, and injurious designs of his enemies, and from the heathenish rituals of necromancers, especially such as have recently been contrived by several persons (it is said) for his destruction and overthrow.[11]

This request for prayers, which was said to have come originally from the king, is likely to have been the result of the regency council's foreknowledge of a supposed plot against him, details of which burst out only two days later when the council deprived Dowager Queen Joan of her dowry and possessions, and then, four days after that, arrested her and had her confined (though comfortably) in one of the royal manor houses in Surrey. The ostensible reason for this was that she was accused of plotting to kill the king, her stepson. As a contemporary chronicle explained, 'This same year Friar Randolph, a Master of Divinity, who used to be Queen Joan's confessor, made plans, at the instigation of the foresaid queen, to destroy the king by sorcery and necromancy [nygromancie].'[12] Two other male members of her household were implicated, so here perhaps we have an explanation for the plural 'necromancers' in the archbishop's ordinance. There can be little doubt that, as has often been said, Henry's shortage of money to fund his wars in France, a shortage felt acutely in 1419, caused the regency council to lay its hands on the queen's extensive wealth, and the fact that she was not charged with treason – the natural concomitant of suborning necromancers to do away with the monarch – suggests that neither Henry nor his regent took the accusation seriously. On the other hand, it may have been lent a certain colour by the fact that her father, the King of Navarre (known as 'Charles the Bad'), had had the reputation of being a magician, or at the very least someone actively interested in magic. The future Charles V of France accused him in 1358 of using ritual magic against him, since Navarre himself had a collection of talismans, and his personal physician had been found with rings, powders, and other *instrumenta* interpreted as magical.[13] Randolph fared less well. He remained at liberty for a while, eluding capture, but was eventually arrested in Guernsey, taken to Mantes to be examined by the king, and then returned to London where he was imprisoned in the Tower. There he lived for another ten years before meeting a violent end.

Round about the Feast of St Barnabas [*11 June*], the sun glowed hot upon the spirit of a priest, a man full of rage, who was living in the Tower of London. Goaded by this rage, he killed Brother Randolph, a Franciscan, a Professor of Sacred Theology, and (it was believed) a necromancer [*nigromanticum*]. He killed him with a large stone and afterwards kept beating his head with an axe, with the result that he breathed his last. The [priest] hid his body under excrement and sand.[14]

The implication of 'necromancer' in this episode seems to be that Randolph was, perhaps among other things, a ritual magician who called upon demons to fulfil his commands and intentions. Certainly his being a cleric serves to suggest that this type of magic may have been his special interest or talent. When we reach the reign of Henry VI, however, we find the term *maleficae* ('female workers of harmful magic', i.e. 'witches') used in a text relating to yet another treasonable moment. 'Round about Christmas this year [*1430*], certain witches, seven in number, from various parts of the kingdom, were arrested in London and imprisoned in the Fleet. They had devised the destruction of the King.'[15] Since Henry VI was only eight at the time, this seems a little harsh, but it was not the first time this had happened, for in the previous year 'a group of knights, gentlemen, and clerics, plus a housewife, Agnes Burgate of Exeter, were accused of placing a wax image of a small boy, representing Henry VI, to burn on a spit of alder, so as to weaken the King's body and cause his death'.[16] Now, it is interesting to note that the magical operators of 1430 were women – so far, as we have seen, the majority of those reaching the records have been men, and many of those clerics – because women's magic seems largely to have been that of the home, the workplace, and the immediate neighbourhood. To have women other than noble instigators or wealthy practitioners stepping into the field of national politics is therefore noteworthy. So too is the information that these seven from various parts of the kingdom were arrested in London. Had they converged there after being sent for? If so, who had sent for them? Or were they pilgrims, travellers, or women newly arrived in the city to look for work? Or were they London residents who happened to have been born elsewhere? The *Annales* give us no further clue, but if it is true they had been plotting the king's death, it seems odd that seven disparate women should have had the same idea and indeed, even if they were Londoners, it appears likely they lived in the same area or parish and therefore knew each other, otherwise the 'disparate' objection would still apply. On the other hand, had they been commissioned by some person or persons not mentioned in the record, we can see that, while they could have been contacted as a group, they could also have been suborned individually by more than one employer; and actually this last makes better sense, since it is not altogether likely that something as serious as murderous treason would have remained in the hands of a single disaffected individual, as is illustrated by the plots of 1419 and 1429.

The early 1430s seem to have been years in which female magicians seized the notice of chroniclers. On 23 May 1430 St Jeanne d'Arc was captured by the English and put on trial the following January, the charges against her including that of being a woman trained in various forms of magic. 'When she was young,' said her trial record,

> This Joan was not taught or instructed in the belief or the basic tenets of the Faith, but was habituated to and steeped in the use of sorceries [*sortilegiis*], divinations, and other superstitious practices or magical arts by some older women. Many of the inhabitants of the villages [in the area] were well known of old to use the foresaid acts of harmful magic [*maleficiis*].[17]

Here *sortilegia* are differentiated from divinations and other magical arts, as they are also in a résumé of the summons from the Bishop of Beauvais, which talks of 'sorceries, idolatries, invocation of evil spirits, and many other instances touching and opposed to our Faith'; so it is difficult to tell now as these texts proceed whether *sortilegium* is beginning to shift its centre of meaning from 'a form of divination' to 'a genre of magical practice', and is being used with consciousness of its meaning and implication, or whether some writers at any rate are merely throwing it into the mix as an emotive term, like 'necromancy', without considering its original and distinctive sense. What we cannot do, however, is translate it as 'witchcraft' *tout court*, since it had not yet attained that particular set of associations.

In November 1430 the role of the female practitioner was further emphasised by the arrest and imprisonment of Margery Jourdemayne, the so-called 'Witch of Eye', in Windsor Castle. She was kept under guard until May 1432 when she and two clerics were brought to Westminster and examined on a charge of 'sorcery', which is how the record describes it: '*De sortilegiis cancellario deliberandis*' (acts of *sortilegium* to be considered by the Chancellor).

> On 9 May 1432 Margery Jourdemayne, John Vitley, a cleric, and Brother John Ashwell of the Order of Crutched Friars in London, recently imprisoned in [Windsor] castle for *sorcerye*, were brought before the King's Council in Westminster and there, by order of their lordships, discharged upon custody.[18]

Margery's discharge, however, was conditional upon her not practising magic arts again, 'using no sorcery nor witchcraft', as the *Close Rolls* express it. Sorcery is here distinguished from witchcraft. Is this merely an example of lawyers' verbosity, or are we to understand that Margery practised some form of divination as well as what was seen as harmful magic, in which case the *sortilegium* will refer to that? The practices most closely associated with her were actually love- and fertility-magic. After she had been arrested for a second time, in 1441, one of the charges against her alleged that for a long time 'by her sorcerie and wicchecraft' she had supplied Eleanor Cobham, who hoped to become Duchess of Gloucester, with 'medicines' and drinks intended to force the Duke to fall in love with her and marry her – which he duly did. A second charge related to a wax image of the king. The prosecution maintained that Eleanor had had it made by Margery and others with a view to bringing about the king's death. Eleanor, on the other hand, said its object was to help her become pregnant by her husband.[19]

Now, it seems to have been true that she and the duke were having problems with fertility. His doctor wrote to him, 'Your loins and genitals are being weakened by the unrestrained frequency of your love-making, as the wateriness and scarcity of your semen indicate,' and he urged the duke to alter his diet, adding,

> Take great care never to try to please any woman at the climax of the act of love because, as the Book of Proverbs and the teachings of [natural] philosophers tell us, it is not possible for any man to satisfy the appetite of a strong, healthy, virile woman at the climax of that act.[20]

This appears to tell us almost as much about Eleanor as it does her husband, but one cannot help thinking that the details of the wax image are important. Was it that of a child, as one might expect in fertility-magic, or did it look older? More importantly, did the conspirators intend to roast it at a fire, as the 1429 plotters had done, in which case there would have been no question of its being a fertility figure? Had its age been indeterminate and its substance undiminished, perhaps there was no way of telling. Wax images, indeed, could be ambiguous artefacts. When Richard Wyche, a Lollard, was burned on Tower Hill in 1440, people started coming to the spot at night and praying, as though to a saint, and brought with them offerings of money and wax images. This sounds as though they attributed miraculous cures to him and were bringing wax figures of the parts of their body which had suffered and were now cured, a common practice at shrines of the saints.[21] As always, however, context is paramount, and Margery's and Eleanor's wax image was firmly situated in that of some kind of magic. The likelihood of its being fertility-magic was not high, either, because, in spite of Margery's apparent skill in that form of the art, her associates – Roger Bolingbroke, clerk to the duchess herself, John Home, one-time secretary of both the duke and duchess, and Thomas Southwell, a well-connected priest who was also a physician – were accused of plotting against the king's life. Harmful rather than fertility-magic, then, seems to have been the purpose of the puppet.

The seriousness of this can be gauged by the state of the royal succession at the time. Had Henry VI died, the Duke of Gloucester would have become king – of France as well as of England, in English eyes – and therefore Eleanor, queen. For unless or until Henry married and produced heirs, the Gloucesters were the only Lancastrian claimants to the throne. Richard of York and his wife, by contrast, were remarkably fertile – thirteen children in fourteen years, eight of them boys. So the characters and reputation of the Gloucesters were of the highest moment, and the characters and reputation they actually had made them ripe for conspiracy. The duke, for example, was interested in the theory and practice of medicine, and in astrology, both capable of being given a sinister interpretation if that were required, especially, perhaps, the latter in his case, since one of his astrological books was written by a Brother Randolph, who was almost certainly the Randolph of the 1419 conspiracy, whom the duke had taken under his protection, which caused the Bishop of Winchester to say later 'that my lord of Gloucester took upon himself further than his authority stretched unto, and caused him to doubt and dread [that], had the Tower not been strong, [the duke] would have proceeded further' – in other words, liberated him from imprisonment altogether.[22] This is very notable patronage, particularly for someone thought, indeed known, to be a magician. However, the duchess also had at least one dubious book and connection, a volume on the principles of geomancy, written by Roger Bolingbroke and dedicated to her. So it could be, and was, said that the interest of both duke and duchess in magic went beyond what might be regarded as the normal and relatively harmless consultation with wise men and women on questions of love and childbirth, accepted by the majority of their countrymen.

Once charges were uttered, events began to move and moved quickly. Eleanor made a grand entrance into London on 28 June 1441, but on that night or the next she was told that Bolingbroke, Southwell, and Home had been accused of plotting to harm the king. She learned that one of these charges alleged that Bolingbroke had cast her horoscope to see whether or not she would become queen, an action which inevitably involved predicting (if only tacitly) when King Henry was going to die. Another charge clarified this by saying that in October 1440 Bolingbroke and Southwell, with Eleanor's active consent, spread the rumour, clearly based on some kind of astrological information, that the king would either die soon or pass through a dangerous crisis. On 10 July 1441 Southwell was arrested and imprisoned, accused of meeting Bolingbroke and Home on more than one occasion after April 1440 in three separate parish churches in London, where Bolingbroke and Home, wearing special vestments, had worked ritual magic with figures and *instrumenta*, and invoked evil spirits with a view to bringing about the king's death through 'the craft of nygromancie', while he (Southwell) celebrated Mass for their protection. Next, Bolingbroke was arrested and examined, once before an ecclesiastical court, once before the council, and during the course of these interrogations gave evidence against Eleanor, saying that everything had been done at her request and direction. After he had given his evidence, he was made to undertake a public repentance, surrounded by his magical paraphernalia which apparently included images made of metal and of wax.[23] The duchess fled to Westminster Abbey for sanctuary, but the authorities had by no means finished with Bolingbroke. On 26 July he appeared before an ecclesiastical court again and, in Eleanor's presence, repeated his allegation that she had instigated the acts of magic with which both of them were charged. (The *Chronicle of London* refers to these acts quite simply as 'witchcraft', which should serve to remind us of what a broad range of occult activities can be contained in that simple term, although another record is more expansive, referring to the accused as 'a superstitious sect of necromancers and persons charged with witchcraft and incantations'.)[24]

Eleanor now implicated Margery, who may have been under arrest already, and decided to plead guilty to five of the twenty-eight charges, after which the court allowed her to return to sanctuary. She was, after all, a duchess, and this immense social status may have given a room full of clerics pause before they decided what further measures to take. Allegations of treason, however, were too serious to let her remain at comparative liberty for long, and on 11 August she was committed to Leeds Castle in Kent from where she was brought in October to be charged again with sorcery and witchcraft directed against the king's life. Both Margery and Thomas Southwell were present on at least the second of these occasions and repeated their defence that it was Eleanor who had asked them to carry out the astrological inquiries and the image-magic. The defence proved worthless. Margery was burned – as a heretic and a witch: one notices the combination – on 27 October, and four days later the king authorised payment of £20 'to be distributed among the scholars, lawyers, and clerics who were striving to destroy the superstitious sect of necromancers [*nigromanticorum*], chanters of spells [*incantantium*], and *sortilegi*, along with their activities'. Southwell died in prison. Jessica Freeman speculates he took his own life there. Days later, the Archbishop of Canterbury declared Eleanor's marriage to the duke annulled on the grounds that, as she had used magic to induce him to marry her in the first place, the marriage could not have been valid; three days after that she was pronounced guilty of sorcery and witchcraft, but not (interestingly enough) of treason or heresy; and four days after that she was obliged to undertake a series of public humiliations to atone for her offences of encouraging and participating in various acts of magic. People at the time seem to have regarded the whole affair as a politically motivated conspiracy aimed at damaging the duke. 'Venom will once break out,' wrote the chronicler Richard Grafton, 'and inward grudge will soon appear, which was this year to all men apparent, for divers secret attempts were advanced forward this season against the noble Duke Humphrey of Gloucester afar off, which in conclusion came so near that they bereft him of life and land.'[25]

Recognising a possible political conspiracy, however, does not necessarily mean that one dismisses people's belief in the reality of the potential harm magical attacks might be able to cause. We are here dealing with a perceived misuse of magic, not a dismissal of magic itself, although that is not to say that sometimes the very notion of magic's validity did not suffer dismissive criticism, usually by the Church. This can be seen in the problem in France with the illness of Charles VI at the end of the fourteenth and beginning of the fifteenth century. From 1392 the king was occasionally subject to what Famiglietti has called 'psychotic episodes', which were characterised by babbling, staring, forgetting who he was, even down to his name, irrational hatred, and paranoia. In 1393 a magician brought from Guyenne to cure him declared that his illness was caused by witchcraft, and two years later the Duchesse d'Orléans and her father were accused of being responsible for it – another instance of magic's being drawn into royal politics and, indeed, influencing foreign opinion, because Richard II was convinced that the charge was true. It was repeated in 1398 when two monks, also from Guyenne, who had tried to cure the king by means of magic, failed in their task, were arrested, and put to death: but not before they had accused the Duc d'Orléans of using *maleficia extrinseca* ('acts of harmful magic coming from somewhere at a distance') to cause Charles's illness; and long-distance magic, this time curative in intent, was tried in vain in 1403, resulting in the execution of the two magicians from Dijon who had essayed it. The situation changed somewhat in 1409 when the Duke of Milan was said to be holding the king in magical subjection by means of a silver image; but by this time it is not surprising that Brother Michel Pintoin, a monk of the Abbey of St-Denis, who wrote a contemporary chronicle of these events, observed testily that only fools, necromancers, and the superstitious believed in magic, and that physicians and theologians both said it had no power whatsoever.[26]

The prevalence of harmful magic in high places, however, must not cause us to forget how common an experience magic and the occult sciences were in the lives of everyone, regardless of rank or profession, and if one looks at both ecclesiastical and secular court records for the thirty years following the Eleanor Cobham-Margery Jourdemaine episode, one finds evidence of the kind of magical hum running through life all over England. Thus, in London in 1444 a man was put in the pillory for invoking 'Oberon' (that is, a demon, not the King of the Fairies), 'and the manner of his process and working' was written and hung about his neck when he was in the pillory; Thomas Curteys from Hertford or the neighbourhood was talked into 'nigromancy and heresy' by Thomas Hull, as Hull confessed to the Bishop of Lincoln in the presence of witnesses on 22 June 1457; in January 1466, Robert Barker was brought before the Bishop of Ely for possessing a grimoire, a 'chart' with hexagonal and pentagonal figures and characters on it, six engraved metal plates, and a gilded wand, all of which point to his being a ritual magician. John Hope, we are told, had offered to buy all these from him because he wanted to raise spirits who would tell him where treasure was buried, but Barker must have refused because he still had them when he was ordered to do public penance for owning them, and probably watched when they were burned in Cambridge marketplace.[27] The following year, William Byg, also known as Lech, from Wombwell, a village in south Yorkshire, was convicted of claiming to detect thieves by using a crystal stone. Part of his subsequent penance involved his wearing paper notices round his head and on his chest and back, proclaiming his offence: '*sortilegus*', said two of them, and '*invocator spirituum*' the third. In other words, he was a diviner and an invoker of spirits, *sortilegus* here being used in its principal, not its extended sense.[28]

Women, of course, were not overlooked by courts trying magical offences. Durham, for example, saw several such processes during this same period. In October 1446, Mariot from Belton was accused of being a *sortilega* and of telling unmarried (or perhaps divorced) women who wanted to marry that she could bring it about that they had the men they were keen on and wanted to have. She denied the accusation, but was obliged to provide compurgation by finding twelve people to swear she was innocent. Isabella Broome was accused of similar offences. She too denied them and had to provide four witnesses for compurgation. The *sortilegium* here, to judge by Mariot's other service as a go-between or furnisher of love-magic, is perhaps more likely to have been a positive activity, such as divination, rather than a negative one, such as doing magical harm. Likewise, Agnes Bowmer, who was summoned, but did not appear, before the court in October 1450: she was censured in her absence on account of her *sortilegium* and for slander, both of which offences she denied. Again, her *sortilegium* may have been divination rather than harmful magic, as we may guess from the case of Alicia Davison who appeared on 23 March 1452, accused of 'using the practice of *sortilegium*, that is to say, a healing technique [*arte medica*] with lead and with a comb [*pectine*] and with iron'. These represent three different ways of doing the same thing, rather than a single action with three constituent instruments, and we know that magicians would pour molten lead into cold water as a mean of divination, and interpret the shapes formed thereby. This may also be the type of *sortilegium* with which Agnes Thomson slandered Joan Smithson and which brought both of them to court in August 1452. Mariot Jackson, on the other hand, was a 'chanter of spells' [*incantatrix*], an allegation she successfully refuted in February 1448 by means of five compurgators.[29]

However, magic could be fun as well as sinister or useful, as the anonymous ballad, 'A Merry Jest of the Friar and the Boy', first published in around 1510, illustrates. It tells the story of a young boy who was subject to the cruelty of a stepmother.

> The stepmother she hated him
> And so malicious grew,
> That sure I am she was a limb
> Of the infernal crew.

One day, however, the boy was kind to an aged pilgrim who, after hearing the lad's complaint about his treatment at the hands of his stepmother, promised to give him three things in return for his generosity: a bow, a pipe, and the fulfilment of his wish that whenever his stepmother frowned or glowered at him, she would be obliged to fart. These three wishes the old man granted, and when the boy had gone home and was eating a hot capon at dinner, his stepmother frowned and glowered at him as usual.

> With that, a cracker she let fly,
> Which seemed to shake the ground.
> She blushed as they made pleasant sport,
> [And] the little boy replied,
> 'My mother has a good report,
> You hear at her backside,
> Sure had [that] been a cannonball
> (With such a force it flew),
> It would have beaten down the wall,
> Perhaps the chimney, too.'[30]

There was, however, not much occasion for laughter during the fifteenth century. To be sure, these court records give us glimpses of the patterns of everyday life, and even if we make allowances for malicious accusation, allegations against the wrong party, official acquiescence in the face of local insistence that something be done to deal with a particular circumstance, deliberate fraud by the defendants, or any of the other excuses one may have for not taking these accusations seriously, there remains a not inconsiderable stratum of behaviour – from genuine practitioners actually practising magic they believe is real and valid in both its forms and effects, as well as from the genuine belief, in their communities and among the authorities called on to deal with them, that the practitioners were sincere and their magic substantially authentic in its potential outcomes – to warrant our accepting the widespread prevalence in all ranks of society of magic in all its multiple guises and conditions. While the behaviours themselves may not have changed all that much, even sometimes in detail, over centuries the contexts in which they happened certainly had, and the fifteenth century in England was one of uncertain government leading at last to civil war. From the dethronement of Richard II in 1399 to the accession of Henry VII in 1485, England was disturbed by raids from Scotland (resolved temporarily by a treaty in 1475), serious unrest in Wales and, apart from the respite of Henry V's reign (largely owed to his absences in France designed to settle his claim to the French throne), deterioration in the effectiveness of central government, a deterioration which served merely to emphasise the actual separateness and distinctness of the regions that made up the geographical and political concept 'England'. Heresy, too, had raised its head in the form of Lollardy, which had stemmed, at least in part, from the writings of John Wycliffe in the previous century, and had received a degree of noble protection until the 1380s. Some Lollard support for the Peasants' Revolt of 1381, however, and then the passing of an Act of Parliament in 1401, *De heretico comburendo* ('Burning a Heretic'), meant that increasingly both Church and state linked interests in rooting this heresy out of the body of England.

In the middle of the century, almost in anticipation of the dynastic wars which would follow soon, a rebellion broke out in Kent in May 1450 and quickly gathered both numbers and pace. Based on disparate grievances over perceived injustices, corruption in high places, and the continuing wars in Normandy, the insurrection reached London and caused havoc (not to mention beheading the Lord High Treasurer and several others), until the government – after falsely agreeing to meet the demands of the rebels' leader, John Cade – rallied and struck back. Nevertheless, the signal for unrest had been given, and from that time onwards the country was scarcely quiet until the accession of Henry Tudor by military conquest put an end to the blood-letting.[31] Needless to say, Cade's reputation was a target for government propagandists, and a proclamation issued on 10 July noted that

> [he] was a false traitor to God, that is to say that he set in the craft and in the help of the Devil, as it appears openly by the books that were found with him at the taking of his person, the which was even last passed, being at Dartford, in the chamber that he was lodged in [he] reared up the Devil in semblance of a black dog.[32]

Cade was not a man from the educated or upper reaches of his local society, but seems to have been well spoken and intelligent, so it is at least within the bounds of possibility that he could have possessed some kind of grimoire. On the other hand, the books may have belonged to the owner of the house in which Cade was captured, and not to Cade himself.[33] Certainly that particular claim in the proclamation may have been entirely fraudulent and intended simply to blacken his character further, but, in the light of what we know about magic and the use of magic during this period, we cannot afford to dismiss entirely the notion that Cade may have possessed such things.

The same kind of problem attends accusations made against Jacquette, Dowager Duchess of Bedford, in 1471. The year is significant. Edward IV had been king since 1461, but had succeeded in alienating his supporters, especially the Earl of Warwick, who then combined to initiate a rebellion against him in 1469. The rebellion was successful, and Henry VI, who had been dethroned by Edward and kept in the Tower since 1465, was now restored in 1470, Edward's unfortunate allies being scattered, captured or done to death during July and August that year, while Edward himself was kept in what amounted to semi-royal captivity in Warwick Castle. Now, the following February, Thomas Wake, a squire from Northamptonshire who had lost a son at the battle of Edgecott on 26 July, was said to hold a grudge against the duchess and so,

> of his malicious disposition towards [her], of long time continued, intending not only to hurt and impair her good name and reputation, but also proposed the final destruction of her person ... to that effect caused her to be brought in a common noise and slander of witchcraft [*wychecraft*] throughout a great part of this realm, alleging that she should have used witchcraft and sorcery [*sorcerie*].

The charges he brought were those of image-magic for harmful purposes, and he made them to Edward and the remnants of Edward's council in Warwick. Accompanying his written accusations, he sent what he alleged was one of the duchess's puppets, 'an image of lead made like a man of arms ... the length of a man's finger and broken in the middle, and made fast with a wire'. However, he alleged more (and cited as his witness John Daunger, parish clerk of Stoke Brewern in Northamptonshire), saying that there were two more images also made by the duchess, one representing the king and the other Queen Elizabeth, the duchess's daughter, but for what purpose Daunger neither could nor would say, although a later Act of Parliament settling the English crown on Richard III maintained they had been used to make Edward fall in love with and marry Elizabeth.

The duchess immediately appealed to Edward to have Wake and Daunger examined, a request he granted, and four members of his court were delegated to see to that task. Their reports summarised what the two men had told them.

Thomas Wake: The image – only one is mentioned – was shown to someone in Stoke, who then handed it over to the parish clerk, who then showed it to others including the parish priest, after which it was seen by some nuns and various other people. Wake said he knew nothing of all this until the said parish clerk (John Daunger) sent it to him, along with the details that Wake had passed on to his examiners.

John Daunger: It was Wake who had asked him to send him the image – again only one is mentioned – and so Daunger had done so. At that time, he (Daunger) had heard nothing about the duchess's being involved in or connected with witchcraft. He himself had received the image from one Harry Kingston who had found it in his house after soldiers (presumably billeted upon him) had left and gone. However, after Wake had returned from seeing the king, he went to Daunger and tried to throw the blame for the whole episode on to Daunger's shoulders, at the same time asking him to say there were two other images, one of the king and one of the queen. But this Daunger said he refused to do.

Clearly the two accounts are incompatible, and the council which considered the evidence decided to dismiss the case altogether. One image certainly existed. The king and council had seen it. Shaped or dressed like a man-at-arms, broken, and repaired with wire, it sounds more like a broken toy than a magical image, although if Daunger had had children and the toy had been one of theirs, he would surely have known about it. It would be easy, of course, to draw from the council's dismissal of the case a conclusion that the whole thing was no more than a piece of malice from

Thomas Wake, who had tried to suborn Daunger into supporting his fraudulent tale, and such indeed may have been the situation. We know nothing of Wake's motives for embarking upon the potentially dangerous course of accusing the king's mother-in-law of practising hostile magic against her monarch, nor can we say the council found her innocent. It seems to have set aside the case as 'not proven' because the evidence amounted to one man's word against that of another. Still, if Wake was right in saying that several people had seen one of the images before it came into his hands, one wonders why we do not hear that those others had been questioned and their evidence weighed. Neither are we told what, if anything, happened to Wake as a result of the council's action. Such a serious accusation against someone of such importance should surely have had consequences, but we hear of none. All in all, therefore, the incident is something of a puzzle. What is worth noting, however, is that an accusation of image-magic could be made and taken seriously by such people as the Archbishop of Canterbury, the Archbishop of York, the Chancellor, the bishops of Ely, Rochester, Durham, and Carlisle, and several secular lords, an action which, not surprisingly – bearing in mind that none of them was a modern sceptic – indicates their absorption in the prevailing mindset of the period, which meant they regarded the accusation as being at least possible even if, on the evidence, they found it unlikely.[34]

However, King Edward's brushes with magic were not yet over. By 1477, relations between himself and his younger brother George, Duke of Clarence, had deteriorated for a variety of reasons to the point of bitterness, and in May that year a trial took place which touched the unfortunate duke and put him in danger. Thomas Burdett was a country squire, a Member of Parliament, a Justice of the Peace, and a servant and personal friend of Clarence. According to his indictment, in April 1474 he had approached John Stacy and Thomas Blake, both Oxford scholars, and asked them to cast the horoscopes of both the king and his heir, Prince Edward. This they did, and foretold an early death for both of them. Such an act in itself could be construed as treasonable, but when in May the following year Stacy and Blake told other people what they had discovered, the treason was beyond doubt. Two years after that, Burdett exacerbated their situation by disseminating rebellious leaflets and ballads among the people of Holborn, but worse perhaps than the astrology and the pamphleteering was the charge that they had 'imagined and encompassed the King's death by sorcery', or 'had worked and calculated [it] by the art of magic, necromancy, and astrology'. *Imagined* here is not so much the modern sense of 'forming a mental image' as the older 'forming a physical image' – that is to say, making a puppet for use in image-magic. All three men were put on trial and found guilty, Burdett and Stacy being hanged while Blake was saved by the intervention of the Bishop of Norwich. Burdett and Stacy protested their innocence and one is bound to admit that the episode is peculiar. It will have suited anyone who wanted to undermine the Duke of Clarence and therefore may have been fabricated, as Dominic Mancini suggested. On the other, if the plot was a real one, we might expect the participants to have behaved in very much this fashion: astrology to calculate the chances of success or failure, image-magic to harm and ultimately destroy the king and Prince Edward at a distance, and incantations and other magical formulae or rites to empower the image and cause the deaths to happen.[35]

Now, so far the bulk of our discussion has involved English magicians. This is because evidence from elsewhere in Britain is not available, the records having disappeared over the course of time. An example of this relates to Scotland in 1479. James III was then twenty-eight and, according to the sixteenth-century historian George Buchanan, began to turn into a tyrant with the result that when his youngest brother, John, 'more heedless than everyone else, had spoken rashly and too freely about the state of the kingdom, he was forcibly removed from Court, thrown into prison at the instance of the King's Council, and forced to die, having had a vein slit open'. This sounds remarkably similar to the deaths of certain Roman patricians who were obliged by Imperial command to commit suicide in just this way, except that Buchanan's Latin leaves it ambiguous about who opened John's vein, John himself or others. The common people were told, presumably by proclamation, that the reason for John's death had been his secretly consulting *foeminis veneficis* ('women who practised poisonous magic') – that is to say, female magicians who specialised in herbal concoctions, which could be made to produce a fatal result – with a view to causing the king's demise; and to make it look as though the charge were true, twelve women from the lowest ranks of society were tortured (*decreta questione*) and then burned.[36] Such an accusation, if Buchanan is reporting a true incident, will not have struck contemporaries as impossible or particularly unlikely, although they may not have believed it on other grounds. Nor is the witness of twelve unfortunate women likely in itself to have caused doubt in the minds of the public, who probably did not know the women had been tortured and who would, in any case, almost certainly have accepted this as a legitimate means of extracting the truth. Again we lack so many details essential to a proper understanding of the case that it is impossible for us to say whether John was guilty as charged or not. Consulting witches was not in the least unusual behaviour, and consulting those who specialised in poisonous substances was one of the obvious things to do if John had it in mind to do away with his brother as a solution to the problems of the kingdom, which he clearly thought was being misruled. We can, therefore, torture of the women or not, make a case for John's having tried to poison his older brother. Whether he actually did so or not is another matter.[37]

Buchanan also tells us why King James succumbed to the supposed tyrannical aspects of his character. Envoys had been sent to Flanders to try to settle some trading disputes with the Duke of Burgundy, and one day at dinner they met Andrews, 'a medical practitioner and someone considered to have great skill in astrological prediction'. The envoys told him why they were there, and he took them on one side and said they need not be in any rush, because a message about the duke would arrive; and, sure enough, three days later they learned the duke had been killed in a battle with the Swiss. This successful prediction impressed the envoys, who told King James about Andrew when they returned to Scotland, and as a consequence the king, who was already well inclined to the occult sciences, sent for Andrew to come to the Scottish court. He did so – the rewards were substantial – but warned the king that he was in danger of death from his own people: the Latin says *a suis*, an ambiguous phrase. It could mean 'from his own family', 'from his own household', or 'from the Scots in general'. Now, James was immoderately given to consulting witches (*maleficarum mulierum*, 'women who work harmful magic') and they had already told him something similar, namely, that 'a lion would be destroyed by his own cubs'. This fixes the meaning of Buchanan's *a suis* and tells us why James then sought the source of assassination among his own family members.[38] Did James or his brother really consult witches? Again we lack supporting or contradictory evidence, but we should not dismiss the possibility. Magic was certainly a feature of life in the highest as well as the lowest circles – one has only to think of the Countess of Atholl's resorting to it in an effort to ease Queen Mary's pains during her difficult and prolonged labour with the future James VI – and James III's personal interest in astrology, for example, can be gauged from, among other things, *The Buke of the Sevyne Sagis*, which was adapted from an earlier Latin text in ways which the author clearly hoped would appeal to the king.[39] In the end we are circumscribed by Buchanan's text. This was published in 1582 (very late, one may think), but seems to have owed a great deal to Hector Boece, who was twenty-three when King James died, and wrote a history of Scotland up to James's accession. We should also bear in mind Giovanni Ferrerio, who continued that history to the end of James's reign. Hector was old enough to have been able to hear the gossip of 1479, and, as he left two books of his *History* unfinished at his death, it is possible these contained information used by Ferrerio, and were thus passed on to Buchanan. Ferrerio also knew Henry Sinclair, Dean of Glasgow, who collected manuscripts, including those of Boece, and so Sinclair may be regarded as another possible source of information. Buchanan, therefore, may have been a reliable conduit for these stories about King James, and the stories themselves not inaccurate.[40]

In England, the political situation had deteriorated further as a result of the minority of Edward V. He was twelve when his father died in 1483, protected to some extent by powerful allies within the nobility, including the Woodville family, relatives of Edward IV's wife Elizabeth. However, the young king's safety was more apparent than real, and he and his younger brother disappeared into the Tower of London while their uncle, Richard of Gloucester, seized the throne. Almost immediately, the new king resurrected the charge that Edward IV's marriage had been invalid because of his mother-in-law's use of magic to make it happen,[41] and added further allegations against Queen Elizabeth and Margaret Beaufort (mother of the future Henry VII). One principal source for these later charges is St Thomas More's *History of King Richard the Third*, written both in Latin and in English, and published first in 1543, containing the famous scene of the morning of 13 June 1483, when Richard, in the presence of the council, accused Queen Elizabeth and Elizabeth Shore of deforming his arm by magic. 'What are they worthy to have that compass and imagine the destruction of me, who am so near of blood unto the king, and Protector of his royal person and realm?' he is supposed to have said. 'It is yonder sorceress, my brother's wife, and others with her. Ye shall all see in what wise that sorceress and that other witch of her council, Shore's wife, with their kind, have by their sorcery and witchcraft wasted my body'. Thereupon he pulled up his left sleeve, and exhibited 'a werish withered arme and small'.

St Thomas's *History*, however, is not quite history as we understand it, but a work of propaganda, satire, and moral comment, and the general inclination of historians has been to discount the whole episode as a rhetorical invention, intended to increase the drama of St Thomas's account of the summary execution of Lord Hastings, a major player in what More painted as Richard's growing paranoia.[42] The earliest sources are the work of an anonymous contemporary, the Crowland Chronicle, and *The Seizure of the Kingdom of England by Richard III*, a version of events by Dominic Mancini, a visitor to the country, who spoke no English and tended to report city gossip rather than informed news. Neither of these mentions sorcery or witchcraft, and neither does the near-contemporary John Rous in his *History of the Kings of England*, although Rous tailored his version of events to suit the ruling party, producing a Yorkist account under Richard III and a Lancastrian one under Henry VII. It is the later Italian historian, Polydore Vergil, in England on a diplomatic mission in 1502 and therefore not too far removed from some of the events he describes, who mentions a charge of harmful magic levelled against Elizabeth Woodville. Vergil's choice of words is significant. 'The evil in me,' says his Richard, 'stems from that evil-doing woman [*ab illa malefica muliere*], Queen Elizabeth, who has infected me with her [magical] poisons [*suis veneficiis me infecit*]. These have damaged me and little by little I am being destroyed [*dissolvor*].'[43] *Malefica* means 'evil-doing', but also carries the sense of 'witch', and so when Richard mentions *veneficia* a few words later, this word, which can simply mean 'poisons', takes on the colour of magic – as it frequently does in any case – and suggests that poison of some kind, strengthened by incantations or other magical formulae, has been employed against him. Such a possibility, as we shall see in a moment, appeared not uncommonly in magical plots to kill a monarch. Vergil's verbs *infecit*, *laesus*, and *dissolvor* also continue the theme of poison. *Inficio* means 'stain, dye, discolour, taint, infect, spoil, corrupt'; *laedo* means 'wound, injure, damage'; and *dissolvo*, 'unloose, dissolve, melt, destroy'. We thus have a picture of the queen's 'poison' spreading through Richard's body and causing it to fall or come apart – a slow and painful death in which the body becomes discoloured and melts away. In its fashion, therefore, Vergil's account may be as carefully calculated a piece of drama as St Thomas's.

However, is it, for that reason, implausible as a piece of historical record? Elizabeth, we may recall, had been involved in a charge of image-magic earlier under Edward IV, and it appears that 'the common opinion of the people and the public voice and fame ... through all this land' at the time believed these charges against Elizabeth and her mother were true.[44] There is strong circumstantial evidence, too, which suggests that both women may have used astrologers, perhaps simply to find out the future course of events – a desire which could easily be seen as sinister, since it was likely to involve discovering when the reigning monarch might die, a political offence in itself – but perhaps also, more worryingly, to assist in the consecration of magical images or the gathering of 'herbs' for concoctions of one kind or another. There was, for example, a Welsh astrologer, Lewis Caerleon, who numbered Queen Elizabeth as well as the future Henry VII and his mother among his clients, and who, as a Lancastrian supporter, was arrested in 1483 when the Duke of Buckingham tried to overthrow Richard; Thomas Nandyke, a priest and physician, described as a necromancer in an Act of Attainder dated 1483, who may also have been deeply involved with Richard's opponents; and John Argentine, Edward V's personal physician, who was known to have cast horoscopes for both young Edward and his father. So Richard's suspicions about Queen Elizabeth were certainly not without foundation, and even if we feel we cannot rely on the exact wording of either Polydore Vergil or St Thomas More for an accurate understanding of the king's alleged behaviour in the council chamber that June morning, we may certainly allow that, if he did have suspicions of magical plotting against him, he need not have been mistaken or paranoid therein, since his suspicions could well have contained more than a grain of truth.[45]

This, however, was not the end of the matter, for the century had one more magical plot against royalty to add to its collection, an involved and rambling scenario worthy of a Victorian novel. In March 1496 a Frenchman, Bernard de Vignolles, living in Rouen, made a startling confession anent a conspiracy to kill Henry VII and other members of the royal family and court. It was a confession read by the king himself, who endorsed the document in his own hand, and its story was as follows.[46] Two years earlier, in 1494, John Kendal, Grand Prior of the Order of St John of Rhodes; John Thong, his nephew and a knight of the Order; and William Horsey, Archdeacon of London, were all in Rome, looking for someone to murder King Henry, his mother, and his children, along with close friends and members of his council. With this in mind, the three men got to know a Spanish astrologer called Radigo, and Archdeacon Horsey actually went to stay in his house. Radigo, however, did not know how these murders could be carried out, so the three turned to another Spanish astrologer called Juan who said he had a very good idea how to accomplish their intentions. They hired him, and he, to prove he knew what he was doing, murdered one of the servants belonging to the Turkish sultan's brother, who was a prisoner in the papal palace in Rome at the time. The three conspirators then left Rome for England, leaving behind one of their servants, a Sardinian called Stefano, to keep an eye on Juan's progress, and sent money to both men to cover their expenses. However, Juan complained it was not enough, and de Vignolles had to explain to him that he was not going to get any more for the time being.

Two years went by and nothing happened, so Kendal, Thong, and Horsey decided to send Bernard to Rome to murder Radigo, who had been unable (or unwilling) to help them in the first place and was now blabbing about their intention to murder the English king. They also told Bernard to speak to Juan and tell him to get on with what he had promised to do, saying he would not receive any more money in advance. So Bernard had a conversation with Juan, urging him to do as the plotters wanted, and to do it from where he was, because he might be recognised if he came to England. Juan replied that he would come to England disguised as a friar, and because he had two teeth missing he would have two replacements made from ivory, stained to look like the rest. He would come by sea, he said, under the pretence of going on pilgrimage to Santiago di Compostela. He never did come, however, and Bernard believed this was because he lacked the money to do so. Bernard then left Rome, and as he was leaving Juan gave him a small wooden box containing ointment, which he was to smear along and across a door or gate through which the king would pass and thus walk over the smear. If this were done, said Juan, those who now loved the king would be the ones to murder him. When Bernard went back to his lodging, he opened the box and found something foul and stinking; so he closed the box and threw it into a lavatory, and the next day started his return journey to England. On arriving in Orléans, he began to worry in case Juan had written to Kendal, saying he had sent him a box via de Vignolles, so to prevent his being blamed for not bringing a box, he went to a local apothecary and bought a box similar to the one he had been given by Juan, and a small quantity of quicksilver. Then, back in his lodging, he took some dry earth, some soot, and some water and mixed them together with the quicksilver, so that the whole thing resembled the contents of the original box.

Back in England, he reported to Kendal and handed over the box, but told him not to touch it because it would bring great danger to anyone with wicked intentions, and he added that, if Kendal kept it in his house for twenty-two hours, it would be at his personal peril. So Kendal told Bernard to take it a long way from the house and throw it away where it would not be found – which Bernard did. Three or four weeks passed. Kendal visited Bernard and found him very ill. He suggested he get on a horse, if he could, and leave England on the excuse of going on pilgrimage or of returning to his father's house to get well again, and promised Bernard some money and a horse (actually he wanted Bernard out of the way in case Bernard told anyone about the conspiracy). Bernard agreed to leave, although his illness lasted another six months, during which Kendal urged him to go by sea; but when at last Bernard recovered, he asked Kendal permission to go home to his parents, intending, once he was there – because he did not dare make the attempt while he was still in England for fear of being assaulted by the conspirators – to warn the king what was being planned for him. Permission was granted, and Bernard promised to return as soon as he could.[47]

Was this a real or fictitious plot? Frederic Madden suggests that the plotters were clergymen, and many of the English clergy were disaffected towards King Henry at this time. Several, indeed, were arrested along with other supporters of Perkin Warbeck and the Yorkist cause, and although Kendal and Horsey seem to have escaped serious punishment once the whole Warbeck incident was over, this may not argue their innocence but rather suggests their craftiness or good luck. So the fact of a plot, he thought, may not be impossible.[48] The proposed method of magical assassination can also be paralleled from Scotland where a group of witches was said to have met in 1589 with a view to murdering James VI, and to have prepared a venomous concoction from a toad, urine, an adder skin, and *hippomanes* (either an excretion from a mare in heat, which Vergil said was poisonous, or possibly a plant). This liquid was to be introduced into one of the royal palaces and 'laid in his Majesty's way, when his Majesty would go in over [it], or out over [it], or in any passage, that it might drop on his Highness's head or his body, for his Highness's destruction'.[49] Magical poisons, or poisons with their effect signally intensified with the help of magic, seem to have been one of the hazards of kingship. In 1401, an allegation was made by someone who had turned king's evidence that there was a plot, supported by the clergy, 'to arrange by necromancy and spell to make an ointment with which to anoint the saddle of the King ... and before he had ridden ten miles he would be quite swelled up and die suddenly, sitting upright in his saddle'.[50] As is so often the case, then, our verdict upon the reality of the plot described by de Vignolles must be 'not proven'; but if it was genuine, it shows that the tradition of clerical use of and participation in magic had by no means faded by the end of the century, and that no one, no matter how exalted, could escape being the target of some kind of malefice.

But beyond the rarefied confines of the court the London commissary continued to deal with a wide variety of offences, several involving *sortilegium*, but few with harmful rather than helpful intent. John Stokes in 1480 was arrested for 'using chanted spells to deal with fevers, [incantations] which had been given to him by a *sortilega*'; in 1482 Joan Beverly, herself a *sortilega*, sought the services of two married *sortilegae* – the phrase may also mean 'two complicit *sortilegae*' – to make Robert Stanton and another man of higher social standing fall in love with her and no one else. The *sortilegae* were successful, because the two men committed adultery with Joan and then fought over her, one of them almost killing the other. Her husband, meanwhile, did not dare stay with her because of her two lovers, although the final note in the record gives the impression he had other reasons for leaving the marital home: 'she is a common prostitute and a bawd, and wants to poison the men because her [magical] art has failed'. Another woman with whom it would have been uncomfortable to live was Elena Dallock, 'a slanderer of her neighbours'. She was in the commissary's court in 1493 to answer nine varied charges:

Item: [She is], as it were, a chanter of spells [*incantatrix*], and says that whatever she curses always departs this world.

Item: She says she curses a good many people who have never afterwards lived in this world.

Item: She says that if she has Heaven in this world, she doesn't care about Heaven in the next one.

Item: She expressed the wish to be in Hell as long as God will be in Heaven, so that she can take revenge with infernal hooks on one John Gybbis, now deceased.

Item: She slandered a respectable woman while the woman was alive, and [says that] because she was not able to take her revenge on her while she was alive, she would, in monstrous fashion, be happy to take her revenge on her now she was dead.

Item: She always behaves in a devilish, not a godly way.

Item: She has never been to confession with her own priest with the result that, as he says, her parish priest has no knowledge of her spiritual life.

Item: She said that if she commanded it to rain, it rained on her command.

Item: She says she has a book which tells her all about the future.[51]

This last makes her a *sortilega* in the restricted sense, but clearly her claimed abilities to exercise a death-curse and to perform weather-magic suggest she was a combination of *maga* ('magician') and *malefica* ('worker of harmful magic'), just the kind of person to whom the English were applying the word 'witch'. One wonders, then, what lay behind the complaint that Joan Corbett was a *sortilega* 'and makes use of acts of *sortilegium* [*utitur sortilegiis*]'. Were these acts all the same type, or were they different, as in Elena Dallock's case? Were they benevolent or, as in Joan Bennett's case, malicious? Joan 'alias Ward', cited to come before the court on 10 and 11 June 1490, is described in the same terms as Joan Corbett: 'she is a *sortelega* [sic] and makes use of acts of *sortelegium*'. Here, however, we are given an example of the kind of thing she did. She would measure a man's height, have a wax candle made the same length, and then have it offered in front of a statue or painting (*coram imagine*). Once it was lit, the man would waste away just as the candle did. Presumably the painting or statue was in a church, so Joan was practising malevolent image-magic under the guise of piety. A 5- or 6-foot candle would not have been cheap, so this suggests that Joan (or her client, if she was acting for someone else) was quite well off.[52]

Magic certainly did not always come cheap. A case from 1492 is worth quoting *in extenso*, partly because the record includes a conversation in English between a heretic and sorcerer, and a woman he may have been trying to con.

As a result of public gossip, a report was made to our department concerning one Richard Laukiston from the parish of St Mary Magdalene in Old Fish Street, Margaret Geoffrey, a widow, recently from the parish of St Bartholomew the Small, and certain articles touching the crime of heresy and sorcery. Namely, that in the months of January, February, March, and April 1480 (or in one of them), this same Richard said the following (or words very similar) in English to the said Margaret.

'Thou art a poor widow, and it were alms to help thee to a marriage, and if thou wilt do any cost in spending any money, thou shalt have a man worth a thousand pounds'.

Then the foresaid widow, Margaret, replied, 'How may that be?'

Then Laukiston said, 'My wife knoweth a cunning man, that by his cunning can cause a woman to have any man that she hath a favour to, and that shall be upon warranty. For she hath put it in execution before, and this shall cost money'.

Then the foresaid Margaret said, 'I have no goods save two mazers [*large drinking cups*] for to find me, my mother, and my children; and if they were sold and I fail of my purpose, I, my mother, and my children were undone'.

Then the said Laukiston said, 'Deliver me the mazers and I will warrant thine intent shall be fulfilled'.

Then the foresaid Margaret handed him the two mazers which were worth five marks and ten shillings.[53]

Both Richard and Margaret turned up to the next court hearing – something which did not always happen, for example, Joan Bennett did not – took the oath, and then confessed that the charges against them were true. Both were sentenced, Margaret to do public penance, and Richard to give her back the mazers or the equivalent of their monetary worth, along with other penalties, details of which were postponed to a later date.

Was this a fraud? It is impossible to tell from the bare record, but of course the potential for fraud was always there, and in the sixteenth century, Protestant writers enjoyed attributing such practices as thief-detection to Catholics, calling them 'Popish trickery', even though they had been and continued to be part of magical behaviour all over Europe for centuries. So Reginald Scot, referring to the Danish Lutheran theologian Nils Hemmingsen, records the technique of divination by psalter and key.

Popish priests (saith Hemmingsen), as the Chaldaeans used the divination by sieve and shears for the detection of theft, do practise with a psalter and a key fastened upon the 49th Psalm to discover a thief. And when the names of the suspected persons are orderly put into the pipe of the key, at the reading of those words of the Psalm, 'If thou sawest a thief, thou didst consent unto him', the book will wag and fall out of the fingers of them that hold it; and he whose name remaineth in the key must be the thief. Hereupon Hemmingsen inferreth that although conjuring priests and witches bring not this to pass by the absolute words of the Psalm, which tend to a far other scope, yet Satan doth nimbly, with his invisible hand, give such a twitch to the book, as also in the other case to the sieve and the shears, that down falls the book and key, sieve and shears, up starts the thief, and away runneth the Devil, laughing.[54]

But on 26 April 1497, we find John White indicted for exercising 'the forbidden craft of magic by psalter and key', which he used to uncover the thief who had purloined a silver spoon from John Ryan's property. It was, he said, Elizabeth Doland, an accusation which her husband believed, for he threw her out of the house and beat her. When questioned in court, John White admitted he had been paid eight pence by John Ryan's wife to find out who had stolen the spoon, and that when Elizabeth's name was put into the book, the key turned, thereby indicating she was guilty. Master Robert, rector of St Mary at Nax, also performed thief-detection 'by means of his acts of *sortilegium*', and seems to have named the wrong person more than once, especially Alice Hall, whom he accused of stealing two rings from Robert Draper. What these sortilegious acts entailed, however, we do not know. Nazareth Jarbrey, on the other hand, at the request of Thomas Barley in 1480, used a beryl-stone to show him who were the culprits.

In it, on one occasion, he saw a man dressed in a particular way, who brought back a small box which had been stolen from his [Jarbrey's] mother's house along with pearls, [precious] stones, and other things; and on another occasion, at the request of the clerk of St George's church, he came once more to Thomas's house and there, using the beryl-stone again, he saw a man and a woman dressed in a particular way. He did not know who they were, but once he had described their clothing and appearance, the clerk said he knew who the woman was. Her name was Longbell. This (said Jarbrey) was all he had done.[55]

What, then, can be said of magic in this century? Perhaps one of its most notable features here is that, in spite of the rebellions and civil wars' creating heightened tension throughout the social strata, there is no evidence that accusations of and prosecutions for harmful magic (what would later be understood by the term 'witchcraft') increased in either ecclesiastical or in secular courts. Attempts, or at least alleged attempts, at magical assassination of prominent individuals do appear to have been more frequent than in previous centuries, but as far as the middling and lower classes are concerned, allegations of magical behaviour exhibit the same patterns and traits as those of the previous century, cases finding themselves in court largely because they had failed in some way to fulfil their part of a contract, or the practitioner had been denounced to the court for heresy or suspected heretical leanings. The theory that magical workers, witches in particular, were part of a widespread army of Satan, who was seeking to corrupt individuals and overthrow organised society in preparation for the advent of the Antichrist and the Last Days, a theory gaining ground among many theologians and lawyers elsewhere in parts of Europe, does not seem to have made any headway in those parts of the British Isles whose witchcraft history we know. This, given the obvious intellectual links between Britain and the rest of Europe, and therefore the opportunities for the theory to flow through these available conduits, is noteworthy. Noteworthy, too, is the prevalence of men among those accused in both types of court. Women, certainly, were beginning to make a somewhat larger showing, charged with crimes of this sort, but not in sufficient numbers to warrant our particular notice. More prevalent were men in holy orders, but not all of them ritual magicians as one might expect. So the face of magic in this largely English century appears to be conservative and low-profile. However, with the onset of the sixteenth century and the emergence of records from other parts of Britain, not to mention major religious upheavals all over Europe, from which the separate kingdoms, principalities, and provinces of Britain were by no means exempt, magic in all its aspects entered a new and much more dramatic phase of its history, and witchcraft emerged from the linguistic shadows of Latin and redefined itself in its largely negative sense.

3

BUSINESS NOT QUITE AS USUAL:
1502–1542

Time does not divide itself into centuries, and so the 1500s began very much as the 1400s had ended. On 13 July 1502 Eleonora Doolin came before the London commissary court (held on that occasion in old St Paul's Cathedral), because, it was alleged, she had plotted to use the arts of divination (*artes divinatorias*) to kill her husband by poisoning him. She was permitted to purge herself of this accusation with the help of two other women, Anna Marys and Agnes Winchcomb. The clerk's use of *divinatorias* here is somewhat unusual, but he may have been thinking of *sortilegium*, which, as we have seen, had by now both a basic meaning relating to divination and a developed one relating to other forms of magic. We may take it, then, that harmful or poisonous magic was what the clerk had in mind. Three days later, on 16 July, Anna Miller, with a reputation for slandering her neighbours, came to court on a charge of defaming Eleonora by saying she had given her (own) husband medicines with the intention of poisoning him. In answer to the court's questions, she said that, about a year before, John Davely, Eleonora's husband – women did not necessarily change their surname on marriage at this period – felt the need to take a purge because his stomach was heavy. So he sent Anna, his servant at the time, to Bucklersbury to get the appropriate ingredients for the purge. This she did, and came home and made up the medicine. However, then Eleonora handed her some poisonous substances, obviously wanting Anna to add them to the mixture, which, Anna told the court, she was unwilling to do. Next morning John called for his medicine and Anna said to him, 'Sir, it has lain uncovered all night and I don't know what may have fallen into it. I'll make you another one.' Eleonora, who had come into the room, heard her and said, 'You great whore! Have you been telling him I put something in it?' This made John suspicious and he made his wife eat some of it, as a result of which she became ill and had not fully recovered her health at the time of the hearing.[1]

Superficially this may look like a straightforward case of alleged poisoning, but there are one or two points to bear in mind. First, medicines contained a variety of substances, and if one or more of them was potentially toxic, an incorrect mixture could easily kill the patient or exacerbate the condition for which the medicine was being taken. In John's case, his wanting a purge would have resulted in vomiting or excreting, or both, in quantity, and if the medicine had indeed been poisonous, John's reactions might not have been immediately suspicious. Nor, if the medicine was no more than a purge, was Eleonora's illness necessarily anything more than a strong reaction to the purgative qualities of the contents. Interpretation of their symptoms would have depended on whether other people had reason to think there was more to the vomiting or excreting than simple purgation. Secondly, it would not have been unusual for someone to seek to improve or strengthen the quality of the medicine by saying a charm or a prayer, or chanting a spell, while the mixture was being put together, and one notices it was Alice, not the apothecary, who made up the remedy.[2] Thirdly, as the charge Eleonora faced on 13 July makes clear, Anna (or perhaps someone else) thought or said she thought that hostile magic was involved. This, whether true or not, altered the context of the whole episode. Fourthly, had it been a simple case of attempted murder by poisoning, the reference to 'divinatory arts' would have been pointless, because an allegation of poisoning was quite sufficient in itself to destroy Eleonora's reputation, and possibly to take her life if she were found guilty. So we may take it that 'divinatory arts' had indeed been mentioned at some point in the initial incident. We may also suggest that it is possible, even likely, that the case actually did involve magic in the form of charms or spells at some point during the course of its early events.

Defamation again was the stimulus for a case brought in 1509 against Alicia Ancetyr, who, like Anna Miller, had a reputation for slandering her neighbours. This case involved her alleging that Christopher Sandon had stolen from her house a rosary made out of coral. She named him, apparently, because she had gone to a man living in Charterhouse Street, 'who made use of the art of magic', and with the help of a magical drawing let her see a vivid likeness (*picturam et imaginem*) of Christopher in a mirror. Christopher, she said, was standing by a window made of glass, and saw Alicia putting the rosary in her straw mattress. Then she went out, and Christopher came into the room, found the rosary where she had put it, and took it away with him.[3] This is thief-detection, but in a somewhat more elaborate form than that we have met before. The magician's doing some kind of magical drawing (*figuram artis sue*) before turning to his mirror is a detail not usually given. What may it mean? One possibility is that he was consecrating the mirror before putting it to divinatory use, not very likely in this instance; another, that he was drawing up an astrological chart to see if the moment was propitious to consult the mirror; or that, as William Perkins explained in 1608, it was a charm without words, part of a magical preparation for the act of scrying.[4] It is noteworthy, too, that Alicia says she herself could see the images in the mirror – the usual practice was for the magician to use a medium, often a small boy, who would then describe to others what he could see in the reflective surface – and that the images she saw were moving. This is reminiscent of crystal-gazing done by Edward Kelley for John Dee during the 1580s. At nine in the morning of 2 January 1584, for example, Kelley was describing to Dee what he was seeing in the crystal and what he heard the figures therein say to him.

The curtain appeareth, but more deep into the stone [*i.e. the crystal*]. At length cometh one very tall in a long white gown, all open, and his hair of his head hanging down to his legs. He hath wings upon his head, arms, back, and legs. He seemeth to descend from the clouds, and upon clouds which lie stoperwise for his descending. He speaketh as followeth ... He turneth now back again (as before) speaking. He seemeth now to

lean against a pillar of copper, great and round: and he is become less than he was. Now
he standeth on the top of the pillar. Now he kneeleth down, his back being turned.[5]

Catoptromancy, crystallomancy, and any of the other common methods of scrying by
means of a polished or reflective surface were held in deep suspicion by the Church,
partly because scrying represented an unlawful and potentially blasphemous attempt
to pry into what God had chosen to keep secret, and partly because one could never
be sure that demons had not entered the instrument of divination (or had been put
there by magical constraint), and that whatever one saw therein was anything more
than demonic illusion. Hence Pope John XXII's bull of 1326, tellingly beginning with
the words *Super illius specula* ('Concerning his mirrors'), which noted that

> many who are Christians, but Christians in name only, make a covenant with death,
> and are in agreement with Hell, for they sacrifice to demons, worship them, make or
> have made for them images, rings, mirrors, phials, or some other thing in order to bind
> demons magically therein.

In connection with this we should bear in mind, perhaps, that images seen in
Mediaeval mirrors were not the clean-lined, instantly recognised and recognisable
reflections to which we are accustomed, and which appear to act as efficiently as
modern glasses in paintings showing them, such as Jan van Eyck's *Arnolfini Portrait*
(1434), Hans Memling's *Vanity* (*c.* 1500), or Quentin Metsys's *Moneychanger and
His Wife* (1514). In the middle of the thirteenth century, mirrors were either sheets
of steel, copper or highly polished marble, or glasses 'silvered' with lead – later tin,
pewter, or mercury. In consequence, images seen therein were imperfect, sometimes
to the extent that, as a fifteenth-century observer noted, 'one sees someone else there
rather more than oneself'. Distorted, cloudy, unrecognisable images, therefore, may
have helped to intensify distrust of mirrors and also to have assisted the notion that
those images were not so much reflections from without as projections from within,
although of course they do not explain (that is, explain away) the phenomenon of
apparitions of future events, or the location of hidden treasure for which mirrors
were often used.[6]

Conjuration of spirits lies at the heart of a case of ritual magic and treasure hunting
investigated by the Archiepiscopal Court of York, and it is worth looking at this
case in some detail, since it illustrates the nature of some of the ritual magic of the
time, the deep involvement of the clergy and the culture of male-dominated magic as
opposed to that which women usually practised. It also raises the question of whether
the *sortilegium* involved should be regarded as a form of witchcraft or whether it
represents a quite different kind of activity. In May 1510, James Richardson, a priest
from Bingley in Yorkshire, and John Steward, aged forty-eight, a schoolmaster for
sixteen years in Knaresborough, were arrested, preparatory to their being examined
in June by the Archbishop of York himself, on charges of having a reputation for
heresy and *sortilegium*.[7] The first item on Fr Richardson's indictment established that
he was indeed a priest. The second said,

You, knowing that John Steward of Knaresborough is a practitioner of pretended and criminal conjurations, invocations, and acts of *sortilegium*, and that he has been publicly censured and widely condemned for this kind of thing, consulted and had dealings with this same John so that, by his magical, criminal art, he might recover something which had been stolen and discover the whereabouts of one Christopher Scarsborough who has recently run away from the service of Thomas Jameson,

Jameson being a man of standing and substance in York; he had been its lord mayor in 1504.

Fr Richardson answered that when Thomas Jameson had asked him for help, he told him he had heard that John Steward would reveal the whereabouts both of Scarsborough and the stolen articles. So they both rode over to Knaresborough after Epiphany, and Jameson gave Steward 6s 8d, in return for which, according to Fr Richardson, Steward promised to tell him very early next day where to find his servant. According to Jameson, however, Steward took the money but said, 'Let God, the Devil, and me alone,' and then changed the subject. An immense treasure, he said, had been hidden in Mixenden, a village near Halifax, and, with Fr Richardson's assistance and advice, and that of others, he would like to work the spot. According to the testimony of William Watson, servant to William Ottwell, both of whom became involved in the episode early on, and two priests, Richard Greenwood and John Wilkinson, this treasure consisted of a chest full of gold, 'every noble as thick as five', a sword of maintenance on top of it, and a book covered with black leather; and according to Steward, it was these two priests who had written to him twelve months earlier to tell him about the treasure and offer him a partnership in their enterprise to get it. Attempts had been made even before that, apparently, both by the priests and by a Robert Leventhorp, but these had been unsuccessful. Leventhorp, according to Henry Bank, a chaplain at Addingham, reporting a conversation he had overheard between Christopher Hardwick and the parish priest of Bingley, had actually seen the chest, 'and the Devil sitting upon it'. Leventhorp had tried to remove the Devil by brandishing a sword at him, but the Devil had broken it in two, as though it had been a bean-stick. Letters were exchanged between Fr Richardson, John Steward, and the two priests in Bingley, and it was agreed that 'it were a good deed to get that good with the power of God', and that it would not be against the law to do so because no ground would be broken. At first the priests were uncertain that Steward's help would be needed because 'he was not as cunning [*magically competent*] as they were'; but then the parish priest of Addingham said another priest had told him that Steward kept three bees under a stone, 'and called them out one by one, and gave each of them a drop of blood from his finger'.

This very early reference to spirits in creature form, who would later be known as witches' familiars, marks Steward as someone straddling the roles of cunning man, witch, and ritual magician, and clearly it was sufficient to persuade the priests that he was a suitable person to work alongside them in what was to be a complex magical operation. It was certainly enough for Fr Richardson, who promised his assistance, making clear that the way to get this treasure was to make use of 'conjurations and invocations of evil spirits, as well as other illicit and criminal divinations and acts of *sortilegium*', and the priests quietened any reservations the laymen might have about this use of magic by saying that all except one would be standing within a circle – Steward maintained he was sufficiently confident in his own magical abilities not to need this precaution – and so everyone would be safe.[8] So they all met in a house in Bingley belonging to someone simply called 'Ottwell'. Whatever else he may have been in private life, Ottwell was also clearly a ritual magician, for in his bedroom he had a parchment circle 20 feet wide (another witness said there were three circles, one of them 30 feet across); a large book – Wilson calls it a 'Mass book', but as we are told they wrote in it, it is more likely to have been a grimoire; two stoles; a gilded object which reminded Wilson of a holy water sprinkler; some incense; and a number of grimoires. Fr Richardson had brought along eighteen small birds, which he gave to Wilson, explaining that if the spirit would not obey, he would consecrate them and hold them up in front of the spirit, which would then assume the form of a two-year-old child and be obedient.

Preparations went ahead. Fr Richardson, assisted by another priest, John Wilkinson, a canon of Drax priory, who provided a grimoire of his own, supervised the making of a *lamen* (a piece of metal, inscribed with magical words, signs, and characters). This *lamen* was made from lead, and was engraved with a human figure to the accompaniment of genuflections and prayers from Fr Richardson, Thomas Jameson, and Steward himself.[9] Characters and signs were written on the parchment circle, and when asked by the court what the characters and signs engraved on the *lamen* were Fr Richardson answered, 'The figure of the demon Oberion and four names, whereof "Storax" was one, and the other three were taken from the book.' Steward also gilded a sceptre or wand, thereby completing the magical impedimenta required for the operation. Now, according to Fr Richardson's indictment, all the treasure seekers were due to meet at Mixenden on 28 January 1510,[10] but night supervened before they were all assembled, and either the next day or a week later (the record is not clear on this point), they all set off separately in order to divert suspicion. A group of nine men leaving together would have caused unwelcome gossip and speculation. Their intention was to reassemble at a cross on the outskirts of Northowram at sunset, and to perform their ritual by moonlight; but a dense fog rose, causing them to miss their way, and they ended up a mile from the cross at a town called Cockin. Realising their mistake, Wilkinson, Ottwell, and another of their company, Lawrence Knowles, volunteered to try to find the right cross. They asked a local man the way, but although he tried to guide them, the fog was too thick and so they wandered round for a while before finishing where they started.

There they found that the others had gone back to Cockin, so finally all the treasure seekers were reunited. But harmony, already abraded by the disappointments of the day, did not last long, for Fr Greenwood had brought along his father and his brother, since the two of them had heard of the treasure and knew the locality well. Their contribution, however, was not altogether helpful. Edmund, the father, drew Thomas Jameson to one side and advised him to forget the whole business. Many had tried before, he said, and failed, and in any case, should not Jameson consider the consequences for his reputation should his part in these proceedings become public knowledge? So the mood of the company deteriorated further and they started squabbling about the distribution of spoils, even though they had none as yet to divide between them, at which Thomas Jameson was so angry that he took down their names and threatened to report them to the king and his council, a threat which Fr Greenwood's father heard with sufficient seriousness to change his name, just in case.

This treasure-hunting attempt, then, may have ended badly – indeed, it ended with Steward and Jameson in court, with the others, and all of them sentenced to punishment of various kinds – but the evidence given during their investigations produced more details of their previous magical practices. Canon Wilkinson, for example, confessed that when he was only twelve he had been used as a medium by a scholar from Orléans, and had seen in a mirror a woman with a rosary in her hand, and a spirit crowned like a king, seated on a chair of gold; and James Steward told the court that Thomas Laton had once come to him 'to seek remedy for a vexation that he has in his mind by night and by day' – an interesting example of someone's seeking help for a psychological rather than a physical problem – for which Steward prescribed medicines compounded of spices and herbs and a reading of the Ascension Day gospel: 'And he says that he believes steadfastly that these things, with other prayers and good deeds that he bid them do, did ease him.' The Gospel for Ascension Day comes from Mark 16.14–20 and, significantly in this context, describes how Jesus appeared to the Apostles and gave them His commission to go out and preach the Gospel, along with the ability to cast out devils and to lay hands on the sick and make them recover. So far so traditional, but Steward also confessed that when people came to him about lost or stolen articles, he would impress them by opening a book of astrology, a book whose contents he admitted he did not understand: 'and some would give him money, and some wax wherewith he kept certain lights in the church'. This, of course, is not enough to make him a complete fraud, as Kittredge implies,[11] merely that he liked to enhance his reputation by a little showmanship. If he knew nothing of astrology, as he says, it is likely to be that his mathematics were not good enough for him to be able to draw up a chart. Nevertheless, he was certainly prepared to use the psalter and key method to detect a thief. He says he used it only once, but this may be part and parcel of his otherwise blanket denial of keeping bees, making a *lamen* or a parchment circle, baptising or sacrificing animals, and invoking demons – 'he hopes he does not know how to do so'. Of course not. He was standing in front of the Archbishop of York on charges of heresy and *sortilegium*, and if he were brazen or foolish enough to admit to being a professional cunning man or magician, the penalties could be severe. It is thus interesting that, in answer to the question whether he was standing outwith the magic circle during the parties' invocations, he says not that he never took part in such a ritual, but that he does not remember whether he was inside or out.

Here, then, we have a detailed account of what passed for usual and widely acceptable behaviour, even if it was not an everyday occurrence, in which saying or hearing Mass as a preliminary to taking part in ritual magic was taken for granted as a desirable precaution, and baptising small animals before sacrificing them to demons because the magic required the loss of a Christian soul apparently presented no problems to the clergy or the laity involved. (Both these are mentioned in the evidence of this case, along with all the other details.) Perhaps a dozen people took part, some directly, some indirectly, in this incident, most as active participants in the magic; so when Reginald Scot, writing in 1584 of cunning men and women that they were both prolific and popular, and that 'they attain such credit as I have heard, to my grief, some of the ministry confirm that they have had in their parish at one instant 17 or 18 witches', neither he nor his informants appear to have been exaggerating much, if indeed at all.[12] Such perceptions, even if this expression of them comes from the end of the century, were troubling those in authority very early in Henry VIII's reign. *An Act Concerning Physicians and Surgeons*, for example, promulgated in 1511, expressed disapproval – perhaps not entirely unwarranted – of the large number of magico-medical practitioners to whom people could and clearly did turn in time of need.

> For as much as the science and cunning of physic (and surgery), to the perfect knowledge whereof be requisite both great learning and ripe experience, is daily within this realm exercised by a great multitude of ignorant persons, of whom the great part have no manner of insight in the same, nor in any other kind of learning … So far forth that common artificers, [such] as smiths, weavers, and women, boldly and customably take upon them great cures and things of great difficulty in which they partly use sorcery and witchcraft, [and] partly apply such medicine unto the disease as be very annoying, and nothing meetly (therefore to the high displeasure of God, great infamy to the faculties, and the grievous hurt, damage, and destruction of many of the King's liege people – most specially of them that cannot discern the uncunning from the cunning): be it therefore, to the surety and comfort of all manner of people, by the authority of this present Parliament enacted, etc. [*provisions and penalties for unauthorised medical practice follow*].[13]

Evidently this is aimed principally at cunning men and women, and the reference to sorcery *and* witchcraft suggests that these two practices were perceived as different, the simplest explanation being that 'sorcery' referred to divinatory techniques intended either to diagnose the source of the problem or the most suitable and effective answer to it, and 'witchcraft' to those charms, incantations, or ultimately harmful remedies chosen to deal with the matter in hand. Singling out smiths and weavers is interesting. That women practised both domestic medicine and certain kinds of magic was well known, and so it is not surprising to find them classed here as undesirable intruders into the complex field of learned medicine. However, why mention smiths and weavers as examples of the unlearned sort? In the late 1480s there had been a revival of the Lollard heresy, and by 1510 it had turned into a major problem which the Convocation of Canterbury decided to deal with in 1511. In consequence of the assembly's discussions, and following the lead of the Bishop of London, who had already begun to initiate prosecutions, the Archbishop of Canterbury gave his authority to an extensive deracination of Lollards and other heretics in his diocese. Now as it happened, Lollards by and large were actually hostile to magic and the notion of magic – they were vehemently opposed to many of the Church's practices, describing them as no better than magic – but it also happened that many of these people were artisans and cloth workers. So it is possible that, given the new and intensive moves against them (and other heretics) in London and the immediate area of the English capital, moves which quickly spread to other parts of the kingdom, smiths and weavers were uppermost in Parliament's mind when it was thinking of undesirables from the working classes, and hence they made their way as exemplars into the subsequent Act.[14]

While one end of the social spectrum was becoming the focus of official disapprobation, royal targets for occult practices of one kind or another, for example, had not faded away with Henry VII. The Tudor dynasty promised to blossom during the early years of Henry VIII's reign, but the marriage of Henry and Queen Katharine, productive of several children, only one of whom, a daughter, had survived, by the 1520s reached a stage where further appearances of children, never mind healthy and male, were clearly not going to happen. In the minds of the ruling classes, therefore, the question of what might be the state of the English kingdom should Henry die with no more than a female heir began to formulate, and those with royal blood outwith the Tudor family (such as it was) could perhaps be forgiven if the thought of their acceding to the English throne whispered quietly to their ambition. One of the most obvious of these potential claimants was Edward Stafford, 3rd Duke of Buckingham, a man with the blood of Edward III in his veins, who might be expected to have an interest in when Henry Tudor would die; and sure enough, in April 1521 he was accused of high treason, arrested, and lodged in the Tower before being put on trial and executed. Among the articles of his indictment appeared the following:

> [On] the tenth day of March in the second year of the King's reign (1511), and at divers times before and after, [the Duke] imagined and compassed the King's death and destruction at London ... and for the accomplishment of the wicked intent and purpose, the 24 of April in the 4 year of the King's reign (1513), he sent one of his chaplains called John de la Court unto the priory of Kenton in Somersetshire, which was an house of Carthusian monks, there to understand of one Nicholas Hopkins, a monk of the same house (who was vainly reputed by way of revelation to have foreknowledge of things to come), what should happen concerning this matter which he had imagined.

The monk swore the chaplain to secrecy except to the duke himself and then said that Stafford would be successful and that, to further his success, he should try to win the people's favour. On 22 July, Stafford sent de la Court to the priory again with letters, asking for further clarification, and again received the same answer. Further letters the following year asked what would happen during the coming war in France and whether the King of Scots would invade England during Henry's absence, to which the monk replied that Henry was going to have no male heir. That Stafford would indeed be the next King of England Hopkins made explicit in a conversation with the duke on 16 April 1515, and his priory was duly rewarded with the promise of annuities in future, while Hopkins himself received various sums of money at different times. The two men had further converse on several more occasions, but the plot (if plot there were) now began to go wrong, partly because the secrecy enjoined by Hopkins was breached as the duke failed to keep his mouth shut and told Charles Knevet, a member of his household, and someone who later testified against him at his trial, how he had sent his chaplain to Hopkins and what Hopkins had said.[15] It is a pity the record does not mention the method by which Hopkins obtained his foreknowledge, other than to call it 'revelation'. This could mean anything from his using one of the usual magical methods of divination to his going into a trance or receiving messages or visions via dreams, but if we want suggestive guidance, we may find it in the religious trances of Elizabeth Barton, the so-called 'holy maid of Kent', who was arrested only a few years later for prophesying after much the same politically dangerous fashion. On the other hand, Hopkins was a cleric, and many of those in holy orders were prepared, as we have seen, to practise both magic and divination; so we cannot rule out the possibility that Hopkins did employ some kind of ritual – unless, of course, he cast astrological charts, but this we should have expected to hear about more clearly than the vague 'by way of revelation' which we are given.

Stafford seems to have been remarkably indiscreet. Putting treasonable questions on paper was almost asking to be found out. These letters were not produced at his trial, but the indictment, which the historian Stow claimed to have seen and read, recorded the verbal evidence about the duke's trafficking with Hopkins, which was given by several of the duke's present and past household and by Hopkins himself; and it also provides a further charge that the duke had said Cardinal Wolsey was an idolater because he had consulted a spirit about the best way to retain the king's favour, an allegation which is just as likely to be true as those about his own consultations with Hopkins.[16] For the simplest thing might be given a preternatural explanation. In 1523, the Earl of Surrey wrote to Wolsey about a stampede of horses in Lord Dacre's troop on active service against Scotland. 'I dare not write the wonders that my Lord Dacre and all his company do say they saw that night, six times, of spirits and fearful sights. And universally all their company say plainly, the Devil was that night among them six times.'[17] 'All their company' will have included men from the shires whose consorting with and consultation of magicians would have been a natural part of their lives back home, and if their horses had fallen sick there, someone such as William Brown would have been available to help them. Brown was prosecuted in February 1528 for using the art of magic (*arte magica*), and for curing horses by giving them herbs and reciting prayers in the manner of spells (*incantatione*). 'He confessed he collects certain herbs and buys others and says the Lord's Prayer five times, the Hail Mary five times, and the Apostles' Creed three times, and with these medicines he cures a horse of the disease known as 'fasshyns' [*i.e. farcy, a form of glanders*].' Similarly, Elizabeth Footman misused religious symbols when she healed a carrier's horse which was sick with botts (the larvae of the gadfly) by taking a reed and making crosses on the horse's belly with it.

Had the men themselves been ill, they could have visited a woman such as Margaret Hunt, prosecuted in May 1528, who could have assisted them, for she was in trouble with the law for the way she cured various disorders. Elizabeth Martin, who testified at Margaret's trial, told the court she had known Margaret for three years, and that the first time she visited her house, she showed Margaret her sore arm; then Margaret asked her her name and advised her to collect certain herbs and rub their sap on her arm while reciting the Lord's Prayer five times, the Hail Mary five times too, and the

Apostles' Creed once, in honour of the Holy Trinity, the Holy Spirit, Saint Ive, and a saint whose name is missing from the record. Then she was to wrap her arm in a light-blue cloth – blue very likely because the colour was associated with the Virgin Mary and thus with purity. When questioned by the court, Margaret explained her procedure. The record begins in Latin, but deviates into English.

> She says that first she asks the sick person's name, and then she kneels down and prays the Blessed Trinity to save them and heal them from all their wicked enemies. Then she teacheth them nine nights for to say five Paternosters, five Aves, and a Creed, and three Paternosters, three Aves and Creeds in the worship of the Holy Spirit; and when they take their chamber and go to bed at night, to say one Pater, one Ave, and one Creed in honour of St Ive, to save them from all envy. Then for them that lie sick of the ague, she teacheth them to gather herb grace, pennyroyal, red sage, red fennel, and the bar root, before sundown, so that it be the last drink that the sick drinketh at night. For them that hath any sores on their bodies, she teacheth them to gather herb grace, dill, vervain, [and] marigolds, put a little holy water to them, and say some prayers: and when she [*the person preparing the medicine*] stampeth, to say three Paternosters, three Aves, and a Creed in worship of Our Lady, if it be a woman that stampeth; and if it be a man, he must say three Paternosters, three Aves, and a Creed in the worship of Jesus. She says she learned this body of teaching in Wales from a woman called Mother Emmet.[18]

The reference to healing people 'from all their wicked enemies' suggests that Margaret may have thought their physical problems were caused by witchcraft (or demons, which in this case would amount to the same thing), and 'to save them from all envy' underlines this interpretation, since envy was held to be one of the distinguishing characteristics of a witch's character and lay behind the concept of the 'evil eye'. Consequently, we may infer that Margaret's prayers, while undoubtedly Christian and pious in their intent, actually acted as counter-magic and thus represented an illicit use of religious behaviour. This mixture of religion with magic, however, while very common and quite traditional, was coming under critical scrutiny from the Tudor government. At a time when the régime was engaged in political and religious revolution – the so-called 'Reformation Parliament' began in 1529 with removal of the clergy's legal privilege to be tried in its own courts, and ended in 1536 with an Act for the dissolution of the English monasteries – the behaviour of the clergy in particular was having hostile, or at least unsympathetic, official eyes turned on it, and the close connection between magic and unorthodoxy was troubling to politicians, who were keen to impose stricter controls on people's morals, beliefs, and actions in answer to imperatives coming, in part at least, from the throne.

Nor was this concern entirely unwarranted. Friars, monks, and parish clergy were notoriously involved in the practice of magic and divination – Thomas Sall, precentor of Norwich Priory, for example, had several houses to which the neighbourhood resorted to receive the benefits of his special arts; William Stapleton, a former Benedictine turned parish priest, helped raise spirits in people's search for buried treasure; Friar John Colsell was arrested in 1535 for practising magic and astrology

– so reformation of clerical behaviour in this regard might well be, and indeed was, regarded as highly desirable.[19] The case of William Stapleton, in fact, illustrates the kind of thing that not infrequently faced the authorities.[20] In a letter addressed to Cardinal Wolsey, he explained that in 1528, while he was still a monk, one Dennis from Hofton brought him a book called *Thesaurus Spirituum* ('A Treasury of Spirits') and then another, *Secreta Secretorum* ('The Secrets of Secrets'), along with a little ring, a metal plate, a circle (perhaps drawn on parchment, perhaps made from wood or metal), and a sword, all connected with the business of treasure hunting. These books and instruments were sold to him and a John Carver for two nobles, Dennis apparently acting as a middleman between the vendor, the vicar of Watton, and Stapleton and Carver. Now, Stapleton wanted to leave the monastery because he was tired of being punished for staying in bed instead of getting up and going down into the church to recite the Divine Office at the proper times. In order to leave legally, however, he needed a dispensation, which had to be paid for, and as he had no money, he thought he would seek some way of gaining the necessary cash. (Presumably this is why we hear of John Carver. He must have put up the cash to buy the vicar's books and equipment on Stapleton's behalf.) Stapleton managed to arrange an agreement that he would pay for his dispensation by the end of the next six months, or return to the monastery if he found he could not do so. 'I went that night to Dennis of Hofton,' he wrote,

> and showed him my licence and desired him to help me towards the purchasing of my said dispensation: who asked of me how I did like the said books, and I said, 'Well'. And then he said, 'If you be minded to go about anything touching the same, I will bring to you two cunning men that have a placard for treasure-trove, by whose means, if I had any cunning, I might the better help myself.

Stapleton agreed to the proposition, met the two men, who provided him with some more books, and the three of them went off to look for treasure. At first they looked on private land and were quickly told to move; then Stapleton and the two cunning men parted company, and Stapleton went first to Norwich, where he met someone called Godfrey. Godfrey knew a man called Anthony Fuller, and Godfrey's servant, a young boy, acted as a medium for him. Together they went to Felmingham and scried for suitable land on which to dig, but found none; so they all went back to Norwich again, where they tried but failed to summon the spirit of the treasure to appear. Having managed to pay for his dispensation, Stapleton was urged by Richard Thorny, whom he had met in Norwich, and some of Thorny's friends to take up treasure hunting again. However, he said he needed better books than those he had. 'Whereupon they informed me that one Leech had a book, to the which book, as they said, the parson of Lesingham had bound a spirit called Andrew Malchus.' So Stapleton went to see Leech, who readily handed over *instrumenta* made according to the book's instructions, and told him that the parson and two other priests had recently evoked the spirit Andrew Malchus, as well as one called 'Oberion' and another called 'Incubus'.

At this point in his narrative, Stapleton makes an extraordinary claim, potentially dangerous for him, as it involved the Cardinal himself.

And when [the spirits] were all raised, Oberion would in no wise speak. And then the parson of Lesingham did demand of Andrew Malchus, and so did John Leiston also [*one of the other priests*], why Oberion would not speak to them. And Andrew Malchus made answer, 'For because [Oberion] was bound unto the Lord Cardinal'. And also they did entreat the said parson of Lesingham and the said John of Leiston that they might depart as at that time; and whensoever it would please them to call them up again, they would gladly do them any service they could. And so they were licensed to depart for that time.

Matters seemed to come to a standstill, but Stapleton continued with his efforts to uncover treasure. A lord from Walsingham contacted him with a view to his digging on his land, offering to make him his personal chaplain if he were successful, but Stapleton failed a preliminary test. The lord buried some money in his garden, and Stapleton had someone scry for him, but he was unable to locate the money, and he was no more successful when he and two more priests went off to a place near Creke Abbey where one of the priests invoked the spirit of the treasure and still 'all came to no purpose'. Not that these failures put people off, for Stapleton seems to have gained some kind of reputation in this field, and the following Lent he received an invitation from a Master Cook of Calkett Hall to find out money which, Cook was sure, lay in the neighbouring area. At this point we learn that the Duke of Norfolk had had Stapleton's grimoire removed from him – why and when we do not know – but for whatever reason it was now restored to him, and Stapleton wrote to John of Leiston, asking him to come and invoke the spirits. John, however, did not turn up, in spite of saying he would, and so Stapleton went off to Calkett Hall with the parish priest of Gorleston to try his luck. But as usual, he had no success at all. He went to London with his brother, but was there arrested at the instance of Lord Leonard from Walsingham because, said Lord Leonard, he had left his service without permission, and his magical impedimenta were confiscated and ended up in the hands of St Thomas More.

Stapleton's letter ends with a peculiar farrago involving the Duke of Norfolk and Cardinal Wolsey. Lord Leonard apparently decided to have Stapleton released from custody, and Stapleton, realising his book and magical instruments were gone, applied to a West Country priest for a job, which he did not get. He was thus stranded in London, and managed to get himself into serious trouble, the fault for which he maintained rested with one of the Duke of Norfolk's servants, a man called Wright. Wright, said Stapleton, told him that the duke was being troubled by a spirit that had been sent by Wolsey to vex him, but Stapleton replied that he should not say such things as 'it was too high a matter to meddle with'. Wright, however, went to the duke and told tales, as a result of which the duke sent for Stapleton and, in his presence, asked Wright if Wright had said anything to Stapleton. Wright denied he had, but when they were alone told Stapleton he had done him a favour with the duke by suggesting that 'by reason of the cunning that you have', Stapleton could rid the duke of the troublesome spirit inflicted on him by the Cardinal. Stapleton protested he did not know how to do such a thing – his expertise, if he had any, one may remember, lay in treasure hunting, and even in this he relied on others to scry and summon spirits for him – but Wright and Stapleton's own brother persuaded him to lie and say he could help. So Stapleton told the duke he had made and consecrated a wax image in his likeness, 'but whether it did him any good for his sickness or nay, I could not tell'. The duke then pressed for details. Did Cardinal Wolsey have a spirit at his command or not? Stapleton replied he did not know, apart from the reason the spirit Oberion was said to have remained silent when they raised him. So was the duke suspicious or intrigued? Stapleton says the duke questioned him further on another occasion, this time assisted by 'a cunning man named Doctor Wilson' – the 'Doctor' suggests he was a scholar from Oxford or Cambridge – and in consequence the interrogation may not have been a comfortable one for Stapleton, especially as the duke ordered Stapleton to write down everything and send the result to Wolsey. Was this out of malice towards the Cardinal, who would receive thereby an insult second-hand, or was it policy? In either case, Stapleton would have had good reason to be terrified. 'Considering the great folly which hath rested in me,' he concluded his report, 'I humbly beseech your Grace to be good and gracious lord unto me, and to take me to your mercy.' Whether Wolsey did or did not remains a matter unknown.[21]

One notes the interest of the aristocracy and landed gentry in these magical attempts to uncover supplements to their wealth, and their apparent acceptance that spirits could be raised or sent to do someone's bidding, as though they were servants. This helps to explain why Thomas Cromwell bothered to send his own secretary, a London alderman, and Thomas Starkey, an Oxford scholar, to investigate the discovery on 7 January 1538 in a London churchyard of the wax image of a child, stuck with two pins and wrapped in a piece of cloth. Fulk Vaughan, a witness to the discovery, who was later questioned by Cromwell's investigators, said the image came from the churchyard opposite his master's house, and that people first thought it actually was the body of a child – an indication that the image was not particularly small. (One recalls Joan Bennett's wax candle the length of a man, intended to waste him as the candle burned away.) After the parish clerk had picked it up and ripped open the cloth in which it was wrapped, Vaughan seems to have taken charge of it and took it to a public document writer called Pole. Pole, however, dismissed the object as a piece of magical amateurism. 'But can someone be killed this way?' asked Vaughan. 'Yes,' answered Pole, and there the conversation ended. Now, it seems that Cromwell knew about Pole and his expertise in magic, because he had had Pole's books removed on an earlier occasion, a slightly surprising move, perhaps, since Pole specialised in finding buried treasure. Indeed, he and Vaughan had already had at least two conversations in which they had agreed to go to Yarmouth to look for treasure troves. However, Cromwell's confiscation of his books, said Pole, had not really interfered much with his magical activities. He could still do a great deal without them, and had friends outwith London who possessed all kinds of books to help in their endeavours. What was this great deal more? The investigators certainly had either their suspicions or prior information, because they asked Vaughan whether he had heard Pole speaking before about what they called 'conjuring matters', and that is why Vaughan told them about his earlier conversations with Pole. 'Conjuring matters' clearly imply evocation of spirits, and it may have been this rather than the actual treasure hunting (although, as we have seen, the two seem to have been allied) that had caused Cromwell to have the scrivener's books removed.[22]

However, Cromwell's nerves had been on edge in regard to all forms of occult activity for several years already. The episode of the London churchyard came at the end of a line of incidents from the 1530s, which coincided with some of the most momentous, not to say destructive, events in English history since the Norman Conquest, and Cromwell was at their heart, assisting at one stage, directing at another. In 1532, for example, he was obliged to take note of the case of William Neville, one of the fifteen younger brothers of John Neville, Lord Latimer. William was fascinated by magic – at one point he tried to make himself a cloak of invisibility – and in consequence got to know a number of magicians, astrologers, and alchemists. One in particular, recorded simply as 'Nashe', knew how to discover missing articles, and in December 1531, when some spoons went missing from Neville's lodgings in London, William consulted Nashe, who claimed to be able to foretell the future (through astrology or scrying in a stone or mirror, perhaps, these being the common methods of divination). Nashe seems to have had nothing to say about the spoons, but he did tell William that his (William's) present wife would die soon, that he would then marry a wealthy heiress, and that within five years his brother, Lord Latimer, would be dead and he (William) would succeed to the barony. This alluring future was confirmed in more detail not long afterwards by Richard Jones, a magician and alchemist, in the presence of two of William's brothers, George and Christopher. Jones also suggested that William have a ring made, which would be imbued with magical properties. These would make him a favourite with the king, said Jones, adding that Cardinal Wolsey had one, and see how important and favoured he had become! Not content with all this, however, William consulted another cunning man, William Wade, like Nashe a caulker by trade, who mentioned the Earl of Warwick, and this apparently random allusion was taken up by Jones, who hinted yet more strongly that William might yet succeed to that title.

By now it was summer 1532 and William was beginning to talk openly of his inheriting the earldom, his belief in his magicians' prophecies leading him further and further into dangerous political waters. For now their talk turned to the king himself – his reign would end in 1533, a Yorkist prince would succeed him, the King of Scots would become the King of England, too, there would be battles on English soil, King Henry would be driven out of the country by the English commons – and by December, Edward Legh, William's chaplain, and Thomas Wood, one of his close friends, were sufficiently disturbed and frightened to have Legh write to Comwell, denouncing his master. Cromwell acted immediately, rounding up everyone involved, and within about a fortnight the whole sad story was in the council's hands. Nashe and Wade disappeared. The rest found themselves in the Tower, although Jones offered to reveal incriminating evidence against the Warden of New College, Oxford, in return for his being released. The release duly happened, but not for quite a while.[23]

Prophecies of one kind or another abounded at this time, and it might be thought that Cromwell had enough to do without sparing attention for magicians, astrologers, alchemists, and witches. In March 1532, Parliament banned payments to Rome from the English Church; in May, St Thomas More resigned as chancellor over the king's seeking annulment of his marriage to the queen so that he could marry Anne Boleyn; in September, the new marriage was a certainty, and Boleyn became queen in January the following year. So all the talk of an earldom's changing hands, the present royal dynasty's coming to an end, and the renewal of civil war, all apparently stemming from a group of magical workers who were, at least in part, playing a young aristocrat for a fool, was certainly enough to make sure that Cromwell would take an interest. Yet it is also worth noting that neither this incident, nor that involving the Duke of Buckingham earlier, set off any official persecution of magical operators. Joan Sergeant from Minehead could cut her sick child's belt into five pieces, go to church and say five Paternosters and five Aves, and then bury the five bits of belt in five different places in the hope of effecting a cure, without danger of being hanged as a witch.[24] Ecclesiastical penance would be sufficient to expunge her fault. However, the politicisation of magic that we have seen happening, gradually but increasingly, at this time, along with changes in the English religious landscape, would, sooner or later, prove sufficient to alter that semi-tolerance. The case of Elizabeth Barton suggests how that process worked. At about Easter 1525, she fell ill, and while incapacitated entered into trances, during which she made predictions. These were accurate enough to be believed at the time, and she successfully survived examination by the Archbishop of Canterbury, on whose estates she and her family lived, so she gained both a reputation and a following. Not long after, she was restored to health and became a Benedictine nun. Her prophecies continued, and included the perilous assertion that the king's marriage to Queen Katharine was good, something she later said to the king himself. This chimed with what a large number of people thought, but, as it ran counter to the flow of contemporary English politics, Elizabeth was inevitably seen by the ruling circles as seditious; and so her examination towards the end of 1533 by Henry's tool, Thomas Cranmer, and the unfavourable reservations of St Thomas More, who had also seen her, meant that she was almost bound to be arrested sooner or later. It is worth noting that the council spent three days discussing the matter – another example, along with Cromwell's concerns over magicians and diviners, of governmental unease in the face of almost anything that smacked of either the preter- or the supernatural. Nevertheless, by February 1534 her fate was decided, and she was arrested, tried without being allowed to make any defence, and hanged at Tyburn on 20 April.[25]

Now, Elizabeth might be seen as just another clairvoyant or fraud, or a mixture of the two, were it not for some of the reactions to her. St Thomas More was wary, not surprisingly perhaps in view of her telling him in the spring of 1533 that

> of late the Devil, in likeness of a bird, was flying and fluttering about her in a chamber, and suffered himself to be taken; and being in [her] hands, suddenly changed in their sight that were present into such a strange, ugly-fashioned bird that they were all afraid and threw him out at the window.[26]

It was a distinctive mark of English witches that they were supposed to have attendant-demons in the form of creatures such as dogs, cats, frogs, or birds, and so it would not be difficult for any hostile party to regard such an incident as proof, or at least as a strong indication, that Elizabeth was a witch; and indeed the anonymous author of *The Image of Ypocresye* called her a witch and said she was sent from the Devil, while Reginald Scot included her among those witches who 'spake hollow, as in the bottom of their bellies, whereby they are aptly in Latin called '*ventriloqui*'.[27] Elizabeth's whole story, including her alleged confession to fraud, is difficult to assess, because she later became a stick with which Protestant writers could beat Catholics, and supporters of Henry's second marriage could belabour its opponents; but we can at least see two things distinctly. There was a political imperative to discredit and silence her – 'If credence should be given to every such lewd person as would affirm himself to have revelations from God,' wrote Cromwell, 'what readier way was there to subvert all commonwealths and good order in the world?'[28] – and such was the febrile atmosphere of Henry's reign from the late 1530s onwards, with its incidents in high places of foretelling the future, demon-assistants, treasure hunting, misapplication of religious ritual and sacramentals, that fear of what people's involvement with preternatural forces might bring, no matter how harmless their involvement might appear to be, or how much sanctioned by centuries of tradition, was almost bound to lead to their official suppression.

People kept up their spirits with laughter. Joke books and collections of stories provided a safety valve and reassurance for those whose fears were real enough, and gave everyday living an undercurrent of nervous apprehension. One such tale, for example, recounts how John Adroyn was playing the part of the Devil in a stage play in one village, and afterwards went home to his own village 2 miles away, still wearing his costume. En route he ran into a priest and two or three others illegally hunting rabbits. It was getting dark and, when they caught sight of him, they thought he actually was the Devil, and ran away. John, not looking where he was going, tripped over one of their hunting nets and then noticed a horse left behind by one of the poachers. So he mounted it and rode to the nearest squire's house, intending to return the horse to its owner. He knocked at the door and a servant opened it, took one look, slammed it shut again, and ran to tell his master that the Devil was at the door. Daunted, the squire sent for a priest to exorcise him, but when John had a chance to explain who he was, they recognised him and let him into the house. Then comes the moral. 'By this tale ye may see that men fear many times more than they need, which hath caused men to believe that spirits and devils have been seen in divers places, when it hath been nothing so.'[29]

However, while the lower orders were able to continue, for the immediate present, much as before, they were subject to scrutinies if they went too far and annoyed the wrong person, and to ecclesiastical penances, which embarrassed or humiliated the individual in front of his or her community, but did not deprive people of life. So Margaret Chancellor from Suffolk was perhaps lucky not to be punished further for slandering Anne Boleyn in February 1535 by calling her a 'naughty whore' and 'a goggle-eyed whore', but offered the excuse that she was drunk and 'under the influence of an evil spirit',[30] which may mean she was egged on by someone else, or that she was ill at the time ('spirit' in the medical terminology of the time referring to a type of fluid in the body), or that she was prompted by a demon. If she meant this last, it is an interesting example of how some people conceived the relationship between responsibility and wrongdoing, and its acceptability as a legitimate excuse. Demons, after all, were everywhere, and their hand might therefore be seen in any incident. Hence, for example, in January 1534, during a violent storm in Shrewsbury, the Devil appeared in St Alkmond's church and carried off part of the steeple, leaving the imprint of his claws on one of the bells. (More or less the same kind of thing happened in Calais, when a spirit in human form suddenly appeared while a party was going on, and as suddenly vanished, taking part of the house with it.)[31] In fairness to Margaret, too, one must allow that she was not the only person to abuse Anne Boleyn. According to a piece of gossip he picked up from the Marchioness of Exeter, Eustace Chapuys, Imperial ambassador to the English court, 'the King had said to one of his courtiers, by way of a great secret and as though he were at confession, that he had made this marriage [*to Anne Boleyn*], seduced and constrained by *sortilegia*, and that for this reason he considered the said marriage void'.[32] Shades of Edward IV and Elizabeth Woodville. If Henry actually did say this, he knew his royal history.

So did James V of Scotland. Nearly sixty years earlier, his predecessor, James III, had accused the Earl of Mar of consulting *feminae veneficae* ('women specialising in poisons and poisonous magic') with a view to assassinating him, and now in 1537 Janet Douglas, Lady Glamis, was charged with trying to poison the king. This is the wording of the verdict against her,[33] and the note, with the Latin *per pessimum venenum*, 'lie poison', makes it clear that poisoning rather than anything else was the chosen means of causing the king's death. The whole thing was false. This is obvious from the record, which not only notes the people's scepticism, but also Janet's defence. The king hates both her and the Douglas family, she says, so how could she gain sufficient access to him to administer poison? A guilty verdict, however, was a foregone conclusion, and the poor woman was burned alive in Edinburgh Castle on 17 July 1537. Now, this would not warrant inclusion here were it not for the rumour of witchcraft which entered the case. It is mentioned by David Hume of Godscroft, who was twenty-one at the time of Lady Glamis's death, and wrote *History of the House and Family of Douglas and Angus*, based, at least in part, on family papers. After noting that Janet had been 'accused by false witness, condemned, and execute', he adds, 'The point of her accusation was that she and her [second] husband, and her son, and an old priest had gone about to make away the King by witchcraft.'[34] Why would Hume say that? He may have been repeating contemporary propaganda that he found in his sources; he may, from his experience of living in France for a decade during the early seventeenth century, have assumed there was some connection between Lady Glamis's being executed by burning, and witchcraft, even though this was not the means of executing witches in Scotland; or he may have connected the crime of poisoning (*veneficium*) with the crime of poisonous magic (also *veneficium*). We may note, too, the arrest and torture of a priest, along with the rest of the supposed conspiracy. Since many clergy were known to be deeply involved in magic, does his presence suggest, however tenuously, a suspicion of the kind in the minds of the Scottish authorities? On the whole, we can probably say not, but the incident does show how quickly the notion of witchcraft could raise its head, even in royal circles and even if the available evidence pointed in quite another direction.[35]

Meanwhile, in England the dissolution of the monasteries was under way, disrupting communities and local economies, and throwing an extra number of clerical magicians into society to find a living either as parish priests – if they could stomach the concomitant break with Rome – or in some other way, which might include selling their services as professional workers of the occult sciences. This extended further than the mainland, too, for in July 1537, John Butler, Cromwell's commissary in Calais, wrote to Cromwell about two priests, one of whom warranted further official notice. 'I have heretofore certified your Grace of his doings, and at one time he should have been punished for using of sorcery and other things; but there was made such importunate suit made for him at that time that nothing was done.' This importunity seems to have stemmed from Lady Lisle, wife of the governor of Calais, so it looks once again as though magic had friends in high places.[36] Nevertheless, it is at this stage that we begin to hear rather more of women and magic. In 1538, the Bishop of Salisbury felt obliged to write to every parish in his diocese, telling his clergy to admonish midwives not to recommend women in childbirth to undertake traditional Catholic practices of making a vow to a saint or of going on pilgrimage to such and such a shrine, or 'to use any girdles, purses, measures of Our Lady, or any other such superstitious things, to be occupied about the woman while she laboureth, to make her believe to have the better speed by it'.[37] A fuller list of the female witch's range of accomplishments (but one which echoes that of the Bishop of Salisbury, too) is given in John Bale's *Comedy Concerning Three Laws of Nature, Moses, and Christ*, written that same year.[38] Bale was a Carmelite turned layman turned Protestant parson, and was later dubbed 'bilious Bale' because of his forthright, not to say crude, manner as a controversialist. His witch, tellingly called 'Idolatry', appears in Act Two of his *Comedy*, and it seems that an immediately recognisable image of a witch existed in people's imaginations, for a stage direction says, 'Let Idolatry be decked like an old witch.'

The theme of the play is straightforward. The three laws of nature, Moses, and Christ have been corrupted in various ways by faithlessness, and Bale shows that in the end faithlessness will be defeated and that God's three laws will be restored to their proper place in the history of things and the life of the true Christian. The character 'Faithlessness', in pursuit of his wrecking ways, summons up Sodomy and Idolatry, 'the Devil's own kitchen slaves', to assist him in that task.

> I will cause idolatry
> And most vile sodomy
> To work so ungraciously
> Ye shall of your purpose fail.

So they are evoked by magic.

> I conjure you both here
> And charge you to appear
> Like two knaves as ye are ...
> By Tetragrammaton
> I charge ye, appear anon,
> And come out of the dark.

Sodomy and Idolatry then make their entrance, a monk and a witch together. Next, Faithlessness asks the witch, 'Is not thy name Idolatry?' to which Sodomy chooses to answer with a few preliminary remarks.

> Yes, a wholesome woman verily,
> And well seen in philosophy.
> Men's fortunes she can tell.
> She can, by saying her Ave Mary
> And by other charms of sorcery,
> Ease men of toothache by and by,
> Yea, and fetch the Devil from Hell.
> She can milk the cow and hunt the fox,
> And help men of the ague and the pox,
> So they bring money to the box
> When they to her make moan.
> She can fetch again all that is lost,
> And draw drink out of a rotten post
> Without the help of the Holy Ghost.
> In working, she is alone.

Then Faithlessness asks an interesting question. 'What? Sometime thou wert a he?' to which Idolatry answers:

> Yea, but now I am a she,
> And a good midwife, perdy.
> Young children can I charm
> With whisperings and wishings,
> With crossings and with kissings,
> With blazings and with blessings,
> That sprites do them no harm ...
> With holy oil and water
> I can so cloyne and clatter
> That I can at the latter
> Many subtleties contrive.
> I can work wiles in battle
> If I do once but spittle.
> I can make corn and cattle
> That they shall never thrive.
> When ale is in the vat,
> If the brewer please me not,
> The yeast shall fall down flat
> And never have any strength.
> No man shall tonne nor bake,
> Nor meat in season make,
> If I against him take,

> But lose his labour at length.
> Their wells I can up dry,
> Cause trees and herbs to die,
> And flee all pullerie.
> Whereas men doth me move,
> I can make stools to dance,
> And earthen pots to prance,
> That none shall them enhance,
> And do but cast my glove.
> I have charms for the plough,
> And also for the cow.
> She shall give milk enough
> So long as I am pleased.
> Apace the mill shall go,
> So shall the cradle do,
> And the mustard quern also,
> No man therewith diseased.

There follows her claim that she never fails to go to Mass or say her rosary every day (clearly, in context, indicating that she is both superstitious and hypocritical), and then she offers recommendations anent which herb to use for which illness, and which saint to address in each circumstance. Faithlessness applauds the list of her wickednesses.

> It is a sport, I trow,
> To hear how she out blow
> Her witch's crafts in a row.
> By the Mass, I must needs smile![39]

Apart from the anti-Catholic propaganda, then, which links the old faith with magic – a connection which was to become a staple of Protestant controversy – we find that this witch is female and that her magic is largely domestic. She misuses prayers as charms (a feature we have come across before), is knowledgeable about the different properties of herbs (something expected of any housewife, whose duty it was to care for the health of her family), is prepared to use her magic for malevolent as well as beneficent purposes, claims to foretell the future, and works illusions. She is thus a combination of *sortilega*, *malefica*, and *praestigiatrix*, this last being the equivalent of our 'conjuror' or 'illusionist'. It is interesting that Bale offers no explanation for her extraordinary abilities; even the reference to fetching the Devil from Hell is just one more in the list of unusual things she can do. Perhaps there was no need for him to do so, as everyone would assume she was in league with the powers of darkness. However, in view of later insistence that witches consorted with evil spirits in the form of familiar creatures and that these were the source of her power, it is perhaps noteworthy that Bale makes no mention of them. His reference to Idolatry's being a midwife should not be misunderstood. He is not implying that witches tended to be midwives, merely that assisting at childbed was one of this witch's activities, and one observes that his description of what she does there describes Catholic piety rather than magical performance.

Perhaps the most striking part of this dialogue comes in the exchange between Faithlessness and Idolatry when the former says, 'What? Were you at one time a man?' and the latter replies, 'Yes, but now I am a woman.' What does Bale mean by this? He himself gives the appearance of having a high regard for women, and his comments and glosses on the writings of Anne Askew, a Protestant burned at Smithfield in 1546, and Elizabeth Tudor make it clear, as Krista Kesselrig says, 'that Bale expects women to be capable of the same emotional, spiritual, and mental strength as their male counterparts'.[40] Why, then, does he appear to suggest that a witch may be identified as a personification of idolatry and as a new phenomenon, that of female exemplar of worshipper of false deities? The first we have met already, since from the earliest times magical operators had been liable to find themselves accused of demon worship in addition to their other offences, and the sacrificing of small creatures to spirits appears to have been practised in Bale's own day if, for example, we remember the claims of William Stapleton. However, Bale's commendations of women are actually limited. Those of whom he approves must be Protestant, literate, and conformable to Protestant male expectations of how women should behave. So if his commendable woman is God-fearing, her opposite will be Devil-worshipping and, if the former is representative of reformed religion, the latter is a stereotype of the superstitious adherent of the old faith. Hence, on the one hand, 'Idolatry' is a key figure in his anti-Catholic polemic, but on the other is something rather more.

Bale had been a Carmelite since he was twelve, and in 1533 was elected Prior of Ipswich. He was still prior in 1536, but had absorbed Protestant ideas (allegedly in Cambridge), and at some time in 1536 or 1537 gave up his monastic duties, married, and, with the help of Cromwell who appreciated and used his talent for religious controversy, became the parson of Thorndon, a small village in Suffolk, where he remained until Cromwell's fall from power in 1540 sent him into exile in Flanders. His *Comedy* was thus written in the heat of his abandoning the Ipswich priory and going to live in a small country community. In 1801 Thorndon had a population of 526 persons, with sixty-three inhabited houses, and had grown in size since the sixteenth century. Its earlier size might therefore be compared with that of the Essex village of Boreham, which had a population of between 350 and 400 persons in the second half of the sixteenth century. Between 1566 and 1593, four people from Boreham, all women, were accused of being witches,[41] so if we suggest (very tentatively) that the numbers from Thorndon may not have been all that different, we can also suggest that Bale's personal experience of witchcraft in Thorndon was not likely to have been great, and his animus against the witch may thus have been a derivative either of his reading or of his experiences in Norwich and Ipswich, neither of which places seems to have had any noticeable problem with witches at this time.

However, Bale's witch was not a portrait drawn so much from Bale's own experiences as a composite intended to appeal to and be recognised by the audience that watched his play, and that audience was sharply alive to the removal of images from churches in accordance with the royal injunctions of September 1538. 'Such feigned images as ye know of in any of your cures to be so abused with pilgrimages or offerings of anything made thereunto, ye shall, for avoiding that most detestable sin of idolatry, forthwith take down and delay [*destroy*].'42 So to see Idolatry on stage in the guise of a female witch, and in the constant company of Sodomy, as though the two were bosom companions or husband and wife, served merely to emphasise the association between the notion 'female = superstitious' and 'female = sexually degenerate', which echoed all the misogynistic clichés Bale's audience had probably heard a thousand times before. Yet 'Idolatry' here presents another, slightly less obvious, image. Because of the theatrical convention that prevented women from acting on a stage, Idolatry will have been played by a man dressed as a woman. Thus, the notion that idolatry, and by metonymy Catholicism, feminises men and turns them into parodies of what men ought to be unmistakeably suggests to the audience that a witch destroys the natural order of things and subverts God's laws (not to mention those of the king). A male witch, of course, would actually do the same, but his maleness on the stage would not be able to make Bale's point. For that, a feminine image was essential, and the theatrical convention may also help to explain that exchange between Faithlessness and Idolatry: 'What? Were you at one time a man?' 'Yes, but now I am a woman.' There in front of its eyes, the audience could see the man playing the woman, the man in women's clothes, the man changed into a woman.

It may also not be entirely an accident that Bale's instinct here mirrored a change that was taking place in the social psyche. The Protestant versions of Christianity that were now beginning to take root in the English governing class, and that both Edward VI and Elizabeth Tudor would impose on the English people – with varying success, but with constant official pressure – tended to stress the Lutheran ideal of Woman as wife, mother, and submissive housewife.43 Abnormality in female behaviour – that is to say, behaviour which did not conform to the expectations of her own community anent how a woman should comport herself – was disturbing, as much perhaps to the woman herself as to her neighbours and family, and can be seen, in at least some instances, to have led to suspicions that the woman in question was a witch. However, what constituted 'normality' as well as 'abnormality' in behaviour is a question not yet well understood. General expected norms there certainly were, of course: both the Church and the state provided guidance. The witch, however, tended to be a local phenomenon, a person in a community whose speech and behaviour that community judged, estimated, commented on, and sometimes complained about, and its tolerance of one individual might not be the same as its tolerance of another, just as its tolerance of one individual's behaviour might break down if or when circumstances changed. Now this, of course, could be as true of a man as of a woman, so gendered witchcraft, in which the female was more likely than the male to be suspected, criticised, complained of, arrested, investigated, and tried, was a matter of her crossing boundaries set for her by men and, perhaps more importantly, crossing them at the wrong moment.

In the local context, where virtually all witchcraft suspicions or accusations started, this would be a matter of local timing. In a regional or national context, this might depend on other, broader factors; and in the England of the 1530s, so many changes, revolutionary and highly disturbing, whether welcome or not, came hurtling through people's lives that stability, whatever form that might take, became more than a desideratum: a necessity. The old faith, traditional practices, behavioural norms thus retained their attractions. It was not easy, as Eamon Duffy has pointed out, to turn the English from their adherence to the old faith, and indeed the attempt was never entirely successful. However, if one tradition goes, another may be seen as a guarantor of desired stability; and so when the old faith became mere 'superstition' and its rituals and prayers repositories of and adjuncts to magic, a cold official eye was turned upon anything which seemed to prolong its beliefs and usages, and in as much as men expected themselves to be 'rational' and behaviourally controlled, they expected women to be the opposite. Hence male magicians were likely to be seen as unnaturally feminised, and women as irrational, behaviourally uncontrolled individuals in need of boundaries, and needing to have those boundaries policed and enforced. To an extent, of course, this was not new, but the patriarchal emphases of the Protestant confessions underlined it, and the upheavals of contemporary society made it more desirable; and those women who were anxious to conform to the highlighted boundaries were therefore more likely to police their known sex, and pull offenders back into line or expel them from the community altogether via complaint to the courts and the law. Thus, more women than men denounced other women as witches, and so male practitioners of magic, who had hitherto been somewhat more prominent in the record, receded from official view, and female practitioners began to step forward to take their place.[44]

The change, needless to say, was not immediate, but in the same year as Bale's *Three Laws*, the case of Mabel Brigge, a widow aged thirty-two from the East Riding of Yorkshire, came before the authorities.[45] According to Agnes Lokker, who was examined on 28 January 1538, Mabel came to her house, having been sent there by a previous employer. After a while Agnes and her husband John noticed that for three days Mabel fasted until after Mass. Asked why she did so, Mabel explained that she had once undertaken a fast against a man, and that he had broken his neck before her fast was over; so she was now engaged in repeating what was clearly a hostile magical operation against the king and the Duke of Norfolk. She had been hired for that purpose, she said, by Isabel Buck. John was angry, as well he might have been, since Mabel's action amounted to treason. So he put Mabel out of the house and went to have words with Isabel. The matter was hushed up for the time being, and Mabel went to work for another employer, but there she undertook another 'black fast', as she called it, and was accused of stealing some money; and although she denied the theft, she was beaten and thrown out of the house. This, then, was her version of events. The various people named and involved were arrested and held for questioning, and on 4 and 5 February the parties had their chance to explain their positions and try to blame each other. Isabel Buck, for example, denied she had hired Mabel to fast to shorten the lives of the king and duke, but Ralph Bell, the local priest, said that

> John Lokker and Agnes his wife had told him (under seal of confession) that Mabel Brigge did fast what was called 'Black Fast' or 'St Trinian's Fast' in their house to consume and shorten the reign of the King and my lord of Norfolk, and about St Katharine's day last they had told him that William Buck's wife of Hompton had provoked the said Mabel to it.[46]

Mabel, however, said that Isabel had indeed hired her to fast, but when asked the reason, was told that Isabel had lost some money and was desperate to have it found again. It was not Isabel who wanted her to fast against the king's life, but John Lokker, who offered to pay her seven shillings if she would fast for that intent. Thomas Marshall, chantry priest of Hompton, on the other hand, alleged that Mabel had said to John and Agnes that her fast was for mischief, and that he himself had rebuked all three of them for slandering each other.

On 11 March, the principals in the case were brought to York and lodged in separate prisons, where they were re-examined.[47] They appear to have stuck to their previous stories, although Agnes expanded hers by saying that Isabel had gone to her and,

> for fear her husband should be in danger, languished and made great sorrow, meeting with the said Mabel in a stable at [her own] house. They swore hand in hand, foot upon foot, and kissed upon the same, never to discover [*disclose*] the same fast, not even to her [confessor].

The Lenten assizes then heard the case, and altogether four individuals from the assizes were found guilty of treason, one of whom was Mabel. She was executed, along with two of the others. It is a comment on the way gossip could take hold, at a time when communication was necessarily slow between various parts of a country, that on 29 June a conversation between the parish priest of Kirkby Moorside and his parish clerk was reported to the local authorities. Robert Lyon, the clerk, referring to Mabel, noted that her fast must have worked because the king was dead. To this, Robert Keriby, the priest, replied, 'Vengeance must needs light upon him because he hath put so many men wrongfully to death,' and the clerk added that it would be a good thing if Cromwell died as well. It would actually not be long before Cromwell was indeed dead; he was arrested on 10 June 1540 and decapitated on 28 July. Along with him, on the same day, Lord Hungerford also lost his head. William Byrd, vicar of Brodford in Wiltshire, had called the king a heretic for his attack on the monasteries, in spite of which Lord Hungerford had chosen to bring Byrd into his service as his chaplain. For some time Hungerford had also employed three magicians – High Woods, a chaplain, Dr Magdalen, and a woman known as 'Mother Roche' (presumably local) – to conjure spirits in order to find out how long the king was going to live. There is also mention in the record of 'an old woman called Mother Huntley' who was to be examined 'on certain grave misdemeanours alleged against Lord Hungerford'. Now, Hungerford was also being accused, under the Buggery Act of 1533, of practising 'the abominable vice of buggery with William Maister, Thomas Smith, and other his servants', but since it is not clear what Mother Huntley would have to report to the council on that subject, it is perhaps more likely she was being summoned to comment on the conjurations of spirits.[48]

Nor was this all the magic to come before the council in 1540. On 26 August,

> John Heron, the bastard brother of Giles Heron, was sent to the Council from Sir Richard Long, knight, with a letter ... [concerning] the apprehension of him, and of

a sceptre, and certain characters on a plate [*i.e. a lamen*], [and] touching conjurations
found in the house of the said John Heron at the time of his apprehension.[49]

The record of the following day mentions 'his knowledge, suspicion, and consent as
well of the treasons whereof his brother Giles was attainted', and on 28th he was
'committed to the porter's ward' until this line of questioning could be pursued further
and he could be 'examined upon the practice of necromancy'. He remained in custody
until 4 September, when the council asked him about 'his practice of astronomy [*i.e.
astrology*] and necromancy since the prohibition of the late Earl of Essex [*Cromwell*]'.
Heron seems to have given vague answers, because he was then 'remitted to ward
again and charged to put in writing all his practice since the said prohibition, and
the names of them that have required his working in it, and the names and dwelling
places of all such as he knoweth [to be] practitioners of the said craft'. This he must
have done to the council's satisfaction, because on 16 September, 'after examination
... acknowledging his folly in using of fantastical practices in astronomy, [he] was set
at liberty and was bound in recognisance of one hundred marks'. By this arrangement
he was forbidden 'at any time from henceforth [to] practise, use, or exercise any
manner of necromancy, astronomy, calculations, or other experiments', and was also
obliged to report to the council any other occult practitioners he discovered or heard
about.

Not long after the council had dealt with John Heron, however, it had to pursue
a Thomas Walpole from Norfolk.[50] Apparently he had been part of a ring engaged
in distributing an English translation of one of Melanchthon's letters, contrary to
Henry's *Act of Six Articles*, and had implicated others, including one of the Bishop
of Ely's chaplains and a Fleming called Deryck. But he had also conspired 'with one
Ford of East Dereham, touching certain conjurations', so on 4 January 1541 the
local authorities in Norfolk were told to arrest Ford, 'a physician dwelling in East
Dereham, and to fetch from his house for instruments of conjuration, and to send
him up, and such instruments as can be found in his house, unto the Council with
convenient diligence'. Meanwhile, Walpole was committed to the Fleet Prison along
with four others, but for the moment this probably had more to do with his helping
to circulate Melanchthon's letter than his conjurations, since the council did not yet
know what those conjurations had been for. Unfortunately, neither do we because the
record mentions neither Walpole nor Ford again.

Only a year later, on 16 January 1542, the English Parliament printed its *Act against
Conjurations, Witchcrafts, Sorcery, and Enchantments*. It was the first of its kind in
England and is therefore worth quoting in full, but I have modernised the text with a
view to making its provisions more immediately comprehensible.

(i) Where divers and sundry persons unlawfully have devised and practised invocations
and conjurations of spirits, pretending [*claiming*] by such means to understand and
get knowledge for their own lucre, in what place treasure of gold and silver should or
might be found or had in the earth or other secret places:
(ii) and also have used and occupied witchcrafts, enchantments, and sorceries to the
destruction of their neighbours' persons and goods:

(iii) and for the execution of their said false devices and practices have made or caused to be made divers images and pictures of men, women, children, angels or devils, beasts or fowls:

(iv) and have also made crowns, sceptres, swords, rings, glasses [*mirrors*], and other things:

(v) and, giving faith and credit to such fantastical practices, have dug up and pulled down an infinite number of crosses within this realm:

(vi) and taken it upon them to declare and tell where things lost or stolen should be [found]:

which things cannot be used and exercised but to the great offence of God's law, hurt and damage of the King's subjects, and loss of the souls of such offenders, to the great dishonour of God, infamy and disquietness of the realm;

for reformation whereof, be it enacted by the King, our sovereign Lord, with the assent of the lords spiritual and temporal, and the commons in this present Parliament assembled, and by the authority of the same, that if any person or persons, after the first day of May next coming, use, devise, practise, or exercise, or cause to be used, devised, practised, or exercised, any invocations or conjurations of spirits, witchcrafts, enchantments, or sorceries:

(a) to the intent to get or find money or treasure,

(b) or to waste, consume, and destroy any person in his body, members, or goods,

(c) or to provoke any person to unlawful love,

(d) or for any other unlawful intent or purpose, or by occasion or colour of such things, or any of them,

(e) or, in contempt of Christ, or for lucre of money, dig up or pull down any cross or crosses,

(f) or by such invocations or conjurations of spirits, witchcraft, enchantments, or sorcery, or any of them, take upon them to tell or declare where goods stolen or lost shall be [found],

that then all and every such offence and offences, from the said first day of May next coming, shall be deemed, accepted, and judged felony: and that all and every person and persons offending as is above said, [and] their counsellors, abettors, and procurers, and every [one] of them, from the said first day of May, shall be deemed, accepted, and adjudged a felon and felons: and the offender and offenders contrary to this Act, being thereof lawfully convicted before such as shall have power and authority to ear and determine felonies, shall have and suffer such pains of death, loss and forfeiture of their lands, holdings, goods, and chattels as in cases of felony by the course of the common laws of this realm, and also shall lose privilege of clergy and sanctuary.[51]

The brutality of the Act is noteworthy, and while its targets are those which we have seen raising their heads during Henry's reign – invocation and evocation of spirits, treasure hunting, malefice, image magic, the making of magical *instrumenta*, and the detection of lost or stolen articles – it is interesting to see that one more is appended in the second half of the Act – love magic – as though the legislators or the drafter of the original Bill had had their attention drawn to the omission after the initial targets had been identified. Digging up wayside crosses to find treasure was clearly a problem and, indeed, continued to be so. In 1519 Robert Tales was accused before the Bishop of Lincoln for removing a number of crosses in pursuit of treasure; a Dominican, Christopher Threder, was arrested in 1536 for possessing magical books and for digging under crosses to look for treasure; in his *Latter Examination of Mistress Anne Askew* (1547), John Bale lumped 'cross diggers' together with 'sorcerers, charmers, enchanters, dreamers, soothsayers, necromancers, conjurors [*evokers of spirits*], devil raisers, miracle doers, dog leeches, and bawds'; and even as late as 1615, William Sharples, John Brooke, and Richard Jackson were in trouble for this same offence.[52] Now, while the Act concentrates on conjuration of spirits, largely in connection with treasure hunting, malefice, and the recovery of lost or stolen goods, the emphasis is upon conjuration of spirits and this makes one wonder whether the recent cases before the Privy Council, those of Lord Hungerford and John Heron, and their alliance with divination, did not have some influence upon the minds of those introducing and drafting the Bill. One notices, too, that the magic of the Act, especially where a particular offence is specified, refers to the kind of thing practised more by men than by women – the passing mention of love magic is an exception – and while harmful magic is included in the sections clearly aimed at malefice, the helpful, curative magic of home and village is not, at least certainly not by means of specified example. So although female practitioners could certainly fall foul of the 'witchcrafts, enchantments, and sorceries', and 'the intent to provoke any person to unlawful love', one has the impression that women were not at the forefront of the legislators' minds, and that it was the behaviour of their own sex which was the principal target of their intended reformation of manners. This is underlined by another afterthought appended at the end of the Act. Priests, as we have seen, were frequently employed in magic and could perhaps have tried to claim benefit of clergy to spare them the full effects of the Act. So whatever the motives behind the Act, it is clear that the legislators were determined to eradicate these behaviours from the general population and to bear down hard on male practitioners in particular.

John Morris, therefore, should have counted himself lucky to escape the draconian penalties laid down only eight months earlier when in October he received 'a pardon of all felonies, being the crimes of the magic arts, divinations, and *offensiones ariolarum*, committed since 1 May, with release of forfeitures'.[53] *Ariolus* was one of the Latin terms for 'diviner' and is here given in its feminine plural form. So Morris had been consulting cunning women or female witches in addition to practising magic and divination himself, or hiring someone to do it for him. Why he was so favoured, we do not know, but his advocates to the council must have been very influential or very persuasive. Henry Neville, son and heir of the Earl of Westmoreland, was almost as fortunate.[54] He was a somewhat feckless young man, married very young, with some military experience during the early 1540s and a serious gambling habit. This last made him a target for London's fraudsters and one of them, Ninian Menville, told him that there were people who could make him a magic ring which would ensure his success at the gambling table. Warned that involvement in this would be breaking the 1542 Act, Neville decided to ignore the danger and go ahead; whereupon he was introduced to one Gregory Wisdom who promised to make him a ring, and the two men struck a deal very favourable in its provisions to Wisdom. Wisdom then played Neville for a fool and, probably without malicious intent, drew him further into serious danger by performing a pseudo-rite of ritual magic in Neville's house on 26 December 1544. But when neither the ring nor its attendant magical ceremonies worked, Neville became angry and nearly walked away from the whole business.

His credulity, however, got the better of him and he began to listen to tales of treasure hidden beneath a wayside cross on the Neville family estates, gullible to the extent of agreeing to pay Menville and Wisdom to go north and dig for it. Nothing was found, of course, but during Lent 1545 the two conmen approached Neville with a new idea. If he agreed, they would kill his wife by magic and he would be free to marry another more congenial to his tastes (and presumably richer, too). It seems probable he agreed and three weeks later the two men told him they had cast the requisite spell. Whether realisation of the enormity of what he had consented to finally struck him, or whether nerves in the end got the better of him is not clear, but Neville seemed at last to have had enough of Menville and Wisdom and sought to free himself from their web. There followed a brief period of soldiering in Scotland during the autumn of 1545, followed by an even briefer sojourn in France in July 1546; but too many people, his own servants included, knew about at least some of his business with magicians, and by 1 October he had been arrested and charged under the 1542 Act. That he was guilty there was no doubt. The Act made anyone who consulted an occult practitioner a felon as much as the practitioner him or herself, so on this ground alone Neville ought to have been executed as the Act provided. But he had also taken part in the conjuration of spirits and consented to the overthrow of a wayside cross during treasure hunting, as well as to malefice against his present wife. It is almost as though the framers of the Act had people such as Henry Neville specifically in mind when they drafted it. Each one of these offences was also enough to have made Neville a felon and so subject to the death penalty and loss of everything he owned. That he did not suffer these penalties is almost certainly owing to the fortunate chance that the king died in January 1547 and thus did not have the opportunity to exercise his vicious taste for butchery on the naïve young man. Henry had no qualms about executing members of the nobility, so Neville's title would not have saved him. As it was, he lingered in prison until March and emerged into a new reign which had other things to think about and other principal targets for its displeasure, but which was not prepared to forgive and not inclined to forget.

4

WITCHES TO THE NORTH, SOUTH, AND WEST: 1549–1563

With the death of Henry VIII and the accession of his son to the English throne, official animus against occult workers of all kinds became more intense and reformers blasted them with increasing, if repetitious vigour. Typical was Roger Hutchinson, a Fellow of St John's College, Cambridge, who in his *Image of God or Layman's Book* (1550) put words into Satan's mouth: 'I think our Sadducees will be edified more by a conjurer than by the words of godliness. Wherefore I send them to conjurers, sorcerers, enchanters, charmers, witches, which will learn and persuade them that there be devils, and that they be not lusts of the flesh, but spiritual substances and spirits created for vengeance; which now, in the end of the world, shall pour out their strength to pluck the Lamb of God out of the minds of all men.'[1] The government may well have had cause to feel uneasy. Everywhere it looked, it seemed to find magicians of both sexes, astrologers, alchemists, cunning men and women, and diviners whose willingness to engage with the spirit-worlds appeared to be undiminished by threats, admonitions, or punishments. Perhaps they felt freer after the English Parliament had repealed Henry VIII's Witchcraft Act along with other legislation under the terms of a new 'Act for the repeal of certain statutes concerning treasons, felonies, etc.' in 1547. Nevertheless, they continued to be harried, as we can see from the signed confession of William Wycherley, a tailor by trade, who, along with his partner, John Clerk, was examined by Sir Thomas Smith on 23 August 1549. His record is worth quoting in extenso because of the vivid picture it provides of divination and magic in London at this time, and the number of practitioners Wycherley can cite.

Item: he says that about ten years ago he used a circle called *circulus Salomonis* at a place called Pepplesham in Sussex to call up Baro, whom he takes [to be] an oriental or septentrional spirit. Where was also one Robert Bailey, the scryer of the crystal stone, Rev. John Anderson, the master operator, Rev. John Hickley, and Thomas Gosling, in the which their practice they had sword, ring, and holy water. [In this endeavour] they were frustrated, for Baro did not appear, nor [any] other vision of spirit; but there was a terrible wind and tempest during the time they were working in the circle. And since that time he has used no consecrated circle, but has used the crystal to invocate the spirit called Scariot, which he called divers times into the crystal, to have knowledge of things stolen, which the spirit has given him knowledge [of] a hundred times; and thereby men have been restored to their goods. And this practice by the crystal he has, at the commandment of my Lord Protector, executed in the presence of Master Thynne, Master Halley, Master George Blagge, and Master Chancellor, and one Weldon. And by this mean my Lord Protector's plate was found where this deponent told his Grace that it was hidden. And about a month ago, at the change of the moon, he did use this practice with the crystal and invocation of the spirit to know whether he could find things that were lost, and about two months [ago] likewise, at Holyoak, for hidden treasure. But he has found none by his art. [*Signed*, William Wycherley].

Item: he says he can invocate the spirit into a crystal glass [*mirror*] as soon as any man, but he cannot bind the spirit so sure as other people falsely claim they can.

Item: as concerning the sword and the use thereof, he says he has not used the same, except that about two months ago he used holy water [and] an unconsecrated sword (and therefore was unsuccessful) at Holyoak beside Fulham where they dug for treasure and found none. But as they were working at their magic, there came by them along the highway a black, blind horse, and made this deponent and others with him run away, for it was in the night. Otherwise, he has not worked with sword, sceptre, crown, ring, or any other thing.

Item: he says that within this week, one Humphrey Locke, from near Windsor Forest, and one Potter, from St Clement's parish outside Temple Bar, came to this deponent for a sword and a sceptre going upon joints – which have been consecrated and are now polluted – and a ring with the great name of God written thrice, Tetragrammaton, which this deponent delivered them. And they two, with a priest, intend at this or the next lunation to conjure for treasure hidden between Newbury and Reading.

Item: he says that about nine years ago he did conjure, at Yarmouth, in the great circle with the consecrated sword and ring, but nothing appeared unto him because an old priest who was there was so sore afraid that he ran away before the spirit called Ambrose Waterduke could appear.

Scryers

Item: he knows that one Louth in Fleet Street, an embroiderer, uses this crystal stone and goes about daily to dig for treasure. Thomas Malfrey of Goldstone next to Yarmouth [and] a woman beside Stoke Clare, whose name he does not know, are scryers of the glass [*mirror*].

Conjurors

Meyer, a priest and now Assay Master of the Mint at Durham House has conjured for treasure and stolen goods. Rev. John Lloyd, a priest, who formerly lived at Godstone next to Croydon has also used it. Thomas Oldring of Yarmouth is a conjuror and has very good books of conjuring, and a great number [of them]. Rev. Robert Brian of Highgate, priest, formerly a hermit, conjures with a sieve and a pair of shears, invocating St Paul and St Peter. And he also uses the psalter and the key with a psalm, *Deus humani generis* ('God of human kind') or *Deus deorum* ('God of gods').[2] One Thomas Shackleton makes use of the sieve and shears, and he lives in Aldersgate Street, a labourer. [Wycherley] says, by St Saviour, that the man has done many remarkable things therewith, and has essayed many truths. One Christopher Morgan, a plasterer, and his wife, living in Beech Lane next to the Barbican, makes use of the sieve and shears, too. *Item*: one Croxton's wife in Golding Lane in St Giles parish, makes use of the sieve and shears, but speaks only with the fairies. John Davy, a Welshman, recently living with my Lord Protector's Grace, is a prophesier and a great discoverer of things lost. John Turner, living at a place within two miles of Lynne, and his son, conjures a spirit. One Durant, a painter in Norwich, uses invocation of spirits.

And this deponent says that that he thinks there are within England more than five hundred conjurors (but he does not know their names), and a great number especially in Norfolk, Hertfordshire, Worcestershire, and Gloucestershire. [*Signed*, William Wycherley].[5]

We notice that Wycherley, Clerk, and most of the others specialised in thief detection (including discovery of lost articles) or the rather more complex conjuration of spirits to find out buried treasure, both practices specifically described and punished as felonies under Henry VIII's Act. Three points mentioned in his confession are interesting. First, the mention of fairies in connection with thief detection. Whether this means that the spirits raised by Mrs Croxton were interpreted as fairies, or whether fairies were the kind of spirit Mrs Croxton sought to raise is not altogether clear, but thief detection was not their usual role. Secondly, mention of the Lord Protector, the Duke of Somerset, is intriguing. Was John Davy living in his household as a servant, or had he been given lodging there because of his gifts as a prophesier and finder of stolen goods? Wycherley's claim that the duke employed him to use magic to discover some lost (silver) plate may be an idle boast – Wycherley hoping that his supposed engagement by the effective ruler of the country might go a long way to afford him some protection from the lesser authorities who were questioning him – or it could have been the truth. The case of Davy suggests that it may not have been a fiction, and so we may have found another example of the near-highest secular authority's being prepared to condone and use magic, presumably either believing or hoping that the magic would be efficacious. Nor did the duke apparently try to keep his query a secret, since Wycherley says he conjured in the presence of the duke's steward and chamberlain and two others, one an MP and one an important statesman. Thirdly, and perhaps most suggestive, if we believe him, Wycherley claims there was a great number of evokers of spirits all over England and in four of its counties in particular. Unless he had travelled extensively during his earlier years, he cannot have had sufficient knowledge to be able to put even an approximate number on these practitioners, so he may have extrapolated either from his knowledge of London or from knowledge of the four counties he named. So did he travel in them, or was there some kind of network of such people who knew of one another by repute, gossip, or letter? Wycherley's trade of tailor was not really a travelling one, but we do not know what he did for a living before he settled in London. On the whole, then he raises more questions than answers, but does provide suggestive evidence that occult workers were both numerous and active both in and outwith the English capital.

Meanwhile the English government was pressing ahead with religious change overtly intending to suppress Catholicism and Catholic practice in the country and substitute forms of Protestant confession and worship. Propaganda, preaching especially, condemned the use of any kind of magic and any kind of divination, including astrology. Demonic possession raised the troubling question of exorcism: the possession itself might be real, but Catholic means of dealing with it were condemned as superstitious. Visions, prodigies, monstrous births, portents posed difficulties of interpretation: were they messages from God, demonic activity, or natural phenomena? Ghosts posed equally difficult questions: if the Catholic doctrine of Purgatory was to be rejected, the dead must be trapped, so to speak, in Heaven or Hell without any chance of appearing in the material world unless, of course, God permitted them to do so, in which case their appearance was in effect a message from God. But how was one to discriminate between genuine ghost and natural or diabolical illusion? With apparently limited means to deal with contacts by non-human entities – prayer, fasting, and submission to the will of God were really the only legitimate methods approved for Protestants – consciousness of the other world seems to have become, at least in some measure, consciousness of threat, and so Protestant writers and preachers, perhaps subconsciously aware of their restricted ability to calm this unease and fear, turned the greater range of means available to Catholics into manifestations of 'superstition' and identified many of the old faith's pious practices with credulity and delusion. The Protestant Bishop of Gloucester, John Hooper, illustrates this mixture of anti-Catholicism and condemnation of all forms of occult working when he lumps them together as simple idolatry in his *Declaration of the Ten Holy Commandments* (1549).

> To pray or trust in any dead saint departed out of this world is idolatry against this [first] commandment ... Such as fear the menaces and threatenings of the Devil or of devilish people, that mindeth the subversion of God's holy word, and persecution of such as follow it ... Such as be given to astronomy, or other, that superstitiously observe the course and revolution of the heavens, [and] think they can do good or harm, give good fortune or ill, as those think and judge that elevate the figure of heaven to judge what shall follow them, when they perceive by their nativities under what sign they were born, offend against this commandment. The which abomination hath not only been used before our time of superstitious persons, but also nowadays of them that hath a right knowledge of God ... Such as give faith unto the conjuration or sorcery of superstitious persons – as to priests that bless water, wax, bone, bread, ashes, candles: or other to witches or soothsayers, where they abuse the name of God to sing [*chant*] out the fire of him that hath burned his hand, to staunch blood, to heal man or beast: or to such as destinieth what shall happen unto man, and what plenty shall follow of grain and fruit in the earth, health, or sickness in the air – committeth idolatry ... So there be among people christened, that know neither art nor science, that take upon them to know [*people's fates and characters*] by their countenance, the lines of their hands, or by their paces or going ... the same doth the Devil show unto many that, by the abuse of God's name, use superstitious conjurations and enchantments when they seek the truth of the Devil and dead bodies.[5]

We see most of these in operation during the rest of the reign of Edward VI and that of Queen Mary. In 1549 Robert Allen, an astrologer, was arrested and lodged in the Tower of London where he remained until at least February 1552, largely because he had been unwise enough to announce, somewhat prematurely, that Edward VI was dead. His private papers contained spells for thief detection, good luck at dice, knowing whether someone is lying or not, whether a traveller will have a safe journey or not, if someone will succeed in getting a benefice, an astrological figure to determine if one would do well to move house or not, ands an astrological guide to answer whether one should undertake something or not. Edward Underhill recorded in his autobiography, 'The King lay at Hampton Court the same time, and my Lord Protector at Sion [House], unto whom I carried this Allen with his books of conjurations, circles, and many things belonging to that devilish art which, he affirmed before my Lord, was a lawful science, for the statute against such was repealed. "Thou foolish knave!" said my Lord. "If thou and all that be of thy science tell me what I shall do tomorrow, I will give thee all that I have."' So Allen was taken to the Tower and there examined by a zealous Protestant 'unto to whom he did affirm that he knew more in the science of astronomy than all the universities of Oxford and Cambridge', a boast which failed to impress one of their scholars who concluded that '[Allen] knew not the rules of astronomy, but was a very unlearned ass and a sorcerer, for the which he was worthy hanging'. Allen was then confronted with a gambler by the name of Morgan whose acquaintance he denied, although Morgan had already told Underhill several accurate details about Allen's magical activities.[6] In September 1550 a Surrey poulterer was arrested for prophesying and offering magical cures free of charge; in Hooper's diocesan court, four people were presented in 1551 for sorcery and thief detection; and on 24 May that same year, William Tassell from Balsham near Cambridge was arrested and detained 'for casting of figures and prophesying'.[7]

Then in 1552, that occasional connection between the nobility and magical operators, which we have noted before, once again becomes apparent. On 4 April, one Richard Hartlepool had his house searched for writings and other such things, and the next day was committed to solitary confinement in the Fleet Prison. This was because he had known about the activities of someone called Clerke and had helped him with them, for on 5 April Clerke was brought before the Privy Council, 'being accused to be a reporter abroad of certain lewd [*wicked*] prophecies and other slanderous matters touching the King's Majesty and divers noble men of his Council'. He was asked about these and also about 'certain characters and books of nigromancy and conjuration found in his lodging, which were brought before him. Whereunto, being unable to make any other answer but stiff denial of the whole, he was by their lordships committed to the Tower till the matter might be better examined and order taken for the worthy punishment thereof accordingly.' Like Hartlepool, Clerke was kept in solitary confinement, and that is the last we hear of him. The connection with nobility concerns Hartlepool's wife who was arrested along with Anne Calthorpe, Countess of Sussex, on 13 April, both women being sent to the Tower, with the provision that they be 'severally kept so as neither they have any conference together, nor any other with them'. The implication, then, is that the two women were acquainted in some way. Anne Calthorpe was a Protestant and a known troublemaker. She had already been examined in 1549 'for errors in scripture', and had separated from her husband (whom she was later to divorce), and when she and Mrs Hartlepool were eventually set at liberty on 27 September, they were both first given a lecture on the inadvisability of practising what the record calls 'sorceries'. This may mean *sortilegia*, 'prophetic divinations', which would fit the kind of activity for which Clerke and Hartlepool had been arrested, and is just the sort of thing the London government detested.[8]

On 6 July 1553, Robert Allen's failed prophecy about King Edward's death became a reality and Mary Tudor succeeded to the English throne. Her restoration of the Catholic faith made no difference to the English government's view and treatment of occult practitioners. The latter continued to operate much as usual, the former to suppress them whenever they were brought to its attention. On 15 July, 1554 the *London Chronicle* recorded,

> A young wench of the age of 16 or 17 years did open penance at Paul's Cross, standing upon a scaffold all the sermon time, and confessed her fault openly: that she, being enticed by lewd counsel, had counterfeited certain speeches in a house in Aldersgate Street, about the which matter the people were wonderfully molested [*troubled*], some saying that it saying that it was a spirit that spake in a wall, some one thing, some another. On this manner she used herself. She lay in her bed and whistled in a strange whistle made for the [immediate purpose]. Then was there (as she confessed) 6 false knaves, whose names she there declared, confederate with her, which took upon them to interpret what the spirit spake, expressing certain seditious words against the Queen's Highness.[9]

As so often, our difficulty with these confessional accounts lies in assessing whether they are true confessions or not. It is obviously quite possible, even likely, that this young woman, Elizabeth Croft, was admitting a genuine fraud, but we must also bear in mind the possibility that she had been a real medium, manoeuvred or forced into a public declaration of fraud by pressures about which we know nothing, and our possible reservations about spirits and voices do not entitle us to take confessions of fraud at face value, merely because they suit our mindset.

In the same year William Hazelwood, parish clerk of Hornsey in London, was caught by a general visitation and brought before the London commissary on a charge of using '*arte magica seu sortilegio*, in English, witchcraft or sorcery, with a sieve and a pair of shears'. Now, this actually presents a problem of interpretation. *Seu* can mean 'or' or 'and', and it is not altogether clear what 'or' means in this sentence. There are three possible ways to understand what the recorder is saying: (i) Hazelwood was using *ars magica* 'or' *sortilegium*, that is, he was employing one or the other, the recorder is not sure which, and thus there are two separate occult workings involved; (ii) Hazelwood was using *ars magica*, 'that is to say' *sortilegium*, in which case the recorder is identifying *sortilegium* with *ars magica* and saying that the two things are in fact one; (iii) Hazelwood was using *ars magica* 'and' *sortilegium*, which implies that the two are distinct and, as in (i), that there are two separate workings involved. The description of the charge against him does not, unfortunately, make things clearer:

In July was twelve months last past he, the same Hazelwood, having then lost his purse with 14 groats in the same, and thereupon remembering that, he being a child, did hear his mother declare that when any man had lost anything, then they would use a sieve and a pair of shears to bring to knowledge who had the thing lost. And so this examinate, upon occasion thereof, did take a sieve and a pair of shears and hanged the sieve by the point of the shears, and said these words: 'By Peter and Paul, he that hath it' (naming the party whom he in that behalf suspected). Which thing he never used but once, and also declared it to one of his acquaintance.[10]

The principal offence is obviously that of divination, for which *sortilegium* would be the natural translation. But the act is itself magical and the invocation of St Peter and St Paul is clearly a charm, which brings it within the meaning of *ars magica*. So the natural interpretations of *seu* here is 'and', thereby implying that two separate offences in one are being committed. The recorder, however, has chosen to understand *seu* as 'or', which means we are faced by the possibilities of (i) or (ii) and cannot properly decide which is preferable. One notices, too, that the recorder has chosen to translate *ars magica* as 'witchcraft', a choice which seems to suggest either that constant propaganda identifying magic as the equivalent of malefice worked with the help of demons was having an effect on the public's understanding of magic, or, of course, that the equation of the two stems from the recorder's personal belief.

Indeed, we have further examples of occult working at this time in a Somerset cunning woman who earned her living by employing the knowledge she had been taught by fairies; in Nicholas Butler, also from Somerset, who specialised in thief detection and the recovery of stolen goods, and may or may not have been genuine; John Davis from London, arrested in 1556 for 'soothsaying'; and William Atkinson and John Tassell, described as people who could see into the future and declare what it held in store.[11] But while occult working clearly continued uninterrupted, perhaps the most notable is the case of John Dee, arrested at the behest of the Privy Council on 28 May 1555. He was known to the court of Edward VI as a scholar particularly learned in astronomy, astrology, and cosmology, and had thus had a chance to make important contacts, one of whom was Elizabeth Tudor. In 1555 there was the possibility that Queen Mary might produce an heir, so Elizabeth wanted to know what was likely to happen and therefore what she should be doing to provide for her future. Dee worked magic and probably cast horoscopes for the her, the queen and King Philip at Woodstock Palace in April, and pursued his divinations in Great Milton and London, but was later arrested along with one of his astrological assistants, John Field. Both men were closely investigated and by 5 June Dee and others had confessed to 'lewd and vain practices of calculating and conjuring', but were then accused of 'conjuring or witchcraft', probably because soon after Dee's arrest, two children belonging to one of the informers who denounced him suffered harm: one died, the other lost its sight. Eventually, and after he may have suffered torture, Dee was released from the Tower and free to rescue the remnants of his career.[12] But the episode shows how quickly, in spite of the absence of a Parliamentary Act against such things, magic and divination could turn into 'witchcraft' and, if venturing near the higher circles of society, even with those circles' encouragement and approval, how dangerous these practices might turn out to be for those working them.

With the death of Queen Mary in November 1558 and the accession of her half-sister, Protestant reformists began to try to pick up where they left off at the death of Edward VI. Scotland, too, had been restless in religion and by 1557 her Protestants were agitating for wholesale change, an objective they attained in 1560 when a new parliament, following the death of the regent, Mary of Guise, abolished the old faith and set up (but slowly and with many attendant difficulties) a new religious constitution which, unlike that of England, was heavily influenced by the teachings of Calvin and the Genevan school of theology. At about this point, too, records of magical workers in Scotland, missing hitherto – which is why our concentration has been upon England – begin to give us some notion of what was happening there. The earliest is dated 1510 and refers to a justice air at Jedburgh, which asked whether anyone knew anything about witchcraft or sorcery (presumably *sortilegium*) in the area; on 1 June 1536, the bailiff of the Bishop of Aberdeen received a commission to execute justice upon Agnes Scot who had been found guilty of 'witchcraft', the crime being so designated in the vernacular; and in 1542, Cardinal Beaton issued a commission to the Provost of St Salvator's College in St Andrews to try three suspected witches, called *maleficae* ('female workers of harmful magic') and *sortilegae* ('female diviners').

> Within the last few days it has given me great displeasure to be told by many trustworthy people that certain women (viz. JS, ML, and JG alias S) who are not in the least concerned for the salvation of their souls and have put aside their fear of almighty God, have conspired to contrive on more than one occasion devilish illusions and apostasies such as malefice, divination, and the apostate act of working harmful magic. They have brought, and threatened to bring, various other temporal injuries and physical harm upon the inhabitants of this kingdom and (which is even worse) have taken the opportunity to abuse various faithful Christians of both sexes by means of their incantations, superstitions, illusions, and acts of malefice, striving to draw them away from true Christian piety and religion and so bring them, via the disgrace of heresy, apostasy, and acts of harmful magic, wither they themselves are bent – to ruin and damnation.[13]

These references, however, are scattered and very few and give us very little notion of what the practice of magic was like in late Mediaeval Scotland. From later information, we can guess that it was likely to have been as widespread as elsewhere and to have taken much the same diversity of forms as those in England and the rest of Europe; and we must not forget the attendant presence of fairies, holy or magical wells to which people resorted for cures, 'two sights' (*dà shealladh*), whereby the envisioner was able to see in two worlds simultaneously (the physical world and that of the dead or of spirits), and various means of divination such as physiognomy and palmistry, both of which were mentioned in an Act of the Scottish Parliament in 1574. We must also bear in mind that if the manifestations of magical belief and behaviour were local in England, they were likely to be more so in Scotland, whose population and culture were very much more diverse. The Northern Isles and parts of the mainland such as Caithness were deeply influenced by Norway in particular, while the influence in the Borders both west and east was northern English. In the Highlands and the Western Isles the culture and language were Gaelic; in the Lowlands both language and culture were Scots, the dividing line between Highland and Lowland running, not west to east across the middle of the country, but as a steep diagonal from south-west to north-east. Cultural and societal, not to mention linguistic differences within Scotland were therefore sharply defined, and control from the centre was always tenuous.

During the 1530s and 40s, however, the Scottish government was fighting attempts to introduce Protestant-inspired reform into the country. Its efforts were not particularly successful, partly because after the death of James V in 1542 the political centre was unstable, and partly because decisions made in Edinburgh had intermittent or, indeed, no effect in the Highlands and Islands. The 1550s saw further, more concerted efforts by Protestant sympathisers to capture the reins of government and outbreaks of iconoclasm, and the example of England from 1558 gave heart to the Protestant movement. In this, again, Scotland was different from England in as much as the strongest influence upon her impetus for change came from Geneva and the Calvinist theology formulated there. This envisaged a structure for a national Church entirely different from the English model, with closer control of people's beliefs and behaviour through parish committees known as 'kirk sessions', and while these took a long time to get themselves established in large enough numbers to make a visible difference in people's lives, it was actually through them that a majority of witchcraft complaints and investigations would eventually pass. On 10 July 1560, the so-called 'Reformation Parliament' came into session and began the work of dismantling the old faith and Church, and to accompany its efforts the *Scots Confession* appeared, the officially approved statement of the new doctrines and discipline which laid heavy emphasis on ecclesiastically administered discipline of the laity.[14]

At the very end of 1562, an assembly of the new Church discussed proposals for further legislation, and it seems likely that it was during the sessions of this assembly that a Witchcraft Act took shape.[15] The driving force behind it may very well have been the Calvinist reformer John Knox, and when it was laid before Parliament on 4 June the following year, it passed into law with one likely amendment which probably struck out a clause associating magic with Catholicism in a way too overt for the stomachs of Catholics in the government and, of course, the queen herself. The translated text of the Act, which is quite short, is as follows:

(i) In as much as the Queen's Majesty and three Estates in the present Parliament are informed that the heavy and abominable superstition employed by divers of the subjects of this realm, by using witchcrafts, sorcery, and necromancy, and credence given thereto in times past, against the law of God: and for avoiding and putting away all such empty superstition in times to come:

(ii) it is decreed and ordained by the Queen's Majesty and the three foresaid Estates, that no manner of person or persons of whatever station, rank, or condition they may be, take upon hand at any time hereafter to use any kind of witchcrafts, sorcery, or necromancy:

(iii) or give themselves forth to have any such craft or knowledge thereof, thereby abusing the people:

(iv) or that anyone seek any help or response [from] or consultation with such ofresaid users or abusers of witchcrafts, sorceries, or necromancy:

(v) under the pain of death, to be executed against the user [or] abuser, as well as the seeker of the response or consultation.

The subtext of the first paragraph clearly means to include Catholicism as one of the superstitious and therefore ineffective practices listed there, and I am inclined to regard the 'witchcrafts, sorcery, and necromancy' as references to three different categories of magical activity. 'Witchcrafts' will mean 'acts of harmful magic', 'sorcery' will mean 'divination', and 'necromancy' will mean 'magic involving the evocation of spirits'. The plural 'sorceries' in paragraph (iv) simply mirrors the plural 'witchcrafts' and this refers to more than one act of divination. These three broad categories encompass the generality of magical practices we have seen that was common among English occult workers, but how far we may associate them with those carried out by cunning men and women (in Scotland 'charmers') is not quite clear. Obviously there could be an overlap in individual cases, but on the whole the Act seems to be directed principally, not so much against charmers as against those who were liable to do harm with their magic, those who blasphemously sought forbidden knowledge, and those who deliberately evoked spirits to assist them or answer questions.[16] Included in its targets were those who sought magical help, those who asked questions in anticipation of a response whose validity would be guaranteed by its spirit source (necromancy) or its being grounded in occult knowledge of some kind (divination = sorcery), and those who consulted magical workers for either of those two broad purposes.

The penalty for practising these arts and for being a client of the practitioners was, as in the English Act of 1542, draconian and it is worthwhile asking why it should have been so. Certainly Protestant thinking behind the Scottish Act saw aspects of Catholicism as no better than magic, but there was no direct equation of the two and we cannot suggest that the new prosecution of magicians was prosecution of Catholics under another guise. But just as the genesis and drafting of the English Act seems to have been affected by the contemporary phenomenon of people's conjuration of spirits in pursuit of buried treasure, so, as Goodare suggests, the Scottish Act's provisions about consultation may have been influenced by recent political upheavals in the north. Elizabeth Keith, Countess of Huntly, was a formidable member of a staunchly Catholic family who had fallen foul of the ambitions of Sir John Gordon of Auchindon and had managed to alienate the good will of Queen Mary, fresh from her arrival in Scotland in August 1560. As part of her desire to acquaint herself with the more northerly parts of her realm, the queen made a progress to Aberdeen in late August 1562, where the simmering rivalry between the Huntlys and the Gordons eventually resulted in both the earl's and Sir John's being declared outlaw. Rebellion broke out in October, and the Countess consulted witches to find out what would happen. They told her a partial truth. The earl was captured but suffered what appears to have been a heart attack, and died as he was being brought back to Aberdeen. John Knox records the moment, and the countess's reaction to it.

The Earl, immediately after his taking, departed this life without wound or yet appearance of any stroke wherof death might have ensued; and so, because it was late, he was cast over athwart a pair of creels, and so was carried to Aberdeen, and was laid in the Tolbooth thereof, that the response which his wife's witches had given might be fulfilled, who all affirmed – as the most part say – that the same night should he be in the Tolbooth of Aberdeen without any wound upon his body. When his lady got knowledge thereof, she blamed her principal witch, called Janet. But she [*Janet*] stoutly defended herself – as the Devil can ever do – and affirmed that she gave a true answer, albeit she spake not all the truth; for she knew that he should be there dead, but that could not profit my lady. She was angry and sorry for a season. But the Devil, the Mass, and witches have as great credit of her [*Countess Huntly*] this day, the 12th of June 1566, as they had seven years ago.[17]

Two months later proposed legislation which included the Witchcraft Act was being discussed, and if Goodare is right in thinking that Knox may have played an influential role either in drafting the Act or in encouraging its inclusion in those Acts which would pass on to Parliament the following year, he is also right in suggesting that the Huntly incident may have played a part in drawing Knox's attention both to witchcraft and to its clientele. The stage was therefore set for prosecution. But it did not happen, in spite of the fact that there was widespread famine in Scotland in 1563, especially in the north, a disaster which could have had a dire effect on people's perceptions of magical workers, had they been looking for someone to blame. Three weeks after the Act became law, two women from Dunfermline were banished because charges of practising witchcraft had been brought against them; in July, according to Knox, two witches were burned, the elder being 'so blinded with the Devil that she affirmed no judge had power over her'.[18] (The contrast between these two cases is noteworthy and may suggest that in the latter case there was much more to the accusation levelled against them; perhaps heresy was included.) Then on the very last day of December, four women from Fife in the east and Galloway in the west were referred to the Privy Council on charges of witchcraft, but that is all we know; and in case we think these eight constitute quite a large number, contrast this with a single incident in 1562 when the Earl of Moray went to Jedburgh and arrested fifty thieves, all of whom were executed, seventeen by drowning on the spot.[19] As so often, the nobility was treated differently from the polloi. During a conversation with Walter Melville some time after Easter 1563, the queen remarked that Lord Ruthven had offered her a ring, but that she could have no warm feelings for him, 'for I know him to use enchantment'.[20] Rings, as we known from England and gossip anent Cardinal Wolsey, could be enchanted to give the wearer power. The Ruthvens, too, had a continuing history of practising magic, so one can see why the queen may have been suspicious of such a gift, quite apart from any token of sentiment it may have represented. But the nobility, it seems, was free to exercise its interest in the occult sciences without legal consequences, provided that interest did not threaten or appear to threaten the person or power of the sovereign.[21]

In England meanwhile the new régime of Elizabeth Tudor had had witchcraft on its mind almost from the start, because on 15 March 1559 a 'Bill for conjurations, prophecies, and sodomy to be felony' was read in the House of Commons. On 4 April, 'the Bill against sorcery, witchcrafts, and prophecies of badges and arms' was read and ordered to be engrossed. Then on 25 April, 'the Bill for punishment of sorcery, witchcraft, and buggery to be felony' was read again and passed on to the Lords. In the Lords it underwent yet another change of recorded title, 'the Bill whereby the use and practice of enchantments, witchcrafts, and sorceries is made felony', and was read on 27 and 28 April, but got no further.[22] It is not clear whether these variant titles represent vagaries in the subject matter presented to Parliament, or are simply the result of précis by the clerks or the modern transcriber, but prophecy was certainly hived off later into a separate piece of legislation, 'an Act against fond and fantastical prophecies', aimed in fact at rebellion against the Crown. Sodomy, too, disappeared into a separate Bill brought before the Lords on 5 May, so it looks as though the attempt to punish magical working as a felony simply fell by the wayside, partly because Parliament had more important things, such as the royal supremacy, to consider, and partly perhaps because the drafting of the Bill was poor. One notices, for example, that 'witchcraft' and 'sorcery' also appear as 'witchcrafts' and 'sorceries'. So was the proposed Act to be directed against magical working and divination (if that is what 'sorcery' means here) as abstract conceptions, with the result that someone might be prosecuted for *being* a witch or a sorcerer in much the same way as someone might be prosecuted for *being* a Catholic or an Anabaptist; or was the Act meant to afford means of prosecuting *acts* of witchcraft or sorcery, in much the same way as someone might be prosecuted for attending Mass or taking part in any other illegal religious assembly? Whatever the cause for its lapse, the legislation's disappearance was only temporary because in January 1563 it reappeared in different form and in March successfully passed into English law.

George Kittredge and Norman Jones describe the background to its passage and show that a mixture of magic in low places, and magic and politics in high places influenced Lords and Commons first to try to revive Henry VIII's law and then to formulate a new one.[23] The background begins with the arrest of Lady Frances Throgmorton in August, 1559. She was charged with bewitching and poisoning her husband, and 'certain persons accused of sorcery, witchcraft, poisoning, enchantment, etc.' seemed to have been mixed up in the business. In other words, we appear to have a case of *veneficium* ('poisonous magic') which falls uneasily between straightforward intentional poisoning and unintentional poisoning owing to the administration of a herbal mixture (love potion?) which inadvertently turned out to be fatal or near-fatal in its effect.[24] In this same year, John Jewel, Bishop of Salisbury and an enthusiastic apologist for the new Protestant settlement, remarked to a fellow reformist that during the late Queen Mary's reign, 'the number of female magicians [*magarum*] and female workers of poisonous magic [*veneficarum*] had increased everywhere to an enormous extent'.[25] Notice that he emphasises the gender of these magical workers and that he links one group with the use of poisonous materials. Bishop Grindal's visitation injunctions of 1559 required visitors to ask 'whether you do know any that do use charms, sorceries, enchantments, invocations, circles, witchcrafts, soothsaying, or any like crafts or imaginations invented by the Devil, and especially in the time of women's travail'.[26]

So while neither the Throgmorton episode nor the visitation reports had any direct effect upon the English government's growing conviction that something ought to be done to counter the prevalence of occult workers in society, they must have remained at the back of the authorities' minds and festered there, joined in due course by awareness that the problem was not diminishing. At the Chelmsford summer sessions in 1560, John Samond from Danbury in Essex, a brewer, was accused of being a common chanter of spells [*incantator*] and a caster of the evil eye [*fascinator*], harming both human beings and animals.[27]

> The said John, not having God before his eyes, but moved and led astray at the Devil's instigation, by means of the devilish practice of incantation and casting the evil eye on 28 May 1559 and on various days and in various places before and after that date, in Danbury foresaid, from his premeditated ill will threw the evil eye [*fascinavit*] on [Antony] Grant and Bridget Peacock, and cast a spell on them [*incantavit*]; and because of that incantation and evil eye, the foresaid Bridget was weak and had no energy [*languebat*] from the said 28 May 1559 until 29 August, on which day this same Bridget died at Danbury because of the foresaid incantation and evil eye. The said Antony was also weak and had no energy because of the foresaid incantation and evil eye from 28 May 1559 until 28 May 1560, on which day he died at Danbury because of the incantation and evil eye. Consequently, the jury says that the foresaid John feloniously killed and murdered the foresaid Bridget and Antony on the day and in the year and place foresaid.[28]

Murder by magic was a serious business and it was not confined to the lower classes, as the Throgmorton incident shows and as the case of Sir William and Lady Elizabeth St Loe also indicates. Sir William was Elizabeth's third husband. She married him in 1559 and thereby incurred the suspicion and enmity of his younger brother, for Sir William was a very wealthy man and it was feared his money and estates would pass out of the family's hands and into those of his wife when he died – as indeed they eventually did. At least one attempt to kill both William and Elizabeth by poison came to light from the confessions of two magicians, Hugh Draper and Francis Coxe, and although both men seem to have been cleared of the crime, the accusation served to remind everyone of the potential physical dangers which attended practice of the occult arts.[29] Now, Hugh Draper and Francis Coxe revealed this incident because they were already under arrest, along with seven other people, in connection with an entirely different matter. Sir Edward Coke gives their names, their professions or trades, and an outline of the charges at the start of his *Booke of Entries* (1614): Hugh Draper, a 'merchant' (actually an innkeeper) from Bristol; Leonard Bilson and John Cox, both clerics from Winton in Dorset; Robert Man, an ironmonger and Francis Coxe, a yeoman, both from the parish of St Egidius-without-Cripplegate in London; Rudolf Poyntell, a miller from Fakenham and John Cockoyter, a cleric from Harnington, both in Worcestershire; Fabian Withers, a salter from Clerkenwell in Middlesex; and John Wright, a goldsmith living in Westminster. The wide spread of their origins across the south of England shows what a magnet London had become. They were arrested in the city, says

Coke, for various offences – contempt (of court), conjuring spirits, 'sorcery', and chanting spells in London and elsewhere in the kingdom – and committed to the Fleet Prison. After remaining there for three weeks, they were brought to the Court of Queen's Bench on 23 June 1561, made confession openly and publicly of their abominable acts (*nefanda sua*), and then were made to swear on the Gospel that they would not use 'any invocations or conjurations or spirits or incantations or anything connected in any way with such things'. As punishment for their offences, they were put in the Westminster pillory 'by order of the queen and her council'.

Not long after, Francis Coxe, the yeoman, published a short account of his life in sinful magic: *A Short Treatise declaring the detestable wickedness of magical sciences, [such] as necromancy, conjurations of spirits, curious astrology, and such like.* It is perhaps unlikely that he himself either wrote it or saw it through the press – his apparent disclaimer ('Although I lack such eloquence and learning as is to be required in him which should compile any work to the praise or dispraise of anything') sounds like the real writer's attempt to circumvent any objection that a yeoman would not have been able to pen the broadside as it stands[30] – but it is almost certainly based on Coxe's evidence given in court and perhaps supplemented from his answers to other questions, and thus stands as a work both of confession and propaganda, which contains one or two items of interest to us. He mentions, for example, that there was a widespread belief in prophecies, and that this was noticeable particularly in 1558 when 'the whole realm was so troubled and so moved with the blind, enigmatical, and devilish prophecies of that heaven-gazer, Nostradamus'. The third edition of the *Prophéties* had been published that year and there had been a second the year before, so his fame as a seer had begun to spread, and Coxe's mention of him thus reflects contemporary awareness of his work.[31] With a great deal of pious verbiage, Coxe tells us he will be writing about astrology, geomancy, necromancy, and suchlike sciences 'contained under the general name of "Magic"', but takes a long time to get to any sort of narrative, and spends space and effort on condemning astrology in particular – 'experience therein have I had divers and sundry kinds'. He gives an example:

> The question was moved for stolen goods; the hour was by the instrument exactly taken; the astrologer draweth the form of the 12 houses and so calculateth the time which, [*according to his specifications*], he had now in his foresaid calculation moved with talk, and forgetting himself (as he afterwards confessed) where he should have subtracted, he added, and by that means placed the sign that should have been ascending in the 7th house, and so contrarily, that sign which should have been in the 7th house, placed he in the first, whereby all his work was turned upside down and, as we properly term it, the cart set before the horse. Yet he, not finding this his great error, gave judgement that [*the stolen article*] should be had again. So fell it out that it was recovered; whereupon may easily be gathered that if he had calculated right, according to the rules of his art, he should have quite missed the cushion!

Animus against judicial astrology had long been a staple of both ecclesiastical and secular criticism, and would continue for a very long time, but can one detect a slight edge to Coxe's sarcasm and condemnation? Coxe, as we have noted, was one of nine people arrested in 1561. Hugh Draper was another and both he and Coxe owed their confinement to an informer, a John Man, himself an astrologer, who had implicated both of them in the plot to murder Sir William and Lady St Loe.[32] (Draper, ironically enough, was both an astronomer and an astrologer, as can be seen from his large, intricate, and detailed engraving of an astrological sphere on the wall of his cell in the Salt Tower of the Tower of London.) So Coxe had a particular reason to be resentful of astrologers. His second target (he ignores geomancy) is necromancy, by which he clearly means the ritual evocation of spirits, and he gives an illustration drawn from his own experience.

> For that stars and skies are not sufficient for their future prediction, but they must adjoin thereunto most detestable parts or societies with spirits. Which thing, when they go about it and would have anything brought to effect, they do it by one of these 2 means: either, besides the horrible and grievous blasphemies they commit in their conjurations, they must fall to some composition with the Devil – that is, to promise him for his service [they] will abstain from wines, or some certain meats or drinks. As I myself knew a priest not far from a town called Bridgewater which, as it is well known in the country, was a great magician. In all his life-time, after he once began these practices, he never would eat bread, but instead thereof did eat always cheese: which thing, as he confessed divers times, he did because it was so concluded between him and the spirit which served him, for at what time he did eat bread, he should no longer live. Yea, he would blush to say that after a few years he should die and that the Devil for his pains that he took with him, should have in recompense his soul ... The second way, which is as evil as the first, or rather, worse, is thus. When the spirit is once come before the circle, he forthwith demandeth the exorcist a sacrifice, which most commonly is a piece of wax consecrated or hallowed after their own order (for they have certain books called 'books of consecration') or else it is a chicken, a lapwing, or some living creature which, when he hath received, then doth he fulfil the mind of the exorcist; for unless he hath it, he will neither do, neither speak anything ... I mind not here to speak of the trumpery which they have in this their work, [such] as hallowed chalk, water and palm, circle, pentacles and plates [*lamina*] used for defence, crown, sword, and sceptre as a token of power, fire, oils, and powders to make fumigations: [or to speak] of their tedious fasts, washings, and shavings: of the consecration of their invocations, constructions, ligations,[33] maledictions, and other their foresaid instruments wherein is contained such horrible blasphemies as my heart quaketh to think thereon.

If Nostradamus was Coxe's principal bugaboo in connection with astrology, Agrippa was his equivalent when it came to necromancy. 'Cornelius Agrippa, of whom all the world speaketh, whose works remain unto this day, of whose end are divers opinions, some rumours have been that when he rode abroad, he had always a black dog waiting upon him, which dog one day in journeying carried him away, body and soul.' Agrippa was perhaps the doyen of occult studies in the early part of the sixteenth century – his *Three Books of the Hidden Philosophy* (1531) is an immense compendium of the theory and practice of magical working – and while his supposed bad end was fairly recent (1535), Coxe cannot resist adding another anecdote to drive home his point. 'What may we say of Stanshold of late time, which was expert in these sciences, which for robbing of a college in the University of Oxford, was hanged at the town's end for his demerits?' If you are a practising magician the Devil will have you away, or you will turn to crime and die at the end of a rope.

But while Draper, Coxe, and the others were abjuring their transgressions in June 1561, a far more serious, though allied, incident was occupying the attention of the Privy Council. On 14 April that year, a Catholic priest, John Cox, also known as John Devon, was arrested at Gravesend on his way to Flanders. Under interrogation, he revealed the existence of a network of Catholic families in Essex and of a plot to marry the Earl of Northumberland's sister to Arthur Pole, the nephew of Cardinal Pole, thereby creating an alternative Catholic succession to Elizabeth Tudor. Magicians, it appeared, had 'conjured to have known how long the queen should reign, and what should become of religion', a piece of information which resulted in the arrest and imprisonment of some six or eight clerics for invoking spirits with a view to killing Elizabeth thereby. Horoscopes for Elizabeth and Robert Dudley, her favourite, were found among their confiscated papers; so altogether it is not surprising that in a letter to the English ambassador in Paris, a clerk of the Privy Signet could write of 'a nest of conjurors and Mass-mongers', and that Elizabeth herself was convinced that the men were conjuring and conspiring against her. A crucial point, however, is that in spite of these discoveries and allegations, the magicians could not be charged with conjuring Elizabeth's death because Henry VIII's Witchcraft Act, which would have designated their actions felonies, was no longer in existence.[34]

So no wonder that as early as February 1560, in a sermon delivered in the presence of Elizabeth Tudor, Bishop Jewel had lamented that 'this kind of people (I mean witches and sorcerers) within these last few years are marvellously increased within this your Grace's realm. These eyes have seen most evident and manifest marks of their wickedness ... Wherefore your poor subjects' most humbling petition unto your Highness is that the laws touching such malefactors may be put in due execution.'[35] Jewel may have been disturbed then, but by 20 April 1561 so much more had happened that the Lord Chief Justice was moved to write to William Cecil anent the need for a new law for the punishment of witchcraft and sorcery,[36] and Edmund Grindal, Bishop of London, was stirred by his examination of Father Cox to make the very same point to the very same minister of state. So it is likely, as Norman Jones observes, that the government's realisation it had no law wherewith to prosecute these people led eventually to the English Witchcraft Act of 1563. Francis Coxe, in his published *Retractation* of 1561, tacitly explained this official inability to punish magical workers as felons as Elizabeth's mercy towards himself and the rest whom he describes as 'magicians and astrologians, necromantians, witches and sorcerers, blind prophesyers, fortune tellers, a most pestilent infection of a common wealth';[37] but while the supposed magical conspiracy against Elizabeth dragged on through 1562, Thomas Gale, Master in Surgery, noted that many of the disabled men and women he saw in London hospitals had been harmed by the attentions of female magical workers. 'I think there be not so few in London as three score women that occupieth the art of physic and surgery. These women: some of them be called "wise women", or "holy" or "good women"; some of them be called witches and useth to call on certain spirits.'[38] In March that year, the Countess of Lennox and others were arrested and brought before the Star Chamber on 7 May on a charge (one among others) that they had consulted what William Camden calls 'the illegal arts of diviners [*ariolorum*]' to find out when Elizabeth Tudor was likely to die; while in September news also came out that John Prestall and Edward Cosyn, two members of the Pole conspiracy who had fled abroad, had 'practised various incantations and conjurations of evil spirits in working their said affairs, and inquired of an evil spirit how to carry their treasons into effect'.[39]

So all in all, London, the south, and the east of England in particular seemed at this time to be awash with magic and divination or 'prophesying', some of it directed against Elizabeth Tudor herself, and since Elizabeth nearly died of smallpox in October 1562, it may well have seemed possible that maleficent intentions, allied to preternatural powers, were indeed active with alarming hazards for the future. The time for a new Witchcraft Act was thus overdue – the Convocation of Canterbury, meeting on 12 January 1563, heard a proposal 'that there be some penal, sharp, yea, capital pains for witches, charmers, sorcerers, enchanters, and suchlike' – and so on Monday 18 January the *Journal of the House of Commons* recorded that 'five Bills of no great moment had each of them one and the first reading'. This is clarified a little on Thursday 21st – 'the Bill to revive divers Acts to be felony' – and then becomes plain on Thursday 11 February when 'three Bills of no great moment had each of them one reading of which the last, being the Bill for servants robbing their masters, buggery, invocation of evil spirits, enchantments, etc. to be felony, was read the third time and passed the House'. It may be considered odd, after the growing agitation about conjuring spirits and divination which permeated the late 1550s and early 1560s, to find that proposed legislation to deal with the problem is classified as a Bill of no great moment; this, however, was not the comment of the original journal, but of its editor, Sir Simonds D'Ewes, and so we can watch the progress of the Bill without being misled as to the contemporary view of its importance.[40] On Monday 15 February the Bill had been separated into its constituent parts and changes must have been made, because on Monday 8 March 'the Bill against enchantments, sorceries, and witchcraft was read for the first time', and then for a second time the following day. It was next 'brought from the Lords by Master Solicitor' on the morning of Saturday 13 March and was read for the third time, and passed in the Commons on the morning of Thursday 18th, although it is recorded as being read for the third time and passed on the afternoon of Friday 19th, too. On Saturday 20th, it was sent up to the Lords by Master Vice-Chamberlain and recorded as being received there by the *Journal of the House of Lords*. Finally, on the afternoon of 20 April, the Bill received the royal assent and thus passed into law, where it remained until another version was published in 1604.

The modernised text of the *Act against Conjurations, Enchantments, and Witchcrafts* is as follows:

A. Where at this present there is no ordinary or condign punishment provided against the practisers of the wicked offences of

(i) conjurations and invocations of evil spirits, and

(ii) of sorceries, enchantments, charms, and witchcrafts,

the which offences by force of a statute made in the 33rd year of the reign of the late King Henry the Eighth were made to be felony, and so continued until the said statute was repealed by the Act and Statute of Repeal made in the first year of the reign of the late King Edward the Sixth:

since the repeal whereof many fantastical and devilish persons have

(i) devised and practised invocations and conjurations of evil and wicked spirits,

(ii) and have used and practised witchcrafts, enchantments, charms, and sorceries to the destruction of the persons and goods of their neighbours and others subjects of this realm, and (iii) for other lewd [*wicked*] intents and purposes contrary to the laws of almighty God, to the peril of their own souls, and to the great infamy and disquietness of this realm:

for reformation whereof, be it enacted by the Queen's Majesty, with the assent of the Lords spiritual and temporal, and the Commons in this present Parliament assembled, and by the authority of the same:

(a) that if any person or persons after the first day of June next coming use, practise, or exercise any invocations or conjurations of evil and wicked spirits to or for any intent or purpose;

(b) or else if any person or persons after the said first day of June shall practise or exercise any witchcraft, enchantment, charm, or sorcery whereby any person shall happen to be killed or destroyed;

that then, as well every such offender or offenders in witchcraft, enchantment, charm, or sorcery whereby the death of any person doth ensue, [and also] their aiders and counsellors, being lawfully convicted and attainted of either of the said offences, shall suffer pains of death as a felon or felons, and shall lose the privilege and benefit of sanctuary and clergy.

[*The wife or heir of someone so convicted and punished, however, will not be legally affected in his or her rights.*]

B. And further be it enacted by the authority aforesaid,

(c) that if any person or persons after the said first day of June next coming shall use, practise, or exercise any witchcraft, enchantment, charm, or sorcery whereby any person shall happen to be wasted, consumed, or lamed in his or her body or member;

(d) or whereby any goods or chattels of any person shall be destroyed, wasted, or impaired;

then every such offender or offenders, their counsellors, and aiders, being thereof lawfully convicted, shall for his or her first offence or offences:

(1i) suffer imprisonment by the space of one whole year without bail or mainprise;[41]

(1ii) and once in every quarter of the said year shall, in some market town upon the market day or at such time as any fair shall be kept there, stand openly upon the pillory for the space of six hours;

(1iii) and there shall openly confess his or her error and offence;

(2) and for the second offence, being as is aforesaid lawfully convicted or attainted, shall suffer death as a felon, and lose the privilege of clergy and sanctuary [*the wife not*

being affected, as above stated].

[*If the offender is a Peer of the realm and will suffer death if found guilty, trial will be by his or her peers, as in cases of felony or treason.*]

C. And further, to the intent that all manner of practice, use, or exercise of witchcraft, enchantment, charm, or sorcery should be from henceforth utterly avoided, abolished, and taken away, be it enacted by the authority of this present Parliament:

(e) that if any person or persons shall, from and after the said first day of June next coming, take upon him or them, by witchcraft, enchantment, charm, or sorcery, to tell or declare in what place any treasure of gold or silver should or might be found or had in the earth or other secret places:

(f) or where goods or things stolen should be found or become:

(g) or shall use or practise any sorcery, enchantment, charm, or witchcraft to the intent to provoke any person to unlawful love, or to hurt or destroy any person in his or her person, member, or goods:

that then every such person or persons so offending, and being thereof lawfully convicted, shall for the said offence

(3i) suffer imprisonment by the space of one whole year without bail or mainprise,

(3ii) and once in every quarter of the said year shall in some market town upon the market day, or at such time as any fair shall be kept there, stand openly in the pillory for the space of six hours,

(3iii) and there shall openly confess his or her error and offence;

(4) and if any person or persons, being once convicted of the same offence as is aforesaid, do later perpetrate and commit the like offence, that then every such offender, being thereof the second time convicted as is aforesaid, shall forfeit unto the Queen's Majesty, her heirs and successors, all his goods and chattels,

(4i) and suffer imprisonment during life.

There are several points worth noting in connection with this Act. First and most noticeable is the lack of any legal definition of the various actions described as felonies. It seems to be taken for granted that the courts will know what Parliament means by 'witchcraft', 'sorcery', 'enchantment', and so forth. Secondly, the Act deals with deeds, not conditions. That is to say, it prosecuted people for what they did, not for what they were, although, of course, while the commission of a crime does not necessarily rise from a criminal nature, performing an act of magic involving the assistance of demons (which is what the courts understood by the term 'witchcraft') can be understood to argue a pre-existing human will which has allied itself with the forces of evil before any magical act has taken place. Nevertheless, under the Act, 'being' a witch would not have been illegal, since there is no provision made therein for such a condition. Practising 'witchcraft', however, certainly did break both the law's intention and its prohibitions. Thirdly, in spite of what may seem to be a condemnation of magical acts in general, the legislation is fairly specific. It is cast in three stages. First and foremost, as in Henry VIII's Act, evocation of spirits with attendant malefice resulting in death or physical harm is singled out. It appears in the Act because people had been doing this since 1547 and, as we have seen, a common thread to many of the incidents recorded between then and 1563 was precisely conjuration of spirits with the aim of doing harm to others. Reference to 'conjuration' and 'invocation' reflects the difference between the two. Conjuration (or evocation) means summoning spirits to appear visibly under some form or other; invocation, to pray to or address them without the intention they should make an appearance. Scrying in a mirror, for example, falls under the first heading, and we have noted that it was a fairly common practice among male magicians in particular. Invoking a spirit, of course, might well precede its evocation, so the two practices could easily occur in the same operation, but the inclusion of 'witchcrafts, enchantments, charms, and sorceries' here is legal care not to leave open loopholes in case anyone should argue that his or her maleficent results did not include conjuration or invocation. The thrust of *A* is clearly against the summoning of or appeal to spirits for assistance in magical work intended principally to do harm (although 'to or for any intent or purpose' would be legally sufficient to bring an intellectual inquirer after secret wisdom, such as John Dee, within the scope of the Act) and for this particular offence, death was to be the penalty for both practitioner and client.

Fourthly, the Act turns its attention to image magic. The wasting, consumption, or laming of the body clearly has in mind wax images which are made to melt or are stuck through with pins, and once again the reference to goods and chattels (which can obviously not be harmed by image magic) is the keenness of the lawyers to be sure of closing every conceivable loophole. For this offence the punishment is imprisonment and public humiliation – this last an important pressure upon the individual to conform to expected norms of behaviour in future – but for a repetition of the offence, death. The special provision for peers seems to be an attempt, perhaps emanating from the Lords, to keep nobles' dabbling in magic out of the public view, since news that they had done so might provide encouragement and precedent to the lower orders.

Fifthly, the Act forbids three of the most frequently found magical practices: treasure hunting (and as this was usually done with the help of spirits, we find tacit allusion to conjurations and invocations again), thief detection (commonly involving sieve and shears, or key and psalter), and love magic both beneficent and maleficent. (The reference to hurting or destroying anyone in his 'member' surely means causing impotence.) Again, the first offence warrants imprisonment and public humiliation, any subsequent offence, complete loss of property, along with life imprisonment.

Now the Act lists the genres of magical working it wishes to eliminate and punish: witchcraft, enchantment, charm, and sorcery. Is this merely lawyers' verbiage or are these distinct and separate types of magical operation? 'Witchcraft', as we can tell from its prosecution at the time of the Act and later, is intended to refer to maleficent magic; 'enchantment' is incantation, that is, the working of magic which calls for the relevant formulae to be chanted or spoken in a sing-song manner; 'charm' includes magical formulae spoken in an ordinary voice, and the manufacture, bestowal, and use of amulets and similar protective devices;[42] and 'sorcery' covers various forms of divination, such as those referred to in *C* (e)–(g). So the 1563 Act includes and specifies the same magical activities as those designated in the Act of 1542. We may notice that 'necromancy' is not mentioned in either piece of legislation. This may be because it is covered by the references to conjuration and invocation, but it is still interesting to find that the term itself is not employed. A possible explanation is to be found in the care the Parliamentary lawyers seem to have taken over their terminology. If 'sorcery' here means 'divination', as opposed to its looser applications in other documents which perhaps reflect popular usage, 'necromancy' would probably be understood in its basic sense of 'divination by means of the dead', and if this was not regarded as sufficient of an immediate problem to warrant specific inclusion in the law, it may have been felt could be omitted without there being much danger of leaving a major crime uncovered.

Did the new Act have an immediate effect in accordance with its legislators' obvious wishes? In June 1564 in the Archdeacon of Essex's court, Elizabeth Lowys of Great Waltham was accused of bewitching to death John Wodley, Robert Wodley, and John Canell. At the Essex summer assizes, William Rande of Great Totham was said to have bewitched a cow to death. At the Surrey winter sessions, Eden Worsley was alleged to have bewitched and killed Elizabeth Dybye.[43] They were the slow beginning of an increasing tide of prosecution which grew notably greater for the rest of the century. So as far as Parliament was concerned, it had done its job and provided an instrument whereby such wickedness could be detected, punished, and stamped out. As far as the general population was concerned, however, the Act, for all its fierce intentions, was not always quite so helpful.

5

A GROWING WAVE OF WITCHCRAFTS: 1564-1582

The 1560s may have been full of incident in England, but they were no less eventful elsewhere in the British Isles. In Guernsey, for example, Gracyene Gousset, Catherine Prays, and Collette Salmon were executed on 19 November 1563; Françoise Regnouff and Martin Tulouff followed on 17 December; and on 22 December, Collette Gascoing was whipped, mutilated, and banished from the island. All had been refused the royal pardon and all, apart from Collette Gascoing, had been burned (not necessarily alive) for the crimes of witchcraft and sorcery. We get some idea of Martin Tulouff's offences from his admission that the demon who appeared at meetings of witches, which Martin attended four times a week at the crossroad at Les Eturs, took the form of a cat, a clear indication of European rather than English tradition at work. This, however, is precisely the time Guernsey was under pressure from the English government to surrender Catholicism in favour of the new religious régime which at first did not make a great deal of headway against a combination of indifference and sullen resentment. Complaint, indeed, was made that there were 'disturbers of the common quietness in the said isle, moving the people of the same to all insolent disorders and disobediences against God, the Queen's Majesty, and [the] good surety of the said isle'. But contrary to the establishment in England, the Channel Islands were slowly beginning to adopt a Calvinist model of Church government, belief, and worship, since many Huguenots were seeking refuge there from prosecution in France, and Huguenots looked to Geneva for religious direction. A system of close scrutiny of the individual's public and private behaviour started to be adopted and (after a while, of course) this precipitated a greater number of cases of misconduct to be brought before the appropriate courts, magical practice being one obvious form of misbehaviour. There was widespread plague in Guernsey, too, in 1563. Whether the prosecution of three witches that year was stimulated by social unrest, the sudden onset of disease, or a combination of the two is perhaps open to question, and we also have to bear in mind the very recent passing of the new English Witchcraft Act only six months before. What is notable is that the next witchcraft trials in Guernsey took place in 1570, so those three are, to some extent, isolated incidents, which suggests they happened for very local reasons and were not the result of any impulse towards finding scapegoats for the island's troubles.[1]

In 1562 on Jersey, Anne from St Brelade had also been burned for witchcraft, Michelle La Blanche hanged – an oddity of punishment owing to specific local custom in her fief – and Thomasse Becquet was acquitted in 1563. Customary Norman practice anent divination and witchcraft had long been known on the island. *Traités sur les Coutûmes Anglo-Normandes* records both practices as heretical and provides for trial by ordeal as a way of settling a person's guilt or innocence, and although the book consists of a collection of extracts of material not published until 1776, it does contain passages from a thirteenth-century *Mirror of Justices*, one of the chapters including 'the various kinds of divinations [*sortilèges*] or magic, and the punishments which were inflicted by our old customs on those who were found guilty of them'. The various kinds range from interpreting signs in the air or in water or in soil to necromancy, thief detection, astrology, and invocation of spirits, the text overtly stating that 'sorcery is the art of divination'.[2] Once again, however, change in the religious establishment similar to that in Guernsey led to a slow increase in the number of recorded trials and executions for witchcraft on the island. On the Isle of Man, by contrast, things were rather different. Magic had certainly been practised there during the Middle Ages – we hear that one of the island's governors wrote a treatise against it during the 1330s, and the historian Ranulph Higden noted that certain women there would sell wind to sailors, the wind being confined in three knots of thread which the men would untie according to the strength of wind they wanted – but people brought before the island's court on a charge of maleficent witchcraft might easily escape the worst penalties. One woman did so in 1569 because she was pregnant and another in 1598 on a legal technicality.[3] Provision for the arrest of such persons was recorded in the island's spiritual laws and customs.

> Also, all those which are suspected of sorcery or witchcraft, and are presented by the Chapter Quest, then the Ordinary doth examine all such causes; and finding any suspicion, shall appoint another jury of honest probable men within the same parish, and doth commit the party suspected in the mean time to the Bishop his prison; and all the offences and crimes the jury do find or can prove, the Ordinary shall write: and if the jury can bring or prove any notorious fact or crime done by the said person, then the Ordinary doth deliver the same person out of the Bishop's prison to my Lord's gaol and court.[4]

The magic of which these people may have been suspected can be gauged by the case of John the Irishman in 1560, who had a grudge against a farmer from Ballamoar, and one night built a pigsty with a dead weasel in it over a path regularly used by the farmer. He was charged with harmful magic and found guilty but, like the two women we mentioned, escaped execution.[5]

On the mainland, however, life for workers of the occult sciences slowly became more difficult. In June 1564, in the court of the Archdeacon of Essex, Elizabeth Lowys, a married woman aged about thirty-nine or forty, was accused of malicious witchcraft: making her own husband lame, killing two pigs out of spite, blasting a child – 'it lay with the neck twisted, the face under the left shoulder and the right arm clasped with the hand backward and the body lying not right but writhing, and the right leg turned backwards behind the body' – and doing something similar to an adult female. It was common talk in Waltham, the village in which Elizabeth was living at the time, that she was a witch, although on at least one occasion she had advised a woman with a sore arm to go elsewhere and ask someone else for help. The psychological burden her reputation seems to have created for her can be guessed from two incidents, an accusation of blasphemy and an attempted suicide. Anent the first she was asked 'whether she in her yard or house, kneeling, standing, or lying flat, spoke these words: "Christ, my Christ, if thou be a saviour, come down and avenge me of my enemies, or else thou shall not be a saviour."' This could be understood in more than one way. Was she threatening Christ that if He did not aid her to achieve an angry purpose, she would turn elsewhere for assistance? Or was the question about her posture during these alleged remarks taken to be an indication of a ritual action intended to bind Christ to her will and dismiss Him if He did not do her bidding? Either interpretation presented her with a serious personal situation. As for the second, it appears to have been precipitated by her husband's remark to one Thomas Wignall in her hearing.

I may thank my wife for my lameness, for she has bewitched me lame, and when I sent for the cunning man of Witham, he told me it was my wife's doing. And then and there Lowys's wife and her mother who lived with them fell to vexations, and she (the said Elizabeth Lowys) said that, being weary of exercising her witchery because her mother was stronger in bewitching than she was, she would devour herself. And upon that her husband, being in fear of her, went into the street. And when coming home, he found her hanging in the house. She had hanged herself until she was [*nearly*] dead. And her husband cut the rope. And being relieved, Thomas Wignall and others demanded of her why she did so, and she said that she did it to the end that her mother should be hanged because she was the stronger witch.[6]

The man examining her was Thomas Cole, Archdeacon of Essex since 1559, a Calvinist intent on bringing discipline to his district. In June 1564 he heard twenty-three cases of various kinds, of which Elizabeth's seems to have been the only one involving magic. She was not subject to torture – the Archdeacon's court had no authority to apply it – and although many of those instructed to attend such courts failed to do so, Elizabeth did turn up and answered the questions put to her with a combination of boldness and level-headedness. Joyce Gibson suggests she may have been hoping to clear herself of all charges by having people willing to come into court and swear to her innocence – the procedure known as 'compurgation'. But it turned out that if this had indeed been her expectation, it was not to be fulfilled.[7] The crucial event which brought her before a criminal court seems to have been the death of John Canell, the child whose body was so badly twisted awry. Further interrogation of witnesses took place, one of them affirming that 'he hath heard by talk that she hath been suspect of witchery this four years', and as a result, Elizabeth was arrested and taken to Colchester gaol to await her formal trial for murder by magical means. The vicar of Great Waltham where she lived, the Archdeacon of Essex who had initially questioned her, and Lord Rich, the local landowner, justice of the peace, and politician eager to show compliance with the 1563 Witchcraft Act, were all influential men eager to see order established and maintained within their several jurisdictions. Her judges were also men of no mean importance: Gilbert Gerard, the Attorney General, and John Southcote, a justice of the Queen's Bench. It may be said, therefore, that Elizabeth would have been lucky to survive such a formidable combination of determinations and, indeed, she did not. A jury found her guilty, and although execution was deferred for a while because she pleaded pregnancy – no jurisdiction executed expectant women – the delay was temporary; for by March 1565 the child had been born and another woman, Anne Vale, had been brought before the Spring assizes, charged with bewitching eight pigs to death. She, however, turned out to be more fortunate than Elizabeth because she was found not guilty. Elizabeth was hanged along with four other felons the day after the assizes ended.[8]

From now until the end of Elizabeth Tudor's reign, we see what seems to be a growing number of cases covered by the terms of both the Scottish and the English Witchcraft Acts. It is impossible, of course, to draw any meaningful statistical conclusions simply from court records, and it may well be that the appearance of growth in numbers is delusive, that is to say, it may not have been as large as it appears to be. But even if we take into account the necessary caveats, we can reasonably say that the number of investigations and prosecutions of magical offences in the British Isles did not diminish after the Acts, so it is also possible to suggest that if the purpose of the legislation was to eradicate first the use and then belief in the efficacy of magic, it failed because people clearly continued to resort to magical practitioners for the same reasons and in hope of the same services as before. So how was the English Act felt in England, and in Wales where it had supremacy in law as a result of 'An Act for Laws and Practice to be [Ad]ministered in Wales in like form as it is in this Realm' (February 1536) and the Channel Islands where it was likewise the overriding provision for dealing with magical workers and their clients? What, too, was the effect of the Scottish Act within the four different cultural areas which made up Scotland?

The answer anent England is easily given. A series of court cases heard allegations about killing and curing and finding lost articles by the sieve and shears. In Kent, Alice Latter was accused on 1 February 1565 of bewitching Joan Harris to death. She put in a plea of not guilty and was acquitted. On 26 February, a person whose name has not survived was similarly accused, pleaded similarly, and was similarly acquitted. In Surrey, Joan Gourse bewitched a bull to death, put in a plea of not guilty, but was judged culpable by the jury, as was Rose a Borow the following June, having bewitched and killed Alice Lambert, wife of Geoffrey; while in Dorset the local authorities received a letter from the Privy Council 'to cause one Agnes Monday of the county of Dorset to be apprehended and committed to ward, to be further ordered according to the quality of her fault: and further, to make search in her house or other resorting places for all such things as [the authorities] think may tend to witchcraft, and to advertise hither what they shall do herein: which Agnes, besides many other devilish parts, hath of late bewitched one Mistress Chettell [so] that she hath been in peril of her life'.[9]

But one of the noteworthy cases to come before the English courts took place in 1566 in Essex where it was heard in the market town of Chelmsford at the local assize. Our information comes principally from a contemporary pamphlet – the reason for the case's noteworthiness, as this is the first such English pamphlet on this subject – entitled *The Examination and Confession of Certaine Wytches at Chensforde in*

*the Countie of Essex, before the Quenes Majesties Judges, the xxvi day of July, anno
1566.*[10] This falls into three parts: an 'epistle to the reader', accompanied by two sets
of doggerel verses; the examinations of four women (an account clearly based on
pre-trial documents); and a brief 'end and last confession' of one of the condemned.
The 'epistle' consists of an exhortation to the reader to maintain virtue and eschew sin
by avoiding folly and the verses do the same while holding up details of the accused
witches' behaviour and trial as an illustrative warning to avoid all kinds of sin. The
first confession comes from Elizabeth Francis who, with the other accused, lived in
Hatfield Peveral, a village 5 or 6 miles north-east of Chelmsford. A mature woman
at the time of her trial, she told the examining magistrates she first learned the art
of witchcraft at the age of twelve. Her grandmother, now dead, had encouraged
her to renounce God and give some of her blood to 'Satan' whom her grandmother
presented to her in the form of a white spotted cat. The name appears in the pamphlet
via the pen of the recording clerk – 'Satan (as she termed it) ... the said cat (calling it
Satan)' – but the possible reservation in his voice will not have been mirrored in the
voices of the women for whom, clearly, this cat was either the origin or the medium
of preternatural power, and their calling it 'Satan' suggests they were fully persuaded
of its demonic nature. In consequence, we have here, not an example of magistrates'
misreading (deliberately or not) a popular magical practice, but of the practitioners'
conscious awareness that they were trafficking with powers of darkness.

The blood Elizabeth offered the cat-demon appears to have had the nature first of
the sealing of a covenant and secondly of a reward for magical services rendered – a
mere token, it seems, because the familiar required only a single drop in recompense,
its principal food being bread and milk. According to the pamphlet – and there may
have been further information which is lost to us – Elizabeth's instruction in the art
of witchcraft amounted to no more than this: the gift of the cat, with instructions to
call it 'Satan', offer it blood, and feed it on bread and milk. This does not amount to
inherited witchcraft, in spite of the two women's family relationship, and it is notable
that Elizabeth's subsequent acts of magic as described here stem entirely from her
asking 'Satan' to grant her certain wishes. She works no magic for herself, nor does she
betray any knowledge of how to do so. However, once Elizabeth made her bargain, she
set about gratifying her immediate desires. Not surprisingly, her first request was to be
rich and have material possessions. The familiar then spoke to her 'in a strange hollow
voice, but such as she understood by use', and promised her what she asked for. This
voice is interesting and suggests that the spirit may have been conceived as something
similar to the Hebrew *ob*, which the demonologist Johann Wier and, following him,
Reginald Scot explained 'signifies a bag or bottle, [and] therefore the demons who
give responses in obscure voices from the more remote parts of the body ... as though
from a bottle, were called *ob* by the Hebrews'.[11] The context of this explanation is
that of ventriloquism. Some magical workers used this device, explained Wier and
Scot, to give the impression that a demon was speaking through them: as Thomas
Ady expressed it, 'the imposture of a hollow feigned voice, which those witches or
deceivers used in their oracling, by harring in their throats'.[12] There is no telling, in
Elizabeth's instance, whether her demon's voice originated with her in some fashion
such as ventriloquism or imagination (and I am not suggesting that either possibility

is the only one), but the fact that it was not immediately comprehensible to her, becoming so after her ear had become attuned to its modulations and expressions, tends to suggest – unless, of course, we simply dismiss her assertions about the voice as lies or fantasy – that the voice was either muffled or had a way of speaking strange to her, such as a thick foreign accent. The other accused women also claimed to have heard it, although do not say they had any difficulty in understanding what it said – we must remember that in the pamphlet we are reading a précis of the original documents – so on the whole we are constrained to say that the source and nature of the voice remain obscure.

Elizabeth's immediate notion of riches and possessions was sheep, not surprising perhaps in the inhabitant of a village, and her familiar obliged by giving her twenty-eight, his gift proving, in the manner of all such demonic fulfilments, a false largesse, for they 'continued with her for a time, but in the end did all wear away, she knew not how'. Next she wanted a husband and got one, after a fashion, Andrew Byles, 'a man of some wealth', but only on condition that he first abuse her: which he did and then refused to marry her after all. It is not clear whether at this stage Elizabeth was still a girl of twelve or thirteen, or whether we are to suppose that some time passed before she entered into this relationship – if 'relationship' it was rather than a one-night stand – but legally, under legislation of Edward III, the age of consent was twelve (the Elizabethan parliament lowered it to ten in 1576), so Elizabeth Francis could have been considered, by herself and others, as more or less ready for marriage at about that age. Certainly it was not long before she was pregnant and, in anger at Byles's refusal to marry her, 'she willed "Satan" to waste his goods, which he forthwith did: and yet not being contented with this, she willed him to touch [Byles's] body, which he forthwith did, wherefore [Byles] died'. She also, with 'Satan's' advice, procured an abortifacient, drank it, and 'destroyed the child forthwith'; but as abortion was not a felony under English secular law at the time and counted as trespass or misdemeanour if it came before a secular court, it was a matter to be dealt with rather by the Church, and therefore its inclusion among Elizabeth's offences was because of its demonic association.[13] The unhappy experience with Andrew Byles did not, it seems, give Elizabeth pause for reflection, and when she asked 'Satan' for another husband, he gave her Christopher Francis, to whom she was married at the time of her arrest. Fornication had, once again, taken place before wedlock and, again, had resulted in pregnancy. This time, however, a marriage did happen and the daughter born three months thereafter was allowed her life – but not for long. The demonically assisted union did not prosper, Christopher being bad-tempered, and so Elizabeth decided to ask 'Satan' to kill her six-month-old child (which he did) and to render her husband lame. This too 'Satan' granted. 'It came in a morning to this Francis's shoe, lying in it like a toad, and when he perceived it, putting on his shoe, and had touched it with his foot, he, being suddenly amazed, asked her of what it was. And she bade him kill it, and he was forthwith taken with a lameness whereof he cannot be healed.'

After fifteen or sixteen years, however, Elizabeth decided to give 'Satan' to her neighbour, Agnes Waterhouse, who was aged sixty-four at the time of her trial, and was described by Elizabeth on another occasion in 1579 as her sister.[14] Some people apparently said Elizabeth did this because she was tired of the cat, but as 'Satan' seems to have fulfilled Elizabeth's every expressed wish so far, one must agree with her examiners that this explanation vis-à-vis 'Satan' as a demon-familiar is unlikely to have been true. On the other hand, 'Satan' the cat form would have been nearing the end of its natural life expectancy at this time – modern domestic cats tend to live for between fifteen and seventeen years, although some, of course, live longer – and so Elizabeth may simply have decided she did not want to look after an old cat anymore and shuffled it off on her sister. Whatever the truth of the matter, the exchange is described in the pamphlet as Elizabeth's giving Agnes the cat along with the same instructions she had received from their grandmother, in return for a cake fresh from the oven.

That brought to an end any confession Elizabeth was willing to make. Her preliminary examiners who heard this sorry tale were the Archdeacon of Essex and a local justice of the peace, Church and state thus represented from the start. What they appear to have listened to was the account of a mature woman looking back to a time when she was abused by an older man and had taken steps to rid herself of a pregnancy resulting from that abuse. How long after this she entered an abusive marriage we do not know, but her experiences seem to have made her bitter, since asking her demon to kill her daughter looks like an act of spite against her husband. 'After they were married, they lived not so quietly as she desired … *wherefore* [my italics] she willed "Satan", her cat, to kill the child.'

Psychologising the past, of course, is to traverse a minefield, and in any case the pamphlet does not give us the whole story, for in addition to these offences Elizabeth was also charged with bewitching the infant child of William Auger from Hatfield Peverel. The child became 'decrepit', a word which signified 'prematurely aged' and was probably meant to indicate that the child was weak and that its ability to move was badly affected.[15] It is thus clear that it was at least possible that Elizabeth had contravened the Witchcraft Act in such ways – by invoking a spirit and using maleficent magic to destroy both persons and goods – as to merit the death penalty laid down by statute for such offences. Indeed, she admitted her crimes, *cognovit indictamentum*, and yet she escaped the gallows. Her punishment was a year's imprisonment, the penalty for 'wasting, consuming, or laming' someone in his or her body, or for 'destroying, wasting, or impairing' a person's goods or chattels. Elizabeth must, therefore, have been convicted of 'wasting' her first husband's goods, but not of causing his death by magic, and of laming her second husband, but not of magically causing the death of her daughter. Making William Auger's child 'decrepit' will have been considered 'wasting' or 'laming', and thus count as a repetition – a very recent one since it took place in February 1566 – of the earlier laming of Christopher Francis. Why the jury apparently ignored the verbal traffic with 'Satan' which, surely, should have been seen as a kind of invocation and hence an action forbidden by the Act, we cannot reasonably guess. Yet the most notable aspect of Elizabeth's confession, and so the evidence heard in court, is not so much the various incidents of which it is composed, as their causative agency. Elizabeth is quite clear that the power behind them was demonic, and that she consciously and deliberately made use of that power to achieve her will which demanded both harmless benefits for herself (the sheep and husbands) and maleficent ripostes to the harm she received from others. Torture had not been used to elicit her confession and it looks very much as though she was a firm believer in the source of her gratifications and the power which stemmed from their fulfilment, an impression strengthened, as we shall see, by her later history.

Gratification of spite in return for perceived rebuffs was also the principal motive underlying Elizabeth's sister's use of the cat-familiar. We are told that she tested the willingness of 'Satan' to serve her by getting him to kill one of her own pigs.

> Which he did, and she gave him or his labour a chicken which he first required of her, and a drop of her blood. And this she gave him at all times when he did anything for her, by pricking her hand or face and putting the blood to his mouth, which he sucked, and forthwith would lie down in his pot again, wherein she kept him: the spots of all the which pricks are yet to be seen in her skin.

Confidence thus established, Agnes Waterhouse then set about avenging slights from her neighbours. One had three of his hogs killed, another three of her geese, and a third lost her cow by drowning. A fourth refused to give her butter and so 'lost the curds two or three days after', and a fifth denied her yeast and so lost her or his brewing. This loss of livestock would not have been trivial to its owners – the death of a cow in particular must have represented a serious financial blow to its owner – so killing the animals was likely to have had implications beyond the immediate loss of the animal. Even more seriously, however, Agnes turned her malice against human beings, for after she had fallen out with one of her neighbours and his wife, 'she willed "Satan" to kill him with a bloody flux [*dysentery*], whereof he died'. This was probably William Fyne who fell ill on 1 October 1563 and died a month later. Likewise, she confessed that 'because she lived somewhat unquietly with her husband, she caused "Satan" to kill him. And he did so about nine years past, since which time she hath lived a widow'. Agnes also provided information about how she constrained 'Satan' to do these things for her. Apart from the regular rewards of personal blood and a whole chicken, she would say the Lord's Prayer in Latin. Agnes had been born in 1502, well before Henry VIII's break with Rome and the establishment of English as the required liturgical language of the new Church, so she was merely repeating the form of the prayer which had been taught to her as a child and with which she had grown up. Her use of the Paternoster as a magical spell is by no means peculiar to her. It is well known that Latin prayers, exclamations, and individual words or phrases are to be found embedded in, or constituting entirely, very many magical formulae belonging to both 'popular' and ritual magic; and we should also remember that English lay people were now being taught by their parish ministers that Catholic prayers (not to mention the Catholic liturgy itself) were no better than magic – 'Queen Mary's days,' wrote Thomas Ady later, 'when churchmen had more cunning and could teach people many a trick that our ministers nowadays know not. Thus we may see still how the witchcrafts of that grand Witch, that Whore of Rome, hath deceived all people'.[16] It is a confessional point the pamphlet, which was written, among other things, as a call to the newly conceived morality and avoidance of sin, was not slow to point out.

Being demanded whether she was accustomed to go to church to the Common Prayer or divine service, she said, 'Yea'; and being required what she did there, she said she did as other women do and prayed right heartily there; and when she was demanded what prayer she said, she answered, 'The Lord's Prayer, the Ave Maria, and the belief [*Creed*]'. And then they demanded, 'In Latin or in English?' And she said, 'In Latin.' And they demanded why she said it not in English but in Latin, seeing that it was set out by public authority and according to God's Word that all men should pray in English and mother tongue they best understand. And she said that 'Satan' would at no time suffer her to say it in English, but at all times in Latin.

Latin, then, was the Devil's tongue when it came to prayers, and magic was the reason for thinking so. It is not quite clear, however, whether she used Latin or English to turn her cat into a toad. Apparently she used to keep the cat in a large pot lined with wool, but when poverty constrained her to remove the wool, (presumably either to sell it or some article made from it), 'she prayed in the name of the Father, and of the Son, and of the Holy Ghost' that the cat would turn into a toad, and so it did. That liturgical phrase she may have repeated in English, but it is quite likely she remembered '*In nomine Patris et Filii et Spiritus Sancti*' from her childhood and youth. Was the cat, which must have been old by this time, replaced by a toad after its death? Joan Waterhouse, Agnes's daughter, knew only a toad-familiar, not a cat, so something, whether natural or preternatural, had happened to the original gift.

Joan was the third woman to be examined by the archdeacon and the justice. The pamphlet says she was eighteen at the time, which means that if Agnes was her mother, she would have borne her at the age of forty-six, a most unlikely circumstance. So presumably Joan was actually her step-daughter from a second marriage. Joan told her examiners that Agnes wanted to teach her witchcraft during the winter of the previous year (1565), but that she (Joan) refused and did not even know Agnes had a familiar. She found out, she said, once by accident when she came across Agnes holding the toad in her hand, calling it 'Satan', and asking it to do something for her – what is not specified. But curiosity at last got the better of her, apparently, because one day, when Agnes had gone to Braxted, a village about 3 miles from Hatfield Peverel, Joan decided she was hungry and, as there was no bread in the house, went to a neighbour and asked the neighbour's child, Agnes Brown, a girl of twelve, to give her some bread and cheese. The girl was unwilling to do so – her parents may have been out and she did not want to take responsibility – and either gave Joan very little or nothing at all (the pamphlet is not clear on this point). Hungry and annoyed, Joan went back home and decided to call upon Agnes's familiar for help. She called out 'Satan', and from Agnes's shoe, which was under the bed, the familiar appeared – not, however, in the form of a toad, but in that of a large black dog which frightened her. A conversation ensued:

Dog: What do you want?
Joan: I want you to make Agnes Brown afraid.
Dog: What will you give me?
Joan: A red cockerel.
Dog: No, you will give me your body and soul.

This exchange is significant. When Elizabeth and Agnes had employed the familiar, it had been satisfied – according to the record of the pamphlet – with a drop of their blood and (in Agnes's case) the reward of a chicken to eat. To be sure, the offering of human blood implies a contract, but there is no overt mention that they were to suffer loss of their soul and body. In Joan's case, this is made explicit. Had something in the questioning of the two examiners caused the clerk either to introduce this theme or to make the implication of the blood offerings an overt admission of the diabolic compact? Joan says that, because she was afraid and wanted the familiar to go away, she accepted the bargain. It was an age steeped in religion, with an acute awareness of Satan as a real personification of evil. Did Joan, then, offer as any kind of genuine explanation for her actions that she was frightened and wanted the demon to go away? On one level of understanding it seems unlikely. 'What tender heart would God renounce?/Who would His Gospel leave?/What godly one would hate his Lord,/ And unto Satan cleave?' as one of the prefatory poems to the pamphlet expresses it. On the other hand, the fear she felt under these extraordinary circumstances would – if we accept her terms of understanding the situation – be overwhelming, and we may be prepared to agree that a person confronted by an embodiment of evil, which she took to be real, said yes to anything which might end the immediate horror. As I have said elsewhere in relation to early modern encounters with the Devil, 'meeting the Devil did not feel like an hallucinatory experience, no matter how we may care to suggest that experience could have originated. On the contrary, [for early modern people] nothing could have felt more real, more intense, more substantial.'[17]

On 27 July the three accused came before one of the local justices of the peace and the Attorney General for their trial. Agnes repeated the information she and Joan had given the previous day, and then Agnes Brown, the girl who had been frightened by the familiar, was called into court to give her evidence. Her account of events was as follows. She had been churning butter when there appeared something like a black dog with a face like that of an ape, a short tail, a chain and silver whistle (she thought) round its neck, and a pair of horns on its head. It was carrying the key of the milk-house door in its mouth. (We should not over-read these details. None of them is odd except for the pair of horns, and this may simply have been young Agnes's post-identification of the animal as a demon rather than an ordinary dog.) It frightened her initially because it kept jumping up and running round, but at last it stopped and sat down on a nettle.

> Then I asked him what he would have, and he said he would have butter, and I said I had none for him. Then he said he would have some before he went home, and then he did run to put the key into the lock of the milk-house door. I said he should have none, and he said he would have some. Then he opened the door and went upon the shelf, and there upon a new cheese laid down the key. And being awhile within, he came out and locked the door, and said he had made flap butter for me, and so departed.

So it was at this point in the girl's narrative rather than before, with the speech and other human-like actions, that events became unmistakeably preternatural. Agnes Brown went and told her aunt what had happened, and the aunt sent for the local minister, who told her 'to pray to God and call on the name of Jesus'. Next day, the dog-familiar came again – beyond what Joan Waterhouse had asked it to do, for young Agnes had already been frightened, although she seems to have recovered quite quickly from her immediate fear. Indeed, according to the way the story is told in the pamphlet, her fear was of the dog-as-dog rather than of the dog-as-familiar, a possible psychological inconsistency which owes less to the reality of the original situation (whatever that made have been) and more to the requirements of the pace of the narrative. Agnes Brown saw the familiar three more times. On the first, two full days after his initial appearance, he carried the milk-house key in his mouth and when young Agnes and her aunt went inside, they saw the imprint of a decorative butter moulder upon one of the cheeses. A few days later he came again with a bean pod in his mouth. The Attorney General asked Agnes what that was – a strange question, if reported accurately, for it is scarcely an unusual object and the most cloistered lawyer would surely have come across one – but was told that when young Agnes said to the familiar, as she had done on the previous occasion, 'In the name of Jesus, what hast thou there?', the familiar upbraided her for 'evil words in speaking of that name', and so departed.

The third time he appeared was Wednesday 23 July, and the women were arrested very soon afterwards, on the 24th and 25th. According to Agnes Waterhouse, 'Satan' had come to her on her way to Braxted and told her to go back home, 'for she should have great trouble, and that she should be either hanged or burned shortly'. Burned she would not have been, at least not for witchcraft, for which the English death penalty was hanging. Nor, indeed, would she have been branded, if that is what 'burned' was supposed to mean, because branding was a penalty reserved for such offences as vagrancy or seditious libel, not witchcraft. The Wednesday visitation to Agnes Brown was much more ominous than the previous two had been. This time the dog-familiar was carrying a knife in its mouth, and the ensuing conversation took a sinister turn.

> [He] asked me if I were not dead, and I said, no, I thanked God. Then he said if I would not die, he would thrust his knife to my heart [and] would make me to die. Then I said, 'In the name of Jesus, lay down thy knife', and he said he would not part with his sweet dame's knife yet. Then I asked him who was his dame, and he nodded and wagged his head to where Agnes Waterhouse lived.

It was by no means rare for the Devil or one of his demons to tempt a human being to kill herself, but in these cases the individual was usually either a witch in a prison cell, awaiting trial, or someone in the throes of demonic possession. Thus, for example, in 1645 in Suffolk, Susanna Smith combined both situations, as she admitted to Robert Mayhew and the court.

> Eighteen years ago, the Devil appeared to her like a red shagged dog and tempted her to kill her children, but she strove with him 24 hours before he went from her, and would not kill them. But, being desired to relate further of her witchcraft, there rise two swellings in her throat so that she could not speak. But [Mayhew] coming to her

the next night, she confessed that the Devil did again appear to her in [the] likeness of a black bee and told her that she should be attached [*arrested*] the next day, and that if she confessed anything she should die for it. And being demanded why she would eat nothing, there being good meat provided for her, she said the Devil told her she should never eat or drink again. But they then provided and brought her meat, and with much trembling she got some down, and further said that the Devil came to her in the likeness of a black bee and went into her body, and there continued until that [... *paper clipped*] that she would not confess until he went from her again. But after that he was gone, she confessed that she had signed a covenant with the Devil at his first appearance, and signed it with a cross, and after that the Devil wrote her name to that covenant to which she had made that mark. And [she said] that the Devil had so told her where there [was] a rusty knife in the room, wherewith she might kill herself; and they looked in that place and found such an old knife as she described. But she said that she could not kill herself because they were in the room.[18]

Agnes Brown's circumstances, however, were quite different. She was neither a witch nor under suspicion of being a witch, nor possessed, nor melancholic, nor imprisoned. Now, of course we need to make possible allowances for fiction. The child may have been making up the whole story, or embroidering a genuine, frightening experience, as indeed Joan and her mother appeared to suggest in part by accusing her of lying about details. For on the girl's saying that the familiar acknowledged Agnes Waterhouse as his mistress, the Attorney General asked Agnes what she had to say to this. She turned to the girl and asked what type of knife she was talking about, to which young Agnes replied, 'A dagger.'

'I have none such in my house,' answered Waterhouse, 'only a large knife. So she is telling a lie.'

'Yes, my lord,' Joan butted in, 'and she is lying when she says it had a face like that of an ape, because the thing which came to me was like a dog.'

These objections, however, are flimsy details and at best hint at embroidery of a real event. Neither woman appears to have challenged the girl's assertion that she had had several visits from a demon-familiar. Indeed, they could not do so without incriminating themselves as liars, and clearly they did not think they were. The Attorney General may have had his doubts, or simply been intrigued by what he was hearing.

'Well, well,' he said. 'Can you make it come before us now? If you can, we shall despatch you out of prison by and by [*at once*].'

'No,' replied Agnes, 'I cannot. For, in faith, if I had let him go as my daughter did, I could make him come by and by. But now I have no more power over him.'

Letting him go in the manner of her daughter presumably means that if she had sent him on a maleficent errand, he would still be her servant, but once Joan had assumed control by giving him her soul and body and despatching him to work malice, it was she, not her mother, who was now his mistress. The reply has a certain logic, but we are not told whether the same demand to see the demon was made of Joan, a gap in the narrative which may indicate that the request was not made or that the narrator did not consider it a useful or pertinent addition to his story. What we get instead is another question from the Attorney General.

'Agnes Waterhouse, when did thy cat suck of thy blood?'

'Never,' said she.

'No?' said he. 'Let me see.'

The gaoler then removed her head-kerchief and revealed several spots on her face and one on her nose. So the Attorney General asked again, 'In good faith, Agnes, when did he suck of thy blood last?'

Agnes gave in.

'By my faith, my lord,' she said, 'not this fortnight.'

The jury then retired to consider its verdict. Agnes had already pleaded guilty, so this was not her trial and the uncovering of the marks would merely have served to confirm what she had confessed, and Elizabeth Francis, too, had pleaded guilty. The jury was therefore considering whether Joan, Agnes's daughter, was guilty of witchcraft or not. Taken all in all, the experience of accused witches at the Chelmsford assizes during the 1560s had so far been encouraging. In July 1560 Joan Haddon had been found not guilty of witchcraft, although she was convicted of fraudulently receiving sums of money. John Samond, charged in 1560 and tried in March the following year, was found not guilty of murdering by witchcraft. In March 1565 Anne Vale was acquitted of bewitching eight pigs to death, and then in July 1566, at the same assize trying Elizabeth, Agnes, and Joan, Laura Winchester, also from Hatfield Peverel, was acquitted of magically killing a cow, six sheep, and four pigs belonging to William Higham. The only certain guilty verdict had been that of Elizabeth Lowys in 1564. All these assizes had been presided over by John Southcote and Gilbert Gerard, the two justices trying Elizabeth, Agnes, and Joan, so the odds in favour of an acquittal in Joan's case were perhaps fairly high; and, sure enough, the jury brought in a verdict of not guilty, in spite of the extra charge, not recorded in the pamphlet, that she had made Agnes Brown's right arm and right leg 'decrepit'.[19]

Now, we must not allow ourselves to be misled by these not guilty verdicts. They did not express any doubt about the reality of witchcraft and the need to suppress; nor did they express any doubt about the reality of the Devil and his ability to appear in this physical world in a variety of forms. 'Not guilty' meant that the jury did not accept that a particular deed, such as the death of an animal or a human's disability, had been caused by an act of witchcraft perpetrated by the accused. That witchcraft could do such things was not doubted. That an individual witch could do such things by witchcraft was also not doubted. That an individual witch had, on a particular occasion, successfully and deliberately employed magic to accomplish the deed alleged, was open to question and, of course, was what each trial of each witch was about. So this is what Joan's jury will have been deliberating – not whether her mother actually kept a familiar, or whether it appeared in the form of a cat, a toad, or a dog, or indeed all three; but whether she had made use of it to frighten Agnes Brown and to make her arm and leg decrepit. We can perhaps follow their train of reasoning. The damage to Agnes's arm and leg could have had a natural cause; frightening someone by sending her or him a demon did not constitute an offence under the Witchcraft Act, and Joan's calling to the familiar by name, as she had seen her mother do, did not constitute 'invocation' in the sense intended by the Act, although of course a skilful lawyer might have argued to the contrary. Joan, then, seems to have been acquitted on purely legal grounds, which suggests that the jury was doing its business properly.

English law works upon precedent. This trial in Chelmsford is important either because it illustrates the following of precedent very soon after the passing of the Witchcraft Act, or because it set precedent for later courts to follow. What, for example, can be said about the admission of evidence from a twelve-year-old? The *Malleus Maleficarum* (1486) had said that excommunicates, witches' accomplices, heretics, and a witch's family members could give evidence against the accused, and this was referred to by Reginald Scot in his *Discoverie* (1584) and endorsed by James VI in his *Daemonologie* (written around 1590, published 1597): 'Since in a matter of treason against the prince, bairns or wives or never so defamed persons may of our [Scottish] law serve for sufficient witnesses and proofs, I think surely that by a far greater reason such witnesses may be sufficient in matters of high treason against God.' These opinions clearly chimed with English sentiment too, for we find two eight-year-olds providing evidence of familiars in a witch trial in St Osyth in 1582; two children, the elder of whom was ten or twelve, commended for their contribution at the Chelmsford assize of July 1589; and a nine-year-old in the Pendle trial of 1612, similarly praised for her evidence against her mother and others.

> It pleased God to raise up a young maid, Jennet Device, [Elizabeth's] own daughter, about the age of nine years, (a witness unexpected), to discover all their practices, meetings, consultations, murders, charms, and villainies: such, and in such sort, as I may justly say of them, as a reverend and learned judge of this kingdom speaketh of the greatest treason that ever was in this kingdom, '*Quis haec posteris sic narrare poterit, ut facta non ficta esse videantur?*' That when these things shall be related to posterity, they will be reputed matters feigned, not done.[20]

Normally, however, children were not regarded as competent witnesses, so it was the peculiar nature of certain crimes, such as rape, buggery, and witchcraft, which allowed courts to hear them, although some legal theorists still expressed unease, especially when it came to children giving evidence against their parents.[21]

Apart from this particular hesitation, though, people were well aware that children's fantasy might get the better of them, or that because of their youth they might be influenced or manipulated by the adults around them. 'Yea, sundry times,' wrote George Gifford in 1587, 'the evidence of children is taken, accusing their own mothers, that they did see them give milk unto little things which they kept in wool. The children, coming to years of discretion, confess they were enticed to accuse'; and he added in 1593, 'Many go so far, that if they can entice children to accuse their parents, they think it a good thing.'[22] It is not difficult, of course, to manufacture plausible explanations for children's evidence in witchcraft cases, and it is always possible, again 'of course', that these explanations may be wholly or partly valid. But they carry with them the danger that we may ignore the historical context in which the evidence was given – as Christina Larner put it, 'We ... identify with aspects of the past while discarding others. The effect of this is that we cannot see past systems of thought as connected wholes. We single out those aspects which we have inherited for applause and those we have discarded, for special explanation. There ought to be a word for this particular distorting mirror.'[23] The context of the Chelmsford trials, then, is one in which there was a possibility that magic might be real; that the Devil was indeed real and was capable of appearing to people and offering them deadly bargains; that spirits of all kinds were real and, like the Devil, could enter the world of matter and so interact with human beings; and that humans might and did traffic with malevolent entities for the sake of personal advantage and power over and among their neighbours. These were all proven possibilities, even if not every instance was necessarily an example or embodiment of one of them. It is thus not appropriate or valid to argue that because we may not believe in the actuality of these possibilities, our ancestors must have been manipulating child witnesses, and the child witnesses themselves fantasising or lying. Nor is it enough to say that because some children lied and created mischief, as William Somers, for example, notoriously did in 1591 by pretending to be demonically possessed, all must be suspected of doing so. The children belonged to their own historical context as much as the adults did, and in consequence when they described animal-familiars or the magical actions performed by adults, they may have been telling the truth as they (and their audience) saw it, understood it, and interpreted it.

Some reservations apart, then, the sixteenth century viewed witchcraft as a heinous offence of a kind peculiarly difficult to pin down because of the frequent private and solitary nature of its transactions. Without a confession from the witch her or himself, therefore, the courts felt obliged to take secondary accounts from wherever they might be obtained. Hence English law provided for situations when evidence could be given by minors, and not just in witchcraft trials, under certain conditions.[24] The judges and jury in the Chelmsford trials were thus neither naïve nor fanatical, and while allowance must be made for the possible unreliability of the child witness, allowance must also be made for her equally possible reliability. The jury convicted Elizabeth Francis because she had admitted the offences with which she was charged. But they chose to overlook (or did not notice) the implication that her separate dealings with the cat-familiar involved invocation of spirits forbidden by the Witchcraft Act, and so she paid the lesser penalty of imprisonment. Agnes Waterhouse, too, admitted her offences. These involved several instances of deliberate, malevolent damage to persons and property, and while Elizabeth Francis had apparently also done both, the jury may have borne in mind the abuse she had suffered from both her husbands and granted her the doubt that the death of the first and the lameness of the second could have happened through nature rather than because of magic. Agnes had no such excuse. Her malevolence was clear and no allowance was made. Moreover, the physical evidence of marks upon her face from which her familiar had sucked its payment of blood had to be taken into account. Had the jury been inclined to grant her leeway, it might have dismissed these as natural blemishes. As it was, they were interpreted in accordance with her confession that she had indeed practised harmful magic in tandem with a spirit.

Joan Waterhouse was found not guilty. We can obviously not know for certain why the jury came to this conclusion, but we need to bear in mind that the majority of what Agnes Brown told the court had nothing to do with Joan directly. The first appearance of the dog-familiar may have happened at Joan's instance, but not its subsequent harrying of the girl. The pamphlet makes this point clear: 'Now these witches (as they say) cannot call him in again because they did not let him out.' *These witches* must refer to Elizabeth and Agnes, as Joan certainly did let him out. Her object in doing so was clearly malicious, although not intended to kill or damage the person of Agnes Brown, so it may not have been seen as coming within the meaning of the Act. Whether her calling upon 'Satan' could be interpreted as invocation of a spirit is, as we have suggested, perhaps open to some doubt since the familiar had taken the shape of a dog. Did Agnes Waterhouse actually have a dog she called 'Satan'? If so, the jury may have felt disinclined to view Joan's summoning it from under the bed as magical invocation. Her apparent agreement to give 'Satan' her body and soul in return for his performing a magical errand was accompanied, as we have seen, by fear, and here again we may find that the jury was prepared, in the comparatively small light of Joan's malice, which appeared to have been triggered by a single incident rather than to have been an integral part of her character as, apparently, it was in her mother's case, to make allowances and not seek a punitive interpretation of the Act. A similar inclination may have brought them to conclude that the 'decrepitude' in Agnes Brown's right arm and leg was owing to natural rather than magical causes, and so it is possible to suggest that in all three cases the jury was coming to sophisticated conclusions after careful consideration of what the Act meant and how they thought it should be applied to the particular circumstances in front of them.

The trial had taken place on 27 July. On the 29th Agnes Waterhouse was executed. Hangings were done in public and the condemned expected to make some kind of final speech to the crowd. In Agnes's case, these last words are given in the pamphlet, although how much editing may have taken place is unclear. The account is brief. According to it, Agnes confessed she had been a witch for fifteen years, and asked God to forgive her. She said she had several times sent 'Satan' to harm one of her neighbours, a man called Wardle, but that Wardle's faith was so strong, 'Satan' could not harm him. Did she say this on the scaffold, or is this an interpolation by the compiler of the pamphlet to make a confessional point to his readers? It is followed by an apparent question and answer session about whether Agnes went to church and what prayers she used and whether she said them in English or in Latin. Her replies, as reported, suggest she kept to the Catholic Latin of her youth, and are followed by the significant '*for these* [my italics] and many other offences which she hath committed, done, and confessed she bewailed, repented, and asked mercy of God'. The Protestant propaganda is unmistakable, but whether it took placed as reported or was added to the pamphlet later is an open question.

Why did anyone take the trouble to produce this compound pamphlet at this particular juncture? For several months the English ecclesiastical establishment had been coping with discontent over details of the mode and accoutrements of its worship, and in March 1566 Matthew Parker, the Archbishop of Canterbury, had issued his *Book of Advertisements* which, among other things, tried to lay down the required mode of dress for Anglican clergy in church and cathedral. These were not mere inconsequential details at the time. If the English government wanted to make its version of state Christianity a permanent innovation, it would have to ensure that everyone was doing, hearing, saying, and thus conforming to the same thing, and in the 1560s this was far from being uniformly achieved. Agnes Waterhouse's use of Latin for her prayers was only one small example of many deviations, and while many statues, pictures, crosses, and other artefacts of Catholicism had been removed or destroyed very quickly after 1558, there is evidence that in 1566, in some of the more outlying parts of the kingdom, still much remained to be done.[25] The association of Catholic practice with witchcraft and the call to a virtuous life contained in the prefatory poems of the pamphlet thus combine to assist the governmental message. Witchcraft is both a sin and an attack on simple, trusting folk. The duly appointed officers of state and Church are competent to deal with it and will do so effectively. So adherence to the Church was now established in England, and avoidance of the Devil-tainted practices of Popery were to be commended and observed.[26]

If this kind of line was the message, who were the intended recipients of it? An increasing number of pamphlets, essays, and treatises on witchcraft were published in England during the second half of the sixteenth and first half of the seventeenth century – neither Scotland, Wales, nor Ireland produced anything like the same number on this subject – and both tone and content changed over the years. The Chelmsford pamphlet of 1566 is in the nature of a newsletter, put together from pre-trial and trial documents, either to provide factual illustration of magical evildoing in support of its moral message, or to provide moral commentary on its report of a case of witchcraft. Unlike the rest of Europe, England did not have publishing houses in several of its large towns. Publishing took place in London, and therefore information in one form or another – memorised eye-witness or gossip, notes, fully written documents – had to be taken there to be put into print by the time-consuming and laborious methods then available. The run of each pamphlet might be between 600 and 1,000 copies. It obviously depended on how many the printer judged he could sell, because printing was not a speculative business and one did not publish copies of a work in the hope that it might sell, but rather in the knowledge that it would. Extra copies could always be run off if the work were in demand. Unsold copies were thus a waste of time, labour, and materials, for the aim of the publishing business was commercial, as Thomas Dekker makes clear in his 1613 pamphlet *A Strange Horse-Race*: 'The title of this book is like a jester's face, set (howsoever he draws it) to beget mirth, but his ends are hid to himself, *and those are to get money*' (p. 4, my italics).[27]

We must therefore assume that 'William Powell, for William Pickering, dwelling at Saint Magnus's corner' had an audience in mind for his trouble. He seems to have published his pamphlet in three stages: the examination of Elizabeth Francis and Agnes Waterhouse, based on pre-trial documents; the confessions of Agnes and Joan Waterhouse, based on trial papers; and Agnes's scaffold confession, possibly based on eye-witness testimony, but perhaps, in view of its heavily propagandistic nature, 'reconstructed' to make a useful and fitting extension of the original account. Printing in London meant an audience largely envisaged to come from London. Now, news pamphlets obviously carried certain potential dangers in their pages. Contemporary, everyday events might have their appeal, but what if their telling or re-telling ran counter to government policy? The well-known case of John Stubbs tells us what could happen. In 1579 he published a pamphlet vigorously criticising one of the main topics of the day, the proposed marriage between Elizabeth Tudor and the Duc d'Anjou. He, his printer, and his publisher were arrested, tried for sedition, and both Stubbs and his publisher had their right hands cut off with a cleaver. Stubbs himself was further imprisoned for eighteen months. Political events, therefore, carried serious dangers.[28] Witchcraft, on the other hand, steered clear of these perils while offering possibilities of which the government could not but approve: condemnation of wickedness and a serious social problem, promotion of virtue according to official governmental precepts, anti-Catholic propaganda, and entertainment. For people accustomed to public executions that were treated as a combination of holiday, sermon, and warning, the opportunity to read about certain individuals' trafficking with the Devil, their preternatural feats (largely of malice), and their meeting a deserved justice (interspersed with the occasional happy ending of an acquittal), had immense appeal. The Chelsmford pamphlet, therefore, had a potential audience ready to enjoy and be edified by an event which may have taken place several miles away from the capital – and could, for that matter, of course, have seemed the more interesting for it – but which had resonances for everyone, Londoner or not, and could provide matter for thought, comment, and speculation, which were staples of town as well as country gossip.[29]

It may be thought that Elizabeth Francis would have learned a lesson after her escape from the possible gallows. Imprisonment for a full twelve months was by no means an easy sentence, for neglect, ill treatment, and disease, not to mention suicide, carried off many an individual condemned to gaol. But Elizabeth survived and between 27 July 1567 and 25 March 1572 remained quietly at home in Hatfield Peverel. But on that March day, apparently, she bewitched Mary Cocke, wife of Nicholas Cocke, the miller, causing her to be lame and infirm and despairing of her life for ten days, in consequence of which Elizabeth was arrested. She was due to appear before the Chelmsford assize in August that year, but the paperwork had been badly drafted and a new indictment had to be written, which meant that her case did not come up for trial again until 2 March 1573.[30] Meanwhile, fate appears to have struck at the same family, for in August 1572 an Agnes Francis, wife of William Francis of Hatfield Peverel, was indicted on four counts of witchcraft, and if we take it that William may have been the brother of Elizabeth's husband Christopher, we may have a sister-in-law from the same village charged with witchcraft at the same time. Agnes's counts were serious: bewitching to death Alice Wilmot, wife of Alexander Wilmot, in October 1566; killing Clemence Wilmot, wife of Walter Wilmot, in like fashion in 1569; killing a horse by magic in November 1571; and likewise killing Walter Wilmot in March 1572 – a seeming example of inter-familial rivalry or hatred of the kind common in the often febrile atmosphere of small communities. Agnes was found guilty of killing Walter Wilmot as charged, but pleaded pregnancy and was thereafter remanded on three separate occasions at the March and June assizes of 1573 and the assize of March 1574.[31]

Elizabeth's second trial, which took place before John Southcote, who had tried her before, and Robert Monson, saw her plead guilty again but once more escape the gallows. She was sentenced to stand in the pillory and to imprisonment for a whole year, the statutory penalty for a first offence, even though the Witchcraft Act clearly stated that a second offence, involving the wasting, consuming, or laming of a person in her or his body or member, should bring with it death as a felon. So how Elizabeth avoided this after pleading guilty is impossible, at this stage, to tell. The August session at which she first appeared was unusually busy with witchcraft accusations. John Salmon from Danbury was accused of killing two cows by magic and, with his wife's help, of maiming Edward Robinson, a sawyer, while Joan was separately accused of bewitching Richard Pearson, a tanner, so that he became lame in one leg. Nor was this the first time John had appeared before the court. He had, 'being a common wizard', as the record expresses it, been indicted in July 1560 for murdering John Grant and Bridget Peacock by witchcraft, his trial being held over to March 1561 when he was found not guilty. Add to these the trials of Agnes Francis, and of Agnes Steadman from Halstead who was indicted for making four cows and one woman very ill – guilty, but sentence unknown – and we find only one possible death sentence out of five individuals, with the equal possibility that no one was sentenced to death at all. In such an atmosphere, then, it may be that the jury for the occasion was reluctant to see the penalty inflicted, had grave doubts within the law about the culpability of some of the parties – six out of eleven verdicts being 'not guilty'[32] – and Agnes Steadman, like Elizabeth Francis in 1573, may have been imprisoned, or pilloried and then put in gaol for the full year required by the Act.

When Elizabeth actually came to trial, in March 1573, however, the session was a very different occasion. Catherine Pullen from Tollesbury was accused of bewitching Joan Denning to death, and William and Margery Skelton between them were indicted on charges of making a little girl very ill and of magically killing Dorothy Fuller, Phyllis Picket, and John Churchman. All three accused were found guilty and sentenced to hang,[33] and so Elizabeth's escape at this time is perhaps the more notable. Having evaded the hangman, however, she served her time in prison yet again and was back in Hatfield Peverel by 18 March 1574, where she remained quietly enough – although what must her neighbours have thought? – until June 1578 when, so her third indictment said, she bewitched Alice Poole to death. Alice took just over four months to die, but Elizabeth must have been arrested before that happened, on a slightly different charge, because, according to a news pamphlet, *A Detection of Damnable Drifts*, published in April 1579, when questioned she said she had spoken to Alice not long before.[34] The substance of her offence, as reported by the pamphlet, was as follows. One day, during Lent in 1578, Elizabeth called on Alice and asked her for some old yeast. Alice refused and Elizabeth then set out for the house of Mother Osborne – this may have been the Joan Osborne who had been found not guilty in March 1567 of bewitching a six-year-old boy to death[35] – and on the way cursed Alice aloud and wished her harm. Whereupon a spirit in the shape of a shaggy white dog appeared and asked her where she was going. Elizabeth explained that she needed yeast and that Alice had refused to give her any, and so asked the spirit to go and trouble her by plaguing her in the head. The spirit promised to do so, but asked for something in return, and Elizabeth threw him a morsel of white (that is, expensive) bread which she bit off a crust in her hand. The spirit then ate the bread and went away, and some time after that Elizabeth heard from her neighbours that Alice was suffering from severe head pain which lasted right up to Elizabeth's arrest and examination.[36] Three arrests for trafficking with evil spirits to the harm of her neighbours and fellow villagers were too many for the authorities to overlook, and in any case the court that year was noticeably less understanding than it had been during its two sessions the previous year.

So when Elizabeth finally came to court on 8 January 1579, her fate was more or less sealed. According to the pamphlet, she denounced two other women as witches, Elizabeth Lord and Mother Osborne, both from Hatfield Peverel; but whether she was required to do so or hoped, by this means, to avoid the ultimate blow of the law, is uncertain. Neither woman, as far as we can tell, was pursued by the authorities, so if their denunciation was a ploy, or even some kind of personal revenge, it did not work. For a third time Elizabeth was found guilty by her jury of twenty-one, which included two men described as 'gent', and the inevitable followed. She was hanged, probably within a day or two of her being sentenced.

Persistent offenders such as Elizabeth, who were caught more than once and managed to survive the system for a while, do not often appear in the records. Usually the accused turns up once, is found guilty or not guilty and, if the former, duly punished, and that is the last we hear of her. Alice Daye from Boxley in Kent, however, came before the Dartford assizes on 11 March 1574, indicted for murder by witchcraft. The three charges laid against her went back to January and June 1573 and alleged that she bewitched to death Isabel Chylde, Alice Goodwin, and Thomas Chylde (father of Isabel). She was found guilty, but remanded because she was pregnant, and she seems to have remained in gaol well past the twelve-month period laid down by the Witchcraft Act, because her name is included in lists of gaol prisoners for July 1575, March 1576, and February 1577. There is no mention of her in July 1577, so by then she may have been released; but she was back again in July 1578 to appear before the Maidstone assizes on a fresh indictment. This says that in August 1577 she made John Collins very ill by magic, and that in December that year she bewitched two heifers to death. The first of these alleged offences took place in Maidstone, the second in Boxley, but as the two places are only about 4 miles apart, it seems reasonable to suggest that when she left prison in the spring or early summer of 1577, she went back home and either quickly resumed whatever magical practices had caused her to be denounced in the first place, or suffered the results of her damaged reputation. The jury in the 1578 trial found her guilty and she was back in gaol, but a fortnight later John Collins died, and so a new charge of murder by witchcraft was alleged. Once again Alice was found guilty and this time her execution was inevitable. Her pregnancy appears to have helped her evade it in 1574 and in 1578 there had been damage to property, but no human deaths. Even so, it is worth noting that although the Witchcraft Act called for a capital sentence to be passed on any second offence, the court sent her to prison instead. It may be, of course, that the justices were waiting to see the outcome of John Collins's prolonged illness, but as the Act required them to sentence Alice to hang in the case of a second offence, regardless of whether Collins survived or not, it is interesting they did not do so.[37]

What, then, can be said about the effect of the Witchcraft Act in the Home Counties, of which Essex rather more than the others has received a good share of scholarly interest? From 1564 until the end of 1602, Essex saw 172 people, of whom only sixteen were men, charged with one form or another of witchcraft. Of these, fifty were hanged and seventy found not guilty, the rest being imprisoned, pilloried, remanded (usually on a plea of being pregnant), or being 'at large' – in other words, they had run away in order to escape arrest. Now, if we compare this with Sussex during the same period, we find twelve people accused of witchcraft (two men), of whom one was hanged and six were found not guilty. The contrast with Essex is startling and if we compare the figures with those of Hertfordshire, beginning in 1573 when the published assize records for that county begin and ending in 1602, the picture is much the same. Total witchcraft cases: Hertfordshire twenty-seven, Sussex ten, Kent seventeen, Essex ninety-nine. Those hanged: Hertfordshire three, Sussex one, Kent two, Essex forty-five. Those found not guilty: Hertfordshire twelve, Sussex five, Kent ten, Essex sixty-two. It is thus clear that Essex not only tried a larger number of people for witchcraft than its neighbouring counties, but acquitted more of them, too. For some reason, then, Essex appears to have been more acutely sensitive than others towards this kind of magic, and while it is true that in Essex enclosure and new agrarian techniques tended to enhance the problem of poverty, detailed studies of villages and regions within the county do not support the older theories of Alan Macfarlane and Keith Thomas that charity denied played a major part in promoting witchcraft accusations. Nor does the clash of religious confessions – dynamic Puritans with Catholics – explain Essex's peculiar situation, since both Sussex and Lancashire can be said to exhibit similar conflicts, and the disparity between them and Essex at this period is still marked. Frustratingly enough, therefore, Essex's apparent willingness to prosecute and acquit more accused witches than the other Home Counties remains for the moment a puzzle.[38]

We can, however, note that the Witchcraft Act took time to settle down. In Essex, the years which saw most prosecutions for what was almost invariably described as 'murder by witchcraft' (thereby denoting that the offence which most exercised the courts was the killing rather than the method by which the killing was carried out) were 1579 (ten), 1584 (fifteen), and 1594 (eleven). In Sussex, the notable year was 1577 (three), in Hertfordshire 1590 (five), and in Kent 1567 (three) and 1593 (three). With only two exceptions, therefore, the peak years belong to the 1580s and 1590s and suggest that the Act did not set off a wave of prosecutions or, apparently, stimulate in any noteworthy fashion extra interest in witchcraft or animus against its practitioners. It is also interesting to note that the peak years in Essex were not connected with outbreaks of sustained prosecution in specific places, because while it is true that many of the overall 172 prosecutions can be located in the general area of Chelmsford-Braintree-Maldon, the majority come from all over the county, one in one place, two in another, one in a third, and the same can be said for Sussex, Kent, and Hertfordshire as well. Moreover, in any given year in any of these Home Counties, witchcraft (or 'murder by witchcraft') represents a very small fraction of the total number of offences brought before the assize courts, who were preoccupied largely with crimes of theft, such as grand larceny and burglary. It thus looks as though the 1563 Witchcraft Act represented the fears and concerns of its sponsors and the legislators themselves rather than any widespread or pressing unease in the population at large.

Can it be said that this obtains elsewhere in England? There is certainly little evidence of diminution in witchcraft charges in other shires after 1563, and the magical crimes alleged of women and men are largely those familiar from the courts of the Home Counties. In Surrey, for example, Richard and Clemence Marshall, along with six others, killed several farm animals by magic in 1571; Elizabeth Robinson killed a child by witchcraft and then a man in 1572; in 1575 Marion Constable likewise killed two pigs; two years later, Bridget Hitchcock killed a mare. In 1582 Mabel Jackson killed a woman, and Joan Marlow a man; in 1585 Agnes Stevens killed a woman, a man, and a child; in 1589 Sybil Preston killed a mare; in 1596 Alice Marten killed an ox, a ram, a sheep, and a lamb; and the next year Margaret Cooke killed two women – all crimes of 'murder by witchcraft' and damage to livestock.[39] It is the same picture in Middlesex[40] and in Norfolk where, most unusually, Margaret Read was burned for witchcraft in 1590. This suggests, as Gregory Durston points out, that she had been found guilty of the murder by witchcraft of her husband or her employer, in which case the offence would have been classed as petty treason for which burning was the standard penalty. Norfolk, however, was not peculiarly harsh in its judgements and also saw personal affection triumphing over judicial process when friends and relatives rallied to the support of Margaret Grame after she had been accused before the local JP in 1590, a situation reflected elsewhere, showing that witches or accused witches did not always lack the sympathy of the public. Leonard Norgrave, keeper of the gaol in Canterbury, for example, found himself in trouble in July 1570 for letting a convicted witch leave the prison, being heard by several people to remark 'that the witch did more good by her physic than Mr Wood, a minister of God's word'.[41] In Shropshire, 'Mother' Garve tried to enchant a cat to rid a sow of its disease, presumably by magical transference, and in Huntingdonshire 1589–93 saw the outbreak, continuance, and lamentable end of the notorious episode of alleged witchcraft in the village of Warboys, when five daughters of Robert and Elizabeth Throckmorton appeared to fall sick as a result of the personally directed witchcraft of Alice, Agnes, and John Samuel. What probably triggered their execution, however, was the death of a local woman of importance, Lady Susan Cromwell, and so 'murder by witchcraft' loomed large in the various accusations of *maleficia* levelled against all three.[42]

In Leicestershire 'Mother' Cooke was hanged for witchcraft in 1596, and in Nottinghamshire Ellen Bark was presented for the same reason in 1601.[43] But when we come into the north of England, the context changes with a larger number of men being charged with magical offences, while witchcraft accusations are often allied to charges of recusancy. Recusancy, of course, was to be found in every shire, not to mention London itself, but Lancashire and Yorkshire, perhaps along with Devon and Cornwall in the south, represent areas in which the intractability of large numbers of local people who adhered either to Catholicism or to Catholic practices or to both clashed with London's determination to impose its own religious settlement on the whole country. Thus, in the case of Richard Dean, curate of Harewood chapel near Leeds, the ecclesiastical commissioners at York were moved to discipline him in 1571 because he had Papist leanings and was 'a sorcerer and charmer of the people'. Peter Carter, a schoolmaster in Whalley, Lancashire, was also referred to the commissioners that same year because 'he was supposed to be a Papist and to be privy with roving priests, an open professor of astrology and necromancy'. In 1571, too, the commissioners disciplined Robert Clough, curate of Kirkby chapel in the diocese of Chester, because he was 'a sorcerer, a hawker, and a hunter', and Richard Stabler, a physician from Howden in Yorkshire, was accused of hanging written prayers round his patients' necks to the accompaniment of 'superstitious' (i.e. Catholic) prayers.[44] In 1578 Janet Milner had a can thrown at her head by Robert Singleton because, he said, she was a witch and used to heal cattle by means of charms. Three women were tried for witchcraft in Hull in 1583, one of whom was pilloried for it; Anne Acson in Chester was accused of using witchcraft to make two cows fall sick, Grace Anslowe was imprisoned there for two months in 1590 on charges of sorcery, and Thomas Blackbone was charged 'for sorcery about money' – that is, he was said to have summoned spirits to help him find buried treasure, an offence we find repeated several times in various parts of England such as Surrey (1575), Suffolk (1581), and Warwickshire (1590).[45]

Divination, too, remained a common practice. John Walsh from Dorset detected bewitched individuals with the help of fairies of whom he said there were three kinds – white, green, and black, the black being the worst. He would speak to them at noon or at midnight – significant times when demons were reputed to be at large[46] – in the countryside where there were prehistoric burial mounds, and he also possessed a grimoire which he used to summon a spirit which would tell him who had stolen some article and where it was to be found. The pamphlet which describes his case is heavily anti-Catholic in tone and makes much of his having learned his magic, allegedly, from a Catholic priest.[47] Catholicism appears again in the case of Edmund Hartley. In December 1595 Nicholas Starkie from Cleworth near Manchester hired Hartley, a local cunning man, to cure his two sons who were showing signs of demonic possession. Hartley helped them by means of 'certain Popish charms and herbs', but came under suspicion of witchcraft himself and was eventually put on trial at the Lancaster assizes in March 1597. There he was found guilty and sentenced to be hanged. The rope broke. Hartley confessed his offences and was then successfully hanged a second time.[48] But in the latter years of Elizabeth Tudor's reign, people were not going to be deterred from trying to look into the future to see what would happen when the monarch was dead. Elizabeth herself was kept informed about this as, for example, in a letter sent to her by Richard Young on 30 November 1594, referring to one Jane Shelley, a prisoner in the Fleet, who had employed several 'sorcerers, witches, and charmers' to find out the time of Elizabeth's death and the destiny of the state.[49]

Image magic, rather more sinister, is found in Berkshire in 1579. Richard Galis *fils* wrote and published a pamphlet in May that year, *A Brief Treatise containing the most strange and horrible cruelty of Elizabeth Stile, alias Rockingham, and her confederates, executed at Abingdon, upon Richard Galis*. This Richard was Galis *père*, and seems to have been only one of Elizabeth's victims, for according to the pamphlet, she and three other women, along with a male witch, Rosimon, who could shape-change into any animal he wanted, had familiars in the likeness of toads, cats, and rats which carried out their dire commands on at least five people. 'Mother' Dutton, one of the company, also used to make images out of red wax, and would either stab them with a hawthorn or cause them to melt beside a fire. In 1585 Stephen and Jane Kylden from Surrey set their maleficent eyes higher up the social scale, and were indicted 'for engraving my Lord Treasurer's picture in wood and therewith to make his picture of wax to the intent to destroy him in his body and feloniously to bring him to death by art magic and enchantment, and for the like against my Lord of Leicester'. Richard Bate, a surgeon, was accused in 1583 of trying to kill his mother-in-law and her children by means of wax images which he was then ordered to show to the mayor of Nottingham, after which he was arrested. Others found themselves in similar peril in 1590. On 31 January that year, 'information [was laid] against Mrs Dewse who, having heard that Robert Birche was a conjuror [*i.e. raised spirits*] desired one Atkinson to be a mean that she might speak with him. Their conversation: her desire to be revenged of her enemies, one of whom was that thief, Justice Younge who lived by robbing Papists. The others were Sir Rowland Hayward and others, whose pictures of wax she would have made and then prick them to the heart.'[50]

Now, granted that the relative paucity of records from the Midlands and the northern counties of England, in comparison with those available in the south, does not enable us to draw a detailed picture of how much magic of one kind or another was being practised and continued to be practised after the Witchcraft Act – although there are obviously many more examples than the small number given here – it is still clear that the government was not being successful in its declared desire to put an end to 'superstition' (by which it meant magic on the one hand and Catholicism on the other) and that in general people clung to those preternatural methods for answering or dealing with problems, which they had inherited, or learned, or read about, with as much tenacity as before the Act was passed. That there appears to have been an increase in the number of accusations reaching the courts during the 1570s, 1580s, and 1590s, however, is clear enough, and we should not underestimate the effect an increasing flood of pamphlet literature would have been having on people's awareness of the witchcraft around them and at their doorsteps. It raised public consciousness of magic and hoped to shape the way that consciousness operated, and not only made people take a more sophisticated view of the theology involved, but also quickened their legal sense, making some more sceptical, others more inclined to believe what they heard in court.[51]

More than anything, perhaps, these pamphlets and short treatises made readers more aware of the complexities of the subject, even while they were bombarded with what seemed to be an endless succession of different threats and dangers. The 1570s in England saw many more seminary priests and Jesuits coming into the country to stabilise English Catholics and effect conversions when possible. The 1580s were dominated by the wars elsewhere in Europe, culminating in the attempted Spanish invasion of 1588; and the 1590s saw growing tensions as impressment and conscription for military service in the Netherlands, France, and Portugal began to bite hard, especially after 1595 when fighting in Ireland was added to the nation's burdens. Disruption to trade, plague, harvest failures in 1596 and 1597, and a consequent spectacular rise in prices, meant that the country was seething with discontent. Add to this growing unease about Elizabeth Tudor's failure to marry and thus secure the future with an heir, and it is not difficult to understand that an increase of general underlying fearfulness may not have been unconnected with an increase in the number of prosecutions for witchcraft during these decades.

Nevertheless, it should also be noted that the government did not set about any large-scale active programme of suppression of magical workers, either. Catholics and dissident Protestants supplied sufficient targets in their stead. Witchcraft trials continued to be relatively low-key affairs, save for the occasional scandalous outbreak such as those at Chelmsford in 1566 and 1579 and at St Osyth in 1582, and even then the numbers of those prosecuted reached nowhere near the levels of genuine pogroms elsewhere in Europe. Juries, too, tended to abide by the rule of law, and when the Act laid emphasis on the killing of humans and destruction of or harm to property (largely meaning livestock), and these were the charges levelled against the individuals brought before them for trial – as they were in a very large number, if not the majority of cases – they seem to have listened carefully to the evidence and condemned or acquitted according to what they had actually heard. In other words, in England, probably because of rather than in spite of the Act, the rule of law remained strong in witchcraft cases, and justice was both attempted and, as far as we can tell, for the most part achieved. If this was a precedent, was it a precedent followed elsewhere in Britain?

6

THE ISLANDS, ANOTHER WITCHCRAFT ACT, AND A FAMILY FEUD: 1582–1590

The relative paucity of information we have noted anent the Midlands and north of England makes it difficult to assess the situation elsewhere, too, but it looks as though English nervousness may have communicated itself to some other parts of the British Isles. In Ireland, for example, we are told that two witches were executed in Kilkenny in 1578, and this was followed by an Irish Witchcraft Act passed by Dublin in 1586. The Irish Act, however, was merely the English Act of 1563 with one or two slight necessary changes in wording – 'after the end of three months next' instead of 'after the first day of June next coming' – and thus not tailored to any specific Irish situation or context at all.[1] The 1580s were especially grim for the Irish population. In Munster there was a major famine in 1582–83, caused principally by the scorched-earth military tactics of the invading English army, and by the end of that disaster about one-third of Munster's population had died of hunger or disease.[2] Whether these extreme conditions sharpened Irish use of magic or magicians to assist people through their immediate crises and give them some sense of being in control of their day-to-day lives is open to question. Certainly English writers on Ireland tell us that magic was in common use there. 'The inclination of the Irish people,' said Barnaby Rich, 'is to be religious, frank, amorous, ireful, sufferable of infinite pains, very glorious [*boastful*] ... There are many sorcerers and the country doth no less abound with witches; and no marvel that it should do so, for the Devil hath ever been most frequent and conversant amongst infidels, Turks, Papists, and such other.' Fynes Morison agreed in 1617. The Irish were by nature superstitious and given to utter incantations against wolves; old women used to be called in to undo the harm to horses inflicted by some men's eyes; men would employ incantations before they went into battle; and people sought witches' help against diseases.[3]

Most of this could apply to the English, too, but Morison was highly prejudiced against Catholics and so we have to treat some of his observations with care. The Irish may well have used magic, but perhaps no more so than their contemporaries in England, Wales, or Scotland. Something, however, stirred the English authorities to introduce witchcraft legislation into Ireland in 1586 and that something may have been little more than a basic misconception of and prejudice against the Irish, sharpened by the particular political and military circumstances of the 1580s and a determination to forward the objective of 'civilising' the Irish by turning as many of them as possible into docile Anglicans. (The tone and intention of these desires is well expressed in Edmund Spenser's *View of the Present State of Ireland*, 1596.) It is unlikely to have had anything to do with a witch trial in Kilkenny in 1578, as St John Seymour suggested. The fact that two witches were tried there may point to increased tensions in the province of Leinster at the time, as William Kramer opines.[4] On the other hand, two witches do not make a hunt or a pogrom, and it is equally possible that the Kilkenny incident was entirely a parochial affair and arose from disputes between neighbours, as was so often the case. For the fact remains that Ireland showed nothing even vaguely similar to the increase in witchcraft prosecutions in England at this time, a phenomenon which has puzzled historians ever since. Theories have been offered, but what quite probably constrained the English from pursuing witches in Ireland was the more pressing business of trying to conquer the island and impose military control over it – more costly, more time consuming, more politically and indeed religiously significant than fetching Gaelic-speaking peasant women in front of a disdainful and uncomprehending bench – and what quite probably constrained the Irish from having their witches tried in such a court was the simple fact that the court would have been an instrument of the invading, foreign, and heretical English. Moreover, as Elwyn Lapoint has suggested, the Irish seem to have preferred to fight maleficent magic with counter-magic, one ritual with another, and so did not feel the need to resort to alien law.[5]

Wales, too, was regarded by English writers as a place filled with ignorant, superstitious people, and it was claimed, for example, that the country was overrun by swarms of soothsayers and enchanters who maintained they would walk with fairies each Tuesday and Thursday night. Like Ireland, however, Wales seemed to be a place of impenetrable Catholicism shrouded in a foreign language, with laws and customs of its own, and a people who did things the old way in apparent defiance of attempts to persuade or pressure them into the new.[6] Wales was certainly seen as a schoolroom for magic. On 22 May 1528 Margaret Hunt appeared before the London commissioners charged with employing herbs assisted by prayers to heal the sick – five Paternosters, five Aves and one Creed, plus three Paternosters, three Aves and three Creeds for nine consecutive nights – along with the use of holy water. This and the rest, she said, she had learned from a woman called 'Mother' Emet in Wales. On 29 September 1556, the English Privy Council sent a letter to the Lord President and Council of Wales 'to send hither the obligation of one John Davys, who being imprisoned at Ludlow for deceiving of people, taking upon him to be a soothsayer, was bound in £40 not to use like practice henceforth: which nevertheless he hath since attempted to do, and remaineth presently in prison at London for the same'. In 1579 in Montgomery, Gruffyd ap David ap John and various others were charged with working enchantments and witchcraft, and also with invoking spirits whereby they had enchanted an apple. This apple, along with enchanted powder, they had given to a young virgin who, upon eating the fruit, had become bewitched and had run away with John ap Gruffyd, 'a light, lewd, and evil-disposed person and a married man with many children', who had then 'feloniously ravished her'; while in 1588 the bailiffs of Cardiff were in trouble for permitting sorcerers to operate within their jurisdiction.[7]

The bailiffs' attitude certainly seems to bear out L'Estrange Ewen's observation that 'sorcery was either not a prevalent practice or it did not greatly perturb the

Welshmen', and it is also notable that during the sixteenth century there were very few trials for witchcraft at the various Welsh assizes – one in the 1560s, two in the 1570s, one in the 1580s, and three in the 1590s[8] – perhaps in spite of late attempts to deliver propaganda such as the anti-witchcraft tract *Dau Gymro yn Taring* ('Two Tarrying Welshmen'), published in 1595 by Robert Holland, a clergyman who had spent many years in England. Holland's essay contrasts the easy acceptance by one speaker in the dialogue of magical operators and diviners with the anxiety felt by the other, who represents Holland himself. Holland's English experience had obviously had its effect, for what distinguishes the dialogue is that it is clearly inspired, not by books, but by his life in the rural societies of his separate parishes. As Clark and Morgan observe, too, Holland's principal concern was 'not the detection of actual witches and the definition of specific acts of *maleficium*, but with the prevalence in his congregations of the superstitious reliance on demonic remedies for misfortune'.[9] In other words, the anxiety he undoubtedly felt did not translate itself into seeking to bring witches before a court, ecclesiastical or criminal, but into vigorous efforts to overcome 'superstition' with right (i.e. Puritan doctrine), and this religiously inspired concentration upon the reform of thought and manners perhaps helps to account for the relative fewness of Welsh trials during this period.

Indeed, it seems that the first person in Wales to be executed for the offence of witchcraft was Gwen ferch Ellis in October 1594.[10] She was committed to the Fleet prison in June on suspicion of using witchcraft, and then sent to Denbighshire where she remained in gaol until her case came up for trial. Aged about forty-two in 1594, she had been twice widowed and married for a third time just two years before her arrest. She was a spinster – the description given of so many women in the English assize records, too, meaning that they earned money by spinning, not that they were single – and made medicines of various kinds for sick people and animals. Did these involve magic? Her indictment says she was led astray by the prompting of devils and that she employed certain devilish and detestable *venecicales artes* ('poisonous skills'), called 'witchcraft' in English, against Lewis ap John.[11] Gwen acknowledged that she had used charms for ten years past and had learned them from her sister. These charms, of which she provided an example, were a mixture of Catholic-infused prayer and petition to be recited, and the opening words of St John's Gospel written down to be worn or carried as an amulet. It was found in the house of a local JP and seemed to have been written backwards. People suspected, therefore, that its intention was maleficent, and not long after its discovery Gwen was arrested. Witnesses lined up against her, with complaints of illness in humans, loss of farm livestock, and a familiar spirit in the shape of an unnaturally large fly. As a result, Gwen was formally charged with breaking a man's arm, causing a woman to lose the use of her limbs, and killing another man – all by witchcraft. Interestingly enough, the grand jury hesitated over this last charge before admitting it for trial, for murder by witchcraft carried the death penalty under the English legislation then in force.

But if the grand jury had reservations, the trial jury did not and Gwen was duly convicted and hanged. Did this execution take place because a member of the ruling class had been involved? Richard Suggett thinks so, although one should not interpret this in terms of class or status, so much as those of local abrasiveness in which one party had the social clout to vent its own displeasure against another which did not. Thomas Mostyn, the JP in question, was certainly an important figure in the district, 'strong-willed, obstinate, and not altogether likeable',[12] and in 1594 seems to have been at odds with one Jane Conway whose son had provided Gwen with two written copies of the relevant verses from St John's Gospel to be used as charms. (Presumably she herself could not write.) The discovery of one of these in Thomas Mostyn's house may thus have suggested that Jane had commissioned Gwen to bewitch Thomas in pursuit of their disagreement, and as Jane had confided in Gwen about her sense of Thomas's injustice, and had asked, at one point, how long Thomas had to live, the implication that the two women had struck a magical bargain was certainly strengthened. Thomas also had a close relationship with William Hughes, Bishop of St Asaph, who examined Gwen on the allegations against her before sending her for trial, because he married William's daughter two years later. Gwen's downfall, then, owed much to her unfortunate and unforeseen intrusion into a local dispute whose ramifications may not have concerned her directly, but which led in the end to her death.

So neither in Wales nor in Ireland, both of which were regarded by the English as hotbeds of ignorance, superstition, and witchcraft, is there any available evidence that the ruling English took enough notice of magical workers to charge them in any noticeable numbers with offences under the English Witchcraft Act, whose provisions obtained in both countries. Likewise, there is no surviving evidence that more were in danger of being so charged during the last three decades of the sixteenth century than during the previous seven. This is in sharp contrast with England itself, and although one might conjecture that England had enough problems of its own during those last thirty years without being over-concerned with countries outwith its own borders, it is worth observing that even in England there appear to be differences between north and south in particular. In fact it looks as though, while London and its immediate neighbours developed a kind of nervous tic about magic and divination, that nervousness did not communicate itself to anything like the same extent the further one went from the English capital. The apparent unity of the English state – and political, religious, and to some extent social harmony was an aim of the later Tudor government – was something of an illusion. Roads there were, and rivers, but travel was difficult because the roads were hazardous, their condition variable, bridges often dangerous, and their role in cementing 'unity' tenuous and fragile at best.[13] Nowadays we think of travel in terms of hours, which makes our destinations appear to be closer to us. In the sixteenth century, people thought of travel within their own country – when they thought of it at all – in restricted terms of a few miles to and from the local market town, or of days, not hours, with their attendant lengthy disruption, discomfort, and potential danger. Hence, the idea of 'unity' was difficult to grasp and most people were vividly aware of the differences rather than any similarities between themselves and those from some other district. As for peoples who spoke a foreign language – Welsh, Irish, Manx, Cornish – they were quite un-English, even if the English government claimed jurisdiction over them. Perhaps not surprisingly, therefore, in spite of the existence of the 1563 Witchcraft Act, neither Ireland nor Wales was particularly affected by what concerned London and the English south-east.

The same may be said of the Isle of Man at this time. It was a personal possession of the Earl of Derby and had its own parliament, the Tynwald, which passed laws borrowing from both Scottish and English legislative systems. Yet the island's isolation from London and the gap in mutual understanding between its English-speaking officials and its Manx-speaking populace meant that the island was unlikely to be much influenced by southern English practice when it came to its own witches and their witchcraft: and so it proved to be. Only two people appear to have been brought before the island's Court of General Gaol Delivery at this time, one in 1569 and another in 1598. The former, Alice Ine Gilbay, claimed to have a fairy spirit at her command, which she could send at any time to kill. She was found guilty, but was saved from execution because she was pregnant. The other never came to trial because of a mistake in the relevant legal procedure.[14] On 24 June 1594, articles were delivered to officials at the Tynwald, instructing 'that they inquire and present if there be any in the isle do use witchcraft or sorcery',[15] but this gives the impression either of perfunctoriness or of a situation in which magical workers were not raising their heads above the legal parapet. Much further south, in Jersey and Guernsey, however, things were not quite so restrained. Jersey saw trials and executions of witches in 1562 (two women, both executed), 1563 (man acquitted), 1583 (woman's death in prison), 1585 (four women and one man executed), 1591 (four female and three male executions, one man acquitted), 1593 (woman, fate unknown), 1597 (one woman executed, two women released after their juries failed to reach a unanimous verdict), 1599 (one woman executed, one woman acquitted, one woman, fate unknown), 1600 (three executions, two women and one man), and 1602 (two women executed).[16] Here something of an increase in numbers during the 1580s and 1590s can be detected. Their offences can be gauged from the sentence of death passed on Jeanne Le Vesconte on 2 November 1585:

> Whereas common report has long suspected Jeanne Le Vesconte of the diabolical art of witchcraft, charging her with constantly using spells and wicked devices, sometimes against people, sometimes against their goods, making some ill, and curing others; and whereas complaints and scandals have so multiplied that she has been arrested; she has voluntarily submitted the question of her guilt or innocence, her life or death, to an Enquere du Pays. The said Enquere of twenty-four, having been sworn and purged of suspicion, as custom requires, has unanimously voted for her condemnation to death; according to which verdict she is sentenced to be hanged till death ensues, and in detestation of her crime to be reduced to ashes, and all her goods, chattels, and property confiscated to the Crown or the Seigneur to whom it belongs.

These charges sound very similar to those levelled against English witches, but we also find evidence of direct traffic with Satan. In 1585, Jean Morant 'having been so forgetful of his salvation as to make a contract with the Devil, confessed with his own mouth his dealings with the Devil by mark and pact (confirmed by pledge and gift of one of his members) by means of which he had committed infinite mischiefs, crimes, and homicides'; and in 1591, Simon Vauldin confessed that he 'had at divers times held familiar intercourse and talks with the Devil who appeared as a cat and then as a crow'.[17]

Such converse, along with pact, mark, and sacrifice of a part of the body, is much closer to the experience and practice of mainland Europe than to what is generally found in England. But, as we have noted earlier, Jersey had a mixed religious society after 1558 when Elizabeth Tudor came to the English throne, with a large number of Calvinist refugees from France seeking refuge on the island and a Calvinist régime in place to enforce new belief and behaviour, even though officially Jersey was under the supervisions of an English bishop (Winchester) and was supposed to use the English order of worship in its churches. The new order, however, was not readily accepted and 'superstitious' (i.e. Catholic) practices continued to be employed, while night-time parties called *vueilles* happened quite frequently, 'not without great debauchery and dissoluteness', according to the records of the Colloque on Guernsey in 1587.[18] So what we can see in Jersey is a restless populace, with long-established customs and authority more readily informed by European witchcraft theory than the English government was prepared to be, bearing down upon a society unlike that on mainland England in as much as it was much more compact, much smaller, and therefore easier to influence and control as a unitary body. Hence we see that when Jacques Le Brocq's daughter fell ill, Jacques and her two brothers, Mathieu and Jean, were arrested and imprisoned in October 1585 simply for seeking a cure from a woman suspected of witchcraft; and in a similar frame of mind in 1591, the Cour de Cattel, the island's principal court, issued a proclamation redolent of its own fears and determination to deal severely with what it saw as a problem:

> Whereas many have in days gone by committed the heinous sin of seeking aid in time of trouble from warlocks and witches, a thing contrary to the honour of God and His express command, and a grievous insult to the Christian faith and to those whose duty it is to administer justice; and whereas ignorance is no excuse for sin, and no one can tell what depravity and danger may ensue from such practices; in order that henceforth all may turn from these devilish and wicked cures, the use of which merits by God's law the same penalty as is inflicted on warlocks and witches themselves, and that God's wrath may be averted, which now threatens the officers of justice because of the impunity with which these crimes are committed; all who dwell in this island are strictly forbidden to receive aid or advice in trouble from warlocks or witches or anyone suspected of witchcraft, under pain of a month's imprisonment in the castle on dry bread and water, with the reservation that they must declare in court their excuse for such effrontery and, according as this shall appear reasonable, be dealt with as God's law directs.[19]

In Jersey, we note from Jeanne Le Vesconte's sentence, condemned witches were executed as they were in Scotland, being hanged or strangled until dead, after which their body was burned and their property confiscated.[20] The practice on Guernsey is a little more difficult to ascertain exactly. Tony Bellows points out that a record from 1622, detailing the method used for the execution of four witches, says that they were 'sentenced to be executed by being tied to a post on a scaffold, and then burnt to death', and that the mention of 'scaffold' suggests they were hanged before being burned.[21] Being tied to a post on a scaffold is actually more reminiscent of the practice used in Scotland in which the condemned was garrotted before the fire was lit – Goya's pen-and-ink drawing of a garrotted man gives a vivid notion of the procedure – but it is fairly clear, in spite of the phrase 'then burnt to death', that the condemned were not actually burned alive, as is sometimes asserted. The number of those tried on Guernsey at this time, however, seems to be somewhat smaller than that on Jersey, for in 1563 there were six trials, in 1570 seven, and in 1583 one. Of these fourteen, five resulted in execution, three in whipping, mutilation, and banishment, five in banishment alone, the result of the remaining trial being uncertain. It is interesting that most of these should have taken place earlier than in Jersey, but this may be accounted for by the change of bailiffs at a particular moment. Helier Gosselin was sacked early in 1563, partly as a result of his alleged behaviour during the execution of three heretic women on 17 July 1556, and partly for 'other most crafty dealings and deceits'. The burning of the heretics quickly became notorious. According to John Foxe's Acts and Monuments, when Perotine Massey was to be put to death and the fire had actually been lit, she suddenly gave birth and her baby fell into the flames. A bystander rescued it, but Gosselin ordered that it be thrown back into the fire, and so the child as well as its mother became a Protestant martyr. There are so many things about this take which render it implausible that one may easily dismiss it as most unlikely to be true even in part, but the fact that an act of barbarity could be attributed to Gosselin tells us something, perhaps, about the way he was perceived, unless, of course, he was being smeared in the interests of Protestant propaganda.[22]

But by May 1563, Gosselin had been replaced by Thomas Compton, a ship owner who had overseen the dissolution of the house of the Cordelier Franciscans in St Peter Port in 1536, and was appointed to a royal commission in July 1562 to oversee the seizure for the English Crown of concealed Catholic revenues. He then joined the Calvinist consistory intended to ensure the island's adoption of Genevan reform of religion, a body which first met on 17 May 1563.[23] The witch trials, dated 19 November, 17 December, and 22 December that year, therefore took place during the opening stages of his term of office. But although it may look as though he was trying to make a good impression (especially as his immediate predecessor had been ignominiously dismissed from his post) – one notes that the English Witchcraft Act had been passed in April, so not a great deal of time had been lost in arresting, interrogating, and trying the individuals accused – nevertheless, no more trials followed until July, October, and November 1570, and only one of those defendants was executed. Add to this that under the next bailiff, Guillaume de Beauvoir (1572–81), one incident, which did not actually turn into a prosecution, took place;[24] under Thomas Wigmore (1581–88), one extended trial; and under Louis de Vic (1588–1600), two executions, and we seem to have a clear enough picture of little official interest on Guernsey in pursuing and prosecuting workers of magic.[25] The contrast with the south, especially the south-east, of England is thus noteworthy.

The Calvinist settlement in Guernsey was not altogether popular. In 1580 the bailiff remarked that the ministers 'by their preaching ... are the causes of many troubles here and the people desire to be delivered from their discipline', and one can see what he meant from an ordinance promulgated on 7 October 1583:

> In as much as God is offended by the vulgar and detestable abuses committed at dances and illegal gambling, where it would seem the law is flouted, it is ordered by the court that any who allow or tolerate dancing, gambling, or unlawful assembly to take place in their house, or who play any instrument or sing dissolute songs at such dances and suchlike, will be thus punished: that in church on a Sunday, before the whole congregation, in front of the pulpit, with head, legs, and feet bared, wrapped in a white shroud and holding a lighted torch, they will admit their offence. Anyone who dances or is present at a dance will be flogged, as ordered by law.[26]

The witchcraft incident of 15 May 1581 involved Katharine Eustace and her daughter, who were reputed 'by common consent' to be practising witches. They were accused by Mme Cousin of making her cow produce blood instead of milk after she had refused to give milk to the accused, and by Johan Le Roux of afflicting him with pains in his knee as a result of bewitchment specifically by Katharine. Apparently, Mme Le Roux went to Katharine and threatened to bring her to court. M. Le Roux then recovered, and one has to presume the complaint never progressed as far as formal denunciation and trial.

But on 25 February 1583 what turned out to be a lengthy process against Collas de la Rue began, with several witnesses offering evidence for the prosecution. Matthieu Cauchez deposed that Collas had correctly foretold Mme Cauchez's death; James Blanche that Collas had first made Mme Blanche fall ill and had then cured her with herbs; Thomas Behot that Collas had afflicted him with illness because he had refused to give Collas's son some fish.[27] After a long time, during which the illness refused to go away, Mme Behot took her husband's mattress apart and found all kinds of curious objects in it – seeds, sheep treadles,[28] bits of laurel, rags with feathers stuck into them – and when she threw them on the fire, they gave off a dreadful smell. She then put the key of their front door into the fire, and when it was red-hot Collas suddenly appeared, offering to cure Thomas with herbal poultices. These did not work, but poverty (or obstinacy) made him go out fishing again, contrary to Collas's advice, upon which he nearly drowned and returned home as ill as ever. Mme Behot decided to investigate his mattress again and found a small doll made from gnawed bone. This Thomas took to a magistrate, an action which resulted in his recovery from the illness. We have come across this before in the case of Katharine Eustace, and the clear inference is that a threat of initiating a formal complaint could be sufficient either to make the witch stop her or his *maleficium*, or to satisfy the victim that he or she had found a refuge from preternatural attack and thus a cure or feelings associated with a cure soon followed.

A similar kind of situation arose when Collas, who had continuing lawsuits against Pierre Tardif, was alleged to have made one of Tardif's daughters ill. When her mattress was searched, they found several intruded objects – coloured thread, twigs of broom, black beans, and a pin stuck in a piece of rag. Rather than go to the authorities, however, Tardif, 'having taken advice' (one wonders from whom), gave Collas a good thrashing and drew blood, after which his daughter recovered her health. Drawing blood from a witch by violence, usually scratching in the case of a woman, was, of course, a well-known tactic one could employ as a piece of counter-magic to undo the effect of a witch's malevolence. It may have produced the same kind of psychological satisfaction as the threat to go to a magistrate, but was also likely to have signalled to the witch that his or her power was gone or diminished. Contemporary or near-contemporary writers on witchcraft, however, had their reservations about this kind of practice. George Gifford tells the story of a man whose son was covered with sores which were caused by a witch. He went to a cunning man who told him how to summon the witch magically and when she appeared, she told the sick boy to scratch her. 'He scratched her until the blood followed, and whereas before nothing would draw his sores, they healed of themselves'. But to this, the other person in Gifford's dialogue observes, 'Do you think a man may lawfully seek help at the hands of the Devil?' Cunning folk were as bad, in their way, as witches, and counter-magic as sinful as the original witchcraft. 'What virtue [*power*] can the scratching of a witch have to cure a hurt? Where do we find it in any part of the word of God that scratching should be used?' asks William Perkins, and Alexander Roberts is equally scathing. 'This [practice] hath gone as current and may plead prescription for warrant – a foul sin among Christians, to think one witchcraft can drive out another.'[29]

For some reason – the records are torn in various places – Collas's trial was adjourned or even dismissed, but it was resumed nearly three years later in December 1585 when further witnesses appeared against him. One produced a child in court and alleged that its inability to talk properly was because of Collas's magic. Here we learn that Collas had been imprisoned for sorcery before, 'although he had not always been found guilty'. That 'always' suggests his reputation as a witch was long-standing and that more than the complaints here recorded had been lodged against him, and also makes it unlikely that the imprisonment referred to here meant simply that he had been put in gaol after the February 1583 hearing and left there. In 1585, however, his luck ran out. For James Blanche came forward again; and Jehennet des Perques said Collas often went to the harbour and predicted the weather for fishermen, and that one day, when Collas quarrelled with Mme de Bertran, the lady fell downstairs and bruised herself from head to toe. Several people deponed that Collas was in the habit of issuing threats, making people fall ill and then curing them, and that he was called 'sorcerer' to his face by many. This accumulation of witnesses (and to this we should perhaps add his long-standing reputation as an ill-tempered worker of magic) seems to have brought him to trial at last, and then to the scaffold, and he was executed on 25 March 1586.[30]

So here we have Jersey and Guernsey showing signs of increased activity against witches in the 1580s and 1590s, although there were slightly more of these in Jersey than in Guernsey. Jersey, of course, is nearer France and thus perhaps somewhat more open to French influence, although this point cannot be pressed too hard. Both islands were caught up in European tensions – those of the religious wars in France after 1572 and those in the mid-1580s as Normandy battled with Paris and Spain set in motion its grand invasion of England. What is more, the islands themselves were plagued by intermittent, serious quarrels between their governors and local elites.[31] These external and internal tensions, however, merely provide the context in which accusations of and trials for witchcraft took place. They do not act as necessary triggers for such accusations or trials. But it is worth noting that of all French provinces, Normandy stands out as the one which executed the largest number of witches at this time, in spite of appeals to the *parlement* in Rouen: 62 per cent between 1585 and 1589, 50 per cent between 1590 and 1593, 43 per cent between 1594 and 1599, and 64 per cent between 1600 and 1609.[32] If anything can validly be said about Jersey's greater proximity to France, therefore, it may be that Norman anxiety about magical practitioners may have transferred itself thither via Huguenot refugees who are known to have fled there and to Guernsey, especially in the aftermath of the St Bartholomew's Day massacres in August 1572.

But the relative scarcity of witchcraft cases in the islands, Ireland, Wales, and the north of England during the late decades of the sixteenth century was not altogether matched in Scotland where religious, political, and social upheavals were greater than those in England and provided an even more intense context for witch trials of scandalous proportions in Edinburgh. To appreciate how this came about, we should start, perhaps, with the *Catechism* of John Hamilton, Archbishop of St Andrews, which was published on 19 August 1552. This makes it clear that anyone who uses magic sins against the first commandment, and that all magical operations are based upon a pact with the Devil.

Whoever uses witchcraft, necromancy, enchantment, jugglery: or trusts in them, or seeks their help: who depends on words or dreams: who trusts to defend themselves or their animals or [their] property against fire, water, sword, dangerous beasts, superstitiously with certain tokens [*amulets*] or writings, breaks the [First] Commandment. And if any man or woman would say, 'We often see that what diviners say comes to pass. Often lost or stolen property is found again by conjurors, and so clearly to seek for such help is not an evil thing to do' – oh you wretched and blind man or woman who thinks or speaks words such as these! I know well and understand that whenever you ask for or seek any help, counsel, remedy, consolation, or defence from any witch, sorcerer, conjuror, or suchlike deceivers, you do great injury to your Lord God because you take the honour and service which ought to be given to God alone and give it to the Devil who is [a] deadly enemy to your soul. For without doubt, all witches', necromancers', and suchlike works are operations of the Devil under a pact, condition, bond, or obligation of service and honour to be made to him ... And to make an answer to your argument: sometimes the Devil shows you the truth in small matters only so that in the end he may make you believe in his lies and black falsehood in matters of great importance concerning your soul. Sometimes he will help you to recover the goods of this world, but his intention is to make you lose the good things of the world to come. Sometimes he will help you to recover the health of your body, simply so that he may bring you to the eternal death of your soul. Therefore all true Christian men and women should not, by the command of God, use any kind of witchcraft, but also should not seek any kind of help from witches.

Here let us note that the archbishop not only distinguishes between different types of magical operation, but includes 'jugglery', *praestigium*, the deceptive quickness of hand or manipulation of light and shade to produce illusions, which, while recognised by many at the time to be mere conjuring tricks, were also condemned as sitting uneasily upon the border between acceptable entertainment and demon-assisted magic. He also mentions 'conjurors', magicians who summoned spirits to help in the location and recovery of lost or stolen articles, and attributes all such and similar dealings to a pact with the Devil. Following this passage, the archbishop condemns superstition, too – he gives as examples 'certain craftsmen who will not begin their work on a Saturday, certain shipmen or mariners who will not begin to sail on a Saturday, [and] certain travellers who will not begin their journey on a Saturday,' and 'some people who will not bury the bodies of their friends on the north part of the kirkyard, believing that there is more holiness or virtue on the south side'. So it is clear, even from this catechism, that there was a vivid awareness of preternatural forces and constant alertness in people's dealings with them among those Scots with whose beliefs and behaviour the archbishop was most familiar, that is, people from the south-east of Scotland.

Our records for this period are extremely thin, however, and offer only very occasional evidence for the existence and activity of witches. But there are enough glimpses to let us infer their continuity throughout the early sixteenth century. In 1518, a justice air at Jedburgh was instructed to ask if anyone knew anything about witchcraft or sorcery in the area; on 1 June 1536, Agnes Scot 'was convicted of the magical practice known in the vernacular as "witchcraft"'; in October 1542, three female witches were condemned and executed in St Andrews – one notices the references to heresy and apostasy linked to magic, references which may account for the women being burned; on 1 June 1545, Margaret Hay was tried in Elgin for calling Margaret Balfour a whore and a witch – standard insults between women, which may or may not have some foundation in truth; in Elgin again, in 1560, Andrew Edie claimed forty (Scots) shillings from the town council in recompense for his warding accused witches in the church steeple – a common place to be used as a temporary prison; and in September 1562, Janet Lindsay and her daughter Isabel Keir confessed to witchcraft and were banished in perpetuity from Stirling.[33]

Now, in 1560 Protestant reformation came rapidly, not unexpectedly, and violently to Scotland. Attempts at reform had been made during the 1540s, but an English invasion and occupation of the south-east of the country between 1547 and 1549 encouraged Protestant militants, and by 1557 the new faith was gaining favour among some members of the aristocracy, although we must always remember that the Scottish aristocracy always tended to be turbulent and difficult for the Crown to manage; and how far its members' Protestantism was the expression of genuine religious commitment and how far that of political opposition to a French Catholic regent is in some cases perhaps open to debate. By 1559 internal war between Mary of Guise, the regent, and the Protestant 'Lords of Congregation' was throwing Fife especially into turmoil. But then, on 11 June 1560, Mary of Guise died and scarcely one month later, on 10 July, a parliament met in Edinburgh to establish the Protestant confession in its Genevan manifestation as the officially approved form of religion in Scotland for the future. Mary Stuart, Queen of France and Queen of Scots,[34] was thus greeted by a religious fait accompli when she returned to Scotland in 1561. But since none of the 1560 Parliament's Acts had received royal assent, another parliament was necessary and it was this fresh parliament, meeting in 1563, which would pass, among other legislation, Scotland's first Witchcraft Act.

The groundwork seems to have been laid the previous December in a general assembly of the new Protestant Kirk, and although there is no evidence that the assembly itself drafted the Act, there is a strong likelihood that it emerged from a growing concern to purge Scotland of Catholicism root and branch, practice as well as belief. Julian Goodare has made a very good case for the authorship of the Act's resting with a clergyman, and he suggests that the leading, if not the only hand may have been that of John Knox, whose enthusiasm for the Genevan-based settlement of religion in Scotland was both fierce and unremitting.[35] The general assembly was also concerned with topics other than witchcraft, of course – adultery and restitution of manses and glebes to Protestant ministers, for example – but the common and widespread Protestant association of magic with Catholicism meant that any attempt to eradicate the latter would involve eradicating the former; hence Knox could well have given his blessing to the new Act, even if he did not actually pen it himself.

The text was passed into law on 4 June 1563 and shows significant differences from its equivalent in England.

(i) For as much as the Queen's Majesty and three Estates in this present Parliament are informed that the heavy and abominable superstition used by several if the lieges of this realm, the use of witchcrafts, sorcery, and necromancy, and credence given thereto in times gone by against the law of God: and for expelling and putting away of all such empty superstition in times to come:

(ii) it is decreed and ordained by the Queen's Majesty, and the three Estates foresaid, that no manner of person or persons, no matter what their status, degree, or condition, take upon hand in any times hereafter to use any kind of witchcrafts, sorcery, or necromancy, or give themselves forth to have any such craft or knowledge thereof, whereby they abuse the people:

(iii) nor that any person seek any help, response, or consultation from any such foresaid users or abusers of witchcrafts, sorceries, or necromancy:

(iv) under the pain of death, to be executed against the user-abuser, as well as the seeker of the response or consultation.

(v) And this to be put into execution by the Justice, sheriffs, stewards, bailies, Lord of Regalities and Royalties, their deputies, and other competent judges within this realm, with all rigour, having power to execute the same.[36]

The Act begins with the loaded word 'superstition', links it with 'use of' and 'credence given to' three magical practices, and refers to 'times gone by', all of which allows the reader and implementer of the Act tacitly to associate these three practices with Catholicism. 'Credence' implies either doubt on the part of the legislators anent the validity of witchcrafts, sorcery, and necromancy, or dismissal of the false creed of Catholicism to which the Act implicitly links them. This is a point to which we shall return. Whatever may have been accepted belief and practice in the past, however, is now going to be wiped out. No such rigorous wording attends the English Act, which does not express possible disbelief in the reality of magical actions, either, but turns rather to practical means for their control and 'reform'. But both pieces of legislation, one notices, condemn witchcraft as a series of actions and not as an abstract concept or profession. A witch is to be dealt with not because of what she or he is, but because of what she or he does. Hence the reference to *witchcrafts* as a plural noun. By these are clearly meant (as they meant elsewhere under their jurisdictions) acts of magic either overtly maleficent or, (as in the case, for example, of magically curing the sick), acts of magic suspected of deriving their power and efficaciousness from demonic sources.

'Sorcery', however, causes more of an interpretative problem. James VI later quite rightly pointed out that the word is derived from Latin *sortiarius*, meaning 'someone who divines the future or seeks out hidden information by casting lots'. The king gives contemporary examples of the practice – 'the turning of the riddle, [and] the knowing of the form of prayers, or suchlike tokens, if a person [later] deceased would live or die' – before performing a neat segue from divination into magic; 'and in general, that name was given then for using of such charms and freits [*superstitious acts*] as that craft teacheth them' to which he adds that 'many points of their craft and practices are common betwixt magicians and them, for they serve both one master, although in divers fashions'.[37] Magicians and sorcerers, then, are different in spite of their practices' frequently overlapping, and the mention of 'charms' and 'superstitious acts' suggests where the division broadly lies. Scottish 'charmers' were the magical workers referred to in England as 'cunning men and women', and Joyce Miller points to a difference between them and the other operators of magic. 'Charming was the antidote to witchcraft but could also be used to cure some natural diseases. Many of the rituals and practices were common to all three – charming, witchcraft, sorcery – but the intent, and the source of power, of charming were very different.'[38]

So King James was eliding sorcery with charming while at the same time recognising a difference as well as a similarity between them. The Witchcraft Act may be doing the same (in which case its 'witchcraft' will refer to maleficent magic and its 'sorcery' to a combination of divination and acts of benevolently intended magic), or it may not, in which case its 'sorcery' will refer to divination of various kinds, but not to acts of charming. Goodare points out that in a general assembly of the Kirk in 1646 'nobody thought that the witchcraft act might already cover charmers',[39] but as, in practice, charming was likely to be treated as though it were witchcraft – an understandable elision, since accused witches' dittays (indictments) often mention magical acts of beneficence alongside those of maleficence, and both witches and charmers were presumed to derive their power from demonic sources – the Act's 'witchcrafts' may well have included acts of charming, leaving 'sorcery' to refer to acts of divination.[40]

This leaves 'necromancy'. There is evidence, as with 'sorcery', that people were not always precise in their use of occultist terminology. Del Rio, for example, complained that 'theologians such as Grillando reduce all explicit divinations to necromancy and implicit to *sortilegium* and augury. They use these words very loosely and incorrectly, in spite of the fact that these words have a fairly restricted sense which does not embrace just any type of divination.' On the other hand, if one looks at what Grillando wrote, a somewhat different picture emerges. 'Divination is of three kinds,' he said, 'and the first is done through the overt invocation of demons. This type is practised by necromancers ... These people appear to raise the dead by means of their incantations and invocations. The necromancers ask them questions and [the dead] give their replies.'[41] If, therefore, we wish to suggest that the Witchcraft Act did distinguish between 'witchcrafts' and 'sorcery', we are bound to include 'necromancy' as an activity separate and distinguishable from them, and if we bear in mind that summoning the dead might easily be interpreted as summoning evil spirits (as, indeed, Grillando suggests), the activity of invoking spirits to assist in looking for buried treasure – a relatively common practice at the time, especially among men – could have been what the Act had at the back of its mind, as well as the simple process of inquiring about the future. (The English Act does not use the word 'necromancy', but does explicitly condemn the employment of magic to discover the whereabouts of treasure. Does this greater explicitness point to a difference in drafting, the English Act by lawyers, the Scottish Act by a clergyman not expert in the law?)[42]

Another difference in emphasis between the Scottish and English Acts lies in their reference to offenders. The English Act talks about 'many fantastical and devilish persons' and makes special provision for the trial of a peer accused of witchcraft. The Scottish Act damns everyone regardless of rank or social status, and one wonders why the drafter found it necessary to make clear that members of the nobility were to be regarded as equally culpable with the rest of society. If we remember that the legislation was probably discussed during the general assembly meeting of December 1562 – after a feud between George Gordon, 4th Earl of Huntly, a Catholic, and the Ogilvy family, had broken out into violence in August and September and rapidly assumed serious political aspects when the queen became involved – it becomes significant perhaps that the Countess of Huntly had the practice of consulting witches. On 16 October, the earl and his third son were officially declared outlaws, and witches told the countess that her husband's body would soon be lying without a wound in the tolbooth of Aberdeen. This prophecy turned out to be correct, for a fortnight later he suffered a seizure and fell dead from his horse, whereupon his body was take to lie in the tolbooth before being handed over to embalmers.[43] The incident was no local scandal. Indeed, the earl's body was removed to Edinburgh and the following May tied to a chair before a session of parliament and tried for treason. So the general assembly, including Knox, had every reason to remark on the countess's consultations with witches and decide to include the nobility in its condemnation of those who consulted as well as those who professed to be diviners or workers of magic.[44]

Practitioners and consulters were to be treated alike: the death penalty awaited both. This is more severe than the English counterpart, and one notices that it covered anyone who claimed to have esoteric knowledge, whether she or he practised as a result of it or not. So it provided, potentially at least, a window into people's souls and an instrument for close scrutiny of both motive and behaviour, which the Kirk in its new form was keen to have at its disposal. 'Giving themselves forth to have any such knowledge thereof, thereby abusing the people' made the magical practitioner or diviner an 'abuser' as well as a 'user', a doublet which is repeated just after the provision of the death penalty for the magician and her or his client, and one which makes it clear that 'user' and 'abuser' are being treated as synonymous. The user of witchcraft, sorcery, or necromancy is someone who uses other people for her or his own ends – the negative sense of the Latin verb *abutor* – and 'abusing the people' thus means the same thing.[45] As far as the Act is concerned, therefore, even if witchcraft, sorcery, and necromancy are real and valid in themselves, their use by anyone claiming to have knowledge of their techniques is deliberate guilt. It is an implication underlined by the use of the word 'vain' in the early reference in the Act to 'doing away with all such vain superstition', since the Latin *vanus* means 'empty, groundless, deceptive'. But if these superstitious practices are simply meaningless ways to deceive people and are employed for the user's own particular purposes – one thinks, perhaps, of street tricksters conning passers-by out of money by such well-known pieces of legerdemain as 'Find the Lady' – why are they deserving of so draconian a punishment as death? Why, too, under these circumstances should the deceived client be executed? There seems to be some kind of confusion here in the minds of the drafter and legislators. If witchcraft, sorcery, and necromancy are real and offer means whereby Satan can lure people into losing their souls, they are entirely serious matters and the references to abusing and vain superstition forfeit a good deal of their force, or even become redundant; and if witchcraft, sorcery, and necromancy are closely associated with Catholicism, which is, itself, regarded as little better than a conduit for demonic deception of the people, it is perfectly possible to understand why the Kirk and its Calvinist secular supporters should consider death penalty for 'users' appropriate. Heretics were frequently executed, and from this point of view the Witchcraft Act is partly a Presbyterian Heresy Act under another guise. But of course not even the most fervent Protestant would have claimed that witchcraft, sorcery, and necromancy were nothing more than a mask for Catholicism, and so we are back with the ambiguity of the Act's choice of vocabulary. Eager to condemn magic as both undesirable and dangerous, the drafter has not considered sufficiently the implications of his wording – a disconcerting aspect of a piece of legislation which the courts could use to deprive people of their lives and families of their inheritance.[46]

As in England, however, the Act does not seem to have had the effect that Parliament may have envisaged. This is perhaps not altogether surprising, as the estates and general assembly had many pressing things to think about as well as witches, diviners, and charmers: deciding which was to be the predominant power in the state, Kirk or Crown, and the extirpation of Catholicism throughout a not altogether willing or co-operative country, to mention only two. Nevertheless, witches there were, and in no small numbers, and whereas in England the passage of its Witchcraft Act does not appear to have led to much conscious and active exercising of official and governmental minds anent the problem of magic and its practitioners, in Scotland, where witchcraft or perceived witchcraft was mingled much more thoroughly with a hatred of Catholicism, the Act provided the state and Church with a lethal weapon to deploy against those they deemed inimical to the interests of society. One cannot say they did not try. In 1565, the general assembly petitioned the queen to ensure that recent Acts of Parliament were put into effect, including 'such horrible crimes as now abound in this realm ... such as idolatry, blaspheming of God's name, manifest breaking of the Sabbath day, witchcraft, sorcery and enchantment, adultery, incest ... with many other detestable cromes'; and two years later another article was laid before Parliament, seeking renewed investigation and punishment of witches and their clients: 'how witchcraft shall be punished and investigation made thereof, and that the execution of death may be used as well against those who consult with the witch, seeking her support, [or who] furnish aid or defend her, as against [the witch] herself'. This is noteworthy, since it defines a witch as a woman, something the 1563 Act was careful not to do. Then in April 1568, the bailies of Arbroath and others sought permission to bring to trial forty named individuals 'accused or suspected of certain abominable crimes of sorcery and witchcraft recently committed by them'. Magic could be found, as the Act knew well, in the higher reaches of society, and in August that same year, Sir William Stewart, Lyon King of Arms, was reported hanged 'for conspiring to take the regent's life by sorcery and necromancy'.

Witches were being tried in Fife in 1569 and 1572, one of whom was preached at by John Knox himself; but then on 24 November 1572, Parliament felt obliged to legislate yet again in the case of diviners and other practitioners of occult arts, a provision which had to be repeated, word for word, in November 1579:

> It is declared that all idle persons going about in any part of this realm using subtle [*ingenious*], crafty [*skilful, dexterous*], and unlawful performances such as jugglery [*conjuring tricks*], 'fast and loose', and suchlike: the idle people calling themselves 'Egyptians' [*i.e. gypsies*], or anyone else who claims to have knowledge of physiognomy, palmistry, or other abused [*misused*] sciences, whereby they persuade the people that they can tell their destinies, deaths, and fortunes, and such other fantastical imaginings, [*shall be punished as idle beggars, i.e. scourged and branded on the ear, and for a subsequent offence, executed*].

This, however, is clearly aimed at vagabondage rather than fortune telling and the like, for had it been primarily about fortune telling, the gypsies would have been arrestable under the terms of the Witchcraft Act and would have needed no separate legislation.[47]

Witchcraft proper, then (as opposed to conjuring-tricks and divination), kept nagging at the administration of Scotland, like a kind of aching tooth, frequently poked to make sure it still hurt. But 1567 had initiated an even more troubled period for the kingdom. Queen Mary had been forced to abdicate in favour of her infant son, James, and had fled into England. After her departure, a series of unstable governments under four successive regents tried to calm the country, which was suffering intermittent civil war between the supporters of King James and those of his mother. On 23 February 1573, however, a conference in Perth brought settlement. The Earl of Morton was recognised as regent and Mary's supporters surrendered to his authority and were granted indemnity from their former actions, 'incest, witchcraft, and theft excepted'. It is an interesting proviso, and one which was repeated by the Privy Council in a meeting on 17 December that same year, when it considered the illegal purchase of a document of remission made out to three named persons, John Moscrop, advocate, Katharine Liddell, his wife, and Patrick Moscrop, their son. The regent, it was emphasised, did not grant remission for several crimes, among them witchcraft, and so the Moscrops' document had no value or validity.[48] Clearly, then, the Witchcraft

Act may have stimulated official intentions and efforts to reform, but equally clearly it was having no effect on people's behaviour. If we ask ourselves, 'What behaviour?', meaning magical practice, several records from the 1570s and 1580s can give us an outline of an answer. Thus, on 4 May 1577, John Addie turned up in court to act as bail for Edward Kyninmonth, pledging that Edward would appear for trial at the justice air in Forfar 'or elsewhere' to answer the charge of 'frequent repetition and use of incantation and magical tricks [*prestigiarum*] known as "witchcrafts", and various other crimes'. The Scots version of this Latin note, however, speaks of his 'using and seeking of enchantments and witchcrafts in the month of October 1574 when sundry of his cattle were stricken with sickness'. So was he a farmer who went to someone else, such as a charmer, for advice and help, and was given magical formulae to use, as the Scots suggests, or did he know these already, as we might be led to deduce from the Latin alone? (One notes that the recording clerk has chosen to employ the dismissive word *praestigia* for 'witchcrafts'.)[49] Here 'enchantments' and 'magical acts' are clearly separate, so we may be able to infer that the attempted cure consisted of ritual gestures or the use of amulets, accompanied by chanted or spoken words. The amulets may simply have been certain stones which were to be rubbed on a cow's afflicted parts or steeped in water, after which the water would be sprinkled on the cow or given her to drink. This was a common practice as late as the nineteenth century, as J. M. Joass, minister of Golspie in Sutherland, bore witness:

> Rather over forty years ago a case was tried in the Dornoch small debt court when 'a man of skill' from Lairg, prepaid to cure a cow, declined to remit the fee although he failed to effect the cure. The present sheriff-clerk, who writes that he distinctly remembers the case, says that the sheriff pressed hard to find out the usual methods employed by the wizard but could get no other reply than 'that is my secret'. At last a hint of imprisonment (without option) brought out the admission that a glass charm was placed in water with which, after invocation of the Trinity, the head, especially the nostril, was washed and the ceremony concluded by a solemn assurance to the owner of the ailing beast that according to *his* faith it should fare with his property.[50]

Other cases show that magical workers might be hired to curse someone, or slaughter people by magic. One instance of the latter is that of Violat Mar from Perthshire (1577), who was accused of intending to use 'sorcery, witchcraft, and incantation, and invocation of spirits' with a view to killing the regent. Another is that of Tibbie Smart from Kincardineshire, who was kidnapped by members of the Findlaw family, brought to their house 'secretly and under silence of night', and kept there for nearly four days while they persuaded her to murder another family, the Reids, with whom they were at feud, 'most ungodly and unnaturally by sorceries and witchcrafts'. This, under pressure, she did and during the next few months first one, then another of the Reids died.[51] We also find a significant minority of men accused of witchcraft, as in one case from Easter Ross in 1577, when six men and twenty-six women were arrested on the orders of the Sheriff of Cromarty, or another in Ayrshire in 1583 when nine men were indicted for 'crimes of the practice of magic, sorcery, and other offences'. Cases come from the west (Ayr), the central belt (Perth), east (St Andrews), the Borders

(Jedburgh), and north (Montrose).[51] But these are actually very few, especially when one considers they are spread over two decades, and so in spite of the Act and the hostility of both Kirk and state to magic, it cannot be said that Scotland embarked on any serious implementation of its desire to control and eradicate the popular beliefs and practices associated with magic during these twenty years or so.

Features of one or two cases, however, are worth looking at, as they reflect aspects of those beliefs and practices one might otherwise gloss over in one's concentration on witchcraft alone. In 1572, a year in which the Kirk renewed its war against Scottish Catholicism with some vigour, Janet Boyman from Edinburgh was arrested and tried under the Act. The charges against her centre upon Alan Lauderstone, a smith in the Canongate, who had fallen gravely ill. Janet seems to have been consulted anent his cure, and she advised that his shirt be sent to her so that 'by the sight thereof she could know what sickness he had and if she could mend him thereof nor not'. Apparently she was undecided, because she took the shirt to a fairy spring on Arthur's Seat, the principal peak of a range of hills in the centre of Edinburgh, whose Gaelic name, 'High Place of the Arrows', may refer to Neolithic arrowheads found thereon and which were believed to be fairy weapons.[53] Once there, Janet invoked spirits to come and tell her Alan's fate, 'and there came thereafter, first a great blast like a whirlwind, and thereafter came the figure of a man and stood on the other side of the well [spring] opposite her'. Janet spoke to this apparition in the name of the Father and the Son, and of King Arthur and Queen Elspeth, asking him 'either [to] give him his health or else to take him to you and relieve him of his pain': in other words, cure or kill. She then washed Alan's shirt in the south-running spring and sent it back wet to Alan's wife, with specific instructions about its disposal over his body. These instructions went unheeded and the other world made its displeasure known. For 'about midnight came like a great wind about the house, and a very great din which made [Alan's wife] very afraid'. A horseshoe next to the bed began to rattle, and from the empty smithy came sounds of a hammer striking the anvil very fast. In consequence, Alan's wife quickly did as she had been instructed and her husband recovered his health.[54]

From this we may deduce that Janet was a charmer rather than a witch. Her invocation of spirits in a fairy domain is not unique, as we shall see, but it illustrates a thread running through popular belief in Scotland well into post-industrial times, as James Hogg in the eighteenth century and George MacDonald in the nineteenth bear witness. On this, Emma Wilby makes pertinent observations:

> Distinctly folkloristic shamanistic beliefs and practices, such as those relating to fairies and the dead ... despite the disapproval of the Church, because there was a clear need for them ... [and] the fact that so many fairy-related narratives taken down during witchcraft and sorcery interrogations contain themes from fairy stories is not because desperate suspects frantically attempted to fill out their false confessions with half-remembered fairy tales, but because these themes were active on an experiential level, and reflected a living reciprocal interchange through which fairy lore fed into visionary experience and visionary experience fed into fairy lore.[55]

Wilby's perceptions are entirely just. We shall not get anywhere in our attempt to come to terms with and understand magic and witchcraft in the past if we take the facile way out and attribute what we ourselves do not believe or comprehend to the stupidity, malice, or fantasising of those who have left us records of what they believed and did and how it was interpreted. There is in Janet's answers to her interrogators and in the court's record of them something much more interesting than vivid imagination, and since there is no evidence of her having been tortured or subjected to ill treatment – and we are not entitled to assume she must have been, any more than we are entitled nowadays to think that because there is some evidence in some cases of harsh treatment of prisoners by prison guards, all prisoners must therefore be regularly subjected to brutality – we should ask ourselves what it was that Janet was experiencing and deliberately seeking to experience when she went to a fairy location and invoked spirits there.

It is probably worthwhile remembering biblical precedent, because 3 Kings 19.11–12 would certainly have been familiar to everyone from study and pulpit. Elijah went to encounter God on a high mountain and as he stood there, a strong wind blew, followed by earthquake and fire, and then the voice of God.[56] Janet's venturing on to Arthur's Seat and being greeted, after her invocation, by a strong wind and a preternatural apparition therefore may not only have reminded her interrogators and the court of this biblical passage, but may have contributed to fashioning Janet's behaviour and understanding of what she was doing. This 'great blast like a whirlwind' was not a fairy whirlwind because these were transporters, carrying human folk long distances over the earth or into fairyland itself, and were often assimilated with the journeys of witches to Sabbats or places of temporary pleasure. Janet's blast came in answer, as it were, to her invocation and thus presaged the arrival of an entity, just as the blast, earthquake, and fire had preceded God's voice on Mount Horeb.[57] Janet's invocation, then, was intended to produce a non-human presence of some kind, whether fairy or some other kind of spirit, and so she must have expected or hoped to hear or see something in answer to her call. We are told the result was both visual and auditory, a human shape to which she spoke and from which she received answers. The temptation to dismiss this with the word 'hallucination' may prove strong to a modern commentator. But 'hallucination' is not synonymous with 'imaginary and therefore unreal or fictitious episode'. An hallucination is quite likely to be entirely real to the person experiencing it, and she or he, in reporting it, will be speaking personal truth, not fiction, in such a report.[58]

Nevertheless, 'hallucination' is not a particularly helpful term to apply to Janet's experience because of the potentially dismissive undertone of modern, non-specialist usage. One may do a little better to think of what she underwent in terms of her attempting to contact a spirit world while in a state of altered consciousness. Wilby calls this 'fairy shamanism' and refers to similar experiences as 'witchcraft as shamanism', which makes a valid point, although Ronald Hutton has issued a warning about the possible confusion of understanding attending the use of that word.[59] But Holger Kalweit's observation about shamans is pertinent to Janet Boyman's case.

[Shamans] are not sufficiently aware of the mechanisms involved in the transformation of their consciousness or, for that matter, the psychic principles of intercourse with their spirit partners, for their reports to satisfy our scientific and analytical curiosity. The shaman is deeply and unconsciously rooted in his traditional culture and looks upon contact with a spirit being as a relatively normal occurrence.[60]

We may thus be concerned with a charmer consciously or unconsciously imitating a biblical precedent and entering into a state of 'otherness' in which she saw and heard an authoritative presence. As to the means by which she may have done this, we know only what the record tells us – that she invoked spirits. What form her invocation took, whether it was long or short, ejaculatory or complex, accompanied by ritual gestures or not, spoken or chanted, we do not know. What we can reasonably and fairly propose, however, is that when she was arrested and interrogated and provided these details, or something like them, to her interrogators, she was surely not delivering an account entirely novel or surprising to them; for fairies, as well as other non-human entities, were part and parcel of the culture in which both she, her interrogators, the court officials, the witnesses, and the jury lived. Yet it is clear these officials and her jury chose to interpret the Arthur's Seat episode as a deliberate invocation of and meeting with demons – her dittay calls them 'evil spirits'. But it is not difficult, perhaps, to account for the judges' and advocates' attitude to what they were hearing from Janet and, indeed, from other accused workers of magic in other cases. The fervency of their Protestantism and eagerness for reform of behaviour in every walk of Scottish life meant that they viewed the ocean of 'superstition' they saw surrounding them in all parts of the country with a mixture of fear, guilt, and grim determination. I say 'guilt' because they were not immune to the siren voices of that 'superstition'. Some of their kirk ministers, too, 'saw visions, heard the voices of both God and the Devil, foretold the future, and worked miracles', and under these circumstances we can sympathise with their parishioners' indignation when they were condemned from the pulpit for their superstition and fortune telling. Reformers trod a delicate line and knew it. On the other hand, they knew they could rely on that instinctive reverence for men of the cloth, which travellers and strangers noted as characteristic of the Scots. So we can see that judge and advocate, imbued with Protestant fervour, were likely to interpret Janet's talk of invocation, fairies, and apparition as a confession of trafficking with the Devil and evil spirits, and that the jury would be likely to follow their lead, provided no wrong note were struck or sensibility offended.[61]

Here it may be worthwhile to append an observation about confessions and the evidence they contain. It is too easy to dismiss their reports as fantasies constructed either to avoid repetition of the pain of torture, or to please the evident wish of the interrogator to be told what he wanted to hear. I have commented elsewhere on the facile assumption that torture was always used in witchcraft cases, that 'watching' a prisoner was the same as depriving her or him of sleep as a form of torture, and the belief that torture invariably produces lies, fictions, and fantastical imaginings.[62] Interrogation of witches seems to have taken two principal forms: (i) the witch is asked about an action, she denies having done it, the interrogator pressurises her into rescripting her negative as a positive; (ii) the witch provides information about her actions, she is asked, or volunteers, her interpretation of them, she is then pressurised into reinterpreting her actions in accordance with her interrogator's preconception.

Janet's case surely falls into the second category. She said she was invoking spirits, clearly interpreting these as fairies; her interrogators insisted that these spirits were actually demonic. Both sides accepted the reality of the other world, both agreed it could be contacted, both acknowledged the validity of such contacts. Where they differed was in their understanding of what those contacts were, and the concern of both Kirk and state officials was to have *their* interpretation of the other world and the nature of its entities accepted by everyone. This, therefore, has nothing to do with a desired uniformity of scepticism, but much more with a desired uniformity of comprehension and exegesis. There were, of course, problems attendant upon this desire. If the Protestant reformation had replaced the authority of the Church with that of scripture, it did not intend to leave the interpretation of scripture entirely to the uneducated who were unable to read for themselves and thus depended on others for instruction and interpretation, or to the personal guesswork of those who were able to read but had not been trained in the required methods of interpretation. Commentary and teaching should be in the hands of those learned enough to be able to understand the scriptures correctly so that the generality might become, in the words of a sermon notebook, 'Christian professors brought up in the fear and information of the Lord'. We can see a parallel frame of mind in the English Royal College of Physicians, which excluded John Geynes from membership at the end of the sixteenth century because he suggested that Galen might not be altogether infallible; and he was kept out until he changed his mind and signed a recantation of his 'incorrect' ideas.[63]

The glimpse into Scottish popular belief and practice afforded by Janet's case can be repeated by others from the same period. In 1576, Elizabeth Dunlop from Ayrshire was tried for 'the using of sorcery witchcraft, and incantation, with invocation of spirits of the Devil, continuing in familiarity with them at all such times as she thought expedient, dealing with charms, and abusing the people with devilish craft of sorcery foresaid ... used these several years bypast'. The wording of her dittay thus closely follows the intent of the Witchcraft Act. Like Janet, Elizabeth seems to have had dealings with fairies and with an apparition in the form of a man. This apparition took the shape of Thomas Reid, who had died at the Battle of Pinkie in 1547 and, like Janet's apparition, could not only be seen but heard as well. Elizabeth was another charmer. She foretold people's fortunes, distributed herbal mixtures, and may well have been a Catholic, or at least sympathetic to the old faith – an inclination her accusers and judges would have found irritating at best.[64] Then there was Alison Pearson, another charmer, who was accused of sorcery and witchcraft, and of 'the invocation of the spirits of the Devil, especially in the vision and form of one Mr William Simpson, her cousin and mother's brother's son'. Whether William was still living at the time of Alison's trial is not clear. Alison calls him her mentor in the magical arts of curing, but from her testimony it seems that both of them were able to visit fairyland, that is, cross in some way the boundary between their physical world and that of another order of existence, an indication perhaps of their falling into a trance or trancelike state.[65] It is interesting that William told Alison he knew when the fairies were going to come to her, because he was aware of a whirlwind passing over the sea. This presaging wind reminds us of Janet's experience, and it is worth noting what Carol Lederman felt when she had entered a trance under the guidance of a Malay shaman. 'At the height of my trance,' she wrote, 'I felt a wind blowing inside my chest with the force of a hurricane' – not a presaging whirlwind, to be sure, but enough to offer an association between the trancelike sensations of the three women. Again, as in Elizabeth's case, there is the possibility that Alison was a Catholic, or used Catholic gestures such as making the sign of the cross when faced by awareness of the fairies, and this alone would have been sufficient to prejudice the officials at her trial against her, or at least view her behaviour as tainted by 'superstition' in both the ways they chose to interpret that word.[66]

Many of the accusations and trials of the 1570s and 1580s, however, leave us without such details and we can therefore only guess at what their witchcraft and sorcery may have entailed. But it is clear that when those in authority looked outwards from Edinburgh, what they saw was a land riddled with 'superstition' (Catholic or magical) and awash with charms, amulets, the evil eye, 'two sights' (otherwise known as 'second sight'), spirits, ghosts, sacred wells, image magic, and the sacrifice of bulls. Examples of most of these can be found all over Scotland, and they all, without exception, persisted. As late as 1767, for example, a heifer was sacrificed on Mull to drive away disease from the island's cattle.[67] The further north and west the government looked, the more it was disturbed by what it thought it saw, and the more censorious of it. James VI's views on Highlanders are well known. 'I shortly [*briefly*] comprehend them all in two sorts of people: the one, that dwelleth in our mainland, that are barbarous for the most part and yet mixed with some show of civility [*civilised behaviour*]; the other, that dwelleth in the isles and are utterly barbarous without any sort of show of civility.' Edge may have been imparted to James's prejudice by the thought that most Highlanders at the time were Catholic; but even the Jesuit William Crichton had no good opinion of them, dismissing them on his map of Scotland (1595) as 'half-barbarous, half-defenceless'.[68] In consequence, when two witchcraft cases came from the Highlands to Edinburgh in July 1590, they can only have confirmed the authorities' fears that the Highlands were indeed not only barbarous, but also poisonously imbued with those occult arts which so frightened Kirk and government and galvanised them into action.

What made the cases worse in their eyes was the distasteful fact that they involved the nobility. Katharine Ross was the second wife of Robert Munro, 15th Baron of Foulis, whose seat was in the shire of Ross in north-west Scotland. They married in 1563 when Katharine was thirty-one and Robert forty-five. By his first marriage, Robert had three daughters and three sons, and by his second, three sons and four daughters, and after thirteen years of marriage Katharine seems to have conceived the idea of murdering her stepson Robert, the heir to the Foulis title, so that her brother George might be able to marry his widow, a plan which, of course, also required George's present wife, Marjory Campbell, to die as well. But what made this more than a simple tale of murder among relatives were the intended means: 'perverted enchantments, witchcraft, devilry, incantations, and sorcery, with the craft of poison', as it says in her dittay.[69] Katharine's initial attempts began in midsummer 1576 and her plotting continued to the end of 1577. One of her constant tasks was to bribe people to carry to carry out tasks for her and keep their mouths shut – William MacGillivray and John MacNilland, for example, who were to fetch and carry, Thomas MacKane, one of the 'devisers of the said destruction and poison', and several local witches of whom the principals were Christian Ross, Agnes Roy, Christian Malcolmson, and Marion Niven, known by the nickname or alias 'Laskie Lucart' (Gaelic *Losgadh Luchairt*, 'Burning the Castle'). Katharine started by sending Agnes to Laskie to consult her on her behalf. Laskie advised Katharine to go into the hills and ask 'the elf folk' for their prophecy anent the outcome of her designs – an interesting echo of what Janet Boyman did before trying to cure Alan Lauderstone of his illness – and it looks as though the advice was to proceed, for Laskie told Agnes (presumably on a second occasion, when the elves' answer had been relayed to her) that she herself and Christian and Gradach (Gaelic, *gradhach*, 'dear'?) Malcolmson would make clay images of young Robert and Marjory Campbell. (Such a likeness was known as a *corp creadha*, 'clay body', and was made to look as much as possible like the individual it portrayed. It was by no means small and probably took quite a long time to make, the process being lengthened by the recitation of charms or incantations, and by the time it took to harden the clay in a fire.)[70] So Laskie came to Agnes's house where they may or may not have been successful in making their images. But on that occasion they did devise a secret signal 'in case there was any man or woman in the company who was not privy to their secrets', namely, that 'the said Agnes Roy should shake and grip their hands or stamp underfoot'.

But something must have gone wrong – we shall see in a moment what problems might attend the *corp creadha* – because the next we hear of magic, it is Easter 1577 and William MacGillivray is delivering to Katharine 'a small box of witchcraft ... which [she] received from him and put it in [her] own pocket straightaway, the set purpose [of it being] to bewitch the said young Laird of Foulis therewith'. What the box contained, we can only guess. It may have been enchanted objects which Katharine would seek to place under or in his mattress, for example, or ointment of some kind which she would smear on the lintel or threshold of a door. (This last was a device which, it was alleged, witches had arranged to have introduced into one of the royal palaces in their attempts to kill James VI in 1589–90). Success failed her again, so Katharine started to think about straightforward poisoning. But she possessed too little poison and in May asked William MacGillivray if he had any. He said he did not and refused to get her any unless her brother Hector took him into his service, a large and somewhat ambitious request. Katharine smoothed over the awkward moment by telling William her brother knew all about the plot to poison his wife and step-brother. 'Is it better to dish up the poison in eggs, broth, or cabbage?' she asked, to which William replied she should administer it in whatever way she liked. Was William nervous, surly, insolent? It is difficult to catch the tone, although Katharine seems to have thought it sufficient to answer by sending him some bread and cheese and good ale for his supper.

If this was indeed an abrasive moment, however, it did not last and in June William was given eight (Scottish) shillings and some linen cloth as payment for his consulting local gypsies about the best way to go about poisoning young Robert and Marion. He then went to Elgin and got hold of some ratsbane, which he brought back to Katharine. Next, Katharine suggested to Christian Ross that Laskie should come and stay with her so as to be on hand for further consultation. But at the same time, she was not neglecting magic and sent Christian to Dingwall three or four times to contact John MacNilland. Apparently this was to obtain an elf arrowhead, for John came back with Christian to her cottage, stayed overnight, and next day went to Foulis and gave an arrowhead to Katharine, for which he received four (Scottish) shillings. Thus primed, on 2 July Katharine, Thomas MacKane, and Laskie under the direction of William MacGillivray and Donald MacMillan made an image of young Robert Munro out of butter and set it up against a wall in Christian Ross's house. Laskie then shot at it with the arrowhead, but missed. So four days later, the company gathered again and made another image out of clay, resting this one against a wall inside the house, too. Laskie took the arrowhead and tried to shoot the *corp*, but missed, and after a dozen attempts had still failed to hit the image. Had she been successful, we are told, the *corp* would have been wrapped in linen and buried beneath a local bridge.[71]

Meanwhile, George Ross, Katharine's brother, the husband of Marjory Campbell, joined in his sister's endeavours to rid him of his wife. He sent for Thomas MacKane in mid-August[72] and on the 17th Katharine met him and had a long conversation with him, urging him to use his magical craft to murder Marjory and promising to pay him well. In anticipation of his agreeing to do as he was asked, Katharine then sent someone to Laskie Luchart and Christian Smith ('which women are held and reputed [to be] rank common witches in this part of the world'), to obtain another elf arrowhead. Her messenger came back with one and Katharine put it away safely before joining her brother, 'Christian Malcomson's daughter', (perhaps the Gradach Malcolmson we have met already), and Thomas on 24 August in a local kiln. George, we are told, stood with his back to the door, stick in hand, and urged Thomas 'to do that thing which he [*George*] was to put to his charge touching the destruction of his wife and the young Laird of Foulis', and promised him a suit of clothes for his trouble. Since Thomas had already assisted at a ritual of image magic for this purpose in July, one wonders why Katherine and George thought it necessary to take such trouble to persuade him to continue; but since clearly nothing untoward had happened so far, perhaps Thomas was becoming tired of the whole business or perhaps, considering the seriousness of the crime and the number of people now involved, he was simply having cold feet. If so, he was not the only one, for in October William MacGillivray had to be bought off again, this time with a promise of a post in Katharine's employ.

Cold feet among some of the plotters is understandable, for if we can disentangle the chronology correctly, it seems that Katharine was becoming more and more reckless in her murderous attempts. On 2 November she met Christian Ross and Laskie Lucart once again and together they made two more *corp creadh*, which were set up against the north wall of a room in Christian's house. Laskie then took two elf arrowheads and shot them at the images, but the clay broke before the arrowheads hit them – presumably they fell over and cracked or shattered – and so yet again Katharine's magical ventures had come to nothing. The women met once more, but this time there was no question of magic. Poison was going to be the sole method of murder. Yet even here ill luck or incompetence dogged her attempts, for together the women made a flagon of poisoned ale, this time intending to kill young Robert, his brother Hector, and several other members of the family and household, a wholesale slaughter which would ensure that Katharine's own children might inherit the title.

But somehow the flagon was upset or had a leak, and the contents ran out, leaving behind only a small amount of the liquid. This, by way of experiment, Katharine gave to one of her young servants who immediately became very ill, thereby indicating – by not dying – that the mixture had not been strong enough. So three days later, Katharine told Laskie to make another, stronger poison which was then put into a large earthenware container. Young Robert was staying with one Angus Leith at the time, so Katharine sent her own wet nurse to take it to Angus's house. But it was night time: the wet nurse stumbled in the darkness and dropped the container which broke, spilling its contents over the ground. The woman, for whatever reason, decided to taste some of the liquor which remained – perhaps she thought it was fine wine or good ale – and, of course, it killed her.

Nothing perturbed, Katharine bribed young Robert's cook with a present of cloth, a shirt, and 13s 4d to mix ratsbane into a dish of kidney made from a deer killed that day during a hunt. Everyone ate and fell sick, Marjory Campbell in particular, all vomiting and exhibiting such pains that even one of the conspirators was appalled at the sight. (One presumes, therefore, that she was a member of the Foulis household.) Marjory does not seem to have recovered, for she is described at the time at the time of Katharine's trial in July 1590 as 'remaining still incurable'.[73] But nets were closing in. In 1577–78, as we have seen, the Sheriff of Ross and Cromarty ordered the arrest of six men and twenty-two women on charges of witchcraft, and one of these was probably Christian Ross, for we know she was formally questioned on 24 November 1577 and brought to trial four days later. A jury found her guilty and she was executed very soon afterwards. Others, including Thomas MacKane, suffered the same fate and, of course, in giving evidence before and at their trials, aired Katharine's attempts, both magical and venomous, to murder her relatives in shocking detail. Katharine herself, however, evaded the consequences of their testimony. Says her dittay:

A day or two before the burning[74] of [your] accomplices you, understanding that they, being examined, would convict you of witchcraft, sorceries, and poison, in respect [that] many of them knew your secrets and were practisers of your devices, you came to where there were two notaries, with no judge present or any court which might realise what you were doing, and there, before two or three witnesses who were privy to your intentions, declared that you were talked about and slandered with witchcraft and sorcery, and that you were ready to stand trial for it: and seeing there was no one [there] to accuse you, you asked for legal documents [to be drawn up to that effect]. However, for fear of your vicious life, you never came to offer these documents in court and immediately after the documents were drawn up, you had your horse already taken out of the stable and fled with diligence out of the area, as a fugitive, to Caithness where you remained for the space of three quarters of a year.

By August 1578 she had returned home, to what reception can only be imagined, since the evidence of her co-conspirators against her had certainly been heard in open court and accepted, at least tacitly and at least in part, by the juries at their trials. The idea, therefore, that Lord Robert did not know what she had been trying to do is surely untenable. Did he care? Almost certainly he did, because Katharine's loss of reputation would have reflected upon him. Her trafficking with witches may not have troubled him quite so much. To judge by the numbers involved, it is clear that witches were a common feature of society of Ross and Cromarty, and this implies they were frequently consulted and had their services called on. So from that perspective, Katharine had not been doing anything too much out of the ordinary, although one must also bear in mind that Robert was a convinced Protestant – unusual among Highland chiefs at this time – and so may have shared the Kirk's belief that 'superstition' should be eradicated from society as soon as possible. But it was his wife's motives in seeking magical help which would have been seen and felt as dishonourable. Yet Robert did not seek a divorce – perhaps that would have thrown up even more family dirt to taint his name, perhaps a divorce would not have been feasible; Katharine was evidently a strong-willed woman and may have been the more dominant of the two – and the two remained man and wife until 4 November 1589 when Lord Robert died.[75]

But although the scandal does not seem to have affected Lord Robert's immediate conduct, his patience and forbearance may have been tried beyond measure in 1588, for in January that year his son Hector fell ill and set about finding a magical cure for himself. He sent one of his servants to fetch a witch well known in the area, Marion NicIngaroch, and when she arrived, after consultation, she gave him three drinks of water from three stones – these may have been hollow and so acted as cups, or they had simply been dipped in water, thereby imparting their curative power to it, and the water thus infused was then given in a cup[76] – but added that actually no remedy would restore him to health unless his most important blood relative died in his place. Finding a substitute victim by transferring illness from one person to another, or from a human to an animal, or from a human to an object which could be disposed of safely, was by no means an unusual magical technique. But one cannot help being suspicious of Marion's indicating a particular member of the Munro family for potential sacrifice. Moreover, when it was decided, after consultation between Marion and others (called her 'accomplices' in Hector's dittay), that the victim should be George, Katharine's oldest son and Hector's stepbrother, one asks oneself whether this might not be some kind of revenge for Katharine's attempts on the family a decade earlier, or whether something had happened in the meantime to make George a particular target.

George having been chosen, however, Marion gave Hector specific instructions: (i) no one must come into the house until George visited Hector; (ii) when he arrived, Hector was to take his right hand and offer George his left; and (iii) Hector must not say anything until George had spoken first. So Hector sent for George and after five days his messengers found George hunting, delivered their errand, and George then came to where Hector was lying sick in bed. Only three other people were present: Marion the witch, George's foster mother Christian Dalyell, and Christian's daughter. Hector carried out Marion's bidding to the letter, remaining silent (we are told) for an hour before George spoke first and asked him how he was. 'The better now you have come,' said Hector and fell silent once again. This ended the visit and the first part of the magical transference of Hector's illness. Night came and at one hour after midnight, Marion and some of Hector's close associates who were in on the secret took spades and went out of the house to a particular spot where they dug a grave. But at this point Hector got cold feet. Suppose George died suddenly, he said. Wouldn't that give rise to talk which would put all their lives in danger? Could Marion not delay George's death a while? Certainly she could, was her reply, George would not die until 17 April; and so, reassured, Hector allowed himself to be wrapped in a couple of blankets, taken outside, and be laid in the open grave which was then partly filled in. During this time, no one was to say a word until Marion and Christian had spoken to what the dittay calls 'their master, the Devil'. Obviously this is the court's reinterpretation of something, but of what? Are we to understand that Marion and Christian made an invocation at the start of this part of the ritual? The next stage involved Christian Dalyell and Neil, her son. She was to hold him by the hand and both of them were to run the width of nine rigs, that is, across nine alternating ridges and furrows of a field ploughed in the runrig system. Whether Christian's holding her son's hand is an indication he was young or simply that a female and a male were thus linked magically as they traversed the ground is not clear. But they had to perform the run three times, coming back to the grave each time and asking, 'What is your choice?' To this Marion answered, 'Master Hector is my choice to live and his brother George to die for him.' This done and completed, Hector was removed from the grave, everyone went back to the house in complete silence, and Hector was put to bed.

The magic, or nature, proved more potent than the sickness and Hector duly recovered, after which he went to stay in one of his uncle's houses. It is called 'Kildrummody' in Hector's dittay and may refer to Kildrummy, an estate in Aberdeenshire, some 50 or 60 miles from Aberdeen itself. He took Marion with him and lived with her there, we are told, 'as if she had been your spouse, and gave her such pre-eminence in your region that there was none dared offend her', although, for form's sake, he pretended she had been hired to look after his sheep. Needless to say, their scandalous conduct will have become the talk of the neighbourhood, and so it is not surprising that it reached the ears of the king, who was in Aberdeen between 18 and 26 April 1588. Intrigued by the gossip, James asked to see this witch. Hector was reluctant to agree – not surprisingly, given the extent to which both he and Marion had contravened the Witchcraft Act – but Katharine stepped in and persuaded him to comply with the king's request; and so, most unwillingly, he took Marion to Aberdeen and presented her to the sovereign. The king had either heard already about Hector's magical cure or the details emerged during his questioning, and so he wanted to see the stones she had used to empower the water which Hector had drunk. At first Marion demurred, but finally produced the stones, which were then confiscated and passed for safekeeping to the Justice Clerk. Nothing more happened, however: the king had satisfied his curiosity, and Hector and Marion resumed their semi-marital life. The effect of all this on Katharine must have been dramatic: her stepson had tried to kill his own flesh by magic, a method in whose efficacy she must have believed, since she had tried it herself more than once. So if there had not been bad blood between them before (and surely he must have resented her attempts on his older brother's life), it certainly could not have been suppressed for very much longer, and if it festered, its release would be potentially destructive for both of them.

For Hector, things began to go wrong in August. Young Robert fell ill and, to help his brother, Hector turned once again to magic. He sent for 'three notorious and common witches', John MacConnell, John's wife, and the wife of John Bain, all from

Little Alness 5 or 6 miles away.[77] They were put up in a convenient house, without the owner's knowledge, for about five days while Hector consulted them about how his brother might be cured. Their answer involved his getting hold of clippings of Robert's hair, fingernails, and toenails. But he took a long time to procure them – too long, according to the charmers, which meant their magic would not work – and in the meantime Lord Robert had found out what was going on and was preparing to arrest them, from which fate, however, they were saved because Hector, for fear of his father, 'conveyed them away under silence of night'.

Lord Robert's patience had run out. His wife had tried to use magic and poison to kill his son and other members of the family; his second son was living with a witch after employing magic to cure himself of an illness at the expense (as yet unrealised) of his stepbrother's life; the king knew much, if not everything, connected with this business; and now Hector, in seeking further magical help to cure young Robert, had delivered into witches' hands parts of his brother's body, which these people might be tempted to use for evil rather than good. On 27 July, the king had appointed Lord Robert commissioner for the shires of Inverness (which then included Ross-shire) and Cromarty, for the better administration of justice.[78] No wonder he was keen to arrest three charmers who were operating within his own territory, and at the request of his own son. But Lord Robert could be circumvented. He did not have much longer to live and indeed died on 4 November. Thus young Robert inherited the title his stepmother had wished to take from him, although he enjoyed it for only a few months; for in July the following year he died and so made way for his younger brother, who was now in a position to give full vent to his resentment against his stepmother.

In fact, he actively turned against her a month before he became the seventeenth baron, for it was then he applied to the Privy Council to dispossess Katharine of her widow's rights in rents and other monies from the Foulis lands. At first he had tried to provoke her into agreeing to surrender them, by intimidating her tenants and servants, and the level of possible intimidation can be illustrated from the example (admittedly an extreme one) of a complaint, referring to December 1586 and received by the Privy Council on 1 March 1587, that George Munro and about 400 others, armed to the teeth, had invaded a bailie court in Ross and forced an end to the session because they objected to a previous verdict against one of the Munro clan. When that failed to work, however, he decided to ask for a commission which would allow him to try Katharine and four other women for witchcraft and a number of other crimes. His modus operandi is clearly expressed in the Privy Council record for 4 June 158: '[He] intends to proceed against them most partially and wilfully, and thereby to drive the said [women] to that strait that either they shall satisfy his unreasonable desire or then to lose their lives.' Katharine and the others retorted by submitting a complaint to the council that the evidence against them was factually wrong, was motivated by hostility, and had been garnered by force. But they were careful to express themselves willing, like persons genuinely innocent, to stand trial for the alleged offences, and posted bail to that effect. The council listened to both sides and ordered Hector to desist from any further action against the women, while at the same time setting a date for their trial. It was to be a year hence, 'after his Majesty's repairing to the north parts of this realm', perhaps on the assumption that James would take a personal interest in the proceedings.[79] But we are bound to ask why Katharine and the others were prepared to take such a risk in offering to stand trial for witchcraft when they were notoriously guilty of it. The Privy Council record refers to them as 'honest [*respectable*] women, reputed to be so these many years past, spotted at no time with any such ungodly practices', but everyone in Ross and Cromarty at the very least knew they were neither innocent nor respectable. Bluff, then. They had to react to Hector's immediate challenge as though they were wronged innocents, but who could tell what might not be arranged in the future?

It did mean, though, that Katharine would be under house arrest until her trial. On 1 August, Hector bound himself to produce letters from the king, authorising the trial on 28 October at the tolbooth in Edinburgh, and agreed to pay Katharine's expenses while she was in ward from 2 August until the day of the trial. Not that that stopped him from being a threat to his stepmother, because on 5 November John Campbell was obliged to stand bail that Hector would not harm Katharine or her tenants or servants.[80] The two of them continued squabbling – the Privy Council had to hear complaints from both on 11 November about the payment of Katharine's expenses – but at last, on 22 July 1590, both of them came to trial. By this time the king had returned from Denmark with his new queen and had other things on his mind, so he did not attend or preside over the trials as had, perhaps, been envisaged earlier. Nevertheless, he would almost certainly have heard about them, their dramatic exoticism helping to confirm his prejudice against Highlanders. Katharine was pursued (that is, prosecuted) by Hector himself, as he had threatened, with an advocate, David MacGill of Cranston-Riddell, addressing the court on his behalf. For some years MacGill had been Lord Advocate, the chief legal officer of the Scottish Crown and the Crown's official prosecutor, so he was a lawyer of considerable experience. Katharine's defence advocates (proloquitors for the panel) were Thomas Craig and John Cheyne. Thomas Craig was also an advocate of long experience and high standing in the Scottish legal profession, having practised since 1561 and having developed into a notable theorist of the state of Scots law and, important for all concerned in the near future, on King James's claim to the English throne.[81]

The conduct of the trials was based upon the written evidence gathered beforehand from questioning the accused and witnesses on both sides. A detailed summary of their allegations (the dittay) was read aloud, principally for the benefit of the jury (the assize), whose members had not heard them before, and then the pursuer and proloquitor were able to argue about details contained in those written statements. These arguments had to be related directly to that evidence – neither pursuer nor proloquitor could introduce anything new by way of prosecution or defence, for example – so the proloquitor's principal aim was to show that an individual item on the dittay was in some way deficient and should not be admitted for consideration. The pursuer's job was to defend it and persuade the presiding judge that it was relevant. Once the judge had made his rulings on these points, witnesses were admitted and repeated what they had said earlier to interrogators. There was no cross-examination and the witnesses' accounts had to corroborate one another, otherwise their evidence was of no use and was discarded. After all this was complete, the assize chose its chancellor (foreman) and retired to a separate room to consider its verdict.

What it was considering was each point of the dittay individually. A vote was then taken on each point, guilty or not guilty, and these separate decisions were totted up at the end in order to produce an overall verdict on the whole dittay. An accused could therefore be found guilty on several items but not guilty overall, in which case the chancellor would deliver a 'not guilty' verdict to the court. Vice versa, of course, also applied.[82] The fifteen members of Katharine's assize were men fairly local to Foulis Castle – five came from Tain, about 20 miles or so to the north, and three from Dingwall, about 7 or 8 miles to the south, for example – and six were burgesses, which means they were neither servants nor dependants of the family although, of course, they will have been aware of the social influence of the Munro laird. They will have listened to the dittay – how much of it did they actually know already? – and to any points made by David MacGill, Thomas Craig, and John Cheyne, and then waited to have the evidence confirmed by witnesses. Some of the witches involved had already been tried and executed, but the record gives the names of six men (one from as far away as Elgin) who were formally called several times to come into court, but entirely failed to do so. Without their confirmation of the allegations made in Katharine's dittay, the case was bound to collapse, as indeed it did. The chancellor of the assize came back into court and 'found, pronounced, and delivered the said Katharine to be innocent and acquitted on every point of the dittay', as of course he had to do. Whereupon a fresh assize took its place and Hector moved from his pursuer's seat to the dock for the hearing of the case against him.

Like Katharine before him, he pleaded not guilty and said he was ready and willing to stand trial. The dittay was read and David MacGill, having been Katharine's pursuer, now took the same role against Hector. The record does not preserve the name of any proloquitor for him, but in such a case and with such a defendant there surely must have been one. Witnesses there certainly were, but not those one may have expected. Marion NicIngaroch, for example, who had played such an important role in Hector's personal and magical life, had been discarded a week before the trial began, a repudiation the prosecution took as a further testimony of Hector's guilt and which they included in his dittay. But she would not have been permitted to give evidence even if she had wanted to, for this was a criminal trial and women's testimonies were not valid therein as corroboration.[83] The three male witnesses who were due to appear, however – including the man from Elgin, interestingly enough – were summoned several times but, as in Katharine's case, did not present themselves, and so the assize came to its inevitable verdict of 'acquitted and innocent of all the heads of the said dittay', and thus Hector's trial was over.

Why did no witnesses turn up in either case, and who were they? It cannot be said they were unable to make the long and expensive journey to Edinburgh, because both assizes managed it. Had they succumbed to pressure back in Ross-shire and the Black Isle? Testifying against the most powerful family in the area would have required a deal of courage and perhaps they succumbed to intimidation or bribery before ever they set out for the capital. On the other hand, not one, as far as we can tell, played even a minor part in the events to which they were supposed to testify, so what could their witness have been? Testimony of rumour and gossip at best, if they were being truthful. It is the presence among their number of the man from Elgin which strikes one as odd, if not suspicious. He was really nowhere near the location of any of the magic, so we may ask ourselves what he was doing as a witness at all. There are perhaps three possible explanations for the men's non-appearance. First, they did not actually exist and were merely names submitted to the court for form's sake; second, they were real but had been nobbled by Katharine and Hector before the trial began, their non-appearance arranged by threat or bribery; three, they were genuine and had turned up in Edinburgh, but had been prevented from coming to court, again by threats or bribery, and perhaps the promise that their hefty fines for non-attendance would be paid for them. On the whole, the first seems the most likely as it answers the problem of what kind of testimony such people could be expected to offer. All three explanations carry the implication that Katharine and Hector co-operated to achieve their acquittals. It may seem an odd suggestion, given Hector's threat against her, made to the Privy Council. But perhaps realisation that if Katharine were found guilty his own innocence would be difficult to establish, especially in the whirlwind of scandal which would inevitably follow, and cooler counsel suggested that this could, in fact, be an effective way of countering their adverse histories. Certainly the fact of the trial did Hector no harm, for he continued to enjoy the king's favour to the end of his life. Had he or his stepmother been found guilty, that favour might have evaporated.[84]

Both episodes illustrate a number of points. They depend, of course, on whether one believes the evidence, whole or in part, offered to the court, and perhaps the first thing to say is that there is no indication that it was obtained by torture. Much, in Katharine's case, came from direct participants in the events described, and at least some of those participants were tried and executed for their participation and perhaps other charges which have not been recorded. These people were social inferiors giving evidence against the actions of their social superiors, so of course it is perfectly possible that pressure was brought to bear to elicit the full extent of that evidence. On the other hand, so many individuals were involved one way or another that keeping Katharine's various attempts at murder quiet would have been nearly impossible, and if everyone knew the outline, if not the details, of her actions, there may not have been need for any particular pressure to elicit those details from her subordinates. We also have to bear in mind that not all witches were reluctant to confess their actions. Some, not a few, provided their accounts willingly and of their own volition.

Secondly, there is no evidence that the authorities were trying to mould the various testimonies either into a preconceived narrative, or make them accord with some notion or theory of witchcraft and what witches ought to be doing: no hint of a Sabbat, pact, *osculum infame*, sex with the Devil, and so forth. What the court appears to have listened to was an account of home-grown magical practice, similar in certain points to some of the magic practised in England, for example, but distinctively Scottish in its main features. Thirdly, while Katharine's magical workers seem to have been 'witches', as the Kirk and the law would have tried to define them, Hector's appear to have been 'charmers'. (There is a grey area here, of course, and one cannot afford to be precious about how exactly one proposes to define these people, especially as a 'witch' might be a 'charmer' and a 'charmer' a 'witch', depending on the kind of magic they were doing, or their intention in carrying out a ritual. But the courts would almost certainly have perceived a difference between them in these two cases.) So may we credit their evidence as, by and large, a truthful account of actual deed and practice? There seems to be no good reason we should not.

Thirdly, let us note that in both cases we have seen the whole range of Scottish society, from king to landowner to commoner, participating in some fashion in the contemporary realities of witchcraft. Some practised, some had others practise for them, some investigated, but no one appears to have expressed any doubt that there were forces and powers other than human, which could be harnessed to fulfil the earnest desires, good or ill, of those who were willing to reach out and draw them down. When people tried to use them, it was not because they doubted they were real and valid. When the Kirk and state tried to suppress them, it was not out of some 'enlightened' notion that such powers did not really exist except in the heated imaginations of their social and intellectual inferiors. On the contrary, it was because they were real that they needed to be suppressed; and when the law was brought to bear on magical practitioners, it was not because their crimes were imaginary, but because they were entirely real and dangerous to others.

7

PROSECUTION IN A TIME OF UPHEAVAL: 1604–1624

By the time James VI inherited the English throne on 24 March 1603, he had had enough experience of witches and witchcraft to last him the rest of his life. Upon his return from Denmark in 1589 he was plunged, within a few months, into a series of investigations which revealed that the storms which had hampered his efforts to sail to Denmark in the first place had been raised by magic. Witches from East Lothian had put out to sea, received a cat from the hands of Satan who was one of their company, and, on his instructions, had cast the animal into the waves. This same group too, with Satan's help had created a mist at sea on the king's return, hoping thereby to have wrecked him on the English coast. But, these two attempts having failed in their object, further trial was made to end the king's life by magic. Someone, for example, stole a picture of the king and brought it to a convention of witches who then passed it from hand to hand, speaking the king's name as they did so, until it came to the hands of the Devil – a clear intention to enchant the picture and cause it to emanate harm in some fashion, either in the king's presence if it was put back in place, or at a distance as commonly happened in image magic. Magic with a waxen image was then tried. They made a likeness of the king, and this too was passed round a circle and finally given to the Devil, who is described in the record as looking like a priest in black clothing made from roughly woven cloth. Finally, in yet another attempt on James's life, the Devil told them to make an enchanted liquid from a roasted toad, stale urine, an adder's skin, and the lump from the forehead of a newly born foal. This was to be introduced into one of the royal palaces and placed in such a way that the liquid would drip on to the king as he passed through a doorway.[1]

The Earl of Bothwell, the king's cousin and one of the principal troublemakers in the kingdom, now became the focus of attention, as he was named by several parties as the fount and originator of this treasonable conspiracy, even being a candidate for the role of Satan at the various meetings of these witches. He was not the only one. Another, perhaps more plausible, was Richard Graham, a magician on friendly terms with some of the foremost men in government. 'I met him once again,' said Bothwell, 'at the chancellor's house where, in the presence of me and the chancellor, as we were riding, he showed us a stick with nicks in it, all wrapped about with long hair, either of a man or a woman, and said it was an enchanted stick.' King James himself, however, blamed Bothwell for setting the witches in motion and questioned one of the principal witches about her magical activities, but as some of the evidence for what had gone on was obtained from people who had been subjected to torture, it is an open question how far we can trust the details of what they were telling their interrogators. Moreover, it is disturbing that the political and reasonable dimensions of the affair do not seem to have emerged until later in the protracted investigations; so it is possible that what began as purely a matter of local malicious witchcraft, perhaps not even coherent, but a series of disparate episodes later woven together, was then developed into a meaningful narrative aimed at destroying Bothwell as a political figure. The trouble is that even though we have a remarkably large number of surviving records for this whole episode, those documents which might prove or disprove a political connection have either not survived, or were never existent in the first place. So, as Christina Larner observed, 'Whether there was a genuine conspiracy to kill the king, a scare that snowballed, or a government conspiracy to incriminate the Earl of Bothwell, it is now impossible to say.'[2]

Whatever the truth of the matter, though, James had been badly scared, a fright made worse by Bothwell's behaviour. Having been put on trial for treasonous conspiracy and witchcraft, he was acquitted but imprisoned in Edinburgh Castle from which he broke out, evaded capture, and then invaded Holyrood House with a view to capturing the king and killing the chancellor, whom he blamed for devising the witches' plot in order to efface him from public life. The aristocratic turbulence, the internal hatreds, the lack of respect for the Crown, were typical of the ambience in which James was obliged to live. Plots and violence against his person were not uncommon. The ferocity of the witchcraft apparently directed at him, however, was new and unexpected, and one can sense James's fear in his treatise on witchcraft, *Daemonologie*, which seems to have been written in the immediate wake of the affair although it was not published until 1597. 'The fearful abundance at this time in this country of these detestable slaves of the Devil, the witches or enchanters,' he begins his preface, 'has moved me (beloved reader) to write quickly this following treatise of mine ... to endeavour thereby, as far as I can, to resolve the doubting hearts of many, both that such assaults of Satan are most certainly practised, and that the instruments thereof merit most severely to be punished.'[3]

It is interesting he should mention abundance of witches on the one hand and doubters on the other, but the doubters he had in mind – as he goes on to make clear – were the Englishman Reginald Scot, whose *Discoverie of Witchcraft* (1584) identified witches with old, often deluded women who tended to be relics of earlier Catholicism, and Johannes Wier, whose *De praestigiis daemonum* (1563) argued that witches were liable to be insane and therefore should not be executed. As far as James's experience had informed his opinion, however, the women concerned in the magical actions against him were neither insane nor deluded, and were accompanied, assisted, and directed by men who knew exactly what they were doing. Where he does agree with Scot is in the association of aspects of witchcraft and superstition with Catholicism. Thus, he likens a ritual magician to 'a Papist priest dispatching a hunting Mass'; criticises celibate Catholic clergy by observing that the Devil did not 'dissemble ... so far as to appoint *his* priests too keep their bodies clean and undefiled before their asking responses of him'; throws doubt on the ability of witches to shape-change because 'it is so contrary to the quality of a natural body and so like to the little transubstantiate god in the Papists' Mass'; and notes that 'as we know, more ghosts and spirits were seen or tongue can tell in the time of blind Papistry in these countries where now, by the contrary, a man shall scarcely all his time hear once of such things'.⁴ The relevant speaker of these observations in the dialogue is, of course, meant to be conveying James's opinions even if, as in the case of his remark about ghosts and spirits, he nods towards orthodox Protestant doctrine rather than his own recent experience which should have told him that the other world was by no means remote or scarcely contactable.

The situation in Scotland seemed to become worse rather than better after the king's brush with conspiracy. In August 1597, the English ambassador there wrote to Lord Burghley that the king was 'much pestered with witches, who swarm in thousands', and indeed the records show that 1597 was a particularly active year for the courts in their pursuit of this kind of offender. James himself spent several days in St Andrews, during which, as Burghley was informed, 'the number of witches exceed. Many are condemned and executed'; and the whole of Fife and Perthshire and Aberdeen saw many arrests and trials. Once again, it seemed, the king's life was in danger from witches' activities, 'as is acknowledged by some of them', the ambassador wrote, and so it is scarcely surprising that James continued to take a personal interest in such cases as came before him. He was aware, of course, that not everything was as it seemed. An episode of August 1597 involving Margaret Aitken from Balwearie in Fife told him as much.

> This summer there was a great business for the trial of witches, wrote John Spottiswoode, a parish minister in Midlothian at the time. Amongst others one Margaret Aitken, being apprehended upon suspicion and threatened with torture, did confess herself guilty. Being examined touching her associates in that trade, she named a few and, perceiving her delations find credit, made offer to detect all of that sort and to purge the country of them, so she might have her life granted. For the reason of her knowledge, she said, 'That they had a secret mark all of that sort, in their eyes, whereby she could surely tell, how soon she looked upon any, whether they were witches or not.' And in this she was so readily believed that, for the space of three or four months, she was carried from town to town to make discoveries in that kind. Many were brought in question by her delations, especially at Glasgow, where divers innocent women, through the credulity of the minister, Mr John Cowper, were condemned and put to death. In the end she was found to be a mere deceiver (for the same persons that the one day she had declared guilty, the next day being presented in another habit she cleansed) and sent back to Fife where first she was apprehended. At her trial she affirmed all to be false that she had confessed, either of herself or others, and persisted in this to her death; which made many forthink their too great forwardness that way, and moved the King to recall the commissions given out against such persons, discharging all proceedings against them, except in case of voluntary confession, till a solid order should be taken by the Estates touching the form that should be kept in their trial.⁵

That Aitken was a fraud and shown to be one perhaps ought to have shaken James's confidence in these trials rather more than it did, but in September 1597 it was reported he was still keen on pursuing offenders – 'the king has his mind only bent on the examination and trial of sorcerers, men and women' – and the publication of his *Daemonologie* not long after, possibly at the beginning of March 1598, shows how deeply he was preoccupied by the problem.[6]

Now, he may have taken such an interest because he had his doubts about the validity of witchcraft and the accusations levelled against so many of his subjects, and it is true that before the North Berwick affair of 1590–91 he showed little if any inclination to take the subject seriously or devote much time to it. But it is perhaps more plausible to suggest that 1590–91 shook him badly and 1597 renewed his fears and threatened any complacency he may have had that North Berwick had been unusual in its extent, malignity, and choice of directed target, and that the subsequent trials had put paid to the problem in his kingdom. Indeed, the extensive outbreaks may have seemed overwhelming, in the manner of forest fires: deal with one and another breaks out immediately either in the same place or elsewhere. So by the beginning of 1598 James may have had more than enough. The number of prosecutions dropped off dramatically from 1598 onwards, by which time tension between the king and the Kirk for control over people's behaviour had eased somewhat in favour of the king. James also survived yet another assault upon his person in 1600 – the so-called Gowrie Conspiracy – and so between the ferment of hostile magic; the strain of tussling with the Kirk; the recurrent attempts, either of kidnap or murder, upon his person; the recalcitrant unrest of the nobility, rebellion on the one hand and the draining poverty of the Crown on the other; his inheritance of the English throne in the early hours of the morning of Thursday 24 March 1603 cannot have come too soon for his hope and expectation of peace of mind. In going to take up his crown and residence in England, he would leave behind not only constant personal warfare with his nerves, but also the swarms of witches whose malevolence, though under control in 1603, experience told him might burst again without warning at any instant.

But if James hoped to escape witchcraft, he would be disappointed, at least initially, for England was boiling with controversy over both identification of witches and demonic possession. It was an inheritance from the 1580s and 90s during which there had been scandals in Buckinghamshire and Middlesex over Catholic priests conducting exorcisms while, at the same time, a Puritan exorcist, John Darrell, had apparently been equally successful in curing demoniacs by prayer and fasting, and identifying certain witches as the cause of his clients' suffering. The claims of both religious confessions were food for controversy, and even when Darrell's activities came to an end in 1599 after he and his associate were convicted of being imposters by the High Commission, controversy continued because of the complexities of the case. Had the age of miracles ceased or not? Were Protestant exorcisms valid, as opposed to Catholic fraud? Were the symptoms of demoniacs the result of genuine possession, or could they be attributed to natural causes? Were Anglicans or Puritans right in their assessment of these questions? Between 1599 and 1603 the arguments spawned a series of books attempting to provide answers: Samuel Harsnett, *A Discovery of the Fraudulent Practices of John Darrel* (1599); John Darrell, *A Detection of that Sinful, Shameful, Lying, and Ridiculous Discourse of Samuel Harshnet* [sic] (1600); George More, *A True Discourse concerning the Certain Possession and Dispossession of 7 Persons in One Family in Lancashire* (1600); John Deacon and John Walker, *Dialogical Discourses of Spirits and Devils*, 2 vols (1601–1602); and Samuel Harsnett, *A Declaration of Egregious Popish Impostures* (1603), registered in London only a week before Elizabeth Tudor's death. Sermons were preached on the subject in November 1602 and in February and March 1603, too, partly as a result of yet another case, that of Mary Glover, a young London demoniac, whose fits became the matter of medical controversy as some physicians argued for a supernatural cause of her illness and others a natural, and accounts were written about it and published in the spring of 1603.[7]

Into this highly politicised hurly-burly was now cast the English printing of James's *Daemonologie*, entered on the Stationers' Register on 3 April, two days before the king left Edinburgh on his journey south. James's treatise made it quite clear that he had no truck with any opinion denying the reality of witchcraft and the operation of the Devil in the world, so his book could not fail to support one side of the current English controversy rather than the other, a point John Swan was keen to point out in his *True and Brief Report of Mary Glover's Vexation*, printed in 1603 with a dedicatory epistle addressed to the king. Here he makes a direct appeal to James's known opinions – 'who can be a fitter judge in such a cause than a prince whose book (of the like case) proclaims his knowledge?' – and condemns Harsnett outright: 'I could not in silence let pass his speech, wherein he termeth the holy practice of prayer (used on behalf of poor distressed creatures) "Devil-puffing" and "Devil-praying": as also that wherein he compts witches to be but Bul-beggers, and the opinions of witchery to be brainless imaginations.'[8] So what were James's intentions in announcing beforehand that he regarded witchcraft to be a real, not an imagined, phenomenon? In fact, as Clive Holmes has argued, in spite of his recent experiences in Scotland, aspects of those same experiences may have troubled his conviction. He had been bothered in 1597, for example, by local judges' procedures against Scottish witches and the kind of evidence brought against them, and in 1598 the General Assembly of the Kirk complained that the king seemed unwilling to allow those accused of witchcraft by the unsupported testimony of a single self-confessed witch to be convicted on that evidence alone.[9] But James's carefully timed release of his *Daemonologie* into the English reading public was actually not so much to come down on one side of the English debate rather than the other, or to give his new subjects to understand that he was deeply committed to the extirpation of witches from society, as it was to give the English advance notice that, because he had survived witches' combined attacks on his person, he had investigated the subject thoroughly and could now be counted an authority on it. Hence he was at once an exemplar of the godly magistrate against whom the gates of Hell had not prevailed and would not prevail in the future, and an authoritative arbiter of disputes involving Satan, his minions, and the other world. In other words, the controversialists in the demonic possession debates should not look to him as a partisan but as a judge whose authority stemmed not merely from his position as the Lord's anointed, but from personal experience, too.[10]

It was a message some of the English embroiled in their quarrels did not quite seem to read correctly. April and May 1603 were taken up with James's progress into England; July with his English coronation; and thereafter the king moved restlessly around the country, spending quite a large portion of his time, not in London but in Royston, which he particularly favoured. It meant he was away from the English capital for long periods at a time, which allowed the possession/dispossession combatants in these early months of the reign a relatively free hand to pursue their arguments, and a rash of writers and performers to republish books and put on plays dealing with magic and witchcraft, on the assumption that the king had a major interest in the subject and would be flattered by these intellectual and theatrical attentions.

But while the king was on the move, initially from Scotland to England, and then round the Home Counties, he could not fail to notice that witches were presenting scarcely any kind of problem. Mary Pannel was tried at York in 1603 and executed for bewitching a child to death. At the Hertfordshire sessions in June, Agnes Whittenbury was accused of making two people ill and killing two hogs by witchcraft, to which she pleaded guilty and was sentenced to imprisonment and the pillory; and at the Kent sessions in September, Anne Winchester was hanged for a murder by witchcraft, while George Winchester, her husband, was found not guilty of assisting his wife to carry out a similar magical assault on someone else. Essex hanged two female witches during the same month and found a man and a third woman not guilty, while in Norfolk the bailiffs of Great Yarmouth reported to commissioners at the end of September that one Alice Moore was being held in the gaol for witchcraft.[11] Sussex had no such accused during its session of 1603. Nor was the following year any busier. Neither Sussex, nor Surrey, nor Hertfordshire, nor Essex tried anyone for witchcraft. Kent was told of one woman, Frideswide Symons, who was alleged to have murdered three people by witchcraft, but she was 'at large' at the time and when she was eventually brought to trial in 1606, she was found not guilty.[12] So the king may well have found the flurry of interest in London a marked contrast with the rest of the country through which he travelled, and it is worth our bearing this contrast in mind as we look at the passage of a new Witchcraft Act through the king's first English Parliament.

The Bill received its first reading on 27 March 1604. On the 29th it was read a second time and then sent to the Lords, who rejected the draft and proposed one of their own on 2 April. A new reading in the Lords with further amendments took place on 8 May, after which it was sent back to the Commons and the process began all over again, with readings on 11 and 26 May, amendments in committee, and finally a third and last reading in the Commons on 7 June and a reading in the Lords on 9th, after which it passed into law.

It begins with a statement that the previous Act made under Elizabeth Tudor – 'An Act against Conjurations, Enchantments, and Witchcrafts' – will be repealed with effect from the next Feast of St Michael the Archangel (29 September), and continues with its various provisions.

> For the better restraining of the said offences, and more severe punishing the same, be it further enacted by the authority aforesaid, that if any person or persons, after the said Feast of St Michael the Archangel next coming, shall
> (i) use, practise, or exercise any invocation or conjuration of any evil and wicked spirit;
> (ii) or shall consult, covenant with, entertain, employ, feed, or reward any evil and wicked spirit to or for any intent or purpose;

(iii) or take up any dead man, woman, or child out of his, her, or their grave, or any other place where the dead body resteth, or the skin, bone, or any other part of any dead person, to be employed or used in any manner of witchcraft, sorcery, charm, or enchantment;

(iv) or shall use, practise, or exercise any witchcraft, enchantment, charm, or sorcery whereby any person shall be killed, destroyed, wasted, consumed, pined, or lamed in his or her body, or any part thereof;

(v) that then every such offender or offenders, their aiders, abettors, and counsellors, being of any the said offences duly and lawfully convicted and attainted, shall suffer pains of death as a felon or felons, and shall lose the privilege and benefit of clergy and sanctuary.

[The remainder of the Act is the same as that of the 1563 Act.][13]

Now, it should be noted that this new Act was by no means notably more severe than the Act it replaced. Gregory Durston calls it 'far-reaching and draconian', but this judgement is very difficult to sustain, although he is quite right to point out that when it made 'communing with familiars and spirits a capital offence per se, one no longer requiring evidence of maleficium', this made it 'more in keeping with Continental legal practice'.[14] Other novelties are the clause anent the exhumation of dead people so that their body-parts could be used in magic, the addition of the word 'abettors' to the secondary group of aiders and counsellors who are to be executed as felons, and the death penalty for those convicted of second offences. Digging up dead bodies for use in magic was a practice long established in Europe, but there was nothing in either Scottish or English law which made it illegal until now. Why, then, is there specific reference to it in this new Act? Dismembering corpses had taken place during the North Berwick affair, and James refers to this practice in his *Daemonologie* when he explains that this is what necromancers do: '[They] serve themselves with dead carcages in their divinations.' So it is possible that the clause was inserted as a result of the drafters' knowledge of these instances.[15]

But who were these drafters, and did they owe anything significant to James's direction, interference, or known wishes? Given the marked fall in the number of prosecutions in England since 1600, it is hard to see why a new Act should have been envisaged. The king almost certainly did not demand it, and it is by no means as severe in its provisions as the Scottish Act with which James was familiar and which might have furnished a model had James wished to visit draconian measures on English witches. So we should look elsewhere for the Act's originators, promoters, and supporters, and one person immediately springs to mind. Sir Edmund Anderson was Chief Justice of the Court of Common Pleas, an Anglican with experience of trying witches in the 1580s and 90s. 'The land is full of witches,' he said to the jury in Mary Glover's trial in 1602, probably but not necessarily exaggerating. 'They abound in all places. I have hanged five or six and twenty of them. There is no man can speak more of them than myself ... [If we are not careful], they will in a short time over-run the whole land.'[16] Anderson was rendered indignant by the argument that Mary Glover may have been ill in some natural way rather than bewitched, and he was clearly having none of it, arguing that this medical opinion was simply a theory, as open to proof in open court as any other evidence; and after fiercely cross-examining the physician who proffered the explanation, he declared he was not convinced. This may be taken as typical of him. 'I sit here to judge of law, not logic,' he said on another occasion, and it is perhaps because of his rigorous commitment to the letter of the law that he gained a reputation for particular severity, especially when trying Catholics or sectaries. Here, then, was one man who had set opinions, partly confirmed by judicial experience, whose presence on a committee advising the House of Lords would almost certainly have ensured a voice in favour of tightening the law against witches and other magical workers and their clients, whom he saw as a blight on the body politic, social, and religious.[17]

Other members of the same committee had a similar outlook. Sir John Croke, for example, was responsible for staging a number of tests to see whether Mary Glover was faking her possession or not and, having begun them in the belief she was guilty of fraud, changed his mind and became convinced of her innocence. The Attorney General, Sir Edward Coke, also had firm opinions on witchcraft, commenting in 1606 in a preamble to his brief observations on the new Act that 'it had been a great defect in government if so great an abomination had passed with impunity';[18] while two others, Sir William Peryam and Sir Christopher Yelverton, were Puritans and tough, no-nonsense lawyers. So it was these people, along with others, who redrafted the Bill sent to them on 29 March and produced a new version for the Lords on 2 April. Their conviction that witchcraft was real and posed a real threat to society is likely to have been influenced by their experiences of the 1580s and 90s, just as the king's convictions had been influenced by personal experience during the same period, and in consequence their opinion that something effective should be done to scotch the evil before it had time to burst out into virulence again happily coincided with the arrival of a new broom in the shape of the Scottish king who, it was presumed, thought much the same. The time was right, the moment ripe, the iron hot. To these people, therefore, we may incline to attribute authorship of the Bill and the impulse which led to it, and it would have been odd had the English not taken advantage of this particular change of monarchs to press for legislative change. The idea that James himself arrived with a preconceived programme is very unlikely, although it is certainly true that, once in England, he took a close interest in cases of witchcraft, as can be seen from his spending a whole afternoon early in January 1605 questioning a minister from Cambridge about witches and prophesiers recently arrested there.[19]

Until 29 September 1604, convicted witches were sentenced under the 1563 Act. Thereafter their situation was legally somewhat more bleak. In practice, however, the authorities exercised more scepticism and a lighter touch and, just as after the passage of the earlier Act, the courts were largely tranquil since there was no consequent rush to fetch magical workers to judgement. In Essex no witches were tried between September 1603 and March 1607 when Blanche Worman was hanged for murdering three people and making two others ill by witchcraft. In Hertfordshire nothing happened between June 1603 and the two sessions of April and August 1606 when Joan Vaughan was found not guilty, and Christian and Alice Stokes from Royston were hanged for magical murder. In Sussex there was a single case between 1603 and

1616, and this took place in July 1605 when Robert Stockden was found not guilty of making Margaret Carpenter ill by witchcraft. Surrey had to wait until 1607 before it remanded Simon Reade, a physician from London, who had invoked spirits in order to identify a thief, and although Kent tried Charity Hills for magical murder in 1605, she was found not guilty, unlike Mary Mercy who was tried on similar charges the following year and hanged. But thereafter Kent tried no witches until 1611.[20]

Even the London theatre seemed a little slow to catch up with the new legal situation – or perhaps playwrights were not especially interested since there was no rapid outburst of prosecutions to titillate public curiosity and gossip. John Marston's Tragedy of Sophonisba, first performed early in 1606, resurrects the ghoulish figure of the witch Erichtho from the Roman poet Lucan's Pharsalia, but its connections with the Act are tenuous, as are those in Shakespeare's Macbeth (1606), which appear essentially to flatter the Scottish king with allusions to the perpetuity of his royal line. Magical workers of one kind or another, certainly, had appeared on the stage in the 1590s – Joan of Arc in Shakespeare's Henry VI Part 1 (1591), Marlowe's Faust (1594), Lyly's relatively sympathetic charmer, Mother Bombie (1594), and knockabout magicians in Greene's Friar Bacon and Friar Bungay (1594) and Peel's Old Wives' Tale (1595).[21]

But these had, to some extent, mirrored public interest rising from more than a decade of notably more intense prosecution of witches than attended the mid-1600s. Nothing like this characterised the years immediately following 1604, so the extra rigour of the new Act seems to have failed to make any particular impact either on the courts or the organs of popular reaction.

Elsewhere other than England, the situation appears to have followed more or less the same pattern. In 1587 in Wales, for example, John Penry described the country as swarming with soothsayers and enchanters, 'such as will not stick openly to profess they walk on Tuesdays and Thursdays at night with the fairies, of whom they brag themselves to have their knowledge', and recommended they be put to death in accordance with Leviticus 20.27: 'A man or a woman who is a medium or a wizard shall be put to death; they shall be stoned to death.' Penry, it may be noted, was a Puritan and deeply anti-Catholic, openly associating witches' behaviour with the practice of Catholicism. Calvinist in outlook and sympathy, too, were the brothers Henry and Robert Holland. Both were clergymen of Welsh descent and English education, but while Henry was appointed to an English parish and wrote his Treatise Against Witchcraft (1590) from his experience of witches in the south-east of that country, Robert became rector of Prendergast in Pembrokeshire and wrote his anti-witchcraft dialogue, Dan Gymro yn Taring (circa 1595), against a background of witches, diviners, charmers, and other magical workers in his own mixed-language and mixed-culture experience.[22] The 'swarming', however, did not produce any concerted attempt to deal with magic, even after the passage of the Act which, of course, automatically applied to Wales as well.

English writers noted that the Irish were given to witches and diviners, and since the ruling élite in Ireland were Protestants and the indigenous population Catholics, the scene should have been set for prosecution similar at least to that in England during the neurotic decades of the 1580s and 90s, and possibly to the same intensity as showed itself in various parts of Western Europe. Indeed, it is worth remarking that the Irish Witchcraft Act of 1586 (essentially that of 1563 in England) was never replaced by the Act of 1604. So it was under the English Act that John Aston, a clergyman (Protestant, one may note, not Catholic), was charged, 'being wholly seduced by the Devil', with invoking spirits in order to find a stolen silver cup, to uncover buried treasure, and to inform himself of the movements and intentions of the Earl of Tyrone. Aston's case, however, illustrates why Ireland never experienced witchcraft trials in any notable number. The accusations and prosecutions, such as there were, rose among the Scottish and English immigrant communities. The Catholic majority ignored the phenomenon, or was not unduly worried by it. Moreover, since the Irish Catholics were Gaelic-speaking and the courts were English both in language and law, there was no impulse to send a neighbour in front of them; and while the Catholic Church was vociferously opposed to witchcraft, divining, and what it characterised as superstitious beliefs and practices, the Irish clearly preferred to keep these abrasive situations 'in house', so to speak, rather than refer them to a hostile and intolerant foreign jurisdiction. That Anglo-Scots minority, too, by reason of its being a minority, was politically nervous and so more likely to look for cases which could be interpreted as bearing upon disaffection or civil unrest – John Aston's querying the spirits about the Earl of Tyrone clearly comes into this category of suspected offence. But the social and political situation in Ireland, however conducive it might seem to easing tensions by means of large numbers of witchcraft prosecutions, lacked accusations, and without accusations there could be no trials. Frankly, the Protestants had other things on their minds. Rebellion at the end of Elizabeth Tudor's reign had brought military atrocities in its wake, a flood of Scottish Presbyterian settlers after 1603 created further tensions and problems, and increasingly harsh administration from the English government exacerbated the already volatile conditions, and so witchcraft among the largely Catholic Irish was therefore pretty well the last thing the English authorities wanted to be bothered by.[23]

Scotland, of course, was not affected by the new Act, but her prosecution of witches shows the same diminuendo perceptible in England itself. Between 1605 and 1611, the number of cases coming before the High Court of Justiciary in Edinburgh, the Privy Council, and other courts, while quite high – about twenty-six in all, allowing for an unknown plural in the other courts in 1609 – reveals small numbers in any given year and some years with no prosecution at all: 1606 before the High Court of Justiciary, 1607 and 1610 before the Privy Council, 1605 and 1611 before other courts. The rate of recorded execution is around 50 per cent, but there are several cases where the sentence is unknown. Others include non-capital punishment, which will mean imprisonment or pillory or both; and while the majority of cases appearing before the High Court of Justiciary came from the east and west Lowlands, those coming to the notice of the Privy Council included cases from further north, two from Moray and one from Angus, while under 'other courts' we hear for the first time of Shetland with two cases, one dated 7 August 1603, the other 15 July 1604, both of which involved using the sieve and shears as a means of divination.[24]

In the Channel Islands, however, perhaps as one might expect, the course of events was governed by outside circumstances. On Guernsey, Katherine Eustache was tried for witchcraft in March 1583, but not convicted; in May the same year, Collas de la Rue was released for lack of evidence, but burned after a fresh trial three years later; 1594 and 1598 saw Marie Martin and Alichette Queripel burned, and in December 1603 Marie Rolland suffered the same fate. Thereafter, and once the new Witchcraft Act had come into force, there were only three executions in its immediate wake: Anne Gruth, Pierre Manger, and Jeanne le Roulx were all burned in July 1605. On Jersey, too, where the 1580s and 90s had been particularly fierce in their prosecution of witches, with four women and one man being hanged in November and December 1585, three men and one woman being hanged in October and December 1591, one woman garrotted and two released in July, October, and December 1597, and one woman hanged, one imprisoned, and one released in January and December 1599. The situation did not improve in 1600 when three women were hanged in May, or in 1602 when two more were executed in June and October.[25] Why were these two islands, and Jersey in particular, so keen to prosecute witches at this time? To some extent the answer lies in their political situation, both external and internal, for both islands were caught up in France's religious and dynastic wars, and were used as a base for English and Dutch troops on their way to support French Huguenots in Brittany; and internal struggles for power unleashed tensions throughout both Guernsey and Jersey.

It is also worth remembering that the two communities were constantly in flux, with people coming to and fro from both mainlands – English because the environment and cost of living were attractive, and French because they were refugees from religious conflict. But they also became home to English radicals hoping to launch a change in the Anglican establishment in favour of Presbyterian doctrine and practice, and in consequence they saw an increasing intolerance on the part of the English authorities in London towards dissent, actual or perceived. At the same time, the islands' legal jurisdictions, especially the authority of the church courts whose influence on Jersey was particularly strong, were striving to keep their powers intact, and so clamping down on people's behaviour carried an added importance. Nevertheless, we can actually detect a very slight diminution in the numbers executed on Jersey between December 1605 and December 1611 – eight out of seventeen, compared with eleven out of seventeen between October 1591 and October 1602.[26] Guernsey, however, was somewhat different. In 1617, for example, there were fourteen prosecutions for witchcraft in its courts, one of which in particular illustrates the confluence of popular and learned beliefs. Collette Becquet confessed to being taken to a Sabbat by the Devil himself, whom she had first met when she was young, whether girl or young woman is not clear. He had appeared to her during daylight hours in the form of a cat and had induced her to do harm to a neighbour with whom she was at odds. At the Sabbat Collette saw fifteen or sixteen male and female witches along with demons in the form of cats and hares. They all worshipped the Devil, had sex with him in his shape as a dog, danced back to back, drank some rather poor wine, and ate white bread. Then the Devil gave Collette some black powders and told her to use them to cause harm to humans and animals.

So far so conventional, and the judiciary's possible reading of treatises such as those by Henri Boguet or Nicolas Rémy could certainly account for the appearance of this narrative in Collette's confession. Her acts of maleficent witchcraft included making Jeane Totevin's cow ill, killing the parish minister and Madame Manques and Madame Perchard and her children, while other incidents such as managing to be seen in front of her house, taking to her family, when she had been left behind on the road by the witness Collas Le Hurey, too far to have overtaken him except by magic, or rolling around naked on the floor, twisting and turning and crying out 'Je suis brûlée' ('I've been burned'), were taken as evidence of witchcraft or demonic possession. But whereas she might have been regarded as a victim had she simply been a demoniac, the other evidence against her assimilated her possession with her being a witch, and so enabled the apparent possession to be interpreted negatively as another sign of witchcraft. 'I have been burned' could thus be understood as an involuntary confession that someone was employing counter-magic against her. Collete was found guilty along with two other women in the dock with her, and sentenced to be strangled and burned, but before execution she would be tortured to get her to name her accomplices. Torture, then, was not used to elicit a confession in the first place, but was employed on someone adjudged guilty who might be expected to be recalcitrant and unwilling to betray the names of those fifteen or sixteen individuals whom she had seen at the Sabbat but claimed not to recognise.

At this point perhaps it will be useful to ask, who were these people being prosecuted as witches? Sir Robert Filmer made a pertinent point in 1653 when he observed of the 1604 Act, 'This statute presupposeth that everyone knows what a conjuror, a witch, an enchanter, a charmer, and sorcerer is, as being to be learned best of divines', although when it came to distinguishing between these magical workers, we may reasonably think that personal experience would have played as large a part as people's recognition of them as treatises written by clergymen. It is also interesting that Filmer adds that the law requires a close definition, because none of the terms he lists were ever defined by law or commentary upon the law. One difficulty in doing so, of course, was the blurring of lines between these magical operations in practice, since the witch could be a charmer, the charmer a diviner, and a single person all five; so this meant that in practice a jury would be likely to look for a generalised rather a particular figure, one similar to a magical worker they knew from their own local experience rather than an operator sharply defined by the lucubrations of a jurisconsult or theologian. This is not to say, of course, that their expectations could not be modified by treatise or sermon or, indeed, popular entertainment, so a brief review of possible disjunction between literary image and real life is surely a useful digression.

Edmund Spenser gives us a cliché in Part 1 of his *Faerie Queene* (1590):

> There in a gloomy hollow glen she found
> A little cottage built of sticks and reeds,
> In homely wise, and walled with sods around,
> In which a witch did dwell, in loathly weeds
> And wilful want, all careless of her needs.
> So choosing solitary to abide
> Far from all neighbours, that her devilish deeds
> And hellish arts from people she might hide,
> And hurt far off unknown whomever she envied;

And, of course, Reginald Scot's dismissal of witches is notorious:

One sort of such as are said to be witches are women which be commonly old, lame,
bleary-eyed, pale, foul, and full of wrinkles, poor, sullen, superstitious and Papists, or
such as know no religion, in whose drowsy minds the Devil hath gotten a fine seat: so
as what mischief, mischance, calamity, or slaughter is brought to pass, they are easily
persuaded the same is done by themselves, imprinting in their minds an earnest and
constant imagination hereof. They are lean and deformed, showing melancholy in their
faces to the horror of all that see them. They are doting, scolds, mad, devilish, and
not much differing from them that are thought to be possessed with spirits: so firm
and steadfast in their opinions, as whosoever shall only have respect to the constancy
of their words uttered would easily believe they were true indeed. These miserable
wretches are so odious unto all their neighbours, and so feared, as few dare offend them
or deny them anything they ask: whereby they take upon them – yea, and sometimes
think – that they can do such things as are beyond the ability of human nature.[27]

Henry Holland (1590), George Gifford (1593), and William Perkins (1608) followed
suit in describing witches – all female, one notices – as old, silly, credulous, and weak-
brained; and Shakespeare's famous witches in *Macbeth* (*circa* 1606) are hags with
choppy fingers, skinny lips, and beards. But we really have to ask ourselves whether
these literary portraits coincide with reality or are merely part of a literary tradition
which maintained that witches are female, old, and foolish.

Greek and Roman models began with Circe and Medea, neither of whom were
depicted as either old or stupid, so the more likely literary source for such a picture
may be found in Lucan and Horace, both of whom delineate vivid images of old, ugly,
malicious women living on the margins of society. Christian writers of the early centuries
AD, however, often saw the magical worker as male – Arnobius, for example, refers to
them as men, as does Lactantius, while the historian Sozomen tells us that when Julian
the Apostate died, professional philosophers discarded their distinctive fringed cloaks
in case they were mistaken for sorcerers.[28] But these, of course, were not 'witches' in
the later sense of someone who was able to manipulate the laws of nature to her or
his will and advantage by entering into an agreement, tacit or overt, with an evil spirit.
This notion, and the assumption that a majority of such individuals would be female,
emerged gradually during the Middle Ages partly via a series of incidents centred upon
the Dauphiné, the Pays de Vaud, Piedmont, Savoy, western Switzerland, and Geneva,
Lausanne, Neuchâtel, and Sion. These incidents provided material for the formulation
of theological and demonological treatises, and thus the picture of the witch became
fixed and a tradition began. Another classical stream which fed into this portraiture
was the inherited Latin vocabulary expressing the concept 'witch'. Two of the most
common terms were *strix* and *lamia*, the former denoting a kind of night owl and the
latter a mythological child-eating monster. With these are emphasised shape changing,
the ability to fly, and severe danger to small children and babies, all of which became
features of the learned literary description of a witch and her activities. Other texts, such
as laws and penitentials, however, offer no descriptions, assuming that the individuals
and their actions will be well known to everyone through personal experience.[29]

Illustrations of witches, unfortunately, are often difficult to interpret. Various
church wall paintings in Denmark, for example, show women at a milk churn or

a beer barrel, attended by demons who appear to be encouraging the women to steal from the contents. Do these pictures show the temptations to which women may be prone, or do they show witches stealing milk and beer with the aid of evil spirits? Another picture has a woman about to be sexually assaulted from behind by one demon while another demon holds a beaker into which she is being sick. Is this specifically a witch who is being punished for consorting with devils, or a representative woman about to be tormented for sinning through lust and drunkenness, those typically female failings?[30] In neither case is it really possible to distinguish the ages of the women depicted, as is true also of the well-known marginal illumination of two female Waldensian heretics-as-witches in Martin le Franc's *Le Champion des Dames* (1451).[31] Indeed, it is generally true to say that neither manuscript pictures nor woodcuts give us much, if any, help in distinguishing the age of the women in scenes quite clearly of Devil worship or witchcraft. A pen drawing from the first half of the fifteenth century shows a woman turning into a cat and she appears to have pert breasts, as do women shown in two woodcuts from 1486 and around 1495, suggesting that they are probably not meant to be old; but we can scarcely lean too much on these because the medium in which they are depicted does not lend itself to subtle distinctions.[32] Engravings, paintings, pen-and-ink drawings, and woodcuts of the sixteenth century show witches as young women as often as they show them old, sometimes separately, sometimes together in the same group. Occasionally this is because the artist is depicting Circe, who was always young – Dosso Dossi's famous picture of Circe and her lovers, *circa* 1525, is an obvious case in point – but an artist from the beginning of the century, such as Baldung Grien, is happy to paint or draw both types, and this remains true of the 1580s as well, as can be seen from a title-page woodcut illustrating three witches grouped round a cauldron, an image favoured by Baldung Grien, too.[33]

Pictures, therefore, seem to suggest that the witch need not necessarily be old, as traditional descriptions would have her, and if we measure these two general sources against information derived from trials and similar transcripts, we find the reason for artists' inclusion of a fairly wide spectrum of age in many of their depictions. Witches may have tended to be middle-aged or elderly when they were arrested, but they had frequently been operating in, and drawing clients from, their communities for many years before that; for magical services not only provided the poorest cunning folk with an income, but furnished others with enough money to live extremely well, a professional approach to magic which also applied to witches, whose work often overlapped with that of the cunning person.[34] A table of suspects, based upon Scottish information, shows that the most common age for those formally accused of witchcraft lay between forty-one and fifty, with thirty-one to forty being the next most common. If we assume that in early modern Scotland – and this applies elsewhere as well – fertility ceased at about forty and that physical aspects of both menopause and aging after a hard working life were noticeable by about fifty, we can see why witches standing trial can be described as old – *vetulae*, 'elderly', is the frequent term in Latin. Their reputation as witches, however, was likely to have begun well before that, and so the 'young witch' and 'old witch' of art was reflecting reality rather than literary tradition, and should thus be consulted as a somewhat surer guide to one's image of a witch rather than the stereotype virtually invented for, and certainly cultivated and sustained by, literature intended either to press home a message or entertain by reference to that stereotype.[35]

Witches, then, who pursued their habitual methods of offering magical services of various kinds to their immediate communities and sometimes to individuals from further afield, seem to have had little fear, other than the inevitable undernote of unease attending anyone working with magic, of the provisions of the 1604 Act – the Channel Islands, for reasons of their own, being something of an exception. James continued to interest himself in the subject, not because he was a persecutor of witches – clearly he was not – but because his curiosity had been piqued by his earlier Scottish experience and because he was keen to know more about the situation in his new kingdom. This experience and his own authorship of a treatise on witchcraft made him an expert on the subject, and led him not only to investigate and make inquiries about cases which came before him or were brought to his notice, but also to realise the extent to which incidents of witchcraft or demonic possession might be fraudulent. Thus, Sir Roger Wilbraham recorded in his journal on 18 January 1605 that since the king had arrived in England he had uncovered two impostures, one of a physician who pretended to preach in Latin while he was still asleep, the other of a woman who claimed to be bewitched and 'cast up at her mouth pins', while 'pins were taken by various people, in her fits, out of her bosom'. On 21 May James also delegated the Earl of Salisbury to inquire into the young women held in Cambridge who were supposed to be bewitched; and on 27 August at Oxford, in late September at Windsor, and on 9 and 10 October at Finchingbroke he met Anne Gunter, a young woman who, through her trances and regurgitation of pins, had gained a reputation for being possessed as the result of witchcraft by several women, two of whom were subsequently put on trial. Close examination, on the king's instructions, by Richard Bancroft, Archbishop of Canterbury, and Samuel Harsnett, his chaplain, revealed that Anne was a fraud and on 10 October she confessed as much to the king.[36]

Such incidents as these, as well as his own private memories, seem to have helped to keep witchcraft in James's mind, and in consequence the subject could rise to the surface at any moment. In a letter to Sir Amyas Paulet, Sir John Harington recorded a lengthy private conversation he had had with the king in January 1607. At first they talked of personal matters before going on to academic topics in which James displayed his learning, but then James turned to magic. 'His Majesty did much press for my opinion touching witchcraft and asked me, with much gravity, why the Devil did work more with ancient women than others. I did not refrain from a scurvy jest and even said (notwithstanding to whom it was said) that we were taught hereof in scripture, where it is told that the Devil walketh in dry places.'[37] The king was amused, but went on to make Harington uneasy by talking about his mother's death, referring to the Scottish (and indeed Gaelic) preternatural gift of 'two sights' whereby, he said, some people had had forewarning of Queen Mary's judicial murder by the sight of her bloodied head dancing upon the air.

This reference to second sight may serve to remind us that James was well read on magic and other occult themes, as his library bears witness, and that fashionable Neoplatonism as ceremonial magic, and alchemical symbolism, were exploited by writers and artists of the Jacobean Court. When Shakespeare's Tempest was performed before the king on

1 November 1611, for example, he was being shown the figure of a ritual magician by whose lofty actions order is restored to a topsy-turvy world and virtue exalted to her proper place in nature. James could thus be identified with this 'Philosopher King', as he had been almost from the start of his English reign when Samuel Daniel represented him on 8 January 1604, in his *Vision of the Twelve Goddesses*, tacitly but unmistakably, as the embodiment of the creative magical power which banishes the darkness of chaos and summons the goddess virtues of a new creation. Astrology, too, was brought into play to suggest that monarchy was able to command the stars and banish any of their malign influences; and Ben Jonson's *Masque of Queens*, staged on 2 February 1609, begins with the latter, an anti-masque of twelve witches dancing, boasting about their evil deeds, and then dancing again before they are dispersed by the twelve virtues of the House of Fame.[38]

James thus had more than the investigation and trials of witches and demoniacs to keep his mind exercised with the occult in all its various manifestations, and this interest tempered by a growing and renewed scepticism may help to account for one or two of the pardons for witchcraft he issued in the first years of his English reign: 15 February 1608, Simon Reade for conjuration and invocation of spirits; 3 April 1610, Christian Weech, for a second time (the first being 16 April 1604), on a charge of murder by witchcraft; and 7 May 1611, William Bate, who had first been indicted in the 1590s for invoking spirits to find buried treasure.[39] But while these initial years had seen the criminal courts relatively quiet on the topic of witches, a flurry of cases enlivened (if that is the *mot juste*) the 1610s and 1620s in Scotland, the Northern Isles, and England. Essex, for example, tried five women in March 1610 for a variety of offences including making humans ill, killing a horse, and murdering named individuals, all by witchcraft. Four were found not guilty, the other was hanged. Another woman, tried at the July session, was also found not guilty of murder by witchcraft. A husband and wife were accused in March 1612 of bewitching a horse to death and, more unusually, of 'employing, feeding, and rewarding several evil spirits called Jockey, Jack, and Will, with the intention of destroying the livestock of their neighbours'. The husband was found guilty and hanged; the wife seems to have died while awaiting trial.[40] This reference to familiars is a reminder of the characteristic (though not exclusively) English habit of keeping spirits as servants which commonly manifested themselves as some kind of animal; and for reasons not altogether clear, they appear more frequently in East Anglia and Essex than in other parts of England, and enter the records relatively late – 1566 is the first mention of them in a popular pamphlet. The court's phrase 'employ, feed, or reward' is a direct echo of the 1604 Act, which forbade consorting with spirits for any reason at all, and also indicates the fear lying behind that legal prohibition, that fellowship between spirit and human implied a pact similar to, or indeed identical with, the covenant between a witch and the Devil, so familiar from other European witchcraft literature and practice.[41]

The following year, 1613, saw two men, one described as a 'gentleman', tried for acts of magical malignity against a father and son, both confusingly called 'Thomas Brown'. They were accused of killing the son by witchcraft and of making the father seriously ill, the 'gentleman', Robert Parker, employing 'charms and sorceries' in his pursuit of doing harm. He was found guilty and imprisoned, and his partner was acquitted. Spirits make another appearance in Essex at two trials from 1616. Three women 'entertained and fed spirits' in February, and one woman 'consulted and entertained several evil spirits' in March; but all four accused were found not guilty, as was John Godfrey, who was said to have murdered John White by witchcraft, and White's wife Sarah, who was alleged to have killed a horse, a mare, a pig, and a nag by similar means. Susan Barker from Upminster, however, was not so fortunate, being hanged for making a woman ill, killing a father and son, and taking a skull from a grave in Upminster churchyard to assist her in doing magical harm.[42] The 1604 Act had specifically introduced a clause forbidding the digging up and use of human body parts for magic, perhaps inspired by the actions of the witches in the churchyard of North Berwick, but perhaps also mindful that the practice was fairly widespread. Francesco Maria Guazzo gives examples from the 1580s, Pierre de Lancre refers to bodies being torn from their graves and dismembered, and in 1612, during the trial of one of the Pendle witches in Lancaster, one of the accused, James Device, provided further graphic details:

> And he further sayeth that twelve years ago the said Anne [Whittle] at a burial at the new church in Pendle did take three scalps [*i.e. skulls*] of people which had been buried, and then cast out of a grave ... and took eight teeth out of the said scalps, whereof she kept four to herself and gave the other four to the said [Elizabeth Southerns], [James's] grandmother; which four teeth now showed to [James] are the four teeth that the said [Anne Whittle] gave to his said grandmother, as aforesaid; which said teeth have ever since been kept until now found by the said Henry Hargreaves and [James] at the west end of [James's] grandmother's house, and there buried in the earth.[43]

Hertfordshire was also busy during these years. In 1610 and 1612 there were the usual offences of killing people, making them ill, or killing livestock, and in 1613 two pairs of husband-and-wife offenders came before the session in March, each accused of killing someone. But while the man of each couple was found guilty and hanged, the wife was found not guilty. In 1614 we hear of people being summoned to give evidence against John and Elizabeth Parrot, who were suspected of witchcraft, but the two suspects were released on bail and nothing more was heard of whatever case may have been laid against them.[44] Three married couples: was the woman the main target and the man simply caught up in accusations against her, or was it vice versa? Malcolm Gaskill has pointed out, in reference to Kent, that many of the women accused of witchcraft were persons of some significance – personal, business, religious – and in consequence attracted not only accusation but also defence, and that this may help to explain why some of them, at any rate, were acquitted. We need to know many more details than we have preserved in the records, which can often be quite terse, before we venture upon firmer explanation of some of these legal phenomena; but if the wife, for whatever reason, was unpopular enough to draw to herself a formal accusation of witchcraft, it is reasonable to suggest that her husband might share her unpopularity and hence the accusation. The opposite is equally true, of course, and husbands were as liable to be considered witches in their own right as by association with their wives, although the single male witch was accused rather more frequently of necromancy and conjuration of spirits than was the husband-witch of malefice along with his wife.[45]

Now, the magical crimes which appear in the records of the Home County sessions show very little variation, and none relates to any of the learned contemporary European assertions about fight, Sabbat, worship of the Devil, indiscriminate sex, and the murder of babies for their fat. Killing men, women, and livestock by witchcraft or making them ill is almost the sum total of the offences of the accused, with the occasional consultation of spirits or, as in two cases from Essex in 1620 and 1621, fraud, when Gilbert Wakering pretended to identify a thief and Anne Godfrey pretended to have been bewitched – the only variants upon the standard pattern.[46] Sudden, unexplained, or lingering death or illness, then, seem to have been the principal triggers for accusation, and since the accused will not have been chosen at random, she or he will generally have had some kind of reputation already, deserved or not, as a worker of magic. Personal malice between neighbours, a bad name as a troublemaker, jealousy, grudge, the bursting of long years of fear, or being a newcomer to an established community – any of these may have been sufficient to build up tension which was released in an accusation of malefice. As Robin Briggs says, 'Witchcraft was about envy, ill will, and the power to harm others, exercised in small face-to-face communities which, although they could often contain such feelings, found it almost impossible to disperse them ... Witches were people you lived with, however unhappily, until they goaded someone past endurance.'[47] It is thus the ordinariness of magic as one of the threads, along with many others equally commonplace, woven day by day to make the pattern of prosaic lives, which is often forgotten by modern Westerners who see exoticism and bizarreries where actually there were none.

There is also the temptation, not always resisted, to count numbers and talk of persecutions and hunts. In the case of, let us say, the Pendle witches of 1612 and the witches of East Anglia and Suffolk in 1645–48, this may be justified, at least to some extent, since in Pendle the ten executions of people from a small area in Lancashire were driven not only by local feuds but also by one man in particular, the magistrate Roger Nowell, a Protestant in a county full of Catholics: and in East Anglia by the exertions of Matthew Hopkins (assisted by John Stearne), a Puritan whose pursuit of witches was part zeal, part business enterprise. Certainly, Hopkins's trawling for witches over a wide area merits the description of a 'hunt'. But in Essex and Hertfordshire during around 1610–1616 there was no such conglomeration of suspects from a single district or pursuit by a determined individual fulfilling an agendum. In Essex, for example, the accused of these years came from fourteen different places removed, in some cases far removed, from each other, as we have seen of prosecutions during the 1580s and 90s. The picture for Hertfordshire is the same, and the numbers involved in both counties very small, so we cannot talk about 'persecution' or 'hunt' in connection with these witchcraft trials at the local sessions.[48]

Trials held at the Northamptonshire assizes in 1612, however, appear to combine in their totals suspects from various quarters and suspects from a restricted area. Agnes Brown and her daughter Joan Vaughan are described as unpleasant individuals with bad reputations. They came from Guilsborough, a town about 8 miles north-west of Northampton, and it was there one day that Joan's behaviour so irritated 'a virtuous and godly gentlewoman' called Elizabeth Belcher that Elizabeth slapped her, upon which Joan threatened revenge and went home to her mother. Three or four days later,

Elizabeth suddenly suffered severe pains and in the hearing of her friends and neighbours blamed Joan. She also complained to her brother, William Avery, who then tried to get to the witches' house so that he could scratch them and so release his sister from their malign magic. Finding himself unable to move beyond a certain point and thus foiled of his purpose, he had Agnes and Joan arrested; and their subsequent imprisonment in the gaol house meant that he and Elizabeth were able to come and scratch the two women, a process which worked briefly in delivering them from their pain – 'their', because after his effort to beard them in their house, William had been struck by the same ailment as his sister. The counter-magic, however, had no lasting effect and soon brother and sister were as ill as they had been before. But eventually, on 22 July, Agnes and Joan were tried, found guilty of using witchcraft against Elizabeth and William, and executed. Their offence was thus the same as we have seen in other assize records: that of making humans ill by magic.[49] The inclusion of the illegal practice of scratching to draw blood reminds us that people were not helpless in the face of witchcraft, and did not necessarily consider themselves to be so. Counter-magic of various kinds was widely available and frequently used. In 1589, for example, an old woman, Mother Samuel, was accused by the children of the Throckmorton family in Warboys in Huntingdonshire of tormenting them with her witchcraft and making them suffer fits. Mother Samuel was urged to go and visit the children to bring them relief but, says the pamphlet recounting the affair, 'she feared the common practice of scratching would be used on her' – as indeed it was, for she was eventually obliged to go to the house and her hand was thrust by one of the adults present into that of one of the children, 'who no sooner felt the same but presently [*at once*] the child scratched her with such vehemence that her nails broke into spills with the force and earnest desire she had to revenge.'[50]

The other witches from Northamptonshire came from three villages not far apart – Raunds, Thrapston, and Stanwick. Arthur Bill and his mother and father were subjected to the illegal swimming test and all three failed it. Arthur was the one accused of killing a woman by magic and was duly imprisoned, an outcome which seems to have had a dreadful effect on the older man and woman, for Bill senior lost the power of speech for a while, although he later recovered sufficiently to testify against his son, and Arthur's mother cut her own throat. In court Arthur confessed to having three spirits at his command (a variant upon the familiars who attended a female witch and fed on her blood), but refused to acknowledge his guilt of the magical murder or of any other crime, and so went to the gallows protesting his innocence. All three Bills, according to the 1612 pamphlet, were 'of an evil life and reputation'. This they had in common with Helen Jenkinson from Thrapston, who was searched for 'that insensible mark which commonly all witches have in some privy place or other of their bodies'.[51] One notes, however, that this search, illegal in itself, was done before she was even arrested. It seems a Mrs Moulsho tricked her into going 'into a place convenient' where she could be physically seized and investigated, a clear indication of bad blood between the two women, who lived in the same village. Mary Barber from Stanwick appears to have been a woman of little if any self-control, who 'gave way to all the passionate and earthly faculties of the flesh'. Accused of bewitching a man to death and harming livestock, she and Helen Jenkinson were hanged on 22 July on the Abingdon gallows. In spite of these individuals having come from places geographically close to one another, then, it seems clear that their separate prosecutions had nothing to do with each other and were not part of some earnest local attempt to purge the district of witchcraft. Nor were their alleged crimes any different from those regularly claimed of witches at county assizes. 'Hunts' and 'persecutions', then, do not apply here.

What happens if we look far north to Orkney and Shetland, for it is round about this time that their records anent witchcraft, magic, and 'superstition' begin to provide much detail? Orkney had been ruled by Norwegian earls until 1231 and had passed into the full control of the Scottish Crown only in 1468. Many islanders still spoke Norn rather than Scots, and the influence upon their cultures was heavily Norwegian, even though by the beginning of the seventeenth century the Presbyterian Kirk was making inroads into island society and imposing its will upon Orkneyans through local kirk sessions. Shetland, too, had been treated as a province of Norway until it was annexed by the Crown of Scotland along with Orkney and, like Orkney, its inhabitants spoke Norn until the post-Reformation influx of Scots obliged them to become bilingual. James VI had a low opinion of both Orkneyans and Shetlanders, lumping them together with other 'such wild parts of the world as Lapland and Finland', because belief in incubi and succubi was strong among them.[52] Women were prominent in magic and divination in the Nordic traditions which were strong in the Northern Isles, and the notions of a pact with the Devil or worshipping the Devil appear in a variety of Mediaeval texts current in Scandinavia and Iceland.[53] Yet there is not much evidence in the Isles of any of this – notable prominence of women, pact or, indeed, traffic with the Devil, except by inference: he was seen with Marion Richart from Orkney in 1633 in the likeness of a black man; four years earlier he appeared to Janet Rendal like a man dressed in white with white hair and a grey beard; and in 1616 he met Elspeth Reoch several times in the likeness of a fairy. Nor do women figure disproportionately here in comparison with the rest of Europe. Ernest Marwick, for example, lists thirty-four names of witches between around 1595 and 1689, of which eleven belong to men, and while his figures relate to Orkney and are obviously not exhaustive, they do show that the presence of male witches cannot be counted negligible. In spite of their being targeted by the Kirk, too, magical workers were able to operate in their communities – small, intimate, and isolated – without much fear of finding themselves in court.[54] So to that extent their situation is comparable with that in England. (The Scottish mainland was more severe, and there is too little available evidence for us to make useful comment on Ireland or Wales at this period.) Shetland provides fewer figures. Black records more than twelve witches between 1603 and 1700, of whom two were men. The uncertainty comes in 1666 when the Earl of Morton was granted permission to try 'a great number of persons within the bounds of the said sheriffdom of Zetland, who are suspect to be guilty of the horrid crime of witchcraft'. 'Persons' indicates that this number included men; how many, of course, is another matter.[55]

Of what did this horrid offence consist in the Northern Isles? Let us look at one or two trials in further detail. On 7 June 1615 on Orkney, Janet Drever and Katharine Bigland were accused of practising the abominable and devilish crime of witchcraft. The charges against them are interesting.[56] Of Katharine it was said she laid a sickness on one man, then removed it by transferring it to someone else: nothing unusual in that, for it was an ability often imputed to witches. She also cured her master of a magically imposed illness by washing him with salt water: again, nothing unusual except, perhaps, for her manner of doing it, 'practising the said devilish crime of witchcraft', as her indictment says, 'in going out of the house under cloud of night, about Candlemas last, and bringing in to the said William his house of water (as it appears) and washing of the said William his back therewith: and laying him down, saying he would get good rest, and lying down betwixt him and the door, having refused to lie in any other place.' William must have fallen asleep, because he woke in fear, feeling he was being smothered – a brief episode of 'night hag', perhaps – but Katharine reassured him, saying, 'Be not afraid, for it is the evil spirit that troubled you that is going away.' Next evening after sunset, Katharine took William to the seashore and washed him with salt water, repeating this five or six nights running until he recovered his health. Washing in water, salt or not, was certainly used to cure someone of an illness. Katharine Craigie, tried for witchcraft a second time on Orkney in 1643, was said to have brought three stones to the house of a sick man, laid them in the nooks of the hearth, taken them up cold in the morning, put them into water and churned them round, and then washed the invalid with it three times, after which he began to feel somewhat better. Katharine had earlier used these same stones to determine the origin of the man's illness – 'I should tell whether it were a hill-spirit, a kirk-spirit, or a water-spirit that so troubles him.' So it was the stones which absorbed virtue and stirring them round in water transferred that virtue. Janet Forsyth, on the other hand, not only used salt water to wash a sick man and thereby make him well, but also used it to bewitch a man's cattle, having gone out to sea at midsummer, 'when the stars were in the firmament', and filled a can, the contents of which she then enchanted by 'devilish practices'.[57]

Relations between Katharine Bigland and her master seem to have been volatile. Here she is shown curing him, but the episode of her lying on the bed (rather than on the floor, presumably), cannot be interpreted as implying intimacy between them, since William clearly did not want her on or in the bed at all. Lying betwixt William and the door is, rather, the office of a protector, the common night-time position of the husband vis-à-vis his wife, and so Katharine seems here to have been fulfilling a traditionally male function. That she was well able to do so can be gauged from another charge against her; 'for standing the most part of a night in the stile of the kirkyard of the Cross Kirk of Westray with drawn knives in her hand, until Marion Tailor, her mother, and others who were in her company came furth of the said kirk'. Clearly Katharine was on guard. What were her mother and the others doing in the church at night and for so long at night? This was surely not robbery of church ornaments – that kind of theft does not take the best part of a night – and in any case the indictment links the women's activities directly with witchcraft. Now, this may be entirely justified. We know, as we have seen before, that several of the North Berwick witches were said to have held a meeting with the Devil in North Berwick kirk at night and that they dug up corpses, pulling parts off them for use in maleficent magic. We know, too, that this was by no means unusual. Isobel Scudder, for example, who was tried and executed in Aberdeen in March 1597, 'passed to the kirk of Dyce and gathered a number of dead folks' bones, swilled them in water, and took the water and washed William Symmer ... he being sick'.[58] The Orkneyan women, then, may have been holding a magical meeting within the church itself, or have been digging for bones and other body parts in the kirkyard. In either case, Katharine clearly acted as an effective guard and lookout, capable, it seems, of fighting with knives if that became necessary.

Janet Driver, who was tried at the same session, was found guilty of 'fostering a bairn in the Hill of Westray for the fairy folk whom she called "our good neighbours", and of having carnal dealing with them, and frequenting the company of the fairies for the past 26 years'. Fairy lore was strong in the Northern Isles. On 12 March 1616, Elspeth Reoch stood trial for witchcraft and the court heard how she had learned magic from one of two male fairies she had met one day, and how the other had had sex with her. In June that year, Katharine Caray was said to wander among the hills 'at the down-going of the sun [when] a great number of fairy men met her', and on Shetland Katharine Jonesdochter also had sex with a mysterious being who turned out to be a fairy (although the court record calls him the Devil, just as it did in Elspeth Reoch's case) and Barbara Thomasdochter 'saw a little creature in her own house amongst her own bairns, whom she called the bowman's [*fairy man's*] bairn'.[59] The fates of Janet Driver and Katharine Bigland were different. Janet was sentenced to be flogged and then banished from the Islands; Katharine was to be strangled and her body burned.

How far can it be said they are either typical of or different from witches in the Northern Isles, and other witches elsewhere? The case of Marable Couper from Orkney is instructive.[60] She was a married woman who, at some point in the previous few years before her trial on 7 July 1624, had made a bargain with the court which had tried her, namely, that she would consent to be banished from her parish of Birsay in the north-east of the main island, and if she returned to Birsay, she would be prosecuted again as a witch. In spite of this, however, Marable did not leave the parish and in consequence the provision made earlier was activated and she stood trial once more. The points in her indictment form a curious mixture, most relating to offences alleged to have been committed between two and four years previously. These include cursing cattle, causing livestock to die, making a man ill, bewitching a woman to death, stopping a quern from working, and causing oats to be burned. The incidents follow a pattern to be seen elsewhere: harsh words and hostility between the accused and a neighbour or neighbours, followed by economic misfortune as the neighbour's sources of income or day-to-day living suffer damage or disease or death, the perceived human cause of these disasters naturally being hated, a personal hostility returned as the 'witch' replies in kind. Thus, at midsummer 1620, David Mowat and his wife Margaret Corstoun in Birsay had three cows which had recently calved but were not giving them the return they expected. Margaret blamed Marable, came to her house, and launched into an accusation that Marable ('banished witch!') had taken the profit of her cows, to which Marable replied that 'it would be seven years before any witch took the profit from her cows again'; and, sure enough, the following year David and Margaret's cows either died in calving, dried up completely, or refused to be mounted by a bull. So on Candlemas (2 February) Margaret came again to Marable's house and, after many words and harsh exchanges, hit her. Marable's answer was that Margaret and David would lose a lot of money, which indeed they did, for at Beltane (1 May) one of their cows and two other farm animals died.

Let us note: Marable was known in Birsay as a witch and should not have been still resident there. Resentment among her neighbours was therefore probably high.

For Marable to have ignored her sentence of banishment and continue living in such an atmosphere thus may betoken a strong character and probably economic necessity. How would she earn a living elsewhere among strangers who would soon learn why this incomer had tried to settle among them and, in all likelihood, was asking for their charity and assistance? Banishment to another parish would have made Marable in effect a vagabond, and vagabonds were subject to harsh local laws forbidding anyone to help or succour them. She could not have escaped Orkney and gone to Shetland because an ordinance of 7 November 1615 forbade anyone to transport beggars or poor vagabonds thither. 'For as much as there is great repair of poor strangers, idle and vagabond persons that overlays the country, who have not been born nor brought up within the country,' anyone who granted them hospitality was fined forty shillings; and 'in case any such person shall be found going hereafter outwith their said parishes, it shall be lawful to the finder and apprehender to present them to the bailie of the parish to be punished as idle vagabonds in the jougs or stocks'.[61] Marable may have been born in Orkney, but that would probably not have counted in her favour had she turned up, a banished witch, in a parish outwith Birsay. Forced by necessity to run the risk of staying where she was, Marable may have decided to make the best of her reputation and turn it to her advantage. Her indictment makes the point that she openly maintained she knew how to use magic, and it is just as possible that she genuinely believed in her own powers as that she did not, but used people's misapprehension for her own purposes. Indeed, the former is perhaps more likely, since the latter smacks somewhat of modern 'explaining away' rather than explaining.

Margaret's hitting Marable was not the only violent incident she had to endure, for David Mowat struck her, too, after she and he had had high words and he had physically thrust her out of his house. Violence, whether verbal or physical, seems to have been a fairly common feature of Scottish life and one which kirk sessions did their best to control and punish.[62] The flyting and abuse suffered and offered by Marable clearly arose out of her peculiar situation of course, and the strained relationship she had with Margaret and her husband, but what we need to notice more than these peaks of hostility are the phases in between, because these represent subtleties in the course of those neighbourly relations and may change or at least modify the picture we build of them. So let us look again at Marable's story, starting with those incidents we have mentioned already. The charges against Marable are not listed in chronological order in her indictment – this is not in the least unusual – but we can work out a timetable for some of them from indications in the wording of the text (references to Candlemas, midsummer, and so forth). Marable's problems with the Mowats cluster round the years 1619–21. In 1619 one of their cows refused to be mounted by the bull and continued to refuse for the next four years. In late June or early July 1620, three of the Mowats' cows became 'profitless' and Margaret accused Marable directly of causing it. Then in August or September, David was preparing to dry his newly harvested corn and Margaret was grinding some barley in a quern when Marable turned up and asked for the return of something David had borrowed. David angrily denied having borrowed anything and wanted to strike, but found he had no power to do so. Angry words were exchanged instead and Marable left. Margaret then found that her quern would not work and that the barley she had ground already was 'like dirt'. But Marable's brother, who worked for the Mowats as a farmhand, had words with his sister – told her off, in effect – whereupon the rest of the ground barley 'was as good and fair as possible'.

Things seem to have quietened down until the beginning of February 1621 when three of the Mowats' cows failed again, which caused Margaret to turn up at Marable's door, angry and vociferous. The two women quarrelled and Margaret hit Marable, at which Marable said Margaret would suffer serious financial loss. Very soon afterwards, Marable met David as she was coming home with a stoup of ale. At her invitation David drank some, but fell ill that same night. It is interesting that, under the strained circumstances of their relationship, Marable asked if he would like a drink and that he accepted, but we do not know whether their anger was quick to flare up and as quick to die down, or whether Marable meant her invitation to be a gesture of appeasement which David was willing to accept. The drink, however, either made him ill or he fell ill by coincidence that same day. But the charge in Marable's indictment does not quite seem to attribute the onset of the illness to her malefice and there is no suggestion that Margaret, usually quick to blame Marable for misfortune, did so this time. A fortnight later Marable came to visit him – at his request or of her own accord? We do not know – and said she would lay her life for him and that he would either continue sick for another month or get better sooner. It took a week after her visit, during which he scarcely slept, but then David recovered, and it is this recovery 'by your devilry and witchcraft' which the indictment appears to lay at Marable's door. 'Lay her life for him' simply means that she would wager he would get well soon or remain sick for a while. It is the same as the modern 'I'll bet you', etc. One may note, then, that in spite of their fraught relations, neither Margaret nor David sought to blame Marable for the illness, only for the cure, and a marginal note recording the jury's verdict on this point suggests that Marable 'gave herself furth to have skill', in other words, claimed to have power to cure.

While David was lying sick, however, Marable staged a peculiar episode which makes one wonder what she thought she was doing. Marable had quarrelled with Alexander Phillips's wife and on 21 February Margaret Corstoun came to see her. Since she and Marable had had violent words only three weeks earlier and there is no indication in the indictment that Margaret had come in a hostile or accusatory spirit, we may ask where the women's anger had gone in the meantime. Marable was in bed. As Margaret talked to her, Marable pulled back the bed cover and revealed a large bag 'like a pig's bladder, great at one end and small at the other'. This, she said, contained her own guts which Alexander Phillips's wife had trampled out of her with her knees. She told the same story in the same fashion to Oliver Garacoat, who came that same day to summon her to appear before the kirk session (presumably to explain why she and Mrs Phillips had quarrelled), and said that under the circumstances she could not come. A marginal note tells us that Marable later confessed the bag actually contained lamb's entrails. This sounds rather like a desperate ploy to avoid the kirk session, for it may be that the minister and elders would want to explore her conduct further than the high words between herself and Mrs Phillips, and this would raise the unwelcome subject of witchcraft and why she was still resident in the parish, a presence to which the minister and elders had clearly turned a blind eye at least for the present.

It is unlikely the kirk session allowed her to get away with postponement for very long. Kirk sessions were very persistent and kept on summoning people before them for weeks or even months until the offender gave in, made an appearance, and submitted her or himself to discipline. But whatever the Birsay session decided to do about Marable, she was still at liberty a few weeks later at the beginning of Lent when she came to the Mowats' house and quarrelled with David – over what we do not know. This resulted in David's hitting her and pushing her out of the house, to which she replied that he would regret it. Four days later David tried to dry some oats, but his kiln caught fire and when he took the remaining oats to a neighbour's kiln, that too caught fire and the oats were burned. Come the first of May and the Mowats lost a cow and two young animals, deaths which they or the court linked with Marable's threatening Margaret and David with heavy financial loss after Margaret had hit her in February. (Why not, one wonders, with David's more recent abuse?)

The connection may well have been made quite a long time *post eventum*, although relations between the Mowats and Marable rankled, as can be seen from an incident later in the year. In July Margaret fell ill and when no immediately available remedy helped was taken to Kirkwall, as much as a two-day journey away. A long stay in Kirkwall, however, made no difference and so Margaret came home again on 1 November. She was going to Alexander Phillips's house, which meant she had to pass Marable's front door. Marable was standing there and the two women had high words, with Margaret calling her, yet again, 'Banished witch!' and adding that if she died, she would lay the blame on Marable. Marable answered that if Margaret wanted to lay the blame for her sickness on her, she might have done so quietly, having said which, she brought Margaret indoors, took a stone, put it in the fire, heated some ale with it – nothing necessarily magical about that – and then gave Margaret a drink of the warmed ale. Margaret seems to have recovered her health afterwards or, as the indictment puts it, 'by your witchcraft and devilry you cast the sickness [away, and] so by the like devilry and witchcraft she got her health'. Once again, what we are not told is as important as what we are told. If the mere sight of Marable standing at her door was enough to set Margaret's accumulated spleen boiling over, why would she then accept Marable's invitation to come into her house, and why would she take a drink from a known witch whom she had, only a few moments before, accused of making her ill in the first place? Are volatile temperaments really enough to explain this kind of behaviour?

Relations between Marable and the Mowats now disappear from the court record. They refer to a fraught eighteen months between mid-1620 and late 1621, and as Marable's trial took place on 7 July 1624, the gap of two and a half years before Margaret came to Kirkwall and testified against her in court is both puzzling and frustrating. Were there no more incidents of witchcraft about which the Mowats could complain? If there were, why do they not appear in Marable's indictment? If there were not, why not? For Marable did not cease behaving in such a way that people would forget she was actually a banished witch. One further incident can be dated. On the feast of St Magnus (16 April) 1622, Thomas Seatter and his servant Margaret Bimbister were ploughing a barley field when Margaret looked round and saw a woman with 'a black *bruch* about her'. *Bruch* may refer to a rough apron, but also to a halo such as one can sometimes notice round the sun or moon. When Thomas saw her, 'he beseeched God' – probably meaning no more than he said something like 'Oh my God!' – and observed to Margaret it was Marable Couper. Marable told him she wanted help in fixing the coulter to her plough, but that she did not have it with her. So Thomas told her to send her husband or her son and the job would be done.

So far, so ordinary, unless *bruch* is taken to be a sinister sign rather than a mere apron. Now, however, the record takes a potentially curious turn. At Thomas's house a cow was calving and Elspeth Thomson, Thomas's wife, had hung up a couple of sheets to screen it from the rest of the house. Peasants often shared their living space with some of their livestock, but as Elspeth and Thomas had a byre, it may be that this particular cow was having difficulties and had been brought in so that she could be given special treatment. Elspeth was with the cow behind the sheets when suddenly she realised that Marable was there too, looking over her shoulder. Her reaction was the same as her husband's. She 'beseeched God' and then told Marable to go away, whereupon Marable went to the byre and sat down between two of the cows. One of the children followed, then ran to tell Elspeth who came and accused Marable of being there for no good purpose. 'I have come to warn you that your husband's life is in danger and your cattle, too,' said Marable. She actually said they were 'waited on', which means 'ambushed' or 'waylaid', and distinguished between their fates by attaching 'death' to Thomas's ambush and 'evil' to that of his cows. She could do something to save her cows, she told Elspeth, and showed her some grass she had brought for that purpose. Elspeth, reasonably enough under the circumstances, was frightened and went to find Thomas who came home and told Marable to hand over the grass to Elspeth. She mixed it into a dough made of oats and water and gave it to two dogs. Both ran amok. One started humping a cow which began to urinate blood, or pass blood in her urine, and promptly died. But when the dog was hauled off her, he did the same with four calves, each of which also began to pass blood and did not stop doing so until he was removed from their legs. The other dog also behaved in the same frenzied way 'until he was libbed'. That may mean he was castrated, but *lib* is also a charm against the evil eye, a mixture of oatmeal and salt which would be enchanted and then poured down the animal's throat. Within twenty-four hours of the cow's death, Marable turned up at the farm again, saying she was sorry the cow had died, and asking to see where the death had taken place because she wanted to tell Elspeth and Thomas who, living or dead, had been the cause of that death. So if we take each separate part of this extended article of the indictment, we can see it is only this last point which is necessarily magical at all, the combination of these events perhaps coloured by it and thereby becoming sinister, or open to sinister interpretation.

As we have seen, both Thomas and Elspeth knew Marable and did not particularly like her – hence their beseeching God at the sight of her. They cannot have lived far from each other because Elspeth became involved with Marable in another episode, though whether before or after the last one, we do not know. Elspeth, we are told, came to Marable's house to ask for some barm, the foam from fermented liquor used to leaven bread or start a new batch of liquor. Marable said she had neither, but the wording of the indictment is odd: 'You gave both ale and barm to the Devil that was in your house', an expression we may interpret as her swearing by the Devil that she had none. Elspeth reproved her for swearing and lying, and insisted she had both, whereupon Marable knelt down and prayed to God that her soul might never see Heaven if she had either barm or ale. Now comes an oddity. Elspeth went into Marable's cellar, which was pitch black, felt around, and put her hand on a barrel of ale with a pot of barm on top of it, 'which she tested to be ale'. As her eyes accustomed themselves to the gloom, or perhaps as the door to the cellar opened further, letting in more light, Elspeth saw clearly half a barrel of new ale standing on top of a chest.

Here one is surely driven to ask what Marable was doing while Elspeth was fumbling around in her cellar. ('Cellar', by the way, implies a larger house than that belonging to a peasant, so it looks as though Marable did not belong to the poorest class on the island. Does her status have anything to do with the long tolerance of the authorities to her behaviour, and that of her neighbours to her sinister reputation?) There is a blank caused by damp in the manuscript at the beginning of this article, so we cannot be sure when this incident took place, but it is followed by another clearly connected with it dated 1 November, so the two probably took place on the same day or on consecutive days. Elspeth, we are told, reproved Marable for her lying and giving herself to the Devil, to which Marable replied that she had nothing to do with the Devil. Had Elspeth misunderstood the form of Marable's earlier denial she had barm and ale, or was this misapprehension on the part of the recording clerk?

The word 'Devil' has been seized on by somebody because the article ends with the apparent non-sequitur, 'But when you lay giving birth to your son Robbie, your company came and took you away, and they fetch you and you are with them every month.' Lapsing into unconsciousness or convulsing during labour or in the immediate period before or after giving birth is not usual, but certainly possible, and these days would constitute a medical emergency. Neither, of course, may be an appropriate explanation of Marable's being carried away by her 'company', and neither explains the alleged repetition of some kind of trance or loss of consciousness every month. We also need to allow for the possibility that none of this actually happened (unlikely) or that it happened during childbirth and was said – by others, or perhaps by Marable herself – to have been repeated after; or that Marable did fall into some kind of a trancelike state which just happened to coincide with the time she was in childbed. Perhaps this was merely the first time it happened, or the first time that Marable found herself able to make it happen. Who were her 'company'? The implication of the article is that they were demons or other witches, since the allegation follows directly the record's remarks about the Devil, and this mention of the Devil by Marable herself proved fatal to her chances once she came before a criminal court. Fairy lore being so strong in Orkney, however, it is possible we should infer an other-world journey with fairies – Lizanne Henderson and Edward Cowan draw attention to several instances of witches and other women being drawn away from childbed to nurse fairy children[63] – and indeed a marginal note says, 'The pannell confessed the going with the faire [*fairy*] twice'. 'Twice' suggests a much more limited and fortuitous experience than 'every month', but it is noticeable that the formal indictment did not pick up the reference to fairies and neither did the jury at the trial. Instead, the Devil came to the fore and appears to have guided people's interpretation of the incident.

Another undated charge has Marable giving Katharine Fulsetter, a married woman, a piece of bread – probably the traditional Orkneyan beremeal bannock. Shortly afterwards Katharine fell ill and Marable came to visit her, asking her for alms and saying she would recover. (These 'alms' sound rather like payment in advance for a cure because, as we have seen, Marable does not appear to have been a poor woman, and her husband was still alive). Katharine gave her a pint of ale – so the 'alms' were slight, not an offering of support to a beggar – and Marable put the pot beside her chair. Unfortunately, a pig came into the house and knocked the pot over, so Marable asked for another. Katharine, however, refused and Marable lost her temper, saying as she left the house that Katharine would never sell ale again, a prophecy 'which came to pass by your witchcraft and devilry, for shortly after the said Katharine died'.

Here, then, are the allegations made against Marable at her second trial, along with a summary of the points obviously considered most serious by the court. These are interesting: '(i) you are a common witch; (ii) you consort with the Devil who, you confess, takes you away each month; (iii) you claim to have knowledge of superstition, witchcraft, and sorcery, and therefore you abuse the people and harm both humans and animals; (iv) consequently you have the reputation of being a witch; (v) you were convicted as a witch at a previous trial and banished from Birsay, but you have continued to live there, and so the provision agreed at that former trial that this would cause you to be tried again as a witch, now comes into force'. That mention to Elspeth of the Devil, misunderstood or not, clearly struck a raw nerve in the authorities. But apart from that, the general complaint is that Marable has the reputation of a witch, one which she has done nothing to correct or mitigate, and that she has broken the conditions set by her previous trial, conditions to which she willingly agreed. The separate articles of the indictment thus serve to illustrate the alleged truth of the general statement.

Marable was tried in Kirkwall before the sheriff-principal of Orkney and Shetland, Sir John Buchanan, and a jury (assize) of fifteen men drawn from fifteen different places in Orkney, none from her parish of Birsay. The assize was sworn and admitted to the courtroom, but Marable objected – on what grounds we do not know – and the procurator fiscal prosecuting her 'protested for wilful error' – whether Marable's or someone else's is, once again, unclear. Finally, however, things settled and the trial proceeded. Marable's confession to various points will have been heard (there is, incidentally, no indication that torture was used or even contemplated), so will witnesses, and then the assize will have retired to another room, elected its foreman ('chancellor'), and considered its verdict. On returning to the courtroom, the assize delivered a unanimous judgement. Marable was guilty of most charges, but was found not guilty of setting two kilns on fire – fire happened, said the chancellor – and the charges of killing Katharine Fulsetter by witchcraft and swearing and cursing in front of Elspeth Thomson were treated *clauso ore*, 'with closed mouth' – that is, the assize made no decision one way or the other. Scottish assizes voted on each item of an indictment and the total numbers of 'guilty' and 'not guilty' were added up to produce the final verdict. In Marable's case, 'guilty' outnumbered 'not guilty' or '*clauso ore*', and so the sentence of the court that she be strangled and her dead body burned inevitably followed.

The trial, in as far as we can follow it, seems to have been a fair one. If Marable insisted she was indeed a witch, and deliberately broke the conditions of her bail after her first trial, there was little an assize could do other than find her guilty. She was not hounded into the dock. On the contrary, she had lived openly as a banished witch in her own parish and her own neighbours, while disliking her or being wary of her, accepted her presence there for at least four years. The Kirk, keen as it was to exert discipline – Kirkwall had readers to provide morning and evening prayer and daily reading of scripture[64] – tried to summon her in February 1621, but this was almost certainly because she had recently quarrelled with Alexander Phillips's wife, not because she was a witch. Indeed, the fact that an elder came to summon her suggests she was a member of the congregation and not an excommunicate. So both community and Kirk, however reluctantly, accepted her continued presence and treated her, except when high words were flying, as one of their own. Exactly what brought her to court in 1624, we do not know. An episode, a loss of temper, a threat, or a boast too far, and she would have been vulnerable to prosecution, especially as she had been prosecuted before and escaped with her life.

This story of Marable is instructive. It tells us how much we do not know, as well as giving us information, information which is often little more than a set of clues to a mystery, the larger part of which, as that of an iceberg, remains hidden from view, and thus bids us beware how we go about interpreting the little we have been given, or the little which has survived. It draws attention to people's short tempers, understandable in those living with the pressures of a life dependent on hard labour for even the simplest of things such as fresh water, food, clean clothing; a life of danger in which any accident or illness might cripple or kill or make labour difficult, with all the attendant consequences for comfort or survival; a life of dependency on family and neighbours whose intimacy or continuous sense of obligation might prove to be explosive; a life surrounded by unseen forces and transiently visible entities not human, not dependable, often frightening, often fickle, whose presence could be sensed in the slightest of noises or wavering of candlelight. But it also draws attention to people's tolerance, even if it were not always given willingly, in the face of those uncertainties which kept everyone on edge, but which some individuals seemed able to control to some extent and who were thus worth tolerating, using, or exploiting for the benefit of a community or an individual. It shows the pervasiveness of magic, its ordinariness in a context which accepted its existence and its validity as a given fact of nature, and it also demonstrates how far removed from the world of the Sabbat, sexual orgies, Devil worship, flying, and shape changing the witchcraft and magic and divination of people's ordinary experience could be. Marable, in fact, while a magical worker in the particular context of early seventeenth-century Orkney, is much more representative of the witch in the British Isles than the half-witted, marginalised beldame imagined by Reginald Scot or the juggling, covenanted slave of Satan, surrounded by familiar spirits, described by William Perkins and other pamphleteers. Whether this would continue to be true when those same British Isles slid into civil war and political revolution was, of course, another matter.

8

RELIGIOUS STIRS AND CIVIL WARS: 1625–1649

On 25 March 1625, James VI & I died. He had had an eventful but not altogether unsuccessful reign, and both events and his policies left long-lasting marks on the countries and islands he ruled. The Gunpowder Plot focussed English hatred on Catholics; the Plantation of Ulster altered the composition and religious character of large parts of Ireland; the Scottish Kirk was forced to conform, after a fashion, to the model of the Church of England; and no English parliament sat between 1610 and 1621. Some people later seized the opportunity to publish scurrilous portraits of the king, creating an image which still lodges itself in the public consciousness, but witches, while not escaping the law entirely, managed to live, operate, and avoid either imprisonment or execution to an extent much greater than is often realised. We have already reviewed a number of cases from the first two decades of the king's English reign. As for the remaining five years, the Home Counties produced only four trials between them, all in 1621. In Essex, Elizabeth Parnsby was found not guilty of making John Tuer ill with the help of his wife or daughter, Joan Tuer; Anne Hughes was acquitted of killing one man, making an unrelated man and woman ill, and killing a cow, all by witchcraft; while Anne Godfrey found herself on trial for pretending to be bewitched; and in Hertfordshire, Frances Catlyn had been arrested on 8 May on suspicion of witchcraft, but was released at the July assize.[1]

But the positive quiet of the Home Counties was not quite duplicated elsewhere during the 1620s. The occasional flurry happened although, as so often, these stirs were highly local and not set off by any centralised drive from government or Church, and were often broadcast to a wider public through the printing of detailed and somewhat dramatic accounts. Such, for example, was the episode of William Perry, a twelve-year-old boy from Bilson [Bilston] in Staffordshire, who in July 1620 pretended he had been bewitched by someone he first said was an unknown stranger.

> The boy returning homeward from school, an unknown woman met him and taxed him in that he did not give her good time of day, saying that he was a foul thing and that it had been better for him if he had saluted her. At which words the boy felt a thing to prick him to the very heart. In fine, the boy came home, languished some days, and at length grew into extreme fits, that two or three (though he was a child of 12 years of age) could hardly hold him. The parents of the child, seeing the extremity of the fits, and the misery and imminent danger of death every hour the child did lie in, moved with

tender compassion, sought help of Catholics, and with cap and knee, by the means of some friends, did solicit a zealous gentleman who, overcome with their earnest suit, did use some prayers and lawful exorcisms allowed by the Catholic Church, with whose prayers the child eased something, and the force of the spiritual enemy abated.[2]

This extract, however, drawn from an account published two years after the event, and purporting to be the narrative of a local Catholic, is preceded by a lengthy anti-Catholic rant, and its details do not coincide with what follows, which is a Protestant version based upon other documents, including William's unmasking as an imposter by the Bishop of Lichfield and Coventry, to whom he was sent for examination. According to this, when asked how he had learned to fool people, William answered that the previous Lent he had met an old man 'having a grey beard, russet apparel, and carrying a cradle of glasses or pots on his back', who offered to teach him how to exploit people by pretending to be bewitched. He told the bishop the that

being willing not to come at school for fear of whipping, [I] was desirous to learn such tricks. By and by this old man began to teach me: first, how to groan and mourn; next, to roll and cast up my eyes so that nothing but the white of the eye should be seen; after that, to wrest and turn my neck and head both ways towards my back; then to gape hideously with my mouth and grate with my teeth, to claw and draw in my belly and guts, to stretch out my legs and clutch my hands; after that, to put crooked pins, rags, and suchlike baggage into my mouth, that I might seem to vomit them up. And although (said he) that some folk shall put thee to pain by pricking and pinching thee, yet thou must endure all patiently. After this sort he taught and learned me some six several times privately in a close, where none could see us.

Having received instruction, William proceeded to put it into practice and accused Joan Cox of being the magical source of his pains, making a clay image of himself and hiding it in her house where it could be found and prove that she was a witch with a personal grudge against him. Joan was then arrested and tried at the local assizes on 10 August, but released after the judges had decided that 'some slender circumstances which were vulgarly esteemed strong proofs of witchcraft' were no more than 'fantastical delusions'. William went on to describe how Catholic priests had tried to exorcise him, a part of his confession which was clearly either put into his mouth for propaganda purposes or exploited for the same ends after he had volunteered the information of his own free will. One thing he did say rings true, that is, appears to be more or less free from tendentiousness. When asked why he would pick out a woman known to be a Catholic as the person who had bewitched him, he answered that 'he named this woman because she was a woman ill thought of and suspected for suchlike things'.[3] A bad reputation and neighbours' suspicions were frequently enough to turn people into potential targets for accusations of witchcraft although, as we have seen, these might not follow for years and, if they did, might not stand up in court.

Was Joan disliked because she was a Catholic? Possibly. Catholics might well be blamed for leading people into the Devil's hands as happened, for example, in 1616 when Margaret Vincent murdered two of her children. According to a contemporary pamphlet which recounted her sad story, and links it with witchcraft via such words as *bewitching* and *charming*, 'at last there were such traps and engines set that her quiet was caught and her discontent set at liberty. Her opinion of the true faith (by the subtle sophistry of some close Papists) was converted into a blind belief of bewitching heresy, for they have such charming persuasions that hardly the female kind can escape their enticements, of which the weak sex they continually make prize of, and by them lay plots to ensnare others, as they did by this deceived gentlewoman.'[4] Certainly instances of demonic possession as well as of witchcraft itself seem to have been on the increase during the early years of the century, and we have to ask whether the Gunpowder Plot had had the devastating effect of turning, even more than may have been the case previously, common perception of English Catholics into 'enemies within', people naturally and confessionally allied with Satan and therefore peculiarly susceptible to the seductions and allurement of witchcraft which might be, so it seemed, at once an ally of Catholicism and a victim of it. King James himself tried not to join in the general presumption, but a plan, described by some of the Pendle witches, to blow up Lancaster Castle will scarcely have helped this more generous frame of mind and, indeed, will have served to remind people that Catholics, as 1605 had shown, were prepared to use gunpowder as a political tool, and Thomas Potts, in fact, links this with the Lancashire witches' activities in an oblique reference to 'the greatest treason that ever was in this kingdom', a reference which will not have gone unnoticed by Thomas Knyvet, to whom he dedicated his *Wonderfull Discoverie*, since Knyvet had been the man who found and arrested Guy Fawkes on 4 November.[5]

Now, Staffordshire was well known to be an area rife with recusancy. When Stow Heath Manor in Wolverhampton was raided in 1633, it was found to contain four Jesuits and a school for the sons of local gentry, and a list of Staffordshire recusants made in 1641 recorded as many as two hundred names. A Puritan preacher, Richard Lee, who came to Wolverhampton in around 1623, noted sourly in a sermon that the city was a place where 'Rome's snaky brood roosted and rested themselves more warmed and safer and with greater countenance than in any other part of this kingdom'.[6] Bilston, as part of the Wolverhampton mission, will probably have had its share of Catholics – if William Perry's family could find as many as three priests to exorcise him, Catholicism was clearly strong in the district – and so unless Joan Cox's neighbours were particularly resentful or disaffected Protestants, it is perhaps more likely that Joan had garnered a reputation for magic (whether justified or not, we cannot tell) and that it was this rather than her recusancy which William was relying on to capture official interest.

Another case of bewitchment took place in Yorkshire between late October 1621 and April 1623, also described in a published narrative. Edward Fairfax, resident at Fewston near Harrogate, was a member of one of the county's leading families, 'in religion neither a fantastic Puritan nor superstitious Papist', as he expresses himself in his very detailed account describing events day by day throughout the eighteen-month period.[7] His two young daughters, first Helen, aged twenty-one, then Elizabeth, aged seven, began to fall into trances during which they claimed strange things happened to them: 'A white cat has been long upon me and drawn my breath, and hath left in my mouth and throat so filthy a smell that it doth poison me', after which she coughed up or spat out blood. Helen was also visited in trance by a young gentleman who offered her marriage, but refused to hear her name God and later offered her a knife and a rope with which to kill herself. She continued to be plagued by him throughout the first fortnight in November, and then on Friday 23rd the family was gathered in the kitchen and started to talk 'about charmers and lookers-on (as our rude people call them) and the names of many were reckoned up who were thought to be skilful therein, and it was said that such as go to these charmers carry and give them a single penny'.[8] This is worth noting as an almost casual remark. It seems to have taken about three weeks before the family sat down and openly began to speculate whether the children's trances may not have been connected with magic, so witchcraft was not the immediate explanation which sprang to mind. But when it did, the family was able to name a good many magical workers in the neighbourhood, and indeed, when Maud Jeffrey, the fourteen-year-old daughter of one of the family's acquaintances, began to exhibit the same kind of behaviour, her parents went to a local wizard in the hope that he might effect a cure. Magical workers, then, were common in the area and some people were not slow to use them, 'some people' including the gentry, for this is how Maud's father is designated in Fairfax's account.

Magic might also intrude upon people's lives, even if they did not deliberately seek it out. The mention of the charmers' penny reminded Mrs Fairfax that a woman called Margaret Wait had given her a penny with a hole in it, mixed up with the coins with which she had paid for some corn. Was this accidental or deliberate? Margaret asked Mrs Fairfax to keep it safe because she wanted it back – it was an amulet she wore to keep her from dreaming, she said – but when Edward heard about this, he wanted to destroy the coin as an object imbued with and used for evil, and this he actually did two days later. The incident of the penny turned out to be significant. 'Until this time,' wrote Edward, 'we had no suspicion that [the children's trances] should be witchcraft; but the matter of the penny and the fame [*reputation*] of the woman that did bring it to the house gave cause to us to surmise that it might be the action of some witch, many being evil-reputed.'[9] Once the notion of witchcraft had entered Fairfax's head, it stuck there and coloured both his account and that of others anent dealings with Margaret Wait and other women. Helen Fairfax, for example, went down to the nearby river one day to fetch water in a pail and suddenly met Margaret, who said, 'Your band is loose. Let me pin it', and while doing so took a thread from the girl's dress. Neither of these actions, apparently meant as a kindness or courtesy, should have raised suspicion, except for one thing: Margaret was seen as a witch. Hence Edward records the pinning and thread taking as magical actions 'by which she got more power upon her than by the touch'.

Touching or getting hold of something belonging to an individual were, in fact, important ways for a magical worker to provide her or himself with a medium to transmit whatever power she or he intended, whether current of ill will or curative force. Hence, giving a witch or suspected witch any object might be dangerous to the giver, and this may have played a part in the refusal of charity or refusal to lend which appears so frequently in accounts of people's dealing with witches. Fairfax, then, was suspicious of this pinning incident. 'You may gather,' he says to his readers, 'that the Devil prescribeth rules and circumstances by the witches to be observed, in the doing whereof if they fail, their attempt has not the success they designed.'[10] Hence, perhaps, a witch's explosion of anger at the other person's refusal to give or lend her some object, for without its acting as a medium and channel through which her power was directed and concentrated, the effect of her magic would be lessened or even annulled.[11] But simple touching was also enough to have a deleterious effect. On Friday 14 December, Helen was in a trance 'and felt a naked hand touch her eyes, each after the other, and her eyes were thereupon closed so fast that by no means the lids could be lifted up, though we strove much to open them'. Jennit Dibble, too, it was said, 'got power on [Helen] first by touching her at the church, but that touch was not enough. Yet the same Sunday in the afternoon as she came from home ... she touched her again and got power on her.' It is this kind of thing to which Rowley, Dekker, and Ford refer to in their play *The Witch of Edmonton* (1621), where the Devil in the guise of a dog says, 'Now for an early mischief and a sudden! The mind's about it now! One touch from me soon sets the body forward' – whereupon the man against whom he has rubbed himself immediately becomes intent on murder as evil impulses flow through the newly opened channel.[12]

Now, it is worth noting that the children's trances began on 28 October 1621 and that it is not until 9 February 1622 that we learn that Margaret Wait senior and Elizabeth Fletcher had been committed to gaol in York. Three days later the two Fairfax girls were in a trance and later Helen said she saw Jennit Dibble, an old woman, who showed her 'some pictures and a little creeping thing among them. The woman told the wench these were the pictures by which [the witches] bewitched folks.' The old woman then named Margaret and Elizabeth as the two who had arranged for Helen and her sister to be bewitched. This, as Edward Fairfax tells us, was the first time Jennit Dibble had made an appearance. Between 14 and 22 February, Elizabeth Dickinson, Jennit Dibble, and Margaret Thorp were arrested at the instance of John Jeffrey, father of Maud, the other child allegedly bewitched, and on 23rd in a private house in Fewston they were searched for marks – discolourations or 'teats' which would indicate feeding spots for their familiars. Helen Fairfax, brought along to see the women face to face, identified them as the witches who appeared to her in her trances, and the next day received a visit from Margaret Wait junior, who was brought to the Fairfax house because 'many persons were desirous to see the trial of these speeches of the children to the witches'. A piece of theatre followed in which Margaret knelt before Helen and begged her forgiveness and Helen duly forgave her.[13] So from the beginning of the trances to the point of arrest and search had taken nearly four months. We have seen that it took time for Edward Fairfax to consider witchcraft as the possible, then probable, then certain source of his daughters' affliction, and it has now taken time for women (well known to be witches, we are told, although this may have been hindsight: unlikely, but we have to bear it in mind) to be apprehended and subjected to a search (by other women, not by men). It was not Fairfax who had caused three of them to be arrested, however, but another father involved. There was thus no rush to judgement or haste into court.

Nevertheless, once the process started, it gained momentum, even if slowly. On 9 March, a justice of the peace tested Margaret Thorp in the church at Fewston by getting her to say the Lord's Prayer. 'If she were a witch,' he said, 'in the repetition of that prayer she could not say the words, "Forgive us our trespasses"', and, sure enough, she could not, even after more than one attempt. This was a standard test in England, although it served only as an indication, not as legal proof, that a person might be a witch, as Joseph Glanvill made clear in the case of Julian Cox (1663).

> Judge Archer who tried the prisoner told the jury that he had heard that a witch could not repeat that petition in the Lord's Prayer, viz. 'And lead us not into temptation', and having this occasion, he would try the experiment and told the jury that whether she could or not, they were not in the least measure to guide their verdict according to it because it was not legal evidence, but that they must be guided in their verdict by the former evidences given in upon oath only. The prisoner was called for up to the next bar to the court and demanded if she could say the Lord's Prayer. She said she could and went over the prayer readily till she came to that petition. Then she said, 'And lead us into temptation', or 'And lead us not into no temptation', but could not say, 'And lead us not into temptation', though she was directed to say it after one that repeated it to her distinctly. But she could not repeat it otherwise than is expressed already though [she] tried to do it near half a score times in open court.[14]

Edward also considered scratching Margaret as a mean of counter-magic, but rejected the idea in favour of prayer, very much, in its declining to use ritual methods, a Protestant way of doing things.[15]

On Monday 1 April, he and Helen attended the York assizes, where six women who had been arrested in connection with this case underwent questioning, but by Thursday 4th, Jennit Dibble and Margaret Thorp were back at home in Fewston and the Fairfax children's ordeal, self-induced or not, continued. We are told about daily trances, visions of the same witches as before, cats, birds, strangers, and distressing episodes of violence within those visions, throughout the rest of April and May, June and July. Eventually, however, the women appeared once more in person at the York assizes at the beginning of August, and over the next week evidence was proffered against them by Edward, Maud Jeffrey's father, and several others. On the 9th the women's trial proper began. While being questioned in court, both Maud and Fairfax's two daughters fell into their trances and Helen spat a lot of blood. All three girls were carried into another room. 'Sir George Ellis and some other justices from the bench followed,' says Edward, 'and made special trial of them with intention, as it seemed, to find some imposture in the matter', as a result of which Maud's father was arrested, on the grounds that Maud had confessed to fraud and blamed her mother and father for making her act as she did. Helen and Elizabeth Fairfax were not, it appears, implicated, but the presiding judge still stopped the trial and set the accused women free.[16]

Not that this stopped the trances, for in Elizabeth's case they continued until April 1623, at which time Edward's narrative abruptly ceases. On the 17th of the previous November, however, Helen suddenly declared that a deafness which had been afflicting her had gone and that now she heard perfectly well. Moreover, her memory of seeing witches and spirits had disappeared, to the extent that when Elizabeth fell into a trance, Helen asked what was wrong with her and, upon being told she was bewitched, protested that she herself had never seen a spirit.[17] Edward's account, if slightly confused in places, illuminates aspects of contemporary magical belief and practice, and reaction to them, which go beyond the immediate circumstances of his own family's problems. Charmers, witches, people with the evil eye, were common, their identities well known, and their residence in their communities accepted often long before any arrest or trial was envisaged. Their neighbours and acquaintances were thus willing to tolerate them and to use their expertise, and it actually took more than a little effort to have them arrested, examined, questioned, and tried. Indeed, we have an example from Wales in 1618 of a justice of the peace sending for Jane Bulkley to identify a thief who had stolen cloth from one of his tenants. This she did by making the suspects eat a piece of cheese she had enchanted beforehand by speaking charms over it.[18] The law may have been potentially fierce but, whether through restraint of juries or judges, was not necessarily so in practice. Well-educated men were prepared to accept the validity of magic and the existence of genuine witches, even though they might not turn to these at once in a crisis as the answer to the problems which faced them.

Perhaps in our eyes, though, the most unusual feature of the Fairfax case is the apparent absence of medical practitioners. In spite of his daughters' weird behaviour and astonishing tales, it does not seem to have occurred to Edward to seek out a physician, although other people did lend him medical books which he read and then rejected; but, of course, there was no real reason for him to do so. His daughters were falling into trances and later describing what they saw and experienced in them. They were not ill. They were undergoing events which were clearly taking place in the spirit and this meant that those events could be understood and, if need be, countered only by spiritual means. Hence Edward's briefly considering the use of counter-magic and deciding, because of his particular religious confession, to use the power of prayer to sustain himself and his children, and protect them from what was obviously immaterial, not directly physical, aggression. The need for a physician did not come into it. Edward's reaction, however, was not a universal one, for when Elizabeth Jennings, aged thirteen, fell ill in January 1622 and began to suffer convulsions after being frightened by an old woman – was that significant? – she was taken to London and put under the care of a Dr Fox whose treatment had no beneficial effect. Then on 25 April she began to say that several women, whom she named, including Margaret Russell, known as 'Countess', who had visited the house earlier, had bewitched her and all her siblings. Elizabeth's ramblings were reported to a local justice of the peace, Sir William Slingsby, who took the child's accusations seriously enough to send for Margaret and question her. Margaret produced a story that, when she heard about Elizabeth's illness, she told a friend about it and the friend recommended she consult a minister's wife who was a 'physician'. This sounds very like a recommendation to see a cunning woman for the answer this 'physician' gave was that none of the Jennings family could prosper as long as there was bad blood between them and their next-door neighbour. Another woman who possessed a grimoire, she said, might be able to help, but in fact the only person who could do anything effective in this case was a Catholic priest. (How interesting to see that when it was not actually being more or less identified as witchcraft itself, Catholicism was seen as witchcraft's most powerful counter, and that the 'physician' seems to have assumed that 'a seminary priest' could be readily contactable.) Further examination of Margaret by three more justices of the peace resulted in her being sent to Newgate Gaol, but nothing more appears to have come of it, and on 30 July Elizabeth was taken to another regular physician, Richard Napier, who diagnosed *epileptica matricis* and *morbus matricis*, that is, some kind of disease of the womb which produced convulsions.[19]

Both this and the Fairfax case bring us to the role of children and spirit evidence in witchcraft incidents. Most of the extraordinarily detailed daily descriptions of what Helen, Elizabeth, and Maud experienced came from their own accounts once they had left their trances, and Edward was not unaware that some people thought the children were faking both their behaviour and their testimony. There had been no lack of evidence from other sources and cases to justify their doubts. Anne Gunter (1604–5) was twenty; Jennet Device (1612), one of the witnesses in the Pendle trials, was aged nine; Grace Sowerbutts (1612) from Samlesbury in Lancashire, a Catholic stronghold, was aged fourteen when she testified that she had been troubled for years by four women, including her grandmother, who made her faint and subjected her to frightening experiences in both flesh and spirit; in 1616, a twelve- or thirteen-year-old boy called Smith from Leicester pretended to have fits and accused six women of causing them by tormenting him with their familiars, a lie uncovered by King James himself; and William Perry (1620) was twelve.[20] Anne, William, and Grace had been detected as frauds, so the role of young people and children in these affairs tended to be undermined by people's awareness that they could not always be trusted to tell the truth. No wonder, then, that only thirty years or so after Fairfax, Thomas Fuller was able to write in his *Church History* that, 'All this king's reign was scattered over with cheaters in this kind, some Papists, some sectaries, some neither, as who dissembled such possession, either out of malice to be revenged on those they accused of witchcraft, or covetousness to enrich themselves.'[21]

The Fairfax incident also raises, though not directly, the question of personal moral responsibility for one's actions. If Satan appeared, suggesting that one deny God and one's baptism and surrender one's soul to him, and if one did so in return for temporary magical powers, could one argue that becoming a witch had been involuntary, that one had been tempted beyond measure, and that in consequence one could not be expected entirely to answer for one's subsequent behaviour? Opinion was not altogether uniform on the subject. 'Witches are Satan's slaves,' wrote Bernard, 'who cannot do those evils which men accuse them of, but the Devil doth it for them. Therefore the scriptures ascribe the acts to the Devil as his own and not unto the witches.' Juries were to consider, he went on, that if the Devil is the actual doer of a witch's evil, can it be said, in some cases at any rate, that the witch is unjustly prosecuted and condemned? The conundrum was not new. Gifford raised the problem in his dialogue on witches:

We may learn in the holy scriptures that the shedding of innocent blood is a very horrible thing in the eyes of almighty God, and a very grievous thing it is to have a land polluted with innocent blood. And that is one special cause why Satan dealeth by witches. For he laboureth to wrap in many guiltless persons upon suspicions. He suggesteth by his helping witches that there be many hurting witches in all towns and villages, that so he may set the multitude in a rage and to suspect upon every likelihood that he can devise or make show of. And thus whole juries must become guilty of innocent blood by condemning as guilty, and that upon their solemn oath, such as be suspected upon vain surmises and imaginations and illusions, rising from blindness and infidelity and fear of Satan which is in the ignorant sort.[22]

These considerations, however, did not urge accused witches' automatic innocence, for if witches exercised their free will in succumbing to Satan's temptation, they were guilty of co-operating in the commission of sin for which that exercise of free will made them responsible. What witches could not do, ran the argument, was perform magic of their own power. Hence the magical acts belonged to the Devil. But responsibility for willing participation in those acts belonged to the witch. Bernard, too, was not suggesting that accusations of witchcraft were inevitably the result of popular misapprehension or communal fears or panic. What concerned him was that the existence of such misapprehension or fears might interfere in the proper exercise of justice and that juries should therefore be aware, or be made aware, of the context of each case they were called on to try.

It is also worth noting that spiritual conflict affected different groups of people in different ways. For Protestants it took the form of a constant and unremitting struggle with temptation, and whereas Catholics possessed several means, including confession and penance, of isolating their struggles with Satan into disparate instances which could be dealt with separately and then put to one side, Protestants had only prayer and hope as their constant resort during a fight with darkness which never seemed to end. Satan, of course, was the great tempter, and Fairfax's narrative is full of visions of the Devil in many guises and of his agents, the witches, in many shapes and forms, and so Edward seems to take for granted that this long, distressing episode is simply a heightened and more dramatic example of the phantasmagoric battle with evil which every Christian had to endure in one form or another. But while Helen, Elizabeth, and Maud appeared to do no more than name the witches who appeared to them in their visions – an identification which could have turned out to be fatal for the women so named, but does not seem to have been done in malice, as was undoubtedly the case in some other similar instances – a vision of the Devil might easily have serious consequences as, for example, in the case of John Foulkes from Cil Owen. In 1630 he was troubled by night visions of a man with a black beard, who told him that his wife was intending to murder him and remarry. So he killed her and then handed himself in to the authorities.[23] Was this an acknowledgement of personal guilt and personal responsibility, or of personal guilt to be explained by irresistible external spiritual pressures?

Scepticism about the extent to which diabolic temptation, witchcraft, or other forms of magic could compromise a person's exercise of free will circulated among the well educated as one strand in the constant speculation about the exact relationship between the other world and this one. As Sir Francis Hubert wrote in 1629,

Witchcraft may work upon the body much,
But there's no fascination of the mind.
The soul is free from any magic touch,
Nor can enchanting charmers loose or bind
The powers and faculties thereto assigned.
Spirits may suggest, they may persuade to ill,
But all their power cannot compel the will ...

He [*Satan*] may (and doth oft times) delude the sight
By offering strange phantasmas to our eyes,
And then the judgement is perverted quite,
When 'tis seduced by such erroneous spies
As brings us no intelligence but lies ...

Beside, when any error is committed,
Whereby we may incur of loss or shame
That we ourselves thereof may be acquitted,
We are too ready to transfer the blame
Upon some witch that made us do the same.
It is the vulgar plea that weak ones use.
'I was bewitched. I could not will or choose.'[24]

'Strange diseases may happen either to man or beast,' warned Richard Bernard in his *Guide to Grand Jury Men*, 'and the same originally from some natural cause, and neither effected by devils, nor yet proceed from witches. It is the general madness of people to ascribe unto witchcraft whatsoever falleth out unknown, or strange in the vulgar sense.'[25]. But while this may have been true in the eyes of some of the educated, the 'vulgar' in general continued to view the world surrounding them with a wariness born of the traditional conviction that there were forces at work in the world which were beyond normal control and that some people with specialised knowledge or particular abilities were able to exercise an abnormal or preter-normal control over them to the benefit of humanity, even if that knowledge or those abilities could also be used to people's detriment.

But the 1620s were years of increasing tension, as the Thirty Years' War got under way, with James's son-in-law claiming, gaining, and quickly losing the throne of Bohemia. Anti-Catholic fervour dominated the English Parliament in 1621 while religious wars on the European mainland gathered momentum and the government became increasingly suspicious that the French might be planning to invade the Channel Islands and take them over. Hence both Jersey and Guernsey underwent repair to their fortifications and added extra cannons to their ordnance, for by 1625 fighting in Europe was beginning to escalate, and within the islands themselves confessional tensions were heightened, not helped by the fact that the Bailiff of Guernsey, Amias de Carteret, came from a family which supported Presbyterianism.[26] This growing religious tension between Catholic, Puritan (or Presbyterian) and Anglican confessions did nothing to soothe inflamed sensibilities, of course, and if the English looked north to Scotland or south to Guernsey, they would have had the distinct impression that in those two areas, both especially taut with hostility between their Catholic and Calvinist communities, the reign of James VI & I was drawing to an end in spasms of violence against those accused of and tried for witchcraft. On Guernsey, for example, two women were banished from the island in 1620; six people (five women and one man) were executed in 1622, three burned alive, the others strangled then burned, one was banished along with her husband and children, and two (a man and a woman) were set at liberty; in 1623 a man was executed; and in 1624 one woman was burned alive, a man and a woman were strangled and burned, and one woman was set at liberty.[27] By contrast, Jersey seems to have been free from witchcraft prosecutions during these years, although she made up for it during the years immediately after, for the opening months of Charles I's reign saw the island execute three people in 1625 and banish two in 1626.[28] Further north, though, the Isle of Man was quiet. Margaret Ine Quayne and her son, John Cubon, had been burned alive in 1617 on charges whose nature has not survived, but thereafter the island seems to have left its magical workers alone until 1658.[29]

Not so in Scotland, where 1621 saw the Privy Council issue commissions to examine accused witches in Brechin, Inverkeithing, Crail, Culross, Kirkcaldy, Selkirk, Glasgow; Glasgow again, Tranent, Kilpont, Aberdour, Edinburgh, and Large in 1622; Inverkeithing and Perth in 1623; Edinburgh, Culross, Pinkerton, Eyemouth, Borrowstonness, Spott, Birsay (the trial of Marable Couper which we have already examined), and Orkney in 1624.[30] With the exception of the two commissions relating to Orkney, these are all directed at the central belt of Scotland from Glasgow in the west to Eyemouth in the east, but with an emphasis on the eastern rather than the western side, a reflection, perhaps, of the reach of government to its immediate and near regions. These commissions were issued against a total of seventy-three individuals, sixty-six women and seven men, with 1624 seeing more than the previous years – twenty-seven women and four men, as opposed to eleven plus one, fourteen plus one, and fourteen plus one respectively. Two of the men were husbands of accused women, although in one of these cases the commission was issued against the husband, with the wife named as the partner rather than the other way round. The charges, where recorded, contain nothing unexpected: 'the detestable and devilish crime of witchcraft, sorcery, enchantments, and other devilish and wicked abuses'; and 'witchcraft, sorcery, and using of charms and other devilish practices offensive to God, slanderous to the true religion, and hurtful to our good subjects'.[31]

What was frequently meant by 'using of charms' can be seen from the case of Janet Anderson, a cunning woman from Stirling, who confessed to several points of curing and divination. A man from Falkirk came to her, she said, with a child's shirt which he wanted her to charm, the child having fallen ill as the result of the evil eye. Falkirk and Stirling will have been a good day's journey apart, but people were perfectly prepared to travel much further than this to consult a magical worker with a good reputation, and Janet confessed to seeing other clients with similar problems. Clearly counteracting the evil eye was her speciality, and indeed she said she had no charms for any other kind of sickness – 'she confesses she could not help gallstones, but she could give a charm for the waft of an ill wind or forespeaking' – but she did not invariably claim to be able to lift the malefice and thus restore the patient to health. 'You need not seek this charm,' she told Sandy Weir, 'the bairn will be dead by the time you come home.' Sometimes she appears to have contacted the dead as a way of effecting her purpose.

> Patrick Mungwall in Falkirk confesses [*to the presbytery session*] that his wife was sick, sometimes better and sometimes worse; and being informed that there was a woman in Stirling that would do her good, therefore he came to the said Janet Anderson and desired her to mend his wife. They both confess the said Janet asked him for a piece of clothing, to whom he gave two pieces; and when she had done half the charm, she said he was over-long in seeking it, and in the end said his wife would be well enough. She bade him put the shirt she had charmed on his wife when he came home, which he did. After he went to bed in his house, he confesses there appeared to him a white thing like a woman, at which he was frightened; and on the next Saturday thereafter when he came to her [*Janet*], he told her the said apparition and she answered that nothing would harm anyone in his house. On being asked how she knew that nothing would harm anyone in his house, [she] refused to answer. And albeit she has obstinately denied that she used any other words in charming than those [we have] recorded earlier, yet when she was challenged, she confesses that she said the following words of the charm, 'Earthless king and earthless queen, God let thee never get rest in kirk nor have Christian burial until they restore this woman, Janet Wilson, to her health again. In the name of the Father, the Son, and the Holy Ghost.'[32]

The charm is something of a puzzle. The reference to king and queen may suggest fairies, but this does not sit happily with the threat to leave 'thee' without proper burial, as does the adjective 'earthless', so perhaps the greater likelihood is that Janet was appealing to some ghost or similar spirit. Fairies, of course, might be identified with the dead, or be seen as hosts to certain dead people in fairyland, or act as intermediaries between the living and the dead, and several witches and cunning folk claimed to receive information from fairies which enabled them to carry out acts of divination or magic. So we may be prepared to see some such connection between Janet's charm and the purpose for which it was uttered, as also between Janet's possible appeal to the dead, or to fairies via the dead, and Patrick's ghostly apparition.[33]

Now, it is clear that these commissions were issued against named individuals. The practice had arisen partly because of challenges by accused persons that the local courts were not competent to deal with these charges – Patrick Lowrie in 1605 and Isobel Falconer in 1606 had both used this argument to have themselves tried by the Justice Court in Edinburgh where they obviously hoped to get better justice – and between 1611 and 1628 Privy Council commissions proliferated.[34] But in 1624 the council issued an instruction that any new request be examined first by the local bishop.

> For as much as sundry commissions have been sought from the Lords of Secret Council against persons suspect of witchcraft these years bygone, and that upon some dittays

[*list of charges*] and pieces of information given in against the said suspect persons whereby the said Lords have been very often troubled by the importunity of those who sought the said commissions and who constantly affirmed that all the dittays and pieces of information given in against the said suspect persons were true: and whereas many of these dittays and pieces of information in sundry of the special points and heads thereof seemed to be very obscure and dark to the said Lords: and they being careful that in time coming they be truly informed of the nature and quality of such dittays and pieces of information in matters of this kind as shall be hereafter given in to them, to the intent the innocent be not troubled nor the guilty escape punishment: therefore the said Lords have thought meet and expedient, concluded and ordained, that in time coming all depositions, dittays, pieces of information to be given in unto them, whereupon commissions shall be sought against witches, shall be first presented to the bishop of the diocese, to be seen and considered by him and such of the ministry as he shall call unto him: and upon the bishop's report to the Council anent the nature and quality of the crimes contained in the said dittays, depositions, and pieces of information, the said Lords will accordingly grant or refuse the said commissions.[35]

The authorities in Edinburgh, then, were keen to exercise some kind of control over what appeared to be a growing danger of local demands for witchcraft prosecutions. That they did not altogether succeed can be gauged from the even larger number of prosecutions and attempted prosecutions between 1628 and 1630 – approximately 331 suspects in that short period.[36] This far exceeds anything we have seen in England or the islands and suggests that there were peculiar circumstances in the central belt and Fife especially which were contributing this upsurge of personal malice and deeply felt grievance against so many individuals. Plague and famine may suggest themselves as such peculiar circumstances, but neither is actually sufficient to account for this increase in social tension. To be sure, harvest failures in 1621 and 1622 caused a severe famine in 1623 and large numbers of people died – in Dumfries, up to 15 per cent of the population – while plague struck in the same year, Kelso, Dumfries, and Dunfermline being especially hit. But the places named in Privy Council commissions do not appear to coincide with plague or famine centres, and Christina Larner has pointed out that 'it is difficult to make any general correlation between surges of witch-hunting and demographic disasters'. Indeed, outbreaks of plague and famine seem to have happened during relative lulls in witch prosecutions. So it looks as though demands for commissions during the 1620s owe much more to highly localised circumstances than to anything more widely spread.[37]

One factor among several may be the religious views of many of the ministers of the central belt parishes. Alexander Bisset from Brechin, for example, refused to read the English service book in 1637; and Robert Roche from Inverkeithing, Robert Colville from Culross, John Gillespie from Kirkcaldy, and John Malcolm from Perth all objected to the reintroduction of episcopacy into Scotland and made their opinions known by signing declarations to that effect. Patrick Shaw from Selkirk, too, signed a protestation anent the liberties of the Kirk in 1617.[38] Keen Presbyterians all, they will have been eager to establish strict discipline within their parishes, and this will not have included turning a blind eye to the magical activities or consultations of their parishioners. Church courts such as kirk and presbytery sessions could not impose a death sentence on those they found guilty, only secular courts could do that, but ministers and their elders, once moved to take action – and this might not be immediate: the Kirk did exercise a degree of Christian patience up to a point, but only up to a point – took seriously accusations of witchcraft, charming, and divination and made every effort to root out both practitioners and their clients.[39] Alongside this we should note that official preoccupation with the role of the Devil seems to have been strengthening during the 1620s, perhaps as a result of the influence of King James's *Daemonologie*, which emphasised the demonic pact as a particular feature of witchcraft, perhaps because Protestants in general tended to lay stress upon the pact, although Stuart MacDonald has pointed out, in reference to Fife, that 'references to the Devil are more common in documents which came from the central government than they are in the minutes of sessions or presbyteries'.[40] Calvinist teaching, however, stressed how depraved was humankind, and how constantly people had to struggle in spiritual warfare between God and Satan, one expression of which was the waves of terror experienced by individuals as their acute awareness of Satan's nearness and strength advanced and receded within their consciousness.

The inference to be drawn from this is therefore that the Kirk and its important lay supporters, as well as parishioners of lesser influence, were likely to be troubled by the demonic aspect of witchcraft, and so we may look to a heightened fear or nervousness of the Devil as one cause among many of increased numbers of accusation. Sermons, of course, may have helped to inflame sensibilities, but Michael Wasser may also be right in seeing the Scottish government's attempt to establish 'circuit courts' (i.e. 'justice airs') along English lines between 1628 and 1630 as providing a stimulus to the disaffected to accuse their unwary neighbours – 'unwary', of course, because those who consulted witches and cunning folk might well find their visits misinterpreted when or if circumstances turned against them and they were suspected of being guilty by association if not by wilful intention.[41]

If witchcraft in central Scotland was bubbling, however, so were a good many other discontents both there and elsewhere in the British Isles. Charles I became king on 27 March 1625, at a time when wars in Europe raged, religious (or rather confessional) abrasiveness in the various kingdoms and regions of Britain was becoming almost daily more acute, and climate change – that period between the 1640s and 1690s which formed one of the climaxes of what is known as the Little Ice Age – was about to precipitate famine and its consequent wars, diseases, and deaths, along with a sharp conviction everywhere that the world was so distressed and overtaken by disasters, and so overshadowed by omens, portents, and divine minatory signs, that the End of Times might well be imminent. 'Sometimes Providence condemns the world with universal and evident calamities, whose causes we cannot know,' wrote one commentator in 1643. 'This seems to be one of the epochs in which every nation is turned upside down, leading some great minds to suspect that we are approaching the end of the world. We have seen all the north in commotion and rebellion, its rivers running with blood, its populous provinces deserted, England, Ireland, and Scotland aflame with civil war.' 'God Almighty,' wrote another in 1647, 'has a quarrel lately with all mankind, and given the reins to the ill spirit to compass the whole earth. For within these twelve years there have been the strangest revolutions and horridest things happened, not only in Europe but all the world over, that have befallen mankind (I dare boldly say) since Adam fell ... [Such] monstrous things have happened, it seems the whole world is off the hinges.'[42]

Such comments serve to remind us that these earlier periods lived *sub specie aeternitatis* and that everything was likely to have meaning and significance. The weather was thus not merely sunshine, rain, wind, or snow, but potentially at least a series of messages from other worlds, warnings, blessings, exhortations, or trials. A Welsh minister, Hugh Roberts, preaching in England in 1598, summarised this belief:

> Every plague, every calamity, sudden death, burning with fire, murder, strange sicknesses, famine, every flood of waters, ruine of buildings, unseasonable weather: every one of these and of the like adversities, as oft as they happen in the world, are a sermon of repentance to all that see them or hear thereof ... a memento to every one of us to look to ourselves and to call to remembrance our own sins, knowing that it is the same God that will take vengeance of every sin and transgression of men, and that He will strike with a more heavy hand if His warning and example of His justice be not regarded.

People saw armies, flotillas, funeral processions, and angels in the sky; monstrous births or unnatural physical phenomena such as two-headed or misshapen children, or a woman with a horn growing out of her forehead, were increasingly publicised through cheap print, and were interpreted as signs of the times or indications of God's call to repent and abandon false religion; and even a slight sickness might be taken as a reflection of God's intervention in the physical world, as when Margaret Hoby from Yorkshire recorded in her diary that 'it pleased [God] for a just punishment to correct my sins to send me a feebleness of stomach and pain of my head that kept me upon my bed till 5 o'clock: at which time I arose, having release of my sickness, according to the wonted kindness of the Lord who, after He had let me see how I had offended, that so I might take better heed to my body and soul hereafter, with a gentle correction let me feel He was reconciled to me'.[43]

A pamphlet from 1644, *Signs and Wonders from Heaven*, summarises the atmosphere of the time. 'It is a known thing to all Christian people which are capable of understanding how that the sins of the world have in a high degree offended the world's Maker and provoked the Lord to anger. Yet hath the Devil so blinded the eyes and hardened the hearts of many men and women, that they cannot or will not see or take notice of their own iniquities' (p. 1). The result of this is the breach between king and Parliament, along with widespread plague, the birth of deformed children and animals, and the activities of witches in Norfolk – forty witches were arraigned there and twenty executed – Suffolk, and Essex, along with 'some in Stepney parish now in question about witchcraft, [who] being persons of eminence' – an interesting comment which shows that witches did not always belong to the lower or peasant class – 'their names must as yet be concealed' (pp. 2–3). 'God in His mercy give us all a sight of our sins,' the author concludes, 'and grant us grace to acknowledge them and amend our lives' (p. 5).[44]

Street literature, however, was happy enough to whip up emotions by retelling stories from fifteen years before. One such, *Witchcrafts Strange and Wonderfull*, published in 1635, tries to circumvent possible scepticism in its readership by an appeal to trust.

> Because the mind of man may be carried away with many idle conjectures, either that women confessed these things by extremity of torture, or that ancient examples are by this time forgotten, (although the particulars are upon record for the benefit of all posterity), or that they were beside themselves, or subject to some weak device or other, rather to bring in question the integrity of justice than to make odious the lives of such horrible offenders, I have presumed to present on the stage of verity, for the good of my country and the love of truth, the late woeful tragedy of the destruction of the Right Honourable, the Earl of Rutland's children. (p. 5)

Joan Flower, the principal witch in this case, is given a novelist's pen-portrait.

> [She] was a monstrous malicious woman, full of oaths, curses, and imprecations, irreligious, and for anything they saw by her, a plain atheist. Besides, of late days her very countenance was estranged, her eyes were fiery and hollow, her speech fell and envious, her demeanour strange and exotic, and her conversation sequestered, so that the whole course of her life gave great suspicion that she was a notorious witch. Yes, some of her neighbours dared to affirm that she dealt with familiar spirits, and terrified them all with curses and threatening of revenge if there were never so little cause of displeasure and unkindness. (pp. 6–7)

Her malice, while ingrained, was exacerbated by her daughter Margaret's dismissal from the earl's employ for 'some undecencies both in her life and neglect of her business' (p. 7), and thus she and Margaret gave way to the Devil and became his apprentices, learning how to prevent the earl and countess from having any more children, killing their eldest son, and making the countess ill. But 'it pleased God to discover the villainous practices of these bad women and to command the Devil from executing any further vengeance on innocents' (p. 9). So Joan and Margaret, along with Joan's other daughter, Philippa, were arrested and sent to Lincoln gaol were Joan died, choking on a piece of bread and butter, and Margaret and Philippa were hanged.

Further tales follow, one of which contains unusual features. On 1 March 1618, the Earl of Rutland and other gentlemen examined Anne Baker from Bottesford in Leicestershire.

> She saith that there are four colours of planets, black, yellow, green, and blue, and that black is always death; and that she saw the blue planet strike Thomas Fairbarn, the eldest son unto William Fairbarn ... within the which time the said William Fairbarn did beat her and brake her head. Whereupon the said Thomas Fairbarn did mend. And being asked who did send that planet, answered, 'It was not I.' Further she saith that she saw a hand appear unto her, and that she heard a voice in the air [which] said unto

her, 'Anne Baker, save thyself, for tomorrow thou and thy master must be slain.' And the next day her master and she were in a cart together, and suddenly she saw a flash of fire, and she said her prayers and the fire went away. And shortly after, a crow came and pecked upon her clothes, and she said her prayers again and bade the crow go to whom he was sent. And the crow went unto her master and did beat him to death, and she with her prayers recovered him to life. But he was sick a fortnight after, and saith that if she had not had more knowledge, then her master, both she and he and all the cattle, had been slain. (pp. 10–11).

These visual images and auditory experiences are not altogether dissimilar to those in some of the so-called 'shamanic' trance states we can note in other witches, and it is difficult to know how unusual they are in people, especially women, of this kind. It may be argued, of course, that the very frequent witches' reports of seeing Satan in various guises, or of travelling through the air to a Sabbat, or of feeding spirits in the shape of animals, can be taken as narratives of both visual and auditory experience. Arguments that such reports are either fraudulent or fictional in some fashion should obviously not be dismissed entirely; but nor should they be taken as indisputable in every case, and as our surviving records rarely provide enough information to allow us to come to a firm judgement either way, we should at least sometimes suspend dismissiveness in favour of neutral consideration. Thus, for example, we have the case of Margaret Flower who told the court that while she was in Leicester gaol, she had been visited by four devils at about midnight, one of which 'stood at her bed's feet with a black head, like an ape, and spake unto her: but what, she cannot well remember, at which she was very angry because he would speak no plainer, or let her understand his meaning' (p. 19). Are we to infer from this that she was dreaming, or that she was caught between waking and sleeping and had something like a half-dream, or did she have a genuine visual experience which failed in its auditory aspect, thus causing her frustration because she could not hear clearly or understand what was being said to her? All three are possible interpretations and, on the evidence provided, one is not stronger than the others.

The social and political dramas of the civil wars in Scotland and England, resulting partly from Charles I's ruinous attempt to impose a religious settlement on a Scotland which, by and large, was unwilling to receive it, and partly because invasion of England by Scotland in 1640 produced talk, (not altogether unjustified), of the king's readiness to use Catholic soldiers from both there and Ireland to force his will upon those who opposed him, infuriated the English into taking advantage of a new English parliament to attack Charles's power and position in both Church and state. War immediately politicised portents and prodigies, and both sides of the divide poured pamphlets from their presses, purporting to show that the avalanche of extraordinary phenomena threatening to overwhelm the skies, the land, and the sea was permitted and indeed sent by God to recall His people (whichever side of the conflict they might be on) to their senses and to the practice of religion as He wished it to be done. In the midst of these wars and dire monitions from on high, heterodox notions flourished, some intellectually respectable, at least in some quarters – not by chance is this period the golden age of alchemy in England, with astrology vying with it for that elevated status – but others, such as those of Anabaptists, Familists, Grindletonians, and Ranters, being considered too radical to be accommodated in either the old or new dispensations. Many of them, interestingly enough, had doubts about the reality of either Hell or devils, and this, of course, undermined one of the key beliefs necessary to the concept of witchcraft at this time. 'There is no other devil or spirit or familiar spirit for witches to deal withal, or to work any enchantments by, but their own imagination,' wrote Lodowick Muggleton, one of the founders of a new sect named after him.[45]

But nor, one should add, was a certain level-headedness altogether missing from the orthodox and learned who had long been aware that nature could produce, of herself, oddities and peculiarities which were not necessarily vehicles of signs and admonitions. Yet cabinets of curiosities, or 'museums of the preternatural' as Lorraine Daston calls them, containing such things as abnormally large bones, ostrich eggs, rhinoceros horns, and elaborately carved nuts, provided visitors with a theatre of the world which, while diverting and eliciting astonishment also instructed them in the remarkable abundance of God's creation and drew attention to the multiplicity of objects which might be found, through significant colour or shape or association, to provide further illustrations of the links between this and other worlds.[46] These 'curiosities', then, hung midway between material portent and cold fact, and any propensity to regard them as purely the latter might well be subverted by the traditional inclination to see them as the former. Outright rejection of any supernatural element in certain physical objects or natural phenomena was thus for many a step too far, and the tide of the times was against it. Indeed the very fact that dismissive opinions had their origin in highly unorthodox and dubious sources meant that they would scarcely be received with any degree of seriousness. It was such a febrile atmosphere, for example, that enabled propagandists to suggest that the dog belonging to Charles I's nephew, Prince Rupert, was actually 'a very downright devil ... or a spirit sent to nourish division in Church or state ... Certainly he is some Lapland lady who by nature was once a handsome white woman, and now by [*magical*] art is become a handsome white dog and hath vowed to follow the prince to preserve him from mischief'. This, of course, made the dog a familiar and in consequence made the prince a witch, a set of suggestions which would not have seemed entirely unbelievable to many who read the relevant pamphlet or heard the gossip, since popular English literature about witches had been describing witches' familiars in the shape of dogs for nearly a hundred years.[47]

But we have to ask whether the civil wars which produced this and similar stories, combined with the unusually hostile climatic conditions of the 1640s and 50s with their consequent increases in death and disease, had an effect on the number of accusations of witchcraft in the various parts of the British Isles – the 'search for scapegoats' theory.[48] There had been flurries during the 1630s as the political situation in England deteriorated, and many Presbyterians in Scotland banded together in a solemn league and covenant to reject all innovations in religion brought in since 1580, a religio-political alliance which had significant results for Church, state, and witchcraft only a few years later. In Guernsey, 1631 saw the prosecution of sixteen people, mainly women, of whom two were executed, ten banished, and four set at liberty – scarcely a bloodbath – while on Jersey one woman was executed and another imprisoned.[49] These prosecutions, however, do not represent the beginning of persecution in the islands, and the rest of the 1630s were almost free from legal action against suspected witches. The same may be said of Scotland, in spite of religious tension in Edinburgh. Tension spilled into action during the 1640s. Even during plague years in the south of Scotland and the north of England – 1605–1609, 1625–1626, 1628–1629, 1635–1637, 1645–1647, 1650 – when the Scottish government issued segregation and quarantine orders to prevent or contain the problem, there is no correlation between these periods and increase in witch prosecutions.[50] One should also note that while plague affected the eastern and southern parts of Scotland, it hardly touched the west and north. This is because the west and north were cooler and wetter, and so provided discouraging conditions for disease-bearing fleas.[51] England fared much worse, with severe outbreaks of plague in the 1620s (1625 being a particularly bad year) and the early 1630s (with 1631, 1636, and 1637 being the worst years). Yet again, there is no correlation between these years and any noticeable increase in the number of prosecutions for witchcraft, and the same can be said in relation to famine and prosecutions.[52]

Christina Larner has noted that 'while witchcraft was sometimes held to be responsible for rather vague general conditions such as an increase in sin, rebellion, or disturbance, and occasionally for storm raising, it was rarely held to be responsible for large-scale disasters in which the suffering might be random'.[53] Thus, for example, the plague in London in 1665 was blamed on malevolent stars or poisonous vapours, and the fire of 1666 on Catholics or foreigners, rather than on witches. Witchcraft, in fact, was highly personal, its magic aimed in a particular rather than a general direction. Even storm raising can be seen in this light, for the intention behind the magic tended to be directed against an individual or a family, as when Lothian witches raised a storm to wreck James VI's ship as he returned with his bride from Denmark.[54] Famine and plague might well increase anxieties within a community or in communities over an area, of course, and elsewhere in Europe in those places where the belief in a conspiracy between witches and Satan to destroy whole swathes of humanity was strong, there could be a correlation between bad weather, loss of crops, and intense prosecution of witches, but this was not the case in any part of Britain.[55]

Civil wars first in Scotland, then in England meant that social tensions were increased, but 'war' of itself, like 'plague' and 'famine', did not act as the immediate cause of witchcraft prosecutions. Indeed, as far as those are concerned, the 1650s were worse than the 1640s, when the majority of the fighting took place, but even so the numbers of those accused cannot be said to have reached anything like the magnitude of some of the other European pogroms, except perhaps for the notorious episode of hunting in Essex, Suffolk, and other parts of East Anglia, directed and orchestrated by Matthew Hopkins and John Stearne between 1642 and 1647. Hopkins and Stearne, however, are unusual figures in English witchcraft, in as much as the extent of their activities has no real parallel elsewhere in the British Isles. To be sure, there were professional witch prickers elsewhere – people whose employment was to sink pins into physical blemishes on the suspect's body to see whether they bled or were insensible to pain (either an indication, though not proof, that the suspect was a witch). The best-known of these others was John Kincaid who operated principally in the Lothians during the late 1640s and 1650s, and Scottish prickers acquired a reputation for efficiency, which frequently caused them to be hired by authorities in the north of England, too, to test suspects this way. Pricking, in fact, was a business and treated as such, and was undoubtedly abused by those who wanted to increase their income by faking results or suborning people to make false accusations. Kincaid himself was guilty of this, as was another pricker, George Cathie, who operated mainly in Lanarkshire. But fraud was by no means universal or undetectable, and one is not entitled to assume that because it could be and was practised sometimes, it was therefore always practised.[56]

The accusations levelled against individuals during the war years were little different from those before and after. A London man called Hammond was tried in 1641 for killing someone by means of a wax figure, and in St Albans in 1649, John Palmer and his kinswoman, Elizabeth Knott, 'encompassed the death of Goodwife Pearls of Norton, framing a picture of her in clay, which they laid upon the fire, and while it was consuming and mouldering away the woman suffered torments, and with its complete destruction, died'.[57] Murder by witchcraft, whether of humans or animals, and making people ill, continued as before, with varying outcomes for the accused. In 1643, Nicholas Culpeper, gent, from Shoreditch, was found not guilty of bewitching Sarah Lynge to death, as was Elizabeth Smyth of London in 1650, accused of killing Jane Gwynne by magic, while Elizabeth Peacock, tried at Hertford assizes in March 1641, was found not guilty of murder by witchcraft, but was obliged to stay in prison until she could find sureties for her future good behaviour.[58] Interestingly enough, however, accusations of using spirits to find lost or stolen goods or buried treasure seem more or less to disappear during the war years, although they appear again in the 1650s, with Christiana Weekes from Wiltshire being indicted in both 1651 and 1654 for professing to be able to tell someone where lost articles could be found; John Haye of Handley in Cheshire, a schoolmaster, being tried in 1655 'for professing himself one called a wiseman, and that he can inform others where to have their goods that are stolen and lost'; and John Bennet from Oxfordshire, released from gaol on 23 July 1659 after a jury could not make up its mind whether he was guilty of 'witchcraft in telling of stolen goods' or not.[59]

But what we may note about witchcraft cases during the decades of war and the interregnum is the violence frequently offered to the accused either before or after arrest, and the exotic or sensational details appearing in the records. (It is not, of course, that violence and exotica were not reported at other times, merely that records from this period seem to note them rather more often. Thus, in Yorkshire three women were accused of killing two children and six pigs by magic in 1646. Apparently after his infant son died, Henry Cockcroft suspected witchcraft by one Elizabeth Crosley, a reputed witch who had actually been employed by Henry's wife to cure their pigs. Henry went to Mary Midgley to test his suspicion, because Mary confessed she herself had some magical ability – set a witch to catch a witch, in fact – and she identified Elizabeth Crosley and two other women, Elizabeth's daughter Sarah and Mary Kitching, as the culprits responsible. Henry had brought some friends with him, and as he was clearly not satisfied with this answer, he and the other men set about beating a confession of personal guilt out of Mary, an aim in which eventually they succeeded. Elizabeth Crosley, meanwhile, had her own problems to bear. For John Shackleton, an infant, had fallen ill with convulsions, and it may have been the coincidence of this and his own son's fits before dying which had made Henry suspicious of witchcraft and of Elizabeth in particular, since she had made a fuss about the alms she was offered by Henry's wife. Henry must have called on the local minister at some point, because the minister observed that while Henry and his servant were going home, they might meet someone, and if they did so, they might feel a strong desire to beat him or her round the head. It is an extraordinary remark. Are we to take it that the minister was prescient in some way, knew they would run into Elizabeth, and was thus advising Henry to shed blood as a means of counter-magic? Was he aware that Elizabeth would be coming along that particular road and so was urging Henry and his servant to take some kind of vengeance? Or was he merely advocating that Henry beat someone up as a way of relieving his obvious frustration? (This last is most unlikely and in any case is redolent of twenty-first-century psychology.) Whatever the answer, Henry did indeed meet Elizabeth and his servant hit her with a candlestick, after which the child's health improved somewhat, although the child died about three months later.[60]

Violence was in the air, of course, since war was raging up and down England at this time and the arrival of soldiers in an area was always an unmitigated disaster for the local population as food was stolen, houses burned, women raped, men and children murdered, and disease spread.[61] Once again, the major battles from Edgehill (1642) to Worcester (1651) do not correlate with any outbreaks of witchcraft accusations in the same area, but in one or two cases the army does make an appearance in the written record. On 19 September 1643, for example, the day before the First Battle of Newbury, some Parliamentarian troops had fallen behind the main army, lured by the profusion of fruits and nuts in the nearby countryside. One soldier had climbed a tree to escape the boisterous behaviour of his companions and from there caught sight of a woman apparently walking on the water of a nearby river. Upon further investigation, the soldiers found she had been manoeuvring upon a plank, but the woman herself had vanished and either this or her dexterity in riding the water's surface convinced some of the men, including their commanders, that she was a witch. Orders were given for her arrest, and when she was found and brought before the officers, she refused to answer their questions or say anything of consequence. As a prisoner she would be a nuisance to men about to fight a battle, so they resolved to shoot her then and there, but 'with a deriding and loud laughter at them, she caught their bullets in her hands and chewed them'. Thoroughly irritated by this disdain, one soldier put his carbine to her chest and fired. But the bullet rebounded, and when another man tried to run her through with his sword, he was no more successful than his companion. 'Yet one among the rest had heard that piercing or drawing blood from forth the veins that cross the temples of the head, it would prevail against the strongest sorcery and quell the force of witchcraft.' He must have urged this aloud upon his fellows, for the woman began to weep and cry out, after which someone shot her beneath her ear and she fell down dead.[62] We need not spend long on the details of this story. Mark Stoyle is clearly right in suggesting that the author of the pamphlet (published in 1643, a year after the battle in September) had probably seized on a genuine killing and worked it up with a number of sensational incidents to provide a piece of propaganda in the form of entertainment. A Royalist witch – she was reported by *Mercurius Civicus* as a person sent to blow up the local Parliamentarian commander's magazine before the battle – had been caught and dispatched by Roundhead troops. Her prophetic words, uttered just before she died, that the Parliamentarian Earl of Essex would win the ensuing conflict, made clear the purpose of the pamphlet – to link the king's army, and through them the king himself, with witchcraft and therefore Satan.[63]

Fanciful though some of the details may be, however, the casual violence is clearly not, and an example from German fiction may serve to illustrate the kind of treatment regularly meted out to the civilian population all over Europe by soldiers on their way to or from a battlefield.

A number of soldiers began to slaughter, to boil and roast things, while others, on the other hand, stormed through the house from top to bottom. Others still made a large pack out of linens, clothes, and all kinds of household goods. Everything they didn't want to take with them they destroyed. A number of them stick their bayonets into the straw and hay, as if they didn't already have enough sheep and pigs to stick. Many of them shook out the feathers from the bedcovers and filled them with ham. Others threw meat and other utensils into them. Some knocked in the oven and the windows, smashing copper utensils and dishes. Bedsteads, tables, stools, and benches were burned. Pots and cutting boards were all broken. One servant girl was so badly handled in the barn that she couldn't move any longer. Our servant they tied up and laid on the ground and rammed a funnel in his mouth and then poured a ghastly brew full of piss down his throat. Then they started to torture the peasants as if they wanted to burn a band of witches.[64]

Having the reputation of a witch was thus likely to be especially dangerous in conditions such as these, as Alice Elger from Malmesbury in Wiltshire found out around 1643. Alice is described as 'audaciously obnoxious' to many of the town's inhabitants, meaning presumably that she had a strong personality and did not mind expressing anger or resentment. On 21 March 1643 the town was assaulted and fell into Parliamentarian hands, so the triumph of the unco guid may have helped to exacerbate the dislike or hatred many felt for Alice, a dislike which broke into sudden violence ('an instant emergent') one day when she was in the marketplace. We are told that 'the soldiers and some of the lowest of the people did … use her very roughly' and that, fearful of receiving such treatment again, she went home and poisoned herself. Witches did commit suicide sometimes, but usually in prison after arrest and interrogation. Alice's despairing action is somewhat unusual, but the presence of soldiers in a town under martial law is likely, in effect, to have increased lawlessness, encouraged arbitrary violence, and so made Alice's situation worse.[65] Children might be encouraged by these precedents to behave as adults did. In 1649 a boy from Worcestershire (we do not know his age) lost his speech after being frightened by an old woman and later, seeing her eating with other people, 'ran furiously upon her and threw his pottage in her face and offered some other violence to her'. Whereupon the woman was arrested and jailed until she said the Lord's Prayer and begged the boy's forgiveness, after which (he said) she came and sat in his bedroom window, grinning at him, until he picked up a piece of wood 'and therewith gave her two good bangs upon the arse, as she would have scuttled from him'.[66]

Some of the violence we read about was connected with counter-magic or searching for proof of witchcraft. In 1650, Anne Hudson from Yorkshire was charged with making a man ill through witchcraft and was deeply scratched, after which he recovered; and when Margaret Morton, also from Yorkshire, was blamed in 1651 for making a child sick, the child became well again after Joan Booth had scratched Margaret with a pin. Margaret was then arrested and searched, and one of the searchers, Frances Ward, testified that they found two black spots on her inner thigh. 'They were like a wart,' she said, 'but it was none; and the other was black on both sides, an inch broad and blue in the midst.' In spite of her long reputation as a witch, however, and those of her mother and sister, both deceased, the jury found Margaret not guilty of the charges brought against her.[67] Now, these, of course, were counter-measures with a long tradition behind them and not peculiar to the war or interregnum. But they help illustrate the violence which could break out at any moment against a suspect, whose anticipation of ill treatment must surely have increased in proportion to the anxiety felt by her neighbours, especially if their beliefs, suspicions, or expectations were inflamed by popular pamphlets, sermons, or ill-natured gossip. Several people were said to command evil spirits to work their harm – Anne Camell from Suffolk in 1646, for example, and Ellen and Elizabeth Stubbs from Cheshire in 1653 – while an unnamed man from Boston confessed on 24 July 1650 that he had a familiar in the shape of a chicken which used to peck his nipples until they bled; and John Palmer from St Albans (according to a pamphlet published in 1649), who said he had been a witch for sixty years, made a pact with the Devil, who gave him two familiars, 'one in the form of a dog called George, the other in the likeness of a woman called Jezebel'.[68]

Stories of shape changing were heard before the courts. On 14 October 1654, John Greencliffe of Beverley in Yorkshire gave testimony that

> Elizabeth Roberts appeared to him in her usual wearing clothes, with a ruff about her neck, and presently vanishing, turned herself into the similitude of a cat which fixed close about his leg and, after much struggling, vanished; whereupon he was much pained at his heart. On another occasion, a cat struck him on the head, upon which he fell into a trance. After he received the blow, he saw Elizabeth escape upon a wall, in her usual wearing apparel. Again she appeared in the likeness of a bee which threw his body from place to place, notwithstanding five or six persons were present to hold him down.[69]

On one occasion at least, the witch was accompanied by a ghost. Dorothy Rhodes from Yorkshire told the local JP that 'her child, Sarah, taken with pains and numbness complained of visits from [Mary Sykes, and] also from Kellett's wife who, she was told, had been dead two years. Sarak, quite unabashed, rejoined, "Ah, Mother, but she never rests, for she appeared to me the foulest fiend that ever I saw, with a pair of eyes like saucers, and stood up betwixt them [*presumably herself and Mary Sykes*] and gave me a box of the ear in the gapstead, which made the fire to flash out of my eyes.'[70]

Needless to say, the Devil made frequent appearances in these and other episodes. In Norfolk he took the form of a gentlewoman on horseback in July 1645, and in March 1646 the likeness of a young man accompanied by two puppies, one black, one white. In this instance, confessed by Elizabeth Weed from Huntingdonshire to magistrates during the Hopkins-Stearne witch hunt, 'about ten o'clock at night, he came with a paper and telling [me] the covenant must be sealed, pricked [me] under the left arm and scribbled with blood ... He [then] entered the bed and had carnal knowledge of [me], the other two spirits sucking parts of [my] body where [I] had teats.'[71] The provenance of this information, coming as it did from the midst of local tensions between gentry and their tenants and under the watchful eye of Stearne's supervision may lead us to be wary of its details. But torture was not used to elicit the confession, and there is a consistency in Elizabeth's reference to the Devil and demons-as-puppies with other confessions from the same area at the same time. Frances Moore had a familiar in the form of a black puppy, and Joan Wallis two attendant spirits in the likeness of bristle-backed dogs. Elizabeth and Frances knew one another – indeed, Frances said Elizabeth had supplied her with familiars – and the near hysteria of that springtime as the English war drew to a close. Local animosities flourished, and a rash of celestial phenomena (a meteorite, hailstones, visions, and thunderous drumrolls in the sky) produced a more than usually acute awareness of the impact of the other world upon this one and almost, one might say, an eagerness to give voice to preternatural experiences as one way of relieving intolerable tension.[72]

Similar confessions burgeoned during these mid-1640s. Dorothy Ellis said in 1647 that thirty years previously, the Devil had come to her in the form of a large cat demanding blood and had then worked harmful magic in return. Why wait thirty years before saying anything? If she was speaking the truth about some kind of psychic experience, it looks as though the peculiar and particular circumstances of 1647, especially the Hopkins-Stearne hunt, had created conditions in which she was prepared to be frank, whether with lies or truth. Over and over again in these hunt records from East Anglia and Suffolk we find the Devil making a physical appearance, a feature which, while not confined to this episode, does seem to reflect the special concerns of both Hopkins and Stearne who, themselves, were able to flourish because of the unusual nature of people's psyches at this particular juncture. Elsewhere, by contrast, some people felt able to joke. George Buchanan was presented to the Chester sessions on 17 September 1649, partly for making political statements in his cups and partly 'for that he being offered a candle to light him home, he answered he needed none, for the Devil would light him home'.[73] On the other hand, Isabella Billington from the town of Pocklington in the East Riding of Yorkshire was executed in 1649 along with twenty other malefactors, fourteen men and six women. Their crimes had been nothing out of the ordinary, a mixture of rebellion, arson, and murder, but hers had been to crucify her mother with the aid of her husband (who was later hanged), and to offer a calf and a cockerel as a burnt sacrifice, one presumes to the Devil, but perhaps not. It would be too easy to assume she was insane (although that is always a possibility, of course), and we should not do so without further evidence. But while human sacrifice, usually of babies and small children, was a regular feature of some witchcraft confessions, principally of those alleging attendance at a Sabbat – not a feature usual in British witches' revelations – it was different in kind from that confessed by Isabella, being intended principally to provide fat and grease for flying unguents and other instruments of malefice. Pocklington had executed two witches before in the recent past, Old Wife Green in 1630 and Petronel Haxby in 1642, both despatched in the town's marketplace, and there is a notice in the parish records that Thomas Dobson, buried on 24 March 1643, had been bewitched. But Isabella's case is obviously unusual and either represents an act of possible madness, or a magic ritual intended to ward off some disaster, obtain Satan's favour, or worship the Devil.[74]

Ritual magic and evocation of the Devil were not altogether uncommon among men, and at least one legal commentator in 1645 specified differences between various magical workers, which nevertheless make the presence and co-operation of the Devil the link between them.

The difference between conjuration, witchcraft, and enchantment etc is this: viz. conjurors and witches have personal conference with the Devil or evil spirit to effect their purpose (see 1 *Samuel* 28.7, etc.). The conjurors believe that by certain terrible words they can raise the Devil and make him to tremble, and by impaling themselves in a circle, (which, as one saith, cannot keep out a mouse), they believe that they are therein ensconced and safe from the Devil whom they are about to raise; and having raised the Devil, they seem, by prayers and invocation of God's powerful names, to compel the Devil to say or do what the conjuror commandeth him. The witch dealeth rather by a friendly and voluntary conference or agreement between him or her and the Devil or familiar to have his or her turn served, and in lieu thereof the witch giveth or offereth his or her soul, blood, or other gift unto the Devil. Also the conjuror compacteth for curiosity, to know secrets or work miracles, and the witch of mere malice to do mischief and to be revenged. The enchanter, charmer, or sorcerer, those have no personal conference with the Devil, but without any apparition work and perform things, seemingly at the least, by certain superstitious and ceremonial forms of words, called 'charms', by them pronounced, or by medicines, herbs, or other things applied above the course of nature: and by the Devil's help and covenants made with him. Of this last sort likewise are soothsayers or wizards, which divine and foretell things to come, by the flying, singing, or feeding of birds: and unto such questions as be demanded of them, they do answer by the Devil, or by his help, that is, they do either answer by voice, or else do set before their eyes in glasses, crystal stones, or rings, the pictures or images of the persons or things sought for.[75]

These conjurors or wizards did not necessarily have to be learned, although learning of some kind, usually in the form of prayers or formulae in Latin, tended to come into it. Hence Giles Fenderlin, not a learned man but a soldier serving in the Low Countries in around 1640, had the assistance of a Jesuit when he sacrificed a cockerel and a cat to Satan in return for protection from bullets – a piece of covenant magic which, according to Fenderlin, proved successful.[76] But similar ritual evocations by a woman are found only seldom, although one example from 1653 is worth noting. It concerns Anne Bodenham from Wiltshire. She was an old woman aged eighty at the time of her trial, and had been a servant as well as a cunning woman, curing disease by magic and discovering lost or stolen articles the same way. Two pamphlets published in 1653 provide details of her activities, trial, and execution, and allege that in addition to her selling her relatively harmless magic, she was prepared to wreak harm as well, mainly through poison which she advised should be administered in different ways. Anne was said to have been servant to John Lambe, a learned cunning man (he had the title 'Dr'), who had practised astrology and necromancy for his principal patron, the Duke of Buckingham, from about 1625 until his trial and death in 1628. Anne used a crystal ball in some of her consultations, as she demonstrated to Anne Styles, the woman who would later be the principal witness against her at her trial.

> The witch put on her spectacles and, demanding seven shillings of [Anne Styles], which she received, she opened three books in which there seemed to be several pictures, and among the rest the picture of the Devil ... with his cloven feet and claws. After [Anne Styles] had looked over the book, [Anne Bodenham] brought a round green glass, which glass she laid down on one of the books, upon some picture therein, and rubbed the glass, and then took up the book with the glass upon it, and held it up against the sun, and bid [Anne Styles] come and see who they were that she could show in that glass; and [Anne Styles] looking in the glass saw the shape of many persons, and what they were doing of in her master's house.

Anne Styles was, in fact, a persistent customer and consulted Anne Bodenham several times, at first to discover lost articles, then to obtain counter-magic against her mistress's being poisoned, and finally to get a mixture which would make her mistress's daughters-in-law very ill. During the course of these visits, Anne Bodenham's ceremonies became more and more complex until one day, in an effort to persuade Anne Styles to become her apprentice in magic, Anne Bodenham shape-changed into a large black cat and then forced her to make a covenant of silence about what she had seen – in effect by making her a witch.

> She forthwith made a circle and, looking in her book, called Beelzebub, Tormentor, Lucifer, and Satan [to] appear. Then appeared two spirits in the likeness of great boys with long shagged hair and stood by her, looking over her shoulder; and the witch took took [Anne Styles's] forefinger of her right hand in her hand, and pricked it with a pin and squeezed out blood, and put it into a pen, and put the pen into [Anne's] hand, and held her hand to write in a great book; and one of the spirits laid his hand or claw upon the witches whilst [Anne Styles] wrote; and when she had done writing, whilst their hands were together, the witch said, 'Amen' and made [Anne Styles] say 'Amen'; and the spirits said, 'Amen, Amen'; and the spirit's hand did feel cold to [Anne Styles] as it touched her hand when the witch's hand and hers were together writing; and then the spirit gave a piece of silver (which he first bit), to the witch who gave it to [Anne Styles], and also stuck two pins in [Anne Styles's] head-clothes, and bid her keep them, and bid her be gone.[77]

Anne Bodenham was executed, of course. Her crimes were too many and the evidence against her too compelling for her jury to come to any conclusion other than 'guilty'. Moreover, she was not typical. Most of the witches, male or female, who came before the English courts during the 1640s and 50s conformed to earlier patterns of magical activity. It cannot be said that prosecutions intensified at this time, either. With the exception of the hunts organised by Hopkins and Stearne, incidents of complaint or prosecution are scattered in much the way one might expect, in ones and twos at a time throughout the English counties, although if we look only at the cases noted by Ewen, we see not only the scattering but also what appears to be a slight rise in numbers (but only slight) during the 1650s.

1641: London
1642: London, Yorkshire
1643: Berkshire, Wiltshire, Yorkshire
1644: Essex
1645: Essex, Norfolk, Suffolk
1646: Northamptonshire, Worcestershire, Yorkshire
1647: Cambridgeshire, Middlesex
1648: Middlesex
1649: Cheshire, Hertfordshire, Yorkshire
1650: Leicestershire, Lincolnshire, Middlesex, Norfolk, Northumberland, Yorkshire
1651: London, Wiltshire, Yorkshire
1652: Durham, Kent, London, Middlesex, Warwickshire, Worcestershire, Yorkshire
1653: Cheshire, London, Northumberland, Somerset, Suffolk, Wiltshire, Yorkshire
1654: London, Wiltshire, Yorkshire
1655: Cornwall, Dorset, Lancashire, Somerset, Suffolk, Wiltshire, Yorkshire
1656: Cheshire, London, Sussex, Yorkshire
1657: Cheshire, Gloucestershire
1658: Cheshire, Devon, Gloucestershire, Northamptonshire, Somerset, Wiltshire
1659: Cambridgeshire, Cheshire, Gloucestershire, London, Norfolk, Oxfordshire, Shropshire, Westmorland

Now, it is perfectly true that people of this period were hardly static. Movement of many different kinds between individual villages and towns and, indeed, localities was common enough, especially if one takes into account 'vagabonds' of one kind or another who, by choice or necessity, were rarely resident in one place for long. By them tales, gossip, insinuation, eyewitness accounts, and exaggerations could travel and so spread. Nevertheless, there are no indications that the majority of the suspicions and accusations from these decades amounted to a concerted hunt rather than a series of highly localised, small upsurges such as one might expect to happen anywhere and at any time. Even so, it is perhaps noteworthy how often Yorkshire appears throughout the two decades, while other counties such as Leicestershire or Kent or Devon make no appearance until the 1650s. But while this may be explained, at least in part, by the advent of a Puritan régime in London, military rule via majors general in the rest of the country, and an official eagerness to frogmarch England into a Promised Land of religious radicalism, the impression of greater numbers of suspects and accused in the North may be misleading. Local pastors, to be sure, were more likely than not to keep a stricter eye than before on their parishioners' deviant beliefs and behaviour, and clamp down on both, and this may help to account for the prosecution of, for example, two Quakers from Cambridgeshire in 1659, who were said to have transformed Jane Phillips into a mare and ridden her to one of their meetings.[78] Yet in spite of the fact that the north of England had many Catholics – more Catholics lived in Yorkshire and Lancashire than in the rest of England altogether – thereby inviting the warm distaste of Presbyterians and other Nonconformists alike (not to mention orthodox Anglicans), whether members of the cloth or not, to communicate itself to pamphlets, diaries, and characterise popular adherence to the use of charms and amulets as 'the knavery of the Popish priests that gull their superstitious and credulous votaries with such fopperies';[79] and in spite of the fact that Catholics suffered legal disability and adverse propaganda, and the early 1640s saw anti-Catholic panics in centres of strong Parliamentarian, and so largely Presbyterian/Puritan, activity, there is actually no correlation between Catholics and the objects of witchcraft accusations.

This is interesting, for there had been a slow, small increase in Catholic numbers all over Yorkshire. Holderness in the East Riding, where Anne Hudson was charged in September 1650 with bewitching a man into sickness and scratched to make him recover, had 413 Catholics, over half the total in the Riding.[80] We should therefore expect to see an intensification of confessionally inspired discipline in these areas and hence a greater awareness of anything resembling witchcraft. Yet the places from which accusations emanated during the 1650s are scattered all over Yorkshire, each place prosecuting only one person or two in any given year (exactly the frequency and geographical spread one might expect at any other period), and the accusations themselves almost entirely alleged making people and animals sick. Nothing unusual, untoward, confessionally or politically biased there. What is more, at least two of those accused were acquitted – one after marks had been found on her body – one was freed by proclamation in July 1658, and another reprieved after capital sentence had been passed. So it cannot be said that the situation in the county produced anything which looked remotely like an organised pursuit of magical workers.[81] This is somewhat surprising, since we need to remember the deluge of pamphlets, printed ballads, and popular newspapers such as *The Moderate Intelligencer*, *The Starry Messenger*, and dozens of others, dealing with portents, visions, prophecies, and prodigies of nature, which poured down on the English public during the war years and beyond. *Strange Newes from Brotherton in Yorke-shire*, proclaimed one ballad from around 1648, *Being a True Relation of the Raining of Wheat on Easter Day last, to the Great Amaizment of all the Inhabitants*, adding,

> Our Chronicles report,
> if it be understood,
> A little before a civill warre,
> one day it rained blood,

Hailstones as big as Eggs,
another time then fell,
Which did much hurt to countryfolks
our Chronicles doth tell ...

Within the firmament,
two suns hath often bin,
And armed men presaging warre,
to scourge the world for sin:
The sea did overflow,
and man and beast did drowne,
A Child within a Cradle then
alive the people found ...

When the Scotch and English jarr'd,
about eight years agoe,
The like did hap at Knottingley,
as many people know:
Strange Apparitions too,
of armed men did traine,
On Barkestone Moor not farre from thence
as many will maintain.[82]

A world which was full of wonders and intrusions from the other world became even more disturbingly marvellous – a situation exploited for political purposes by politicians and clergy alike, but one which could not have been so used had the generality of people not accepted that anomalies in nature were meaningful and under divine control. The tendency, however, was to blame society as a whole rather than particular individuals for incurring God's anger. 'Our sinne is cause of our strife', as an earlier verse in *Strange Newes* puts it, and so witches in general escaped blame for the actual strife and some of its attendant disasters, although of course individuals did sometimes bear the brunt of people's anxiety and frustration, which was expressed through complaints about personal harms and envies.

The situation in Wales during the 1650s was not dissimilar in certain ways. Ewen records nine instances of accusations in six years (1654–1659) with six sentences of 'not guilty', one case in which there was not enough evidence to bring the accused person to court, one where the accused was bound over, and one whose verdict is not known. Again, these cases are scattered – Carmarthenshire, Flintshire, and Monmouthshire – and there is no evidence of any concerted local persecution.[83] Nor is there evidence to link these incidents with abrasiveness between Catholics and their Protestant neighbours. Catholics were by no means uncommon in Wales – there were certainly Jesuits working in the country, with one mission opening at Cwm near Monmouth in 1622, for example, and by around 1675 Monmouthshire had nine priests who were saying Mass publicly and regularly. But it cannot be said that Wales was at all comparable with Yorkshire or Lancashire in the density of its

Catholic population, and thus confessionalism seems to have played no part in its witch trials.[84] In Ireland, of course, the situation was entirely different. The country suffered the horrors of civil and external wars between 1641 and 1653, widespread famine and bubonic plague in 1650–1651, and subsequent loss of life, exacerbated by large-scale deportation of Irish men and women to the American colonies. These disasters, however, were not blamed on anyone except the English and Scots who were, self-evidently, some of the principal causes of the catastrophe, although when a severe hailstorm battered the tents of the English army on 8 May 1642, 'our soldiers and some of our officers too (who suppose that nothing which is more than ordinary can be the product of nature), attributed this hurricane to the devilish skill of some Irish witches' – a comment which says as much about the English soldiers as it does about the Ireland they were invading.[85]

The wholesale destruction of Irish legal records in 1922 leaves us in the unfortunate position of not being able to determine how frequently or infrequently Irish individuals were accused of witchcraft at this time, or brought to court for it, but one or two cases suggest that, as one might expect, there was a rich substratum of magic in Irish society, signs of which made their way to the surface every so often. In Limerick in 1640, for example, one correspondent wrote,

> For news we have the strangest that ever was heard of – enchantments in the Lord of Castleconnell's castle 4 miles from Limerick, several sorts of noise, sometimes of drums and trumpets, sometimes of other curious music with heavenly voices, then fearful screeches, and such outcries that the neighbours near cannot sleep. Priests have ventured to be there, but have been cruelly beaten for their pains and carried away, they knew not how, some two miles and some four miles. Moreover were seen in the like manner, after they appear to the view of the neighbours, [an] infinite number of armed men on foot as well as on horseback ... One thing more by Mrs Mary Burke. [She] with twelve servants lies in the house, and never one hurt: only they must dance with them every night. They say, 'Mrs Mary, come away', telling her she must be wife to the enchanted Earl of Desmond ... Upon a manor of my lord Bishop of Limerick, Loughill, hath been seen upon the hill by most of the inhabitants abundance of armed men marching, and these seen many times; and when they come up to them, they do not appear. These things are very strange, if the clergy and gentry say true.[86]

In the same year, too, the English Catholic Countess of Antrim complained to Dublin that she had been bewitched by several poor Presbyterian women living near Dunluce Castle, but her case was dropped, as was another in July 1647 brought by the Templepatrick session against Janet Wilson and an accusation of witchcraft alleged in February 1656 by the Antril presbytery against Elizabeth Kennedy, while in 1656, Marion Fisher from Antrim had her conviction for witchcraft from the previous year overturned on the grounds that she was mentally unstable and the victim of her maleficent magic had actually died of natural causes.[87]

There may be a suggestion in these cases – but from so little evidence one cannot make anything like an argument – that the judiciary in Ireland either had far too much else to bother about at this period than complaints from kirk and presbytery sessions, or that it was not inclined to take the complaints with undue seriousness, although it is undoubtedly clear that from 1641 onwards, fear of witchcraft was beginning to infect the combatants.[88] In Scotland, however, it was not so much the effects of civil war (though these must be taken into account) as the influence of the Kirk which counted most in a sharp and notable increase in the investigation and prosecution of witches during the 1640s and 50s. There had been a major flurry of investigations and trials between 1628 and 1631, largely in the central belt and the Borders, involving more than 130 individuals. This episode can be attributed partly to the zeal of certain authorities – the bailies of Musselburgh and the Presbytery of Haddington are two examples – along with the denunciations of large numbers of people by a few accused. William Davidson, a charmer, and Alexander Hamilton, a vagabond, played an important role in this – Hamilton, indeed, denounced as many as forty-one men and women, mainly women – and did so at least in part under instruction and encouragement from Alexander Howe and James Mowat, the former a servant to Sir George Home who pulled his strings to coach confessions out of certain suspects, the latter officially Sheriff Clerk of Berwick but a man whose personal character and conduct left a great deal to be desired. A combination of religious enthusiasm supported by the secular arm and individuals motivated by fear, hatred, or a craving for personal power, thus set in train a series of events which resulted in nineteen executions, six of men, with perhaps two more of women, and one death before imprisonment. In the majority of cases the fate of the suspect or accused has not been recorded.[89]

This unhappy pursuit illustrates Ian Whyte's observation that the degree of social control exerted by kirk and presbytery sessions probably reached one of its peaks at about this time, and adds to evidence for Brian Levack's note that the clergy were the source of much of the eagerness to hunt down witches during the 1630s and 40s.[90] Undoubtedly the most powerful fillips to the success of this eagerness lay in the National Covenant of 1638, essentially a declaration of the independence of Scottish Presbyterianism from the Anglican Church, and the Solemn League and Covenant (1643), an agreement between the Scots and English to guarantee Scottish support for Parliamentarians during the English Civil War and (as far as the Scots were concerned) a reaffirmation of their own Presbyterian system of Church government, which they hoped to see extended into England and Ireland. Euphoria spread among the supporters of the Covenant and thus gave the Kirk, through its sessions and presbyteries, a greater impulse to impose Calvinist theology and discipline more strictly than before where that could be done, although one must note that large swathes of the Highlands and Islands at this time were more or less impervious to Lowland enthusiasm. As one may expect, therefore, the pressure against witches was most intense in the south of the country. Still, this does not mean that suspects were automatically handed over to the secular authorities for trial. On the contrary, the Kirk was more frequently keen to deal with such cases itself, and for the suspects concerned this was certainly preferable as, if they were not handed over, the worst they could expect was a period of humiliation in front of their friends and neighbours – bad enough in itself, of course, given the close proximity and long memories of the communities in question, but not as bad as prolonged imprisonment and possible execution, which were the legal alternatives.

The years 1643 and 1644, then, were bad for magical practitioners. The records of the Scottish Privy Council alone reveal the determination of local authorities to manage what they clearly saw as a deep-rooted and growing problem in their communities. In January 1643, justice courts were appointed to be held in Jedburgh and Dumfries to deal with a mixture of named crimes – theft, slaughter, depredation, and witchcraft among them (which shows how seriously witchcraft was taken by the council's petitioners). Further commissions to investigate witches were issued on 19 January and again on 13 June, and reports on witch trials came in a steady stream throughout both years: from Elgin, where Agnes Grant had been found guilty of murdering three men, a father and his sons 'by sorcery and witchcraft'; from Cromdale, where Katharine Burgess was to stand trial 'for witchcraft, sorcery, enchantment, and using of charms'; from Culross, where Margaret Hutton, a burgess's wife, was to stand trial likewise; and from Perth, Queensferry, South Ayrshire, and Lanarkshire.[91]

Two trials from Lanarkshire in 1644 catch the tone of the Scottish fight against Satan at this time. On the last day of December, Margaret Watson and Jean Lachlan from the parish of Carnwath were tried 'for witchcraft, consulting with the Devil, renouncing their baptism and giving themselves over to Satan and of their soul and body totally to his service, charming by the Devil's means, and who themselves are possessed by the Devil and having of familiar spirits, and for practising, using, and frequenting with the Devil and of his charms, arts and parts of witchcraft'. This heavy emphasis upon the Devil and possession by him underlines not only the distinctive view that witchcraft was a religious as well as a secular crime – a religious offence involving secular criminal acts, if you will – but also the current preoccupation with Satan as a powerful force to be reckoned with in personal lives and, through them, the life of the state. Hence we find that the preface to Margaret and Jean's dittays begins by invoking biblical condemnations of witchcraft before passing on to a résumé of the 1563 Witchcraft Act and a repetition of the two women's alleged relationship with the Devil and the dreadful example they offered thereby to the Christian community. While similar in tone, however, the individual charges against each woman were different. Margaret was accused first of meeting other witches on various occasions in the high kirk of Lanark and Carnwath parish kirk. They met at night, arriving on a variety of creatures and objects – a cat, a cockerel, a thorn branch, a bundle of straw, and an elder – and once there 'did lift corpses of deceased persons from whom [they] took bits and pieces to accomplish [their] devilish designs upon men and women, whereby [Margaret] and [the others] took several lives'. The witches also blasphemed, drank, and danced. Margaret met Satan three times. The first time, he appeared to her in the form of a black man (which may mean what it says, or that he had black hair and a dark complexion, or that he was dressed entirely in black),[92] gripped her left breast (which should have left a mark, but no mention seems to be made of this), and then had sex with her, promising in return that she should be avenged of those who had wronged her, especially one William Simpson who had allegedly stolen some land from her. Margaret appears to have benefitted from the covenant – a loaded word in Scottish texts – she made with the Devil, for she was able to use her newly acquired powers to kill some of William's horses and cows, a loss he understandably felt keenly.

These are the first five points of her dittay and it is noticeable that they concentrate heavily on the Sabbat and her physical relationship with Satan, which are described quite in accordance with current demonological theory found more commonly on the mainland of Europe.[93] Jean Lachlan's dittay is longer (twelve points). She, too, is said to have met the Devil and attended witches' meetings in the same places as Margaret, but this, the second point of her dittay, rested upon a confrontation between herself and Margaret at Carnwath in the presence of two ministers, and Margaret's added contention that 'Jean Lachlan was more guilty than herself' suggests a bad-tempered or frightened attempt to divert blame and attention. The rest of the dittay makes it clear that Jean was a charmer, one of whose remedies was an infusion of 'fox tree' (foxglove) leaves, accompanied by a spoken charm – not her own, but one well known in different versions all over Europe.

> Our Lord forth rode;
> His foal's foot slipped;
> Our Lord down lighted;
> His foal's foot righted,
> Saying, 'Flesh to flesh, blood to blood,
> And bone to bone
> In our Lord His name.'[94]

This infusion Jean had given to William Denholm, warning him that it would either cure him or kill him; and, sure enough, within six hours of drinking it he was dead. Fifteen minutes after that Jean visited Bessie Lindsay and told her William had died. Asked how this had happened, Jean said it was because of the foxglove infusion, adding that she had administered the drink with the permission and encouragement of William's sons, and that if she had not given him the drink he would have lived another six or seven years and been a nuisance. This last both the kirk session of Carnwath and the presbytery of Lanark interpreted as sinister, inferring from it that William's death was actually murder by means involving magic. This incident clearly made a deep impression on Jean's examiners, for her dittay returns to it over and over again, using it as a condemnatory preliminary to other accusations of charming. Usually, however, her charms did not involve potentially death-dealing herbs, and they were intended to cure. 'She said she could mend any that were sick, either beast or body, even though they were not present, if they believed and asked health for God's sake', although she admitted that if people had no faith in her, she could not help them. Thus she successfully charmed James Leishman's daughter, who recovered from her illness almost immediately, and restored William Somerville's wife, who had been unable to produce breast milk for her child. But when it came to doing the same for Helen Hide, the cure did not last long and Jean had to recommend that Helen go elsewhere (to a man in Dunsyre, some 6 miles from Carnwath), advice Helen followed and through which she duly found assistance.

Jean was no newcomer to this art of healing. She had, by her own admission, been practising for the past twenty years – her success with James Leishman's daughter had taken place twelve and a half years previously – but her method involved more than merely reciting a charm or giving someone a drink. According to what she told her examiners, 'When [she] charmed either beast or body that was forspoken [*bewitched*], the sickness came upon [herself] so that [she] would gape and yawn and sweat for a time.' This, if we are not to dismiss it as play-acting, seems to indicate some kind of trance, and indeed we are told that at one point in her confession of charming and witchcraft, '[her] evil spirit came to [her] and hindered [her] from making this confession, and thereby came upon [her] a horrible trembling and shaking'. The adjective *horrible* is here likely to have its Latin meaning of causing her listeners' hair to stand on end with fear and amazement, so the performance, genuine or not, was clearly dramatic. It would certainly have looked akin to demonic possession, and so it may not be surprising that both officials and others assumed Jean was in the grip of Satan and that her powers of curing or hurting were rooted in diabolic assistance.

As so often, however, interpretation of the limited amount of surviving information is not easy. In Margaret Watson's case, the trigger for complaint and prosecution may have been a quarrel between herself and William Simpson over land; in Janet's case, it may have been William Denholm's death. On the other hand, two of the witnesses against Margaret were Helen Stewart and Katharine Schaw, two penitent witches who had been executed in Lanark not long before; so Margaret may simply have been unlucky enough to have been swept up in denunciations rather than targeted for prosecution by one of her disgruntled neighbours. The same can be said of Jean, who was also named witch by Katharine Schaw (who had herself been delated of witchcraft by others arrested for the same offence), and then accused by Margaret in a confrontation before witnesses. To these possibilities one must add the name of James Douglas, the local minister at Carnwath, for it is notable that in addition to Helen and Katharine, the principal witnesses against Margaret and Jean were James and Robert Birnie, a minister in Lanark. James Douglas arrived in Carnwath in 1640 and was deposed in the late spring of 1646 for 'malignancy', which points to an unpleasant character. He clearly had some kind of animus – personal or general, we do not know – against Margaret and Jean, because when the day of their execution arrived, he should have been rebuking the Marquess and Marchioness of Douglas for their failure to take communion (they were Catholics, hence their non-attendance) or take part in family worship, but chose instead to attend the execution. For this he was sharply rebuked by the presbytery, but it is an interesting example of his priorities. Robert Birnie was a more distinguished figure, noted for his piety and learning, and appointed a member of the commissions of the General Assembly in 1645 and 1647. He had been present at the examinations of Katharine Schaw and other witches as they denounced both Margaret and Jean, and his evidence, along with that of James Douglas, was clearly important in persuading the Privy Council to grant a commission for the women's subsequent trial.[95]

The part played by clergy at this time in the drive to root out undesirable behaviour among the laity thus imparted an edge to witchcraft prosecutions, and on 1 February 1649, the Parliament passed an 'Act against consulters with devils and familiar spirits, and against witches and consulters with them'. This made it clear that the Act passed by Queen Mary was to be implemented in full, and Parliament proceeded to emphasise the point by granting commissions for the trial of witches in May, June, July, August, November, and December that same year. Some of these underlined the role played by the Devil. 'It pleaseth the Lord for His own glory and the good of His Church daily more and more to discover among us the works of darkness and the servants of that prince who rules in the children of disobedience'; 'there was one [witch] that confessed she had been of late at a meeting with the Devil, at which there were above 500 witches present. So far had that wicked enemy of mankind prevailed by these illusions of practices on these poor, wretched, miserable souls.'[96]

Among those incorporated into his satanic company was Katharine Schaw, who met him first in the likeness of a large dog which spoke to her and later had sex with her in the form of one of her neighbours' sons. Agnes Clarkson from Dirleton (1649) saw him as a black dog and then as a 'black' man who had sex with her; Agnes Hunter from Penston (1649) met him first ten years previously, when he appeared to her as a gentleman, a greyhound, a man in green clothes, and then as a 'black' man; Manie Haliburton from Direlton (1649) saw him as a physician, Isobel Brown in Edinburgh (1649) as a large man, and Margaret Dobson from Coldingham (1649) as a dog and then as a man.[97] These encounters with Satan often took place at a time of crisis in the material or spiritual life of the individual concerned, but Calvinist theology taught that humanity as a whole bears the image of Satan within it because of its original revolt against God, and is therefore corrupted and enslaved to evil. 'The Devil is called the prince of this world,' wrote Calvin, 'not because he has some kingdom distinct from God (as the Manichees imagined), but because by God's permission he exercises his tyranny in the world. Therefore, when we hear this title applied to the Devil, let us be ashamed of our miserable lot. For however proud men may be, they are the possession of the Devil until they are regenerated by the Spirit of Christ. For in the word *world* is here embraced the whole human race.'

So what was the nature of people's encounters with the Devil? We can include rationalisation of some of them as internal events expressed in terms of physicality, or as a device to shift responsibility from the self to some posited external agency. We can include explanation of some as lies to hide possible acts of adultery or fornication with a real human being, as, for example, when Isobel Watson from Glendevon in Perthshire told the presbytery of Stirling that twelve years previously she had been taken away by fairies, and that in order to recover her child whom the fairies had stolen, she promised to serve them and allowed Thomas MacCray, who was with them, to mark her upon her head and have sex with her. Or we can try saying that the suspect may have endeavoured to satisfy the suspect's examiners by providing them with what they wanted to hear. None of these, however, is applicable to every instance and all ignore to a greater or lesser extent the entirely different perspective on the preternatural and supernatural held by people of periods earlier than our own. We should remember, perhaps, that while the Devil was frequently on people's lips as a simple curse – Macbeth's cry, 'The Devil damn thee black, thou cream-faced loon!' is an obvious example – and that an apparent exclamation of ill wishing was not necessarily meant or understood as a maleficent invocation, the verbal recourse to his person indicates an acute awareness of his presence in society and his place in the forefront of contemporary psychology, just as the omnipresence of sexually based swearing in our own times signifies our Western preoccupation with coitus and its importance in our culture. Allowance, therefore, must be made for suspect witches' volunteering descriptions of their meetings with Satan, which they took to be plausible, valid, and rational, and which were perceived and received similarly by their examiners.[98]

Given the peculiar circumstances of the time, especially as experienced in the south of Scotland, we might therefore expect the year 1649 to be a high point in the search for witches. In January the king was beheaded in London, the new king was in exile, constitutional uncertainties followed – England had no fewer than four separate constitutions between 1649 and 1659 – while the Scottish Kirk, having seized power in 1648 with the help of a Cromwellian army which invaded Scotland in September to make sure that more radical voices would drown out any compromise with Charles I, then proved somewhat too radical for English tastes and precipitated a further invasion and occupation in 1650.[99] In the spirit of the new lack of toleration and renewed zeal for moral reform, the General Assembly also urged fresh measures upon the Scottish Parliament – 'against witches and consulters, against fornication, against remissions for capital crimes, against swearing, drunkenness, scolding and other profaneness, against clandestine marriages, scandalous persons, going of mills, saltpans, and fishing on the Sabbath day'[100] – and implemented them itself, all too aware of Scotland's laxity in effectively punishing sin since the heady days of the National Covenant.

But these efforts, while creating added anxiety on the one hand and mounting fervour on the other, also helped to create a situation in which charlatans could flourish and make money out of suspicion. At least ten prickers are known to have travelled about, employed by both kirk and presbytery sessions and by secular authorities to examine the bodies of suspects for marks imprinted thereon by the Devil, and to sink long pins into them when found as a test.[101] Lack of blood therefrom and the individual's insensitivity to pain were taken as strong indications (or, in the heated atmosphere of the time, as proofs) that the suspect was a witch. Prickers were especially active in the 1640s and 50s – the best-known, John Kincaid from Tranent in East Lothian, had a career spanning both decades – and operated over the border in England, if requested, as did Kincaid in spring 1649 when he went to Newcastle to examine thirty suspected witches, twenty-seven of whom were later convicted on trial. A contemporary account is worth quoting fully for the vivid picture it gives of such an incident:

> John Wheeler of London upon his oath said that in or about the years 1649 and 1650, being at Newcastle, [he] heard that the magistrates had sent two of their sergeants … into Scotland to agree with a Scotchman who pretended [*claimed*] knowledge to find out witches by pricking them with pins, to come to Newcastle where he should try such who should be brought to him, and to have twenty shillings a-piece for all he could condemn as witches, and free passage thither and back again. When the sergeants had brought the said witch-finder on horseback to town, the magistrates sent their bell-man through the town, ringing his bell and crying all people that would bring in any complaint against any woman for a witch, they should be sent for and tried by the person appointed. Thirty women were brought into the Town Hall and stripped, and

then openly had pins thrust into their bodies, and most of them was found guilty, near twenty seven of them by him, and set aside. The said reputed witch-finder acquainted Lieutenant Colonel Hobson that he knew women, whether they were witches or no, by their looks and when the said person was searching of a personable and good-like woman, the said Colonel replied and said, 'Surely this woman is none and need not be tried.' But the Scotchman said she was, for the town said she was, and therefore he would try her; and presently, in the sight of all the people laid her body naked to the waist, with her clothes over her head, by which fright and shame all her blood contracted into one part of her body; and then he ran a pin into her thigh and then suddenly let her coats fall, and then demanded whether she had nothing of his in her body, but did not bleed. But she, being amazed, replied little. Then he put his hand up her coats and pulled out the pin and set her aside as a guilty person and child of the Devil, and fell to try others, whom he made guilty. Lieutenant Colonel Hobson, perceiving the lateration of the foresaid woman, by her blood settling in her right parts, caused that woman to be brought again and her clothes pulled up to her thigh, and required the Scot to run the pin into the same place; and then it gushed out blood, and the said Scot cleared her and said she was not a child of the Devil. So soon as he had done, and received his wages, he went into Northumberland to try women there, where he got of some three pound a-piece. But Henry Ogle, Esquire, a late Member of Parliament, laid hold on him and required bond of him to answer the sessions. But he got away for Scotland, and it was conceived if he had stayed, he would have made most of the women in the North witches, for money.[102]

As always, however, we need to be careful not to make sweeping generalisations on the strength of separate pieces of evidence which may or may not be connected. It would be entirely wrong, therefore, to say that because prickers were active in certain parts of Scotland, it was their actions which precipitated witch hunts. Hunts (to use an emotive word which may not be justified in every instance of the arrest and examination of witches: two or three arrests do not a witch hunt make),[103] were started by disgruntled individuals, angry because their social relationship with the suspect had broken down, or by suspects under arrest and examination, who named others as witches who would then be arrested in their turn. Prickers were brought to administer a test and thus provide further evidence, much as paediatricians were brought in to make physical tests on alleged victims of child abuse in North America and Britain during the 1980s and 1990s.[104] But the fact that some of these prickers were rogues does not mean the other examiners, kirk ministers, and judiciary were simply fools. They were relying on the accredited expertise of the prickers, just as the police and the judiciary, not to mention the general public, were relying on the expertise of paediatricians, therapists, and social workers in the child abuse cases, and in fact once a pricker had been unmasked as a fraud, he was quickly punished. We also have to beware of how much weight we place on the notion that the use of torture caused multiple accusations of witchcraft. The nature of the source material needs to be examined carefully and taken into account, as Stuart MacDonald has illustrated in the case of a supposed sixty men and women tried before Cromwellian administrators in Edinburgh in 1652. The 'sixty' on such examination turn out to be seven, the source being a partisan English newspaper concerned to denigrate Scottish justice and its supposed barbaric treatment of those witches as worse than that employed by Catholics.[105]

The seventeenth century was thus proving to be a dangerous time for witches and charmers, but not in equal measure over the British Isles. For while parts of Scotland laboured under a Kirk-inspired purge, the north of England suffered less, in spite of incidents such as the trials of the Pendle and Newcastle witches. These incidents, while relatively large in scale, were precipitated more by certain local individuals with personal motives than by any state ideology, and the same can be said of the serious outbreak of witch pursuit in East Anglia. Wales, Ireland, and the Channel Islands were more or less free from such concerns, and while Orkney saw a small rise in the number of its witch trials in 1643 – six women and two men were tried that year, Katharine Craigie being executed after this her second trial – but thereafter the Northern Isles resumed their accustomed calm.[106] 'Calm', however, is not a word which can be applied to the middle of the century, as both Scotland and England were on the verge of finding out.

1. Witches' activities
included making a wax or
clay image of someone they
wished to hurt, and either
sticking pins in it or putting
it near a fire so that it would
melt or become red hot.

2. Witches were said to carry
out their magic by the aid
of the Devil, who appeared
to them in both human and
animal form. This composite
picture illustrates those two
possibilities in one.

3. The intermediary acting on behalf of Satan in helping the witch was an evil spirit referred to as her familiar. 'Familiar' is derived from a Latin word meaning 'close friend'. The familiar could take the shape of any living creature and imprisoned witches were often watched to see if their familiar would visit them in gaol with a view to helping them escape.

4. Among the nefarious activities attributed to witches was interfering with the weather, causing storms at sea to wreck ships or summoning hail to destroy other people's crops or vineyards.

5. Body parts taken from corpses were said to be used in witches' magic. Fingers and toes from the bodies of hanged men and women were readily available because executed criminals were often left on the gibbet where they died as a warning to onlookers and passers-by.

6. Witches were said to fly to meetings with demons and the Devil, sometimes on brooms, sometimes on people or demons in the shape of horses. These meetings were called 'synagogues' in the Middle Ages and 'Sabbats' later on. There witches worshipped the Devil, danced, ate, and received instructions for further deeds of evil.

7. At the Sabbat, the witches danced, often facing outwards from their circle, the opposite of what would happen at normal gatherings such as weddings. They moved in a distorted fashion to discordant music, but dancing for pleasure, not as part of a magical ritual.

8. In 1589–90, James VI of Scotland suffered three magical plots against his life from a large number of witches in East Lothian. They whipped up a storm to wreck his ship as he returned from Denmark with his new queen, Anna; they manufactured a poison from a toad and other material, which was meant to drip upon him as he passed through a doorway in one of his palaces; and they made a wax image to represent him and placed it near a fire so that it would melt, and the king with it.

9. Anne Bodenham was executed as a witch in 1653. She had been a servant to a 'Dr' Lambe who told fortunes, used counter-magic against witches, practised astrology, and found lost or stolen articles with the help of a crystal ball. Anne had learned her craft from him and was alleged to have worked the same range of occult practices.

10. In the mid-seventeenth century in East Anglia, Matthew Hopkins and John Stearne operated as self-appointed witch finders, identifying large numbers of people as witches and causing many to be put to death in what was England's worst incident of witch persecution.

Left: 11. Matthew Hopkins produced a pamphlet in 1647, outlining a number of his witch detection methods, partly for other people's benefit, partly to justify himself in the face of a growing tide of criticism. *Below left*: 12. In Scotland, witches and other malefactors might be chained to a wall to prevent their escaping. This device was meant to go round the neck and was known as the 'jougs'. This example comes from Duddingston church in Midlothian. *Below right*: 13. Sir Matthew Hale was an important and influential English judge who presided over the trial of Amy Duny and Rose Cullender in Bury St Edmunds in 1664. Despite disagreement among learned counsel about the quality of evidence presented to the court, both women were convicted and hanged.

A
TRYAL OF WITCHES,
AT THE ASSIZES
HELD AT
BURY ST. EDMONDS
FOR THE
COUNTY OF SUFFOLK;
ON
THE TENTH DAY OF MARCH, 1664.
BEFORE
Sir Matthew Hale, Kt.
THEN
Lord Chief Baron of His Majestie's Court of Exchequer.

REPRINTED VERBATIM
FROM THE ORIGINAL EDITION OF 1682.

WITH AN APPENDIX
BY C. CLARK, ESQ., OF GREAT TOTHAM, ESSEX.

London:
JOHN RUSSELL SMITH,
4, OLD COMPTON STREET, SOHO.
1838.

¶ The Apprehenſion and confeſſion
of three notorious Witches.
Arreigned and by Iuſtice condemned and
executed at *Chelmſ-forde*, in the Countye of
Eſſex, the *5. day of Iulye, laſt paſt.*
1 5 8 9.
¶ With the manner of their diuelliſh practices and keeping of their
ſpirits, whoſe fourmes are heerein truelye
proportioned.

IOAN PRENTS
& his Bid

JACK

Right: 14. The regular capital
punishment for witches in
England and Wales was hanging.
In Scotland they were garrotted
and their dead bodies burned. In
the Channel Islands they were
sometimes burned alive, but were
usually strangled first. Burning
alive was most unusual. Witches
in Britain were not drowned.
Below: 15. Isobel Gowdie
was a witch from Auldearn in
Moray. She was arrested in 1662
and made a series of detailed
confessions involving fairies,
shooting people with elf-arrows,
changing shape, and ploughing
the land with a plough held by
the Devil and pulled by toads.
This nineteenth-century engraving
gives an idea of the extraordinary
material contained in her accounts
to the local ministers.

16. A battle for acceptance or dismissal of belief in witches, magic, spirits, and apparitions arose in the mid-seventeenth century and was still in full flood a century later. Joseph Glanvill (1636–1680) collected material for the Royal Society in the form of anecdotes and reminiscences so that they could form the basis of a new study of these phenomena.

The Surey Inspector.

Above left: 17. In 1697, Christian Shaw, daughter of the laird of Bargarran near Paisley, accused seven people of being witches and tormenting her into prolonged fits. Five of the seven were tried, found guilty, and executed. One died in prison, the other committed suicide. It is still disputed whether Christian was a fraud or not.

Above right: 18. Richard Dugdale from Whalley in Lancashire suddenly began to fall into a series of violent fits which were taken to be caused by witchcraft. Several ministers took them as genuine, but Lord Chief Justice Holt dismissed them as fraudulent, and soon afterwards they stopped.

9

MAGICAL REMEDIES AND WITCHCRAFT UNDER ASSAULT: 1650–1668

In dark times, people usually try to lift their spirits with a little light-heartedness and a touch of humour. Lawrence Price, a writer of earnest pamphlets, amusing poems, and diverting tales, managed to do this for his audience with his diverting story, *The Witch of the Woodlands: or, The Cobbler's New Translation*, which he published in 1655. This is a pseudo-moral narrative about Robin, a cobbler from Romney Marsh, who gets three women pregnant and runs away to escape his responsibilities. Making for London across country, he loses his way and ends up in woodlands in the wilder parts of Kent. There, after a cold day spent wandering all over the place, he discovers a house and knocks at the door. An old woman answers and he begs for shelter for the night in return for sixpence. The old woman, however, has other ideas and says that as she has only one bed, she will indeed give him shelter, but he will pay her with sex. 'Robin, beholding and taking notice of her person all the body over, saw that she was long-nosed, blear-eyed, crooked-necked, wry-mouthed, crummy-shouldered, beetle-browed, thin-bellied, bow-legged, and splay-footed' (p. 7). He tries to lie his way out of the arrangement by saying he has never lain with a woman before, but a hollow voice from the top of the chimney cries out three times, 'Robin the cobbler is mine', and, in fear of the Devil, he gives in and has sex with the witch.

When he wakes the next morning, the witch (she is overtly called this in the text) is not in the house, but she soon returns with three others who bring with them familiars in the shape of a bear, a wolf, and a long-bladed knife. These three witches then dance while the 'landlady' plays a tabor and pipe, after which the familiars begin to demand food. Robin, who has been hiding under the bedclothes all this time, hears his landlady describe him as a hypocrite who pretends to be godly but seduces women and has got three of them pregnant. 'These things he thought that witches had not known,' she adds, 'but my imps spent not their time in vain. For every night I sent forth my familiar imp, Madge of Wakefield, in the likeness of a black cat, which told me of everything that Robin the cobbler did do' (p. 11); and one of the more foolish things Robin had done, apparently, was to promise a widow marriage if she would lend him money, 'and [he] wished that if he did not do according to his promise, that he might be torn in pieces with wolves and bears' (pp. 11–12). This excites the other witches and their familiars who look forward to feasting upon him. But before that happens, he is to do penance for three days by being transformed into a fox to be pursued all day by dogs, a horse to be ridden without ceasing until he is exhausted, and an owl which will be attacked and mutilated by other birds. So he undergoes these penalties and is finally restored to human shape, but in a pitiful condition. The final part of the tale sees him take up with a conman, learn his tricks, inherit the man's ill-gotten wealth, and return at last to Romney to do the right thing by his children and the women he had seduced.

That there are inconsistencies and oddities in the tale would not have troubled Price's readers, but we should perhaps note his description of the witch as old, ugly, and deformed. It is worth pointing out that this 'portrait' is fiction, not a verbal photograph. The witch's ugly exterior mirrors her ugly soul and is a metaphor, not a portrait. It was a literary convention among certain writers on witchcraft to portray witches in this fashion, and so we cannot rely on treatises or pamphlets (whose principal task was to make a moral point in the midst of their instructing or entertaining) to furnish us with any accurate notion of what real witches looked like. Reginald Scot tells us that a witch was 'old, lame, blear-eyed, pale, foul, full of wrinkles', but his witches represent the superstitious (i.e. Catholic) past and so his portrait of them is motivated, at least in part, by his confessional bias. So too William Perkins, who says that witches are aged persons of weak brain, troubled by melancholia: old, silly, and sick, remnants of the past and symbols of past folly and ignorance – the same message as Scot's, in fact. Reports of actual cases do not make these symbolic points. When a boy gave evidence against Elizabeth Wright and Alice Gooderidge in 1596, for example, he said he had met a little old woman with three warts on her face, but that, along with a description of her clothes, is the only mention made of her appearance. Clearly the facial warts are intended to help identify this old woman, not to class her as some stereotype or make a moral point. When turned into popular literature, however, the ugliness or supposed ugliness of a witch becomes a literary device. Thus, the pamphlet account of a murder accompanied with witchcraft, published in 1606, sets the scene in a public house where several men are drinking and playing cards. The 'witch' comes in and stands nearby, looking at them. One of the men, who is drunk, calls out, 'Do you hear, witch? Look t'other ways. I cannot abide a nose of that fashion, or else turn your face the wrong side outward. It may look like raw flesh for flies to blow maggots in!' Obviously this is not a description but an insult passing itself off as a joke; an insult, too, which may have been coined for the pamphlet by the anonymous writer to raise a laugh from his readers.

Now, certainly it is true that many of those arrested were middle-aged, having practised their trade very often for years or decades – although witches were not always old: John Stearne, for example, refers to Elizabeth Deekes as a silly, ignorant young woman – but neither middle-aged nor old necessarily imply deformity or ugliness, and whether the middle-aged or old were actually targeted in any outbreak of suspicion or prosecution is a complex question which needs much more investigation than it has received so far. The association made between witch and ugliness also usually assumes that the witch is female, an unwarranted assumption which merely indicates that further work needs to be done.[1]

Diversions such as Price's story may well have lightened an atmosphere made oppressive by civil wars and the imposition of a religious culture which was, for many, both alien and disagreeable. But his unusual picture of the witch as an instrument of moral rectification cannot disguise the fact that the 1650s, as we have seen already, were not an easy time for magical practitioners. Scotland and Ireland were both countries under military occupation and England was torn several ways by the demands of Cromwell's 'assembly of saints' to advance the country towards godly reformation and the Promised Land of a new Jerusalem upon earth. Civil authority was thus inherently unstable, for in spite of the unity of purpose between state and community in attempting to purge society of Satan's agents in the shape of witches and other undesirables, those very attempts carried within them the seeds of people's manifold discontents and thus via the trials gave a series of platforms on which grievances, complaints, and rebellious words and deeds could be given airing. They also provided conduits for anti-Catholicism, as Peter Elmer has pointed out. 'At all levels of society, discussion of witchcraft and the prosecution of witches accompanied a wider commitment to moral, religious, and political renewal. Society was cleansed of its Catholic past not so much by an attack on Catholics as witches, but rather through the elaboration in pamphlets, sermons, and charges to grand juries of the inherently diabolical and superstitious nature of the old faith'.[2] Elmer here is talking of late Elizabethan England, but his point remains valid for the 1650s. Conformity to the demands of the London régime was seen as a powerful desideratum, although in Ireland it remained a wish rather than becoming a reality and in Scotland internal religious fissiparousness meant that the stranglehold of the Kirk was never absolute. But on 3 September 1658 Oliver Cromwell died and a period of political volatility ensued until Charles II (who had been in exile since his Scottish coronation on 1 January 1651) was invited to return and assume his English throne. In Scotland these disturbances, affecting the Lowland psyche in particular, along with the Kirk's drive for reform, may have helped to precipitate a serious outburst of witch prosecuting between 1658 and 1662. We can see the connections in the diary of John Nicoll, an advocate and writer to the signet, who noted in March 1658,

Frequent executions against malefactors and horrid and unnatural sins. Among others, a young boy of the age of fifteen years was burnt upon the castle hill of Edinburgh for bestiality with a cow. This execution done upon the 17 of March, being Wednesday, anno 1658. It has been formerly recorded how that this land was filled with odious and crying sins, bringing down heavy judgements upon the same and on all sorts of people therein. Among many other executions at this time there was one very remarkable: two witches and a warlock imprisoned within the tolbooth of Edinburgh in February 1658. One of the witches died within the tolbooth of Edinburgh. The warlock was burnt on the castle hill, and the third, being a young woman called Anderson, newly married within three months or thereby before, was condemned to be burnt. Yet she was spared for a time, being suspect to be with child, which was the cause of the continuation and delay of her execution. Her confession was that she did marry the Devil and had committed sundry adulteries, and after she was contracted with her present husband and going to the kirk to be married, she changed her mind and would have turned back again; and confessed that at her marriage Satan appeared unto her in the kirk, standing behind the pulpit.[3]

He also noted the unseasonably cold weather which made people ill and caused the crops to fall behind in their growth; and 'what extortion was now used (it was devised by some of our own people), even at such [a] time when the land was reduced to greatest penury'. A combination of factors, then, produced moods in which consciousness of sin (one's own or other people's), discontent, physical hardship, and fear, coupled with the practical decision of the Privy Council to resume the practice of granting commissions to local authorities to investigate and try witches – something the council had not been able to do while it was suspended as a functioning body by the Cromwellian administration – enabled individuals to express certain of their personal grievances through the courts, local authorities to demonstrate to their districts and to central government their enthusiasm for moral reform, and central government to feel that its programme of creating a godly society was having some effect.

Some individuals entrusted with the task of carrying out that programme were fierce in their determination. One such was James Dalrymple, Viscount Stair, appointed one of the commissioners for the administration of justice in Scotland on 1 July 1657, and later author of *The Institutions of the Laws of Scotland* in which he noted that crimes such as witchcraft, blasphemy, and bestiality warranted the death penalty whether anyone had been harmed by them or not.[4] This animus seems to have motivated a number of ministers from the west of Scotland in particular. But investigations and trials across the central belt during the late 1650s and early 1660s show a similar determination to do battle with Satan, a determination which also betrays a fascination with and a curiosity about the workings of this devilish underground, which bear some of the hallmarks of mainland Europe's experience of and learned disquisitions upon the Satanic conspiracy against humankind.[5] But the animus was not entirely confined to the clergy, however much their sermons may have excited it. A report on the death of Janet Saers, who was executed for witchcraft in Ayr on 23 April 1658 and died protesting her innocence, adds ominously that 'the people in this country [*i.e. Ayrshire*] are more set against witchcraft than any other wickedness, and if once a person have that name and come upon an assize, it's hard to get off with less than this poor creature'.[6]

One of the features of these witchcraft trials was the looming presence of Satan over them. He appeared most often as a man dressed in black or green, but sometimes as an animal, by the waterside, or on a road, or in the fields, or in someone's house, often the bedroom; and he appeared to a woman when she was alone, or in bed with her husband, or in company. In other words, he was everywhere, not in the least threatening, and able to induce the women to become his servants with scarcely a pause for thought.[7] This near-immediate acquiescence in seduction is obviously exaggerated by the form of our surviving records, but it gives the impression, which may or may not be entirely accidental or a quirk of the narrative form, that women yielded to Satan either because they were content to do so or because they were too weak to do otherwise. Proclivity to sin or inability to resist it were seen as inherent female characteristics because of which, as Johann Wier explained, '[they] are much more subject [than men] to the Devil's deceits. He insinuates himself into their imagination, whether they are asleep or awake, and inserts therein all kinds of

shapes, cleverly stirring up the humours and the spirits in this trickery.'[8] Willingness
to be seduced, and rapid capitulation, owed much to women's petty vengefulness, too,
and at the beginning of the seventeenth century Alexander Roberts summarised this
aspect of their character.

> This sex, when it conceiveth wrath or hatred against any, is unplacable, possessed
> with unsatiable desire of revenge and transported with appetite to right (as they think)
> the wrongs offered unto them: and when their power herein answereth not their will,
> and [they] are meditating with themselves how to effect their mischievous projects
> and designs, the Devil taketh the occasion, who knoweth in what manner to content
> ulcerated minds, windeth himself into their hearts, offereth to teach them the means by
> which they may bring to pass that rancour which was nourished in their breasts, and
> offereth his help and furtherance herein.[9]

Men therefore, while forming a not negligible proportion of those accused at this
period, were nonetheless regarded as less likely to fall prey to Satan's wiles, and the
heavily patriarchal psychology of Calvinist administration at this time meant that
women were going to be seen as the principal weak spots through which the Devil
would try to undermine Scotland's godly citadel.

By 1659 Satan was ravaging East and West Lothian in particular, assisted by the
activities of John Kincaid, and by 1660–1661 he was running amok in the villages
round Edinburgh, with excursions into East Lothian, Midlothian, the Borders, Fife,
Angus, and Glasgow. But did this spiritual whirlwind make an appreciable difference
to the nature and content of witch trials during these years? In August 1661, eleven
witches, mostly from Duddingston, a village in Midlothian very near Edinburgh,
perhaps a couple of miles or so east of Arthur's Seat, were tried for witchcraft. Their
number included one man, and Janet Miller from Auldliston, a village about 10 miles
from the centre of Edinburgh, who had first been delated as a witch in 1650, and then
appeared before the kirk session until August 1659 when she confessed to various
witchcraft offences. Confined to the Edinburgh tolbooth, she was brought before
judges in 1661 along with the witches from Duddingston, presumably in an effort to
clear a judicial backlog.[10]

The charges laid against her in Kirkliston in the presence of Gilbert Hall, the
minister, two kirk elders, and the parish constable of Auldliston, began with what
had become the standard formula of breaking the Witchcraft Act, accusing her of (a)
making a pact with Satan, renouncing her baptism, and having sex with the Devil, and
(b) of using charms, sorcery, and witchcraft to harm people. Specifically, she was said
to have met the Devil in the likeness of a young man in various places and had sex
with him; to have attempted to steal a newborn child in around 1646 after entering
Janet Thomson's locked house at night; to have caused John Dundas, with whom
she was in dispute, to fall ill and remain sick for nine months; and to have killed
several of James Wilkie's animals out of spite because he had refused to let her see
one of his horses. (If he knew she had a reputation as a witch, he may well have been
nervous of her casting the evil eye on his horse and so damaging it.) Janet confessed
to these points on 15 August and next day added that in around 1656, 'after the

passing of daylight, on a moon light night, she and several others with her were near the new bridge, and the Devil with them: and that he was cloven-footed, like an ox: and that they all went from the new bridge end up Cliftonhall side of the water'. Someone's fantasy has intruded with the detail of the cloven feet, otherwise there is nothing inherently unlikely in a number of people being out of doors in the middle of the night. Sleep patterns in Mediaeval and early modern Europe were different from ours. The night fell into two parts, bridged by an hour or two of wakefulness during which people got up and fulfilled various tasks or allowed themselves leisure solo or in company both indoors and out.[11] Ten days passed and then Janet appeared before the kirk session again, this time with two local justices of the peace in attendance. Her two confessions were repeated, stress being laid on the fact that they were confessions made by her in the presence of the kirk session, but now Janet retracted them. Asked if she had been tortured before confessing, she said she had not, but that the constable, Robert Wilson, had told her that if she confessed freely, she would be allowed to go home (presumably instead of being locked up in the church steeple or in a cellar in someone's house, which were the usual places of confinement in the absence of a local gaol).

On 31 August, the justices ordered Janet's removal to Edinburgh because we find her there in the tolbooth on 6 August 1661, begging the royal justice deputies to bring her to trial quickly so that she might either be set free or at least have her expenses in prison paid by the parish (this last being customary), for ever since her arrest and imprisonment she had been wretched and likely to die of starvation. Her petition had an effect, because on 8 August the minister and elders of Kirkliston were instructed to bring their charges against her into court, and on 6 September twenty-six witnesses and twenty-five potential jurors were warned to present themselves for Janet's trial on the 10th. Why, it may be asked, had there been a delay of two years before Janet was brought to trial? The Privy Council may not have been operative again until 1661, but local justices had been active in pursuing witches during the last years of the Protectorate, so we cannot lay blame on the judiciary. Gilbert Hall, minister in Kirkliston, however, had the reputation of being a great preacher but also, in the eyes of the Edinburgh authorities, of being a great nuisance. A committed Presbyterian who had acted as a military chaplain in April 1650, he was listed with others on 8 August 1654 as one of those godly and able men considered suitable to hold a living, in spite of his having fallen out with his presbytery, withdrawing from it in 1651, indeed, to form a protesting presbytery closer to his notions of what the Gospel demanded at the time. In August 1659, as we have seen, he was hearing evidence against Janet Miller, but only a year later he was himself arrested and committed to Edinburgh Castle before being suspended from his living by the synod in May 1661 and deprived altogether by the Privy Council in October 1662.[12] Delays in justice were by no means unusual, but here we can see that Hall was in no position to bother about a witch who was out of sight and evidently out of mind. But once the directive from Edinburgh ordered him and his kirk session to prepare for a rapid trial, he and his elders clearly set about obtaining more evidence against her in case the original charges seemed a little flimsy: either that, or evidence had accumulated during the intervening period and was now sent forward along with its witnesses.

The cover of the records for Janet's trial notes that these are new accusations against her. They begin with a notice that in 1650 seven witches – five women and two men, one of whom was known as 'the Devil's general' – who had been convicted and executed that same year had delated Janet as a witch. She was also said to be 'of an evil report and fame and reputed to be a witch many years before', and, in addition to meeting the Devil in company on various occasions, having sex with him (a charge repeated from 1659), and receiving his mark on top of her shoulder (so she had obviously been searched), she had met him in her own house in Auldliston. There she removed her son to another house and had a violent argument with the Devil, who then threw her over the wall of her yard and hurt her arm. Why did she send or take her son elsewhere? So that she could have sex with the Devil undisturbed? Was this, and the subsequent violence, an episode of adultery or fornication disguised or explained away by calling her lover-assailant 'the Devil'? Before we leap to any such conclusion, let us remember that both Janet and her contemporaries knew the difference between sex with a human and sex with the Devil. Accusations of and convictions for adultery, for example, far outweigh those of sex with the Devil in the records, so the two experiences were obviously distinguishable from one another. Moreover, admitting to adultery or fornication would have been far less dangerous to Janet than confessing to sex with Satan, and as the account is more likely than not to have come from her own lips, it is difficult to see why she would have laid such a charge against herself or admitted to it unless she thought it was true. Nor should the physicality of the episode cast doubt upon her admission. There was a long, indeed an ancient tradition of physical contact of one kind or another between humans and the Devil (not to mention between human beings and other non-human entities such as fairies), which makes Janet one of a very long line of people to have undergone this very particular kind of experience, and to have undergone it in such a way that her description would not have surprised her hearers or been given and received as a potentially accurate, not a fanciful account.

There follow in the court paper six charges of malefice. First, James Dundas from Auldliston contracted 'a lingering and deadly sickness, whereof he never recovered till the said Janet was apprehended'. Secondly, James was in one of his fields, binding some corn, when Janet appeared in the shape of a cat and stared at him. He threw his bonnet at her, but his bonnet disappeared, at which he was frightened and mounted his horse to ride home. But his horse then bolted, carried him to a river or pond, and threw him in, 'to the danger of his life if he had not been rescued'. Shortly afterwards he lost eleven horses and cows to sudden sickness, even though there were no instances of disease among the local farm animals. Thirdly, Janet quarrelled with Thomas Peacock, also from Auldliston, upon which she knelt down and ritually cursed him.[13] A day or so later, one of his cows became ill and Thomas threatened to take its corpse and dump it at Janet's door if it died. So Janet sent a charmer to him and the cow recovered. (It is interesting that she either would not, or could not lift the curse herself.) Fourthly, because James Wilkie had refused to let her hire a horse from him, Janet magically killed three horses and a cow belonging to him. Fifthly, Janet confessed to David Lindsay, one of the elders of Kirkliston kirk session, that she was a witch and offered him 200 merks to look after her children. (200 merks was a considerable sum, roughly the equivalent of a year's wages for seventeen agricultural servants or cooks or baxters or brewsters. Janet, however, did not have this kind of money herself. She was relying on a local landowner, Sir Alexander Inglis of Ingliston, who had stood guarantor for her bond.)[14] Sixthly, Janet quarrelled with Mungo Steill and cursed him, and next day he contracted an illness which kept him bedridden until he died.

The charges against Janet, then, fall into four categories: (a) she was delated as a witch by other witches; (b) she had the reputation of being a witch; (c) she trafficked with the Devil and bore his mark; (d) she performed certain acts of vengeful magic against humans and animals. The complaints of malefice were almost entirely local, that is, they arose from inhabitants of her own village. The delation by confessing witches had happened nine years before Janet's examination by Kirkliston kirk session and she would almost certainly have been investigated at the time, as David Lindsay, one of Kirkliston's elders, was noted as a witness to this charge. But nothing judicial could have come of it (except, perhaps, ecclesiastical penance of some kind), as Janet had clearly been at liberty since. Her confession to being a witch seems to have taken place under pressure from David Lindsay, who had been appointed by the session to watch her during her imprisonment. (This 'watching' is often taken to mean the same as 'depriving of sleep', but the two are not identical. Watching was done partly to see whether she or he was visited by Satan or called upon a familiar spirit to effect her or his liberation. Nor was watching a process confined to witchcraft cases.) Lindsay was therefore taking an opportunity to elicit a confession, or at least more information, to help her ease her conscience and save herself from damnation – in other words, he would have seen himself as a spiritual guide and counsellor wrestling with the Devil for Janet's soul, as happened, for example, in the case of Janet Man from Stenton in March 1659. 'She could not get a heart to repent, for the Devil was locked in her heart, till once, after prayer made by the minister, she got freedom to confess her other sins, and then she thought her heart was something lifted up, and now she thanks God she hath gotten a heart to confess the sin of witchcraft, too.'[15] Thus David Lindsay: 'I was speaking to her anent the sin of witchcraft,' he recorded. 'I desired her that she would confess her sin of witchcraft and get mercy. She said she had something to say, but she could not get liberty [*permission to say it*]. The next day thereafter, she was brought to a confession by the minister and elders.' While she was being tried alongside a number of alleged witches from Duddingston, the jury listened to the evidence against her, retired, and then delivered its verdict. 'The assize, by plurality of voices ... find the [accused] Janet Miller to be clean and not guilty of the crime of sorcery and witchcraft contained in her dittay in respect of non-probation.' It was thus to a certain extent a limited verdict. Some assizers had adjudged her guilty of at least some of the charges, but the 'fylit' votes had been outnumbered by those registering 'cleansit'. Hence the reference to plurality of voices. Nor did the assize declare her innocent. They said merely that the witnesses against her had failed to prove their case. Still, under Scots law it meant she was free and could not be tried again on those same charges.

Janet's case is interesting because it hints at a disjunction between the officials of the Kirk and the laity. Aspects of Janet's confession reveal the usual petty flare-up between neighbours, which frequently resulted in charges of witchcraft if some damage, illness, or death occurred later on and could be tied to the original outburst, especially if that outburst had been accompanied by words of ill wishing or cursing. What imparts a flavour of the period is the relationship with Satan, the meeting and dancing of witches, the renunciation of baptism and giving of a mark. These aspects speak of clerical interest, perhaps informed by some knowledge of demonological theory from elsewhere, perhaps not, but an interest in the role played by Satan in corrupting a Christian soul and turning it to evil. Now, the lay jury will certainly not have discounted those features of the case – far from it. The sermons they heard every Sunday and the church discipline to which they were subjected all emphasised the Devil's power, human weakness, and the perpetual daily battle to earn or stay within the grace of God, and so there is no reason to imagine the jury members will have ignored Janet's confession of meeting Satan and having sex with him and attending witches' meetings. Without a record of the results of their deliberations, such as we have in some other cases, it is, of course, impossible to tell, and we need to make allowance for the possibility that the jury could have been divided as easily as being united on the subject. The same may be said with regard to Janet's malefices, too. For what we do know is the jury's majority decision to reject the charges against her as unproven, in spite of the confession drawn from her by the minister and elders. Fearsome the kirk session may have been in its drive for moral cleansing, but it could be resisted, even in these fraught days so potentially dangerous for witches, and these reservations about the evidence laid before them tell us that Janet's jurors were indeed divided.

Cases which had built up in 1659 and 1660, and continued to accumulate in the last days of the Protectorate and the first months of the English Restoration, burst into the Scottish courts throughout 1661 and 1662, again coming principally from the Lowlands, although one of the most intriguing, that of Isobel Gowdie in 1662, originated in Auldearn, a small town midway between Inverness and Elgin in Moray, on the border between Highland and Lowland cultures, meaning that elements of both might reveal themselves in Isobel's confessions and activities.[16] There, in the parish church of Auldearn in 1647, Isobel met Satan – 'a large, black, rough man' – at night and formally renounced her baptism, receiving from him a new name, 'Janet', and his mark. Thereafter, she had sex with him and met him again several times, meanwhile embarking on a series of actions reminiscent of other witches' activities and yet different in their detail. Using a corpse's body parts for magic, for example, was not unusual – blood, flesh, bone, fat, brains, and skin were all used in contemporary medicine, so actually the charge that witches were doing something similar was far less charged with horror or disgust than we may be inclined to think[17] – but Isobel describes how she and three others (including a man) met in the kirkyard of the church in Nairn, 'raised an unchristened child out of its grave', and then 'took the said child, with the [pared] nails of our fingers and toes, seeds of all kinds of grain and colewort leaves, mixed them altogether and chopped them very small: and did put a part thereof among the dung-heaps of [Mr] Bradley's land and thereby took away the fruits of his corn'.[18] This is more detail than we are usually given and, similarly, Isobel tells us about ploughing a field one February with a plough constructed from ram's horn and drawn by three frogs, guided by the Devil and driven by John Young, a member of a group of witches Isobel calls her 'coven', a word simply meaning 'meeting'. Such extraordinarily poetic images suggest that Isobel may have been in a dream, or trancelike state, when she saw and experienced these things; outright dismissal of her narratives as fantasy inspired by fear or torture is far too crude a reaction and is not supported by the available, highly detailed evidence – and she clearly fascinated the kirk session to whose members she described them in four separate confessions between 13 April and 27 May 1662. The minister and elders also heard about the witches leaving brooms in their beds to deceive their husbands while they were out at night, flying through the air, eating with the queen and king of the fairies – '[she] finely dressed in white linen and white and brown clothes, [he] a good-looking man with a broad face' – stealing cows' milk, spoiling ale, making magical images of people, shape changing, having attendant spirits, raising the wind, killing people with elf-arrows, and both curing and causing illness.[19]

Throughout it all, the Devil is a near-constant companion, frequently having sex with the women, which some of them enjoyed very much: 'the youngest and lustiest women will have very great pleasure in their carnal copulation with him, yea, much more than with their own husbands, and they will have an exceeding great desire of it with him, as much as he can have with them, and more, and never think shame of it. He is [more] able for us that way than any man can be (alas, that I should compare him to a man), only he was very heavy, like a malt sack [and his penis] very cold as ice.' He also assists them in their activities, sends them on errands, and provides them with the elf-arrows with which they kill their victims. Isobel's ultimate fate is unknown to us – the assumption that she must have been executed is unwarranted – but it is noteworthy that the Auldearn minister of the time, Harry Forbes, who was sure he had been the victim of witchcraft at his first arrival in the parish in 1655, and Hugh Rose, the minister from nearby Nairn, both of whom were zealous for the moral reform of their flocks, were clearly fascinated by the wealth of detail Isobel was providing and pursued her many exotic revelations to see where they led. That the Devil was so important a figure in that narrative also intrigued a local landowner, Alexander Brodie of Brodie, an ardent Presbyterian and a judge in witchcraft trials. He, too, was convinced that witchcraft had been directed against him via his family, as he recorded in his diary on 24 March 1662, lamenting on 15 June 'the prevailing of the Devil by witchcraft ... As if Thou [God] hadst given up that place where I had my residence, and the inhabitants of it, to be the Devil's property and possession.' By October that year he was almost in despair: 'I am this day under new exercises and trials. The condition of many who fear God in these lands, and their distress, straits, and temptations: the overflowing of sin, profaneness, and looseness, declining, darkness, untenderness ... The sin of witchcraft and devilry which has prevailed and cannot be gotten discovered and purged out, Satan having set up his very throne among us.'[20] As one may expect, Brodie ascribed this dire situation to God's anger at the people's conduct. In June 1655, long before Scotland's circumstances worsened and Moray in particular saw such an outbreak of witchcraft in its territory, Brodie had discussed these matters with a friend and relative. 'After supper we spoke of familiar spirits, divination, and witchcraft, and were inquiring into the reasons of the Lord's great jealousy against that sin above any other. It was a high degree of undervaluing the Lord, discontentedness, pride, curiosity, unbelief, open joining hands, conjunction, and familiarity with His enemies, preferring their counsel, communion, [and] help to His. It were no wonder that He should take this ill.' Hence it is not surprising to find that when Isobel Elder and Isobel Simson were executed at Forres, refusing to the end to acknowledge their guilt, Brodie observed, 'The Lord seems to shut the door, so that that wickedness should not be discovered or expelled out of the land. Oh! Let the Lord glorify Himself, bring down this kingdom of Satan, and deliver us.'[21]

Brodie's fervour and dejection in the face of what seemed to be overwhelming Satanic odds characterises the mood of Scottish authorities both clerical and lay towards the witchcraft problem of this time. It contrasts with that of England which was much less zealous, much less dark, and tinted with a prevailing anti-Catholicism not nearly so evident at this time in Scotland. In Ireland, the restoration of the monarchy, proclaimed in Dublin on 14 May 1660, brought an uneasy peace, but the religious freedom promised by the Declaration of Breda (1660) was soon undermined by two later Acts of Parliament which made the Protestant Book of Common Prayer compulsory (1662) and forbade all meetings in conventicles (1664), a provision aimed largely at Independents, Separatists, and Presbyterians. Despite its troubled history, however, Ireland as we have seen, appears to have escaped any large-scale pursuits of witches, so the arrest and investigation of Florence Newton from Youghal, a coastal town in County Cork, on 24 March 1661, represented a somewhat unusual event. Why did this happen? It may be that Presbyterian anxiety over the restoration of a king who seemed to be prepared to envisage a balance of toleration between Ireland's bitterly hostile religious confessions temporarily produced a quiet interlude in which people felt they could turn their attentions against witches, as William Kramer has suggested:[22] or, since there is no surviving evidence that witchcraft trials broke out elsewhere in Ireland at this time, it may simply be an accident that Florence Newton's behaviour caused reactions which came to a head in 1661 and thus occasioned her trial.[23]

Florence was tried for two offences, both committed that same year. The first involved Mary Longdon, a servant in the household of John Pyne, the town bailiff. According to Mary's evidence, she had known Florence for about three or four years and at Christmas (presumably Christmas 1660), Florence had come to the house, asking for a piece of salted beef. (Christmas was upon them, so perhaps Florence was too poor to provide beef for herself or her family). Mary refused – after all, the beef was not hers to give – and Florence went away, irritated and grumbling. But a week later, the two women ran into one another as Mary was going to the sea or a nearby stream to do some laundry. Florence knocked the dirty linen away and gave Mary a hearty kiss, saying, 'Mary, I pray thee let thee and I be friends, for I bear thee no ill will, and I pray thee do thou bear me none.' This sounds like a straightforward attempt at reconciliation, an apology, but according to Mary there were disturbing consequences. For a few days later she saw a veiled woman and a little old man dressed in silks standing by her bed. The old man removed the woman's veil, revealing her to be Florence Newton, and he himself tried to lure her into accepting his future advice in return for future prosperity, an offer Mary said she refused. Why should Mary have reacted this way to Florence's overture? The gap of a few days between their last meeting and her night-time vision suggests she had been brooding, and one of the things she may have been thinking about was that kiss; because, as three aldermen of Youghal attested at Florence's trial, not long before Florence had kissed their children and the children had died soon after. Florence's kissing Mary had been, or so anyone might take it, a gesture of reconciliation, but if Florence had a reputation as a witch – and the children's deaths under these circumstances would have given her one, even if she was not so considered before – Mary's reaction would not have been one of acceptance so much as suspicion. Such brooding may well have triggered the vision which seemed to confirm that Florence was a woman with preternatural connections. Her unveiling uncovers her identity and makes it certain. The little old man could have been a fairy – hence his short stature? – but his offer to Mary smacked more of Satan, and it is clear that this is the conclusion to which she came, since (as she told the court) she answered she would have nothing to do with him because her trust was in the Lord.

Scarcely a month after this, Mary began to have fits and behave in the way common to those possessed by demons – exhibiting unusual strength so that three or four men could not hold her, vomiting various objects such as pins and wool – while at the same time being subject to a phenomenon closely associated with poltergeists, that is, showers of small stones raining down on her whenever she moved. Some of these she and John Pyne caught, but most vanished the moment they hit the ground. During these fits, she said, she was completely unaware of what was happening to her, an extraordinary circumstance since it seems she was bodily removed to other places within the house, some of them most uncomfortable, such as a plank between two beams in the solar at the top of the house. Teleportation of individuals in poltergeist cases is less common than apportation of objects, but it is by no means unknown. Christina of Stommeln in the thirteenth century, for example, was hurled by some unseen force into furniture and dragged out of her house one night and tied to a tree; the little grandson of William Morse was flung violently about his grandfather's room in December 1679; and on 10 March 1722 Hans Dunckelmann and his wife watched in horror as their youngest child was carried up several times into the air before their eyes.[24] (In none of these cases can we rule out the possibility of deception, of course, but neither are we entitled to assume it.) These phenomena, coupled with those of possession and Mary's clear association of them with the incident of Florence's kissing her, produced the accusation, and perhaps the personal conviction, that she could see Florence sticking pins deep in her arms. So people fetched Florence and made her face Mary – standard practice in such cases – and while the two of them were in the same room, Mary's fits were worse. Respite came only after Florence had been arrested and sent to prison in Cork – again a familiar pattern – but Mary began fitting again until Florence was 'bolted', that is, made to wear a collar which was then bolted to the wall so that she could not move.[25]

Both before she went to prison and after, Florence was subjected to tests to prove whether she was a witch or not. One involved taking a roof tile to Mary's house, heating it in the fire, and dropping some of Mary's urine on it. While the urine sizzled Florence suffered severe pain; when it evaporated, Florence was well again. This is a variant upon the well-known use of urine in counter-magic and, like other aspects of counter-magic, had its parallel in curative medicine.[26] Another test, however, carried no such medical association. Edward Perry, Valentine Greatrakes, and a Mr Blackwall (likely a Church of Ireland minister), having visited Mary, sent for Florence at Greatrakes's request and sat her upon a stool. A shoemaker with a strong awl tried to stick it into the stool, but was unable to do so until his third attempt, after which he found that half an inch had broken off his blade and yet no one could see the mark of its entry into the wood. Next they gave Mary another awl, took hold of her hand, and ran at Florence with it, proposing to run her hand through. The awl bent, but did not pierce Florence's flesh, so they tried yet again, this time with a lancet. Not surprisingly, perhaps, this did succeed, making a cut an inch and a half long and a quarter of an inch deep; and yet the wound did not bleed. So Mr Blackwell cut her other hand and this time both hands bled.

These experiments appear to be variations upon two separate themes. One is that if a witch shape-changes and is wounded, the wound will show upon her when she resumes her human form. The other is that pricking her 'mark' will test whether the mark bleeds or not, the latter being an indication that she or he is a witch. The use of the awl and lancet, however, was unusual and was tried at the behest of Valentine Greatrakes, who said he had read about them. From this one might think Greatrakes was a pricker along the lines of Kincaid in Scotland or Hopkins in England. In fact he was a landowner, justice of the peace, and Clerk of the Peace for County Cork, and a man who had been strongly attached to the Cromwellian régime in Ireland – an ostensibly respectable figure, then, who was relying on literary precedent to allow him to test Florence's character. Soon after Florence's trial, though, Greatrakes would become a faith healer and achieve considerable fame in both Ireland and England for his cures (but not universal credit in them). That time, however, had not come in 1661. Indeed, anything which might smack of personal eccentricity may well have been far from his mind, for he had only just recovered his lands and offices after being deprived of them at King Charles's English restoration and would be more likely to want to reassure his patron, the Earl of Orrery, and through him the English government that he could be trusted to do his duty and fulfil his civic obligations.[27]

Was Florence a Catholic? There is every chance she was, and the fact that she had annoyed someone as important as the Bailiff of Youghal by magically attacking his servant may have combined with her religion to provide the authorities concerned with a chance to impress Dublin and London.[28] Her removal to Cork for imprisonment and trial would have shifted her to a town from which its Catholic Irish inhabitants had been expelled in 1644 and on a number of occasions afterwards, while the Protestants who had replaced them remained in situ even after 1660. The town would therefore have been an uncomfortable place for any Catholic witch. While she was in prison, Florence had been visited by Nicholas Stout who tried her with another test. Could she recite the Lord's Prayer? This was a common enough test in England and suspected witches tended to stumble or halt at certain phrases such as 'Forgive us our trespasses' or 'Lead us not into temptation'. Florence did her best but kept missing the word 'trespasses' when she was asked to recite the prayer in court, and explained her inability to get it right by saying she was old and had a bad memory. She may have been right, of course, but if she were a Catholic she would have been more familiar with the prayer in Latin or Gaelic. Hence the slightly unusual English word 'trespasses' might fail to lodge with her, especially if she was frightened and her spirit had been broken by the treatment she had received already.

Among the frights to which she had been subjected was the threat of being swum. Upon her arrest Richard Myers, the mayor of Youghal, had sent for her and during his examination of her, Florence had accused two other women, Mrs Halfpenny and Mrs Dodd, of causing Mary's fits; whereupon Myers had them arrested too and brought all three to a suitable stretch of water into which they could be thrown, hands and feet tied in a particular manner, their body attached to ropes held by men on the banks, to see whether the water accepted or rejected them. Had it rejected them by allowing them to float, it would have provided a sign of their guilt. But the swimming did not take place because Florence, clearly terrified, confessed to casting the evil eye on Mary. Mary then exonerated Mrs Halfpenny and Mrs Dodd, and so Florence was left to be taken to gaol in Cork. There she was visited by Nicholas Pyne (an old associate of Greatrakes and also a relation of John Pyne) and by several other men, and repeated her affirmation that she had not bewitched Mary but 'overlooked' her, and now begged her forgiveness for the wrong she had done. She added, however, that she herself could not undo the harm, but that others such as Mrs Halfpenny and Mrs Dodd had the ability to do so, unless one of them had done the harm in the first place. Was Florence saying the first thing that came into her head? If all this had taken place on the same day, as Glanvill's text suggests, Florence may well have been sufficiently frightened and disorientated to blurt out apparently disparate remarks; but none of this necessarily means she was not telling the truth. Her distinction between bewitching and overlooking is significant, in as much as the one was as bad as the other in the eyes of the law, so Florence had nothing to gain by insisting upon the difference. Her reiteration of the names of Mrs Halfpenny and Mrs Dodd, too, was not a renewal of her former accusation, but an avowal that there were workers of counter-magic in Youghal, among whom were Mrs Halfpenny and Mrs Dodd.

There is nothing inherently unlikely in any of this, nor in an incident which followed soon after. Towards evening, the prison door shook and a loud noise, 'as if somebody with bolts and chains had been running up and down the room', made Florence get to her feet. She called out, 'What are you doing here at this time of night?' but when questioned about it said she had no idea what had caused the noise or if she had said anything at all. So far, so plausible. It is not unknown, for example, for earth tremors to be felt in Cork – 1755 and 1761 provide historical examples – and if Florence had been asleep or dozing, she may well have been startled into saying something incoherent but apparently meaningful.[29] Next day, however (and under what pressure, if any, we do not know), she said it was a spirit, her familiar in the shape of a greyhound. This is very much an English rather than an Irish idea, so her confession sounds rather like acquiescence in a suggestion put to her by someone else. But however much these tests and admissions may have contributed to the prosecution's case, two incidents more than any others would surely have loomed large at Florence's trial. One was her behaviour and that of Mary during the trial itself. Mary had just finished giving her evidence, closing with the remark that she had never had fits before Florence kissed her and that therefore it was the kiss which had caused them (a conviction strengthened, she said, because Nicholas Payne and others had told her Florence had confessed as much), when Florence raised her manacled hands and shook them at Mary, saying, 'Now she is down!' Whereupon Mary had a violent fit and had to be carried out of the court into a nearby house where she vomited pins, pieces of straw, and wool. Florence meanwhile sat alone in her place, pinching her hands and arms.

How much of this is true? The fit and vomiting, certainly, even if one is going to suggest, without evidence, that they may have been faked. That Florence lifted her hands was observed by the court. Her words were sworn to by two men, Roger Moor and Thomas Harrison. Did she actually say them? She was said to have uttered others a quarter of an hour later when a messenger came from the house to report that Mary was feeling better. 'She's not well yet,' many heard Florence say angrily, although Florence denied saying anything and explained anything she may have said as a result of her old age, fear, and suffering. The whole incident was most dramatic. Those present were certainly inclined to interpret Florence's alleged words and actions as proof of malefice, perhaps not unsurprising if one compares the behaviour of Isabel Thompson from Northumberland. She lifted up her hands to Mark Humble's back as she passed him in the street, and for years afterwards, he said, he was ill with violent fits.[30] Whether she did say anything is difficult to tell. It is quite possible she did, either if she suspected Mary of faking ('Now she's down' and 'She's not well yet' can be interpreted as sarcastic comments on a histrionic performance) or if she believed that she was genuinely causing these reactions. It shows how very difficult it is for us now to interpret the records, since so many indicators – tones of voice, relationships between individuals, the personal, political, or religious motives of those involved, their states of health, and so forth – are missing and cannot usually be supplied from other sources.

The second incident took place in April 1661. Florence had been in prison for about a month when she received a visit one night from David Jones and Francis Beesley. They went because rumours were flying about that Florence 'had several familiars resorting to her in sundry shapes', and they were curious to see 'whether [they] could observe any cats or other creatures resort to her through the grate, as it was suspected they did'. This was the principal purpose of witches' being 'watched' – not to deprive them of sleep, as is often said, but to make sure they could not escape with the help of their familiars, or to indulge a curiosity about a witch's behaviour when she was in confinement. Expectation of remarkable phenomena could have been high. Anne Foster, for example, committed to prison in 1674, was chained to a post at one point, but then released '[so] that the Devil might come to suck her, the which he usually did, coming constantly about the dead time of the night, in the likeness of a rat, which at his coming made a most lamentable and hideous noise ... which caused many to come and see her during her abode there, and several hath been with her when the Devil hath been coming to her, but could see nothing but things like rats'. Still, the possibility of greater wonders was always there.[31] The two men stood outwith the door of her cell and began to talk to her. David said he had been told she could not say the Lord's Prayer. Florence answered that she could but was unable to do so because she was old, whereupon David tried to teach her, without immediate success. He and

Francis stepped out of earshot and began to talk about this when Florence called them back: 'David, David, come hither. I can say the Lord's Prayer now.' Against his friend's advice, David went back to the door and listened while Florence repeated the prayer, stumbling as usual upon 'Forgive us our trespasses'. So David tried to teach her again, and in thanks for his apparent kindness Florence asked to kiss his hand. He put it through the grating and Florence kissed it. At about dawn the two men left the prison, and not long afterwards David fell ill, so ill, indeed, that he was clearly delirious and when Francis went to visit him, blamed Florence for his affliction. 'Don't you see how the old hag pulls me? Well, I lay my death on her. She has bewitched me!' A fortnight later he was dead.

This was the evidence Francis gave the court. The words he attributed to David sound rather like his own interpretation of the reason for his friend's illness, but they were supported by an earlier conversation David had had with his wife on his return from the prison.

'Where do you think I've been all night?' he asked her.

'I don't know,' she said.

'Frank Beesley and I have standing sentinel over the witch all night.'

'What's the problem with that?'

'Problem? I have the feeling it's never going to do me the slightest good. She kissed my hand and I have a great pain in that arm. I'm convinced she's bewitched me, if ever she bewitched anyone.'

To which his wife replied, 'The Lord forbid!'

Now, we can go in for rationalisation and say that prisons in those days were such unhealthy places, it would not be surprising if during his visit David caught a disease which turned out to be fatal. But this is neither helpful nor, indeed, explanatory since conjecture based on scarcely anything contributes nothing to our understanding of the episode. What matters is the impact of David's health on the court at Florence's trial. She may well have kissed his hand out of nothing more than gratitude for what she perceived, and what may have been offered, as an act of kindness, although it is true she did not attempt to kiss Nicholas Stout, who had also endeavoured to teach her to say the Lord's Prayer. (Perhaps the two men had adopted different tones of voice with her.) But that kiss, following the kiss which was supposed to have bewitched Mary Longdon and the three kisses which had allegedly killed three aldermen's children in Youghal, was unwisely given at best, unless, of course, we accept with the court that it was given in malice by someone who believed she was a witch and knew, or thought she knew, exactly what she was doing.

The case was prosecuted by the Attorney General and heard before Sir William Aston, an Englishman recently appointed to the King's Bench, whose notes, if we trust Glanvill, form the basis of Glanvill's record of the trial. The verdict and therefore sentence remain unknown, a great pity because we should like to known how the court viewed two intriguing aspects of the case: the showers of stones which attended the start of Mary's fits and her vomiting of objects in the manner of someone demonically possessed. The combination of fitting and lithobolia is unusual, though not unique – in 1704 a teenage boy was subject to fits caused by visions of spirits, and these were accompanied by showers of stones, and in 1914 an eleven year-old boy suffered a fit also accompanied by stone-throwing and violent displacement of various objects[32] – and if the theory that individual frustration arising from a particularly strong degree of stress is capable of creating those peculiar circumstances in which poltergeist activity may arise, then it is easy to see why Mary Longdon (whose age we do not know) could have been at the centre of those unusual phenomena. Her vomiting and reportedly unnatural strength are typical of the demoniac, and connection was often made between possession and witchcraft.[33] So it would not be surprising to find that Mary's fits and their physical crises may have been taken as strong proofs that Florence had bewitched her and was continuing to do so in the courtroom.

Even so, one cannot help wondering about this. The Irish authorities trying Florence and the Kirk in Scotland shared a Calvinist culture, for example, and they might be expected to exchange views and reading matter with a degree of ease. But in fact Scotland did not really connect the two phenomena before the notorious Bargarran case of 1697, and while England can certainly provide examples from both the sixteenth and the seventeenth century, there is no good reason to think that these influenced the conception of witchcraft in Ireland or Florence Newton's case in particular.[34] So this episode, which seems to have been uncommon enough to draw some of the most eminent lawyers in Ireland to conduct it, possesses features which make it distinctive, distinctive enough perhaps to have attracted the attentions and curiosity of those lawyers. Did Mary's fits convince them she was really bewitched or did Sir William Aston find himself sceptical? Several cases of possession-cum-bewitchment in England had been uncovered as simple fraud. On the other hand, the combined evidence of a number of important members of Youghal's civic establishment may have been hard to resist. Sir William is described as a man of ability and integrity, so he is unlikely to have been swayed by hysteria or exaggeration; but he was also a committed royalist and so aware of the required official attitude towards the need for peace and tranquillity in a town where the Protestant élite was very much a minority.[35] The atmosphere in Youghal at the time was undoubtedly febrile, and so Florence's proven guilt and execution – if that is what happened – would have served to make the godly minority feel better for having eradicated a source of evil from their midst and demonstrated to important figures such as the Earl of Orrery and Sir William Aston himself, and through them even more important figures in London, that rebellion against authority (in this case the authority of God) would not be tolerated.[36]

But just as Ireland appears to have been largely free from witchcraft trials during the 1650s and 60s, so too does Wales. We meet one or two instances of formal cursing, men falling briefly into a trance after meeting a witch, and consultations for a lost article, a love charm, or an abortifacient. Apart from these, however, Wales seems to have accepted the continued practice of divination and magic by its people without feeling the need to bring them before a court of law. Adherents to radical Protestant confessions, it is true, aroused suspicion. People in Montgomeryshire crossed themselves at the sight of a Quaker and in 1668, after one Hugh Lloyd died after losing his wits and blaming Quakers for it, over thirty of them were arrested and gaoled. But this was because they had been caught attending an unlawful conventicle rather than because of any witchcraft, and no one actually seems to have been prosecuted for witchcraft in connection with Hugh's death.[37] The same kind of willingness, within limits, to live and let live anent magical workers can also be seen on the Isle of Man. The last executions for witchcraft there had taken place in 1617, but thereafter, although charming and divination continued more or less unabated – we know of presentments for these offences in 1664, 1665, 1706, and 1713, for example[38] – what seems to have concerned Manx people more was being slandered as a witch or a charmer. In 1658, Jane Caesar, wife of the island's Attorney General, was alleged by one of her servants to have put certain herbs in water to protect her cattle and ensure them good luck and increase, and to have sent servants to stick twigs of rue into her cattle and sheep on the eve of May (presumably again for protection, since rue had long been used as an apotropaic). She was, in addition, said to have asked a servant to get hold of the parings from a cow's hooves, and to have shaken oats over her sheep on the eve of May. A jury of six men heard the case and declared that Jane had been slandered, adding, however, that they were ignorant of the law touching this kind of accusation. It sounds like a proviso – Jane was innocent, as far as they could judge from what they had heard. (It reminds one of the 'not proven' verdict in Jane Miller's case.) The decision was referred to the governor of the island who, on 10 September 1659, made an interesting order. Jane was innocent *as charged during the trial*, but she must renounce her witchcraft in church – that is, in public – the following Sunday, and warn others not to practise magic. So she was a magical practitioner (like so many others on the island), but officially at least had not done those things her servants had said she had done.[39]

The same judgement was made a few years later in 1666 when Elizabeth Kewin was accused of witchcraft by some of her neighbours who complained of her to the local kirk session.[40] Elizabeth had been in prison before at some time between 1651 and 1660 along with another suspect witch, but as the record for that occasion is missing, we do not know whether she was tried and released or tried and served a sentence. In June 1666, however, she was in trouble again, although this time she was released on bail. The charges against her were mixed: she prevented milk from churning into butter and then reversed the magic; she had, by her mere presence, a dire effect upon one man's crops and cattle; a woman could not rear a calf or make butter or cheese during a twelve-year period while Elizabeth visited her house; and several witnesses gave evidence that she used to shape-change into a hare. On the other hand, people also used her to put wrong things right or cure someone who was ailing, a process which might prove expensive, for on one occasion, we are told, at her direction, a calf was burned in one man's limekiln. The wording of the text implies that this was some kind of sacrifice and one is reminded of Isabella Billington's sacrifice of a calf and a cockerel in Yorkshire in 1649. (Animal sacrifices were still being made in the Highlands and inner isles of Scotland, and in Ireland, at the end of the century, so Elizabeth's remedy was by no means peculiar to her.)[41] Popular animus, however, ran high against her, for she was scratched more than once.

When [John Norris's wife] could not make butter nor cheese, and suspected the said Elizabeth to have done hurt to her, she went one day purposely to the Priory to draw blood upon the said Elizabeth, and having met her in the entry of the said Priory, fell upon her and scratted her nose and face, and drew blood. Then the said Elizabeth asked the said Katharine and said, 'What do you want or would have?' Who answered, 'I would have my own restored me again.' And the said Elizabeth replied and wiped the blood off her face and nose and threw it to her and said, 'If that do thee good, take it, and much may it do thee.'

Elizabeth was tried on 25 October and the six-man jury came to its interesting conclusion. 'In as much as we have not had any proof that she is positively a witch, therefore we do clear her and say (being questioned) that she is not guilty of death.' Once again, therefore, a jury tells a court that the prosecution witnesses have failed to be convincing. Nevertheless, 'the proofs already taken by us, taken into consideration of the spiritual officers, we leave her to be punished at their discretion'. In other words, yes, she is a witch, but the evidence offered to us at this trial is lacking. The ecclesiastical officers took the point and sentenced her to do penance in the usual Calvinist fashion for three Sundays in three separate churches: that is, she had to wear a placard confessing her practice of charming and witchcraft, and beg the congregation's pardon upon her knees. In addition, however, she had to enter into bonds of £3, 'not to use hereafter the said unlawful means, either in her own house by enticing and drawing ignorant people thither, or going abroad to any other houses near or far off to that intent, or sending of her charms abroad privately or openly'. Failure to observe these terms would result in imprisonment.

If we now turn to the Channel Islands, we see that the number of trials for witchcraft during this same period is not great. On Jersey, for example, Jeanne Machon was banished in 1650 and Jean Le Riche died in prison. A note in his parish church register reads: '25 November 1656. Jean Le Riche, son of Edouard, was buried, having been [*illegible*] before his time. He was committed to prison and indicted as a criminal on a charge of witchcraft by the constable and officers of the parish. The officers of the court had caused many witnesses from different parishes to be called, who accused him of this despicable crime, and he was committed to the Castle as a criminal, till the next meeting of the Cour de Cattel. He was found dead in prison.' In January 1660, Marie Jean was executed and in October 1661, Sara Lucette was banished.[42] This trickle of prosecutions may represent the slow retreat before the onset of Anglicanism which gradually replaced the Calvinism of the largest islands – Sark remained obstinate – and thus relieved the kind of pressure seen where attempts at Presbyterian religious settlement were most fierce and most successful. French influence, too, such as it may have been once France's confessional wars had run their course and diminished the flow of Huguenot refugees to the islands, would not have favoured intensive prosecution. Automatic appeals from lower French courts to the parlements, and the growing scepticism of many French lawyers, doctors, and clergy saw a notable diminution in the number of trials for witchcraft and a dramatic fall in the number of executions.[43] So exemplars and pressures from both sides of the Channel may thus have played some part in tranquillising the islanders' hostility towards the magical practitioners in their midst.

In England, the situation was somewhat more complicated. The Commonwealth had seen large numbers of executions for witchcraft, although scepticism along the lines of Reginald Scot and Johann Wier's contentions that witches were merely old and foolish, or sick, or both, could be found even among small-time Parliamentary sympathisers such as Francis Osborne, who wrote to his son in 1656,

> Be not easily drawn to lay foul imputation of witchcraft upon any, much less to assist at their condemnation, too common among us. For who is sufficient for these things, since we are as ignorant in the benevolences as malignities of nature? Madmen, presenting in their melancholy ecstasies as prodigious confessions and gestures [such things] as are objected to [in] these no less infatuated people. And if this humour hath so far prevailed with some, as to take themselves for urinals, wolves, and what not, can it seem impossible for those invaded by all the causes of discontent to imagine themselves authors of what they never did? Most of these strange miracles they suppose, being hatched by the heat of imagination, or snatched out of the huge mass of contingences, such a multitude of individuals as the world produceth cannot choose but stumble upon; neither may it be admitted, with due reverence to the divine nature, that prophecy should cease and witches so abound, as seems by their frequent executions, which makes me think the strongest fascination [*exercise of the evil eye*] is encircled within the ignorance of the judges, malice of the witnesses, or stupidity of the poor parties accused.[44]

The years following King Charles's restoration to his English throne, however, did indeed see prosecutions for witchcraft continue, but they also fell in number considerably in comparison with the 1640s and 1650s.[45] The Devil was still cited as the major instrument in a person's becoming a witch, but noticeably at the beginning rather than the end of the decade. The aged Julian Cox from Somerset protested in 1663 that she had often been tempted but had never consented, although this did not prevent her being found guilty of witchcraft and executed for it. Alice Huson in Yorkshire confessed on 28 April 1664 that three years earlier the Devil had appeared to her 'like a black man on a horse, with cloven feet', and that he was standing beside her even as she was being questioned by the local minister, and supplying her with answers; and in 1665 Elizabeth Style in Somerset told a committee of clergymen headed by a JP that ten years earlier the Devil had come to her first in the shape of a handsome man with whom she had signed a twelve-year contract, and then used to appear as a dog or a cat or a moth, and so suck her blood.[46] In return for this feeding – and once again I think we need to place this vampirism in the medical context of the day, which had long permitted and encouraged the use of human blood as a cleansing and rejuvenating agent[47] – he assisted her to torment Elizabeth Hill by thrusting thorns into her flesh and to kill several of Walter Thick's farm animals. Only a month before her arrest and examination, said Elizabeth, she and three others had met a man dressed in black, accompanied by other people, at nine o'clock at night on a nearby common. There they performed image magic to harm Elizabeth Hill and then ate, drank, and danced. This was the form taken by several other such meetings, and before going to them the witches would smear a strong-smelling oil on their foreheads and wrists and so be carried through the air to their destination.[48] Elizabeth clearly identified the man in black as the Devil, and it may be thought that the picture of those meetings owes something to learned versions of the Sabbat. But, as Jonathan Barry has pointed out, by the mid-seventeenth century elements of those versions are likely to have been so well known that Elizabeth (and the other women accused along with her) could have proffered them without the need for any prompting or suggestion from her examiners.[49]

The offences with which women and men were charged during the 1660s and 70s are, as one might expect, very similar to those of earlier periods, but with variations, as in the development of a sonata or symphony. 'Incantation' was quite a common accusation. We find trials based on that offence in Worcestershire, Herefordshire, Gloucestershire, and Oxfordshire: fourteen altogether, thirteen of which ended in acquittal, the other being dismissed.[50] The 1670s, however, saw only one case, that of Maria Baguley, who was tried on 26 April 1675, found guilty, and executed. She had killed Robert Hall, who died after a short illness, and it looks as though she had cast the evil eye on him as well as employing incantation, since the record includes *per fascinationem* as well as *per incantationem*.[51] Death and illness caused by magic may have remained a common source of complaint, as did laming, but accusations of causing people to fit and vomit up objects such as pins actually seemed to be on the increase. In early March 1665, for example, Rose Cullender and Amy Duny, two widows from Lowestoft, were arrested and searched because it was said in thirteen separate articles of their indictments that they had bewitched seven children between them.[52] Samuel Pacy, who initiated the prosecution, testified to the court that the previous October Amy Duny had come to his house to buy herring, but was refused. 'Immediately,' his daughter Deborah, who had suddenly become lame a week earlier, '[was] taken with the most violent fits, shrieking in a most terrible manner, like unto a whelp.' Samuel then had Amy put in the stocks, whereupon two days later neither of his daughters could breathe properly, began to have fits and vomit up pins, and were unable to pronounce the words 'Jesus' or 'Christ'. Their aunt, called to give evidence, at first thought the children were feigning illness but, after removing every pin from their clothing, noted that they still managed to vomit thirty pins between them. Edward Durent testified that his daughter Anne also vomited pins and had visions of Rose Cullender, while Diana Bocking gave similar evidence anent her daughter Jane, who had also been afflicted in February. Mary Chandler, one of six women who had searched Rose and Amy and discovered 'teats' on Rose's body, told the court that the morning after the search her own daughter, aged eighteen, started vomiting pins, seeing Rose accompanied by a large dog, and losing her sight and speech from time to time. Other witnesses then told the court about past instances which suggested that Rose and Amy had been the cause of various peculiar incidents, such as the deaths of horses, cattle, and pigs, the fall of a chimney, and the loss of a firkin of fish which fell into the sea before it could be landed.

The court was in two minds about the evidence relating to the children's fits. There was melodrama in the room as Susan Chandler fell into a fit and started shrieking, 'Burn her, burn her!' and when Elizabeth Pacy, supposedly unable to see or speak, was brought to Amy, she suddenly jumped up and scratched her till she bled. Further tests carried out in court showed the children in the midst of their fits shrieking when Rose touched them, and opening their hands, which until then had remained stubbornly closed. But a variation on the test produced similar shrieking and opening while they were touched by someone else. Hence, argument ensued among the lawyers about whether the children were genuinely bewitched or not. Medical evidence was sought from Thomas Browne (author of *The Religion of a Doctor*), who was considered to be a person eminently qualified to give an expert opinion.

> In Denmark, [he said], there had been lately a great discovery of witches who used the very same way of afflicting persons, by conveying pins into them, and crooked, as these pins were, with needles and nails. The Devil in such cases did work upon the bodies of men and women, upon a natural foundation, that is, to stir up and excite the humours superabounding in their bodies to a great excess, whereby he did in an extraordinary manner afflict them with such distempers as their bodies were most subject to, as particularly appeared in these children. [I] conceive, [he said], that these swooning fits are natural and nothing else but that they call the 'mother', but only heightened to a great excess by the subtlety of the Devil co-operating wth the malice of these which we term witches, at whose instance he doth these villainies.[53]

This 'on the one hand, but on the other' approach to the problem was mirrored, to some extent, in the judge's summing up. Sir Matthew Hale, a judge of some experience on the Home and Norfolk Circuits and a man of intense religious conviction, told the jury that he would not repeat the evidence because he might thereby do an injustice to one side or the other, and that only two questions were pertinent: were the children bewitched, and had the two accused bewitched them? He then went on to observe that scripture, the laws of nations, and English law had no doubt that witches did exist, before directing the jurors 'to observe their evidence, [and praying] the great God of Heaven to direct their hearts in the weighty thing they had in hand. For to condemn the innocent and to let the guilty go free were both an abomination to the Lord.'[54] Interpretation of these directions, for which we are dependent on a pamphlet published in 1682, is not altogether easy and will clearly be influenced by one's assessment of Hale himself. Gilbert Geis, for example, regards him as a misogynist and a 'pedant with power' who had pre-trial contact with the principal complainant and was swayed not only by his own Puritan beliefs, but also by a local contest for fishing rights in which victory in a legal case would send out political signals. Moreover, Hale and Serjeant Keeling, who carried out the experiments of having the children touched first by the accused and then by someone else, were competitors in the race for legal advancement, so one might infer that if Keeling said one thing, Hale would say the opposite.[55]

Nevertheless, we are not entitled to assume prejudice, wrong-headedness, and (in effect) misdirection of the jury on Hale's part any more than we may assume his impartiality. The jury, like others in the courtroom, had opinions about the existence of witches and the validity or otherwise of their powers. English law assumed both existence and validity and Hale was pointing this out to the jurors, as he was bound to do. The experiments carried out in court caused confusion in the audience's minds and therefore (one may presume) also in those of the jurors, for those who conducted the experiments 'returned, openly protesting that they did believe the whole transaction of this business was mere imposture, [and so] this put the court and all persons into a stand' [*i.e. brought proceedings to a halt*]. The impasse was addressed by Samuel Pacy, who said that his daughter might believe the witch had touched her, even though she had not, because the children were aware of what was going on round them, even though they were in the midst of one of their fits. This attempt at explanation served merely to generate further argument. Some people said the experiments demonstrated that the fits, and therefore presumably the children's accusations, were fraudulent. Others argued that they confirmed the children were genuinely bewitched, and added further arguments that this kind of fit could not be manufactured, especially by children; that those concerned could not or would not have concocted a conspiracy; and that there was no benefit – the legal point *cui bono* – to anyone in accusing two poor old women who would be executed if found guilty.[56] These disagreements expressed in open court, as well as the testimonies of the various witnesses, comprised the evidence which Hale directed the jury to consider. In effect there were two somewhat different groups of evidence for them to weigh: the accusations of bewitchment of a number of children (including one eighteen-year-old), and charges of various acts of malefice against other individuals and their property. The guilty verdict on thirteen out of the fourteen points of indictment shows that the jurors had not been swayed by the experiments. Whether it can be said they were 'judicially elbowed' in this direction by Hale is open to debate. Those who dislike or disapprove of him will blame him for prejudicial steering; those do not will allow him more integrity.[57]

One of the children involved, Anne Durrent, claimed that while she was in a fit, she saw Rose Cullender. Such sights were by no means uncommon. The husband of Dorothy Hearon from Newcastle testified in 1664 that, after reproving Jane Simpson for greed, Dorothy fell sick and suffered from fits.

> On Saturday last, about three of the clock in the morning, she took a most sad fit, crying out to [Anne] who was in bed with her that one Isabel Acheson and Jane Simpson did torment her, and were about the bed to carry her away. And he had much to do to hold and keep her in bed. And she did cry, 'Do you not see them? Look where they both stand.' And the said Dorothy putting aside the curtain, he did clearly see Isabel Acheson standing at the bed side, in her own shape, clothed with a green waistcoat. And he, calling upon the Lord to be present with him, the said Isabel did vanish.[58]

In July 1687, Nathaniel Storch gave evidence that after he had smoked some tobacco given to him by Deanes Grimmerton, he became ill and saw her apparition clothed in green, red, and white and a long-crowned hat, perched upon the upper beam of his bedroom window. An eighteen-year-old woman also testified to having suffered fits for the past three years, during which brass pins were removed from various parts of her body. She said she could see Deanes and that Deanes was holding her down and lying on top of her on the bed – a complaint which sounds like 'the Old Hag'. Deanes, however, was tried only for bewitching Nathaniel – an interesting case of a grand jury's examining the evidence presented to it before the case was allowed to proceed to trial, and then issuing an *ignoramus* ('we do not know') on the eighteen-year-old's complaint, which meant that Deanes would not be tried on that charge.[59] The court, having heard the evidence relating to Nathaniel's grievance, then found Deanes not guilty and released her from gaol.[60] But sometimes things did not go well for anyone. In October 1665, Oliver Heywood, a Nonconformist minister, was holding a fast in Wakefield for Nathan Dodgson, who was suffering fits attributed to witchcraft and during which he saw the apparition of a woman. This was enough for a local witch to be identified as the cause of his suffering, whereupon a lynch mob took matters into its own hands and killed her.[61]

Murder was not the only remedy sought by afflicted people and their friends, of course, for there were several other sources of aid available. One could turn to counter-magic, as did a gardener's daughter from a village in Wiltshire in around 1658. In her case, she went to the woman she thought had bewitched her, a Mrs Orchard, whom she had had arrested and committed to gaol in Salisbury. The reason was that, having failed to provide Mrs Orchard with bread and cheese fast enough for Mrs Orchard's liking, she washed her hands and immediately found her fingers distorted and racked with severe pain. The local landowner then had Mrs Orchard fetched to the gardener's house where the young woman – she was aged seventeen or eighteen – accused her of witchcraft and the bystanders threatened her with hanging.

> But Orchard stood stoutly in it, that she was not bewitched but that she had washed her hands in unwholesome water, and that wholesome water would cure her. Whereupon some of the same sort of water which she washed in before was brought, which [Mrs] Orchard desiring to see, that she might judge whether it was wholesome or not, she put one of her fingers into it, and carried her finger so that she made three circles in it contrary to the course of the sun, and then pronounced it wholesome water and bid the maiden dip her hands in it: which the maiden doing, her fingers recovered their due posture and the extreme pains ceased. But, the tone of the nerves being for the present lost, her fingers had no strength in them at the time of the trial and were not without some pain.[62]

Thomas Stretten, a wheelwright from Ware in Hertfordshire, used counter-magic himself in around 1669 when his daughter (aged twenty) started having peculiar fits as the result of the malice of a local magician. Pins, hair, and flames proceeded from her mouth and she became troubled by hordes of toads and mice. But when the foam she would spew was burned, the counter-magic led people to a magician's wife who admitted the force of the magic which had been used against the young woman. (This is also a case in which, we are told, large numbers of doubters who went to see the afflicted woman came away convinced of the reality of witchcraft.) Thirteen years later in London, Jane Kent was indicted for bewitching pigs to death and similarly killing a five-year-old girl. The father then went to a magician in Spitalfields, who advised him to take some of his wife's urine along with her nail parings and cuttings from her hair, and boil them together. The effect was to produce swelling and bloating of Jane's body and pain enough to make her come and scream at his door. Despite this, however, and the discovery of a 'teat' on her back, Jane was found not guilty by her jury, which was impressed by character witnesses testifying to her respectable life and regular going to church.[63]

Counter-magic, then, could be used by the witch herself to undo her own work, and by others to uncover a witch's identity or to force a witch to identify herself. Physicians, of course, might find themselves called on for assistance, but they too might advise counter-magic if they suspected the illness was not natural. William Drage, author of *Daimonomageia* (1665), a medical treatise on illnesses caused by magic and other preternatural means, tells the lengthy story of Mary Hall from Little Gaddesden in Hertfordshire. She fell ill in autumn 1663 and appeared to be possessed by evil spirits who caused her to fit, and spoke through her mouth, blaming her condition on certain witches. Prayer did no good, neither initially did the counter-magic of hanging her nail parings in the chimney. The sixteenth-century herbalist Nicholas Culpeper had observed that mistletoe was good against witchcraft, so people applied a sprig to her body, but it failed to expel the demons. A physician from Berkhamsted, Dr Woodhouse, boiled various remedies for her to no avail, and Drage, who had been called in for advice, told the family that natural remedies would probably do no good. He himself visited Mary in December and then went to see Dr Woodhouse, who told him that he and two other doctors who had attended her were convinced she was possessed. Mary's parents and friends were obviously keen to try every means to assist and relieve her, for they had also called in an astrologer who seems to have advised the use of an amulet, while a friend of his (once again, perhaps, relying on Nicholas Culpeper) suggested tying the herb bittersweet (*Solanum dulcamara*), gathered when Mercury's influence was strong, round her neck. Mary's demons, apparently willing to be helpful, joined the conversation in their turn and said she should go to a Mr Redman from Amersham (a man who had already served a prison sentence for practising magic), and he would cast them out. Drage, however, was wary of using Redman's services. 'Redman, as I am informed,' he said, 'pretends [*claims*] to do these things and the like feats by astrology. Much indeed may be done lawfully by astrology, but there be many that make that their pretence [*claim*] and defence, and probably use other arts that may be unlawful, that go beyond astrology.' So was Mary cured by any of these methods? We do not know. Was she a genuine demoniac or a fraud? Drage considered the latter possibility but rejected it, observing cautiously, 'If Mary Hall is falsely possessed, it doth not prove another not to be truly possessed; or if Mary Hall be truly possessed, it doth not prove that there are no such counterfeits.' In other words, considered on a case-by-case basis. 'Neither are all diseases natural, curable by natural remedies; nor are all diseases supernatural incurable by natural remedies.'[64]

The physician-astrologer Joseph Blagrave, called in to deal with a case of bewitchment resulting in fits, employed a combination of distilled herbal waters, fumigations, and intensive prayer, an effort which turned out to be successful in more ways than one, for not only did the demon possessing her depart from her body, but the human causes of her affliction were unveiled and dealt with. ''Twas observable,' Blagrave wrote, 'that during the time that I was employed about this business, there was seen by my people and servants three women to walk about the house, and more especially near the window where I was employed; which women her father did judge were three suspected witches who had spoken some words and were afterwards prosecuted by the maiden's father. One of them died, as I was informed, at the prison in Winchester, and what became of the other two I know not, for I never inquired more after them.'[65] This treatment, then, involved a form of Protestant exorcism which, when practised, depended principally on the fervent prayers of those involved. A case from Newcastle, dating from around August 1664 until February the following year, however, employed Catholic sacramentals as well as other means to divine the cause of an illness and effect a cure. Robert Pyle fell ill and sent some of his urine to a Mrs Pepper, a midwife who clearly had other skills to offer clients. She came to see him and gave him something to drink, whereupon he fell into a fit, 'with his legs trailing upon the ground ... and was in the fit by the space of one hour and a half'. Next Mrs Pepper threw water in his face and pressed two babies close to his mouth. Margaret Pyle, Robert's wife, asked why she was doing this and Mrs Pepper answered 'that the breath of the children would suck the evil spirit out of him, for he was possessed with an evil spirit'. Then at some point in the proceedings, Mrs Pepper asked for a bottle of holy water and, upon receiving it, sprinkled some on a red spot on the back of Robert's hand, after which she took out a silver crucifix (the record says 'out of her breast', so this was probably a cross she wore round her neck, perhaps concealed under her clothing), laid it on the red spot, and finally put it in Robert's mouth.[66] Catholic, Protestant: people often consulted both if they were desperate enough. John Barrow, in a piece of evident religious propaganda, published the narrative of the delivery of his son from a two-year demonic affliction, and apologises to his readers for his having consulted cunning folk, astrologers, physicians, apothecaries, and Catholic priests before realising that the Puritans were right, 'a poor despised people whom the Lord owned as instruments in His hand to do this great work. To His eternal praise I speak it, for the Lord saw their fastings and heard their prayers on the behalf of my poor child, at a wonderful rate.' It is good to know that one of his attempts was successful, but one notices he consulted everyone else first.[67]

This battle of the confessions (not forgetting the part played by Anglicanism as it sought to establish itself as the official religious orthodoxy, and by particular groupings such as the Quakers, who frequently acted as whipping boys in the midst of Anglican-Catholic-Puritan sniping and struggle) reminds us that the second half of the seventeenth century in England was a period of immense public anxiety. Sectarians, republicans, Jesuits, foreigners in general and the French in particular, all contributed to the suspicion that plots were afoot to upset England's new-found stability and usher in once more some kind of chaos followed by some kind of unwelcome dictatorship such as the country had endured in the 1630s, 40s, and 50s. It was an anxiety which could easily have led to more pursuit of deviants than it actually did. Nevertheless, one notices that prosecutions of witches, cunning folk, and magicians all over the country, while by no means as intensely pursued as during 1630–1660, were still far from negligible. There was the odd accusation involving high politics – a woman from Looe in Cornwall was arrested in 1671 for hindering England's efforts against the Dutch fleet, making the queen barren, and causing a bull to kill a local JP because he prosecuted Nonconformists[68] – otherwise charges alleged witchcraft in episodes of illness, sudden and unexplained lameness, and death, as had always been the case. Sometimes these charges visited other provisions of the Witchcraft Act, such as discovering stolen goods and image magic[69]; others were more more specialised, such as Peter Banks's guarantees of magically engineered good luck – one promised to keep Cuthbert Burrell safe from storm and shipwreck for a year – or Kitchell Harrison's evocation of spirits to provoke Joyce Massey to illicit love.[70]

The number of those charged during the period 1663–1699 (using information supplied by L'Estrange Ewen) is 144, the outcome of whose investigations and trials we do not know in the overwhelming majority of cases. Where verdicts are recorded, we find that ten were executed, eighteen acquitted, three died in gaol, two were found guilty but were pardoned, and one had the prosecution dropped. The likelihood is that more accused were found not guilty than guilty, but as we do not actually know what happened in a hundred of these cases, that likelihood can be no more than a guess, although it is also true to say that if executions had been frequent, someone would probably have noted it, and we do know from other evidence that officialdom was becoming more tentative in its judicial assessments, while not leaning altogether towards outright scepticism. As Orna Darr has observed, 'Supernatural methods of proof, thriving at the fringes of the official legal system, were reconstructed as rational experiments and then underwent co-optation that neutralised the subversive potential of these means of popular justice. The relative openness to concepts and practices of other social players, and the procedural, evidentiary and structural mechanisms that enhanced flexibility in proving witchcraft, helped to maintain the sense of a just and cautious justice apparatus while rendering convictions possible.'[71]

Another cautious observation which can be made is that the proportion of women prosecuted for witchcraft seems to have risen after 1660, as did popular violence against them, which may mirror people's frustration at the tendency of those in authority to drag their heels in dealing with such cases. In Wiltshire in 1694, for example, a suspect witch was seized by a group of 'unauthorised persons' and swum in the local river until she was nearly dead, and Mrs Common from Coggeshall in Essex was swum three times in July 1699 by villagers dissatisfied with the efforts of their local minister to get her to renounce her pact with Satan and with the counter-magic of scratching her arm till she bled. It is a resort to violence which can be seen in Scotland, too, especially in the notorious episode of witchcraft in Pittenweem in 1704 when one accused witch, Jane Cornfoot, was murdered by a local mob, and in Ireland where a nine-year-old girl started fitting after eating a sorrel leaf given to her by an old beggar woman. Physicians were called in, so was the minister, and the result was that the old woman was accused of witchcraft. She confessed as much, upon which she was attacked by a mob and murdered.[72] (It was a violence which lasted a long time. In the mid-nineteenth century, racehorses on the Wiltshire Downs were being troubled by a local witch until some of the locals attacked her with a horsewhip and drew blood, thereby countering the effect of her malefice.)[73]

Wiltshire, Fife, and County Antrim were strongholds of religious nonconformity, which may help to explain their animus in these particular cases. The Isle of Man, on the other hand, seemed only too eager to please its Anglican clergy, 'seemed' being an important proviso, because although the ministers held what George Waldron (1690–*c.* 1730) called 'a kind of tyrannical jurisdiction' over them, people retained a psychological distance between themselves and an alien English culture through their adherence to the Manx language. Their prayer books and Bibles may have been in English, but church services had to be conducted in Manx, and clearly any denunciation of magic and 'superstition' fell largely on deaf ears, for Waldron lamented 'the excessive superstition which reigns among them', and gave many examples of the islanders' belief in and encounters with fairies (from whom they claimed to be descended), ghosts, and other mysterious beings. He also noted that copies of a paper discovered under a stone cross were widely used as amulets. '[The people] tell you that they are of such wonderful virtue to whoever wears them that on whatever business they go, they are certain of success. They also defend from witchcraft, evil tongues, and all efforts of the Devil and his agents, and that a woman wearing one of them in her bosom while she is pregnant shall by no accident whatever lose the fruit of her womb.' Interestingly enough, Waldron scarcely mentions witchcraft as such, but he does give an example of the Devil's appearance to a widow from Douglas. She had spent the night with a Welsh sailor and robbed him of his money. He complained to the authorities, who then came and searched her house, finding, among other things, a small parcel of bones under her bed. The woman admitted they were those of three of her children, whom she had killed after giving birth because she was too poor to look after them; and when asked why she had kept them instead of throwing them away, answered that she had indeed intended to throw them in the river and was going thither one night with the bones in her apron, when 'she was met by a tall black gentleman who bid her go back, adding she was safe while she kept them at home'.[74] This may sound like a bizarre excuse until one puts it in context. Encounters such as this were commonly reported in witchcraft, so the widow was not actually saying anything unusual. In consequence, while Waldron hedges by saying he does not know whether the meeting did happen or not, he does not and cannot dismiss it outright as fanciful. (It is also worth remembering that witches were said to kill children and to use babies' bodies in the manufacture of magical *instrumenta*, and one has to ask, as Waldron did, why the woman kept these bones under her bed. Pleading infanticide because of poverty may thus have been, or appeared to her to be, a less heinous matter than admitting murder for magical purposes.)

Context, as I have said before, is most important when one is assessing the place and impact of magic and allied behaviours in any given period, and what we have been discussing so far is the context in which intellectual discussion of witchcraft in particular during the second half of the seventeenth century was taking place. By 'intellectual discussion', I refer to an exchange of disputatious essays and treatises between various eminent and not so eminent figures, some of whom sought to attack the concepts of 'supernatural' and 'preternatural' in various of their manifestation, others who defended them vigorously. This debate, however, has nothing to do with any supposed advance of 'science' and retreat of 'superstition', even though this was how many at the time and later liked to view it and describe it. Such a crude Whiggish theory of historical movement – 'ever onwards and upwards' – has been and should be discredited in favour of a more nuanced appreciation of what was going on, and since 'science' has been mentioned, let us begin with the Royal Society, proposed first as a 'college for the promoting of physico-mathematical experimental learning' on 28 November 1660, founded on 15 July 1662, and finally established on 23 April 1663 with the title 'The Royal Society of London for the Improvement of Natural

Knowledge'. From the start, then, members of the society met each week to discuss 'science' and conduct experiments, although the 'science' they were discussing was not our physical and experimental branches of knowledge excluding those related to theology and metaphysics, a definition not in vogue until the nineteenth century, but Isaac Watts's 'whole body of regular or methodical observations or propositions ... *concerning any subject of speculation*' (my italics).

Two points, however, should be borne in mind. Individual Fellows of the Society had their private interests: for Isaac Newton and Robert Boyle this meant alchemy, for Joseph Glanvill witchcraft, for Elias Ashmole Rosicrucianism and Freemasonry. But these personal investigations played little or no part in the official proceedings of the society. Secondly, the institutional role taken by the society had, as Michael Hunter says, 'a substantial influence on contemporaries' perception of what science did or did not comprise'.[75] Thus, when Glanvill proposed that the society investigate witchcraft, the society ignored his suggestion, not so much, perhaps, because some members were anti-magical in their outlook and opinions – others were quite the opposite – as because by concentrating on topics which were not particularly controversial the society avoided a disharmony which could have damaged both members' contributions to the society's activities and the society's reputation. The society almost certainly also wanted to avoid becoming embroiled in the religious debates of the period, when arguments about magic and miracles in general, and spirits and witchcraft in particular, were aired in a highly public battle against what some people saw as the prevailing 'atheism' – largely what we might call 'agnosticism' or 'deism'. The scepticism of individual members of the society therefore played little part in creating an atmosphere of intellectual aloofness among the great and the good, although the society's consistent unwillingness to participate in the prevalent debates will not have gone unnoticed. Apparent scepticism flourished in café society anyway, and one person's enthusiasm to pursue witches might be thwarted by another's reluctance to help him do so.[76]

This 'mechanical atheism', as it was called, meaning a growing inclination towards the kind of materialist approach to natural philosophy, was exemplified by Thomas Hobbes who, in an interesting mélange of intellectual condescension and anti-Catholicism, said that uneducated ('rude') people were unable to distinguish between dreams and sense impressions, which made them susceptible to superstition, and that witches should be punished for claiming they had power to do harm, when in fact they had not.

> Because in sense, the brain and nerves, which are the necessary organs of sense, are so benumbed in sleep as not easily to be moved by the action of external objects, there can happen in sleep no imagination, and therefore no dream, but what proceeds from the agitation of the inward parts a man's body ... From this ignorance of how to distinguish dreams, and other strong fancies, from vision and sense, did arise the greatest part of the religion of the Gentiles in times past, that worshipped satyrs, fauns, nymphs, and the like, and nowadays the opinion that rude people have of fairies, ghosts, and goblins, and of the power of witches. For, as for witches, I think not that their witchcraft is any real power, but yet that they are justly punished for the false belief they have that they

can do such mischief, joined with their purpose to do it if they can, their trade being nearer to a new religion than to a craft or science. And for fairies and walking ghosts, the opinion of them has, I think, been on purpose either taught, or not confuted, to keep in credit the use of exorcism, of crosses, of holy water, and other such inventions of ghostly men [*priests*].[77]

But this brand of opinion was dismissed by others. 'Men otherwise witty and ingenious,' wrote Joseph Glanvill, 'are fallen into the conceit that there is no such thing as a witch or apparition', and in his preface to the second edition of Glanvill's *Saducismus Triumphatus*, Henry More, a man whom Isaac Newton acknowledged as an influence on his own ideas, was equally trenchant.

That I am thus very industrious and zealous to support the belief of spirits and apparitions, and of whatever is true that contributes thereto, may seem strange to some and therefore to want an apology [*defence*]. Yet considering the Saducism of this present age, and atheism too if you will, it were a great neglect in me, or anyone else of my profession, not to have a great zeal and indignation against the stupor and besottedness of the men of these times, that are so sunk into the dull sense of their bodies, that they have lost all belief or conceit [*notion*] that there are any such things as spirits in the world.[78]

This dispute, however, is not an example of forward-thinking rationalism *versus* backward-looking superstition. As we have seen, in England at large, as in the rest of the British Isles, magic of all kinds was flourishing as much as ever, and in London, metropolitan sophisticates were perfectly prepared to laugh at the solemn approach of the Royal Society towards investigating nature. Thomas Shadwell offered a sharp estimation of this in his 1676 comedy *The Virtuoso*. Sir Nicholas Gimcrack, his caricature of a member of the Royal Society, carries out a series of bizarre experiments, learning to swim, for example, even though he admits he never goes near water, by tying some string round a frog, lying on his stomach with the string in his teeth, and imitating the frog's movements while a swimming master stands by with applause and encouragement. But Shadwell's satire could also be quite pointed. In the Royal Society's *Philosophical Transactions* for Monday 11 February 1666, Robert Boyle proposed transfusing blood out of one live animal into another, and listed sixteen queries in connection with the experiment – 'whether by this way of transfusing blood, the disposition of individual animals of the same kind may not be much altered: As whether a fierce dog, by being often new stocked with the bood of a cowardly dog, may not become more tame, and vice versa' (p. 386). This Shadwell parodies, as Sir Nicholas explains, 'I have transfused into a human vein 64 ounces *Haver du pois* weight from one sheep. The emittent sheep died under the operation, but the recipient madman is still alive. He suffered some disorder at first, the sheep's blood being heterogeneous, but in a short time it became homogeneous with his own ... The patient from being maniacal, or raging mad, became wholly ovine or sheepish. He bleated perpetually and chewed the cud. He had wool growing on him in great quantities and a Northamptonshire sheep's tail did soon emerge or arise from his anus or human fundament.'[79]

During the early years of the Royal Society, then, its tendency to stress utility and empiricism, and to compartmentalise knowledge, both of which would be very successful later on, had little or no effect on the continuing engagement with and interest in the various occult sciences. This is partly because magic and witchcraft had important contributions to make to current debates about the nature of revealed religion and the position of God (and therefore the Devil) within the created universe, and partly because magic and witchcraft, not to mention ghosts and spirits, were becoming politicised – useful propaganda tools against Catholics and Nonconformists – as the new party alignments of the 1670s onwards, known as 'Tories' and 'Whigs', adopted positions anent religion and irreligion. Here, context is important. The civil wars had left their mark in more ways than one. Puritans and other Nonconformists refused to accept the proffered embrace of the Anglican Church, a situation which ended in 1672–1673 in the defeat of Charles II's attempt to introduce religious toleration to a society which did not want it. Catholics, on the other hand, seemed to enjoy a degree of royal favour – Charles's mother, wife, brother, and favourite sister were all Catholics, and he himself seems to have converted on his deathbed – and the Titus Oates plot of 1678, supposedly intended to murder Charles and put his Catholic brother James on the English throne, resulted in an exclusion crisis as Whig politicians tried to bar James from the succession. A Pope-burning procession on 17 November 1680 (officially commemorating the accession of Elizabeth Tudor in 1558) marched through London, both making a point and inflaming public opinion. Things only became more frantic with James's accession on 6 February 1685 until a coup dispossessed him in 1688. We may therefore expect to find echoes of these disturbing events in the magic-witchcraft-spirit debates of those troubled times, and indeed anti-Catholicism – a strain which had long appeared in English witchcraft treatises, but was now given extra resonance – was openly expressed in equating Catholicism with magic and Catholic practice with superstition. Thomas Ady, for example, had written in 1656 in a vein we shall see repeated several times in the succeeding decades of 'the Popish religion which is altogether upheld by witchcraft'. '[It] is still a common practice among the Papists,' he went on, 'to carry charms about them (to make them shot free) when they go to war, as also hath been found by experience in the late Irish wars ... many of the poor idolatrous Irish rebels being found slain with charms in their pockets, composed by the Popish clergy, the witches of these latter times.'[80]

It was the question of 'atheism' generated among the educated classes by study and pursuit of the mechanical pilosophies represented by Descartes and Hobbes, however, which loomed larger in the eyes of witchcraft apologists, although if debate allowed incorporation of sectarian and political points, these were not to be passed by or overlooked. 'Attributing diabolical powers to the radicals,' as Thomas Jobe observes, 'was a resource for the Anglicans in power', and so in 1664 Samuel Butler did not hesitate to suggest that Puritans were hypocrites, happy enough to use witches while at the same time hanging them.

> Quoth Hudibras, This Sidrophel
> I've heard of, and should like it well

> If thou canst prove the 'Saints' have freedom
> To go to sorc'rers when they need 'em.
> Says Ralpho, There's no doubt of that
> Whose principles I quoted late,
> Prove that the godly may allege
> For anything their privilege,
> And to the Dev'l himself may go,
> If they have motives thereunto.
> For, as there is a war between
> The Dev'l and them, it is no sin
> If they by subtle stratagem
> Make use of him, as he does them.
> Has not this present Parliament
> A ledger to the Devil sent,
> Fully impowr'd to treat about
> Funding revolted witches out?
> And has not he, within a year,
> Hanged threescore of 'em in one shire?
> Some only for not being drown'd.
> And some for sitting above ground
> Whole days and nights upon their breeches
> And feeling pain, were hanged for witches.[81]

In this same year, Robert Hunt sent to his friend Joseph Glanvill a copy of or extracts from his 'book of examinations' of certain witches he was trying in Somerset. Glanvill saw in this an opportunity to counter the scepticism which attended both these trials and other instances of witchcraft, and used Hunt's information as the basis of a treatise which would put together sufficient examples of this and other manifestations of interaction with spirit worlds to form the basis of a proof that such worlds and such interactions with them were real and not fanciful. Two years later, after collecting further materials for his project, he published *Philosophical Considerations Touching the Being of Witches and Witchcraft*, which proved popular enough to go into several subsequent editions under the title *A Blow at Modern Saducism* (1668) and finally *Saducismus Triumphatus* (1681). In these, he adopted what was, in effect, a combination of storybook narratives and observational data intended to show, in the spirit of the new 'scientific' methodology, that the evidence for the reality of preternatural phenomena was overwhelming, and in January 1663 he went to the house of John Mompesson, a landowner from Tedworth in Wiltshire, to see and hear for himself the activities of a spirit drummer who, it was alleged, had been sent by witchcraft to plague Mompesson and his family in reprisal for his having charged a local drummer with obtaining money under false pretences. The nuisance consisted not only of drumming, but scratching and other noises, unpleasant smells, strange lights, apported objects, and a variety of manifestations reminiscent partly of haunting, partly of magical attack, and partly of poltergeist activity, all of which had been going on for several months before Glanvill arrived. Glanvill was much impressed both by what he had been told beforehand and by what he saw and heard, and added:

> None of those numerous inquisitive persons that came thither purposely to criticise and examine the truth of those matters could make any discoveries [*i.e. of fraud*], especially since many came prejudiced against the belief of such things in general, and others resolved beforehand against the belief of this; and all were permitted all possible freedom of search and inquiry; and after things were weighed and examined, several that were prejudicated enough before went away strongly convicted.[82]

Many of the narratives which went into the later editions of Glanvill's book were provided by his coadjutor, Henry More. More was one of the leading English theologians of the time and a distinguished member of a loose group generally known now as the 'Cambridge Platonists', clergymen who maintained that reason and religion were not antagonistic but harmonious, and that physical sensation alone was not enough to comprehend the complexities of creation. Like Glanvill, then, More was convinced that the current fashionable insistence upon purely mechanical interpretations of natural phenomena was mistaken both in philosophy and method, and described his way of conducting controversy as imitating, *mutatis mutandis*, that of his opponents. 'That [the atheist] might not be shy of me, I have conformed myself as near his own garb as I might without partaking of his folly and wickedness, and have appeared in the plain shape of a mere naturalist myself, so that I might, if it were possible, win him off from downright atheism.'[83] Nevertheless, his tone was trenchant, as was the custom and practice of the day. 'I look upon it as a special piece of Providence that there are ever and anon such fresh examples of apparitions and witchcrafts as may rub up and awaken their benumbed and lethargic minds into a suspicion, at least, if not assurance that there are other intelligent beings besides those that are clad in heavy earth or clay.' Glanvill himself was no less forthright.

> I have no humour nor delight in telling stories, and do not publish them here for the gratification of those that have; but I record them as arguments for the confirmation of a truth which hath indeed been attested by multitudes of the like evidences in all places and times ... But after all this, I must confess there is one argument against me which is not to be dealt with, viz. a mighty confidence grounded upon nothing, that swaggers and huffs and swears there are no witches. For such philosophers as these, let them enjoy the opinion of their own superlative judgements and enter me in the first rank of fools for crediting my senses and those of all the world before their sworn dictates. If they will believe in Scott, Hobbes, and Osborne, and think them more infallible than the sacred oracles, the history of all ages, and the full experience of our own, who can help it? They must not be contradicted, and they are resolved not to be persuaded.[84]

The fierceness of tone is not simply a matter of fashion. Glanvill and the others were convinced they were taking part, not in a cool intellectual to and fro between scholars, but in a fight for truth in the face of intransigent falsehood or misperception, and so although their debate was confined to a small section of educated society, its ramifications reached deep into everyone's lives and were likely to alter fundamentally the way people viewed themselves, the world around them, the workings of the universe, and the possibility of existence in forms and on planes beyond the material, a possibility which hitherto only theology and metaphysics had ventured to take within their discursive compass. When considering these debates, we need to remember that it was not simply magic under attack. Two of the longest-standing physical sciences, alchemy and astronomy-astrology, were falling into disfavour among the same intellectual circles that were rejecting the validity of magic. In the case of astronomy-astrology, a split between what had hitherto been equal parts of a single science was almost bound to happen as the vogue for concentration upon the physicality of the universe gathered momentum. But astrology also had its own internal difficulties, not the least of which was the transition from a Ptolemaic to a heliocentric system, while infighting between astrologers during the 1690s and 1710s gave fuel to its critics. Alchemy, too, found itself in a parlous condition at the same time, for some of its major practitioners were dead – George Starkey in 1665, Robert Boyle in 1691 – and there was no one of their calibre left to continue their alchemical explorations save Isaac Newton, and Newton's highly individual religious views meant he felt obliged to keep his devotion to alchemy (which he pursued as much for religious as for practical reasons) a very private matter.[85] Neither science disappeared altogether, of course, and both, like magic, had their many supporters and enthusiasts; but influential intellectual circles were not in favour, and this had a dampening effect on their credibility and status.

The appearance of a comet between November 1680 and January 1681 precipitated further intensive debate. Comets had long been interpreted as meaningful signs of God's anger, for example, or of impending disaster. Pierre Bayle published a treatise on this appearance in 1682, his title providing the reader with his thesis: 'Letter to M.L.A.D.C., Doctor of the Sorbonne, in which it is proved by various arguments drawn from philosophy and theology that comets are not the harbinger of any misfortune.' In spite of this reference to theology, however, Bayle's contention was subversive and he used history to argue that the belief in comets' portentousness was merely pagan baggage foisted upon their religion by early Christians. This was a point of view which had been expressed in somewhat different form by a Cambridge don, John Spencer, in a treatise, *A Discourse Concering Prodigies*, published in 1663. He speaks of a 'religion of prodigies being conceived in the womb of gross ignorance' (p. 9) by which he means pagan times, and he laments that 'the superstition of prodigies commits no small waste upon religion in regard the fears it creates abuse the minds of men, proving generally but *e vitro fulgura* ("lightning flashes from glass"), vain as the shadows of night' (preface iii). He then goes on to divide prodigies into different kinds under the general headings Natural. Preternatural, and Supernatural. Natural prodigies, such as comets, should not be regarded as prognostics and there is 'no need to call in the extraordinary assistance of Heaven to solve these unusual phenomena' (p. 10). Most people do not know what causes prodigies and so become afraid of them – 'ignorance calls every unaccountable symptom in the patient witchcraft, and every strange accident a prodigy' (p. 21) – and are both impatient and vain enough to want to know the future in advance (hence their trust in astrology as well as divination).

These traits can be and are exploited by the Devil, 'and as it is the design of religion to cast out fear and to introduce a spirit of true freedom and confidence towards God, so it is the work of the Devil to call on a spirit of bondage and fear, that so he may see in men the more lively and express images and portraitures of himself' (pp. 23–24). Superstition is handed down from generation to generation – pagans used to 'look upon their gods as a kind of fairies which would throw firebrands and furies about the house for the omission of some petty criticisms in their rites' (p. 30) – and the propensity of human nature is to credit unusual sights and events to God's intervention. As scripture shows, when God does speak to humanity through signs and wonders, their meaning is unmistakable. It does not depend on the vagaries of human interpretation, and when we are told that 'by removing of the received opinion of prodigies and signs, we remove a main pillar whereupon [is based] the faith of a divine Providence of a God concerned in all the affairs of the world, and that we thereby strengthen the hands of atheism and throw pillars under the elbows of secure and sleepy wickedness, I answer it is rather the way to make men atheists, to tell them these are God's signs of things which they see seldom or never come to pass' (p. 41). On the other hand, properly viewed and understood, prodigies can rouse atheists from their intellectual torpor into a sense and realisation of 'some mighty power which runs through the world and commands the forces of nature which way He pleaseth' (p. 42); and even though scripture shows that God has been known to use earthquakes (for example) as a sign of His displeasure, that does not mean to say that every earthquake must be interpreted thus in the future.

Preternatural prodigies – 'apparitions whether in the air, of armies, of cities, or by any particular application, of angels good or bad, in a way of counsel and conference, (reckoned among prodigies preternatural, no power transcendent to [a] created being [being] exerted in them)' (p. 56) – are to be treated the same way as those which are natural. Some of them, in fact, may have a natural explanation, and all of them invite us, if we are not careful, to indulge our fancies in trying to interpret them. So we must also remember that 'impure spirits, like jugglers, may often do strange tricks to call upon themselves the regard of the world … To receive, therefore, the apparitions, voices, drummings,[86] or antic noises of spirits in any place whatsoever, as presages of some approaching evils … is to consult shame to ourselves and our religion' (pp. 62, 64). Supernatural prodigies are also to be treated with caution, and things should not lightly be labelled 'supernatural' merely because they appear to exceed the limits of what we understand nature to be capable of producing. God has given us the means to be able to judge the reality or unreality of prodigies, and we should make use of them, always bearing in mind that human reason and argument have their limits (p. 103). For the truly sensible person 'is not so vain as to measure the wisdom and goodness of all the results of God's counsels by the reference they bear to the little ends, interests, or opinions of so inconsiderable a piece of the world as himself' (p. 105).

The implications of this kind of argument were, of course, many and various. If comets were not signs sent by God, what of other *mirabilia* in nature? Were deformed births, to take one example, simply accidents? Were miracles no more than events not yet understood, and was this how one should interpret miracles in the scriptures? If God did not suspend or manipulate in some arbitrary fashion the laws He had

imposed on His own creation, could it be said that there were non-material entities
such as ghosts, spirits, demons, or any other kind of spiritual life form, all of which, by
their very existence, appeared to contradict the norms of physically based being? Even
if they did exist, how could human beings know it, if knowledge depended on sense
impressions (as John Locke argued in his *Essay Concerning Human Understanding* in
1689), when spirits of any kind were not apprehensible by the senses? If the accepted
interpretation and understanding of miracles, ghosts, and the rest were called into
question, what of the Devil, and if the Devil were doubted, what of God Himself?
Defenders of tradition (by which they meant a modified tradition, since they were
not blind to the manifold changes in thought which were taking place around them)
were usually keen to begin at the other end of the sequence of inferences. Witchcraft
was a form of magic and witches were dependent on the Devil. Abolish witches and
you abolish their craft and, with their craft, their diabolical source of power. Do away
with one form of spirit and you do away with all. So it is little wonder that those
seeking to defend the reality of witches and witchcraft sought to defend the reality of
ghosts and other apparitions, too. Defence of the parts meant defence of the whole,
and nearly a century later we find John Wesley occupied with the same fundamental
task. 'While I live,' he wrote in his journal for Thursday 23 May 1776, 'I cannot give
up to all the deists in Britain the existence of witchcraft till I give up the credit of all
history, sacred and profane.'[87] He had a fight on his hands but, interestingly enough,
not one of which the result was a foregone conclusion.

10

THE FIGHT FOR WITCHCRAFT, A NORTHUMBERLAND VISIONARY, AND FEARS FOR NATIONAL SECURITY: 1669–1684

Debate having begun, it soared along with the increasingly febrile politics of the 1670s and 80s, intent upon its mission of restoring intellectual order and harmony after a period of what seemed to most people to have been social and sectarian anarchy. It was difficult for some of the participants in that debate to understand why people, learned and unlearned alike in their different ways, would willingly and heedlessly cast aside the traditional certainties in favour of trafficking with phantasms on the one hand or embracing the new religion of materialist thought on the other. Meric Casaubon, an Anglican clergyman who had been deprived of office under the Commonwealth, strongly disapproved of the occult sciences and in 1659 forcefully expressed his distaste for them in his preface to an edition of John Dee's detailed account of experiments in scrying over a number of years. Casaubon condemned Dee's narrative as 'a work of darkness', adding,

> All men may take warning by this example, how they put themselves out of the protection of Almighty God, either by presumptuous unlawful wishes and desires, or by seeking not unto devils only … but unto them that have next relation unto devils, as witches, wizards, conjurors, astrologers, (that take upon them to foretell human events), fortune tellers, and the like: yea, and all books of that subject, which I doubt [*I am sure*] were a great occasion of Dr Dee's delusion. That men are commonly cheated by such is sure enough, and those that are not very fools would take heed how they deal with them, and avoid them, to avoid the imputation of [being] fools.[1]

He followed this in 1668 and 1670 with a treatise, *Of Credulity and Incredulity in Things Divine and Spiritual*, which Euan Cameron has called 'a bricolage of enormously recondite erudition combined with mostly second-hand (and occasionally first-hand) supernatural tales'. Casaubon was fascinated by *mirabilia*, preternatural happenings, sympathetic magic, and astrology, and included a section in his book, devoted to supporting the belief that witchcraft and magic in general are not fantasies but realities. 'That they who are so grossly conceited as that they cannot conceive anything to be really, that is not corporeal, are generally atheists, I think will easily be granted,' he wrote in what was becoming a standard observation on Hobbesians on the one hand and the Royal Society on the other, a remark he reiterated in 1669 in a published letter on the subject of natural experimental philosophy.

> Hitherto nothing has been said to impair the credit or usefulness of natural or experimental philosophy but that we would not allow it to usurp upon all other learning as not considerable in comparison. Now I crave leave to tell you that it is (as all good things, more or less) very apt to be abused and to generate into atheism. Men that are much fixed upon matter and secondary causes and sensual objects, if great care be not taken, may in time, (there be many examples), and by degrees forget that there be such things in the world as spirits, substances really existing and of great power, though not visible or palpable by their nature – forget, I say, and consequently discredit supernatural operations: and at last, that there is a God, and that their souls are immortal.[2]

One book which roused his ire was John Wagstaffe's *The Question of Witchcraft Debated*, first published in 1669 and again in a much enlarged edition in 1671. Wagstaffe came from a well-to-do family and was known as a hard drinker, not much regarded as a person by his contemporaries. Why he should have chosen this particular subject for attention is not clear, but at the time of publication he was living in Oxford and seems to have frequented scholarly circles; so as the 'debate' was rapidly becoming fashionable as a topic of conversation, it may well have suggested itself as a way for him to make his academic mark. He had already published a virulently anti-Catholic work, *Historical Reflections on the Bishop of Rome*, which had been well received, and his dismissal of witchcraft as a mistranslation of biblical and classical terms on the one hand and a fable invented by the Inquisition as a way of acquiring private profit on the other repeats his anti-Catholic train of argumentation. As for the usual modern anecdotes told to prove the existence of witches, he says '[these] are founded partly in the juggling delusions of confederated imposters, partly again in the errors or ridiculous mistakes of vulgar rumours', and he reiterates the assertions of Reginald Scot and Johann Wier that witches were old and mentally ill.

> I do not doubt but some poor, silly, melancholic old wretches have really believed themselves witches, and not to be guilty of those actions which not only their follish neighbours, but worshipful men in the world have charged them with. Nor is it to be wondered at by anyone that considers the strange effects of melancholy, especially if it hath been heightened by poverty or want of good diet, by ignorance, solitariness, and old age: for that such kind of people take their very dreams to be real visions and truths.[3]

As for Glanvill's story about the drummer of Tedworth, he is contemptuously dismissive.

> When they are got to their castle of defence, they make a great noise and cry out upon the unreasonableness of those men who will not believe what so many worshipful persons in the world have heard and seen. And what is that, I pray? Why, they have heard trumpets sound and drums beat, when neither trumpeter nor drummer have

been near the place. They have seen chairs and stools move up and down a room when nobody has touched them, and many other things as strange. Thus will they tell stories of this nature from morning to night, if you please, though when they have done, they say nothing to the purpose. For suppose that all these stories were unquestionably true, yet they would not suffice to prove witchcraft.

In this, of course, Wagstaffe is correct – it may prove the existence of spirits, but not specifically of witchcraft – as also when he goes on to say that those who defend the realities of witchcraft (principally Glanvill again) also defend the realities of spirits, apparitions, and demoniacs.[4] But when it comes to the causes of people's mistaken beliefs, he cannot help blaming them on the machinations of priests, first pagan, then Catholic, for inventing and perpetuating the figure of the witch – the same general thesis proposed by the Dutch Calvinist minister Balthasar Bekker, whose *Die Betooverde Wereld* ('The Bewitched World') was later translated into English in 1695 – and there is thus a vein of anticlericalism as well as scepticism running through his work. But he actually goes further and implies – he is not misguided enough to state it openly – that religion, and Christianity in particular, was at the root of all this witchcraft nonsense, an implication which undoubtedly fed the commonly expressed fears that casting uncertainties on the reality of magic meant taking several steps, if not in the direction of atheism, then surely of the theism prevalent in certain circles.[5]

Wagstaffe's treatise was answered not only by Casaubon, but also by an otherwise anonymous 'R. T.' who published *The Opinion of Witchcraft Vindicated* in 1670. First he accuses Wagstaffe of making himself the only judge of what Biblical and Classical terms for magical workers actually meant, 'refusing any translation that suits not with his fancy, merely for that reason'. To the charge that witchcraft allows the Devil too much power, omnipotence in fact, R. T. observes,

Let [Wagstaffe] observe that many times such changes are seen in nature, serpents being bred of the corruption of other bodies, even of rotten trees and sticks: and the Devil, having had time enough to search into the ways of nature, might probably follow the same steps which she treads in changes of this kind, though he might go faster and be sooner at his journey's end. And seeing no man has yet attained to that perfection in natural philosophy as to know the thousandth part of what may be done by natural means, it is but vanity in anyone to measure the time which is requisite for such a production being wrought by supernatural agents, especially seeing no man knows the means by which it is done.

This is a theme he develops, passing over one of Wagstaffe's major contentions, that the Catholic Church and the Inquisition in particular were behind the notion of witchcraft and the widespread execution of witches, and ends with the reasonable point, anent witches being deluded, that even if some of them were, it does not follow that all of them must have been.[6]

The venom of scholarship, however, did not represent the only way some people approached the subject. One provided a warning not to make use of either. Thus, in 1669 there appeared *The Hertfordshire Wonder: or, Strange News from Ware,* from which we learn that Thomas Stretton, a wheelwright, managed to lose a Bible – perhaps an unlikely detail, but its oddness could be a mark of authenticity – and asked a cunning man if he would tell him who had stolen it. The cunning man hedged – 'I could if I wanted to' – and so the two men quarrelled. Four weeks later, Thomas's daughter Jane began to have fits and for six months apparently ate nothing. Flax and hair fell down from nowhere on to one of her bedsheets, and people who came to gawp were certain the cause of her illness was witchcraft. Very gradually, however, she seemed to recover by nature, and the author thereupon draws his intended conclusion.

> Some are of that belief that stories of witchcraft are but idle chimaeras, but we know that no part of scripture was spoken in vain, and one place thereof saith, 'Thou shalt not suffer a witch to live.' Those who are so, I wish them grace to repent and get out of their damnable estate, and should admonish all persons whatsoever not upon any loss or disaster to go to these soothsayers, wizards, or cunning men. For, as the scripture saith in one place, 'Cursed be the image and the image maker.' So I say there can no blessing be to those who are either wizards, or go to them for help and counsel. (pp. 11–12)

But not every approach was earnest. Others resorted to humour. In 1673, for example, there appeared a satire entitled *A Magical Vision*, which purported to be the account of a spirit meeting between 'a holy sister' and a ritual magician. It begins with a couple of jogging poems and then gets down to business. The writer, she says, had been reading John Dee's accounts of his conversations with angels. Wanting a rest from this, the holy sister wandered into a small wood where she fell asleep and, in her sleep, mounted a broomstick and flew to a vast desert. Noon turned to midnight, and suddenly she had her first sight of the magician, which she describes in terms clearly derived from the mechanics of contemporary theatre.

> I saw ascending out of a vast grotto or cave situated at the foot of a craggy rock o'erspread with ivy and bushes, a tall, venerable old man clothed in a party-coloured vest of white and green, with an austere countenance and swarthy face. His eyebrows, thick as a copse and long as a horse's mane, were curiously turned back and wound up about his ears. A wall [*milky blue*] and and frightful eye he had, sunk above two inches into his head, his beard carelessly thrown over his left shoulder, and his temples anointed with oil of nightshade. On his head he had a large hood of vervain, and about him a girdle of may-fern, artificially woven in tresses. Upon his gown, near his heart, was fastened a bat and a toad, both half dead, and about his collar he wore a collar set with seven several precious stones, each of which wore the character of that planet that governed it.[7]

This pantomime figure then draws three magical circles, writes mystic names, lies down in the circles, goes to sleep, wakes up again, and begins to chant a nonsensical invocation. This produces dreadful noises, a hailstorm, and the appearance of a brisk young man in a flame-coloured mantle, mounted, with his right leg on an eagle and the other on a lynx. The youth and the magician exchange gifts – three small vials containing an unknown liquid, and three hairs – after which the episode is over and the writer about to go home, when the magician takes her to his castle and starts to explain the wonderful things he can do or make others do. These consist principally of the activities usually attributed to witches: divination, control of fairies, raising ghosts, finding treasure, making amulets, magical cures, love magic, shape-changing, gathering bits from corpses, doing harm, arranging Sabbats, and much else. But the joke had gone on long enough, and the holy sister brings it to an end. 'So he would have proceeded with a tedious harangue of his power and titles, had not a small spiritual officer in the shape of a flitter-mouse interrupted him by a whisper in the ear, which obliged the magician to tell me he must omit the rest he intended to have said till another opportunity, for at present he was summoned for by a gang of Lapland witches that came to treat with him about a new bargain of bottled wines ... and saying thus, he mounts a flying dragon that presented itself ready bridled and saddled, and in the twinkling of an eye disappeared.'[8]

It is an amusing and diverting squib, spraying its sarcasm in every direction as it pretends to support the claim that witches are real. 'Henceforwards none need doubt of it, that have but faith enough to credit our relation of the following adventure' (p. 1). Nor was *A Magical Vision* the only such publication that year, for another anonymous pamphlet, *A Pleasant Treatise of Witches*, was issued by someone calling himself 'A Pen' from 'near the covent of Eluthery'. 'Covent' is simply an older form of 'convent', and 'eluthery' is the Greek word *eleutheria* meaning 'freedom', so the author was someone with pretensions (justified or not) to learning. He sets out his stall in his preface:

There is an inward inclination and desire of knowledge, gentle reader, which hath moved many grave and learned authors, amongst the rest of their inquiries, to search into the nature of those things which, because they are beyond the reach of common capacity, seem to the vulgar fables only, and poetical ficitons. Amongst the rest of those things there is nothing hath been more cried down by some and upheld by others: nothing has had more defendants on either side, than the possibility of Man's having familiarity with demons. This general curiosity drew me in among the rest that were ignorant of such matters, and caused me, for my own recreation as well as satisfaction, to allot some spare hours to a stricter inquiry into these things. But their scope being so large and so far extended, so many arguments stand on the one side, so many on the other, that I fell shrot of any just determination. Nevertheless, like that merchant that misses sometimes his designs, yet always comes home well laden, I have found many things by the way and filled this small treatise with the pith and marrow of above a hundred ancient and modern authors, whose pleasant relations have not only been delightful to myself in their collection, but have wrought so effectually on the ears of some that have heard but two or three of them, that not through any desire of mine, but by their frequent and earnest entreaties, I have used these means to satisfy them and to present thee with this compendious treatise. And that thy acceptance of it may be kind, according to my desires, you shall find nothing here of those vulgar, fabulous, and idle tales that are not worth lending an ear to, nor of those hideous,

saucer-eyed, and cloven-footed devils that grand-dams affright their children withal,
but only pleasant and well-grounded discourses of the learned, as an object adequate to
thy wise understanding.

He does not mean a word of it, of course. In spite of his promise of sober-minded
discussion, the author actually uses the opportunity to tell a series of diverting stories,
and his readers certainly get their money's worth, for they are treated to a sequence of
tales, short and very short, taken from both classical and sixteenth-century literature,
dealing with witches, familiars, Sabbats, demoniacs, ritual magicians, incubi and
succubi, other spirits of various kinds, fairies, ghosts, frauds – most of whom, as one
comes to expect from this kind of literature, are Catholics – and a final selection of
anecdotes which show the wicked coming to a bad end, and the welcome ministrations
of a guardian angel.

But while London giggled and argued, witchcraft was by no means vanishing, or
indeed diminishing, in the British Isles, even if the number of prosecutions showed
a downward turn, and slandering, cursing, calling up spirits, causing illness and
debility, and killing by witchcraft continued much as ever.[9] In that same year of
1673, for example, Northumberland saw the trial of Margaret Milburne on 17 May.
Dorothy Himers from Morpeth alleged that about three years previously she had
quarrelled with Margaret and ever since had never had the strength to do her usual
work. The condition had continued until the night of 25 April last when, 'she being
very sick, lying in her bed, did apprehend she see a light about her bed, like stars;
and then she did apprehend that she did see the said Margaret Milburne, widow,
standing on an oat scepp [*basket*] at her bed feet, thinking she was pulling her heart
with something like a thread'. Isabel Fletcher, also from Morpeth, brought events
forward to 12 May, when she and some other women were washing clothes at night
on the 'stanners', small stones in or near water.[10] Isabel went to fetch a cloak she
had left elsewhere and saw 'a white thing coming through the water, like a woman,
and she stood still till it came to her'. Isabel did not recognise the apparition at
first, but then realised it was Margaret. The two had a brief conversation, Margaret
suggesting Isabel should go and see her master and mistress, Isabel refusing to do
so at that time of night, and then the apparition left. Isabel joined the other women,
but a renewed sight of Margaret made her faint and begin to fit. She had a similar
reaction the following afternoon when she was tidying a room in her house and
Margaret put her head in at the window.[11] Visions and fitting, as we have seen, were
by no means uncommon features of certain alleged victims' reported experiences
of witchcraft, and there is no call for us to dismiss them as either fantasies or lies.
Isabel, for example, 'formerly heard [Margaret] reputed for a witch', and if she
believed this reputation, it must have affected the way she viewed Margaret and any
relationship, however casual, between them. Dorothy also informed the court that
'she verily believes Margaret Milburne is the cause of her grievances', a conviction
which may have arisen because of foreknowledge that Margaret was supposed to
be a witch, or conviction *post eventum*. If we lay aside the possibility that Dorothy
and Isabel were bringing their action out of spite or enmity – always a possibility,
of course, but the evidence we have does not warrant such an explanation – we can

and should be prepared to accept the two women's evidence as a true account of their personal experiences, however unusual they may seem to us.

The same may be said of an extraordinary episode of Sabbats, shape-changing, and harmful magic from a case in the same town and area in the same year and in the very same months. In April and May, magistrates sitting in Morpeth and Newcastle heard detailed evidence from Ann Armstrong, a spinster from Birches Nook in the Tyne Valley,[12] who also worked as a servant at Burtree House which lay a few miles from Stocksfield, west of Newcastle. Ann was first examined in Newcastle on 5 February before Ralph Jenison, a prominent figure who had been High Sheriff of Northumberland in 1660 and lived at Elswick Hall (now swallowed by the city); so it was probably there she was taken to be questioned.[13] The story she told was not unprecedented, but contained some unusual details. Her mistress, she said, had sent her the previous August to Stocksfield to get some eggs from Anne Forster, 'but as they could not agree for the price, the said Ann [Armstrong] desired her to sit down and look at her head, which, accordingly, she did' (p. 192). This has nothing to do with phrenology, a technique of determining the relationship between a person's character and the morphology of his or her skull, which was not developed until the late eighteenth and early nineteenth century. It is perhaps more likely that Anne Forster was doing Ann Armstrong a personal service by picking out and destroying head lice. Three days later, Ann Armstrong was out in the fields soon after dawn to see to her cows, when she met an old man dressed in rags, who asked her where she had been the previous Friday. 'In Stocksfield, seeking eggs,' she replied, to which the old man answered that the woman who had 'looked at her head should be the first that made a horse of her spirit, and who should be the next that would ride her, and [described] into what shape and likeness she should be changed if she would turn to their god'. He went on to tell Ann more about what to expect from 'them'. They would ride in her empty wooden dishes and in eggshells, obtain whatever they wanted by pulling on a rope, and tempt her with food and drink. But provided she did not eat any of their food, he said, they couild not harm her. This immediately makes one think of fairies. They were known to be mischievous, small in stature, to feast and drink, and to pose danger for humans who ate their food. The informative and kindly old man in rags is also reminiscent of a brownie or hobgoblin.[14] We are thus reminded of Isobel Gowdie from Auldearn who had extensive dealings with fairies in the midst of her visions, interpreted by her listeners as witchcraft, since her actions were largely malevolent and harmful to others.

As a final warning, the old man said that when she lay down in the field to sleep, she would find a piece of cheese nearby and if she ate it, she would be unable to keep her experiences secret. The old man then left and Ann fell down in a faint or, in view of its continuing the rest of the day and night, more likely a trance. She came to at about six the next morning and went home, but from that moment she had these fits almost every day, sometimes two or three times a day, lying as if dead from evening until the following dawn. Then not long before Christmas 1672, she was lying in one of her trance-fits at night when she saw Anne Forster come with a bridle, change her into a horse, and ride her to the end of the bridge at Riding Mill.[15] There she was restored to human shape and saw not only Anne Forster, but twelve others, two of whom she knew, and 'a long black man riding on a bay galloway, as she thought, which they called their protector'. At this point it is clear we are no longer dealing with fairies but witches, the 'black' man being the Devil. Now, it is interesting, in view of Margaret Murray's somewhat ill-judged comment that witches met in covens consisting of thirteen individuals – twelve witches and the 'god' – that Ann claims she saw thirteen witches (the Devil not included), and she repeated this during her examination on 9 April, claiming that at a meeting on 3 April there were 'five coveys consisting of thirteen persons in every covey' (p. 193), but she is not consistent about this, and other meetings she attended clearly numbered more than thirteen.[16]

Once arrived at the bridge end, the witches tethered their horses and, while Ann was obliged to sing, 'danced in several shapes: first, of a horse, then in their own, and then in a cat, sometimes in a mouse, and several other shapes' (p. 193), after which Ann was re-bridled and ridden home, following the Devil. This account of the mesmeric sight of humans transforming into animal shapes as they danced strongly suggests that Ann was experiencing a trance similar in certain respects to those of 'shamans'. The length of her periods of unconsciousness certainly implies more than a fainting fit or epileptic seizure, neither of which goes on for hours, as does the sensation of a journey in animal shape. Her evidence to Ralph Jenison did not take the usual form of witchcraft accusations or confessions, and it is clear from the way she was called before several sessions and subject to questioning by her examiners that they were intrigued by what she had to say, and gave her room to expand her answers in much more detail.[17]

For six or seven nights in succession, Ann went through the same experience of being shape-changed and ridden to a Sabbat. The final night, however, turned out to be a little different. Instead of meeting in the open air as previously, they assembled at Riding House (newly built in 1660, and now the Wellington Hotel), and Ann saw not only the usual faces, but also 'their protector which they called their god, sitting at the head of the table in a gold chair, as she thought'. Each person then touched a rope hanging from the ceiling three times, and whatever anyone wanted to eat and drink appeared on the table. Whoever was last to finish 'drew the table and kept the reversions', that is, cleared everything away and took home food or drink that was left. This reference to touching a rope to obtain food may initially make one think of pulling a bell rope to summon servants, here translated into something magical by the visionary experience. But these devices tend to belong to the eighteenth century and later when servants' quarters were separated from those of the family by some distance. Earlier times had them much closer. When Samuel Pepys's wife rang a bell on 6 October 1663 to summon the maids, for example, they were sleeping only in the next room, so we should look elsewhere for an explanation of Ann Armstrong's rope. In an appendix to his treatise *The Displaying of Supposed Witchcraft* (1677), John Webster reproduced the deposition of Edmund Robinson, aged eleven, given at the trial of the Lancashire witches on 10 February 1633. It contains certain points similar to those offered by Ann. Two greyhounds, one black, one brown, he said, fawned on him, but when he tried to make them chase a hare, they refused to run. So he tied them to a bush and beat them.

Instead of the black greyhound, one Dickenson's wife stood up, a neighbour whom [he] knoweth, and instead of the brown one, a little boy whom [he, Edmund] knoweth not. At which sight [he, Edmund], being afraid, endeavoured to run away: but being stayed by the woman, viz. Dickenson's wife, she put her hand into her pocket and pulled forth a piece of silver like to a fair shilling, and offered to give him it, to hold his tongue and not to tell: which he refused, saying, 'Nay, thou art a witch.' Whereupon she put her hand into her pocket again and pulled out a thing like unto a bridle that jingled, which she put on the little boy's head: which boy stood up in the likeness of a white horse, and in the brown greyhound's stead. The immediately Dickenson's wife took [Edmund] before her upon the said horse and carried him to a new house called 'Hoarstones', being about a quarter of a mile off. Whither when they were come there, there were divers persons about the door, and [Edmund] saw divers others riding on horses of different colours towards the said house, who tied their horses to a hedge near to the said house. Which persons went into the said house, to the number of three score or thereabouts ... And presently after, seeing divers of the said company going into a barn near adjoining, he followed after them, and there he saw six of them kneeling and pulling, all six of them, six several ropes which were fastened or tied to the top of the barn. Presently after which pulling, there came into [Edmund's] sight flesh smoking, butter in lumps, and milk as it were flying from the said ropes. And after that these six had done, there came other six which did so likewise. And during all the time of their several pulling, they made such ugly faces as scared [Edmund], so that he was glad to run out and steal homeward.[18]

It is unlikely, however, that these two accounts are connected. They are thirty-nine years apart, geographically located on opposite sides of England and different as well as similar in many of their details. But the Lancashire evidence does show that Ann's description of ropes and food was not unique to her.

On two occasions during this session of evidence, Ann is recorded as having said something, 'as she thought': she met the little old man, the Devil was sitting on a golden throne. This is an interesting phrase. It may mean no more than it says, of course: Edmund says the same thing during his evidence. But he did not fall into trances, and was very much younger than Ann, even though we do not know her exact age. So we may wonder whether 'as she thought' – deliberate fictionalising apart – suggests that she was doing her best to remember the details of an oneiric or trancelike experience which she will almost certainly have taken to be some form of reality. As Carolly Erickson says (writing about the Middle Ages, but with continued relevance for the seventeenth century), 'The perceived reality of the enchanted world predisposed Mediaevals to special habits of sight. Put another way, belief in a densely incorporeal population that could be glimpsed under special conditions affected the quality of their visual perception. Their sight was different from ours in kind; accepting a more inclusive concept of reality, they saw more than we do.'[19] Ann's listeners, of course, may have interpreted her narrative differently, depending perhaps on their reading. In 1605, for example, Francesco Maria Guazzo had conjectured that sometimes witches were physically present at a Sabbat, but sometimes not, in which latter case they were subject to delusion by the Devil; while for those who wanted explanations based on sense-impressions, Philip Goodwin, rector of Liston in Essex in

1673, had published a treatise on dreams, which explained that things seen in dreams were vivid, but not real.

> [The dreamer] thinks he sees the sun, though the sun he sees not. As there may appear some things to our eyes, as armies in the air, fighting-men, and flying horses, which are no realities, only apparitions, so to a man in a dream such things and persons appear, but they are no realities, only fictions in his fancy. Philo observes that some awake are like men asleep, [and] while they think they perceive such things, do but deceive themselves, taking the sings of things for the natures of things, mere shadows for substance. In a dream are thoughts of things, not the things thought.[20]

So as far as her audience was concerned, Ann could really have been present at this meeting, or she could have been tricked by the Devil into thinking she had been there, or she could have had a most vivid dream (or something similar) which had led her to believe she had been present. In any of these cases, she would have been telling the truth, and that made her testimonies intriguing and worth listening to.

But Ann did not go willingly to these meetings of witches, and in everyday life tried to avoid the people she recognised there – Anne Forster from Stocksfield, Anne Dryden from Prudhoe, Lucy Thompson from Mickley, all villages within a few miles of each other. These witches, however, did not easily give up their efforts to make her come and worship the Devil, visiting her 'in their own shapes' and threatening that 'the last shift should be the worst', an ambiguous phrase meaning either that their final stratagem would be worse than the others, or that her or their last shape-change would be more frightening than those which had gone before. They had shot their bolt, though, because 'from that time they have not troubled her'. It was on 'St John's day last' that Ann went into a field, looking for sheep, felt tired, and sat down to rest, throwing her apron over her head. When she got up again, she found a piece of cheese lying near her head. She took it home with her, ate some, and, in accordance with the old man's prediction, then found she could not keep silent about her experiences. This 'St John' is more likely to have been the Evangelist whose feast is kept on 27 December than the Baptist who is celebrated on 24 June. The sequence of events Ann describes puts the Sabbats just before Christmas 1672, and so the December feast day and her suddenly starting to talk fits better than talking in June and visiting six months later. It also helps to explain why Ann was brought before Ralph Jenison on 5 February 1673. Extraordinary claims of being taken to Sabbats will have aroused gossip, and that gossip will have reached official ears very quickly, possibly via one of the local parish ministers.

On 2 April, Ann was brought or came before Humphrey Mitford (who died in October that same year), probably at his residence in Mitford not far from Morpeth, where she named Anne Baites, wife of a tanner in Morpeth, as a participant in meetings held at Barwick, Barrasford (a somewhat isolated village north of Hadrian's Wall, quite a distance from the cluster of Riding-Stocksfield-Prudhoe associated with Ann), the bridge end in Riding, and once indoors in the cellar of Francis Pye's house in Morpeth itself. Anne Baites, she said, rode upon wooden dishes and eggshells in Riding House and in the close next to it, and showed off to the Devil by changing her shape as often as she could. This curious apparent elision of fairy and witch behaviour is at least as old as Reginald Scot, who noted that witches 'can go in and out at auger holes, and sail in an egg shell' (*Discoverie* Book 1, chap. 4).[21] Two days later, Ann appeared before yet a third magistrate, Sir Richard Stote, probably in Stote's Hall which, like Jenison's Elswick Hall, was later absorbed by Newcastle. Clearly local officialdom was becoming interested in this woman and her somewhat unusual narrative. Here she told Sir Richard that since the last time she gave evidence against a number of individuals – meaning since 5 February in Newcastle – she had been ridden more than once by Anne Dryden and Anne Forster to further Sabbats. The last, she said, occurred the previous night (i.e. 3 April), when they rode her to Riding House where there were gathered twelve persons, including Anne Dryden and Anne Forster, eight of whom (including three men) she named in full, another whom she knew only by Christian name, and three whose names she did not know. The Devil was there, too, and after they had pulled the rope and obtained and consumed their food and drink, and danced while Ann [Armstrong] sang to them, each person gave the Devil an account of the harm she or he had done.

On 9 April, however, Ann supplemented this evidence. She was now being heard in Morpeth at the local sessions before six magistrates including Sir Richard, Jenison, and Mitford, who had examined her before, and Sir Thomas Horsley, who had been High Sheriff of Northumberland in 1663 (three years after Jenison had held that office), James Howard, and John Salkeld, whose seat was Hulne Abbey, not far from Alnwick. They obviously wanted to know more about the meeting which had taken place on 3 April at Riding House, and Ann obliged not only with specific descriptions of what kind of food and drink the witches got when they swung on (rather than just touched) the rope. There were sixty-five people there altogether, excluding herself and the Devil, but she named only fourteen (including four men) along with the places from which they came, most of which appear to be in the Newcastle–Sunderland area, representing journeys which would have to be made by horse. Each group of thirteen, she said, had an attendant devil with whom they danced and to whom they gave an account of their wickedness they had been doing. This included bewitching horses to death, making one infant ill and killing another by magic, hoping to kill adults the same way, and destroying people's property. The emphasis upon destruction of horses, mares in particular, underlines the importance of the horse to the rural economy. Horses were used as pack animals, drawers of the plough and other heavy loads, and as the usual means of transport, and as the population of England more than doubled between 1500 and 1700, horses were needed in ever greater numbers. To accommodate the need for more agricultural land, the number of horse-breeding areas shrank, meaning that those which were left became even more vital to help satisfy the country's growing demand, and, of course, under these combined pressures, prices rose. A colt, for example, which might have fetched £1 or £1 10s 0d in the mid-seventeenth century was capable of fetching £12 2s 0d or £13 5s 0d thirty years later. So the witches' alleged bewitchment of their communities' horses represented quite an attack on their neighbours' economies.[22]

Such attacks tended to be pointed and personal rather than general. Thus, Michael Ainsley told the Devil about what he, Anne Dryden, Anne Forster, and Lucy Thompson had done to spite Thomas Errington.

Michael Ainsley and Anne Dryden confessed to the Devil that they had power of Mr Thomas Errington's horse, of Riding mill, and they rode behind his man upon the said horse from Newcastle like two bees, and the horse, immediately after he came home, died. (And this was but about a month since). The said Anne Forster, Michael Ainsley, and Lucy Thompson confessed to the Devil, and the said Michael told the Devil that he called three several times at Mr Errington's kitchen door and made a noise like a host of men. And that night (the Devil asking them how they sped) they answered nothing, for they had not got power of the miller. But they got the shirt off his back as he was lying betwixt women, and laid it under his head, and struck him dead another time in revenge [that] he was an instrument to save Ralph Errington's draught from going down the water and drowning, as they had intended to have done. And they confessed to the Devil that they made all the gear of the mill [break down], and that they intended to have made the stones all grind till they had flown in pieces. (p. 195)

The magistrates also heard about bargains struck with the Devil as long ago as 1633 for length of life, while Ann [Armstrong] herself became the object of some witches' persuasion 'to have taken a lease of three score years or upwards', with the promise that 'she should never want gold or money or, if she had but one cow, they should let her know a way to get as much milk as them that had ten'.

As a result of this session, Michael Ainsley and his wife must have been arrested, because when proceedings were renewed before Ralph Jenison on 21 April, we learn they were both in gaol. Ann herself told Jenison about a meeting 'southward, but the name of the place I do not remember'. The meeting had taken place on 14 April, 'she being at her father's house' – so she was either still at liberty or under her father's guard at the court's direction – and had involved the participants' drawing a circle (their 'compass') next to the end of a bridge, after which the Devil ('a little black man [in] black clothes') put a stone in the middle and they all knelt down, bowed towards the stone, and repeated the Lord's Prayer backwards. This last had been done in harmful magic for a long time and seems to have constituted a common way of trying to hurt others. 'If husbands would say the Lord's Prayer for their wives oftener than they do,' observed the anonymous author of *The Family Prayers of Those Poor Christians* (1675), 'God would keep their wives from saying their prayers backwards for them as oft as many do.'[23] The Devil then called on Isabel Thompson, a widow from Slaley, a village a few miles south-east of Hexham, and asked what service she had done him. Her answer in the court record is brief – 'she had got power of the body of one Margaret Teasdale' – but the court wanted to hear more and listened to Mark Humble, a tailor, almost certainly from Slaley as well, as he told the magistrates that about seven or eight years previously he had been walking in the village and passed Isabel Thompson going the other way. 'She being formerly suspect of witchcraft, he looked back over his shoulder and did see the said Isabel hold up her hands towards his back; and when he came home, he grew very sick and told people in the house that he was afraid Isabel Thompson had done him wrong' (p. 201).

It is a good example of *post hoc, ergo propter hoc* and illustrates the way someone's reputation in a small community was capable of generating specific connections between disparate events, or even auto-suggestion whose results would then fulfil fear and expectation. Mark's illness, described as 'fits', continued for the next three or four years, and at some point, probably near the start, Isabel came to his house to say there was a rumour she had bewitched him. 'If that is true,' she added, 'it will soon be known.' What she meant by that is not clear, but while she was in the house, she took some hair from Mark's mother who was in bed, sick, in order to 'medicine' her, that is, provide a magical cure. Here is remarkable evidence about the complex relationships between villagers. Isabel was known to be a witch and Mark Humble blamed her for his illness. Did she come to complain, find his mother was ill, and offer to cure her; or did she come to cure his mother, and take the opportunity to complain of the rumour in the village that she had caused him to be ill? Since she was clearly allowed to take away some of Margaret Humble's hair, it suggests the latter as somewhat more likely, and her 'it will soon be known' sounds like a protestation of innocence. 'You say I harmed you by magic. If I work magic to cure your mother and succeed, that will contradict the rumour I have done you harm.' We lack the details which would allow an accurate interpretation of this episode, of course, but the juxtaposition of harmful and curative magic in the same person who is, apparently, allowed full rein to come and go in her victim's and client's house, perhaps helps to explain the very long interval between the incidents described and their being reported in a court of law. Had Ann Armstrong not given extensive evidence to the Northumberland magistrates, would Isabel Thompson, regardless of being known locally as a witch, have been brought into court at all?

The answer appears to be 'perhaps not', but other considerations are perhaps against it. Early in May Ann was brought to Allendale, a village in the south-west of Northumberland, quite a long way from her usual stamping ground and nowhere near Morpeth or Newcastle where the magistrates' sessions were taking place. Now, the timing of events at this point is not altogether clear. On 12 May Ann gave testimony about a Sabbat which had been held on the 2nd; on the 7th, according to evidence from Robert Johnson from Riding mill, she was in his house – 'where he had Armstrong', which makes it sound as though she had been arrested. It was common for suspects or accused to be lodged securely in private houses if no other accommodation was available locally – and there she was confronted with Mary Hunter from Birkenside, a woman she had named as a witch during the session of 4 April. What followed is clearer if one adapts it from the somewhat opaque record.

The two women spoke to each other.

> Mary: What have you to say to me?
> Ann: You are a witch. I have seen you at Sabbats.
> Mary: Where?
> Ann: Here in this house last Sunday night [*i.e. 6 May*].

Ann then asked after Mary's son, Anton, and was told that one of the men in the room with them (actually Cuthbert, another of Mary's son) was he.

'No, he isn't', said Ann. 'I know Anton well. I've seen him several times at the Sabbats.'

She asked Mary to 'send him down' (meaning 'downstairs': Birkenside is too far from Ridng to mean she wanted Mary to send for him) along with a girl or young woman Mary used to ride like a horse to those meetings. So Anton 'came down' and asked Ann what she had to say to him. He was obviously aggressive – the record says he threatened her – so Ann refused to talk, simply telling him she would let him know at the next court session, since she had heard he would be there. Privately she told Robert Johnson that Anton had confessed to the Devil that he had made Anne Richardson very ill and killed several cows by magic. Anton had told her this, she said, when he came to see her.

Why should he have come to see her? The record does not say, but testimony given by George Taylor may provide a clue. He told the magistrates that he (George) came to Birches Nook specifically to speak to Ann in response to her several requests to see him. She was asleep when he arrived and was woken by her sister. Again the record does not express itself clearly, but it sounds as though he set her a kind of test, asking if she knew who he was or could give his name.

'If you are the man who has recently lost a foal and you live at Edgebridge,' she replied, 'you are George Taylor.'

George was clearly surprised and asked her how she knew.

'I heard Mary Hunter confess to the Devil at a witches' meeting that she had acquired power over your foal,' she said.

(George gave further details to the magistrates. His foal had sickened and died in March that year. Its head and lips especially were badly swollen, and when he opened it up he found scarcely any blood in its body. The illness seemed unnatural.)

Ann then went on to warn George that Mary Hunter and Dorothy Green had told the Devil they controlled George's farm animals, and certainly George thought they were not thriving and looked like skeletons, even though he was feeding them well. Perhaps this is why Ann wanted to see him, to pass on information obtained in her trance states that his animals were bewitched. This impression is strengthened when we look at the testimony of John March from Edgebridge. He went to Birches Nook, Ann's home village, perhaps looking for her. Ann heard someone mention his name and came to speak to him, asking if he had an ox which was lame in one limb.

'Yes,' he replied, 'how do you know?'

'I heard Mary Hunter and someone whose name I do not know tell the Devil during a witches' meeting that they had lamed it,' she said.

(Like George Taylor, John March provided the magistrates further information about a grey mare Ann said had also been bewitched by these same women and was now dead, its illness apparently having been prefaced by the attentions of a persistent swallow 'which above forty times and more flew through under the mare's belly and crossed her way before its breast'. The magistrates who heard this evidence, Sir Richard Stote and Sir James Clavering, wanted to know the name of the other witch besides Mary Hunter, so they had Ann taken to Edmundbyers, a village perhaps 10 miles or so south-west of Riding, and there she identified Dorothy Green as Mary Hunter's partner in crime.)

Ann's reputation as a visionary or as a witch or both was certainly spreading, if she had not been a well-known figure before. Was this why Anton came to see her, to elicit information? Was this, indeed, why she herself came to Humphrey Mitford in April, not under arrest as a suspect witch, but as a visionary who felt compelled or who thought it her duty to tell people what she saw while she was in a trance? Her evidence, if freely offered in this way, would certainly have puzzled the authorities, but it looks as though they listened to her, intrigued or bewildered, but then decided to treat her like a normal suspect and keep her under close watch and (it seems) house arrest. Hence she found herself in Robert Johnson's house, confronted by Mary Hunter, whom she had named more than once as a witch, and Mary's hostile son. From what John March told the magistrates on Sunday 6 May, when Ann had said there was a witches' meeting in his house, he was frightened by thunder and lightning and by the sight of 'twenty creatures in the resemblance of cats and other shapes, lying on the floors and creeping up the walls' (p. 200). Suddenly he heard Ann singing. (He describes her as 'the girl', the first indication we have of her age, though not a clear one.) There were servants with her, so it appears she was sharing a bed, not an unusual arrangement and one which here served the purpose of making sure Ann did not run away during the night.[24] They woke up and came out of the room, saying, 'Alas, the witches have taken the girl away!' Robert went upstairs into the room and found Ann in one of her trances. She remained absolutely inert for almost an hour until Robert fetched two or three of his neighbours to see her. Then she began to move and open her eyes, but did not speak for a long time, until at last she said that all the witches were there, trying to take her away, but were unable to do so.

At some point in this sequence of events, then, Ann was brought to Allendale, apparently at the villagers' request, to identify any witches in the locality, and because Isabel Johnson was suspected, they brought the two women together. Isabel 'breathed' upon Ann. Was this deliberate, or does it mean that the two women were so close to one another that Ann could feel Isabel's breath, or is it a reference to Isabel's being frightened and breathing heavily? We do not know, but the result was that Ann fell to the ground in a fit or trance and remained in it for three-quarters of an hour, after which, upon recovering, she said that 'if there were any witches in England, Isabel Johnson was one'. (Robert Johnson also told the magistrates about certain incidents from August and December 1672 and March 1673, which struck him as peculiar. He did not overtly attribute them to witchcraft and did not mention Ann in connection with them. Perhaps he thought they were relevant, perhaps he described them in the hope of receiving an explanation or reassurance from the court proceedings.)

What happened to everyone concerned, we do not know. If there had been executions, the likelihood is that at least some would have been recorded. Pamphlets frequently published the details of cases, especially those which contained some point of interest. In 1674, for example, there appeared *Relation of the most remarkable proceedings of the late assizes at Northampton, containing truly and fully the trials, confessions, and execution of a most mischievous witch, notorious highwayman, [and] barbarous murderess. The first being Anne*[25] *Forster who by witchcraft destroyed above 30 sheep belonging to one Joseph Weedon, and afterwards burned to the ground his dwelling-house and two large barns full of corn and hay, to his damage above £300, with her confession of the fact, how and why she did it, and asking him forgiveness for the same, and a wonderful experiment of her devilish skill showed in the gaol after she was condemned.* Anne is interesting not so much for what she did as for her ambiguous position and foolhardy exploitation of it. We are told she quarrelled with a local farmer, Joseph Weedon, because he would not sell her some of his mutton for twelve pence instead of the fourteen pence he was asking. Within a week, more than thirty of his sheep were dead, whereupon Joseph 'was advised by some that suspected it to be done by witchcraft to take one of these sheep whose bones were so broken and shattered whilst it was still alive, and burn [it], for that (according to their tradition) would make the witch come to this place' (pp. 4–5). (Did Joseph think of witchcraft first, or was the idea put into his head by his neighbours?) The magic worked and Anne turned up, asking what they were doing. So Joseph tried to scratch her, but found his nails were too short to draw blood, and slashed her hand with a knife instead. The wound was small, but festered. Anne threatened to sue him, but then they came to an agreement to let the matter drop on payment of twenty shillings, which were duly handed over.

So far, so ordinary. But now Anne made a foolish mistake. Boasting that it had not been she, but the Devil in her shape who had been wounded, she announced she now had power to do Joseph further mischief. (Was 'further' an acknowledgement to others or to herself that Joseph's sheep had died because of her magical will?) Two days later, one of Joseph's barns was set on fire and burned to the ground, while another kept on breaking into flames which were safely extinguished. After a pause of three weeks, however, the barn caught fire again and this time was destroyed, along with Joseph's house. Naturally, under the circumstances, Anne was suspected, arrested, examined, and then officially searched by a group of women who found five 'teats' in her body, signs she had been suckling familiars. Having refused to confess anything before, this seems to have changed her mind. (Had she actually practised magic in some form either recently or for some time past and now recognised she had been found out? Had she not realised or considered the possibility until now that she was a witch? Had she decided that being thought of as a witch gave her status, however dubious, and that therefore she would behave as though she were? The pamphlet gives no hint of any such previous reputation, so perhaps the third of these possibilities is the most likely.) Still, her state of mind is not easy to gauge. On the one hand, she told the examining JP that she had set fire to the barn with the help of the Devil, who carried her to the top of the roof. On the other, when it came to her trial, she denied being a witch at all. The jury, however, which had access to details not available to us, found her guilty of the charges against her. These, it is important to note, were two: (i) killing Joseph's sheep by witchcraft; and (ii) destroying his house and barns by fire. Arson was regarded as a serious offence and, under a statute of Queen Mary, dating from 1553, was treated as a major felony carrying the death penalty. Even without the component of magic, therefore, Anne would have hanged.[26]

But, having been sentenced, Anne made the unusual request to be burned rather than hanged. This had actually been the penalty for arson in earlier times, although it is scarcely likely she would have known that. Nor were witches burned, as witches, in England – 'Mother' Lakeland who had been burned in Ispwich in 1645 had been found guilty of killing her husband by witchcraft, but she suffered the statutory death for her petty treason (husband murder), not for her witchcraft – and neither adulteresses nor heretics had been burned in England for at least a couple of generations.[27] So what made Anne ask for this death? Bravado? Madness? Contempt? The clearest association in England between criminal activity and the death penalty of burning was that of religion, especially perhaps Catholicism. Did Anne want to be a martyr? It is only one aspect of her behaviour which seems to be puzzling, although if we were now in possession of the facts available to her contemporaries, we might not be so perplexed.

One possibility we should consider, of course, is that she was unhinged, and there is no doubt that between interrogation and trial Anne had been subject to sorry treatment by her gaolers.

> The keepers caused her to be chained to a post that was in the gaol, but she had not been long so tied before she began to swell in all parts of her body, that her skin was ready to burst, which caused her to cry out in a most lamentable manner, in so much as they were forced to unchain her again and to give her more liberty, that the Devil might come to suck her: which he usually did, coming constantly about the dead time of night in the likeness of a rat which, at his coming, made the most lamentable and hideous noise which affrighted the people which did belong to the gaol, which caused many to come and see her during her abode there; and several hath been with her when the Devil hath been coming to her, but [they] could see nothing but things like rats, and heard a most terrible noise.

It is somewhat difficult, however, to see how this is relevant to her request to be burned. Chaining Anne to a post was cruel but not unprecedented. Her physical reaction to it was severe, but she was then released after a certain time (whatever 'not long' means here). Rats were an unpleasant feature of gaols and other dwellings. Being stared at by curious visitors was not uncommon, either. But was the combination of chaining, unchaining, rats, and visitors enough to sap her sanity? It is possible, of course. We do not know what she was like either before or after her trial, and so have nothing, other than our own preconceptions, to help us gauge her psychological condition, and it is worth remembering that there are many instances both past and modern of people who have been subjected to worse and yet retained their minds and character intact.

But Anne's request is only one enigma among several. Another is the 'wonderful experiment of her devilish skill' promised in the pamphlet's title, 'experiment' here meaning 'experience', in the usual seventeenth-century usage. It took place while she was in prison, awaiting execution.

> After sentence, a citizen of London being there, went out of curiosity to visit her as scarce believing any such thing as witches in nature. After much discourse, he desired her to show him some trick or experiment of her skill, which at last she condescended [*agreed to do*], bidding him get a large basin, but be sure not to wet it. He, going out, wets a basin on purpose and, wiping it dry again, brings it. She gets in it, standing upright, and after muttering a few unknown words, was carried several times round the room and at last up the chimney. But being about half way up, the basin fell down

and she after it without hurt. But [she] scolded the gentleman for wetting it, saying that
otherwise she had got clear out of the chimney. (p. 5)

What was going on here? We have two possible extremes which will give us a definite
answer: the whole episode is fiction, or the episode happened just as described. In
between is confusion. What was printed may have been a garbled version of the
original report, in which case the question is to what extent and in what detail was
the report altered? For what purpose was it changed – to amuse, to make a point of
some kind? On what were any changes focussed? Anne's pantomime with the basin
is significant. Witches were known to travel in strange and unusual objects: sieves in
the North Berwick episode, wooden bowls or eggshells, according to Ann Armstrong.
Why did Anne stipulate that no water should come into contact with the basin? When
the pamphlet says 'she was carried', what does it mean? Did Anne carry it herself
round the room, pretending to travel, or imagining that she actually was travelling in
it? Why did she put it up the chimney? To give herself an extra ledge or foothold in
the hope of easing her way to climb to liberty? Was her performance produced by an
eagerness to please a visitor who clearly wanted some demonstration of 'magic' from
her? Was it done in genuine expectation of success, misguided hope, or contempt for
the man's gullibility? There is so much we cannot tell, but that very proliferation of
uncertainty means that opting for either of the easy certainties is not altogether wise.

Such oddities and entertaining details, coupled with the execution of the principal,
then, were what provided material for popular pamphlets, and the cases presented
in Morpeth and Newcastle by Ann Armstrong were surely full enough of incident
and peculiarity to satisfy a pamphlet audience. Without executions, however, such
cases were of less interest to the general public, and so in spite of the presence of the
Devil, the transvections, shape changings, dancing, magical harm doing, and mutual
recriminations, it seems quite possible, in the absence of evidence to the contrary,
that neither Anne herself nor any of those she accused and implicated were hanged,
and that if anyone was punished, it would have been by gaol and pillory rather than
scaffold and rope.

Learned warfare by treatise, however, recognised no ceasefire. In 1673 John Webster,
describing himself as a 'practitioner in physic', completed a lengthy treatise, *The
Displaying of Supposed Witchcraft*, which he published in 1677. It was intended, as
may be gauged from the title, to pour scorn on the claim that witchcraft might be
real, an aim he emphasised by adding to the title page, for the benefit of his readers,
a sentence from the Roman physician Galen: 'When people's false notions take hold,
they make them not only deaf but blind as well, with the result that they are unable to
see what is obvious to others.' But Webster was by no means only a physician. Born in
1611, he studied chemistry before becoming a church minister in 1632, a pursuit which
emerged as a strong interest in alchemy in later life, and he had unorthodox religious
views which placed him well within Nonconformist groupings and led to his being
deprived of his curacy in the parish of Kildwick in Yorkshire in 1637. This is where
he met Edmund Robinson, the lad whose accusations set in motion the trials of the
Pendle witches in 1634. Edmund was being taken round various parishes by his father
and some others, 'that the boy might reveal and discover witches, pretending [*claiming*]

that there was a great number at the pretended meeting, whose faces he could know'.[28]
In 1643 Webster became a schoolmaster in Clitheroe where he stayed for the rest
of his life, with the exception of three very short intervals in 1647, 1648, and 1653.
During the few months of 1653 which he spent in London, he revealed some of those
individual notions which had made him suspect to the Church authorities: freedom
of personal interpretation of the scriptures, rejection of belief in a physical Devil, and
opposition to any role for the state in religious affairs. He also turned his attention to
reforms of the universities, of whose curricula he disapproved and suggested, among
other things, that they study alchemy and natural magic.[29] Webster was thus not a man
of orthodox, or even comfortable, opinions, and yet not so heterodox or abrasive as
to be deprived of his living a second time, or beckon in any dangerous way the wrath
of those he criticised. It comes as no surprise, therefore, to find that his final work,
Displaying, is a mixture of old-fashioned argumentation and personal interpretation
of scripture, making use not only of the fruits of many years' reading, but also his
own experience, the whole being salted with a mixture of scorn and anti-Catholicism,
which would have gone down well with much of his readership.

We can see some of these traits in chapter 6, which deals with the alleged
mistranslations of Hebrew and Greek terms for 'witch', 'diviner', 'magician', and so
forth – a long-standing topic of dissension among scholars – during which he discusses
the use of ventriloquism to feign the voice of a demon in possession of an individual,
and gives there examples:

(i) I myself also have seen a young man about 16 or 17 years of age who, having
learned at school, and having no great mind to his book, fell into an ague in the
declination of which he seemed to be taken with convulsion fits, and afterwards to
fall into trances, and at the last to speak (as with another small voice) in his breast or
throat, and pretended to declare unto those that were by what sinful and knavish tricks
they had formerly acted, or what others were doing in remote places and rooms; so
that presently his father and the family with the neighbourhood were persuaded that
he was possessed and that it was a spirit that spoke in him: which was soon heightened
by Popish reports all over the country ... A long time I expected to have seen him in one
of his fits, but the Devil was too timorous of my stern countenance and rough carriage.
[The boy and his father] went that night to a Popish house where were a concourse of
people sufficient, and many tales told of the divinations of the spirit in the boy, but not
one word either of me or against me.
(ii) I myself knew a person in the West Riding of Yorkshire, who about some forty
years or above, in order to make sport, would put a coverlet upon him and then make
any believe (that knew not the truth) that he had a child with him, he would so lively
discourse with two voices and imitate crying and the like.
(iii) I have also sometimes seen a person that lived in Southwark near London who,
holding his lips together and making no sound or noise at all, would notwithstanding
have, by the motion of the muscles of his face and the agitation of his head and hands,
and other gesticulations of his body, made any of the beholders understand what tune
he had modulated in his fancy: which was very strange and pleasant to behold, and
that which I could not have believed if I had not seen it. (pp. 124, 125, 126)

Anecdotes from Catholic sources are, needless to say, disparaged. 'This is a story from one single person, a lying Carmelite,' he says at one point, 'one that for interest and upholding of superstition and idolatry had feigned and forged it' (p. 56). Modern judges and juries, however (one tacitly understands 'being Protestant'), were free from bias and ulterior personal or corporate motive, having no 'sinister and corrupt ends to wrest the laws, or wring forth and extort feigned and false confessions, because they have no such ends, as to uphold and maintain idolatrous and superstitious tenets – [such] as praying to saints, magnifying of holy water, or setting up of Purgatory – as had the Popish inquisitors and the demonographers and witchmongers that writ for those ends' (p. 72). But Webster was not an unsubtle controversialist. To be sure, he recycled the old arguments that witches were either frauds or individuals suffering from melancholia or people with a vivid imagination, and denied flatly that witches could do any of the things they claimed to do. This, however, does not place him in the camp of the materialist sceptics. On the contrary, evil spirits ('fallen angels') and the Devil, he said, are real enough, although in what form and with what abilities is not clear. Certainly they can do nothing without God's permission. But in seeking to explain both their nature and their modus operandi, we shall probably do better to await the extension of human knowledge to see whether certain phenomena have a natural explanation or not. There is still so much human beings do not know or understand that it is wiser not to behave like 'those that seem to idolise human abilities and carnal reason [which], though proving ineffectual to find out the true notions and knowledge of natural things, have ... notwithstanding invaded Heaven and taken upon them to discover and determine of celestials, wherein it is in a manner totally blind' (p. 201).

As illustrations of what he meant by things humans do not know or fully understand, he discussed 'divers creatures that have a real existence in nature and yet, by reason of their wondrous properties or seldom being seen, have been taken for spirits and devils' (chap. 15), suggesting that satyrs might be a kind of ape, fairies pigmies and mermaids fish. Apparitions of one kind or another were also real after a different manner, he said (chap. 16), and he provided a large number of anecdotes drawn from recent sources to substantiate his claim. He also accepted the long-standing notion that the body of someone murdered will bleed in the presence of its murderer (pp. 302–309), and that charms could work even if, most of the time, they were little more than placebos recited for the benefit of the patient (p. 329). 'Most', but not 'all' the time, for

> what is here fully explicated, as also what we have formerly in this treatise proved both by reasons, authorities, and examples, doth sufficiently manifest the great power of celestial bodies upon inferior matter, and that, according to the aptitude and agreeableness of the matter prepared and the configuration of the heavens at the time elected, the powerful influence of the stars and planets is received into the subject, according to the purpose it was intended for. So that from hence it will clearly follow that if fit and agreeable words or characters be framed and joined together when the heavens are in a convenient site and configuration for the purpose intended, those words and characters will receive a most powerful virtue [*power*] for the purpose intended,

and will effectually operate to those ends by a just, lawful, and natural agency, without any concurrence of diabolical power, superstition. (pp. 340–341)

As far as Webster was concerned, then, both past and present were awash with instances of deliberate or self-deception which accounted for so much of the accumulated evidences of witches' supposed abilities, ghosts, demons, and some of the more remarkable prodigies seen and reported from nature, scripture, and sound reason should be the only reliable bases for determining the truth about Satan's activity in the world, the nature of spirits, and the operation of magic. But while scripture and sound reason could eradicate much of the detritus of superstition which lingered in society, not every marvel, not every inexplicable sight or event or working should be dismissed.[30]

The ultimate effect of Webster's treatise, however, whether he intended it or not, was to bolster scepticism, and so we should not be surprised perhaps to find that it was condemned by the Church on the one hand, and licensed by the Royal Society on the other, a contrast of judgements mirroring Webster's own ambiguous stance. Ian Bostridge summarises it. 'The implication [of his work] seems to be confusingly double-edged. Witchcraft is no special crime, but merely imposture instigated by counsel of the Devil. On the other hand, all crime is witchcraft, in that all crime involves a league with the Devil.'[31] So witchcraft is both a delusion and a crime, but not a special sort of crime. Not the clearest of definitions.

Webster was partly answered in 1678 by Benjamin Camfield, rector of Aylston near Leicester, in an appendix to his *A Theological Discourse of Angels*. In his dedicatory epistle to the Earl of Rutland and Lord Roos, Camfield observes that his subject matter is 'too suitable to that atheistical and degenerate age we live in, wherein the general disbelief of spirits, divine and human, angelical and diabolical, may well be thought ... the ground and introduction of all that irreligion and profaneness which naturally enough follows upon it'. Webster (he objects) says God is a spirit, but reduces Him to 'a bare and empty name' (p. 174) and, while disapproving of people's intellectual laziness in 'resting satisfied in the sleepy notions of general rules and speculative philosophy, by which means a general prejudice hath been created against the more occult [*hidden*] operations of nature and natural magic', Webster chooses to ignore the experience common to everyone of 'the incorporeal spirit within him, actuating and moving of the body' (p. 204).

Camfield's lament of a 'general disbelief' reflected the situation as it appeared to intellectuals and scholars, of course, rather than the way it was seen by the majority of people. As far as they were concerned, magic worked, witches were as active as ever, and one needed to look no further than one's own doorsteps and the law courts for proof of it. So people in Yorkshire knew that in August 1674, Mary Moor reported to the York assizes a detailed conversation she had overheard between Susan Hinchcliffe and Susan's daughter Ann Shillitoe as they plotted to bewitch Thomas Haigh to death, and Susan boasted she had already lamed his mother and had done her best to make his horse throw him near water so that he would either break his neck or fall into a dyke and drown. Ann's father, too, was a witch and could not only produce butter from thin air, but also ruined two tradesmen, making them unable to work. 'If anyone won't let us have what we want,' Susan was supposed to have said, 'we'll take his or her life.'[32] People in Wales were aware that a similar malice obtained as John Parry cursed Mary Lloyd into illness and death in 1674, while on the Isle of Man, they knew that a vicar cast the evil eye on sheep in 1672 and killed them, and in 1673, 1675, and 1678 that the death curse was invoked, the *skeab lome*, intended to annihilate, had been invoked against various individuals: 'May the besom of destruction come upon thyself, upon thy hearth, upon thy health, upon thy possessions, and upon thy children.' Scandal is evident, too, in the administration of love magic. When Thomas Hughes gave Jane ferch Edward 'some enticing or other enchanting or bewitching powder' in 1675, for example, thus enabling him not only to father two children upon her (who afterwards mysteriously died), but also to get her to make over her property to him, it was only one among several such similar crimes, for Thomas was a serial seducer and tried his luck again in 1678, only to be arrested and brought to trial.[33]

In Scotland, the 1670s saw trials or executions of witches every year, mostly, again, in the central belt from Renfrewshire to East Lothian, the busiest year being 1678 when about thirty-two witches were garrotted and burned in various places. It is worth noting, in case we forget some of the realities underlying these simple phrases, that executing witches was expensive and a charge upon the individual community which did not undertake these extra financial burdens in any light or unconsidered way. The costs of carrying out the death sentence on Isobel Elliot, Marion Meitch, Margaret Dods, and Helen Laing in Peaston, East Lothian on Friday 20 September 1678, for example, were as follows:

> Item: to the dempster [*court official pronouncing sentence*], £2.
>
> To the hangman, 13s 4d.
>
> More to him to give back their plaids, 6s.
>
> To the officers, £1.
>
> Item: for 8 cartfuls of coals at 14s the cart, is £5 12s 6d.
>
> Item: for trees [*pieces of wood*] and nails to the gallows and scaffold, £2 5s 6d.
>
> Item: for 4 tar barrels, £2 9s 4d.
>
> Item: to the wright and his men for building the gallows and scaffold, £1 10s 0d.
>
> Item: for the hangman's wages, and the expenses at Haddington two several times before he came out, and at the sending of him back with a merk to him to buy tows, in all £22 7s 4d.
>
> Summa is £38 3s 0d.
>
> Divide £38 3s 0d in four parts, each part will be £9 10s 9d.[34]

Comparisons are difficult, of course, but figures relating to Linlithgow in Midlothian for 1673 show that a best farm servant would earn £26 13s 4d per year (with board), an able farm woman £16, and a female domestic £8.[35] Executing each of these women was therefore more expensive than hiring a domestic servant for a year.

The motives, however, were compelling. As we have seen before, Scotland experienced waves of reforming zeal from its Calvinist establishment, which was fixed upon cleansing the country of 'superstition' and imposing religious conformity on behaviour, minds, and morals. But in the 1670s the Calvinist establishment was not in control of the state. Episcopacy after the English model had been introduced after 1660 and was immensely unpopular, especially in the south-west where Presbyterianism was strong. In order to worship as they wanted, people met in unofficial and illegal groups known as conventicles, and by 1670 attendance at these had become treasonable, while preaching at them carried the death penalty. Numbers attending them, however, could be huge: 7,000 in Ayrshire and 3,000 in Berwickshire in 1678, for example, and 6,000 in Kirkcudbrightshire in 1679. Needless to say, the government in Edinburgh was determined to suppress these hotbeds of dissent, and during the 1670s tensions were ratcheted so high that in early 1678 soldiers were brought from the Highlands to be quartered in the areas most suspect, where they created mayhem. A Nonconformist minister lamented the dissenters' sufferings: 'It would require several great volumes to record the many instances of horrid barbarities, bloods, and villainies of that wicked expedition, so that what by free quarterings, exactions, robberies, thefts, plunderings, and other acts of violence and cruelty, many places were ruined almost to desolation.'[36] Not long after, in 1679, the two sides clashed in battle and from 1680 to 1685 atrocities dominated certain areas in south-west Scotland and informed, indeed poisoned, relationships between the various parties. It may therefore come as no surprise to find that animus against witchcraft, while not at the forefront of people's consciousness at this time, nevertheless ran as a deep stream throughout southern and Border Scottish society. Sir George MacKenzie who became Lord Advocate in 1677, published his influential legal summary, *The Laws and Customs of Scotland in Matters Criminal*, in 1678, and from this we can gauge the attitude of at least some of the Scottish legal establishment towards witchcraft and therefore the witches who appeared from time to time before them. MacKenzie himself was very hostile to Covenanters, as the religious dissidents were called, but showed a nuanced approach to witchcraft, partly at least because his experience as a justice depute of trying witches had led him to doubt the legal validity of certain aspects of these cases. His review of witchcraft, Title X in *Laws and Customs*, came to the following conclusions:

(i) 'That there are witches, divines cannot doubt, since the Word of God hath ordained that no witch shall live, nor lawyers in Scotland, seeing our law ordains it to be punished with death' (p. 81).

(ii) Witches are no more deluded by melancholia than murderers are by rage or revenge (p. 83).

(iii) Witches' charms cannot produce the effects of which witches are accused and for which they are punished, and when they do work, or appear to work, it is by the Devil's agency (p. 84).

(iv) Because the crime of witchcraft is so dreadful, it requires, of all crimes, that evidence offered be of the clearest relevance and most convincing probation (p. 85).

(v) Miscarriages of justice can take place for a variety of reasons, as MacKenzie knows from his own experience (pp. 86–87).

(vi) Valid reasons for arresting a person suspect of witchcraft – it is noticeable that

MacKenzie uses female pronouns throughout this Title – are that she has been named by other witches, has an evil reputation, has been found practising magic, and magical *instrumenta* have been discovered in her house (p. 89).

(vii) The Devil's mark used to be an important piece of evidence, but not now. Prickers, too, are frequently cheats (pp. 91–92).

(viii) Consulting witches, diviners, and the rest is an offence under the law (p. 96).

(ix) The Devil can delude people into thinking they can do things such as fly or change shape (pp. 98–100).

(x) The evil eye is irrelevant to proving witchcraft (p. 103).

(xi) Images made of wax or clay work, if they do work, via the Devil's agency (pp. 103–104).

(xii) Confessions before a kirk session may be legally valid (pp. 104–106).[37]

This tentative approach perhaps signals uncertainty rather than scepticism, for on the one hand MacKenzie is clear that witches do exist, that they are not necessarily mentally ill, and that some of their magic works because of the Devil's agency. On the other hand, he insists that proof of their malevolent activity be thoroughly convincing because there is too much room for miscarriage of justice.

We catch a glimpse of this caution in action from MacKenzie's account of one of his cases. Five years before publishing his *Laws and Customs*, he had issued *Pleadings in Some Remarkable Cases before the Supreme Courts of Scotland since the year 1661*, which includes his defence of a witch he calls 'Maevia'. The charges against her were straightforward. She had changed shape, flown through the air, laid on an illness and taken it off again. MacKenzie begins with a personal declaration. 'I am not of their opinion who deny that there are witches, though I think they are not numerous' (p. 185). He then employs Webster's argument that there are things in nature we do not yet understand, adding that putting someone to death because of this ignorance of ours is indefensible (p. 186). He mocks the idea that Maevia's cure was unnatural. It was effected by applying a plantain leaf to the patient, and as the illness was a fever and the plantain leaf is known to be cold, there can be no question of unnaturalness in its application (p. 190). As for flying with the help of the Devil, why would God permit this to happen when the people so transported will only blaspheme Him upon their arrival (p. 194)? Shape changing, too, is simply a witch's fantasy caused by the Devil's acting upon her imagination (p. 194). Finally, MacKenzie allows himself an emotional plea to the reader. 'Judges allow themselves too much liberty in condemning such as are accused of this crime, because they conclude they cannot be severe enough to the enemies of God; and assizers [*jury men*] are afraid to suffer such to escape as are remitted to them, lest they let loose an enraged wizard in their neighbourhood. And thus poor innocents die in multitudes by an unworthy martyrdom, and burning comes in fashion' (p. 196).[38]

Such, then, was his approach to the subject, influenced by his own experiences in the courtroom, and it may be observed that this caution reflected growing legal opinion. After 1670, a new system of circuit courts began to operate efficiently and the result was that while an increased number of witchcraft cases came before them, the number of acquittals rose, too. So local tensions, however caused (and there were many contributory factors at this time, as we have seen), ran their heads against the wall of judicial reluctance to allow matters to get out of hand, or to allow trials to take place when the evidence brought before them might be dubious or improperly gained, by which may be meant torture, legally or illegally administered. In 1662, the Privy Council had noted more than one instance of this leading to miscarriage of justice, and had proclaimed its use illegal without the council's express permission. Unfortunately, this did not stop its covert use for a long time afterwards.[39] Official nervousness in the face of the possibility that once witches started naming accomplices they might not know where to stop can be seen from an incident dated 1678, the year MacKenzie published his *Laws and Customs*.

> Eight or ten witches, all (except one or two) poor miserable-like women, were pannelled [*accused in court*]. Some of them were brought out of Sir Robert Hepburn of Keith's lands, others out of Ormiston, Crighton, and Pencaitland parishes. The first of them were delated by those two who were burned in Saltpreston in May 1678, and they delated and named the rest, as also put forth seven in the Lonehead of Lasswade, and if they had been permitted, [they] were ready to file by their delation sundry gentlewomen and others of fashion. But the justices discharged them, thinking it either the product of malice or melancholy or the Devil's deception in representing such persons as present at their field meetings, who truly were not there.[40]

The justices' decision, however, went against the grain of the jury and audience. 'This was cried out on as prelimiting them from discovering these enemies of mankind.' Popular tension, therefore, was as great as ever and did not bode well for the coming decade, and if the accused confessed to the crimes alleged against them, there was little or nothing even the most sceptical or cautious judge could do about it. We can see this in an English case from 1682. On 25 August, Temperance Lloyd, Mary Trembles, and Susanna Edwards, all from Bideford in Devon, were hanged – Temperance apparently unconcerned as she ate all the way from the gaol to the gallows, Mary with difficulty after she lay down on or fell to the floor and had to be tied on a horse to get her to move. Temperance had already sustained two trials, one in 1671 when she was acquitted of witchcraft, and the second in 1679 when she was searched for Devil's marks, in spite of which the accusation against her did not proceed to trial. Their trials and executions followed their confession to a variety of offences, principally making people ill or killing them by witchcraft, and giving suck to demon familiars and the Devil. Torture was not used, and the confessions appear to have emerged from persistent questioning by officials, including the rector of Loxbeare, Francis Hann, who was particularly interested in eliciting details about the accuseds' relationship with Satan.

As it happens, however, this case also illustrates some of the problems we meet in assessing the surviving evidence. Jonathan Barry has warned us about the unreliability of much of the record of these three cases since, apart from such sources as the Bideford session book and the gaol books, it consists largely of three popular pamphlets dated 1682 and a private letter from one interested party to another. The way those latter sources report proceedings suggests that their authors either understood what they were reporting in different ways which coloured the way they presented the evidence, or that the authors had different agenda and so told their tale with their separate ends in view. It is also worth our bearing in mind that, as far as we know, Temperance, Mary, and Susanna were the last English women to be executed as witches and this, if we are not careful, may incline us to over-interpret their situation, as appears to have happened, for example, in John Watkins's account from 1792 which refers to the 'ignorance, prejudice, and superstition' of those concerned, or in a late nineteenth-century fulmination against 'the Moloch of popular delusion', and delineation of the three women as 'the last victims to gratify the appetite of a degrading credulity'.[41] Denigrating the past congratulates the present by implication, and thus a myth of linear historical progress is perpetuated. Thus, the three women are described as old and poor, in one version of events, 'decrepit, despicable, [and] miserable': in another, 'as to sense or understanding, scarcely alive': and in a third, 'overwhelmed with melancholy and waking dreams, and so stupid that nobody could suppose they knew either the construction or consequences of what they said'.[42] These may coincide to form an accurate picture, of course, but that picture stems from Roger North, brother of an assize judge, Sir Francis North, who was keen to establish both his and his brother's credentials as men deeply sceptical of witchcraft, and so it may have suited him to depict the three women as the foolish and confused victims of local uneducated superstition. Hence our necessary caution in accepting his version of the parties concerned and of the trials themselves as unvarnished truth, and it is worth bearing in mind Barry's conclusion that 'we have no direct evidence of what the three women confessed during the trial at the assizes'.[43]

What does seem to be clear, however, is that the trials were driven by particular individuals alleging they had suffered at the hands of these witches, and that because those individuals were well connected, the magistrates who heard the original depositions and then the judges trying the cases had to steer a difficult course between yielding to local emotions stirred up by the accusations and keeping those same emotions under control. In as much as Temperance, Mary, and Susanna were executed, the steering failed. But in as much as the number of accused remained limited and no other people were caught up in any popular spasm, it was successful.[44]

A ballad 'to the tune of "Doctor Faustus" or "Fortune my Foe"' was quickly churned out before the executions. *Witchcraft Discovered and Punished* jogs jauntily through the women's guilt and crimes before coming to a pious conclusion.

> At the last assizes held at Exeter,
> Three aged women that imprisoned were
> For witches, and that many had destroyed,
> Were thither brought in order to be tried
> For witchcraft, that old wicked sin,
> Which they for long time had continued in,
> And joined with Satan to destroy the good,
> Hurt innocents, and shed their harmless blood ...

So these malicious women at the last,
Having done mischiefs, were by justice cast:
For it appeared they children had destroyed,
Lamed cattle, and the aged much annoyed,
Having familiars always at their beck,
Their wicked rage on mortals for to wreck:
It being proved they used wicked charms
To murther men and bring about sad harms;
And that they had about their bodies strange
And proper tokens of their wicked change,
As pledges that, to have their cruel will,
Their souls they gave unto the Prince of Hell ...

But now the hand of Heaven has found them out,
And they to justice must pay lives, past doubt ...

[One] said the Devil came with her along,
Through crowds of people and bid her be strong,
And she no hand should have. But, like a liar,
At the prison door he fled and ne'er came nigh her.
The rest aloud craved mercy for their sins,
Or else the great Deceiver her soul gains,
For they had been lewd livers many a day,
And therefore did desire that all would pray
To God to pardon them while thus they lie,
Condemned for their wicked deeds to die:
Which may each Christian do, that they may find
Rest for their souls, though wicked once inclined.

This same year also saw the trial of Jane Jent, who was accused of bewitching to death Elizabeth Chamblet, aged five. Jane was brought to her accuser's door by the common counter-magic of boiling urine and nail clippings, then searched, a teat being discovered upon her back 'and unusual holes behind her ears'. A coachman testified at her trial that after he refused to carry her and her luggage, his coach overturned, 'but she producing evidence that she had lived honestly and was a great painstaker, and that she went to church, with many other circumstances, the jury found her not guilty'.[45] Likewise, Joan Buts, tried at the Surrey assizes in 1682, was accused of bewitching to death Mary Farmer, a child, and making Elizabeth Burridge, a servant, ill.

The witnesses being sworn, the parents of Mary Farmer swore that their child being taken ill in an extraordinary and violent manner, the neighbours told them it was bewitched and persuaded them to go to Dr Bourn, which they did, and Bourn told them that their child was under an ill tongue, and advised them to save the child's water and put it into a bottle, stopping it close and bury it in the earth, and to burn the child's clothes, assuring them that then the witch which had done her the hurt would come in; and that accordingly they did so; and when the child's clothes was burning, Joan Buts came in and sat her down upon a stool, looking with most frightful and ghastly countenance; and being asked by a woman that was there present what she ailed, she answered she was not well, not had been out in seven weeks before. 'Why would you come out now, then?' said the woman. 'I could not forbear coming to see you,' said she, and with that, she threw down her hat and tumbled down, wallowing to the ground, making a fearful and dismal noise; and being got up, she fell a-cursing in a most horrid manner.[46]

Elizabeth Burridge was also subjected to hails of stones and a wad of clay stuck full of pins, which was thrown at her back from inside the house. One witness testified that Joan had said anent Mary Farmer that even if she [Joan] had not bewitched her, 'if all the devils in Hell could help her, she *would* bewitch her', an unfortunate outburst she explained to the judge, saying, 'I am a passionate woman and, they having urged me, I spake those words in passion, my lord. But I intended no such thing.' The trial was long and the jury divided, but after long discussion it gave in a verdict of not guilty.

Joan may have been lucky. Not so Alice Fowler from the parish of Wapping in London, an old woman who 'had always been a malicious, ill-natured woman and for many years had been reputed a witch'. She scraped a living by selling biscuits to brothels, but depended on the charity of Trinity House, her late husband having been a sailor. For a while she had been foster mother to a girl who was convinced she was a witch and remained frightened of her even when she had become an adult. Alice's son, too, who was hanged in Barbados for murder and housebreaking, said his mother was a witch. None of which, perhaps, would have called for the attention of a pamphleteer, but after Alice died, her body was found naked upon the floor of her room, her two big toes tied together and a blanket thrown over her. It was probably this peculiar circumstance which drew the writer's attention, for tying the toes together was a detail reminiscent of the process involved in swimming someone to test whether or not she was a witch.[47] As late as 1689 this was still being done. Two young people from Beckington in Somerset had started vomiting pins, nails, and other metallic objects, and an old woman who lived in the almshouse was blamed by both. So a JP ordered her to be searched and several purple spots insensible to pain were found on her person. This, perhaps, precipitated what happened next.

This old woman was had to a great river near the town to see whether she could sink under water. Her legs being tied, she was put in and though she did endeavour to the uttermost (by her hands) to get herself under, yet she could not, but would lie on her back and did swim [*float*] like a piece of cork. There were present above twenty persons to attest the truth of this, yet could not gain credit in the minds of people. Therefore she was had to the water a second time and, being put in, she swam as at first; and though there were present above two hundred people to see this sight, yet it could not be believed by many. At the same time also, there was put into the water a lusty young woman who sank immediately and had been drowned, had it not been for the help that was at hand. To satisfy the world and to leave no room for doubting, the old woman was had down to the water the third time and, being put in as before, she still did swim. At this swimming of her were present such a company of people of the town and country, and many of them persons of quality, as could not well be numbered, so that now there is scarce one person that doubts of the truth of this thing.[48]

Such, then, was the popular atmosphere which might surround an arrest and trial and which local officials had to contain if they did not want to see emotions run high and spiral out of control, regardless of whether they sympathised with popular opinion or not; and whatever the personal views on the validity of witchcraft, which magistrates and judges may have had, of course, they were irrelevant to the administration of the law, and the law still maintained there were indeed witches, and if witches committed certain crimes and were found guilty thereof, they should be punished by execution. But doubts and certainties among the learned continued to occupy time, effort, and printer's ink, and the fight against uncertainty or outright denial went on more or less without interruption.

In 1680, for example, John Brinley, describing himself as 'Gent', published a slightly odd treatise, *A Discovery of the Impostures of Witches and Astrologers*, which is actually, as its title suggests, two essays in one. The cheating and superstition implied by his title and referred to in his preface, however, turn out to refer to astrology more than to witchcraft, and although Brinley does not deny the existence of witches or the contracts they make with Satan, he tends to dismiss the reality of much of the evildoing ascribed to them. Most people, he says, are inclined to be superstitious, and when they suffer any kind of affliction, they should remember that it has been sent either by God Himself or with God's permission, and consequently they should sustain it in humble patience, not go running off to workers of magic for a remedy. 'Let no man think it lies in the power of enchanters, witches, or any of their associates or assistants, the devils, to cure those whom the Lord hath smitten, or to hurt any person whom the Lord is pleased to bless' (pp. 14–15). Several diseases, he adds, are natural, not the result of devils' activity, and devils do not need human agents to be able to do harm. Therefore people should hesitate before ascribing their ills and afflictions to witchcraft. So far, one may think, so sceptical. But then suddenly Brinley announces, 'That there are witches and such persons as form contracts with the Devil have undertook, and seemingly performed, some strange things (though denied by some sensual men of this age, whose interest it is there should be neither Heaven nor Hell, and who have therefore proceeded from the denial of the soul to the denial of spirits, and from thence even to the denial of the existence of God Himself) is yet deducible from several reasons' (p. 29). The reasons, he says, are scriptural, which should be sufficient for doubters, even without modern instances to support what scripture says. Witches are real; covenants with the Devil are real; demonic possessions are real caused either by the unmediated working of Satan or the mediated operation of witches; and 'when learned physicians can find no probable reason or natural cause of such grief, pangs, and violent vexations as the patient does endure, it may lawfully be concluded that the Devil's finger is there' (p. 60). Despite some people's attempts to divide witches into good types and bad, therefore, one should avoid them altogether.[49]

Brinley's purpose in writing this part of his treatise was, as he says, to confront the irreligion and 'atheism' of his day and this, too, was the intention of Henry Hallywell whose *Melampronoea* ('Black Forethought') appeared the following year.

> This age hath produced too many over-confident exploders of immaterial substances, and he that shall talk of the existence of devils and evil spirits, their possessions of the bodies of men, of ghosts and apparitions and the fear and practices of witches, shall be confuted with a loud laughter or a supercilious look, as if these things were only the delusions of a distempered imagination, and owed all their being and reality to the dreams and fancies of melancholic persons. Or, if the matters of fact be too notorious to be gainsaid, then these corporealists will not stick to affirm with a late author that they believe there are many thousands of spirits made of incorporeal matter, too fine to be perceived by the senses of men, and that these spirits may play mad pranks amongst us. A thing much more worthy of laughter and the character of folly, and all one as if a man should go about to persuade that the little motes or atoms that fridge [*rub together*] and play in the beams of the sun shining through a cranny, should by a common consent unite themselves into a living heap, and speak and act either ludicrously or mischievously with the standers-by. (pp. 3–4)

To achieve his stated purpose, Hallywell begins by describing the fall of some angels from contemplation of God to a lapsed state of absorption in materiality which affords them no pleasure or satisfaction. 'They being all embodied spirits, that is, vitally united to matter, they must of necessity be capable both of pain and pleasure, the sense of which is more or less acute and vigorous according to either the tenuity or grossness of their bodies, and by consequence they are liable and obnoxious to harm and injury from those of their own society' (pp. 15–16). There is a great diversity among these fallen angels, but they are divided into ranks and orders in the manner of human society, and governed by the more powerful spirits among them, performing a variety of mischievous and damaging tasks under their leadership and governance. Since fallen angels are rational, they can formulate their wicked intentions into coherent designs and it was to thwart these that Jesus became incarnate. The disunity of present-day Christians merely encourages them and the Devil in their efforts, and the spate of demonic possessions throughout history, 'so fully attested by unprejudiced persons in all ages', means that anyone who denies their reality 'cannot escape the suspicion of having imbibed some atheistical principles'. Irresolution in religious belief is what causes people to doubt the existence of such spirits and therefore of wizards, witches, and magicians, all of whom are spoken of in scripture (pp. 47–48).

Having thus brought his readers smoothly to the presence and agency of witches in society, Hallywell now turns to answering five of the principal objections he says are frequently offered. First, it is impossible that witches be simultaneously present at Sabbats and in their own homes. No, it is not, for there is plenty of evidence that souls may be withdrawn from the body, 'a thing which is credibly reported of the Lappians who, lying as it were in a trance for some hours, will give a perfect account of affairs at three hundred miles distance, and by some evident token give assurance of their being in such places' (p. 73).[50] Secondly, these spirits are too remote to have contact with humans. Demoniacs illustrate that this is not so. Thirdly, witches cannot work miracles, even with spirits' help. There are good, bad, and false 'miracles', and one needs to exercise caution in assessing their reality or otherwise. Fourthly, the actions attributed to witches presume they have an incredible power over both elements and humans and animals. But nothing happens without God's permission and He ultimately controls the extent of their activities. Fifthly, it is difficult to believe that demons suck witches' blood. Classical and early Christian literature show that this has happened. Finally, all this should teach us to have a strong faith in God; to watch what we say about evil spirits and how we say it, but not to be afraid of them; to suppress our vices such as pride, malice, and the tendency to quarrel among ourselves; and, after contemplating the kingdom of darkness, to have trust in God's providence.

These calm lucubrations were all very well, but England was now passing through a time of crisis and constitutional upheaval. Not only was a Catholic threat to political stability seen in the accession of James VII and II, but Protestant sects of one kind or another were proliferating, the march of materialist philosophy was as popular as ever among much of the educated class and as much a perceived threat to the Anglican establishment, and the emergence of political parties associating themselves with each of the religious and political divides all contributed to a febrile atmosphere in which defence or repudiation of the other world and magic and witchcraft was rapidly becoming a badge of political and religious reliability or a token of shiftiness or even fanaticism which threatened the nation's security. This threat was perceived as real even if it was more chimaera than genuine danger. The so-called 'Popish Plot' dreamed up by Titus Oates and Israel Tonge in 1678, for example, alleged the existence of a widespread conspiracy to assassinate Charles II, and while it raged it not only intensified anti-Catholic feeling in both England and Scotland, but left a legacy of bitterness which lasted well into the nineteenth century. Twenty-one Jesuits died, nine by execution, twelve in prison, many priests were arrested, and there were big Pope-burning processions in London in 1680 and 1681. The Green Ribbon Club, a Whig club founded in 1675 by individuals hostile to the court, was keenly anti-Catholic and helped stimulate public outrage over the Popish Plot. How one viewed and treated witches, therefore, had developed a serious political aura.

The extraordinary atmosphere of the time can be glimpsed in a play by one of the Greek Ribbon Club's members, Thomas Shadwell. *The Lancashire Witches and Tegue O'Dively, the Irish Priest*, described as a 'comedy', was first performed in 1681 at the Duke's Theatre in London. Its plot is complicated and need not concern us here in detail. Two young women are supposed to marry women they do not like and are in love with two other men who are not their parents' choice. One of the parents, Sir Edward Hartfort, has a household curate called Smerk – 'foolish, knavish, Popish, arrogant, insolent, yet for his interest, slavish' – who allies himself with an Irish priest – 'an equal mixture of fool and knave' – when it becomes necessary to deal with witchcraft taking place in Sir Edward's cellar (this in spite of the fact that Sir Edward does not believe in witches). Mother Demdike, one of the principal witches, fools some of the play's characters by shape changing in a knockabout scene intended to illustrate their silliness, and then summons her sister witches in song.

The owl is flown from the hollow oak.
From lakes and bogs the toads do croak.
The foxes bark, the screech-owl screams.
Wolves howl, bats fly, and the faint beams
Of glow-worms' light grows bright a-pace.
The stars are fled, the moon hides her face.
The spindle now is turning round.
Mandrakes are groaning underground.
In the hole in the ditch our nails have made
Now all our images are laid,
Of wax and wool, which we must prick
With needles urging to the quick.
Into the hole I'll pour a flood
Of black lamb's blood, to make all good.
The lamb with nails and teeth we'll tear ...

(Demdike) The hollow flint stone I have got,
Which I over my shoulder throw
Into the west, to make winds blow.
Now water here and urine put,
And with your sticks stir it about.
Now dip your brooms and toss them high
To bring the rain down from the sky.
Not yet a storm? Come, let us wound
The air with every dreadful sound,
And with live vipers beat the ground.

(*They beat the ground with vipers. They bark, howl, hiss, cry like screech-owls, holler like owls, and make many confused noises. The storm begins.*) (pp. 10–12)

These 'women', of course, according to the theatrical convention of the period, will have been acted by men, whose cross-dressing, unfeminine voices, and dissonant music imitating the confused and bestial noises they make in their magical incantations, draw attention to their unnatural appearances, their disruptive roles, and their intention to create disorder in place of harmony.[51] This intention is then later illustrated when each reports to the Devil the wicked deeds she has done during a night's mischief-making.

(Devil) What have ye done for my delight?
Relate the service of the night.

(Demdike) To a mother's bed I softly crept,
And while the unchristened brat yet slept,
I sucked the breath and blood of that,
And stole another's flesh and fat,
Which I will boil before it stink:

The thick for ointment, then for drink
I'll keep.
From a murderer that hung in chains,
I bit dried sinews and shrink veins.
Marrow and entrails have I brought,
A piece of the gibbet, too, I got,
And of the rope the fatal knot.
I sunk a ship, and in my flight
I kicked a steeple down to night.

(Devil) Well done, my dame! Ho, ho, ho!

(Dickenson) To gibbets I flew and dismal caves,
To charnel houses and to graves.
Bones I got and flesh enough,
From dead men's eyes the gluey stuff.
Their eyeballs with my nails scooped out,
And pieces of their limbs I've brought.
A brat in the mother's womb I slew.
The father's neck I twisted, too.
Dogs barked, cocks crowed, away I flew.

(Devil) A good servant. Ho, ho, ho!

(Hargrave) Flesh from a raven in a ditch
I snatched, and more from a ravenous bitch.
Amongst tombs I searched for flesh and bone,
(With hair about my ears, alone).
Fingers, noses, and a wen,
And the blood of murdered men,
A mad dog's foam and a wolf's hairs,
A serpent's bowels, adders' ears,
I put in my pouch, and, coming back,
The bells in a steeple I did crack.
I sent the murrain into hogs,
And drove the kine into the bogs.

(Devil) 'Tis well, 'Tis well. Ho, ho, ho!

(Spen) To make up love cups I have sought.
A wolf's tail, hair, and yard [*penis*] I've got,
The green frog's bones, whose flesh was ta'en
From thence by ants: then a cat's brain,
The bunch of flesh from a black foal's head,
Just as his dam was brought to bed,

Before she licked it. And I have some
Of that which falls from a mare's womb
When she's in lust. And, as I came home,
I put a women into fits
And frighted a parson out of his wits. (pp. 25–26)

This is a curious collection of the actions popularly attributed to witches and well known to the audience from a large number of sources. But it is also deliberately over the top, rather like Lucan's portrait of Erichtho the witch in his epic *Pharsalia*, and reminds us of Dickens's Fat Boy – 'I wants to make yer flesh creep.' Shadwell's audience will have laughed rather than shuddered. Nevertheless, one should remember that whatever the reaction of the sophisticates in the boxes, some of the gallery at least are likely to have had some personal experience of witches, diviners, magicians, and so on, either as their clients or the objects of their unwanted attentions, and that some physicians – expensive and therefore employed by the circle rather than the gallery – were happily manufacturing and using medicines harvested from human flesh and blood. Shadwell's language may thus be exaggerated, but not quite to the extent it may seem to us.

Sent by Sir Edward's Catholic neighbours to help deal with these witches, Tegue O'Divelly now makes an appearance and from the very start, he and Smerk show themselves to be two sides of the same coin. But Tegue is also shown to be no better than a witch himself, for when a constable complains that he cannot urinate after seeing a large hare at his back door, Tegue offers to cure him. 'Take one of the tooths of a dead man and burn it, and take the smoke into both of your noses, as you take snuff, and anoint yourself with the gall of a crow. Take quicksilver, as they do call it, and put upon a quill, and plash it under the soft pillow you do sit upon. Then make some water through the ring of a wedding, by St Patrick, and I will say some Ave Marys for thee, and thou wilt be sound again' (p. 37). As others come to seek his advice about their ills and problems, he offers more of the same, and so the audience is left in no doubt that he is both irretrievably superstitious and stupid, an impression assisted by the weird pseudo-Irish accent the actor is directed by the text to employ. Eventually, as Smerk believes the witches have cast a spell on him, Tegue endeavours to rid him of it by means of an exorcism consisting of a good dousing with holy water and the performance of an extraordinarily offensive parody of part of the canon of the Mass. This is witchcraft as farce, although the wider social unrest rendered it more sinister than perhaps Shadwell intended. For overt mockery of Catholic exorcism by equating it with witchcraft was not merely amusing for a Protestant audience but was also, given the circumstances of the time, an incitement to discrimination, hostility, and violence against certain sections of society, an incitement we must regard as one of Shadwell's aims, since at the end of the play he has Tegue arrested on a charge of being mixed up in the Popish Plot.

Witchcraft and contemporary politics appear again in 1684 in Richard Bovet's treatise *Pandaemonium: or, The Devil's Cloyster*. 'Cloyster' is a word meaning 'human excrement', as well being a possible variant upon 'cloister', a monastic courtyard, and as the work is virulently anti-Catholic, the double meaning will not have been lost on

Bovet's readers. Bovet, in his guise as 'A Person of Quality in the County of Devon', had already edited *A Narrative of the Demon of Spraiton* in 1683, which is directed against 'sons of the atheistical *Leviathan*', Hobbes's influential work, and hopes that 'if the Great Deceiver, for the security of his dominions, keep the resolute debauchees and obstinate Hobbians in incredulity of relations of this nature ... [this narrative] will have other impressions on the more rational part of mankind'. After which hope, Bovet tells the stories of two ghosts, that of an old man and that of a young woman, both of whom interact quite violently with humans, the latter showing signs of poltergeist-like activity. *Pandaemonium* ('An Entire Assembly of Demons') seeks likewise to convince its readers of the reality of the spirit world and owes something to the example of Glanvill and More – indeed, it is dedicated to More – in its collection of anecdotes about witchcrafts, demons, and spectres which makes up the second part of the book. These are largely contemporary – 1667, 1669, 1678, 1680, 1682, and 1683 are the dates provided – and come principally from Somerset and Devon, although four come from Scotland via 'Captain George Burton, my worthy friend', and other acquaintance.

Before reaching these stories, however, the reader is obliged to plough his or her way through one chapter on the history of divination, in which it is made clear that the Catholic Church is the heir to ancient idolatry, three others which continue the theme before concentrating on clichés in defence of the reality of witches and witchcraft, and then a return to the main message of the first part: 'Confederacy of several Popes and Roman priests with the Devil. Such [are] the principal encouragers and promoters of idolatry in the Church.' *Pandaemonium* is thus a highly political work, attacking the Catholicism Bovet sees at the heart of monarchy and government and stirring up the passions of his readers on the side of dissent in favour, if not of outright rebellion, at least of opposition to what the monarchy and government stood for, an aim which, in the feverish atmosphere of the time, might be regarded as irresponsible and contrary to the proper interests of national security and the wellbeing of the state.[52]

But something more general can also be observed happening at this period, most clearly, perhaps, in the theatre, where witches were given a fairly complex role. We can see in the dances allotted to them not only potential amusement at their uncouth movements, described by Ben Jonson as 'preposterous change and gesticulation' and 'dancing back to back and hip to hip, their hands joined, and making their circles backward, to the left hand, with strange fantastic motions of their heads and bodies', but also an identification of witches as peasants whose morris dancing was offensive to good order and whose jigging was considered bawdy and deviant. This identification was perpetuated in such plays as Heywood and Brome's *The Late Lancashire Witches* (1634), Davenant's version of *Macbeth* (*c.* 1663), Shadwell's *The Lancashire Witches* (1681), and Purcell's *Dido and Aeneas* (*c.* 1687), and indeed turned into something of a cliché.[53] Society was drawing apart within itself. Before the sixteenth century, witchcraft had been associated with a religion everyone shared. During the sixteenth century that religion split and witchcraft became a stick with which to beat one's confessional opponents, and so witchcraft remained a religious concern, but not one which was yet class based. The seventeenth century, however, saw a much deeper cleavage between the educated and uneducated, which in practice meant between the aspiring middle class and the peasantry. The upper classes, when they gave thought to the matter at all, sided with 'modernity' of thought rather than tradition – ironic, considering their reliance on social tradition to maintain their position in the secular hierarchy – and so witchcraft in particular increasingly became something ignorant peasants did, an identification of this kind of magic with the countryside rather than the town, which lodged deep in people's imaginations and subconsciousness even while fact contradicted it, as the late eighteenth and nineteenth centuries were to demonstrate.

11

WITCHCRAFT AND WONDER STILL ON THE RISE: 1685–1697

Danger to the state or not, witchcraft, magic, strange events, and unexpected apparitions continued to frighten and divert the public in almost equal measure. Astrology, for example, largely via popular almanacs which sold in huge numbers, tended to link appearances in the heavens, especially those of comets, to disasters on earth.

> While the common people have admired to see the two superior planets, Saturn and Jupiter, continue so near this whole year, and our astrologers have affrighted them with fearful predictions of direful events to succeed this appearance, the more judicious are desirous to know how often and at what time their conjunctions happen, that by comparing their tables of those planets' motions with their observed appearance, they may be the better able to correct them.[1]

But astrology was also linked closely in both popular and learned imagination with witchcraft, whereby we see that the lines between various occult sciences were by no means distinct and unequivocal. In 1680, a clergyman, John Butler, who entered into a defence of astrology against various opponents, noted that the Bishop of Norwich had remarked of it that '[it] lies in the midway betwixt magic and imposture, and partakes not a little of both', and he himself opined that certain people were astrologically inclined to succumb to the Devil's seduction and become witches. These were the malicious, the needy, the learned – 'who, being afflicted with a vehement desire to know strange things (and that without the knowledge of God) in time do meet and comply with the insinuations of Satan which seem to flatter them with enjoyment of their desires' – and finally, prognosticators, 'who would make the world believe as if they were errand sorcerers by their practices, pretend to astrology by profession'. Butler seems to be acutely aware of this blurring of borders between occult activities. We must be careful to honour theology before astrology, he says in his preface to *Hagiastrologia*, otherwise 'our astrological skill would become rank poison to us, as such a thing would lead us to the Devil sooner than to God, and draw us into sorcery and other evil arts, whereby we should be entangled with diabolical familiarity ere we are aware, even as are witches and conjurors'. Yet even saying this, he was not quite sure he wanted to dismiss every instance of magic as unlawful and listed six examples, all of which had been mentioned by the Bishop of Norwich as 'savouring of witchcraft', of whose efficacy he was prepared to entertain something less than outright rejection: namely, rubbing warts with raw flesh to cure them; the ability of a seventh son to cure sickness by laying on of hands; the use of astral magic in the form of images to cure certain illnesses; anointing a weapon in order to cure the wound it has made; heating an iron to drive out an evil spirit; and judicial astrology.[2]

Butler's concern that astrology withdraw the hem of its garment from the taint of popular superstition, however, is understandable in the light of the fear of the learned classes that their attempts to understand, formulate, and codify knowledge of the natural world and to withdraw that knowledge into a fortress of its own building, might not quite prove impregnable to the shafts the beliefs and practices of the uneducated majority continued to supply to less Cartesian controversialists. But they need not have worried, for the further the classes drew apart from one another mentally and psychologically, the more those popular beliefs and activities began to look quaint rather than dangerous, and this was an attitude which would eventually seep downwards into the lower classes themselves, which then ended up in the situation, such as that described by Jeanne Favret-Saada, in which a newspaper (*Le Monde*) felt able to poke fun at witchcraft in the countryside, raising its eyebrow at 'a primitive society, in spite of the car parked by the gate and the television in the living room'. As Favret-Saada observes, 'The urban reader is thus reassured that even if he is not a great scholar, the gap between an ordinary man and a peasant is infinite.'[3] But in the 1680s and 90s that time was not quite yet and the battle for 'modernity' still had a sharp edge to it. Nature was a book in which God had not written only a single narrative but continued to write, altering or adding to the text as He saw fit, especially when He wanted to teach humankind a lesson. Thus, on comets and blazing stars, William Turner, vicar of Walburton in Sussex, wrote in 1697:

> Whatever they are generated of (for I will not meddle here with the physical consideration), their meaning is something. The God of nature, who is so wise as to make nothing in vain, without all doubt puts them in the heavens for some sign or other. Nor dare I be peremptory to [assign] the particular signification. I humbly conceive the most that we can read in those celestial hieroglyphics is that God is going to do some great thing in the world, and that at the hanging out of those flags, it behoves men to inquire into their lives and search their ways more narrowly and prepare to meet their God who is coming to judge the world in equity, and maketh these flames of fire His harbingers to prepare His way and give notice of His coming.[4]

Monstrous births, too, were interpreted and reinterpreted in accordance with both sides of the political divide, and despite the attempts of some intellectuals to relegate them to the superstitious past, continued to provide fodder for pamphlets and prophets of doom. The anti-Catholic strain underlying so much of the controversial literature can also be seen in the quarrel between two professional astrologers, John Gadbury, a Catholic convert, and John Partridge, who lambasted one another in print during the late 1680s and 90s. No wonder, then, that as early as 1660 collections of this kind of literature had been condemned as socially and politically dangerous on the grounds that the stories they contained were designed 'to infatuate men's minds and set their brains once more a-madding, that they be the more apt to kindle into combustions and break forth into another horrid rebellion'.[5] In 1685–1688, when the threat of constitutional change and religious upheaval not only seemed, but actually turned out to be real, this must have appeared to the powers that be even more true than it had been nearly three decades earlier.

But there was still room for humour and a sense of proportion. In 1681, the Tory newspaper *Heraclitus Ridens* published a satirical squib against the Whig editor of *Domestick Intelligence*.

> If any person out of natural curiosity desire to be furnished with ships or castles in the air, or any sorts of prodigies, apparitions, or strange sights, the better to fright people out of their senses, and by persuading them there are strange judgements, changes, and revolutions hanging over their heads, thereby to persuade them to pull them down by discontents, fears, jealousies, and seditions, let them repair to Ben Harris at his shop near the Royal Exchange, where they may be furnished with all sorts and sizes of them at very cheap and easy rates.[6]

Less political, but no less sarcastic, was the pamphlet *News from Pannier Alley* (1687), which begins with a reference to Henry More's preface to *Saducismus Triumphatus* (an interesting indication that the author thought some of his intended readership would have read that book), before proceeding to tales of the unexpected. On Saturday 3 December 1687, Mary Webb, a servant, met an old woman who told her fortune; instructed her to put a bowl of water in a hole in a certain cellar and leave it for three hours, after which she would find three gold pieces in it; sold her a love powder with instructions she should sew it into her clothes; and then said she was going to an alehouse to cast a horoscope, but that she would meet Mary again to collect one of the three miraculous gold coins. Needless to say, she did not turn up and all Mary found in the bowl was 'what the cat left in the malt' (p. 6). At night, her mistress had gone to the theatre and suddenly found her dress bedaubed with something like wet plaster. The same thing happened to several other people, and early one morning afterwards, when people heard a noise 'like the falling of water emptied out of a pot in the yard, they found a parcel of this stuff dashed on the stones; and though they have had several to watch at night to see if they could discover whence it should come, hitherto it hath been in vain' (p. 7). The sheer banality of these instances, coupled with the initial literary reference, tells us this was a joke at the expense of those who saw spirits and witchcraft in everything and failed to have a sense of proportion when it came to unusual events, no matter how slight.

In the real world, however, witches continued to operate, children to be bewitched into fits, people to killed by hostile magic or to fall ill through malefice. John Tonken from Penzance was one such unfortunate, as we are told in a pamphlet by 'R.P.', *A True Account of a Strange and Wonderful Relation*. In April 1686 he started having fits and in May he began to see 'a woman in a blue jerkin and a red petticoat with yellow and green patches, [who] told him he would not be well before he had brought up nutshells, pins, and nails' (p. 2). With great difficulty he then vomited some shells and pins. The woman continued to appear to him, though invisible to anyone else, sometimes in her own shape, sometimes in that of a cat, and this precipitated such fear and convulsions in the boy that two men were deputed to sit on the bed beside him. Next the woman told him to fetch up straws, which he did, and nails, one of which was found stuck in his foot and another elsewhere in the bed. Some people, of course, were suspicious and 'put their fingers into his mouth to search if he had any pins or rushes, thinking he might put a trick on them, but found none, though some came every day from him' (p. 4). The fits continued throughout May, and in his last he saw three women; but they promised not to come again and two days later he recovered. Two old women, Jane Nowell, known as 'Nickless', and Elizabeth, alias 'Betty Sneeze', were named in affidavits as his tormentors and sent to Launceston Castle, which housed the gaol and courtroom. It seems people may have been right to be suspicious, for only Jane actually came to trial and when she did, she was found not guilty, and similar hesitations can be deduced in the cases of Eleanor Harris, Susanna Harris, Maria Harris, and Anna Cheeke from Somerset in 1684, Mary Stevens from Wiltshire and Jane Vallett from Devon, both in 1685, and Abigail Handford from Devon, Deanes Grimmerton from Dorset, and Elizabeth Langley from Somerset, in 1687, all of whom were acquitted by their juries.[7]

Doubts, scepticism, and hesitation, however, did not always work in the suspect's favour. In March 1686, for example, Christopher Crofts wrote to Sir John Perceval from Cork about his son's illness.

> My poor boy Jack to all appearances lay dying. He had a convulsion for eight or nine hours. His mother and several others are of opinion he is bewitched, and by an old woman, the mother of Neil Welsh, who is reputed a bad woman; and the child was playing by her that day she was upon her examination, and was taken ill presently after she was committed to Bridewell. But I have not faith to believe it was anything but the hand of God. I have committed the girl to Bridewell where she shall stay some time.[8]

Nevertheless, Jack's mother and the several others were in the majority. John Brinley had lamented in 1680 that there were 'swarms of fortune-tellers, geomancers, diviners, [and] interpreters of dreams, who possess the common people with apprehensions that they know all their fate, the number of their days, the casualties of their life, and even their natural inclinations and thoughts of their heart, by this means cheating the poor innocent souls into the grossest superstition imaginable'.[9] But defence of the objects of their activities, if not the activities themselves, continued unabated. Under the initials 'R.B.', standing for 'Richard Burton', a pseudonym used by the printer and bookseller Nathaniel Crouch, there appeared in 1688 *The Kingdom of Darkness*, purporting to be a history of demons, ghosts, witches, and various *mirabilia*.[10] In fact, it is a collection of anecdotes rather in the style set by Glanvill and More, intended to show by an accumulation of reported data that all these things are real. 'Prodigious accidents [*unexpected events*] that have happened in our times in several parts of the world make it manifest beyond contradiction that there are devils infesting this lower world, besides the evidence of scripture which is fully convictive to all sober Christians' (preface, p. 3). 'In our times' here means 'modern, as opposed to Mediaeval or Classical', since several of his tales go back to the sixteenth century, but a good many are taken from accounts published in the 1660s and 1680s. It is also interesting that Crouch includes one or two from New England, his source being Cotton Mather's *An Essay for the Recording of Illustrious Providences, wherein an account is given of many remarkable and very memorable events which have happened in this last age, especially in New England* (Boston, 1684).[11] Since Crouch was a bookseller, it will not have been difficult for him to scour the library ready-made upon his own bookshelves to extract varied and diverting anecdotes for his compilation. As a treatise, however, it cannot be taken seriously, since in effect its argument is: 'Certain people these days deny the reality of witches and spirits. Here are a good many stories drawn from a good many authors, which say the opposite. So there you are.'

Still he does end with three disparate but interesting remarks. 'Extreme poverty, irksome old age, want of friends, [and] the contempt, injury and hard-heartedness of ill neighbours' make people spiteful and those on the receiving end of their spite then prosecute them and hang them as witches. (Crouch clearly does not mean to imply that the spite is spite alone and not witchcraft, but that is the unintended meaning of the way he expresses himself here.) Secondly, 'we may further inquire why spirits so seldom nowadays appear, especially those that are good'. Since his collection of anecdotes from the 1670s and 1680s alone demonstrates that spirits (not, it is true, good spirits) do indeed appear nowadays, it is difficult to see why he should single this out as a question to be asked at this point. His answers are not altogether coherent: (i) people are prejudiced against spirits when they do appear and call them devils; (ii) people are frightened by spirits; (iii) people cannot always tell a real spirit from a fancy of their imagination; (iv) spirits may actually find it difficult to become visible, 'it being as troublesome to them to continue visible for some time as it is for men that dive to hold their breath in water'. This last is at least a worthwhile observation, as it acknowledges the potential difficulties inherent in a non-material substance's becoming material, a problem which had long exercised theologians and natural philosophers as they debated how, for example, an incubus which was, by definition, non-corporeal, could impregnate a woman who then gave birth to a child: or how, if spirits are incorporeal, they can take up time and space, as they do if they occupy a human body for a length of time, a difficulty which Webster tried to solve by arguing that spirits are actually corporeal, and which Camfield answered by referring to the risen Jesus in Luke 24.39. Thirdly, 'our adversaries say [witches] are all melancholy old women who dote and bring themselves into danger by their own fancies and conceits'. Doting they are not, says Crouch, because he has talked to several of them and they were as coherent as one may expect of persons of their class and lack of education to be (pp. 181–182). We ourselves may note that he denies they are foolish but does not qualify the expectation that they will be old. More research needs to be done to establish, if possible, whether old people were really finding themselves targeted as witches, whether a literary tradition that witches were old, and old women in particular, was influencing people's expectations and perceptions, or whether the reality of witches in the courtroom was at variance with what was actually a myth rather than observable fact.

In addition to stories from English, German, French, and New England authors, Crouch also recounted several from Scotland. Witchcraft in Scotland, particularly in the central belt as we have seen, was a more serious business than it appeared to be in other parts of Britain, and the dozen and more stories about Scotland included in Crouch's collection were pilfered from George Sinclair's *Satan's Invisible World Discovered*, which appeared first in 1685. Sinclair was for many years Professor of Philosophy at Glasgow University before being appointed Professor of Mathematics there in 1691, and his published interests encompassed gravity, hydrostatics, the history of coal, and the principles of astronomy and navigation, and how to drain water from coal seams. Not the most obvious person, then, to produce a book on witches and ghosts. But in 1684 he published a translation of an earlier Professor of Divinity's lectures on faith as his own work,[12] so he was not above seizing the chance of what he perceived to be a publishing opportunity, and this may be why he strung together some arbitrarily chosen tales and anecdotes in the manner of Glanvill's *Saducismus Triumphatus* published only four years earlier. Sinclair's instinct turned out to be accurate, for *Satan's Invisible World* was continually reprinted until well into the nineteenth century and was, as one commentator noted, 'for a long time a constituent part of every cottage library in Scotland'.[13]

In his preface to the reader, Sinclair gives his own explanation of why he undertook this work. 'My purpose is only by some few collections to prove the existence of devils, spirits, witches, and apparitions ... especially now, while atheism and Quakerism, that sink of folly and madness, as one calls it, out of which there is not great leap into the other, doth now so much obtain' (p. xv).[14] He gives three principal reasons for the presence of disbelief in society: first, an affectation of superiority in certain circles, leading them 'to droll, scoff, and mock at all such relations' (p. xviii); secondly, the prevalence of atheism; and thirdly the common belief that many of those who had suffered death as witches in the past had been innocent (p. xix). Sinclair then denounces Hobbes, Spinoza, and Descartes for their materialist philosophy, and ends with a reference to the contest between Moses and Pharaoh's magicians (Exodus 7.9–12) in which he ridicules the consequences of materialist attempts to explain it, and describes it as a true battle between light and darkness.[15] About half his collection of stories come from Scotland, principally from the central belt, as one might expect, but chapter 35 gives a brief account of 'some prayers, charms, and Aves used in the Highlands', and interestingly, perhaps significantly enough, considering his stated intentions in writing the book, Sinclair's tone in this chapter is one of unmitigated contempt. He clearly equates the Highlander's Catholicism with ignorance and pagan superstition, the former illustrated by his recording of Highland pronunciation of the Latin Paternoster and Ave Maria, the latter by his use of 'ridiculous', 'ignorance', and 'very bad practice' in describing some of their beliefs and magical working. But the chapter itself is a peculiar mishmash and includes a charm from Galloway and a grace from East Lothian, neither of which places had retained much connection with Highland traditions at the end of the seventeenth century. So it seems like a gratuitous page or two of contempt thrown into the mixture, so at variance with the rest of the book that one wonders what Sinclair thought he was doing.[16]

By this stage, the controversialists were not only beginning to repeat themselves, but also to lose much sense of what their anecdotes were for. Glanvill may have had a serious purpose in collecting data on witchcraft and spirits, but Sinclair was merely a pseudo-short story writer, collecting his entertainments instead of inventing them himself and effectively meaning no more by them, in spite of his protestations about combatting atheist materialism, than putting a few extra shillings in his pocket. It is notable, however, that beyond this flimflam, people were still being fetched into court on charges which were potentially fatal to them and, indeed, still killed a few, regardless of frequent acquittals by some juries. The number of witchcraft trials in Scotland had diminished somewhat after 1662, but started to grow again in the 1670s. Thus we find nineteen people accused in Prestonpans in 1678, of whom eleven were executed, five executed in Edinburgh, three more in Falla sentenced to death, and four executed at Peaston. The next year saw six more executed and one banished, but then there was something of a lull in 1680 and 1681 when Margaret Comb was released from the Edinburgh tolbooth on her promise to appear in court for trial, while Elspeth Kirkland from Aberdour in Fife was discharged because the case against her was ridiculous. This last, in fact, got no further than the kirk session. Bessie Lamb's husband had become mentally ill and violent, and on one occasion Elspeth went into the Lambs' house and removed a rope, whereupon (according to Bessie) her husband recovered his tranquillity of mind and demeanour. Therefore Elspeth must have put the rope there to bewitch her husband. Bessie and Elspeth were not on good terms – Bessie frequently called Elspeth a witch and referred to her children as 'witch-birds' – and this, apart from the sheer coincidence involved in Mr Lamb's recovery, seems to have weighed with the kirk session which ordered Bessie to come and stand before the pulpit and beg Elspeth's pardon for her slanderous remarks.[17]

Political events of the time affected everyone even in the most apparently unconnected of circumstances. The winter of 1683–84, for example, was particularly harsh and many died, and this was taken to be a portent of the so-called 'Killing Time' when persecution of the covenanters was at its height, and when tensions were made worse by the death of Charles II in February 1685 and his brother's accession. A case from Monzie in Perthshire that same winter illustrates the point vividly. Donald MacGregor's ten-year-old daughter began to have visions of a man and a woman who wanted to take her away. These changed around 6 January, when two women appeared with a horse's skull.

> They made a picture [of this], covering it with clay. Then immediately appeared a black man, and sometimes he appeared like an ox. They desired him to make them a nail to put in the head of the picture, and he should have the child for whom the picture was being made – which he did, the child being all this time exceedingly affrighted and calling to those that were in the house to take them from her. But they saw nor heard nothing. Then the child thought she saw them put the picture betwixt two fires for some space, during which time she was sore tormented. Then they removed [it] a little and she had some ease. Then they put it in the fire again and the child was in a sore torment, and exceeding hot and affrighted. Thus she was five or six times that night, and this she was from that night, being the 8th of January until the 10th of February, taking some nights eight fits, some nights ten or twelve, and was ordinarily from seven or eight to ten or twelve at night, seeing them and tormented by fits.

The adults round her resorted to prayer, but on 10 February the child's visions changed significantly, for she started to converse with angels and report what they said to her.

'What folk are these that go not to the kirk?' she asked the angels at one point, thinking of her father who was a Nonconformist.

'They may be much better than those who go to kirk,' came the reply, 'and ye ought not to call them Whigs, but of the true Catholic Church' (by which, of course, was meant the Episcopal Church of Scotland, not the Church of Rome).

As the child's visions became more vivid – she was carried off to Heaven where she sat beside Jesus and saw Adam and Job ('who,' she said, 'was most beautiful of all') – she was told to ask specific political questions of the angels. 'Whether the indulged ministers, [*those who were permitted to retain their posts without subscribing to episcopacy*], did well in accepting the indulgence, or those that refused to hear them did worse in so doing, or those they called "Cameronians" [*covenanters led by Richard Cameron*] in that they did?' This, however, proved too pointed a query, for the angels did not answer. Ought they (meaning ministers) to take the Test Act, since so many landowners had done so? No, came the answer. Will they be executed if they refuse to take the Test Act? They are not obliged to take it, the angels replied, and not long after this the visions ceased.[18]

The episode, whatever we make of it, not only illustrates how such occurrences were accepted by and acceptable to people, but how people might be prepared to use them to clarify immediate pressing questions, in this case political and religious. But incidents of a preternatural kind were frequent, and if their messages were not reported widely to the public through print, their impact upon their local community can easily be gauged or imagined. So we find Janet Fraser, a Presbyterian from Dumfries, who had a number of puzzling visions between 1684 and to 1691. These consisted of her seeing something like a bee at various times, and at others, a black man. This black man appeared to her once while she was at prayer, 'he being upon the one side of me, and there appearing upon the other side a bonny hand and a rod in it, and the rod was budding'. This rod, which Janet saw more than once, she clearly associated with the rod of Aaron – 'it put forth buds, produced blossoms, and bore ripe almonds' (Numbers 17.8) – and then it doubled, 'and after that time I was never troubled with the black man any more'. Janet also saw three human figures clad in white, walking *deiseil* round her, and quoting and commenting upon scripture; and on another occasion, when reading the Bible in a field not far from her father's house, she went to get a drink of water and came back to find her Bible covered in what seemed to be blood, a blood which could not be removed. This happened more than once. A neighbour examined the book and reported, 'It is not blood, for it is as tough as glue and will not be scraped off by a knife, as blood will. But it is so like blood as none can discern any difference by the colour.' All this was quite enough to have her summoned to the presbytery (although one notices that seven years passed before the ministers took action), and there she confessed (perhaps under compulsion, perhaps not) that she had been deluded by Satan and was possessed by an evil spirit. The black man may have disappeared as far as Janet was concerned, but he clearly lingered in the suspicions of the ministers, too like the Devil who appeared to witches to be dismissed or ignored or glossed over.

But visions were always suspect to some degree. In 1686 in Lanarkshire, 'there were showers of bonnets, hats, guns, and swords, which covered the trees and ground', and one or two people saw companies of armed men marching and then falling to the ground and disappearing.

> There was a gentleman standing next to me who spake, as too many gentlemen and others speak, who said, 'A pack of damned witches and warlocks that have the second sight, the Devil ha't do I see,' and immediately there was a discernible change in his countenance, with as much fear and trembling as any woman I saw there. [He] cried out, 'O all ye that do not see, say nothing, for I persuade you, it is a matter of fact and discernable to all hat is not stone blind!' And these that did see told what works the guns had, and their length and wideness, and what handles the swords had, whether small or three-barred or Highland guards, and the closing knots of the bonnets, black or blue. And these did see them there, wherever they went abroad, [and] saw a bonnet and a sword drop in the way. I have been at a loss ever since what to make of this last.[19]

Such things were a puzzlement to the Kirk. On the one hand, they suggested the reality of the spirit world and therefore helped bolster belief in the Bible. On the other, they smacked of superstition and were therefore condemnable. By and large, however, many if not most lay people had few doubts, like the man who spoke of witches and the second sight, and did not actually lean to the scepticism increasingly fashionable in learned or polite circles. This, one might think, would lead, if not to an increase in the number of witchcraft cases, at least to there being no fewer. But strange and dreadful though the last years of the 1680s were in the south-west of Scotland in particular, the courts had enough to do in suppressing rebellious covenanters, without adding to their burdens with witchcraft cases, although it is noteworthy that not only in Scotland but elsewhere, while judicial activity against witches was tepid, printed propaganda supporting or attacking them saw no diminution.

We can see this paucity of court cases all over the British Isles in the 1690s. In Wales, for example, there was little beyond Olivia Powell's ill-natured remarks about her neighbours' property and animals, all of which seemed to suffer disaster or death soon afterwards, and for which she was tried in 1693. The following year, strange fires broke out in the Harlech area and were attributed to witchcraft by the local rector, and in 1699 Dorcas Heddin was tried for bewitching two sailors on board a ship bound for Virginia. But this was the last trial for witchcraft in Wales, even though magical practices continued among the people long afterwards.[20] Similarly, in the Isle of Man witchcraft and ritual cursing persisted well into the eighteenth century, but with no major interest in prosecuting offenders. In 1695, we find William Cairn's wife seeking help from a charmer against an illness she attributed to malevolent magic; William Moor presented to an ecclesiastical court for cursing, that is, laying a curse on other people; and Jony Cowle suspected of witchcraft for being in William Lacey's fields on a May morning, a suspicious occurrence because island folklore said that witches would walk in their neighbours' fields before sunrise that day to gather dew which they would sprinkle on their own crops and thus transfer good luck from their neighbours to themselves, just as Henry Kelly did when he got his son to transfer earth from a neighbour's field to his own at the time of sowing.[21]

In England, juries acquitted rather than condemned, although witches continued to be in peril, partly from conditions in gaol, partly from ill treatment. Margery Coombes from Somerset died in gaol in 1690, but Elizabeth Carrier and Anne Moore, accused alongside her, were found not guilty. In 1693, Mrs Chambers died in gaol after confessing to killing two people by witchcraft, even though the relatives of the latter were satisfied the woman in question had died from natural causes. Margaret Elnore (1694), on the other hand, was acquitted, as were Katharine Williams and Dorothea East. So, too, Sarah Roath (1695), Mary Guy, and Elizabeth Harner (1696). Mrs Comon from Essex, however, in a state of confusion after her husband's death, seems to have been pursued by her parish minister into confessing to a covenant with the Devil and causing a Mr Cox to become lame. She was searched, but no Devil's mark was found. She was then scratched by Mr Cox who dipped his handkerchief in the blood he had raised. When he burned it, he reported 'it had not the usual smell of burnt linen', a remark which may have precipitated an unruly crowd into swimming her more than once. The episode would be silly, were it not so unhappy – it shows how easily a hostile group could have its emotions whipped up by one or two determined individuals – and one is not surprised to find that only a few months later, Mrs Comon died.[22]

None of this, of course, remotely equates to anything like a wide-scale persecution, but it does show that the fear of witchcraft was not only alive but flourishing in the general populace and that even if juries in the formal setting of a courtroom, with the eyes and attention of judges and advocates upon them, were inclined to acquit when the evidence put before them was in some way unsatisfactory, outwith that formal setting restraint, judiciousness, and an equitable impartiality could by no means be relied on to govern people's tempers or behaviour. This extramural fear of witchcraft, however, could also be used to advantage by lawyers keen to win a case, and an instructive trial from Scotland illustrates the point.

In 1696 Christian Shaw, the eleven-year-old daughter of the laird of Bargarran, which was then a remote village west of Glasgow, was cursed by one of the family's maids. Not long afterwards, Christian spoke to an elderly widow, Agnes Naismith, who often came to Bargarran House to beg for food, and the next afternoon started to suffer the first of what would be a long series of convulsive fits, crying out that the servant, Katharine Campbell, and Agnes were cutting her open with knives. Physicians were summoned, but their treatments failed to cure her, and soon large numbers of spectators gathered each day to see the sight. This, however odd it may seem to us, was common custom not merely in Scotland, but all over Europe, whenever someone appeared to be suffering demonic possession or convulsions attributed to witchcraft. Such 'performances', if one may call them such without prejudicing the meaning, were involuntary (or, in the case of fraud, voluntary) psychodramas received by the spectators partly, to be sure, as entertainment, but partly as vivid glimpses into the interaction between the physical world in which everyone normally lived and the spirit world, about which they were constantly being told in story and sermon, but actual experience of which was an extraordinary rather than an everyday event. Christian enjoyed a brief respite of three weeks following a visit to a Glasgow doctor, but then her fits began again, and this time she started to cough up bundles of hair, straw, pins, animal bones, and all kinds of other objects. The physicians called in to treat her were baffled and, as Christian blamed Katharine Campbell and Agnes Naismith for her condition, the idea that witchcraft was behind it quickly began to take hold.

Christian herself spoke not only of Katharine and Agnes, but of many witches trying to kill her, and of meeting the Devil at a witches' gathering in the orchard behind Bargarran House, and a notion of what her parents and the rest of the household heard and witnessed can be gathered from a letter written by her mother to Christian's father on 18 February 1697.

My dear, I thought it fit to give you an account of Christian's condition. This day, about two o'clock in the afternoon, she said she saw the Devil in [the] likeness of a man. She seemed to be somewhat feared, and I desired her to say 'The Lord rebuke thee, Satan', but the use of her tongue was taken from her. Yet, recovering it in a short time, she essayed to speak, but was presently seized with a fit, and when that was over, she went about the room deaf and blind, as you yourself have seen her before, but still speaking, as to a bumblebee, [saying], 'With the Lord's strength thou shalt not put straw nor sticks into my mouth', holding her hand fast on her mouth all the while. Then, walking a little faster, she cried out, 'The bumblebee is stinging me', and, sitting down, looked on her leg where [there] was the impression, very deep, of fingernails. The Devil appeared to her again in the bed, like a gentleman. She, standing at the bedside, reasoned with him after this manner. 'Thou thinks to make me a witch, but through God's strength thou shalt never be the better. I charge thee, in the name of God, to be gone and thy papers, too, for I will have none of them. I will not fear thy ill. Stand here! See if thou dare come one step nearer me. I think thou art feareder for me than I for thee.' Then, turning, she went up and down the room as before, and again was bitten with teeth in the hands, very deep, and impressed with nails of fingers more than twenty-four times, which made her cry aloud every time she received them, and showing the place where she was hurt, by getting her hand upon it. But we neither saw nor heard anything about [*around*] her. She continued in this fit from two o'clock till past five at night. She said in the fit [that] Margaret Lang had given orders to torment her.[23]

The episode so far had lasted from August to the beginning of 1697, and at this point events began to move more quickly. A commission consisting of eleven local men of standing and importance was appointed to investigate. Meanwhile, suspects were named and arrested – eventually twenty-four altogether – some identified by Christian herself, others by Elizabeth Anderson who had been named by Christian as one of her tormentors and who succumbed to intensive questioning by the commission. Christian was visited by the commission more than once, and her behaviour in front of it tended to be a mixture of calm reportage and theatrical swooning, and by the time the commissioners and local clergy had done their work of witnessing and interviewing and compiling the results, which were then conveyed to the Lord Advocate in Edinburgh, an extensive trial for witchcraft was more or less inevitable. It opened in Paisley on 13 April 1697 by which time Christian's fits had actually ceased, the imprisonment of her alleged tormentors, as was commonly believed, having broken the magical hold they had over her. All but seven of the accused, however, were released as the evidence against them proved too thin to warrant proceeding further with it. The seven remaining had the benefit of defence (as was usual), although the advocate had a difficult job, since so many witnesses came forward to accuse them and none to speak up for them, but James Robertson, advocate for the panels, did his best. He argued that some of the charges, such as renouncing baptism and covenanting with the Devil, were not mentioned in the Witchcraft Act and were therefore not legally relevant. The *instrumenta* with which the accused were supposed to have tormented Christian had not been produced in court, nor did the various indictments mention specific dates on which the magical crimes had taken place, in consequence of which the accused had no chance to provide themselves with an alibi. The accused had been pricked and the Devil's marks had been found, he said, but these marks were not sufficient proof of witchcraft because they could equally well be natural blemishes, and pricking could easily be done in such a way as to produce no blood. Nor could Christian's naming of the accused be trusted, because she was clearly possessed and the Devil could cause her to identify honest people, not guilty, as witches.

It was a strong performance, but the prosecution advocates, Francis Grant in particular, gave one stronger. He emphasised the peculiar nature of witchcraft and the fact that 'the experience and observation of the wisest divines, lawyers, philosophers, statesmen, judges, and historians, at home and abroad, beside the testimony of witches everywhere, make the apparitions of witches commonly and mostly real'.[24] Having, in effect, thus suggested to members of the jury that they should not get above themselves, Grant piled on appeals to their emotions, emphasising on the one hand the pains which Christian had suffered, and on the other the validity of circumstantial evidence which, in Scots law, he said, was sufficient even to condemn a man for murder. He concluded,

> As you ought to be wary of condemning the innocent, so, if these panels be proven legally guilty, you ought not to spare them, for in doing so, you would be accessory to all the blasphemies, apostacies, murders, torture, and seduction of which these enemies of heaven and earth shall hereafter be guilty when they have got out. So that the question seems simply to be this, whether, on your oath, you can swear that the panels, notwithstanding of all that is proven against them, are not guilty of witchcraft: in the determination whereof, we pray God may direct you to the right course.[25]

Now, we must beware of misunderstanding this. These appeals to emotion rather than reason were not merely legal histrionics. Grant was a man of deep religious conviction, as evinced by his later book on the case, *Sadducismus Debellatus*, published in 1698. It begins with a lengthy preface in which he says that people doubt the truth of witchcraft because of frequent impostures by Catholics. But there is abundant evidence (which he cites) for witchcraft. Satan deludes witches into doing his bidding, and his superior abilities account for many of the extraordinary things attributed to them. He is permitted by God to act as he does in order to furnish human beings with profitable lessons in morality and a test of their humble patience and trust in Him. Grant then gives an account of the Bargarran episode and a detailed, quite possibly verbatim account of his address to the jury, including his own convictions on the subject.

> I must admit that none could be more sceptical as to the truth of such odd things as I had heard, nor [more] inquisitive for cavassing the reality and explications of them than I was before my attendance at Bargarran's house and the several diets of the court, and my conversation with some of those concerned in the matter. But now, after all that I have seen reasoned, and heard, I do acknowledge myself entirely captivated by the dictates of natural understanding and common sense into a firm belief and persuasion that, as there is such a thing as witchcraft, so it was eminent in its forementioned effects, and that the seven prisoners were some of the witches.[26]

Appeal to belief and emotion won the day and the seven accused – three men and four women – were found guilty and hanged on 10 June. Two, John and James Lyndsay, were boys, aged fourteen and eleven; Agnes Naismith cursed the crowd before a drummer drummed out her words; Katharine Campbell, after an impassioned plea to be allowed to escape the noose, struggled violently with the hangman until she was cast from the ladder; John Lindsay protested his innocence; Margaret Fulton spoke cheerfully of going to fairyland; and Margaret Lang prayed for herself, for the Bargarran family, and for the Church.

It may be argued, of course, that Christian Shaw was a fraud and that seven innocent people had been hanged because of her accusations, but Hugh McLachlan and Kim Swales have reasonably argued that the case for her being an imposter is not convincing.[27] Mental illness has also been suggested as the source of Christian's behaviour in the usual modern fashion of presuming there is no more to the world than matter and that therefore a materialist explanation for extraordinary phenomena must be sought.[28] But as far as our discussions are concerned, this is beside the point. The prosecutors were confident there was a substratum of belief in and fear of witchcraft at which they could aim and which would ensure the success of their arguments, even though the quality of the evidence offered during the trial was poor and doubts about the validity of witchcraft were sufficiently known to make Grant feel obliged to counter them in his address to the court. But to label this mere opportunism would be to do the lawyers less than justice. Grant may have known how to aim his arrows, but he was no cynic and no disbeliever himself, and if his was a piece of acting, it was more in the Method style than that of merely learning lines and not bumping into the furniture.[29]

The Bargarran case triggered an imitation two years later. In April 1699, evidence from ninety-one individuals alleged that Margaret Murdoch and Margaret Laird who lived not far from Bargarran were suffering from witchcraft practised by no fewer than twenty-four persons who were causing them to exhibit the same range of symptoms and behaviour shown by Christian Shaw. There can be little doubt that the similarity between the two cases was not accidental, although whether the two Margarets were imitating Christian either consciously or unconsciously, or whether those investigating and recording the latter case were influenced, consciously or unconsciously, by the former is difficult to say. We also have to bear in mind – given that these two cases represent the first times witches in Scotland were prosecuted for causing demonic possession in their victims – that the similar episode in Salem, New England, had taken place only a few years before, in 1692, and that accounts of it had been published in 1693. The case of Patrick Morton from Pittenweem in 1704, which we shall discuss later, shows that people could be, and were, affected by what they read or had read to them. One day Patrick found what he took to be a magical *instrumentum* outwith his door and quickly developed fits which were interpreted as diabolically inspired. Before they developed fully, however, the local minister read to him one of the recently published accounts of Christian Shaw's experiences, and it was after this that Patrick's signs of demonic possession became unmistakeable. *Post hoc ergo propter hoc*? It is difficult to tell.

There was also a recent English case of alleged demonic possession in an eighteen year-old Lancashire lad, caused by witchcraft, which stimulated a skirmish of tracts between supporters and opponents of the principal's veracity. Between 28 April 1689 and 24 March 1690, a group of dissenting ministers led by Thomas Jollie endeavoured to exorcise Richard Dugdale from the parish of Whalley. After much prayer, they claimed to have done so, and Richard's symptoms and behaviour were described by Jollie, who believed he was genuine and published his *Vindication of the Surey Demoniack* in 1698.

> [Richard's father] said he hath seen his son vomit up stones several times, and other things. Once [Richard] declared he must either vomit up gold, silver, or brass rings and an hair button, accordingly he did so. At other times he vomited great stones, also blue stones like flints. One time he vomited a stone as was an inch and a half long and and inch and a half broad, having blood upon the edges, which [his father] and others standing by him apprehended was very painful to him. And further [his father] maketh an oath that one day, a little before night, walking by his said son then in a fit, it growing dark, a candle being brought in, [his father] looking upon him, there was a great stone laid upon his belly, weighing about twelve or thirteen pounds, [his father] not knowing how it came there, nor was there any suchlike stones about the house. Besides, stones have been thrown at the barn side, falling very thick upon the door, yet [his father] could never discover the hand which threw them, not any person employed therein, although [his father's] wife was hit with one of them, but without any hurt. At other times, the said Richard would cast goose dung at [his father] and others standing by, which he seemed to fetch out of the barn side, although neither [his father] nor those that were with him could find any there, nor discover anyone that brought it. Nor were there any geese kept at the house, nor other geese came near it. And lastly, [his father] saith that his said son would run upon his hands and his feet together as fast as most men could run upon their feet alone, and his body would sometimes be so heavy that two or three strong men could hardly lift it up, at others times as light as a bag of feathers. (pp. 49–50)

Other testimonies speak of showers of stones coming from nowhere, pieces of paper suddenly appearing in Richard's hand, extreme contorsions of his body, and dreadful cursing and swearing while in his fits. Zachary Taylor, a minister closely linked with the local Anglicans, poured scorn and criticism on the whole episode in *The Surey Imposter* (1697), maintaining that some of Richard's behaviour might be attributed to illness, but most of it to fraud, a fraud concocted with the help and connivance of local Catholics – and here we come to the context of the whole incident. Lancashire ('Surey' has nothing to do with the English county 'Surrey') had a great mixture of religious confessions at the end of the seventeenth century: the largest dissenting community in England, a large Catholic minority, and an active Anglican population. The whole county was riven by competing religious and political ideologies, and Richard's possession, real or not, provided the dissident groups with an opportunity to demonstrate the superiority of Protestant prayer over Catholic 'superstition', if the possession were real, and to tar Catholic reputation with charges of cheating, if it were not; while from the Anglican camp came Taylor's charge that the dissenters were no more than dupes of the Catholics and tools in their hands.[30]

In both England and Scotland, then, religion and the other world were being called in to express, and perhaps give relief to, intense political and religious emotions which would have sought other, possibly more violent, outlets had these preternatural vents not been available. But we should also not underestimate the intellectual ferment over traditional Christianity, being expressed throughout the end of the seventeenth century and the beginning of the eighteenth. Some people argued that once the faith had been purged of 'Popish' superstition, it would be fine; others, that it was irredeemably superstitious anyway because of its accounts of miracles and demons. These radical positions were certainly attractive to many, but the more widespread solution to faith, adopted by the English upper and emerging middle classes and preached, through them, via pulpits throughout the country, was Latitudinarianism, essentially the notion that one should conform to the practices of the Church of England out of social courtesy, but that what really mattered was the moral state of the individual, which was, at bottom, his own personal business. Calm reasonableness was this philosophy's watchword, and any notion of demons, witches, miracles, and inexplicable happenings was incompatible with it.[30] To whatever extent the battles of the treatises made up a conversation between intellectuals which appeared to no immediate effect on the classes below them, over time, the drip, drip, drip from pulpits and publishing presses either sapped the convictions of congregations and readers, and wore them away into facsimiles of the beliefs of their social betters: or it alienated them and thus, while driving parishioners into outward conformity, it produced an inward dissent and silent, stubborn adherence to old beliefs and traditional practices.

But if appeals to 'reason' and 'reasonableness' informed this latter-day Latitudinarianism, they could also be used by others for different purposes. Robert Fleming, for example, in 1693 noted that 'though there needs divine light to make a right estimate and judgement of things which relate to the present day, yet if men admit reason, it may be too easy to see that there is no slow motion in the visible tendency of things as they now move in these three nations to some fatal and sudden period'. The title of his treatise gives us the context of this observation – *A Discourse of Earthquakes, as they are supernatural and premonitory signs to a nation* – for what Fleming means is that reason tells us that 'natural' phenomena are signs from

God and should be read as such. This is made clear when he comments on a severe convulsion in Jamaica in 1692.

> As to that tremendous stroke on Jamaica, we cannot see but (i) its being directed to a place where the whole country was purely English in its interest and inhabitants, and thus a part of the same nation, though at a distance: so that it can be no more evident that such a strange stroke was real and no imaginary thing than that it hath a proper aspect in a monitory way on this island, and set up as a public beacon and monument of judgement in this respect – to show how terrible a thing it is to fall immediately into the hands of the living God ... (ii) We see its being directed also with a special commission to that one place which alone was the most flourishing populous part of the whole country, and thus made the scaffold on which so dreadful an execution of judgement was acted, as did in two moments swallow up near 2000 of its inhabitants, whilst no part else of the island had any such dreadful effects. And was this a contingent and casual thing only, if men do but exercise reason herein? (pp. 15–16)

Such invocation of 'reason' marks Fleming not only as a writer touched by the new sensibilities of polite society, but also as someone who has been touched by it in a quite different way from sceptics and doubters. It had, indeed, become commonplace for recorders and defenders of preternatural manifestations, especially those connected with witchcraft, to deal with supposed objections that the extraordinary things they were describing had entirely natural causes and explanations by making an appeal, direct or indirect, to reason and reasonableness. Thus, when Samuel Petto issued *A Faithful Narrative of the Wonderful and Extraordinary Fits which Mr Thomas Spatchet (late of Dunwich and Cookly) was under by Witchcraft* (1693), he launched immediately into answering objections before even embarking on his narrative.

> There are atheistical and irreligious persons in this age, which would persuade us that all such matters are cheats or come only from a natural cause. If some be cheats and counterfeits, must all be so? Surely not. It is not imaginable that this [*i.e. Spatchet's experience*] should be a cheat, for the dispensation was so stupendous and terrible that no man would voluntarily have been biased by interest, or hired into such a condition for such a number of years, whatever worldly advantage could be laid before him. If some strange convulsive motions may be from a natural cause, yea even in this person in part, yet it is irrational to think that the principal or chief of his unusual fits should be reducible thereunto. Men might more probably say that the sore boils which Job was smitten with were from a natural distemper and not from Satan (Job 2.7). Many of these motions were beyond Mr Spatchet's skill (as his acting the part of a drummer, a musician). Others were apparently [*clearly*] involuntary, even against his own life. Others not only morally, but naturally impossible (without super added strength), as far transcending his natural power: which, together with the speedy recovery (in a quarter of an hour after the removal of the fits), from such tormenting, racking pains by violent distorting of limbs, sufficiently argue its not proceeding merely from a natural bodily distemper.

To this I might add what I myself and my friend, Mr William Bidbank, a minister, did observe in another famous case at Lowestoft, where divers persons (not only dissenters but also others) had torturing fits and raised or vomited many pins, all wrinkled and bent, so as I could not observe two pins of those which I saw were bent in the same manner. Can anyone imagine that these pins were from a natural cause engendered in their bodies and thus bent? And when divers of them had fits together at the same time, if one recovered and did but go and lay a hand upon the others, they would immediately recover and be well again. Surely these things may be enough to evince that these things were preternatural. (p. i)

The case Petto then describes has some unusual features. Thomas Spatchet was afflicted by severe trembling and contortions of the body during the 1660s, and in 1665 a woman called Abre Grinset confessed she was a witch and had been instrumental in causing Thomas's sufferings.

She confessed that she had made a league with the Devil and was enticed into it by a witch at her wedding, that she had been a witch above twenty years, and she had bewitched John Collet of Cookly and Henry Winson of Walpool to death. And she must see John Collet before his death, and by a wile did get a sight of him. Calling at the house, [she] said that there was the greatest snake in the way that ever was seen (which was not so). They all run out to see it, and she in the interim went up to see him, and he died two days after, or thereabouts. Also she confessed to them that the Devil had drawn blood of her, and that he did appear in the form of a pretty, handsome young man first, and spake to her [in] a hollow, solemn voice. But she would not declare what he spake. And since, [he] appeareth to her in the form of a blackish grey cat or kitling, [and] that it sucketh of a teat (which searchers since saw in the place she mentioned) and hath drawn blood. (p. 18)

She was searched a second time a few days later, and it was then seen that her body was scratched all over – 'it is probable that the Devil did much torment her after her confession' is Petto's comment – and it may have been this that decided Thomas not to scratch her himself, though urged to do so by various people, although Petto attributes his refusal to plain kind-heartedness. It is notable from this narrative that Abre was not arrested or brought to trial, for she died in her bed in 1667. After her death Thomas began to make a recovery, though it was never full and his shaking and trembling continued, if less severely and with periods of intermission, until his death.

The printing presses in both London and Edinburgh were churning out pamphlets and essays of a similar nature throughout the 1690s. Matthew Hale's *Collection of Modern Relations of Matter of Fact concerning Witches and Witchcraft*, which he had put together after his experiences of witch trials in the early 1660s, was reissued in 1693 by Edward Cooke 'to check and correct the impiety, the vanity, the self-conceitedness or baseness of such witch-advocates as either confidently maintain there are no witches at all, making their shallow conceptions an adequate measure for the extent of the powers of nature and of the wisdom and power of God: or, contrary to their duty and their oaths, make light of the examination and trial of them' (preface, p. vi). To Lord Hale's collection Cooke adds an undated 'horrible relation of a trumpeter, his wife, and daughter, debauched by a wicked foul spirit, transcribed from a letter written by a very intelligent [*well-informed*] person in Holland' (pp. 59–61); and 'a relation of a Dutch boy possessed by a German spirit', dated 12 February and 24 April 1690. The connection of these anecdotes with Hale's text is slight. The spirits were sent by witches, but it is the spirits, not the witches, who are the focus of the narratives, and so their relevance must be regarded as minimal except in so far as they add to the overall intention of the treatise, which is to combat scepticism and disbelief.[32]

Similarly, Alexander Telfair's *True Relation of An Apparition, Expressions and Actings of a Spirit* (Edinburgh, 1696) was published at the instance of certain kirk ministers to confute 'the prevailing spirit of atheism and infidelity' which imputed 'the voices, apparitions, and actings of good or evil spirits to the melancholic disturbance or distemper of the brains or fancies of those who pretend [*claim*] to hear, see, or feel them' (p. 3). As was frequently the case, the invasion (in this instance) of Andrew MacKie's house by a poltergeist was attributed to the actions of a witch. For about ten weeks between February and the beginning of May 1695, Andrew suffered from lithobolia within and outwith his house, along with shrill whistling and a voice crying 'Whisht!' every time someone prayed. Something gripped Andrew by his shoulder and hair, whipped bedclothes off his children, and slapped their hips. Then on 6 April, Mrs MacKie lifted the stone from her threshold, which had shaken under her foot the previous day, 'and there found seven small bones with some blood and some flesh, all closed in a piece of old saddled [*folded small*] paper' (p. 10). This will have confirmed her suspicion that witchcraft had served as the catalyst for these phenomena, for the placing of objects under a threshold was standard magical practice either to do harm or to protect, and here the results clearly suggested the intention was the former. Then the house was set on fire, although each time this was attempted, someone noticed and extinguished the flames until finally, having successfully burned down a little sheep house, the entity departed. It was a complex episode, witnessed by many, including five local ministers apart from Alexander Telfair himself, and the local landowner, eight of Andrew's neighbours, and four others from outwith the immediate district, all of whom swore to the truth of what they reported. Alexander played an active part in these events, for he prayed with the family day after day during this period, and actually entered into conversation with the troublesome entity which identified itself as a spirit sent by God to call Scotland to repentance. This last reminds us how frequently at this time politics were making an appearance in this kind of literature, even though the MacKies' spirit was less than specific in its threat and condemnation.

We may probably believe Alexander when he confesses he was reluctant to go into print. Certainly he says he was urged to do so by various ministers – quite possibly those who had witnessed the phenomena with him – but he may also have had a charitable motive, for he mentions malicious gossip which was current at the time: Andrew was a mason and when he was given the 'mason word' upon graduating to full membership of his craft lodge, he dedicated his first child to the Devil;[33] a woman suspected of being a witch had left a few clothes with the MacKies who had kept some of them after the woman died; a previous tenant had consulted a witch to find out why he was not thriving but her answer had gone stray, and it was only when the next tenant lifted the threshold stone that he found a tooth, which he burned at once (pp. 6–7). Apart from the first point, this tittle-tattle is obviously irrelevant – although it does throw light on the casual way people not only used and experienced witchcraft, and also talked about it – but Alexander clearly felt he should deny all three rumours in print to protect Andrew's reputation and, along with it, the truth of the episode as a whole. Certainly Scottish clergy were keen at this time to fight for the reality of witchcraft, but perhaps one of the oddest 'defences' – odd, because it was actually a condemnation – appeared in 1697. Attributed to John Bell, a Presbyterian minister, although his authorship has been called in question,[34] *Witchcraft Proven, Arraigned, and Condemned* sets out to declare at once that credence in the existence of the spirit world is a necessary belief and that authoritative opinion has always supported this. Then comes an awkward glide from saying that if there are spirits, some must be good and others bad, into an assertion that scripture and history tell us that some people have covenanted with the bad and used them for their own purposes, and thence into a tired rehashing of the definitions of the Hebrew words for magical workers, a piece of learning better done by others long before this author's attempt, and a brief guide to the reader on how he or she may recognise a witch by various signs and behaviours.

The definitions cast a wide net, as was common. Astrologers, soothsayers, magicians, sorcerers, necromancers, and charmers are all lumped together under the generic term 'witch', in a fashion which had long been current, and five of the author's seven 'marks' of recognition are equally clichéd: (i) 'the insensible or dead nip [*teat*] of a blue colour, somewhat hard and withal insensible' (p. 14); (ii) the witch's inability to drown while she is being swum; (iii) her inability to shed tears, regardless of the pain or suffering she endures; (iv) her destructive glance, 'which sight is in them above all other men and women in the world most remarkable, for while as in the apple of the eye there is to be seen in all and every one the image of a man (commonly called the babe in the eye), with the head up and the feet down, the quite contrair is to be seen in them, to wit, the feet up and the head down' (p. 15); (v) her inability to repeat the Ten Commandments, the Lord's Prayer, as the Creed. The evil eye was not a new notion, of course, and the idea that a witch had a peculiar formation in her or his iris was equally old. A century earlier, for example, in 1597, Margaret Atkin, a confessing witch, was carted round the west of Scotland to identify other witches by seeing a mark in their eyes, which she was able to recognise as a secret sign of their identity.[35]

The sixth and seventh marks, however, are somewhat unusual.

The sixth mark is that if you put any great or gross salt in the pipe [*oviduct?*] of a cow and put all into the fire, upon hearing the crackling and seeing the bluish low [*flame*] thereof, which is like that of brimstone, instantly they shall let go their urine. But whether this flows from an inward passion and stupefaction of mind, that upon hearing the crackling and seeing the bluish low foresaid, they be brought to remember the horrible noise and sulphurous burning that is abiding them in Hell at the judgement of the great day when soul and body shall be joined together in one, and for ever and ever made liable to the wrath of the ever-living God, or on what other account, as yet

I know not: however, as I am duly informed, the mark is no less true than strange. (p. 16)

The blue flame mentioned here is reminiscent of the light from candles burned at a Sabbat. '[The witches] offer him [Satan] candles which give off a blue-coloured flame,' and, 'Satan commanded him [John Fian] to make homage with the rest of his servants, where he thought he saw the light of a candle standing in the midst of his servants, which appeared blue low.'[36] (This is the pale blue-grey of washed-out woad, of course, closer to the blue of diseased or dead tissue, not the rich blue of lapis lazuli associated with the Virgin.)

> Seventhly, there are not wanting some who be bold to aver that a witch may be known from a peculiar scent or smell which is to be found in them beside all other people in the world, and which neither flows from the nastiness of clothes, vermin, or the like, but a contradistinct smell from any such thing, which may seem the more probable for that the five senses, being the doors of the soul whereby what is within is ordinarily disclosed, and the Devil being in full possession of their soul must needs emit his own scent, even that of the pit. (p. 16)

Bad smells were redolent of Hell and moral turpitude. The *Apocalypse* refers to fire, smoke, and sulphur coming out of the mouths of the plagues released at the sound of the sixth angelic trumpet, and to the lake of fire and sulphur into which the Devil will be thrown at the end of the world (9.17; 20.10). Many saints could tell a heretic from his or her smell, and apparently Pyrenean patois calls male witches *poudouès* and female *poudouèros* [Latin *putridus*] because of their evil odour, and Jean Bodin noted, 'Women, who by nature have a very much sweeter breath than men, upon becoming intimate with Satan, turn hideous, gloomy, ugly, *and stinking to an unnatural degree*' (my italics). This peculiar and offensive smell thus parallels the odour of sanctity emanating from the righteous or, indeed, the specially blessed – one thinks of the sweet smell said to emanate from the body of the healer Valentine Greatrakes, and even from his urine – and is quite distinct from the common odours of normal everyday life.[37]

Witchcraft Proven was published in Glasgow in the same year as the executions resulting from the Bargarran case – surely not a coincidence – but while this caused a flurry of interest, partly because of the executions, partly because of the pamphlets and tracts which were written about it, we should not run away with the idea that it was part of any widespread movement of witch suppression, or that it stimulated fear or curiosity to the extent that persecution followed. Scotland had other things to worry about – famine, for one thing, and relations with England for another – and indeed so did the Kirk, whose principal preoccupations were illicit sex, swearing, and drunkenness rather than magic.[38] Nevertheless, we should also not fail to observe that the south-west of Scotland especially suffered particular levels of death and cruelty during the attempts to suppress covenanters, the 'Killing Times' of the mid- and late 1680s, and this may have left a legacy of heartlessness which can be seen in the treatment of some witches at the end of the century. We may catch a glimpse of this in the disbursement of public monies not only in executing but also in imprisoning witches. In 1698, Elspeth MacEwen, a convicted witch, was executed in Kirkcudbright at a cost of £7 9s 0d, just under half the average annual fee of a male agricultural servant in Renfrewshire of £16 16s 0d and just under the £12 16s 0d of his female equivalent. Seven prisoners left over from the Bargarran trial (reduced to six after only two days when one man died in prison) languished in custody until at least 12 January 1699 when the Privy Council ordered provision to be made for their maintenance. The council was told it had cost £66 8s 0d so far to keep them in prison, which amounts to just over nine and a half pence per day: slightly less than the male agricultural servant's daily fee of around eleven pence, slightly more than the female's nine and a half pence. The council's provision fixed a maintenance payment for their prisoners at the slightly higher level of one groat each per day, that is, around one shilling or twelve pence.[39] Some notion of how meagre this was can be gauged from the eighty pence per day spent on each of the eight prisoners in the Edinburgh tolbooth in September 1698, and while this is high and we may have to take inflation into account, in 1683 the cost per day of maintaining a prisoner in that same tolbooth was three shillings, or thirty-six pence.[40] The likelihood is, of course, that these prisoners or their families were in a position to pay such sums for their upkeep; but the disparity in amounts illustrates how true was the Lord Advocate's report to the Privy Council in September 1698 anent the Bargarran suspects when he said they were starving. It also shows that the slight increase in their maintenance, ordered by the council, was hardly generous.

As the seventeenth century drew to a close, then, what was the position of witches in the various societies in the islands of Britain? In Scotland, as we have just seen, local sentiments still burned fiercely and while the judiciary may sometimes have had reservations about the quality of evidence laid before it, advocates were by no means reticent about using appeals to the underlying fear of witchcraft they knew still informed many members of their juries. The juries themselves were perfectly capable of trying prisoners according to the evidence, and in many cases acquitted them of their charges; but they were equally capable of condemning them in the face of dubious testimony, and both sides of the legal divide might decide not to pay any judicial attention at all to the magic practised in their midst for, with all necessary reservations made, it seems that the Highlands and islands saw very few cases of witchcraft brought to court in comparison with the central belt where these were still not uncommon. In England, acquittals were frequent, especially when Sir John Holt, Lord Chief Justice from 1689 to 1710, was presiding. 'By his questions and manner of hemming up the evidence,' observed one contemporary, '[he] seemed to me to believe nothing of witchery at all.'[41] Holt was a Whig, of course, and surrounded by the chattering classes in London, for whom scepticism was becoming de rigueur; but of much of England at this time it can be said that the situation resembled that of the Scottish Highlands. Magic went on, people used it or endured its effects, and often dealt with any difficulties or inconveniences by shifting the problem elsewhere. In October 1698, for example, the kirk records of Caithness noted that sorcery and witchcraft were common in the parish of Wick, largely because magical workers banished from Orkney were coming across the sea to settle there. Serious consideration, therefore, was recommended to the authorities to banishing such people from Caithness as well, a recommendation which was approved, although with how much successful outcome is open to doubt.[42] Accusations followed by trials, however, were slowly becoming less frequent, and by and large the same can be said of Ireland, Wales, the Isle of Man, and the Channel Islands. So was magic effectively on its deathbed? By no means as far as the majority of the population was concerned. Were Church and state intent on eradicating it? Suppressing rather than eradicating is probably the *mot juste*, although even so suppression had a long way to go yet before it could be counted as successful or even noticeable.

12

PEOPLE *VERSUS* THE LAW:
1704–1730

It is tempting to misunderstand the role of the Kirk and Church in these controversies over witchcraft and the continuing involvement of ministers in cases of alleged malefice or demonic possession. There was no centrally directed persecution of magical workers by either Church or state in the British Isles, and those incidents which came before ecclesiastical or criminal courts in the late seventeenth century were, with the occasional exception of those which may have imitated one another, isolated complaints issuing from a very particular set of circumstances in a particular location. Published controversies between individuals may have sprung from the writers' concerns to defend or promote certain principles they considered vital either to the maintenance or to the reformation of certain aspects of the religious status quo or philosophical innovation, but their impact upon the majority should not be over-estimated. When witches or other magical workers found themselves in court, it was not because those prosecuting them had an ideological axe to grind at their expense, but because a local situation had become intolerable for someone who wanted redress. If other considerations were involved, this is because people do not live in a vacuum and are bound to be affected by external circumstances; but whether these externals play a major or minor role in the process of accusation, investigation, and possibly trial depends almost entirely on chance. The root cause of the dispute is personal, not intellectual.

We can see this clearly in a case from 1699. The Black Isle in Ross and Cromarty was dominated by the clan MacKenzie, which had its principal seat in the Redcastle. One of the laird's tenants, John Glass, quarrelled with John MacKenzie, minister of his parish kirk, because, among other things, he (Glass) had praised Catholicism as the finest of all religions. John MacKenzie was an Episcopalian and slow to promote any form of worship which might be called Presbyterian. Even so, John Glass's remarks were provocative and MacKenzie reacted as one might expect, by combining with his kirk session to demand that John undergo repentance and humiliation in the usual manner, by wearing sackcloth and standing before the congregation as a sinner during Sunday sermon. He was also required to pay a sum of money into the poor-box, as a fine. None of this, one might think, was over-onerous. Indeed, it was precisely the kind of repentance demanded of many suspect witches, too, all over Scotland, including those called before the nearby presbytery of Dingwall during the past three decades or so. But John was obviously not a man to take his punishment quietly, for he was rash enough to declare that someone would pay dearly for treating him so, and not long after, MacKenzie died of a fever.

A local witch, Donald Moir, was questioned about this – once again we see the application of *post hoc ergo propter hoc*, which meant that MacKenzie's sudden death had something to do with John Glass's outburst – and he averred that John had hired him to get rid of the minister, a magical task he had performed by means of images he and others had made under the supervision of the Devil who attended their working in the form of a black man with cloven feet. The assertion that John had hired him is not at all incredible (although whether he had actually done so, we cannot say for certain), for this is just the type of work and just the kind of revenge within a witch's peculiar province and John does not appear to be the sort of man who would not think twice about consulting a witch for this purpose. Some human hair and dish with a hole in its side were found in the house of one of the suspects and these, by the time arrests were made, eventually numbered twelve, nine women and three men, including John himself and his father-in-law who, according to the record, was a person 'always suspected of witchcraft'. Donald Moir was also arrested, of course, but was then found dead in his cell, and John Glass's sons, who seem to have been as hot-headed as their father, were said to have threatened to shoot John MacKenzie's successor in the parish if he tried to say their father was guilty of witchcraft.

In such an atmosphere it is hardly surprising that John suspected a jury formed of local men might be prejudiced against him, so he petitioned the Lords of Justiciary in Edinburgh to have his case heard by a higher court, a petition which was countered by another from the sheriff depute of Ross, who agreed that a locally drawn jury would find John guilty, but argued that as the clear cause of both MacKenzie's and Moir's deaths was witchcraft, and as the whole district was in a state of agitation over the affair, the sooner the guilty were punished, the better. A board of inquiry was commissioned by the Privy Council and, interestingly enough, two of the women, Margaret Monro and Agnes Wrath, confessed to being witches (though not to perpetrating these particular crimes). John himself was out on bail, the man standing cautioner for him being Rory MacKenzie the younger of Redcastle, his employer. After considering the evidence laid before it, the Privy Council came to a decision. John and Mary Keill were to be released because the evidence was not good enough to secure their conviction or execution; but there was enough to warrant John's being fined and banished, which meant that a troublemaker and source of potential abrasiveness was removed from the scene. The other accused, including the two who had confessed to being witches, were to given 'some arbitrary punishment', in other words, as the local law officers thought fit. What happened to them, we do not know. Under the revised Witchcraft Act of 1649 they should have been liable to execution, but there is no firm evidence that anyone was, so perhaps the more likely outcome is that they were imprisoned and pilloried, or simply imprisoned for as long as the officers decided, or (as Roy Pugh suggests) branded on the cheek and banished.[1]

This somewhat unusual behaviour by the Privy Council in effectively ignoring the law and passing on responsibility for punishment to other people is perhaps a signal of growing witch-weariness among legislators and judiciary, if not the rest of the country. In March 1694, Sir Alexander Home of Renton wrote to Lord Polwarth that there had been a great increase in witchcraft in Coldingham since his father's time. His father, then sheriff, had had seven or eight witches executed, but none had been arrested since because of the slackness of judges and 'I know,' he added, 'if some were apprehended, more would come to light.' It took a while for Sir Alexander's complaints to have any effect, but eventually, in September 1698, the minister of Coldingham managed to uncover one or two suspect cases in his parish.

> Margaret Polwart in Coldingham, having a sick child, was using charms and sorcery for its recovery, and Jean Hart, a suspected witch, was employed in the affair, and also Alison Nisbet who had been lately scratched, or had blood drawn above the breath by someone who had suspected her of witchcraft. One of the witnesses declared that she saw Jean Hart holding a candle in her left hand and moving her right hand about, and heard her mutter and whisper much, but did not understand a word that she said. Another declared that she (the witness) did not advise Margaret Polwart to send for Jean Hart, but she heard her say [that] that thief, Christian Happer, had wronged her child and that she would give her cow to have her child better. And that witness answered that they that chant cannot charm, or they that lay on cannot take off the disease, or they that do wrong to anyone cannot recover them.[2]

One notes, however, that Margaret was merely rebuked in public for her conduct, and certainly the punishment of other witches elsewhere at this time suggests that Sir Alexander's fears that the judiciary was losing interest in witchcraft had some justification. Jean Wharrie from Caerlaverock was summoned to the presbytery of Dumfries in 1697 to answer charges of making one of her neighbour's cows vomit grass, causing horses to prance uncontrollably, a woman to cough up a great deal of blood, and magically inflicting syphilis on a man. The presbytery was keen to have the matter taken up judicially, but their representative was unable to find a lawyer who could be bothered, and two years later the ministers were still without a legal prosecutor for Janet and for others who had been complained of in the meantime. Janet, it seems, had been in prison during all this, so she had had no easy time of it; but in March 1700, the Lord Advocate ordered her release and that of the others on the grounds that the things alleged against them 'were not so momentous as to require a commission to put them to trial'.[3]

This unwillingness to allow local enthusiasms to progress as far as trial was evident in 1701, too, when Kirkcudbright was thwarted in its intention to bring Janet M'Robert into court. Janet had been accused by her neighbours in Milburn of a variety of offences closely related to spite and coincidence. She had helped Robert Crichton's wife winnow corn, for example, and was given a small quantity of chaff in her apron for her cow. This, it seems, was not enough and next day Mrs Crichton's breast swelled and she was unable to supply her child with milk for five weeks, with the result that the child lost weight. Her cow's milk lost colour and taste and proved unusable and Janet not only sent John Robertson's dog mad, but made John M'Gimpser's dog useless for hare coursing as well. Mysterious happenings also attended Janet's own house. After John Bodden's son died, a great noise was heard there, and while Janet explained it was simply made by her hen, John declared that 'all the hens within twenty miles would not have made such a noise'. He also told the kirk session that on the Wednesday after Janet was imprisoned, 'he did see, about cock crow, a candle going through the said Janet's house, but saw nothing holding it', and an equally mysterious event frightened Elizabeth Lauchlon when, upon her going to Janet's house while Janet was not there, she looked in at the door '[and] saw a wheel going about and spinning without the help of any person seen by her. She went in and essayed to lay hold of the said wheel, but was beat back to the door and her head was hurt, though she saw nobody.'

On another occasion, when she was in Janet's house,

> the Devil appeared to her in the likeness of a man and did bid her deliver herself over to him, from the crown of her head to the sole of her foot, which she refused to do, saying she would rather give herself to God Almighty. After the Devil went away, the said Janet, who was present with her, laid bonds on her not to tell. And thereafter he came a second time to her, being in Janet's house alone, in the likeness of a gentleman, and desired her to go with him, and thereafter disappeared, seeming not to go out at the door.[4]

Now these, as opposed to the stories about the breast, the dogs, and the self-moving candle and spinning wheel, are remarkable details and make us wonder what was going on. Who was this man or these men? Did they actually exist, was Elizabeth having hallucinations of some kind, or was she simply lying? It is easy to suggest she was lying, of course, but if that is what she was doing, it obviously carried the risk she would not be believed or that her lie would be uncovered for what it was. It is also easy to 'rationalise' the men as men and to suggest that Janet may have been entertaining male visitors, so to speak, in which case one can understand why she would not want Elizabeth to talk about them. But there is no real basis for this 'rationalisation', and indeed, the difficulty any woman would have had in acting as a prostitute without detection in the small, more or less self-contained villages and hamlets which made up the majority of Scottish communities at this time would have been almost insurmountable. It is also difficult to envisage Elizabeth's having hallucinations of this almost material kind out of the blue, as it were, since there is no hint in our information that she had ever had visions of any kind before. In short, there is a puzzle here because of the disparity between this information and that of the other witchcrafts and oddities, unfortunately not a puzzle which lends itself to solution.

It is also worth noting, however, that Elizabeth felt able to visit Janet and that she seems to have had no hesitation in snooping when the opportunity presented itself. But if we ask why people found it so easy to see into Janet's house, or to go in without her being there, the answer may lie in a description we have of ordinary people's houses in Kirkcudbrightshire in the early 1700s.

> They were built of stone plastered together with mud, and they had roofs of straw and turf, often far from providing shelter in rainy weather. The windows ... had no glass. They were mere holes in the wall, through which the smoke from the peat fire

escaped when it failed to emerge through the chimney hole in the roof. The livestock were sheltered under the same roof as their owners. Man and beast entered by the same doorway, and slept in one undivided chamber. An aged woman of my own parish assured me that, as late as the year 1825, she had visited a house in Minnigaff where there was no door at all, but only an old sheet or curtain hung up as a substitute.[5]

Once again, the Edinburgh lawyers rejected the ministers' request for a commission to try Janet for witchcraft, and once again the ground for the refusal was the insufficiency of proof of the accusations – not that that stopped the parish from taking its own steps, for it banished Janet, who then went to live in Ireland. This setback, however, did not stop the presbytery from its task of cleansing the people, for on 7 January 1702 it appointed a day of public fasting to atone for people's 'gross ignorance', 'neglect of the duties of godliness', 'manifold witchcrafts', and 'idolatrous Popery in the land'. A week later, mindful of its list of people's sins which not only included profane cursing, swearing, and scolding, but also 'murders, whereof some are unnatural, uncleanness of all sorts, fornication, adultery, amidst tippling, drunkenness, and revelling, oppression, cheating, and defect of considerateness in dealing and bargaining ... lying, slandering, backbiting', as well as Sabbath breaking, disobedience to parents, and the fearful spread of the notion that the state takes precedence over the Church in ecclesiastical matters, the presbytery lobbied the General Assembly with a view to renewing the Covenants, and called for the suppression of witchcraft, adultery, and incest, not to mention vigorous enforcement of the laws against 'Popery and Quakerism'.[6]

Now, there can be little doubt that, while the presbytery had a particular view of Scottish society's ills and the moral condition of the people, its concern was not misplaced and arose from a real effervescence of criminality among its flock. Infanticide, for example, was by no means uncommon, and even if we allow that extreme poverty and the perceived need to maintain a public reputation for virtue almost certainly account for some of these murders, murders they still are. Illegitimacy and fornication were frequent offences, as was attempted abortion. 'In April 1708, Margaret Shaw told South Leith [kirk] session that when she advised her partner that she was with child to him, he bade her take a drink, as other women did, to put back the child.' Bestiality (usually called 'buggery') appears often in the records of both the ecclesiastical and the criminal courts, and brawling, drunkenness, cursing, and swearing were also rife, to the extent, in fact, that in 1672 Parliament felt obliged to pass an Act against profanity although, since it had to re-enact it in 1690, 1693, 1695, 1696, and 1701, the effect of legislation on behaviour appears to have been minimal.[7] Moreover, as if to exacerbate society's problem, vagrants roamed the countryside in large numbers and were perceived as both lawless and reprobate.

There are at this day in Scotland, besides a great many poor families very meanly provided for by the church-boxes, with others, who, by living upon bad food fall into various diseases, 200,000 people begging from door to door. These are not only no way advantageous, but a very grievous burden to so poor a country. And though the number of them be perhaps double to what it was formerly by reason of this present great distress, yet in all times there have been about 100,000 of those vagabonds who have lived without any regard or subjection either to the laws of the land or even those of God and nature, fathers incestuously accompanying with their own daughters, the son with the mother, and the brother with the sister. No magistrate could ever discover or be informed which way one in a hundred of these wretches died, or that ever they were baptised. Many murders have been discovered among them, and they are not only a most unspeakable oppression to poor tenants who, if they give not bread or some kind of provision to perhaps forty such villains in one day, are sure to be insulted by them, but rob many poor people who live in houses distant from any neighbourhood. In years of plenty, many thousands of them meet together in the mountains, where they feast and riot for many days. And at country weddings, markets, burials, and other the like public occasions, they are to be seen, both men and women, perpetually drunk, cursing, blaspheming, and fighting together.[8]

No surprise, therefore, if drunkenness and cursing led to blasphemy which, allied to the prevalent fears among both educated and devout Christian folk that atheism was on the march, made both Kirk and state question the stability of that society they were trying to govern. Certainly it was this atmosphere of alarm and displeasure which, combined with the plethora of witchcraft allegations placed before the Privy Council in December 1696, and the ramifications of the Christian Shaw episode, helped lead to the trial and execution on 8 January 1697 of Thomas Aikenhead, an Edinburgh student. Hot-headed with youth, he was brought into court because it was said that he

had repeatedly maintained in conversation that theology was a rhapsody of ill-invented nonsense, patched up partly of the moral doctrines of philosophers, and partly of poetical fictions and extravagant chimeras: that he ridiculed the holy scriptures, calling the Old Testament Ezra's fables, in profane allusion to Aesop's fables: that he railed on Christ, saying He had learned magic in Egypt, which enabled Him to perform those pranks which were called miracles: that he called the New Testament the history of the imposter Christ; that he said Moses was the better artist and the better politician, and he preferred Muhammad to Christ: that the holy scriptures were stuffed with such madness, nonsense, and contradictions that he admired [*he was astonished at*] the stupidity of the world in being so long deluded by them: that he rejected the mystery of the Trinity as unworthy of refutation, and scoffed at the incarnation of Christ.[9]

Aikenhead's blasphemy may have been extreme, but there were sufficient other, if lesser, instances to suggest that people's morals were on the slide. 'Nothing,' wrote an anonymous essayist in 1704, 'does so much contribute to the ruin of kingdoms and societies as the abounding of vice and immorality. Wickedness, where it becomes outrageous, challenges Heaven to vindicate its own authority.'[10]

Scotland, therefore, or perhaps one should say certain areas in Scotland, at the beginning of the eighteenth century was in a kind of ferment agreeable to the actual or alleged practice of magic on the one hand and its firm suppression on the other. But can the same be said of other parts of the British Isles? In 1702, London was scandalised by the trial of Richard Hathaway, a blacksmith's apprentice in Southwark, who, in the words of his prosecutor, Mr Conyers, was a cheat 'for endeavouring to impose upon the people a belief that he had been bewitched by one Sarah Morduck and that, as an effect of her pretended [*claimed*] witchery, he vomited up nails and pins: and that he could not speak nor open his eyes: and that great noises were heard in the house where he lay, and there could be no remedy for him but by his scratching and fetching the blood of this Sarah Morduck. And by this means, the poor woman has been very much abused by her neighbours, reputed a witch, and brought to a trial for her life as such.'[11] Dr Martin, her parish minister, was disturbed by this gossip that Sarah was a witch and carried out an experiment to test its truth. He visited Richard while he was claiming to be deaf and blind, and asked him to scratch 'Sarah', whom he had brought with him: only the woman was not actually Sarah, but a Mrs Johnson whom he had substituted for Sarah in order to see what would happen. Richard, of course, scratched her as though she were Sarah, but the subsequent revelation of his mistake or fraud made no difference in the end, because Sarah was forced to go and live elsewhere. Her testimony before the court at his trial explains vividly the chain of events.

> Sarah Morduck being called and sworn deposed to this effect: that in September last, Richard Hathaway came to this informant in Surrey as she was opening her window and, being behind, scratched her face in a very cruel manner and forced out one of her teeth and carried away her clothes. Upon the eleventh of February last, Thomas Osborn, Thomas Hutton, with four other persons unknown, all in disguise, came to this informant's house in Surrey and forced her out of her house, and carried her to the house of Thomas Welling who is master to the said Richard Hathaway. There the said Hathaway, by the encouragement of the said Osborn and Hatton and the rest of the company, did again scratch this informant in a most barbarous manner; and afterwards Elizabeth, wife to the said Thomas Welling, fell upon her and scratched her in a most cruel manner, and tore her face and tore off her headclothes and hair. Then the said Thomas Welling gave this informant two or three kicks on her belly, and threw her on the ground and stamped upon her, and so much bruised her that she was forced to keep her bed for about a fortnight.
>
> This informant further deposeth that in September last, one Elizabeth Willoughby, the wife of Walter Willoughby, came to this informant's house in Surrey and brought a great many persons unknown to this informant with her. The said Elizabeth gave this informant several blows with her fist, and would have pulled her out of her house for him, the aforesaid Richard Hathaway, to have scratched her, he standing at a corner hard by, but was prevented by Mrs Sarah Hall. [She] further saith that in the month of September last, she having occasion to go into Newmarket, a boy (his name is John Hopkins) called out, saying, 'There goes the old witch!' Whereupon a great company of people in a riotous manner flocked about her and threatened to throw her in a horse-pond. And this informant, being got into an alehouse by the assistance of some women, avoided the fury of the rabble, otherwise she had been murdered, as she verily believes. Afterwards, Mr Burrell, her landlord, with others his assistants, came and conveyed her home. (pp. 87–88)

This is a potent reminder of the depth of belief in the validity of witchcraft, which still permeated a large number of people in the town as well as the country. The chattering classes might have their doubts and the working classes their bravado and drunken scepticism from time to time, but in large part traditional beliefs and attitudes held sway, even though, when put to it, juries were sometimes prepared to acquit, as indeed they were in Sarah's case. For the disturbances about which we have just heard resulted in a complaint, an arrest, an investigation, a trial, and an acquittal. Nothing daunted, however, Richard then pretended he could not eat, even though he was observed to be doing so secretly, and was supported (perhaps unwittingly) in his continued imposture by a local magistrate, Sir Thomas Lane, who decided Sarah should be scratched again. Whereupon Richard 'recovered' and Sarah was rearrested and sent to prison. The jury heard evidence from several witnesses, including Dr Martin, servants, and physicians, all of whom testified that Richard was carrying out an elaborate hoax, and not carrying it out particularly well, the result of which was, as the published account tells us, that 'the jury consulted and, without going from the bar, brought him in guilty' (p. 84).

Sarah's acquittals are matched by those of Susan Hannover from Devon (1702) and Joanna Tanner from Wiltshire (1703),[12] but others were not so fortunate. Sarah Griffiths, a poor woman (she lived in a garret), had a bad reputation and when her neighbours' children started vomiting pins and convulsing, people were sure she was a witch. Oddly enough, however, this did not get her arrested until she went to buy some soap and was laughed at by the young shop assistant who said his scales, which were not working properly, must be bewitched. That night the shop was turned upside down and the boy fell ill; but, having been cured by some clergymen's prayers, he and two others met Sarah as they were walking near a river. Hoping to prove she was a witch, they threw her in and watched her float. Eventually she scrambled out and hit the shop boy on his arm, which began to hurt and later turned gangrenous. In consequence of this, he died, and in consequence of that, his master had Sarah arrested. She did her best to escape, but was overpowered and brought before a magistrate who committed her to Bridewell where she was still imprisoned when Thomas Greenwell published a short account of the episode on 26 July 1704.[13]

Once again we have indications that if high-ranking members of a judiciary may have had doubts about the quality of some witchcraft evidence, others lower down the scale did not. But the volatile difficulties which faced lawyers, juries, and local communities when charges of witchcraft raised their heads can be seen in two Scottish cases from the same period, centred upon the coastal villages of Torryburn and Pittenweem in Fife in 1704 and 1705. Lillias Adie was called before the kirk session of Torryburn on 29 July 1704 to hear accusations of witchcraft laid against her at an earlier session on 30 June.[14] She was not at liberty during this set of examinations, for the session sat in the prison where she was being held and this is where the minister and elders heard evidence both from Lillias herself and others summoned for the occasion. Cited along with her were Janet Whyte and Mary Wilson, and the substance of the complaints were that Jean Bizet, servant to Helen Anderson, had been drinking and had then fallen asleep, waking in a sweat with a sore head and crying out upon 'Lilly, with her blue doublet!' and 'Mary, Mary Wilson, Christ keep me!' (p .131) Her husband, James Tanochie, obviously thought she was merely drunk, as he offered to beat her out of it, but other women were not so sure and talked about her 'doing ill'.

This, however, was actually a diversion from the real problem which was Lillias Adie. Since Lillias had been overtly accused of witchcraft, by 28 July she was in custody and next day began her investigation by the kirk session where she openly admitted to being covenanted with the Devil. 'His skin was cold, and his colour black and pale [*i.e. olivine?*]. He had a hat on his head, and his feet were cloven like the feet of a stirk [*bullock*], as she observed when he went from her' (p. 135). She described meeting him perhaps a hundred times in various places in the local countryside, and on the second occasion, after her sexual initiation as a witch, she saw him along with others (twenty or thirty, she said), adding that it was a moonlit night and that they danced for a while before the Devil turned up on a pony, with a hat on his head. The next time after that, 'the Devil came with a cap which covered his ears and neck. They had no moonlight. Being interrogated if they had any light, she replied she got light from darkness, and could not tell what that light was. But she heard them say it came from darkness and went to darkness, and said, 'It is not so bright as a candle, the low [*light*] thereof being blue, yet it gave such a light as they could discern others' faces' (p. 135). This Vergilian darkness visible is reminiscent of Matthew 6.23 – 'If your eye is unhealthy, your whole body will be full of darkness. If then the light in you is darkness, how great is the darkness' – an image repeated in Luke 11.34–35. Lillias may have picked it up from a sermon – she may have been able to read, although if she could, whether she had a Bible in her house is a moot point – but the blue candle flame, as we have seen, is a not uncommon feature of witches' meetings as, to a certain extent, is her description of the Devil's headgear.

'Hat' might suggest he was dressed as a gentleman, and this could imply he had a cocked (or tricorn) hat. But countrymen also wore plain, side-cocked hats, and the cap covering the ears and neck may suggest either the old-fashioned buttoned cap worn by country folk and old men – a soft, round-fitting cap with a brim worn either turned down over the ears, or up and secured with a button – or it may refer to something like the soft Phrygian cap worn by working men and revolutionaries, and clearly depicted in pictures such as John Collet's *The Female Orators* (1768). This, and his arrival on a pony rather than a horse, suggests the appearance of a rustic rather than a gentleman, and the implication is strengthened by the session's pointed question on 31 July, asking if the Devil had a sword. This would certainly mark him out as a gentleman, but Lillias gave the noteworthy answer, 'I believe he durst not use one' (p. 136). Did Lillias recognise an actual person and remark contemptuously that he was too nervous to handle a sword? Did she mean he was someone who had been in trouble with the law and could not afford to be discovered with a weapon? Did she mean he was a conman who had been caught masquerading as a gentleman and was reluctant to repeat the offence? These 'rationalisations' depend on Lillias's describing a real man, rather lying or fantasising; but 'I believe he durst not use one' is perhaps an odd thing to say if she were telling a lie or a fable, so it remains as a remark worthy of comment, even if comment, in the absence of further information, cannot take one further.[15] A further remark by Lillias, too, cannot have done anything other than sharpen the session's curiosity. 'She knew few of them that were at those meetings, especially the young sort, because they were masked like gentlewomen' (p. 138). This feature, like the candle's emitting a blue flame, was not actually an unusual accompaniment of witches' meetings in Scotland and elsewhere, although there is no reason to suppose the session (or, indeed, Lillias herself) must have known that. In 1658, for example, Margaret Taylor from Dollar had mentioned a masked gentlewoman with a black bag, a green waistcoat, and grey clothes, and men and women wearing masks at a Sabbat near Tranent in 1659 were noted by Barbara Cochran, Janet Crooks, and Marion Lynn. If these women were real and not figments of the imagination, they may have worn vizards either to conceal their identity or to conceal the ravages of a disease such as smallpox, or they may simply have turned up with the mask-like make-up of the period: heavy, shiny white paint over the face and shoulders, vermilion or creuse on the cheeks, and soot colouring the eyebrows. The effect, fully intentional, was that of wearing a mask.[16]

The last Sabbat Lillias attended was in August 1701, according to her evidence, held on the minister's own glebe and attended by sixteen or eighteen individuals. The minister, Allan Logan of that ilk (and thus a gentleman), had come to Torryburn in 1695 very much contrary to his will, since he had appealed against the appointment and had to be ordered by the General Assembly to take it up, and would remain there until 1717 when he transferred to Culross and Tulliallan, taking his experience of witches with him. He appears to have been a disciplinarian, as can be gathered, for example, from his second year in Culross when he excommunicated Bessie Thomson for consistently not standing up in church to receive a rebuke for her conduct (*Kirk Session record*, 29 July 1718). The idea, therefore, that a witches' meeting had been held on his own land would scarcely have been welcome, and these meetings continued almost until the sessions investigating Lillias, for James White, called before the minister and elders, said that only ten days before, 'he heard a great screeching when he was in Craigmilne upon the bleaching green beneath the said milne, and heard a second screech much greater, and clapping of hands and laughing, about twelve of the night, in the green on the other side of the burn. And it was observed by the bleachers to be all pastered [*trampled down*], though there was no cloth at the burn, nor bleachers that night' (p. 137). Then on 2 August, Lillias testified that Grissel Anderson had invited her to her house where there were several witches present, 'the morning just before the last burning of the witches' (p. 138). The chronology is not altogether clear, and we do not know to which execution this refers, but it may be to August 1701, which is when Lillias said she last attended a Sabbat. (Grissel was executed not long after, as was Euphame Stirt, who had bidden her come to the Sabbat at which the Devil turned up on a pony.) Lillias continued her testimony on 19, 20, and 29 August 1704. On the 19th, she said Satan had appeared to her some 100 times and would come and go like a shadow which no one could see save herself, and that on the first occasion when he left her, 'she did not hear his feet on the stubble' (p. 139–140). On the 20th, she was asked if she were guilty of witchcraft and freely answered that she was, but 'desired all that had power with God to pray for her' (p. 140). Other witnesses came before the session, too, and named names of several witches apart from Lillias, both in Torryburn and across the Forth in Linlithgow, but by that time Lillias was dead. She died in Dunfermline gaol where the sessions had been sitting, and was buried on the shoreline between Torryburn and Torrie.[17]

Lillias's case, therefore, never reached a court of law, but if it had done so, both advocates, judge, and jury would have faced the determination of Lillias herself to confess to being a witch, and of Allan Logan, the minister, to have her convicted; and even though there may have been dissent here and there – on 30 March 1709, Helen Key said openly in church during sermon that she thought the minister was 'daft' [*over-enthusiastic*] when he preached against witches, and picked up her stool to leave the service – there were still plenty of others who were willing to testify to the activities in their midst. So sceptics on the bench, at the bar, or among the jury would have felt the pressure of Kirk and populace as they argued and deliberated upon the details laid before them. Pittenweem, a better-known episode, suffered from the same kind of thing. Patrick Morton, a sixteen-year-old, became ill and charged Beatrix Laing, with whom he had quarrelled, with causing his illness. His symptoms were the usual – physical convulsions and spasms, shrieks, and accusations, naming names – and the people he accused, Beatrix herself, Isobel Adam, Janet Cornfoot, Nicholas Lawson (a woman), Thomas Brown, Margaret Wallace, and Margaret Jack, soon found themselves imprisoned in the local tolbooth.

Beatrix already had a black mark against her in the Kirk's record. In 1695, she had appeared before the presbytery of St Andrews accused, at the instance of Patrick Couper, the minister in Pittenweem, of using a charm against a son of James Tod. The incident dragged on somewhat, but when the presbytery finally met in Pittenweem in 1696 and looked into the accusation further, the ministers found that James Tod could not prove his complaint and so the matter proceeded no further. But it did not mean that when Patrick Couper, a strict Presbyterian who had been imprisoned more than once during the 1680s for attending conventicles and had had to live abroad for a while, heard that Beatrix had apparently resorted to maleficent magic once again, he was the less inclined to believe it and pursue it further, for this indeed he did.[18] A petition from the magistrates and town council of Pittwenweem to try seven the people in custody was heard in Edinburgh on 13 June 1704 and permission was granted on 21 July to have the cases heard in the capital. Beatrix, Isobel, Nicholas, and Janet had already confessed, and a letter from 'a gentleman in Fife' suggests that Beatrix had been pricked, deprived of sleep, and threatened with death unless she admitted her offence. But while it is quite possible this is true, we should bear in mind that the whole episode sparked the equivalent of a pamphlet war early in 1705 and that in consequence we need to be careful how much trust we put in the veracity of the various contributions and their details. We are told in another pamphlet, for example, that,

> when Beatrix Laing and Nicholas Lawson were first imprisoned, they were ill used by some of the guard without the knowledge of magistrates or minister. The women made complaint [of this] to the minister, whereof he presently [*immediately*] acquainted the magistrates who, with the minister, went to the prison and threatened the guard if they offered the least disturbance to persons in custody. And the minister on the Lord's Day thereafter took occasion in a sermon to discover the wickedness of that practice, as being against the light of nature, scripture, and the just laws of the land. After this, we heard of no more disturbances they met with.[19]

Is this willingness to trust Patrick Couper's sense of justice, and is his apparently high-minded response to the women's suffering consistent with either the situation or Patrick Couper's known character? Maybe, of course, but one does rather wonder and doubt.

Thomas and the two Margarets, however, had not confessed and were in the tolbooth simply on the strength of statements allegedly made by the other four, as a result of which presumptions had been drawn. All seven prisoners were brought to Edinburgh for further investigation and trial. But by 12 August, Thomas had died and five of the others had been bailed.[20] Then on 3 October, the order came to free Isobel Adam. Isobel had confessed to trying to murder Alexander MacGregor by witchcraft and to meeting the Devil at Thomas Adamson's house on 1 January 1704. He was a man in black clothes, she said, sitting at a table, with a hat on his head. He was fearsome, she added, and his eyes sparkled like candles, which is why she knew he was the Devil, and she had submitted herself to him in bed. Yet in spite of this confession, the Lords of the Privy Council dismissed the case against her, 'finding no evidence from their examinations to be the ground of a process', and ordered not only that she be set at liberty, but that her case be dropped and not pursued again.[21] Patrick Morton, the source of the trouble, however, was not done yet. The minister had been reading an account of the Bargarran case to him, which clearly stimulated, if it did not create, his behaviour, and the effects of this continued to inflame certain parts of Pittenweem's population. On 30 January 1705, Janet Cornfoot who had escaped to Leuchars to avoid these people's hatred, was fetched back to Pittenweem by two men who took her first to the minister who happened to be in the town bailie's house. Mr Couper, according to one of the pamphlets hostile to him, ignored her cry for help and virtually abandoned her to a mob which had gathered in front of the house. 'They fell upon the poor creature immediately and beat her unmercifully, tying her so hard with a rope that she was almost strangled. They dragged her through the streets and along the shore by the heels. A bailie, hearing of a rabble near his stair, came out upon them, which made them immediately disappear.' This version of events is played down by an apologist pamphlet which does not deny the presence of the mob, but says Mr Couper knew nothing of it until later, and that Janet had actually gone to seek sanctuary in Nicholas Lawson's house and called to Nicholas to let her in: 'which, if she had done, she in all appearance had met with no more disturbance. But after this, we hear that some few of the rabble stole up secretly and murdered her.'[22]

Certainly Janet died. According to one source she was caught, tied up, stoned, and pressed to death under a door weighted down with stones and driven over by a man with a horse and sledge. These details do not appear in the pamphlet friendly to the minister and town magistrates, but they are repeated, whether justifiably or not one cannot say for certain, in a report to the Privy Council sitting on 15 February, which then ordered that Pittenweem's magistrates be prosecuted for allowing the whole incident to get out of hand, and that five named men be committed to the Edinburgh tolbooth until further notice.[23] The process cost Pittenweem a lot of money: £194 11s 0d, which was £13 14s 4d over the town's representatives' allowed budget. Meanwhile, Beatrix Laing, after a period of violence perpetrated against her, petitioned the Privy Council for protection. She had been five months in prison, she said, cruelly maltreated, and now, having managed to get out of prison and 'having lately returned to her own house at Pittenweem, expecting to have lived safely and quietly with her husband, the rabble there so menaced and threatened her to treat her as they had done Janet Cornfoot a little before ... that she was forced, under cloud of night, to leave her own house'.[24] The lords' reply was not quite all Beatrix may have wished. They told the magistrates to take steps to have the peace kept, and they arranged for a committee to investigate the whole episode, but when two Privy Councillors came to Pittenweem on 11 May in pursuit of this investigation, the town council flatly refused to protect Beatrix, 'in respect she may be murthered in the night without their knowledge'.[25] The council did nothing, even though Pittenweem was brazenly flouting its authority, and so Beatrix left Pittenweem and went to St Andrews where she was later found dead in the street.

As in the Torryburn case, reservations about the quality of evidence initially laid against Beatrix and the others may have caused the Edinburgh lawyers to order their release from prison and, in Janet Cornfoot's case, to instruct no further prosecution be contemplated; but popular sentiment, abetted either by the sympathy or apathy of Pittenweem's officials, overrode these reservations and this instruction and resulted in murder – not an everyday occurrence, to be sure, but one which illustrates the depth of feeling witchcraft and suspicion of witchcraft could generate among ordinary people. Patrick Couper, the minister, must bear some of the blame for encouraging Patrick Morton in the lies (as they turned out) which had done much to intensify popular inflammation, just as Allan Logan in Torryburn was hot to imply the presence of witchcraft in his congregation. 'At the administration of the communion,' noted Chambers, 'he would cast an eye along and say, "You, witch-wife, get up from the table of the Lord," when some poor creature ... would rise and depart, thus exposing herself to the hazard of a regular accusation afterwards.'[26] 'Witch-wife' was a term of abuse frequently employed in heated exchange among people, as, for example, was 'witch-bird' of children; so it may be that Allan Logan meant no more by it than an expression of general disapproval rather than a particular suggestion that the individual concerned was actually a witch. Nevertheless, the term was loaded and could easily have been misunderstood, especially as Mr Logan was known to be hostile to witches. This is a trait which appears elsewhere in contemporary clergy, too, as we can see from Peter Rae, minister of Kirkbride in Nithsdale, who in 1705 called a woman a witch and, when he himself fell ill, insisted she visit him and come within reach: whereupon he scratched her on the forehead, with the words, 'They say you have my health. So give it me again if you have it!'[27]

Still, it would be wrong of us to run away with the idea that relations between social groups were strained because some people were sceptics, ministers were not, and the bulk of the population was both credulous and intemperate. Nor was Scotland especially more prone to prejudice or rage against witches than England. 'Witch', for example, was still a term of abuse in England in 1709 and 1725, witches were being assaulted there in 1710 and 1728, and English people were swimming women to test whether they were witches or not in 1709, 1717, and 1730, the latter with fatal consequences,[28] and all this in the face of some determined denial as, for example, that of Whitlocke Bulstrode addressing the Grand Jury and other juries in Westminster Hall on 21 April 1718: 'As for witchcraft, sorcery or enchantments, which were anciently the common topics under this head of "Offences against God", by the learned of old, I shall not trouble you with them, there being no such practice now, blessed be God, within this kingdom.'[29] One cannot help wondering how Bulstrode managed to close his eyes and ears to the realities around him.

Malcolm Gaskill, however, has drawn attention to an important point connected with this situation. 'Contrary to many modern assumptions, it was quite possible for tradition to exist alongside innovation, and, although rational thought progressed in a discrete intellectual sense, in the course of the eighteenth century its representatives "were capable of ignoring it or of suspending the criteria it implied."'[30]

I should be inclined to modify the word 'rational' here since, as Richard Kieckhefer has observed, there was nothing irrational about the earlier system and concept of magic, merely a difference in the suppositions on which that system and concept were built. But Gaskill's point remains, and can be illustrated by the career and writings of John Beaumont, a Fellow of the Royal Society, notable as the author of a substantial work on geology based on a lifetime of fieldwork in the earth sciences, and internationally famous for his book *An Historical, Physiological, and Theological Treatise of Spirits, Apparitions, Witchcrafts, and other Magical Practices* (1705), which was partly (but only in part) a riposte to Balthazar Bekker's repudiation of the other world in his *The Bewitched World* (1691–93). The ability of a natural philosopher ('scientist') to accommodate belief in the reality of the other world and detailed investigation of physical creation is by no means unique to him. Isaac Newton had, of course, combined his work on gravity and the spectrum with his Arian heresy, scrutiny of biblical prophecy, and experimental interest in alchemy, each interacting with and influencing the others. Richard Boyle, a founder member of the Royal Society, considered his theological activities as at least as important as his alchemical investigations, supported Joseph Glanvill in his mission of collecting and verifying accounts of witchcraft, not to mention his specific interest in the poltergeist case at Mâcon in 1658, and himself amassed accounts of occult phenomena, which he intended to publish as an appendix to his *Experimenta et Observationes Physicae* (1690).[31] So when we talk about the trend toward 'rationalism' of the period, we need to be careful what we mean in this context by 'rational', just as people of the period were actually concerned, whether they expressed it openly or not, with the meaning of 'occult'; and in fact, the methods used by the natural philosophers of the seventeenth and early eighteenth centuries produced an interesting effect. In the words of Christopher Carter, 'Nature became, not a mechanism to be deconstructed or an inanimate machine to be conquered, but a prodigy itself, a sight unusual in a world once thought to Cartesian mathematics.'[32] These same natural philosophers, let us not cease to forget, were the same people who could just as easily turn from the natural world to the preternatural, from mathematical tables, dissecting room, and laboratory to Kabbalah, alchemy, ritual magic, Rosicrucianism, and Freemasonry. Boundaries between spheres of knowledge were still fluid, open-mindedness was still unbolted and unbarred, and curiosity willing to visit bourns of all kinds, not merely those approved and sanctioned by materialist philosophies.

Just as the esoteric interests of Newton and Boyle influenced their pursuits in natural philosophy, then, so John Beaumont's personal experiences of the spirit world stimulated his investigations into the biblical accounts of the Creation and Deluge, and thus into those evidences – fossils and post-diluvial strata, for example – which illustrated his work in what are now called the earth sciences. His account of those visitations from spirits is worth repeating in full.

I declare, then, with all the sincerity of a Christian, that it never so much as entered into my thoughts to use any practice for raising or calling spirits, as some men have done, and that when they came, it was altogether a surprise to me. At their first coming, they did not appear to me, nor come into my chamber, but kept at my chamber windows, and in a court adjoining to one of my chamber windows, and in a garden adjoining to another window. They called to me, sang, played on music, rang bells, sometimes crowed like cocks, etc. and I have reason to believe these to be all good spirits, for I found nothing in them tending to ill, their drift in coming, as far as I could perceive, being only to compose my mind and to bring it to its highest purity. They used no threats to me, but the surprise kept always a terror upon me, and they continued with me about two months.

Their second coming to me was some years after, when at first there came five ... Presently after there came hundreds, and I saw some of them dance in a ring in my garden, and sing, holding hands round, not facing each other, but their backs turned to the inner part of the circle. I found these of a promiscuous nature, some good and some bad, as among men. For some of them would now and then curse and swear and talk loosely, and others would reprehend them for it. Yet none of these ever persuaded me to any ill thing, but all would dissuade me from drinking too freely and any other irregularity, and if at any time I was upon going to any neighbouring town, they would tell me they would go with me: which I found they did, for they would there call at my curtain by my bedside, as they usually did at my house, and talk to me.

Beside these two great visitations, they have come to me now and then for some years, and sometimes have stayed with me a week, sometimes two or three days; and all along, from their first coming, they have very often suggested things to me in my dreams, as now and then they do still. At their first coming I heard no name of any of them mentioned, as I did at their second coming. I had a perception of them by four of my senses, for I saw them, heard them, and three of them had a dark smoke coming out of their mouths, which seemed somewhat offensive to the smell, it being like the smoke of a lamp. Three of them bid me take them by the hand, which I did. But it yielded to my touch, so that I could not find any sensible resistency in it. Neither could I perceive any coldness in them, as it's said some apparitions have had. I did not ask them many curious questions, as I find many men think I should (and, as they say, *they* would have done.) But I always kept me on my guard and still required them to be gone, and would not enter into such familiarity with them. Indeed, I asked them once what creatures they were, and they told me they were an order of creatures superior to mankind, and could influence our thoughts, and that their habitation was in the air. I asked them also several things relating to my own concerns in this world, and I found sometimes, both in their answers and in what they suggested in my dreams, things very surprising to me. One of them lay down on my bed by me every night for a considerable time, and pretended great kindness to me; and if some others at any time would threaten me, that spirit told me they should do me no hurt.

   If you ask me whether I really think these apparitions to be spirits or only an effect of melancholy, I can only say what St Paul said of the nature of his rapture, God knows I know not, but they appeared to me real.[33]

One notes that Beaumont's experiences were both visual and auditory and, indeed, rather more, since he says he perceived these spirits by sight, hearing, touch, and smell on different occasions. Nevertheless, his remark about touching a spirit's hand without experiencing the kind of sensation he would usually get in response from a human hand is significant and says something about the quality of his experience. This vivid tactile hallucination, if that is what he experienced, is not unprecedented – the hypnagogic or hypnopompic 'Old Hag' is an obvious example – and although Beaumont says the unexpectedness of these visitations 'kept always a terror upon me', his reactions to these sights and sounds actually appear to be calm and detached after that initial shock and fright. Indeed, his intellectual detachment prompts him to ask whether they may have been produced by melancholy which 'chiefly happens to persons from the fortieth to the sixtieth year of their age', he being over forty when the phenomena first occurred. He also mentions dreams: 'they have often suggested things to me in my dreams' (p. 395), but as the spirits clearly appeared to him during his waking hours, this reference to dreams is likely to mean simply that he dreamed about them after those waking experiences, partly perhaps to reformulate them into a coherent narrative for himself.[34]

   Beaumont's interests, however, lie with the spirit world rather than witchcraft. He does record material from 1645 anent witches in Essex and, perhaps more interestingly, anent witches in Mexico, whom his source (the Jesuit José de Acosta, 1540–1600) had interpreted very much in accordance with the perceived behaviours and traditions of European witches;[35] but otherwise his treatment of witchcraft is very brief. But one observation of his should be noted. In describing the second major visitation of spirits, he remarks that they danced 'holding hands round, not facing each other, but their backs turned to the inner part of the circle' (p. 394), just the kind of dancing illustrated by Jan Ziarnko in Pierre de Lancre's *Tableau de l'inconstance des mauvais anges et demons* (1613) and an anonymous woodcut designer in Nathaniel Crouch's *The Kingdom of Darkness* (1688). This striking image tends to draw one away from trying to suggest that these creatures may have been seen as fairies of some kind, even though Beaumont does say that on one occasion other than these visitations of spirits, 'I saw a jury of fairies, or ghosts, or what you may please to call them, summoned and pass a verdict on a person known to me' (p. 105). Notice here Beaumont's inability to be exact about the nature of these spirits and notice, too, that they had clearly been summoned by some other party in a manner Beaumont says he never employed at any time. Now, while he may not have been experienced enough to tell the difference between fairies, ghosts, and other non-human entities, the spirits he saw dancing unnaturally back-to-circle in what he himself says was a mixture of good and bad spirits, leads us in the direction of demons rather than other types of entity. So if Beaumont was familiar with some of the traditional descriptions of witches and their Sabbats, it is these which may have come to his mind when he saw his spirits dancing.

Certainly he associates witches with a particular kind of spirit, because he goes on to say that ignorance of what he calls the *scientia umbrarum* ('branch of knowledge dealing with spirits or ghosts'), 'may have been the occasion of many mistakes in judicial proceedings relating to witchcraft, the dispositions of the astral man being knowable only by that science' (pp. 160–161). People who have had genuine ecstatic or visionary experiences, he says elsewhere, have been accused of witchcraft and prosecuted simply because of the judiciary's being unaware that such experiences may be real. 'Men may as well be executed for falling into a fit of epilepsy' is his comment. Public policy, he goes on (by which he implies the officially approved intellectual trend of the time), has been prepared to put up with miscarriages of justice rather than allow open discourse (he calls it 'teaching') on the subject of the spirit world, because it thinks such open discourse more pernicious than the punishment and execution of a number of witches (p. 161). It is, in effect, a sideswipe at the increasingly closed mind of what we should call the scientific establishment of the day.[36]

Meanwhile, politics were in a ferment. In 1707, the two parliaments of Scotland and England were united under treaty; in 1708, James Stuart made an unsuccessful attempt to land in the Firth of Forth with a French fleet, which did nothing to ameliorate anti-Catholic sentiment in either Scotland or England; during the winter of 1708–1709, the whole of Europe froze in a severe plummeting of temperature which meant that lakes and rivers, even the sea in places, froze, livestock died, oaks and ash trees withered beyond recovery, and the winter wheat crop was destroyed. Some fun may have been had briefly by some, as depicted in Gabriele Bella's picture of people sporting on Venice's frozen lagoon, but on the whole the winter left catastrophe in its wake and more than a million people died before 1709 was out.[37] The following winter, in February and March 1710, Henry Sacheverell was tried in a sensational process, accused by the Whigs of criticising the revolution of 1688–89 and therefore of subverting England's political stability. He was found guilty, and the verdict led to outbreaks of violence directed especially at Presbyterian and Dissenting places of worship, thereby restoring to the workings of prejudice a kind of balance, since the mob had now tempered its anti-Catholicism by a few spates of rock throwing at the other end of the confessional spectrum. But we should not forget, either, that between 1701 and 1714 Britain was engaged with other European powers in the War of the Spanish Succession, with all that that entailed anent financial expenditure, taxation, recruitment and loss of life, political infighting, and so forth. For all this forms the environment, the context, in which the continual struggle to define and then to support or suppress the relationship of any spirit world with this one, and to define and support or suppress any actions resulting from any such posited relationship, was taking place with varying degrees of consequence for those concerned.

Ireland provides an illustration of this through a witchcraft trial in March 1711 in Carrickfergus on the east coast of Antrim. Carrickfergus was an Anglican enclave in a largely Presbyterian area, so the possibilities for confessional conflict were always present and bubbling. In September 1710, Anne Haltridge, widow of the former Presbyterian minister in nearby Islandmagee, started to suffer incidents of poltergeistery. These lasted for about three months and then Mrs Haltridge saw the vision of a young boy who danced wildly round her kitchen before disappearing, after which peace and quiet were restored until February 1711 when the boy turned up again and began mischief-making – waving a sword and threatening to kill the household, smashing windows, and suchlike. The poltergeistery started again, too, and so the new minister from Islandmagee was called in to expel the spirit. His prayers, however, did no good and, after a few days of suffering severe pains in her back, Mrs Haltridge died. Not long after this, an eighteen-year-old girl, Mary Dunbar, came to stay with the Haltridge family and the same phenomena which had plagued Anne Haltridge now reappeared and seemed to be centred on Mary. Complaining that hot knives were being thrust into her, she named seven women, all local, who, she said, were causing her torments, and over the next three weeks these women were arrested on charges of witchcraft. Their trial was set for 31 March, and evidence offered to the court consisted of statements from witnesses to the violent fits which Mary had been having and during which she had vomited a number of objects – feathers, pins, bits of cotton, and two very large waistcoat buttons. Mary herself was in court, of course, but apparently so overcome by the threats against her issued, she said, the previous night by spectral visions of the accused, that she was quite unable to give evidence of any kind. The two judges, Anthony Upton and James MacCartney, both directed the jury. Upton advised acquittal, MacCartney conviction, and while Upton was a Tory and MacCartney a Whig, both were directing contrary to the opinions their respective political parties were supposed to have. The jury opted for conviction, and so the women were sentenced to a year's imprisonment and four separate hours in the pillory, according to the provisions of the 1586 statute.[38]

Parallels may be drawn with the case of Jane Wenham from Walkern in Hertfordhsire, who was tried for witchcraft in March the following year. On 11 February, Anne Thorne, a servant, suddenly flung off most of her clothes and started to talk about running out of the house and gathering twigs in her apron. Mrs Gardiner, her employer's wife, found twigs done up in a bundle of Anne's clothes, and according to one of the several pamphlets and tracts produced soon after the case, *A Full and Impartial Account Discovery of Sorcery and Witchcraft practised by Jame Wenham*,

> As soon as this bundle was opened, Anne Thorne began to speak, crying out, 'I'm ruined and undone', and after she had a little better recovered herself, gave the following relation of what had befallen her. She said when she was left alone, she found a strange roaming in her head ... Her mind ran upon Jane Wenham and she thought she must run some whither. Accordingly, she ran up the close, but looked back several times at the house, thinking she should never see it more. [Then] she climbed over a five-bar gate and ran along the highway up a hill. (pp. 3–4)

On the way she met two men who, clearly worried by her evident distress, tried to slow her down, but she broke away from them and next met an old woman muffled in a hood, who told her to snap some twigs from a nearby oak and wrap them in her clothes along with a crooked pin, after which the old woman vanished. Mrs Gardiner immediately assumed Anne had met a witch and flung the sticks and pin on the fire, saying, 'We will burn the witch (alluding to a received notion that when the thing bewitched is burned, the witch is forced to come in)' (p. 4).

Two things may strike one so far. First, there appears to be an element of fairy tale in the meeting between Anne and the old woman, in the sense of youth encountering old age, a symbolic conjunction of naivety with malevolence and of this world with the other world. But the rest of the episode develops as though this beginning had been a factual rather than a symbolic encounter, and it is unlikely, therefore, that interpretation along the latter lines will turn out to be fruitful. What we may have, rather, is an episode of peculiar behaviour by Anne, brought on by some mental or emotional disturbance, witnessed and reported by the two men who tried to stop her (p. 5); or a false story given an aura of verisimilitude by Anne's deliberately acting in a way calculated to draw attention to herself; or a combination of the two. That fraud may indeed be possible is indicated by an incident which had taken place on New Year's day. Matthew Gilston had met Jane Wenham, who asked him for some straw and, on being refused, took some anyway. This was almost repeated at the end of the month when Matthew met an old woman who made the same request and, on refusal, went away muttering. 'And [Matthew] saith that after the woman was gone, he was not able to work, but ran out of the barn as far as a place called Munder's Hill (which is above three miles from Walkern), and asked at a house there for a pennyworth of straw; and they refusing to give him any, he went further to some dung heaps and took some straw from thence, and pulled off his shirt and brought it home in his shirt. He knows not what moved him to this, but says he was forced to it, he knows not how' (p. 2). This incident and Anne's are so similar that one cannot help thinking they may have been connected and, as Matthew's was the earlier, that Anne was either consciously or unconsciously imitating it.

The other noticeable point is that the author of this pamphlet feels the need to explain why Mrs Gardiner threw Anne's twigs and their pin into the fire. Is this merely and unnecessarily dotting the i's and crossing the t's, or did he think his readers did not know or would have forgotten some of the most basic facts of counter-magic? Does his pamphlet, indeed, have something of the journalist's 'Can you credit people still believe this kind of stuff and still behave this way?' But the professed object of the pamphlet, as expressed in its preface and coda, is to validate the opinion that witchcraft is real enough, in which case explanation of 'a received notion' seems superfluous. The use of the indefinite article, too, draws one's attention, as it implies there are other notions and therefore other explanations for this action. Still, the pamphlet was probably written in some haste, so it may be pernickety to ask for consistency of thought and exactitude of expression in a piece rushed out for the public.

While the twigs burned, Jane Wenham turned up at the house, thereby indicating not only that the counter-magic worked, but also more or less proclaiming thereby her own guilt. Nothing happened immediately, but Anne and Jane ran into each other again next morning and reproachful exchanges took place, with Jane saying, 'If you tell any more such stories of me, it shall be the worse for you than it has been yet', followed by a shove with her hand (p. 5). So it was. That afternoon, Anne repeated the performance of the previous day, trembling, racing through the countryside, and talking wildly about sticks. Mrs Gardiner sent two men after her, who caught up with her and brought her back. Having recovered, Anne listened to people who were telling her to go to Jane's house and scratch her to get rid of the witchcraft and, after further incidents, 'William Burroughs, a neighbour who was present, said he would fetch [Jane] if it were possible. And soon after [he] brought her to [Anne] who was speechless and, to all appearance, in a fainting fit.'

As soon as Jane Wenham approached her, Anne flew at her, crying out, 'You have ruined me.'

Wenham answered, 'You are a liar.'

'No,' answered the girl, 'I am not. You threatened me this morning.'

Whereupon Jane left the house (p. 7).

More fits, more stick gathering followed, along with the sticks and another crooked pin being flung into a fire. Further theatrics and another attempt to bring Jane to the Gardiners' house. But Jane had locked herself in and refused to come, so the constable was sent for. He broke into the house and fetched Jane forcibly to confront Anne who was lying speechless, but apparently aware of what was going on around her.

> As soon as Jane Wenham spoke to her, her colour came into her cheeks and she started up, crying, 'You are a base woman. You have ruined me,' and flew upon her to scratch her, saying, 'I must have your blood or I shall never be well.' She scratched Jane Wenham in the forehead with such fury and eagerness that the noise of her nails seemed to all that were present as if she were scratching against a wainscot. Yet no blood followed, Jane Wenham, holding her head still and saying, 'Scratch harder, Nan, and fetch blood of me if you can.' Yet still no blood came, although her forehead was sadly mangled and torn by the girl's nails. (p. 10)

One cannot help being doubtful about this point. A violent and sustained scratching would certainly have drawn blood, so we are being told the quantity of blood produced was not enough (unlikely, because nowhere else in similar accounts is quantity mentioned as a prerequisite to cure), or is this journalistic licence intended to suggest a preternatural rather than a natural behaviour of the blood?

Whichever it may be, no bleeding was, of course, a bad sign, and worse was to follow when Mrs Gardiner tried to get Jane to recite the Lord's Prayer. Jane did her best, coached and encouraged by Mrs Gardiner, who may have been intending to be helpful or may just have been badgering the old woman: we do not know, because we have no indication of her tone and demeanour. In either case, Jane could still not render it word-perfect, so she was kept in custody and the next morning (14 February) appeared before Sir Henry Chauncy, the local justice of the peace. Anne threw one of her fits, witnesses to the events of the last three days were heard, and their testimony suggested, with illustrations from their own and others' experiences, that Jane had long had the reputation of being a witch. So Sir Henry ordered a committee of women to search Jane for unusual teats or marks, but none were found. Once home, Anne fitted again, but was restored to health by prayer, and on the 15th at a further hearing before the justice, Jane begged Sir Henry not to send her to gaol, going so far as to offer to undergo the swimming test to prove her innocence, an offer Sir Henry refused. A clergyman present then asked Jane to recite the Lord's Prayer, but once again she failed to do so exactly, Anne had another fit, and when the two women were confronted, flew at Jane once more with furious reproaches.

Events now moved quickly. On the 16th Jane was again unable to repeat the Lord's Prayer, but now confessed to being a witch. Why she should have done so is a mystery. We can speculate she was tired out by her treatment and wanted to be rid of the whole prolonged episode, but the speculation is unhelpful because it is based on nothing and therefore is best left unpursued. It is equally plausible that she saw a way of lifting the immediate burden from herself by accusing others and thus drawing official attention to them, for in her confession she said that she and three other women from Walkern were responsible for bewitching Anne. If this was the ploy, it worked to some extent, for orders were sent out for those three women to be arrested. But meanwhile Anne had a violent fit and complained of seeing catlike creatures, so Jane was fetched – this was becoming a habit – her presence eliciting the usual enraged response: 'Are you come again to torment me? I'll have your blood and tear you to pieces' (p. 18). But suddenly Sir Henry, who was urging Jane to remove her witchcraft and give Anne some relief, noticed a pin appearing, as it were from nowhere, in Anne's fingers.

At which, he snatched it from her, saying [to Jane], 'Are you going to bewitch her again with this pin?' And [Anne] crying out for her blood, he took Jane Wenham's arm and ran the pin into it six or seven times, finding she never winced for it but held her arm as still as if nothing had been done to it. Seeing no blood come, he ran it in a great many times more. Still no blood came, but she stood talking and never minded it. Then again he ran it in several times more. At last, he left it in her arm, that all the company might see it run up to the head, and when he plucked it out before them all, there just appeared a little thin watery serum, but nothing that you can call blood. (p. 19)

Sunday 17th was almost as eventful, with screaming cats and pins everywhere. An attempt to boil Anne's urine in order to draw out a reaction from Jane, who was elsewhere in custody, was a failure, as Jane did not react at all, and when her own daughter turned up with a prayer book and suggested she make use of it to prepare herself for death, she seems to have remained calm, saying merely, 'Remember what I told you about the flax and hemp and other stuff' before being taken to Hertford prison.

She was tried at 9 a.m. on 4 March before Sir John Powell, a man described by Jonathan Swift, who met him once, as 'the merriest old gentleman I ever saw, spoke pleasing things, and chuckled till he cried again' (Letter to Stella, 5 July 1711). Sixteen witnesses came forward, including Anne, who fell into one of her fits in the courtroom. When she had a second, however, and it was proposed she be prayed for then and there, Sir John was unsympathetic. 'She will come to herself by and by,' he said: and so she did. Sir John continued to be acidic. When he was told Anne had been brought out of her fits by prayer, he said he had heard of exorcism in the Church of Rome, but not in that of England, but adding sarcastically he was glad to find such power in

Anglican prayer. Even more pointed was his answer to Arthur Chauncy, Sir Henry's son, who offered to produce several of the pins which had been found on Anne's person, but was told there was no need for him to do so, as Sir John presumed they would be crooked. To Francis Bragge, who talked of strange cakes made of feathers, which had been taken out of Anne's pillow, he observed that he wished he could see an enchanted feather; and to Elizabeth Field, who said she had not prosecuted Jane immediately after the death of her child from what she believed were magically induced convulsions because she was poor and had no wealthy friends, Sir John replied, 'Have you become rich now, then?'

It is clear Sir John had little patience with what he was hearing, but when the jury came back into court after an hour and a half's deliberation – quite a long time by the standards of the day, suggesting a degree of initial disagreement between the jurors – its verdict was 'guilty'. Obviously astonished, Sir John asked, 'Do you find her guilty upon the indictment for conversing with the Devil in the shape of a cat?' 'Yes,' replied the foreman. So Sir John had no choice under the law but to sentence Jane to death. He did, however, reprieve her, too, until further notice. That further notice came in the form of a full reprieve on 22 July, and although Jane did not return to Walkern, she lived quite happily, it seems, in Gilston and Hertingsfordbury, villages a good 20 and 30 miles away, for the next twenty years. Francis Hutchinson went to visit her. 'I have very great assurance that she is a pious, sober woman,' he wrote, and 'she is so far from being unable to say the Lord's Prayer that she would make me hear her say both the Lord's Prayer and the Creed, and other good prayers beside.' Hutchinson also observed that 'the whole country [*i.e. county*] is now fully convinced that she was innocent, and that the maid that was thought to be bewitched was an idle hussy'.[39]

Yet again we see a disjunction between a key legal official and popular opinion. We may also note again that this does not represent a difference between the educated and uneducated classes per se, since the clergymen and JP involved in this case were closer to popular opinion, if not entirely at one with it, so mere education was by no means enough to create a sceptic. Country folk and country JPs were, of course, by definition less likely to rub shoulders with those metropolitan groups whose disdain for 'superstition' was becoming entrenched. But the printing press had long made access to speculation and comment available to as wide a public as could read or listen, and so one cannot argue with any conviction that lack of contact with up-to-date views and theories will have created a difference between country and town, either. Legal textbooks, certainly, had become more cautious in their view of what constituted reasonable proof or indication of a crime, but judges differed in the way they were prepared to hear and assess the evidence put before them. As Phyllis Guskin points out, 'Sir Matthew Hale (1609–76) firmly believed in witchcraft and found nearly all he tried guilty; Sir John Holt (1642–1710) never had a conviction on the charge.'[40] So the fact that Jane's was to be the last English trial for witchcraft before the repeal of the Act was a matter of chance rather than the last gasp of a dying belief and tradition. Her village of Walkern was full of Dissenters; Jane was probably a Dissenter herself; Walkern was close enough to London to attract an overspill of infighting between Tory and Whig – 'superstition' and 'atheism', as each liked to think and say of their opponents – and while it is most unlikely that politics had anything to do with the case directly, the pamphlet exchanges which sprouted immediately afterwards and the intense interest shown in the trial while it was going on indicate a seizure of the moment by Tories and Whigs alike in their guises as supporters or opponents of witchcraft.[41]

Between 1710 and 1714, of course, the Tories were in the ascendant. Their star had risen under Queen Anne and died with her, and during these years of ascendancy, while witchcraft trials were by no means frequent, those which did occur, as we have seen with those of Islandmagee and Jane Wenham, had politics simmering in the background almost as warmly as the continuing debate on the nature of spirits and magic, which was tinged with the same politically charged stream. While Beaumont urged a greater, if cautiously governed, understanding of the nature of the other world, it may be expected that the contrary view, cautiously expressed or not, would also be heard; and sure enough, it was in Joseph Addison's now well-known essay no. 117 in the 14 July issue of the *Spectator*, a daily journal founded in March 1711 'to enliven morality with wit, and to temper wit with morality', and 'to bring philosophy out of the closets and libraries, schools and colleges, to dwell in clubs and assemblies, at tea-tables and coffeehouses' (Monday 12 March, no. 10).

> I cannot forbear thinking that there is such an intercourse and commerce with evil spirits as that which we express by the name of witchcraft. But when I consider that the ignorant and credulous parts of the world abound most in these relations, and that the persons amongst us who are supposed to engage in such an infernal commerce are people of a weak understanding and crazed imagination, and at the same time reflect upon the many impostures and delusions of this nature that have been detected in all ages, I endeavour to suspend my belief till I hear more certain accounts than any which have yet come to my knowledge ... I believe in general that there is and has been such a thing as witchcraft, but at the same time can give no credit to any particular instance of it.

Addison's appeal is thus not to reasonableness, but to a mixture of xenophobia and snobbery: 'We may hear about the practice of witchcraft, but only among foreigners and the stupid peasantry, so no thank you!' He then provides an anecdote illustrative of this, describing a meeting between himself, his fictional squire, Sir Roger de Coverley, and a village witch, Moll White, whom he describes, one may note, not directly, but with a quotation from the Restoration dramatist Thomas Otway.

> In a close lane, as I pursued my journey,
> I spied a wrinkled hag, with age grown double,
> Picking dried sticks and mumbling to herself.
> Her eyes with scalding rheum were galled and red.
> Cold palsy shook her head. Her hands seemed withered,
> And on her crooked shoulders had she wrapped
> The tattered remnants of an old striped hanging
> Which served to keep her carcase from the cold.
>
> (*The Orphan*, Act 2, scene 1)

This is not a portrait but a caricature. The figure of the witch, it seems, has now assumed its fixed delineation in literature – female, old, ugly, poor, repellent[42] – and while Addison ends his essay with an appeal not to withhold charity from such omnipresent individuals – 'I hear there is scarce a village in England that has not a Moll White in it' – his tone is, at best, detached and his words lip service to the concept of Christian virtue. 'I hear' is significant. The phrase distances him physically, intellectually, emotionally from any real Moll Whites, and allows him the contempt and distaste he clearly feels beneath his 'enlightened' and gentlemanly exterior. This contrasts sharply with the more robust view of Daniel Defoe who, journalist himself, was not afraid to voice an opinion in the October of that same year. 'There are, and ever have been, such people in the world, who converse familiarly with the Devil, enter into compact with him, and receive power from him, both to hurt and deceive, and these have been in all ages called witches; and it is these that our law and God's law condemned as such. And I think there can be no more debate of the matter.'[43]

In 1712, as if to underline Defoe's general point, London was diverted by the appearance of Duncan Campbell, aged fourteen, seemingly deaf and dumb, who relied upon the second sight to be able to prophesy, describe facts hitherto unknown to him, and cure bewitchment. In his *Secret Memoirs*, published posthumously in 1732, Campbell maintained that witchcraft was real and gave at least two examples of his own ability to detect and remove it, one of which involved boiling the sufferer's urine, this time as a cure for the affliction rather than as an allurement of the witch herself.[44] Addison enjoyed himself immensely at Campbell's expense, publishing an extract from the cod diary of a vacuous young lady and two supposed letters from Campbell himself in the *Spectator*: (a) 'Went in our mobs [*ladies' caps*] to the dumb man, according to appointment. Told me that my lover's name began with a G. *Mem*: The conjuror was within a letter of Mr Froth's name!' (Tuesday, 11 March 1712); (b) 'I interpret [dreams] to the poor for nothing, on condition that their names may be inserted in public advertisements to attest the truth of such my interpretations. As for people of quality or others, who are indisposed and do not care to come in person, I can interpret their dreams by seeing their water. N.B. I am not dumb' (Thursday 9 October 1712); and (c) 'From my cell' (Monday 28 June 1714), which leaves the question, monk's cell or convict's, open to the reader. Campbell's biography, *The Supernatural Philosopher: or, The History of the Life and Adventures of Mr Duncan Campbell*, by William Bond, which appeared in 1720, contains not only what was by that time a clichéd defence the existence of spirits – so many people from so many countries over so long a time have accepted it that 'I think it a violation of the law of nature to reject all these relations as fabulous, merely upon a self-presuming conceit' (p. 269) – but also an equally clichéd set of observations upon certain claims made by witches: demons create delusions, and there is also a theory that such phenomena as the flight and the Sabbat are caused by narcotic medicines (pp. 273–274).

Amusing though readers of the *Spectator* may have found these examples of witchcraft and the second sight, and however much transitory sensation figures such as Campbell may have created, defenders of witchcraft and magic in general were by no means done, and in 1715 and 1716 a physician, Richard Boulton, with a recent publishing history on blood-heat, the action of the lungs, gout, scrofula, venereal diseases, and fevers, released the two parts of his *Compleat History of Magick, Sorcery, and Witchcraft* 'to put us in mind of the delusions of Satan and the ill consequences that attend such who serve so bad a master as the Devil', and '[to] put us in mind to arm ourselves both against the temptations of the Devil, and to implore God Almighty's assistance, that the Devil may have no power over us' (preface, ii). *A Compleat History* is composed mainly of witchcraft, spirit, and possession anecdotes, after the manner of Glanvill's work and intended for a similar purpose, so he spends little time on analysis or discussion of the topic as a whole. But he does review the principal reasons for people's practising magic.

> There are two sorts of persons that may be enticed to the pursuit of this art, viz. learned and unlearned, and two methods also of exciting them to this forbidden curiosity, viz. the Devil's school and his rudiments. The Devil's school is a too eager desire and pursuit of knowledge and natural causes where, when men begin to find themselves proficients in some measure, and that they can account for several things by natural causes, they are apt to advance too high; and where lawful arts and sciences fail of giving them satisfaction, they are apt to apply themselves to the black and unlawful science of magick; and finding that several kinds of circles and conjurations added to them will raise several kinds of spirits to resolve their doubts, attributing these effects to the power inherently inseparable from the circles and several words of God confusedly wrapped together, they flatter themselves that they are masters and can command the Devil, though at the same time they enter themselves as his slaves, and lose Paradise, as Adam did, by eating of forbidden fruits. The rudiments of the Devil are such unlawful charms which old women often make use of to produce effects without natural causes, [such] as charms to prevent evil eyes etc., and by knotting round trees several kinds of herbs, also curing of worms or stopping of blood, by healing of horse-crooks, or turning the riddle, or merely by words, without the application of medicines. For though by such practices they often to what they pretend [*claim*] to, yet it is not through any inherent virtue [*power*] in the thing done, but by the power of the Devil, by which he deceives men; and this he allures them to seek reputation by this deceitful art, or entices them to it through ambition or the hopes of gain, and makes a firm contract with them upon that account. (1.7–8)

Certain aspects of the occult sciences he condemns, such as judicial astrology, chiromancy, physiognomy, and fortune telling, and he reviews further ways in which the Devil seduces people into the performance of ritual magic – 'not only unlawful, but dangerous' – before taking the actual existence of witches for granted and then giving a conventional survey of the kind of things they do – flight, attendance at Sabbats, using dead body parts for magical purposes, making wax or clay images, inflicting and curing diseases, raising storms, and sending people mad (1.11–18). Magicians and witches also communicate with spirits of different kinds: (i) '*lemures* or *spectra* which sometimes appear in the form of dead persons'; (ii) spirits which haunt persons rather than places; (iii) incubi and succubi which impregnate people or make them ill by what is usually called diabolic possession; and (iv) fairies. 'These were most frequent in the time of Papistry here in England, and though it was esteemed odious to prophesy by the name of the Devil, yet those that these kind of spirits carried away and informed were thought to be the best sort of persons' (1.22). Finally, how does one find out who is a witch? By means of the mark, as well as the wickedness of the person's life and mode of speaking, and also by swimming her or him (1.23).[45]

Boulton's treatise does not really advance the argument for the validity of witchcraft and the spirit world any further than it had been pushed already during the previous six decades. These collections of narratives may originally have been intended to provide data for discussion, elucidation, and the formulation of theories in the manner of the experimental natural philosophers of the early days of the Royal Society, but by Boulton's time the mind of the 'scientific' establishment was more or less closed as far as this subject matter was concerned, and so 'complete histories' in the Glanvill mode had, in effect, dwindled into entertainments. This, at any rate, was the great danger facing those with a serious purpose, who insisted on producing their works of controversy in this same format. Francis Hutchinson published *An Historical Essay concerning Witchcraft* in 1718. Ostensibly it is a collection of anecdotes in the style of his predecessors in the subject matter, but he does vary the format with a strong appeal to his readers' sense of history – chapter 2, for example, gives a chronological sequence of the trials and executions of witches, starting with biblical times and coming forward to modern, his last illustration taken from 1701, the fraud of Richard Hathaway. Hutchinson was the curate of Bury St Edmunds and from 1715 one of the royal chaplains, before being elevated to the Irish bishopric of Down and Connor in 1720. He was thus an Anglican, and a Whig by political sympathy, although this last had clearly not saved him from being promoted into what was then regarded as an exile for the unreliable, and both his temperament and convictions meant he would regard witchcraft and its attendant sciences as both unbelievable and undesirable. 'The credulous multitude will ever be ready to try their tricks and swim the old women, and wonder at and magnify every unaccountable symptom and odd accident,' he wrote in his dedication, but was also candid enough to add, 'We clergymen are not thought to have kept our order altogether free from blame in this matter. In our last famous trial of Jane Wenham in Hertfordshire, some of our gown, though otherwise men of no ill character, were so weak as to try charms and give way to scratching and promote the prosecution.'[46]

This acknowledgement of distasteful superstition on the part of some clergy, who should have known better, sets the tone for his *Essay*, which is cast in the form of a dialogue between a clergyman and a man who had been called to serve on a jury dealing with a case of witchcraft. The bulk of the work thus consists of the clergyman's attempts to show that witchcraft is in fact dangerous nonsense. History, he says, presents us with a catalogue of grievous errors of judgement when it comes to our taking accusations of witchcraft with any degree of seriousness. Witches and magicians mentioned in the Bible were actually fraudsters and false prophets. It is 'a vulgar error' to think that the laws of other nations on the subject have been and are the same as those of Britain, since so many other nations are Catholic and therefore benighted and superstitious. British history, too, provides an unhappy sequence of impostures (Hutchinson furnishes examples), and so the best way to approach the subject and avoid egregious mistakes of judgement is to ground oneself in a proper understanding of the Christian religion. To help the fictional juryman do this, Hutchinson ends his book with two sermons: one, 'the Christian religion demonstrated', and the second, 'Concerning angels', which will help give a balanced view when people talk of spirits, demons, and other such entities.

> There is a lesson to be learned from what the holy writers teach us concerning good and evil spirits, and that is, unity under government. Order and government are so necessary to all reasonable beings that even the wisdom and virtue, even of good angels, would be defective without it. Nor doth the perverseness even of the evil spirits make either superiors or inferiors amongst them break the bonds of order that are needful to preserve their state. How inexcusable, then, must we be if we let our minds grow too stubborn to be in due subjection, and how surely must confusion and misery be the consequence! (p. 268)

Hutchinson's scepticism is, in fact, traditional. As Andrew Sneddon points out, his grounds for rejecting the reality of witchcraft were threefold: there is no foundation for it in scripture whose terms for practitioners have been misunderstood or mistranslated; the evidence offered in witchcraft trials is frequently poor and unconvincing; and individual instances of apparent bewitchment can be explained away as stemming from illness, imposture, or demonic possession.[47]

None of this is new, although in Hutchinson's case it is based on fairly extensive reading on the subject, as we can tell from the catalogue of his personal library; so he had done his homework. Yet he hesitated to publish for some time – 'I humbly take leave to present your Lordships with the following historical collections and observations which have lain by me several years,' he says at the beginning of his dedicatory epistle – anxious to make sure he would not offend anyone of importance by his discussion and conclusions, an interesting comment on the delicacy with which the topic was perceived to balance between religion and politics. He had actually completed the manuscript by 1706, and circulated it among friends in high places, but was persuaded not to send it to the press on the grounds that the Scots, among whom scepticism was less strong than among the English, might take offence during the crucial months before union of the Parliaments was effected. He tried again in 1712 when interest in Jane Wenham's trial was fervid, but once more hesitated in the face of difficulties produced, one should note, by disagreement among the educated about whether witchcraft could be regarded as valid or not.[48] When he did go into print, however, he was gratified, perhaps mildly surprised too, to find that his book sold sufficiently to warrant a second impression in 1720, although maybe he should not have underestimated public interest in the subject, for he himself had ruefully noted it earlier. After listing the title and authors of several contemporary and near contemporary tracts and essays on magic and witchcraft in the dedication to his *Essay*, he remarked on their popularity. 'These books and narratives are in tradesmen's shops and farmers' houses, and are read with great eagerness, and are continually leavening the minds of the youth who delight in such subjects; and considering what sore evils these notions bring where they prevail, I hope no man will think but that they must still be combatted, opposed, and kept down' (p. xiv).

In view of this interest, it will or should come as no surprise to find that Hutchinson's *Essay* was by no means the last controversial word on either witchcraft or magic or the spirit world to be uttered as the eighteenth century gathered pace and started hurtling towards the technological innovations for which it is famous. Richard Boulton, whose *Compleat History* had not been so well received, published a rebuttal of the *Essay* in 1722. *The Possibility and Reality of Magick, Sorcery, and Witchcraft Demonstrated* undertook to answer the points raised by Hutchinson and to demonstrate that non-physical substances can indeed affect physical substances including the human body – a clear attempt to deal with the centuries-old problem of interaction between two unlikes. 'I insist,' he emphasised, 'on nothing but reason, moral proof, and the testimony of the Old and New Testament,' and, 'the design [of my argument] is to prove what scripture says, consonant to reason and natural philosophy' (pp. xiv, xv). There is no need here to rehearse Boulton's detailed comments on Hutchinson's objections to him, and his second set of arguments can be summarised in his own words.

> How immaterial substances may affect one another and alter disposition of the mind, we have already observed, viz. by loading it with ideas of an ill or irregular kind which may either incline it to wicked practices, as those wretched creatures are that practise witchcraft: or by the consent or the request of those witches, these evil angels may convey such ideas into the mind of the person who is disordered by the Devil and his agents as may occasion irregular symptoms, and create unusual pains and tortures. And that immaterial spirits may not only disorder the mind and thus disquiet the soul, but disorder the body also will be evident if we seriously reflect upon the great disorders that happen in human bodies only by the influence of our own soul when disquieted with irregular passions of the mind. Some with grief and sorrow pine away and die, and others, though their flesh is almost consumed and wasted away, yet when that uneasy passion is removed that before disordered the soul, they presently recover their strength and grow strong and lusty again. And that the soul of man, which is an immaterial substance, hath so great an influence as to alter the disposition of human bodies so much, not only the common observation of the world testifies, but even the scripture, as Proverbs 15.13: 'A merry heart makes a cheerful countenance, but by sorrow of the heart, the spirit is broken. (pp. 174–175)

He also reiterates his call for the punishment of witches. 'Since it then appears that the art of witchcraft is not impossible, but hath the testimony of reason as well as other proof, all I shall add is that, as God spared not angels that sinned, nor Adam that transgressed, and hath strictly commanded that a witch shall not live, the laws against such persons ought to be put in execution, lest we disobey God and, in excusing horrible crimes, suffer the world to be overrun with wickedness' (p. 184).

Boulton, then, was a sensitive fellow, attached to traditional views on witchcraft, and expressed them in such a way as to suggest his emotional involvement with the subject. Expressed and expressive emotion on religious topics was not encouraged in the polite milieu of the day, being dubbed and dismissed as 'enthusiasm', a pejorative word on the lips of clergymen and politicians alike. (This in an age when it was fashionable to swoon or shed tears at the drop of a sunset.) Hurchinson, on the other hand, adopted (perhaps by nature) a restrained and more distant tone, certainly one which would have eschewed and disapproved of 'enthusiasm'. Daniel Defoe, on the other hand, may have adopted Hutchinson's tone, but he was clearly closer to Beaumont in opinion and feeling, and in his own tri-weekly journal, the *Review* (1704–1713), he cut to the chase by ignoring the to and fro indulged in by many of the other witchcraft writers and asked simply, what is a witch, what is the scriptural authority for believing in witchcraft, and what are instances of witchcraft in everyday life? These were, of course, the essential themes of every contemporary tract on the subject, and Defoe adds nothing new. But he does here put to one side, as he does not later on, the accumulation of illustrative so typical of the genre and comes to the simple conclusion that witches have existed and continue to exist, and so 'I think there can be no more debate of the matter'.

The *Review* was perhaps an unusual organ in which to find an essay on witchcraft. Its usual topics were Britain's commercial empire, domestic politics, and relations between England in particular and France. Essentially, however, the article's subtext called for a reassertion of Christian values in the face of their potential disruption from various sources, notably the trial of Henry Sacheverell for what the House of Commons, on 13 December 1709, called 'malicious, scandalous, and seditious libels' designed to whip up factional and divisive politics by sermons which, in effect, inflamed the mob against Dissenters and Nonconformists of all kinds.[49] 'There are and ever have been such people in the world, who converse familiarly with the Devil,' wrote Defoe, 'enter into compact with him, and receive power from him both to hurt and deceive.' Acknowledgement of this simple fact, he implies, will put an end to divisive arguments and unite people in a recognition not merely that there is a common enemy, Evil, in the world, but that ultimately God is in control of His creation and so restraint, balance, and virtue, those three Anglican desiderata can be made to triumph over faction, atheist doubt, and enthusiasm.

But Defoe's interest in the other world was by no means exhausted by this foray, and in 1726 he returned to the subject with *The Political History of the Devil* and *A System of Magick: or, A History of the Black Art*. He seems to have been responding to a number of recent publications which raised questions about and cast doubts on the origins and teachings of Christianity and contemporary debates about the power and credibility of the current Church of England.

The problem is that the Deists want a God who is limited in His power, a God without a Devil, according to Epicurus: a God wise and powerful, but not infinitely so, not omnipotent, not self-sufficient: a God that, having created the world (and 'tis with difficulty they go so far), has not power to guide it, but has abandoned it to the government of itself, to that foolish nothing called 'Chance': or, like the followers of Zeno, the Deist philosopher, a God depending upon (they know not what, of a) blind destiny: a God who, not being able to break the chain of second causes, is carried away with them Himself, being obliged to act by the course of natural consequences, even whether He will or not.[50]

The Devil, says Defoe, is real enough and active in the world, but is not its ruler and these days manifests Himself more as a state of mind than anything else, and can be seen in certain historical individuals of notorious cruelty or wickedness, or in the human proclivity to warfare, but generally acts as an observer rather than a participant in human life, although His very presence serves to stimulate people's baser instincts.

> Pride swells the passions, avarice moves the affections, and what is pride and what is avarice but the Devil in the inside of the man? Ay, as personally and really as ever he was in the herd of swine ... In a like manner, avarice leads him to rob, plunder, and destroy for money and to commit sometimes the worst of violences to obtain the wicked reward. How many have had their throats cut for their money, have been murthered on the highway, or in their beds, for the desire of what they had? It is the same thing in other articles. Every vice is the Devil in a man.[51]

By the end of the year, Defoe's impulse to write further about the Devil resulted in his historical review of activities attributed to the Devil's inspiration and power, and he is scathing about the various magical practitioners of his own day.

> In the first ages they were wise men; in the Middle Age, madmen; in these latter ages, cunning men. In the earliest time they were honest; in the middle time, rogues; in these last times, fools. At first they dealt with nature, then with the Devil, and now not with the Devil or with nature either. In the first ages, the magicians were wiser than the people; in the second age, wickeder than the people; and in our age, the people are both wiser and wickeder than the magicians. I see no great harm in our present pretenders to magick if the poor people could but keep their money in their pockets; and that they should have their pockets picked by such an unperforming, unmeaning, ignorant crew as these are is the only magick that I can find in the whole science. The best course I can think of to cure the people of this itch of their brain, the tarantula of the present age, in running to cunning men, as you call them, and the most likely to have success, is this – of laughing at them.[52]

Laughing at them is certainly what Addison and Steele were doing, and Defoe's *System of Magick* contains enough good stories to divert as well as instruct, but it is notable that Defoe concerns himself more with intercourse between the Devil and male magicians, and with ritual magic rather than witchcraft. This may have something to do with the period's general perception of witches as women, and Defoe's well-known misogyny – 'Magicians are a most necessary generation of men,' he says at one point, 'that without them, the miserable world would be robbed of the assistance of all those beneficent good spirits in the invisible world, which wait to do us good' (p. 402) – although, to be fair, one must also allow that the book contains a good deal of satire on people's credulity and superstition, 'people' here meaning 'men' as often as the young girls who are tricked by fairground diviners and backstreet conjurors.

From these scenes we get vivid glimpses of the large role still played by magic in the everyday life of a majority of people, and Defoe reminds us of popular beliefs still vibrant elsewhere in Britain outwith the confines of the English capital of Home Counties: the browny of the Highlands and Islands, the omnipresence of the second sight, the charmers of Orkney.[53] This robust magical life seems to have been flourishing in Wales, too, where Erasmus Saunders complained in 1721 that the Protestant reformation had made little headway.[54] He was complaining about the prevalence of Catholicism, of course, but elision of Catholic devotional practice and popular magic into one and the same, which was frequently made by many Protestant ministers, means that Saunders was likely to have been as worried by the latter as by the former, and evidence of Welsh belief in witches and cunning folk as late as the 1830s suggests that his criticism may not have been misplaced. The Isle of Man, too, as we shall see, was still rich in magic well into the eighteenth century, and Scotland, quite apart from the islands, still had plenty of witches as operative as they had ever been.

In 1719, for example, the kirk session of Thurso in Caithness assembled on 8 February to hear Margaret Nin-Gilbert tell the minister and elders that one evening, some time before, as she was out on the road, the Devil in the likeness of a man met her and 'engaged her to take on with him', and that she had met him again 'in the likeness of a great black horse, and other times riding a black horse; and that he appeared sometimes in the likeness of a black cloud, and sometimes like a black hen'. She had also been in William Montgomerie's house in Scrabster in the shape of a cat. His house was infested with cats, she said, and he had laid about him with a sword, a dirk, and an axe, and had so badly cut her leg with his dirk or axe that it had subsequently parted from the rest of her body. Six others were there, too, including Margaret Olsen in the form of a cat who had tried to defend her when William swung at her with his dirk. Asked how she could be physically present somewhere and yet remain invisible, she answered that the Devil threw up a dark mist to screen them from sight. Margaret Olsen was then searched for the Devil's marks and pricked several times in the shoulder, 'where there were several small spots, some red, some bluish. After a needle was driven in with such force, almost to the eye, she felt it not.' Why were they in William Montgomerie's house at all, Margaret Nin-Gilbert was asked. 'We were doing no harm there,' came the evasive reply.[55]

The Sheriff Depute of Thurso was informed about all this on 12 February and was presented with Margaret's gangrened leg. Immediately afterwards, 'she being under bad fame before for witchcraft', he ordered Margaret's arrest and imprisonment, along with that of the other women she had named in her confession. The whole affair ended badly. Margaret died in prison two weeks after her arrest – presumably her gangrene had spread and, allied to deprivation in prison, killed her; Helen Andrew, 'being so wounded and crushed and bruised with either sword, axe, or dirk, died the same night of her wounds, or a few days thereafter'; and William MacKay's wife, 'in a few days thereafter was cast, or cast herself, from the rocks of Borrowstoun into the sea, since which time she was never seen'. William Montgomerie wrote in December 1718 to the Sheriff Depute, confirming he had been troubled by cats and had killed at least two of them. His letter contains the interesting phrase, 'this looking like witchcraft', so clearly the unusual appearance of several cats he did not recognise as local triggered this automatic response which both kirk and state officials then treated seriously.[56]

At the other end of the country, in Mid Calder near Edinburgh, the twelve-year-old third son of the 7th Lord Torphichen, Patrick Sandilands, declared he had been bewitched by an old woman and a man in Calder, and started falling into trances during which he 'prophesied', pee'd black urine, and was lifted into the air by invisible hands. Sharpe's account dismisses this as the fraud of a mischievous boy or as the result of a malady originating in a disorder of his brain,[57] but since we are told that horsewhipping could not rouse him from his trances, there is a good chance his condition was real, whatever it may have been. Black urine may happen for a variety of reasons: the inherited genetic disorder alkaptonuria (perhaps unlikely here, as none of Lord Torphichen's other ten children appeared to have suffered a like symptom), excessive melanin secretion, copper of phenol poisoning, or large ingestion of rhubarb, fava beans, or aloes. What the 'prophesying' consisted of one cannot tell, but other people in trances have been reported as doing the same or something similar – twelve-year-old John Starkie, for example, in the 1590s 'did in his trance declare the strange sins of this land committed in all estates and degrees of people, and denounced the fearful judgements of God due to them'[58] – and the lifting up into the air by invisible hands is ambiguous. Levitation was not uncommon, but tended to be experienced by saints rather than children – Francis Xavier, Ignatius Loyola, John of the Cross, Teresa of Avila, Joseph of Cupertino are the obvious examples – but of course there is the possibility that Patrick, if he was not lying, may have been describing the sensation of being uplifted rather than an actual bodily levitation, which would surely have been witnessed by others and caused a sensation.

The local minister took Patrick's condition seriously and ordered a fast, at the proclamation of which John Wilkie, minister of the nearby parish of Uphall, delivered a sermon on 14 January 1720. There seems to be disagreement about the number of witches allegedly involved. Sharpe, relying on a pamphlet entitled *Strange and Wonderful Discourse concerning the Witches and Warlocks in West Calder*, speaks of four, three women and a man, two of whom were present at Wilkie's sermon; George Sinclair, on the other hand, writes of only one, 'this horrible slave of Satan', who had devoted the body and soul of one of her children to the Devil and who, when examined by her parish minister, turned out to be 'brutishly ignorant and scarce knew anything but her witchcraft'.[59] Frankly, neither Sharpe's nor Sinclair's sources can be trusted, at least not entirely, but we do know that Lord Torphichen had had a brush with a local witch fifteen years previously, because the Mid Calder kirk session record for 1 July 1705 tells us, 'This day Bailie Sandilands complained to the session of Barbara Aikin that she went down on her bare knees at the place where the stocks lies and cursed Torphichen and wished his family extinct, and wished all the woes and curses she could mind might come on the family, saying "The curse of the everlasting God come on him and his wife!"' But whether Barbara Aikin was one of Sharpe's four or Sinclair's only one, we do not know. The waters of information are muddied by the intrusion of William Mitchell, author of the *Strange and Wonderful Discourse*, known as the 'mad Tinklerian Doctor', who published a number of pamphlets on various subjects and who seems to have operated from a shop in the West Bow in Edinburgh. News of Patrick's supposed bewitchment reached him – not surprising, since the demonic possession of a child belonging to the aristocracy would have provided much meat for the capital's gossips – and he sallied forth to Calder to exorcise the evil spirits, with what qualification is unclear, although he told Lord Torphichen that he was sent by the Lord to cast out devils. He got no further than the temporal lord, however, and the confessing witches with whom he managed to have a conversation before being hustled away by Lord Torphichen's servants.

Accusations, trials, and executions for witchcraft continued in Scotland throughout the 1720s. Canisbay in Caithness saw Margaret Bain accused before the kirk session on 18 February 1724, and several witches from Ross in 1726 – not all of them prosecuted, apparently – confessed to blinding an Episcopalian minister by magic in one eye.[60] Meanwhile, we are informed by Edmund Burt, an officer of engineers based in Inverness from 1730, who noted that 'witches and goblins are ... pretty common among the Highlanders', that at the beginning of 1727 a mother and daughter from Sutherland were tried and condemned for witchcraft. Sharpe says that one of the items alleged of Janet Horne, the mother, was that Satan had transformed her daughter into a pony and had shod her, and that she herself had ridden the girl, and experience which left her lame in both hands and feet. The daughter managed to escape from prison (how, we are not told, and we wonder how indeed she managed it with deformed hands and feet; but if the story is true, it illustrates why witches were watched in their place of confinement), but the mother was executed 'in a pitch barrel', says Burt. But was she really burned alive? This was a most unusual form of execution in Scotland, the norm being strangulation before burning of the dead body. Tar barrels were used in the construction of such fires – one such was employed, for example, in the execution of Elspeth MacEwen in 1698 and cost £1 4s 0d – because it is actually rather difficult to burn a human body and the fire must be very hot: so this may account for Burt's reference.[61] The tired story about Janet's warming her hands at the fire without realising what the fire was for is unlikely to be true. Janet will have been tied to a stake, standing or sitting, in the middle of a ready-built fire which will therefore not have been lit until she was dead. On the strength of this anecdote, Janet is often described as 'insane' or 'doting' because she was supposedly an old woman; but these, too, are details we can ignore since there is no evidence for them.

Janet's, it seems, was the last execution for witchcraft in Scotland. In England, warfare between Tories and Whigs, complicated after 1715 by the first Jacobite rising against the Hanoverian settlement in favour of James VII and II and the subsequent suspicion that one party supported King George and the other the Jacobite cause, allowed the underlying tendency of each party to identify itself with religious and philosophical orthodoxy and its opponents with religious dissension and superstition to flourish and grow even more intense. Ian Bostridge has shown how the figure of the witch – old, female, ugly, malevolent – was manipulated in popular print for just these purposes,[62] and in the March 1716 number of his biweekly newspaper, *The Freeholder* (No. 24), Joseph Addison sneered that Jacobites 'are reduced to the poor comfort of prodigies' and 'begin to see armies in the clouds, when all on earth have forsaken them. Nay, I have been lately shown a written prophecy that is handed among them with great secrecy, by which it appears their chief reliance at present is upon a Cheshire miller that was born with two thumbs on one hand.'[63] This detail is, of course, likely to be fictional, but the slur makes its point and derives its strength from its believability. There is no point in calling someone superstitious if people don't think he is or, at least, that he could be, and that such superstitiousness is reprehensible. So it is not actually surprising to find that by the early 1730s witchcraft legislation was either going to remain in place, even if modified, or be repealed in favour of something more 'modern' and sceptical. It depended on how this politico-religious struggle worked out in the British Parliament and that, in turn, depended upon the mood of the moment perhaps rather more than the sweep or tide of history.

13

THE ACT REPEALED, AND WITCHCRAFT'S AFTERLIFE: 1735–

In March 1732, the *London Journal*, a propaganda sheet favouring the Whig government of Sir Robert Walpole, published an account of vampires which were terrorising a village in Serbia. This in turn stimulated replies and comments – '[it] hath occasioned many controversies in conversation,' wrote one contributor, 'whether in reason we ought to yield any belief to it, or no' – and while it was agreed that many other reported phenomena relating to other things, such as the magnetic properties of the lodestone, had occasioned disbelief when they were first brought to people's attention, this talk of vampires, however well attested, was a sensation too far. 'We may admit that those who attest it tell truth as far as they are judges of truth, but we are not therefore to sink our judgements to the same level with theirs and receive as an object of belief a matter utterly repugnant to reason and our senses.'[1] In a word, 'foreign nonsense'. But the interest aroused by the report illustrates, if further illustration were needed, that legislators in the London Parliament would not be seeking to free a sceptical and impatient public from a witchcraft statute people in general found either burdensome or foolishly outdated. While one physician could still loftily observe that 'those who have credulous women [in labour] to deal with advise the wearing of a lodestone, eaglestone, the *cranium humanum*, or the like, and this sometimes to the great consolation of the patient', his colleagues were happily prescribing medicines made from or including mummies, human skulls, or moss grown upon a skull, and continued to do so for the rest of the century.[2] Attributing credulity to women while being prepared to prescribe bits of a human body as medicine for a range of physical ailments shows a split in the eighteenth-century psyche, as does, for example, the case of Valentine Greatrakes, who woke up one morning with the conviction he could heal people by stroking them and went on to attract the attention and clientship of poor and rich, educated and non-educated alike. Far from being 'the age of reason', the eighteenth century was the age of credulousness tempered in places by a combination of curiosity and doubt. This, then, puts the repeal of the Witchcraft Act in context.

Witches, however, were subject to a slight shift of emphasis in the public's perception. Their literary image was beginning to take over from that which had for so long been the norm and they were no longer active accomplices of the Devil in his project of undermining and destroying humanity so much as malevolent old women who could and did harm their communities at will. This downplaying of the Satanic element in their activity opened the door for the view of journalists and the chattering classes to gain a more ready entry – that witches were little more than silly old women playing tricks on a gullible peasantry or artful men deliberately gulling the public out of its ready cash. Richard Walton, 'a student in astrology and physick, commonly called "The Conjuror"', was one such, hanged at Warwick on 10 August 1733 for, among other offences, casting horoscopes, some of which were genuine, but others bogus. That he was principally an astrologer is no cause to omit him from the category of witches because by this time witchcraft could be defined as 'astrology, fortune telling, and all other pretences of that kind which, if they had any reality in them, yet they are truly diabolical'.[3] The same dismissive tone can be found in the *Cambridge Chronicle*, which was founded in 1762: 'So long as ignorance and superstition exist among us, so long will there be persons sufficiently foolish to repair to fortune tellers; and hence the profession of these wicked people will be perpetuated till the dawn of more intelligence ... Fortune tellers are often persons of the most abandoned character, and (as such persons generally be) they possess a certain tact, without which it would be difficult to conceive their breathing the air of any place but a prison.'[4] It is therefore this approach towards the occult sciences and their practitioners that we can expect new legislation to adopt.

Religious controversy broke out with renewed vigour in the 1730s, and this meant that witchcraft and its related issues once more came to the forefront of people's consciousness. Curiously enough, however, as Ian Bostridge points out, 'the problem with the 1736 repeal is that it seems to emerge from nowhere'.[5] This is because our records are particularly sparse at this point. The Bill's three sponsors were all Whigs, of course, and seem to have had in common an opposition to anything which smacked of religious non-conformity. But they were not unopposed in their endeavours, and counter-argument came from a Scotsman, James Erskine, Lord Grange, the brother of one of the Jacobite leaders of the 1715 rebellion. Erskine's opposition was based partly on his wish to attack Sir Robert Walpole, leader of the government in Westminster, partly on his growing adherence to the rights of the Kirk in Scotland as the established organ of Scotland's particular religious confession, and partly in opposition to political chicanery in London, which Erskine saw as an attack on Scottish rights in general. He was thus the spokesman of what Bostridge calls 'a specifically Scottish tradition trying to operate in an English arena' (p. 190). But Erskine, while not alone in his opposition to repeal of the Act, had misjudged the extent to which the new 'rationalist' deism had been absorbed by the English political classes, who either despised or affected to despise belief in witches, witchcraft, magic, and the rest of the occult sciences as both ridiculous and vulgar.[6] In consequence, his speech in the House was greeted with tittering and contempt, and the Bill to repeal the Act sailed through its various stages. It was first presented to the House of Commons on 27 January 1736 and then raced away in the House of Lords: read for the first time on 13 February and a second time on 16th; it entered the committee stage on 24th; a few small amendments were discussed and agreed on 26 February and 2 March, with a third reading by the House on the 3rd. Further amendments by the Lords and the Commons were agreed on the 5th and 9th, and the Bill received royal assent on the 24th.[7] The text of the Bill is as follows:

[An Act to repeal the statute of James VI and I in England and in Scotland, the Act of Queen Mary.] Be it enacted by the King's most excellent majesty, by and with the advice and consent of the Lords spiritual and temporal, and Commons, in this present Parliament assembled, and by the authority of the same, that [King James VI and I's statute] shall, from the twenty-fourth day of June next, be repealed and utterly void and of none effect ... And be it further enacted by the authority aforesaid that, from and after the said twenty-fourth day of June [Queen Mary's Act in Scotland] shall be and is hereby repealed.

And be it further enacted that from and after the said twenty-fourth day of June, no prosecution, suit, or proceeding shall be commenced or carried on against any person or persons for witchcraft, sorcery, enchantment, or conjuration, or for charging another with such an offence, in any court whatsoever in Great Britain.

And for the more effectual preventing and punishing of any pretences to such arts or powers as are before-mentioned, whereby ignorant persons are frequently deluded and defrauded: be it further enacted by the authority aforesaid that if any person shall, from and after the twenty-fourth day of June, pretend to exercise or use any kind of witchcraft, sorcery, enchantment, or conjuration, or undertake to tell fortunes, or pretend from his or her skill or knowledge in any occult or crafty science to discover where or in what manner goods or chattels supposed to have been stolen or lost may be found. Every person so offending, being thereof lawfully convicted on indictment or information in that part of Great Britain called England, or on indictment or libel in that part of Great Britain called Scotland, shall for every such offence suffer imprisonment by the space of one whole year without bail or mainprise, and once in every quarter of the said year in some market town of the proper county upon the market day there stand openly on the pillory by the space of one hour: and also shall (if the court by which such judgement shall be given shall think fit) be obliged to give sureties for his or her good behaviour in such sum and for such time as the said court shall judge proper, according to the circumstances of the offence, and in such case shall be further imprisoned until such sureties be given.[8]

It is interesting that the particular offence singled out by the repeal Act was the endeavour to uncover a thief's identity by magical means. Whereas treasure seeking had once been uppermost in legislators' minds, now it seems detective work had impinged on their consciousness, perhaps because both Houses were concerned by vagrants, including gypsies, and had been coalescing and revising the statute law dealing with them since 1713, and would continue to do so until 1744. Indeed, as Owen Davies points out, this section of the Act was taken at the time to be specifically aimed at gypsies, who were seen and described as idle, deceiving, and manipulative of people's superstitions.[9] By this new legislative arrangement, then, there were to be no more prosecutions for witchcraft as witchcraft because witchcraft, magic, and divination were now to be identified in law as fraud. As for the punishment by imprisonment and standing in the pillory, they had been required under the old legislation for a first-time offence of actual witchcraft, and indeed the writer of a tract, *The Witch of Endor*, written some years before the repeal, but now timeously reprinted, observed that 'the continuance of [the Act] would be justly interpreted a law of extreme severity, or rather, cruelty – to punish a poor hocus pocus vagrant that has, you know, a proper punishment allotted him already by the Common Law'.[10]

The repeal of the old Act did not mean, of course, that witches and the rest were now free to operate as they pleased or that, without prosecutions, witches would quietly fade from the law courts into the harmless haven of fictional literature. On the Isle of Man magic was continuous throughout the 1730s, regardless of the repeal. So, on the one side of the Act, encouraged perhaps by the presence of Thomas Wilson, Bishop of Sodor and Man, who was known to be hot against witches, a charge was brought against Dan Cowle in 1733 for saying that the rector had an evil eye, and for employing counter-magic against him; and in the same year, James Kelley and his wife were prosecuted for divining by the sieve and shears, and Isabel Sale practised counter-magic against John Moore. In 1733, too, Isabel Quayle was told, 'as long as you are in favour with the sorcerers, you are safe enough', advice which would have seemed sensible in the light of the continuous tradition of cursing by the *skeab lome* which, according to our records, happened at least as late as 1735 and 1744. In 1741, testimony was given to the church court that a man had gone 20 miles on foot over the mountains to consult a cunning person about the chances of his sick wife's recovering from illness, and in 1750 William Corlett was severely censured for alleging that Mary Callow had been behaving in a way which suggested witchcraft.[11]

Consultation continued in Wales, too, with Robert Darcy, a cunning man, telling fortunes and restoring stolen goods in 1740 with the help of astrology; and Thomas Morgan who in 1758 showed Anne David the house of a thief who had stolen some money, and the figure of the thief himself with a pipe in his mouth; while in 1764, David Lloyd was given a similar sight of the men who had murdered Benjamin Price. John Price announced in 1788 that he was going to a 'conjuror' to find out who had stolen money from a box in his bedroom, and in the same year a farmer, worried by the strange appearance of his cows and blaming it on witchcraft, sent his son to consult a cunning man miles away. The man's remedies proved unsuccessful, and a second consultation was needed to obtain a description of the offending witch. A similar case and consultation took place in 1832, so nearly 100 years after the repeal of the Witchcraft Act people were still confident in the reality of magic, practising it, and resorting to its practitioners as they had done for centuries.[12]

In Ireland, Mary Batters, 'the Carmony witch', was tried in Carrickfergus in March 1808. Alexander Montgomery had a cow whose milk suddenly refused to turn into butter and this misfortune Alexander's wife attributed to witchcraft. Mary Butters was then consulted, came to the Montgomerys' house, and proceeded to conduct a magical war against those who might be responsible.

> [She] ordered old Montogomery and a young man named Carnaghan to go out to the cowhouse, turn their waistcoats inside out, and in that dress to stand by the head of the cow until she sent for them, while the wife, the son, and an old woman named Margaret Lee remained in the house with her. Montgomery and his ally kept their lonely vigil until daybreak when, becoming alarmed at receiving no summons, they left their post and knocked at the door, but obtained no response. They then looked through the kitchen window and to their horror saw the four inmates stretched on the

floor as dead. They immediately burst in the door and found that the wife and son were actually dead, and the sorceress and Margaret Lee nearly so. The latter soon afterwards expired. Mary Butters was thrown out on a dung heap and a restorative administered to her in the shape of a few hearty kicks, which had the desired effect. The house had a sulphurous smell, and on the fire was a large pot in which were milk, needles, pins, and crooked nails. At the inquest held at Carmoney on the 19th of August, the jurors stated that the three victims had come by their deaths from suffocation, owing to Mary Butters's having made use of some noxious ingredients, after the manner of a charm, to recover a sick cow. She was brought up at the assizes, but was discharged by proclamation. Her version of the story was that a black man had appeared in the house, armed with a huge club with which he killed the three persons and stunned herself.[13]

If Mary had really been using noxious substances for her ritual, it may well be, of course, that she did indeed see a black man with a huge club and was thus telling the truth as she had experienced it, but neither the trial nor her discharge seem to have done her much harm, although a local Presbyterian poet was happy enough to poke fun at her afterwards.

> In Carrick town a wife did dwell
> Who does pretend to conjure witches,
> Auld Barbara Goats or Lucy Bell,
> Ye'll no lang come through her clutches …
>
> The sorceress opens the scene
> With magic words of her invention,
> To make the foolish people keen
> Who did not know her base intention.
> She drew a circle round the churn,
> And washed the staff in south-run water,
> And swore the witches she would burn,
> But she would have the tailor's butter.
> When sable night her curtain spread
> Then she got a flaming fire.
> The tailor stood at the cow's head
> With his turned waistcoat in the byre,
> The chimney covered with a scraw,
> And every crevice where it smoked.
> But long before the cock did craw,
> The people in the house were choked …
>
> If Mary Butters be a witch,
> Why, but the people all should know it;
> And if she can the Muses touch,
> I'm sure she'll soon descry the poet.

> Her ain familiar off she'll send,
> Or paulet [*chicken*] with a true commission
> To pour he vengeance on the man
> That tantalises her condition.[14]

But it is in England that we find most vivid evidence of the continuance of witchcraft and magic and popular attitudes towards them. Almost as soon as the Act had been repealed, a Latitudinarian clergyman, Arthur Sykes, published *An Enquiry into the Meaning of Demoniacs in the New Testament* (1737), a treatise proposing that the demons which appeared therein were actually the souls of the dead rather than devils. This was answered by Thomas Hutchinson in 1738, who was himself rebutted by Gregory Sharpe in 1739, and so the controversy took fire and raged for the rest of the century.[15] Clerical retreat into biblical exegesis and textual criticism thus freed the way for witches to be reduced to figments of the imagination in a flat refusal to see that what was going on outwith the parson's study was no figment, but a living and continuing tradition. Cast adrift from its position as a *casus belli* in theologico-political circles, witchcraft could be dismissed the more readily as the silliness of uneducated peasants, although, it was also lamented, these might have got rid of their fears of the witch were they not still prey to diviners and fortune tellers who were happy to pick people's pockets. Thus the *Middlesex Journal*, on 19 November 1737, clearly if tacitly identified such fortune tellers as gypsies, who were actually still being regarded as witches in 1753.[16]

Particularly notable, however, is the way people, mainly women, continued to be swum as witches throughout the eighteenth century. George Kettredge lists seventeen instances between 1704 and 1795, only five of which took place before the repeal of the Act,[17] and we may take a Hertfordshire case from 1751 as not untypical. An elderly woman, Ruth Osborne from Long Marston, quarrelled with a local farmer and publican, John Butterfield, who refused to give her some milk. There appeared to be consequences. First his calves became ill, then John himself suffered a series of fits which he feared the doctors could not cure; so upon taking advice from someone whose name has not been recorded, he sent for a Northamptonshire witch, who advised him to have six men armed with staves and pitchforks and the witch's charms to guard him and his house from evil. Naturally, this drew local attention and Ruth's reputation for witchcraft grew; but as nothing particular happened as a result of the Northamptonshire witch's protective custody, someone (perhaps more than one person) thought it would be a good idea to profit from the crowds of sightseers and swim some witches. (As a publican, John Butterfield himself could certainly hope to profit from this arrangement, but there is no direct evidence he engineered the swimming and it may be smearing his reputation to draw such an inference.) Details of the swimming of Ruth and her husband were given in the *Gentleman's Magazine* for April 1751.

At Tring in Hertfordhsire, one Butterfield, a publican, giving out that he was bewitched by one Osborne and his wife, harmless people above 70, had it cried at several market towns that they were to be tried by ducking this day, which occasioned a vast concourse. The parish officers having removed the old couple from the workhouse into the church for security, the mob, missing them, broke the workhouse windows, pulled down the pales, and demolished part of the house: and seizing the governor, threatened to drown him and fire the town, having straw in their hands for that purpose. The poor wretches were at length for public safety delivered up, stripped stark naked by the mob, their thumbs tied to their toes, then dragged two miles and thrown into a muddy stream. After much ducking and ill usage, the old woman was thrown out, quite naked, on the bank, almost choked with mud, and expired in a few minutes, being kicked and beat with sticks even after she was dead: and the man lies dangerously ill of his bruises. To add to the barbarity, they put the dead witch (as they called her) in bed with her husband and tied them together ... The poor man is likewise dead of the cruel treatment he received.[18]

The details are dreadful but, as so often, journalists exaggerate and we cannot take every detail at face value. Evidence from the trial of the ringleader, Thomas Colley, for example, indicates that the Osbornes were neither kicked nor beaten nor tied to each other in bed, and that John Osborne – who was in his late fifties, not seventy – was not dead as the magazine reported. But there is no doubt the two suspects were very badly treated and that Ruth died as a result of what she had suffered. This is why Thomas Colley was arrested and tried for murder. Found guilty – under the circumstances, the verdict could hardly have been anything else – Thomas was hanged on 24 August to the resentment of the large crowd which 'stood at a distance to see him go, grumbling and muttering that it was a hard case to hang a man for destroying an old wicked woman that had done so much damage by her witchcraft'. John Osborne, who survived the ordeal, perhaps because he was about thirteen years younger than his wife and apparently in good health, was unable to find work again and had to go to the workhouse, where his reputation as a witch stuck to him. 'Even to this time,' reported one of the pamphlets dealing with the affair, 'a great number of people in that part of the country think the man a wizard, and that he can spew up pins as fast as he pleases.'[19]

This reaction is more or less what one expects. When Richard Giles's family was afflicted by what seems to have been a poltergeist in December 1761 and January 1762 in the Lamb Inn in Bristol, witchcraft was suspected and acted upon. According to an account published by Henry Durbin, 'Mr Giles had asked my opinion whether they should not go to those called white witches to have these troubles stopped. I told them if they could stop it, it must be done by the power of the Devil, therefore I thought it not lawful to go to them, but to trust the providence of God for deliverance. But as it continued above the year and was hired for another year, they were determined to go to the woman at Bedminster to see if she could stop it. The morning they went, it was very violent and spoke aloud and called Mrs Giles, and said they should not be much the better for going to the cunning woman; and as they were going out at the door, [it] pinched Molly in the cheek till the blood came. I saw the mark of it.'[20] London, too, had (one might almost say enjoyed) the sensation of the Cock Lane ghost in 1762, which attracted huge crowds of sightseers and thrill seekers until it was shown that the whole haunting was a fraud. Witchcraft was not blamed in this instance, but the episode did throw up yet another treatise in the skirmish with superstition waged, it may seem endlessly, by *bien pensants* against the ignorance of the multitude.

An anonymous tract published in 1762, *Anti-Canidia* – a reference to a witch in the Roman poet Horace's *Epodes* – pours scorn on magic, witchcraft, and divination and makes constant appeals to 'reason' and 'rationality', while skating on thin ice when it comes to the Apostles and their perception of Jesus. 'Prompted to this undertaking by a sally of indignation at the contemptible wonder in Cock Lane that has lately made so much noise' (p. 4), the author observes and emphasises that 'to see a spirit, in the very terms implies an absurdity and contradiction' (p. 10), and when scripture talks of witches and sorcerers and diviners, it does not mean to suggest these people have real powers, and indeed mentions them at all 'in conformity only to the ignorance of those times and in compliance to prevailing custom' (p. 13). When the disciples saw the risen Jesus, 'they were troubled and supposed they saw a spirit. Their fright was of the same vulgar kind as their notions of seeing a spirit – arguments indeed of their human infirmity, but none at all for the reality of apparitions' (pp. 17–18). The idea that God interferes with the order of Creation merely to frighten people, or 'to discover a butter pot full of money buried in the cellar: or a deed or a will of which the heir has been defrauded, hidden in a rotten chest or behind the wainscot … can only excite the indignation rather than the attention of a sober, serious, and rational mind' (p. 23). Demonic possession described in the New Testament referred to epileptic or convulsive illnesses (p. 26), and to this day possession is often offered as an explanation for such diseases (p. 30). There are fewer witches and demons in Britain now than there are in Catholic countries because 'we have happily ever since [the Reformation] improved the means afforded us to eradicate these prejudices and vulgar errors. And we experience every day that, as science [*knowledge*] and learning increases, the vulgar notions of spirits, apparitions, witches, and demons decrease and die of themselves' (pp. 33, 34). Charms, amulets, incantations, and all methods of divination, including astrology, are 'gross importures' and 'delusive trumpery' (p. 44), and all one needs is 'philosophy and the exercise of a rational understanding', such as one found in the age of Augustus, 'to detect and expose … rogueries and fallacies, and to shake the very foundations of the imposture' (p. 56).

It was not exactly the last hurrah in the battle for people's perceptions of the occult sciences, but the sneering and tittering, perhaps more than force of argument, were slowly doing their work, and witchcraft and magic were retreating from the public eye to hide themselves in the pages of fiction or travellers' tales about places and communities far removed from the salons and public houses of London. Not for nothing did the author of this tract call it *Anti-Canidia*. Only those with a classical education will have recognised the allusion, and as Canidia herself, as described by Horace, was a hideous old female, somewhat absurd, somewhat grotesque, but full of malice, she provided a literary figure of the witch calculated to raise a shudder and a patronising smile, but not to be taken seriously by People Like Us. Perfect for the eighteenth century.

Still, while the sneers and titters had some effect upon those with learning or pretension to learning, older beliefs and practices proved sufficiently resilient to weather much of the disenchanting storm. Witches and cunning folk did not disappear at the behest of their social superiors' disbelief. On the contrary, they continued to perform their historical services for their clients and to be the traditional target for their neighbours' fears and discontents. William Brewer was active in Somerset from the 1830s to December 1890 when he died, consulted as a magical healer, detector of lost property, and worker of counter-bewitchment. Frederick Culliford found himself on trial in 1876 in the same county under the Witchcraft Act of 1736, which had repealed earlier statutes assuming the reality of magic and witchcraft, and substituted the notion that they were merely a pretence whereby offenders elicited money by encouraging false expectations. Found guilty at the quarter sessions, Frederick was imprisoned for a year, a fate which could equally well have awaited James Stacy, 'the wizard of South Petherton', who in January 1883 complained to the petty sessions that he had been assaulted by nine men and women from the village of West Chinnock, angered because his counter-magic against the bewitchment of the husband of one of the women had failed to prevent his death. But James was more fortunate than Frederick, for the magistrates decided he deserved his beating and so dismissed his case against all nine assailants. On the other hand, ten years later, Harriet Carew from Yeovil was forced to seek police protection after a local bus driver accused her of bewitching his sister and threatened to beat her brains out if she did not lift the spell.[21]

The notion, then, that increasing literacy and learned disapproval undermined belief in and acceptance of magic by spreading a certain kind of rationalism is unfounded and mistaken. Indeed, Lady Rosalind Northcote was moved to observe in 1900 that advances in education actually produced more rather than less witchcraft, because the subsequent encouragement to read offered an increasingly large audience for the flood of cheap books and pamphlets dealing with all kinds of occultist subjects.[22] Nor were books and pamphlets the only sources to which people might turn. Newspapers, too, while taking care to preserve their sneering credentials – 'It will hardly be credited that in this year of grace [1867], in a country which boasts of its education and common sense, that anyone can be silly enough to believe in "witchcraft", but so it is' – were still happy enough to report accounts of preternatural happenings, including counter-magic against alleged witches.[23] Almanacs, with their astrological tables, predictions, and advice, were wildly popular, and vampire stories enjoyed a heyday, beginning with John Polidori's *The Vampyre* in 1819 and reaching a climax with Bram Stoker's *Dracula* in 1897, indicate a popular thirst for excursions into bourns of the other world. The twentieth century, of course, just as much as the nineteenth, ran away with the mistaken idea that it had escaped this cast of mind; but it was just as much mistaken, for films and then television stepped in to supplement a hunger which was as sharp as any in the rest of the world (where belief in and practice of magic in all its forms is both widespread and common) but which the rest of the world was not, and is not, so quickly hypocritical to pretend does not exist.

Far from being the end of an old story and the start of a new rationalism, then, the repeal of King James's Witchcraft Act and its replacement under George did little to disturb people's fascination with extraterrestrial intelligences and the possibility of trafficking with them in one fashion or another. The law might adopt one stance and people with influence bend their efforts to cajole, drag, educate, or mock everyone else into agreement with it, but as far as the silent majority was concerned, capitulation to those domineering forces was merely apparent. In 1993, four members of a jury in Hove in Essex, who were engaged in trying a case of murder, used a Ouija board in an effort to contact the murder victim's spirit and thus gain pertinent information which would help them make up their minds.[24] There speaks the authentic voice from beneath the veneer. The person named by the spirit was the person convicted, too. Coincidence or revelation?

NOTES

Preface

1. *Opera Omnia*, Basel 1557–1573, Vol. 1: *Oratio de hominis dignitate*, para. 38.

2. *De la démonomanie des sorciers*, Paris 1580, 1. Interestingly enough, Bodin uses the masculine form of the word for 'witch'. A useful compendium of attempted definitions of magic, from the ancient world to the present, may be found in B-C. Otto & M. Stausberg (eds), *Defining Magic, A Reader*, Sheffield: Equinox Publishing Ltd 2013.

3. For an example from the 1990s of envy leading to witchcraft and the destruction of trust between neighbours hitherto friendly, see C. M. Couniham, *A Tortilla is Like Life: Food and Culture in the San Luis Valley of Colorado*, Austin: University of Texas Press 2009, 164–167.

4. *Witchcraft, Violence and Democracy in South Africa*, Chicago & London: University of Chicago Press 2005, 64.

5. I. Niehaus, *Witchcraft, Power and Politics: Exploring the Occult in the South African Louveld*, London: Pluto Press 2001, 115.

6. J. Favret-Saada, *Deadly Words: Witchcraft in the Bocage*, English trans. Cambridge: Cambridge University Press 1980, 65–75. See also Perle Møhl, *Village Voices: Co-Existence and Communication in a Rural Community in Central France*, Copenhagen: Museum Tusculum Press 1997, 76–77.

7. *The End of Magic*, New York & Oxford: Oxford University Press 1997, 115. Cf. B. Kapferer, 'More generally, sorcery practices and beliefs are assertions of human potency. They are declarations of the power of human beings and that the potency of other human beings is vital to the life chances of human beings in their life worlds. Sorcery beliefs and practices spring from the awareness (both unconscious and reflected on) that human beings participate in fields of consciousness that are also fields of force. This is neither a mystification nor an irrationality: it is a fact of human existence', *The Feast of the Sorcerer: Practices of Consciousness and Power*, Chicago & London: University of Chicago Press 1997, 267.

8. *Exorcism and Enlightenment: Johann Joseph Gassner and the Demons of Eighteenth-Century Germany*, New Haven & London: Yale University Press 2005, 6.

Introduction

1. Spitting tends to be associated with healing – e.g. Mark 8.23 and John 9.6 – but is also a ritual gesture, one of a series, in a spell for a good memory, Betz, *The Greek Magical Papyri in Translation*, 2nd ed., Chicago & London: University of Chicago Press 1992, 29. This spell also involves an offering of cow's milk, *op. cit.*, 35, 194. Part of another spell requires the practitioner to 'hiss a great hiss, that is, one of some length', *op. cit.*, 187. In the fourth century, Julian the Apostate described Christians (who were often dismissed as mere magicians) as hissing at demons, *Contra Galilaeos*, epistle 19. Perhaps, as Charles Bolton suggests, this arose from the notable sibilance of the name Iesous Khristos, likely to have been invoked during any exorcism, 'The Emperor Julian against "hissing Christians"', *Harvard Theological Review* 61 (1968), 496–497.

2. *The Education of Edmund Randolph*, New York: W.W. Norton & Co. 1979, 15.

3. *The Rise of Western Christendom*, 2nd ed. Oxford: Blackwell Publications 2003, 358.

4. One can see how neither Christianity nor paganism turned out to be wholly triumphant over its rival from Pope Gregory's advice anent pagan temples. They were not to be demolished, he said, but after their idols had been destroyed, the shrines should be sprinkled with holy water, altars built, and relics placed therein, Bede, *Historia Ecclesiastica* 1.30. Folk memory, despite the Holy Father's evident wish to the contrary, was thus bound to retain certain ties with older beliefs and practices.

5. Griffiths, *Aspects of Anglo-Saxon Magic*, 174, 187 (quotation), 188 (quotation).

6. Lewis, *Dreaming of Dwarves*, 39–44. For earlier comments, see M. L. Cameron, *Anglo-Saxon Medicine*, Cambridge: Cambridge University Press 1993, 152 and Pollington, *Leechcraft*, 455. It is worth noting that, while illnesses were sometimes conceived as stemming from elves, they were not associated with dwarfs, and so the explanation of the fever's originating with a dwarf may not be not altogether convincing, although MacLeod and Mees say there is a well-attested tradition in Germanic folklore of a dwarf's being an agent of disease, *Runic Amulets*, 26. On elves and illness, see Cameron, *op. cit.*, 141–142; Meaney, *Anglo-Saxon Amulets*, 109–113; Hall, *Elves in Anglo-Saxon England*, Woodbridge: The Boydell Press 2007, 96–118; J. McGowan, 'Elves, elf-shot, and epilepsy', *Studia Neophilologica* 81 (2009), 116–120. A. Hall, however, has reservations, 'Calling the shots: the Old English remedy gif hors ofscoten sie and Anglo-Saxon elf-shot', *Neuphilologische Mitteilungen: Bulletin of the Modern Language Society* 106 (2005), 195–209.

7. Cf. the second charm quoted above which includes the names of the Seven Sleepers of Ephesos.

8. See G. Brandon, *Santería from Africa to the New World*, Bloomington & Indianopolis: Indiana University Press 1997, 74–78.7.

9. MacLeod & Mees, *Runic Amulets*, 120.

10. MacNeill & Gamer, *Mediaeval Handbooks of Penance*, 198, 274, 288, 330–331. It is noteworthy here that secular law was likely to put people to death for practising magic. See, for example, Alfred the Great's civil code: 'women who are accustomed to practise enchantments (*galdorcraeft*), and magicians (*scinlaecan*), and cunning women (*wiccan*), do not let them live', quoted in Crawford, 'Evidences for witchcraft in Anglo-Saxon England', 107–108. Cf. the slightly different version which invokes the death penalty for those who receive magicians into their homes, *Ibid.*, 110 and the two-year penance imposed for the same offence by the Church, MacNeill & Gamer, *op. cit. supra*, 329–330.

11. Quoted in Griffiths, *Aspects of Anglo-Saxon Magic*, 48. Aelfric also said, 'No one should enchant herbs with incantations, but bless them with God's words, and then eat them', *Catholic Homilies: The First Series*, Text, ed. P. Clemoes, Oxford: Oxford University Press 1997, 450.

12. Isidore, *Etymologies* 11.3.2, 4. Cf. Bishop Patrick, 'God in His mercy, the Lord of the world, has given us many wonderful signs which are signifiers of future ill or good', *The Writings of Bishop Patrick, 1074–1084*, ed. A. Gwynn, Dublin 1955, 57. Silvestris, *Cosmographia* 2.1.3, ed. P. Dronke, Leiden: Brill 1978. Hildegard, *Scivias* in Migne, *Patrologia Latina* 197.404–405.

13. As, for example, Luke 21.11: 'There will be dreadful portents and great signs from heaven', and Luke 21.25: 'There will be signs in the sun, the moon, and the stars'.

14. Roger de Howden, *Chronica*, ed. William Stubbs, 4 vols. London: Longmans, Greek & Co. 1869, 2.171, 136. Such phenomena were not altogether uncommon. See further J. S. P. Tatlock, 'Mediaeval cases of blood-rain', *Classical Philology* 9 (1914), 442–447. On changes in explanation, see Watkins, *History and the Supernatural*, 27–38.

15. Bede, *De rerum natura* 13, *Corpus Scriptorum Christianorum*, Series Latina 123, p. 126. Roger de Howden, *op. cit. supra*, 2.29. My italics.

16. *Tractatus de sphaera*, ed. L. Thorndike, *The Sphere of Sacrobosco and its Commentators*, Chicago: University of Chicago Press 1949, 117.

17. Corrector of Burchard of Worms in McNeill & Gamer, *Mediaeval Handbooks of Penance*, 337.

18. *Chronica* 2.10–11.

19. Roger de Howden, *op. cit.*, 2.302–303.

20. On these contrasts, see further P. G. Maxwell-Stuart, *Satan: A Biography*, Stroud: Amberley Publishing 2008, 59–67, 109–119.

21. Fifth century: mosaic of the Annunciation in Santa Maria Maggiore, Rome. Cf. Bartolo di Fredi, *The Murder of Job's Servants* (1367), fresco in San Gimignano cathedral. Various colours of robes: Fra Angelico, *The Universal Judgement* (*c.* 1431–5), now in the Museo di San Marco, Firenze. For a statue, see St Michael winged and clad in a long robe, Cathédrale de Saint-Étienne, Bourges. Originally this would have been painted.

22. *Vita Sancti Cuthberti* in B. Colgrave (ed.), *Two Lives of Saint Cuthbert*, Cambridge: Cambridge University Press, pbk 1985, 177–179.

23. Another example from Bede's *Life of St Cuthbert* has an angel arrive in the form of a man dressed in white, riding a horse. St Cuthbert had a badly infected knee and the 'man' gave instructions on the preparation of a hot poultice. After he had gone, St Cuthbert made and applied the poultice which effected a cure, and then he realised that the 'man' had been an angel. Biblical references to similar cures follow, so any thought that Bede could be using the word 'angel' metaphorically must be dismissed. See Colgrave, *op. cit. supra*, 159–161. Illustrations of this incident show the angel with wings and a halo. M. Baker, 'Mediaeval illustrations of Bede's Life of St Cuthbert', *Journal of the Warburg and Courtauld Institutes* 41 (1978), 25 and illustrations 3a & c, 4b.

24. *Vita Merlini*, Charleston, SC: BiblioBazaar 2008, 24–25, 67–68.

25. Angels had long been divided into nine orders, as we see from St Isidore of Seville, *Etymologies* 7.5.4. Demons, he says, having fallen from their former pure air, now occupy the denser, murkier regions, *Ibid.* 8.11.17.

26. *Hamartigenia*, 514–520.

27. St Robert: quoted by Martín del Rio, *Disquisitiones Magicae*, Louvain 1608, Book 2, question 28, section 3. Étienne de Bourbon, *Anecdotes Historiques*, ed. A. Lecoy de la Marche, Paris 1877, 47–48. Guibert de Nogent, *A Monk's Confession*, trans. P. J. Archambault, Pennyslvania: The Pennsylvania State University Press, 113–116, 206–207.

28. Richalm, *Liber revelationum*, ed. P. G. Schmidt, *Monumenta Germaniae Historica*, Quellen 24, Hannover 2009, 46, 145. Guibert, *op. cit. supra*, 207.

29. Quoted in Tomlinson, *Demons, Druids, and Brigands*, 103.

30. Hieronymus Radiolensis, *Miracula Sancti Joannis Gualberti*, 51–54 in Migne, *Patrologia Latina* 146, 811–970.

31. *Dialogus Miraculorum*, ed. J. Strange, 2 vols. Köln 1851, 2.52–53. Demonic possession had long been described as both noisy and dramatic. Cf. Bede's account of a woman 'seized on by a demon and most cruelly afflicted, with the result that she gnashed her teeth and uttered pitiable cries, flinging her arms and legs about in agitation, and thus inspiring no little horror in everyone who saw or heard her', *Vita Sancti Cuthberti*, 202–207.

32. On Anglo-Saxon death rites, see further H. Williams, 'At the funeral' in Carver, Sanmark, Semple (eds), *Signals of Belief in Early England*, 67–82. For the story of a newly dead Christian corpse which reanimated and prepared hospitality for the pallbearers at its own funeral, see T. A. Dubois, *Nordic Religions in the Viking Age*, Philadelphia: University of Pennsylvania Press 1999, 89–90. The episode is translated in Joynes, *Mediaeval Ghost Stories*, 108–110. For the story of a corpse which returned to be an unpleasant nuisance to its former community and had to be burned to ashes and scattered in the sea, see Dubois, *op. cit.*, 88.

33. William of Newburgh, *Historia rerum Anglicarum* 5.24. *Chronicon de Lanercost*, quoted in Caciola, 'Wraiths, revenants, and ritual', 23. Simpson, 'Repentant soul or walking corpse?' 390–391, 393. Cf. Thomas of Cantimpré, 'Since the structure of a dead body remains behind, just as a human being can [use] a structured body as though it were a garment, so the Devil can sneak into it and mould its mouth to voices and speech again, and call the tendons back to the movements of its bodily parts', *De Apibus* 2.49.6; 2.57.8. Thietmar & Gervase, quoted in Joynes, *Mediaeval Ghost Stories*, 13, 78.

34. Joynes, *op. cit. supra*, 26–28, 60–61.

35. Rudolf Glaber, *Historiarum libri quinque: The Five Books of the Histories by Rodolfus*

Glaber, trans. J. France, Oxford: Clarendon Press 1989, Book 5, chap. 1. Orderic Vitalis in Joynes, *op. cit. supra*, 49–52. See further C. Lecouteux, *Phantom Armies of the Night: The Wild Hunt and the Ghostly Processions of the Undead*, English trans. Rochester & Vermont: Inner Traditions 2011, 33–54.

36. Quoted in Caciola, 'Wraiths, revenants, and ritual', 10.

37. Henderson & Cowan, *Scottish Fairy Belief*, 16–17. See also N. Williams, 'One of the key notions which links usage of *fairy* from its earliest proto-usage seems to be that of "fatedness", but we cannot trace this notion to any particular culture, tradition, style, register, or period, and we cannot even specify what that notions entails', 'The semantic of the word *fairy*: making meaning out of thin air' in Naváez (ed.), *The Good People*, 457–478; quotation, 472.

38. *The Secret Commonwealth of Elves, Fauns, and Fairies*, New York: Dover Publications 2008, 47–49.

39. Purkiss, *Troublesome Things*, 56–62, 68–70. Ralph of Coggeshall & Lanzelet quoted in Briggs, *The Fairies in Tradition and Literature*, 8–9, 5.

40. See further Saunders, *Magic and the Supernatural*, 179–206.

41. Wilson, *The Magical Universe*, 408–409, 48, 8, 134. Jonson, *A Particular Entertainment of the Queen and Prince, their Highness, at Althrope, 25th June, 1603*, 29–46. Cf. the physical afflictions fairies ere believed to visit upon human beings, B. Rieti, 'The Blast in Newfoundland fairy tradition' in Narváez (ed.), *The Good People*, 284–297.

42. McNeill & Gamer, *Mediaeval Handbooks of Penance*, 335, 350. Gui, *The Inquisitor's Guide*, ed. & trans. J. Shirley, Welwyn Garden City: Ravenhall Books 2006, 150. K. Sullivan, *The Interrogation of Joan of Arc*, Minneapolis: University of Minnesota Press 1999, 7, 12–16; quotation, 15.

43. Bates, *The Real Middle Earth*, 101–102, 105–106, 108–109. Pollington, *Leechcraft*, 456–461. Griffiths, *Aspects of Anglo-Saxon Magic*, 50–53. Jolly, *Popular Religion in Late Saxon England*, 134–138. Hall, *Elves in Anglo-Saxon England*, 98–103, 115–117; quotation, 162. Wilson, *The Magical Universe*, 172. On elves as forms of temptation or mental deception akin to attacks by demons, see further K. L. Jolly, 'Elves in the Psalms? The experience of evil from a cosmic perspective' in A. Ferreiro (ed.), *The Devil, Heresy and Witchcraft in the Middle Ages*, Leiden-Boston-Köln: Brill 1998, 19–44.

44. Quoted in J. Harte, 'Hell on earth: encountering devils in the Mediaeval landscape' in Bildhauer & Mills (eds), *The Monstrous Middle Ages*, 187.

45. Thus Athanasius in his *Life of St Anthony*: 'Formerly everywhere was filled with the deceit of oracles … Demons cheated men with their illusions, taking possession of springs or rivers or wood or stones, and thus by their tricks stupefying the simple. But now that the divine manifestation of the Word has taken place, their illusions has ceased; for someone has only to make the sign of the cross to drive away their deceits.' Quoted in Harte, *op. cit. supra*, 191.

46. Friedman, *The Monstrous Races*, 202–205. The Râby frescoes were whitewashed over in 1918 and can be seen now only in photographs. A. Pluskowski, 'Apocalyptic monsters: animal inspirations for the iconography of Mediaeval northern European devourers' in Bildhauer & Mills (eds), *The Monstrous Middle Ages*, 162–165. R. Mills, 'Jesus as monster' in Bildhauer & Mills, *op. cit.*, 37–45.

47. St Isidore, *Etymologies* 11.3.2, 7. *Beowulf*, ed. & trans. J. L. Hall, Boston-New York-Chicago: D.C. Heath & Co 1892, Stanza 2, verses 50–62.

48. Quoted in P. Brown, *The Rise of Western Christendom*, 2nd ed. Oxford: Blackwell Publishing 2003, 483.

49. *Fasciculus Morum*, 578–579.

50. Cf. Watkins discussing an early thirteenth-century priest's reworking of Geoffrey of Monmouth's *Historia*: 'Here an ordinary churchman, writing for an audience of middling status, introduced *incubi*, elves, and other ambiguous supernatural *dramatis personae* as if they were elements of a shared culture, needing little explanation and less defence. This seems to have been the sort of thought world with which Gerald of Wales, William of Newburgh, and Gervase of Tilbury were also becoming increasingly engaged during the decades around the end of the twelfth century', *History and the Supernatural in Mediaeval England*, 65–66.

51. Meaney, *Anglo-Saxon Amulets*, 44, 45.

52. MacLeod & Rees, *Runic Amulets*, 130. Meaney, *op. cit. supra*, 110.

53. Everyday objects: Meaney, *op. cit. supra*, 186, 187, 189. Biblical names: MacLeod & Mees, *op. cit. supra*, 158–159. Bells: *Ibid.*, 188–189. Other objects: Meaney, 71 (quotation 73), 77–78 (quotations, 106, 107). See also Pollington, *Leechcraft*, 419–452.

54. Schulz, *Beschwörungen im Mittelalter*, 80.

55. B. Tovey, 'Kingly impairments in Anglo-Saxon literature: God's curse and God's blessing' in J. R. Eyler (ed.), *Disability in the Middle Ages*, Farnham: Ashgate 2010, 138.

56. Schulz, *op. cit. supra*, 147, 117.

57. Griffiths, *Aspects of Anglo-Saxon Magic*, 173–178.

58. *Summa de praedicandi*, ed. F. Morenzoni, *Corpus Christianorum Continuatio Mediaevalis*, Vol. 82 (Turnhout 1988), 166.

59. Quoted in Peters, 'The Mediaeval Church and state on superstition', 212. This process of intensification can be followed further in Bailey, 'Concern over superstition in late Mediaeval Europe', 115–133.

60. St Isidore, *Etymologies* 8.9.28. McNeill & Gamer, *Mediaeval Handbooks of Penance*, 275–276, 350. De Nogent, *A Monk's Confession*, 105–106. Lots: T. C. Skeat, 'An early Mediaeval Book of Fate: the Sortes XII Patriarcharum', *Mediaeval and Renaissance Studies* 3 (1954), 41–42.

61. Peters, *The Magician, the Witch, and the Law*, 91.

62. Watkins, *History and the Supernatural*, 149–150, 151. Cf. the diagrams of the right shoulder blades of a sheep with the significance of its various places marked for easy reference. C. Burnett, *Magic and Divination in the Middle Ages*, Aldershot: Variorum 1996, XII, pp. 10 & 11. Watkins, *op. cit.*, 160–162. A. Sanmark, 'Living on: ancestors and the soul' in Carver, Sanmark, Semple (eds), *Signals of Belief in Early England*, 173. Lecouteux, *Phantom Armies of the Night*, 47.

63. See further Holzmann, 'Ich beswer dich wurm und wyrmin', 25–47.

64. The etymology of the word 'witch' is disputed. Old English *wicca/wicce* has been traced back to several roots, including verbs 'to see', 'to bend', 'to predict', and 'to consecrate'. In view of the uncertainty, the popular association of 'witch' with 'wise woman', made by Reginald Scot in his *Discoverie of Witchcraft* (1584), cannot be sustained with any confidence.

1 Political Crimes, Divination, and Demons: 1222–1390

1. Book 16, title 18, section 3.

2. Ewen, *Witch Hunting*, 4.

3. *Armarium de serico*. This suggests that the 'box' was made of silk, but *armorium* usually refers to a chest, cupboard, or bookcase, so we may have to imagine a small wooden receptacle covered in silk.

4. Ed. H. R. Luard, London: Longman, Green, Longman & Roberts 1859, 171–172. See also M. Prestwich, *Edward I*, London: Methuen 1988, 339–341. R. C. Stacey, 'Adam of Stratton', *Dictionary of National Biography* 53.38–39.

5. Bartholomew de Cotton, *op. cit. supra*, 173, 180.

6. R. M. Haines, 'Walter Langton', *Dictionary of National Biography* 32.523–525. Prestwich, *Edward I*, 139–140, 548–551. E. Rose, *A Razor for a Goat*, Toronto: University of Toronto Press, reprint 2003, 64–65; quotation, 122–123. Maxwell-Stuart, *Witch Beliefs and Witch Trials*, 19.

7. Maxwell-Stuart, *op. cit. supra*, 22–23.

8. Russell, *Witchcraft in the Middle Ages*, 130–131.

9. M. Jones, *The Secret Middle Ages*, Stroud: Sutton Publishing 2002, 280. See further J. Durrant, 'The osculum infame: heresy, secular culture, and the image of the witches' sabbath' in K. Harvey (ed.), *The Kiss in History*, Manchester: Manchester University Press 2005, 36–59.

10. Russell, *Witchcraft in the Middle Ages*, 187. Cohn, *Europe's Inner Demons*, 181–185.

11. Kieckhefer, *European Witch Trials*, 108–109. Cohn, *op. cit. supra*, 185–192.

12. Kieckhefer, *op. cit. supra*, 109–110. Russell, *Witchcraft in the Middle Ages*, 172–173.

13. N. Fryde, *The Tyranny and Fall of Edward II, 1321–1326*, Cambridge: Cambridge University Press 1979, 162–164. Summers, *The Geography of Witchcraft*, 82–84.

14. M. Lambert, *Mediaeval Heresy*, 2nd ed. Oxford: Blackwell Publishing 1992, 107, 120.

15. See further the remarks of Peters, *The Magician, the Witch, and the Law*, 168–169.

16. W. Page (ed.), *Three Early Assize Rolls for the County of Northumberland*, Durham-London-Edinburgh: Surtees Society 1891, Vol. 88., 343. Kittredge, *Witchcraft in Old and New England*, 46–48. J. B. Given, *Society and Homicide in Thirteenth-Century England*, Stanford: Stanford University Press 1977, 139.

17. *Historia rerum Anglicarum* Book 5, chap. 22.

18. Watkins, *History of the Supernatural in Mediaeval England*, 131. Thomas, *Religion and the Decline of Magic*, 302.

19. Her case is described or discussed in J. T. Gilbert, *History of the Viceroys of Ireland*, Dublin & London 1865, 153–161; Seymour, *Irish Witchcraft and Demonology*, 25–45; Summers, *The Geography of Witchcraft*, 85–91; Cohn, *Europe's Inner Demons*, 198–204; Russell, *Witchcraft in the Middle Ages*, 189–193; Neary, 'The origins and character of the Kilkenny witchcraft case'; E. Colledge, *The Latin Poems of Richard Ledrede, OFM*, xv–xxiii; Williams, 'She was usually placed', 67–83; W. Stephens, *Demon Lovers: Witchcraft, Sex, and the Crisis of Belief*, Chicago & London: University of Chicago Press 2002, 264–267. The fullest account and translation of the principal documents in the case are given by Davidson and Ward, *The Sorcery Trial of Alice Kyteler*. The Latin originals are provided by Wright, *Narrative of the Proceedings against Dame Alice Kyteler*. My translations from the *Narrative* often differ significantly from those provided by Davidson and Ward, and my interpretation of events also differs in some respects from those offered hitherto.

20. R. Frame, *English Lordship in Ireland, 1318–1361*, Oxford: Clarendon Press 1982, 82, 85, 169.

21. S. Payling, 'The politics of family: Mediaeval marriage contracts' in R. H. Britnell & A. J. Pollard (eds), *The MacFarlane Legacy: Studies in Late Mediaeval Politics and Society*, New York: St Martin's Press 1995, 25.

22. Davidson & Ward, *The Sorcery Trial of Alice Kyteler*, 28–29.

23. A. C. Kors & E. Peters (eds), *Witchcraft in Europe*, 2nd revised ed. Philadelphia: University of Pennsylvania Press 2001, 119–120, 123. Cohn points out that 'son of the art' has nothing to do with the proper name Arthur, but refers to the art or craft of magic, *Europe's Inner Demons*, 203–204.

24. Davidson & Ward plausibly suggest that 'fi' may stand for Latin *fiat*, 'let it happen', *op. cit. supra*, 28 note 11.

25. *Decretum causa* 11, question 3, chapter 106.

26. Davidson & Ward, *op. cit. supra*, 78–79. A. R. Ekirch, *At Day's Close: A History of Night Time*, London: Weidenfeld & Nicolson 2005, 300–302.

27. St Augustine, *De civitate Dei* Book 15, chap. 23. St Thomas Aquinas, 'Some people say that demons cannot in any way engender [human beings] in the bodies they have assumed ... On the other hand, many people say the opposite and many think it cannot be entirely false', *Commentum in quatuor libros Sententiarum Magistri Petri Lombardi*, Parma: P. Fiaccadori 1856–8, Book 2, division 8, question 1, article 4, solution 2.

28. *Europe's Inner Demons*, 227.

29. D. Higgs Strickland, *Saracens, Demons, and Jews: Making Monsters in Mediaeval Art*, Princeton & Oxford: Princeton University Press 2003, 85, 86. J. Block Friedman, *The Monstrous Races in Mediaeval Art and Thought*, New York: Syracuse University.

30. Russell, *Witchcraft in the Middle Ages*, 191.

31. Cohn, *Europe's Inner Demons*, 192–194. L. Thorndike, *A History of Magic and Experimental Science*, 8 vols, New York: Columbia University Press 1923–58, 3.19, 23–24.

32. The provision of his appointment noted that he was a man of clean living and a knowledge of letters which, as C. A. Empey points out, suggests 'he had come to the Pope's attention because of his learning and zeal', *Oxford Dictionary of National Biography* 33.42.

33. P. Partner, *The Murdered Magicians*, Oxford: Oxford University Press 1982, 78.

34. Constitutions of Ossory in Davidson & Ward, *The Sorcery Trial of Alice Kyteler*, 74–76, 78.

35. Davidson & Ward, *op. cit. supra*, 10.

36. These were William Utlagh, her son; Robert of Bristol, a cleric; John, Ellen, and Syssok Galrussyn; William Payn of Boly; Petronilla of Meath and her daughter; Alice, wife of Henry, a carpenter; Annota Lange; and Eva of Brownstown. See Davidson & Ward, 53.

37. Davidson & Ward, 31.

38. Davidson & Ward, 47. Williams, 'She was usually placed', 79. Empey, 'Richard Ledred', *Oxford Dictionary of National Biography* 33.42.

39. Davidson & Ward, 49.

40. Davidson & Ward, 52.

41. Davidson & Ward (52) translate 'several women'. The Latin calls them *personae* which is a feminine noun but may refer to both men and women. It is therefore the gender of the noun which accounts for the feminine participles which follow.

42. Not 'relapsed heretic' as Davidson & Ward have it (56). Alice had not been reconciled with the Church and so could not have relapsed. The Latin also makes it clear that *haeretica* and *relapsa* are here two separate nouns.

43. The Latin says *demum deprehensa* ('at long last'), which implies she had evaded arrest for quite a while. Since she was Alice's maidservant, she may have been with her mistress and therefore safe from apprehension until Alice fled to England. Why Alice did not take Petronilla with her, we do not know, but without her mistress's protection Petronilla would have been vulnerable and hence in danger.

44. Part 2, case 33, question 5, chapters 11–19. Gilbert correctly notes the cudgel in his account, although he makes it plural instead of singular, *History of the Viceroys of Ireland*, 161.

45. Worms: worms suggested disease or causes of disease and are often found together with poisons or magico-medical remedies. See Jolly, *Popular Religion*, 125, 126, 128–130. Including worms and poisonous creatures in a concoction therefore indicates intention to do physical harm. Milfoil: See Pollington, *Leechcraft*, 169. Body-parts: See Maxwell-Stuart, *Witch Beliefs*, 49, 72. Cf. modern hunting and killing of albinos in certain parts of the world so that their body parts can be used in magic.

46. He is called a *daemon tertius*. Davidson and Ward (63, note 115) argue that *tertius* cannot here refer to the number three, but should be translated 'infernal'. The precedents they cite, however, are insufficient. Both come from Ovid and refer to the three gods or kingdoms of the underworld, 'infernal' being an added explanation of those phrases by Lewis & Short in their Latin dictionary. So unless one is going to argue for textual emendation to *taetricus*, 'harsh, gloomy, severe' – not a convincing suggestion – one is left with *tertius* in its usual meaning, 'third'.

47. Davidson and Ward (63) say that Alice's husband was included, too, but the Latin is *in maritum proprium*, 'against her own husband', and since the subject of the sentence is Petronilla, only her husband can be meant.

48. See further Maxwell-Stuart, *Satan*, 83.

49. See, for example, the accumulated witness of Templars at their trial in Cyprus in 1310, A. Gilmour-Bryson (ed. & trans.), *The Trial of the Templars in Cyprus*, Leiden-Boston-Köln: Brill 1998, 224, 233, 236, 239, 246 which say that Templars wore a cord night and day either over their shirt or next to their skin. One of the witnesses specifically denies the suggestion that the cord was first wound round the head of an idol, 214.

50. The Templars in Ireland were suppressed in 1308 and their members put on trial just outwith Dublin in 1310.

51. Davidson & Ward, 70.

52. 'She was usually placed', 69 and note 9.

53. Cohn, *Europe's Inner Demons*, 34–35, 56–58. Lambert, *Mediaeval Heresy*, 166–167.

54. Davidson & Ward, 80. My italics.

55. Quoted in Summers, *The Geography of Witchcraft*, 91.

56. Kittredge, *Witchcraft in Old and New England*, 53.

57. *Op. cit.*, 27.

58. There is no warrant for C. A. Empey's remark that 'he introduced the demonic and heretical elements into the Kyteler inquiry', *Oxford Dictionary of National Biography* 33.42. Ledrede's episcopal visitation certainly uncovered heresy and magic, but since this visitation included five knights and a large number of other nobles, it is hard to see the justification for saying that the bishop 'introduced' them into Alice's case. Had his lay fellow inquisitors not been interested or had they wanted the charges of magic passed by, they would have had their way, if only because of force of numbers.

59. Davidson & Ward, 87–89.

60. For the relevant documents, see Maxwell-Stuart, *Witch Beliefs*, 20–23. See also Decker, *Witchcraft and the Papacy*, 23–34.

61. Quoted in L'Estrange Ewen, *Witchcraft and Demonianism*, 33–34.

62. John of Reading, *Chronica*, ed. J. Tait, Manchester: Manchester University Press 1914, 176, 167. The carpenter incident is dated to 1366, the appearance of the Devil to the previous year.

63. Maxwell-Stuart, *An Abundance of Witches*, 150.

64. *Op. cit.*, 17.

65. Ewen, *Witchcraft and Demonianism*, 34.

66. E. Maunde Thompson (ed.), *Chronicon Angliae ab anno Domini 1328 usque ad annum 1388, auctore monacho quodam Sancti Albani*, London: Longman etc. 1874, 98–99.

67. H. T. Riley (ed.), *Memorials of London Life in the 13th, 14th, and 15th centuries*, London 1868, sub. 1382 and 1390.

68. Skemer, *Binding Words*, 194–197.

69. T. Wright, 'The municipal archives of Exeter', *Journal of the British Archaeological Association* 18 (1861), 307.

70. Kittredge, *Witchcraft in Old and New England*, 61, 164–165. Rider, *Magic and Impotence*, 97–98, 144, 157–158, 208. Goodman, 'The female spellcaster in Middle English romances', 46. Watkins Tibbals, 'Elements of magic in the romance of William of Palerne', *Modern Philology* 1 (1904), 356, 357, 364–365. Saunders, *Magic and the Supernatural in Mediaeval English Romance*, 158–162.

71. The *Middle English Dictionary* has examples of this word dating principally from the first half of the fifteenth century. They translate the Latin word *fascennina* which is actually related to the evil eye, although one Latin explanation from 1450 also translates it as 'a woman who knows how to chant spells', which fits this particular context.

72. *Op. cit.*, 576–577, 578–579, 580–581. Four times a year: see further G. W. Bernard, *The Late Mediaeval English Church: Vitality and Vulnerability before the Break with Rome*, New Haven & London: Yale University Press 2012, 25–26.

2 'Sorcery' and Treason: 1401–1499

1. Text given in Wright, *Contemporary Narrative*, x–xi.

2. Acts 16.16. Cf. Deuteronomy 18.11. 4 Kings 21.6 (Vulgate); 2 Kings 21.6 (AV).

3. Galfridus Anglicus, *Promptorium Parvulorum*, ed. A. L. Mayhew, London: Kegan Paul etc. 1908. Wycliffe's Bible translated the Latin *magus*, describing Simon in Acts 8.9 as 'witch'. On *sortilegium* in its developed sense, see C. Rider, 'Magic and unorthodoxy in late Mediaeval English pastoral manuals' in S. Page (ed.), *The Unorthodox Imagination in Late Mediaeval Britain*, Manchester & New York: Manchester University Press 2010, 96–114.

4. *The Register of Bishop Philip Repingdon, 1405–1419*, ed. M. Archer, 3 vols. Hereford: Lincoln Record Society 1963–82, 3.195–196.

5. F. M. Powicke & C.R. Cheney (eds), *Councils and Synods with Other Documents relating to the English Church*, 2 parts, Oxford: Clarendon Press 1964, Vol. 2, part 2, 1349.

6. *Calendar of Patent Rolls, 1422–1429*, 4 Henry VI: Part II, 363.

7. Kittredge, *Witchcraft in Old and New England*, 227. The original Norman-French is given in F. Palgrave, *An Essay upon the Original Authority of the King's Council*, London 1834, 87–88.

Here is preserved the English term 'soothsegger'. It should be added that according to Laurens Pignon's *Contre les devineurs* (1411), the term *sortilegium* covered a variety of practices and superstitions including making signs or saying meaningless words intended to cure human beings or animals, or attaching amulets to their neck or arm; or understanding certain incidents as ominous, such as stumbling when one leaves the house, finding that a mouse has gnawed a hole in one's clothes, encountering a look of hatred, or a monk, or a priest as one goes hunting, or seeing a new shirt or dress at that time, and so forth: J. R. Veenstra, *Magic and Divination at the Courts of Burgundy and France*, Leiden-New York-Köln: Brill 1998, 246–247. The majority of these instances, however, still make *sortilegium* a bridge between the present and the future.

8. See further Kieckhefer, *Magic in the Middle Ages*, 153–156.

9. *Unlocked Books: Manuscripts of Learned Magic in the Mediaeval Libraries of Central Europe*, Pennsylvania: The Pennsylvania State University Press 2008, 41–42.

10. The form *nigromantia* appears in *c.* 1125 and *nigromanticus* in *c.* 1212. These do not refer to a type of magic different from *necromantia*, but are merely variant spellings, perhaps because the Greek root *necro-* was unfamiliar to some copyists who altered it to conform to a Latin root they recognised.

11. *Concilia Magnae Britanniae et Hiberniae ab anno MCCCL ad annum MDXLV*, ed. D. Wilkins, London 1739, 3.392–393.

12. Myers, 'The captivity of a royal witch', 263–265. *Chronicle of London, 1089–1483*, ed. N. H. Nicholas & E. Tyrrell, London 1827, 107.

13. L. Thordike, *A History of Magic and Experimental Science*, 8 vols. New York: Columbia University Press 1923–1958, 3.588–589.

14. J. Amundesham, *Annales Monasterii Sancti Albani*, ed. H. T. Riley, London: Longmans, Green & Co. 1870, 1.38.

15. *Annales Monasterii Sancti Albani* 1.56–57.

16. Freeman, 'Sorcery at court and manor', 345 note 6.

17. J. E. J. Quicherat (ed.), *Procès de Condamnation et de Réhabilitation de Jeanne d'Arc*, 5 vols. Paris 1841–49, 1.209.

18. Text given in Wright, *Contemporary Narrative*, xii.

19. Freeman, 'Sorcery at court and manor', 346, 350.

20. Gilbert Kyme, *Dietarium de sanitatis custodia* = Appendix 9 in T. Hearne (ed.), *Liber Niger Scaccarii*, 2nd ed. London 1774, 2.553, 557–558.

21. E. Duffy, *The Stripping of the Altars*, New Haven & London: Yale University Press 1992, 197.

22. K. H. Vickers, *Humphrey, Duke of Gloucester*, London: Constable & Co. 1907, 181–182, 276.

23. Freeman, 'Sorcery at court and manor', 349.

24. Freeman, *loc. cit. supra*. Kittredge, *Witchcraft in Old and New England*, 82. Wright, *Contemporary Narrative*, xv. Griffiths, 'The trial of Eleanor Cobham', 387–388, 390.

25. T. Rymer (ed.), *Foedera, Conventiones, Literae, et Cuiuscunque generis Acta Publica*, 16 vols. London 1704–1713, 10.852. A. Petrina, *Cultural Politics in Fifteenth-Century England: The Case of Humphrey, Duke of Gloucester*, Leiden: Brill 2004, 149. See also *Ibid.*, 146–150. Freeman, *op. cit. supra*, 350–351. John Home, the other male in the case, was pardoned by the king because he had simply known about the actions of the others rather than being a participant in them, Freeman, 352.

26. R. C. Famiglietti, *Royal Intrigue: Crisis at the Court of Charles VI, 1392–1420*, New York: AMS Press, Inc. 1986, 1–6, 209–210 note 26.

27. One is reminded of John Cans and Robert Hickes from Norfolk who were accused in 1465 of summoning a spirit of the air and offering him a human sacrifice if he would show them where treasure was buried. This it duly did in return for the sacrifice of a red cockerel which Cans and Hickes baptised first, and then showed them in a crystal the location of a hoard of coins. Kittredge, *Witchcraft in Old and New England*, 206.

28. *Historical Collections of a Citizen of London in the Fifteenth Century*, ed. J. Gairdner, London 1876, 185. *Lincoln Diocese Documents, 1450–1544*, ed. A. Clark, London: Kegan

Paul, Trench, Trubner & Co. Ltd, 1914, 259, 260. Saunders, *Magic and the Supernatural in Mediaeval English Romance*, 72–73. Ewen, *Witch Hunting*, 10.

29. *Depositions and Other Ecclesiastical Proceedings*, London 1845, 29, 33.

30. english.byu.edu/facultysyllabi/KLawrence/FRIAR&BOY.pdf. N. Orme, *Mediaeval Children*, New Haven & London: Yale University Press 2003, 293–294.

31. On Cade's rebellion, see I. M. W. Harvey, *Jack Cade's Rebellion of 1450*, Oxford: Clarendon Press 1991, and R. A. Griffiths, *The Reign of Henry VI: The Exercise of Royal Authority*, 1422–1461, London: Ernest Benn Ltd 1981, 610–665.

32. *Literae Cantuarienses: The Letter Books of the Monastery of Christ Church, Canterbury*, ed. J. Brigstocke Sheppard, Vol. 3 (London 1889), 208.

33. Cade's origins are uncertain and at least one rumour had him a physician, in which case he could certainly have read and understood Latin. Griffiths, *op. cit. supra*, 617–619.

34. The text is given in Wright, *Contemporary Narrative*, xvi–xix, xx and in Summers, *The Geography of Witchcraft*, 105–108. See also C. L. Scofield, *The Life and Reign of Edward the Fourth*, 2 vols, London: Frank Cass & Co. Ltd. 1967, 1.498–499.

35. C. Ross, *Edward IV*, London: Eyre Methuen 1974, 240–241. C. L. Scofield, *op. cit. supra*, 2.189. M. A. Hicks, *False, Fleeting, Perjur'd Clarence*, Gloucester: Alan Sutton 1980, 133–136. Leland, 'Witchcraft and the Woodvilles', 278.

36. *Rerum Scoticarum Historia*, Aberdeen: James Chalmers 1762, Book 12, para. 38, 347. There is no mention in Buchanan's text of male magicians being burned as well, although one finds references to this in Sharpe (see next note), Sir Walter Scott, *Letters on Demonology and Witchcraft*, Letter Nine, and Christina Larner (see next note).

37. Christian Larner says this case may be mythical, *Enemies of God*, 65. So it may be, of course, but Larner cites as her source C. K. Sharpe, *A Historical Account of the Belief in Witchcraft in Scotland*, London & Glasgow 1884, 34, which obliquely cites Buchanan but gives no Latin or translation of the Latin, an important omission.

38. Buchanan, *op. cit. supra*, Book 12, para. 37, 347.

39. See M. Robbins, 'Mediaeval astrology and The Buke of the Sevyne Sagis', *Forum for Modern Language Studies* 38 (2002), 420–434. It is a pity, in view of her interesting treatment of the subject, that Robbins feels she has to include, 'A twenty-first-century perspective encourages us to consider James III's interest in astrology as an instance more of superstition than of regard for what we should think of today as modern science', 432. Why an historian should allow her or himself to be encouraged into an historical cul-de-sac is somewhat puzzling.

40. See the two entries by N. Royan in the *Dictionary of National Biography*, 6.418–421, 'Hector Boece', and 19.421–422, 'Giovanni Ferrerio'.

41. Wright, *Contemporary Narrative*, xix–xx. Summers, *The Geography of Witchcraft*, 108–110.

42. Summers, *op. cit. supra*, 110. A. Hanham, *Richard III and his Early Historians*, Oxford: Clarendon Press 1975, 165, 169, 179. Leland, 'Witchcraft and the Woodvilles', 267–268.

43. *Historia Anglica* 25.4.

44. Leland, 'Witchcraft and the Woodvilles', 271.

45. Leland, *op. cit. supra*, 281–287, 273–274.

46. For the text of Vignolles's confession, see *Letters and Papers Illustrative of the Reigns of Richard III and Henry VII*, ed. J. Gairdner, 3 vols. London: Longman, Green, Longman, and Roberts 1861–63, 2.318–323.

47. The rest of the confession is taken up with details of Perkin Warbeck's failure to find enough support in Flanders to enable him to come to England and challenge Henry VII for the throne, and other information incriminating Kendal in Warbeck's enterprise.

48. 'Documents relating to Perkin Warbeck, with remarks on his history', *Archaeologia or Miscellaneous Tracts relating to Antiquity* 27 (1838), 177–178.

49. See further Maxwell-Stuart, *Satan's Conspiracy*, 147. Vergil's observation reads: 'Then *hippomanes*, as shepherds quite rightly call it, trickles down from the groin as a slimy, poisonous liquid: *hippomanes*, which evil stepmothers often gather and mix with herbs to the accompaniment of harmful words', *Georgics* 3.280–283.

50. Ireland, 'Medicine, necromancy, and the law', 57–58.

51. Hale, *Series of Precedents and Proceedings*, 3, 7, 36–37. Slandering one's neighbours was an offence quite often brought before the court, and in the case of John Beer in 1476 this was combined with the complaint that 'he believes in *sortilegium*' (suggesting he credited some people's ability to see into and predict the future), which is a slightly odd way of exacerbating the principal charge of slander, *Ibid.*, 15–16.

52. Hale, *op. cit. supra*, 17, 20.

53. Hale, 32–33. The sum amounts to £3 16s 8d which is almost as much as the annual wage of a master carpenter at the time, and two and a half times that of a guild weaver.

54. *The Discoverie of Witchcraft*, Book 16, chap. 5. Scot goes on to explain how such tricks may be worked without diabolical aid. Hemmingsen, *Admonitio de superstitionibus magicis vitandis* (1575), Question 2, Bix–Ci.

55. Hale, *op. cit. supra*, 61, 63, 10–11.

3 Business Not Quite as Usual: 1502–1542

1. Hale, *Series of Precedents and Proceedings*, 77–78.

2. This is not to say that the apothecary himself may not have used magic in gathering his herbs, for example. 'Have you collected medicinal herbs with evil incantations?' asked the Corrector, Burchard of Worms, McNeill & Gamer, *Mediaeval Handbooks of Penance*, 330.

3. Hale, *op. cit. supra*, 84.

4. *A Discourse of the Damned Art of Witchcraft* (1608), 149: 'the using and making of characters, images, or figures ... a mere practice of enchantment ... a charm, though no words be used'.

5. Dee, *A True and Faithful Relation*, ed. M. Casaubon (1659), Berkeley, CA: Golem Media 2008, 57–58.

6. See further S. Melchior-Bonnet, *The Mirror: A History*, English trans. New York & London: Routledge 2002, 16–17, 188–191; images 123, 202, 15. On mirrors and treasure hunting, see J. Dillinger, *Magical Treasure Hunting in Europe and North America*, London: Palgrave Macmillan 2012, 95–96.

7. What follows is based on the documents published by J. Raine, 'Proceedings connected with a remarkable charge of sorcery, brought against James Richardson and others, in the diocese of York, AD 1510', *The Archaeological Journal* 16 (1859), 71–81. Details of the participants are given by Billingsley, *The Mixenden Treasure*, 6.

8. See further Billingsley, *op. cit. supra*, 30–31.

9. Fr Wilkinson's grimoire, along with the lamen, was later handed over to the Mayor of York.

10. William Wilson, however, recollected a different date: the Monday after Candlemas (2 February).

11. 'He cheerfully confessed himself a trickster', *Witch Hunting in Old and New England*, 208. Dillinger follows Kittredge's lead, 'he coolly admitted that he was a fraud', and seems to overlook the likelihood that the book of 'astronomy' to which the deposition refers was actually one on astrology, *Magical Treasure Hunting in Europe and North America*, 141.

12. *The Discoverie of Witchcraft*, Book 1, chap. 2.

13. *Statutes of the Realm* 3.31–32 = 3 Henry VIII c. 11.

14. On the new wave of prosecutions, see J. Fines, 'Heresy trials in the diocese of Coventry and Lichfield', *Journal of Ecclesiastical History* 14 (1963), 160–174.

15. J. Stowe, *Annales, or a Generale Chronicle of England from Brute until the present yeere of Christ, 1580*, London 1580, 859–862.

16. B. J. Harris, *Edward Stafford, Third Duke of Buckingham, 1478–1521*, Stanford: Stanford University Press 1986, 185. C. S. L. Davies offers no further comment than a reference to 'Hopkind's political prophecies' which gives no indication that both men were, in effect, engaged in a magical discourse, 'Edward Stafford', *Oxford Dictionary of National Biography* 52.42.

17. Kittredge, *Witchcraft in Old and New England*, 62.

18. Hale, *Series of Precedents and Proceedings*, 102, 107–108. Thomas, *Religion and the Decline of Magic*, 283. When a man with an arm 'out of joint' visited Elizabeth Cracklow in 1546, she made her husband preach over it and then she herself signed it with the cross in several places and got her husband to say a prayer, *Ibid.*, 216. 'Stamping' in Margaret Hunt's record refers to pounding the herbs in a mortar along with the holy water to make a compress for the sores.

19. Kittredge, *op. cit. supra*, 210, 65, 189.

20. The following is based on his letter to Wolsey, the text of which can be found in D. Turner, 'Brief remarks accompanied by documents illustrative of trial by jury, treasure-trove, and the invocation of spirits for the discovery of hidden treasure in the sixteenth century', *Norfolk Archaeology* 1 (1847), 57–64.

21. Stapleton's case was by no means the only treasure hunting episode in and around Norwich at this time. In 1521, the mayor and aldermen of the town heard about William smith and two others who met several priests in a private house and there had the priests conjure a spirit in a crystal, with a view to finding the location of treasure; and in June the following year, in the same house, Stapleton held a mirror while a spirit was raised within it. How dubious an experience this was for one of the participants may be gauged from the remarks of one of those present. 'He could not perceive anything thereby, but he says that George Dowsing did arise in a glass [*mirror*] a little thing of the length of an inch or thereabout, but whether it was a spirit or a shadow, he cannot tell. But the said George said it was a spirit', Turner, *op. cit. supra*, 52–53. Kittredge, *Witchcraft in Old and New England*, 20.

22. *Letters and Papers, Foreign and Domestic, of the Reign of Henry VIII*, Vol. 13, Part 1, ed. J. Gairdner, London: Longman, Green 1892, item 41. See also G. Elton, *Policy and Police*, Cambridge: Cambridge University Press 1972, 49.

23. For a full account of this episode, see Elton, *op. cit. supra*, 50–56. See also Kittredge, *op. cit. supra*, 62–64.

24. Thomas, *Religion and the Decline of Magic*, 218.

25. D. Watt, 'Elizabeth Barton', *Dictionary of National Biography* 4.201–204. A. D. Cheney's essay, 'The holy maid of Kent', *Transactions of the Royal Historical Society* 18 (1904), 107–129, is affected by the prejudices of its period and therefore has limited value.

26. Neame, *The Holy Maid of Kent*, 151–152. The quotation comes from one of St Thomas's letters to Cromwell.

27. Kittredge, *Witchcraft in Old and New England*, 64–65. Scot, *The Discoverie of Witchcraft* Book 7, chap. 1.

28. Quoted in Thomas, *Religion and the Decline of Magic*, 177.

29. W. C. Hazlitt (ed.), *Shakespeare's Jest-Books*, London : Henry Sotheran & Co. 1881, 14–17; quotation, 17. The story is taken from a collection called 'Merry Tales' which was first printed in 1525 and reissued in 1558.

30. R. Bigelow Merriman, *The Life and Letters of Thomas Cromwell*, Vol. 1, Oxford: Oxford University Press 1902, 117–118.

31. Kittredge, *Witchcraft in Old and New England*, 156, 157.

32. *Letters and Paper, Foreign and Domestic, of the Reign of Henry VIII*, Vol. 10, January–June 1536, item 284: 29 January, letter to Charles V. But see the comments by E. W. Ives who pours cold water on any interpretation of this remark which might suggest that Anne Boleyn really did use any form of magic, *The Life and Death of Anne Boleyn*, Malden, MA: Blackwell Publishing 2004, 298.

33. For this and an account of the episode, see R. Pitcairn (ed.), *Ancient Criminal Trials in Scotland*, 3 vols. Edinburgh: Bannatyne Club 1833, Vol. 1, Part 1, 187–195. Verdict, 191.

34. *Op. cit.*, Edinburgh 1643–4, Part 2, 261.

35. Witchcraft is not even mentioned in connection with the case by C. A. Gladdery, 'Janet Douglas', *Oxford Dictionary of National Biography* 16.687–688.

36. M. St Clare Byrne (ed.), *The Lisle Letters*, 6 vols. Chicago & London: University of Chicago Press 1981, 4.347.

37. Quoted in Kittredge, *Witchcraft in Old and New England*, 114.

38. This is the consensus of opinion, although J. W. Harris suggested the play could have been written by 1533 or 1534 and perhaps as early as *c.* 1531, John Bale: *A Study in the Minor Literature of the Reformation*, Illinois: University of Illinois Press 1940, 68, 85. The quotations which follow are taken from the edition published in London and Edinburgh in 1908. On the staging of Three Laws, see further T. B. Blatt, *The Plays of John Bale: A Study of Ideas, Technique, and Style*, Copenhagen: G. E. C. Gads 1968, 133–148. On the structure of the play, see L. P. Fairfield, *John Bale: Mythmaker for the English Reformation*, Indiana: Purdue University Press 1976, 57–62.

39. Does 'blow' here mean 'fart'? It would be consistent both with Bale's coarseness and with Mediaeval/early modern amusement at scatological humour.

40. 'Representations of women in Tudor historiography: John Bale and the rhetoric of exemplarity', *Renaissance and Reformation/Renaissance et Réforme* 22 (1998), 48.

41. See MacFarlane, *Witchcraft in Tudor and Stuart England*, 95, 97.

42. Quoted in Gourley, 'Feminised idolatry', 3.

43. The process of imposition can be followed in E. Duffy, *The Stripping of the Altars*, New Haven & London: Yale University Press 1992. The Lutheran ideal in relation to witches is discussed by S. Brauner, *Fearless Wives and Frightened Shrews*, Amherst: University of Massachusetts Press 1995. Brauner's material relates to Germany but, *mutatis mutandis*, has relevance for sixteenth-century England, too.

44. Nothing is as simple as one can make it seem to be, of course. For an overview of some of the relevant complexities, see Gaskill, *Crime and Mentalities in Early Modern England*, 33–78.

45. For what follows, see *Letters and Papers, Foreign and Domestic, of the Reign of Henry VIII*, Vol. 13, Part 1. January–July, 1538, nos 487, 705, 1282, 1350.

46. The black fast was a perfectly orthodox fast of the Church. 'Black' simply indicated that it was severe, especially during Lent which was a fasting period anyway.

47. As there were not four or five prisons in York, what this probably means is either that they were kept in different cells in the same prison, or that some were kept under lock and key in separate buildings, such as the cellars of private houses or church steeples, this being common custom at the time.

48. *Letters and Papers, Foreign and Domestic, of the Reign of Henry VIII*, Vol. 15, no. 498 (para. 59) and no. 784. Buggery, as defined by the Act, had a much wider range of meaning that it has now, so exactly what Hungerford did with his servants is open to speculation. Kittredge, who reports the incident, coyly avoids the question, *Witchcraft in Old and New England*, 65–66. See also M. St Clare Byrne (ed.), *The Lisle Letters* 6.279–280.

49. *Proceedings and Ordinances of the Privy Council of England*, ed. H. Nicolas, Vol. 7 (London 1837), 12. The following quotations and references come from 13, 14, 27, 30, 38.

50. *Proceedings of the English Privy Council, op. cit. supra*, 97, 104, 106–107.

51. The text of the Act may be found in Gibson, *Witchcraft and Society*, 1–2.

52. Dillinger, *Magical Treasure Hunting in Europe and North America*, 117, 154. Bale quoted by Cameron, *Enchanted Europe*, 210. Ewen, *Witchcraft and Demonianism*, 415.

53. *Letters and Papers, Foreign and Domestic, of the Reign of Henry VIII*, Vol. 17, item 1012, para. 48.

54. What follows is based on the detailed account of the episode by Ryrie, *The Sorcerer's Tale*, especially 1–33.

4 Witches to the North, South, and West: 1549–1563

1. Quoted in Kittredge, *Witchcraft in Old and New England*, 68.

2. Psalm 50 begins 'The Lord God of gods has spoken'.

3. Text in J. G. Nichols (ed.), *Narratives of Days of the Reformation*, London: Westminster 1859, 331–335.

4. See further Cameron, *Enchanted Europe*, 174–195.

5. Hooper, *A Declaration of the Ten Holy Commandments*, ed. S. Carr, Cambridge: Cambridge University Press 1843, 307–308, 329. On Protestant propaganda equating Catholic miracles

with the work of the Devil and acts of magic, see further H. L. Parish, *Monks, Miracles, and Magic*, London & New York: Routledge 2005, 45–70.

6. Nichols, *Narratives of the Days of Reformation*, 172–175.

7. Nichols, *op. cit. supra*, 326–329, 331, 335. Kittredge, *Witchcraft in Old and New England*, 71.

8. *Acts of the Privy Council of England*, new series, Vol. 4, ed. J. Roche Dasent, London 1892, 12, 13, 20, 94, 131.

9. Camden Miscellany XII, ed. C. L. Kingsford, London 1910, 36–37.

10. Hale, *Series of Precedents and Proceedings*, 139.

11. Thomas, *Religion and the Decline of Magic*, 296, 290. Kittredge, *Witchcraft in Old and New England*, 230.

12. G. Parry, *The Arch-Conjuror of England: John Dee*, New Haven & London: Yale University Press 2011, 23, 31–36.

13. Maxwell-Stuart, *Satan's Conspiracy*, 30–32.

14. See further M. F. Graham, *The Uses of Reform: Godly Discipline and Popular Behaviour in Scotland and Beyond, 1560–1610*, Leiden-New York-Köln: Brill 1996, 38–44.

15. What follows owes much to Goodare, 'The Scottish Witchcraft Act', 39–67, although I differ from him in certain points of interpretation.

16. Here I differ from Goodare, who lays more of an emphasis upon the charmer as the target because charmers have clients and witches do not, and because the Act also seeks to punish those who consult a magical operator. If, however, one wanted to harm an individual or creature, either directly or indirectly through, let us say, bad weather which would ruin his or her crops, one would go to a witch, not a charmer for this service. So witches, too, could have clients.

17. *History of the Reformation in Scotland*, ed. W. McGavin, 3rd ed. Glasgow & London 1841, 279.

18. Knox, *op. cit. supra*, 283–284, 292.

19. Knox, *supra*, 271.

20. Knox, *op. cit.*, 285.

21. Prominent individuals, however, were quite liable to be accused of working magic. Knox himself complained in 1561 that he had been slandered of magic and necromancy, *op. cit.*, 252.

22. Kittredge, *Witchcraft in Old and New England*, 255–256. E. Jeffries Davis, 'An unpublished manuscript of the Lords' Journals for April and May, 1559', *English Historical Review* 28 (1913), 538, 539.

23. Kittredge, *op. cit. supra*, 257–264. Jones, 'Defining superstitions', 187–203.

24. *Calendar of State Papers, Domestic, 1547–1580*, 137 notes the violent conduct of George Throgmorton, the husband, towards witnesses; 142 notes the examination of those witnesses.

25. Kittredge, *op. cit. supra*, 551, note 50.

26. Ewen, *Witch Hunting and Witch Trials*, 12.

27. *Fascino* means 'enchant principally by means of the eyes'. A *fascinum* was an amulet hung round a child's neck to ward off the effects of harmful magic, mainly that conveyed by the evil eye.

28. Ewen, *op. cit. supra*, 77–78. My translation differs in places from that offered by Ewen.

29. Kittredge gives a slightly confusing account, buried in his narrative of another contemporary incident, *Witchcraft in Old and New England*, 258–259. Clearer are Jones, 'Defining superstitions', 193 and M. S. Lovell, *Bess of Hardwick*, St. Ives: Little, Brown 2005, 153–157.

30. The pamphlet begins, for example, 'Amongst other the godly, wholesome, and profitable sayings of the divine philosopher Plato, I call to remembrance this one as most necessary for all Christians to be had in memory' – which the writer then quotes in Latin, although he provides a translation, too. In fact, Coxe was a former monk who seems to have earned part of his living as a quack physician, so he may actually have been more learned than Coke's designation 'yeoman' would have us believe.

31. William Fulke, 'This Nostradamus reigned here so like a tyrant with his soothsayings, that

without the good lucks [*sic*] of his prophecies it was thought that nothing could be brought to effect ... Except the true preachers of God's holy word had sharply rebuked the people for crediting such vain prophecies, there should have been none ends of fears and expectation', *Anti-Prognosticon* (1560), partly quoted in Ryrie, *The Sorcerer's Tale*, 127.

32. J. Hunter, 'Biographical memoirs of Sir William Saint Loe', *The Retrospective Review and Historical and Antiquarian Magazine*, 2nd series, 2 (1828), 323.

33. Barbara Rosen, who quotes this passage in *Witchcraft in England*, 62–63, questions whether 'ligations' should not be 'libations', but ligatures and magical knots in cord or thread were common features of certain types of magic such as love magic. See, for example, Cornelius Agrippa, *De occulta philosophia* Book 1, chapter 40: 'Bindings, their various kinds and the way they are usually used.'

34. Jones, 'Defining superstitions', 191–192.

35. Quoted in Summers, *The Geography of Witchcraft*, 116.

36. *Calendar of State Papers, Domestic, 1547–1580*, 174.

37. Quoted by Jones, *op. cit. supra*, 196.

38. Kittredge, *Witchcraft in Old and New England*, 259.

39. Camden, *Annales rerum gestarum Angliae et Hiberniae regnante Elizabetha*, London 1607, sub anno 1562. Kittredge, *op. cit. supra*, 260.

40. See D. M. Dean, 'Sir Simonds D'Ewes' Bills of no importance', *Parliamentary History* 3 (1984), 158.

41. A writ addressed to a sheriff, instructing him to take sureties for the prisoner's appearance in court, and to let the prisoner out on bail.

42. On this, see further T. M. Smallwood, 'The transmission of charms in English, Mediaeval and modern' in J. Roper (ed.), *Charms and Charming in Europe*, Basingstoke: Palgrave Macmillan 2004, 11–12. Unfortunately, however, Smallwood sometimes uses 'incantations' and 'charms' as though they were synonymous. So does Elina Bozoky, *Charmes et Prières Apotropaïques*, Turnhout-Belgium: Brepols 2003, 34–36. Neither takes into account the necessity of close definition of terms in a legal document.

43. Ewen, *Witch Hunting and Witch Trials*, 117–118.

5 A Growing Wave of Witchcrafts: 1564–1582

1. See further D. M. Ogier, *Reformation and Society in Guernsey*, Woodbridge: The Boydell Press 1996, 74–81; quotation, 79. Linwood Pitts, *Witchcraft and the Devil Lore*, 13, 34. Bellows, *Channel Islands Witchcraft*, 19. On Tulouff: De Garis, *Folklore of Guernsey*, 168, 169–170.

2. Anon, *The Mirror of Justices*, ed. W. J. Whittaker, London 1895, 15–16. The passage is also quoted by Bellows, *op. cit. supra*, 69.

3. Moore, *Folklore and Witchcraft*, 1. Sharpe, 'Witchcraft in the early modern Isle of Man', 13.

4. *The Lex Scripta of the Isle of Man*, new. ed. Douglas 1819, 58–59.

5. Craine, *Manannan's Isle*, 16.

6. Gibson, *Hanged for Witchcraft*, 115–117, 127–132, 143–149; quotations, 156, 129, 131.

7. Gibson, *op. cit. supra*, 159.

8. Gibson, 164, 166–167, 181. See also Young, 'Elizabeth Lowys', 879–885. On Anne Vale, see Ewen, *Witch Hunting and Witch Trials*, 118.

9. Ewen, *op. cit. supra*, 118–119. *Acts of the Privy Council of England*, London 1893, 7.200–201.

10. The text is given in Gibson, *Early Modern Witches*, 11–24.

11. *De praestigiis daemonum*, translated as *Witches, Devils, and Doctors in the Renaissance*, New York: Binghamton 1991, Book 2, chap. 1. Cf. Scot, *The Discoverie of Witchcraft*, Book 7, chap. 1.

12. *A Candle in the Dark*, 81.

13. See J. M. Riddle, *Eve's Herbs: A History of Contraception and Abortion in the West*, Cambridge, Mass. & London: Harvard University Press 1997, 129. On the kind of herbal

mixtures used to procure abortion, see *Ibid.*, 145–148.

14. Gibson, *Early Modern Witches*, 44.

15. Ewen, *Witch Hunting and Witch Trials*, 120.

16. *A Candle in the Dark*, 65. Cf. Scot, 'The Papists have many conjurations, so as neither water, nor fire, nor bread, nor wine, nor wax, nor tallow, nor church, nor churchyard, nor altar, nor altar-cloth, nor ashes, nor coals, nor bells, nor bell-ropes ... are without their form of conjuration', *The Discoverie of Witchcraft* Book 15, chap. 28. See also Duffy, *The Stripping of the Altars*, 266–287.

17. Maxwell-Stuart, *Satan*, 142.

18. Ewen, *Witch Hunting and Witch Trials*, 296. Cf. a witch from Northamptonshire in 1612 whose familiar kept urging her to kill herself until 'at last she made good the Devil's word, and to prevent the justice of the law and to save the hangman a labour, cut her own throat'. Quoted in Darr, *Marks of An Absolute Witch*, 145. The temptation was also noted by James VI, 'If he [the Devil] find them in deep despair, [he tries] by all means to augment the same and to persuade them by some extraordinary means to put themselves down, which very commonly they do', *Daemonologie* Book 2, chap. 6.

19. See *Calendar of Assize Records: Essex Indictments: Elizabeth I*, ed. J. Cockburn, London: Stationery Office 1978, nos 94, 95, 109, 206, 264. The verdict in another witchcraft case (no. 186 from 1564) is not known. It involved the magical death of a cow. Joan's case is no. 263. Those of Francis and Agnes are 273 and 274.

20. *Malleus* Part 3, question 4. Scot, *The Discoverie of Witchcraft* Book 2, chap. 1. James VI, *Daemonologie* Book 3, chap. 6. Rosen, *Witchcraft in England*, 109–110, 112–113. Gibson, *Early Modern Witches*, 133, 136–137. Potts, *The Wonderfull Discoverie of Witches*, 50–51.

21. Darr, *Marks of An Absolute Witch*, 199–203.

22. Darr, *op. cit. supra*, 202. Durston, *Witchcraft and Witch Trials*, 417.

23. *Witchcraft and Religion*, 99.

24. See M. Dalton, *The Country Justice* (1618), edition of London 1646, 378, quoting the thirteenth-century jurist Henry de Bracton: 'A minor may be a witness or an accuser, but the accused must be attached until the accuser becomes of age.'

25. See further R. Hutton, *The Rise and Fall of Merry England*, Oxford: Oxford University Press 1994, 106–108.

26. Marion Gibson elucidates these points in *Reading Witchcraft*, 160–166. A more virulently anti-Catholic pamphlet dealing with a male witch, John Walsh, who was said to have learned his magic from a Catholic priest, was published in December, 1566, four months after Walsh's trial in Exeter. Gibson, *Early Modern Witches*, 25–32.

27. See A. Pettegree, *The Book in the Renaissance*, New Haven & London: Yale University Press 2010, 339–341. Cf. the situation in Germany, *Ibid.*, 134–136.

28. Paul Voss points out that 'the majority of the printed news pamphlets deal with matters foreign in content and location', 'Print culture, ephemera, and the Elizabethan news pamphlet', *Literature Compass* 3 (2006), 1055.

29. London continued to have its own cases. On 7 September 1566, Margery Skelton appeared before the commissary, 'suspect of the arts of sorcery: concerning which the Master examined her upon the Gospels, that is to say, in these words – [*what follows is in English*] whether she ever used to heal any of her neighbours that were sick or diseased, either women or children. And she said she hath. With praying of her prayers, she hath healed six persons', Hale, *Series of Precedents and Proceedings*, 148.

30. *Calendar of Assize Records: Essex Indictments: Elizabeth I*, nos. 568 and 622. Ewen, *Witch Hunting and Witch Trials*, 125.

31. *Calendar of Assize Records, op. cit. supra*, nos 580, 593, 632, 667.

32. *Calendar of Assize Records, op. cit. supra* (Salmon) nos 95, 109, 571; (Steadman) no. 582.

33. *Calendar, op. cit. supra*, nos 619 and 620.

34. There are problems with the exact dates involved, but these do not affect the substance of what I am saying here. See further Gibson, *Reading Witchcraft*, 55–56.

35. *Calendar of Assize Records, op. cit. supra*, no. 295.

36. Gibson, *Early Modern Witches*, 43–44.

37. *Calendar of Assize Records: Kent Indictments: Elizabeth I*, ed. J. S. Cockburn, London: Stationery Office 1979, nos 716, 919, 931.

38. I am grateful to Professor Clive Homes for discussing this question with me.

39. Ewen, *Witch Hunting and Witch Trials*, 124, 125, 131, 135, 146, 148, 156–157, 166, 184, 185.

40. Middlesex: Ewen, *Witchcraft and Demonianism*, 430 (1574 & 1575); 431 (1576 & 1577); 431 (1582); 431 (1585: this is the case of Joan Berringer who was found not guilty of killing a woman by witchcraft); 431 (1591); 431–432 (1597). Norfolk: Katharine Smythe was accused in 1575 of killing Mary Dogeon by witchcraft, but was acquitted, H. Harrod, 'Notes on the records of the corporation of Great Yarmouth', *Norfolk Archaeology* 4 (1855), 248. Elizabeth Butcher and Cecilia Atkins were pilloried for witchcraft in 1583, and 'Mother' Gabley was accused of killing thirteen men by the same means in the same year, Ewen, *Witchcraft and Demonianism*, 427, 448–449.

41. Durston, *Witchcraft and Witch Trials*, 424–425. B. Mackerell, *History and Antiquities of King's Lynn*, London 1738, 231, 233. Elizabeth Housego, too, was executed there in 1598 on the same charge as Mary, but the means of her death are not described, *Ibid.*, 232. Margaret Grame: *Historical Manuscripts Commission, Reports Various*, 2.243–244. J. S. Cockburn, *Calendar of Assize Records, Kent Indictments, Elizabeth*, London: Stationery Office 1979, no. 537.

42. Ewen, *Witchcraft and Demonianism*, 448. A full account of the Warboys case is given by P. C. Almond, *The Witches of Warboys*, London: I. B. Tauris 2008.

43. Ewen, *op. cit. supra*, 425.

44. Tyler, 'The Church courts at York', 99, 93–94.

45. Tyler, *op. cit. supra*, 100. Pickering, *Witch-Hunting in England*, 204–205. Ewen, *Witchcraft and Demonianism*, 413, 414. Ewen, *Witch Hunting and Witch Trials*, 131–132. Ewen, *Witchcraft and Demonianism*, 428, 426.

46. 'You will not fear the terror of the night, or the arrow that flies by day, or the pestilence that stalks in darkness, or the destruction that wastes at noon', Psalm 91.5.

47. Gibson, *Early Modern Witches*, 25–32. Fairies, as Walsh said, could be dangerous as well as helpful. Cf. the case of Jenkin Pearson's wife who appeared before Durham's ecclesiastical court in the late 1560s. Catherine Fenwicke's cousin had a child who had fallen sick, so Catherine went to Mrs Pearson who said the child 'was taken with the fairy, and bade her send two [people] for south-running water: and these two shall not speak by the way, and the child shall be washed in that water. Dip the [child's] shirt in the water, and so hang it upon a hedge all that night, and on the morrow the shirt will be gone and the child recover health. But the shirt was not gone as she said'. Catherine paid Pearson's wife three pence for her pains. Otherwise, '*she knoweth not whether she was a witch or not*', Quoted in Ewen, *Witchcraft and Demonianism*, 447–448. My italics. Tenno, *Religious Deviance*, 108–113.

48. G. Parry, *The Arch-Conjuror of England, John Dee*, New Haven & London: Harvard University Press 2011, 257–261. Poole, *The Lancashire Witches*, 65. Cf. the curious case of Mrs Malter and Anne Vicars, both from Essex. In 1570 occurred a sequence of events which, starting with an attempt to cure a husband of possible bewitchment, ended in a series of afflictions and deaths which brought both women to court. 'A woman deposed that her husband, "being not well in his wits", Malter's wife advised him that he was bewitched, and "caused a trivet to be set and certain pieces of elder and white hazel wood to be laid upon the trivet across, with a fire under it", and taught him prayers, whereby he should be "delivered of his bewitching, or his witch should consume as the fire did". Examinate having rebuked Malter, the latter bewitched to death two of her husband's sheep. A sow was also found dead with her nose lying upon the groundsel of the suspect's house. Another witness testified that her mistress having displeased Malter's wife, "a speckled bird fluttered among the milk pans, and with her feet and wings slubbered therein". She endeavoured to drive it away and finally calling her mistress "it came downstairs a very toad". For six weeks afterwards no churning was ever successful. A third woman declared that three years last past, being taken with a "strange sickness, her body

disfigured, her lips great and black, and she almost out of her wits", one Cobham of Rumford advised her that Anne Vicars was responsible, but that as long as he lived she should have no power over her, and not until Cobham died did she again suffer. Another woman deposed that coming from Rumford market with Anne Vicars the latter declared that she "smelt either a whore or thief". Upon passing one Maud Ingarsole, Vicars covered her face with her apron, making various crosses. Maud fell sick and lost an eye with a stroke. Corroborated by Maud Ingarsole. Agnes, wife of Thomas Combres, testified that upon a falling out, Anne Vicars cursed her, wishing her eyes out. Within two days she fell down as dead, and afterwards had "marvellous pain in her eyes".' Ewen, *Witchcraft and Demonianism*, 149–150.

49. Ewen, *op. cit. supra*, 450. In 1599 in London, 'an innkeeper learned that the cause of the illness of his child, who had been bewitched to death, was Anne Kerke, she being shown to him in a glass [mirror] by a cunning man', *Ibid.*, 190.

50. Gibson, *Early Modern Witches*, 50–71. Ewen, *Witchcraft and Demonianism*, 449. Honeybone, *Wicked Practise and Sorcerye*, 163. *Calendar of State Papers, Domestic, Elizabeth 1581–1590*, ed. R. Lemon, London 1865, 644.

51. See further Sharpe, *Instruments of Darkness*, 95–100. Gibson, *Early Modern Witches*, 3–7. Behringer, 'Witchcraft and the media' in Plummer & Barnes (eds), *Ideas and Cultural Margins in Early Modern Germany*, 217–236.

6 The Islands, Another Witchcraft Act, and a Family Feud: 1582–1590

1. An abbreviated version of the text is given in Seymour, *Irish Witchcraft and Demonology*, 60–65.

2. Sir Warham Sentleger writing to Elizabeth in 1582, *Calendar of State Papers: Ireland: 1574–1585*, ed. H. C. Hamilton, London: Longmans, Green, Reader, & Dyer 1867, 361.

3. Rich, *A New Description of Ireland*, London 1610, 7–9. Morison, *Itinerary*, London 1617, 314–315.

4. 'English reformation and Irish witches', 26.

5. 'Irish immunity to witch-hunting', 87–91.

6. Thomas, *Religion and the Decline of Magic*, 727, 34, 43. As long ago as 1187, Geraldus Cambrensis had remarked that in Wales, Ireland, and Scotland, old women used to change themselves into hares in order to steal people's milk by sucking their cows' udders, *Topographia Hibernica* 2.19. G. Williams, 'Of the nature of popular belief and devotion it is extremely difficult to generalise ... At its best it was sincere, earnest, and deep-rooted. But within it there was a very large admixture of superstition, credulity, and ignorance. Custom predominated over conviction, and was to prove as resistant to the efforts of Catholic reformers as to those of Protestant reformers', *Welsh Reformation Essays*, Cardiff: University of Wales Press 1967, 39. See also the citations of C. Hill, *Change and Continuity in Seventeenth-Century England*, London: Weidenfeld & Nicolson 1974, 7 and 9.

7. Hale, *Series of Precedents and Proceedings*, 107–108. *Acts of the Privy Council of England*, new series, 5.362. Ewen, *Witchcraft and Demonianism*, 422. Quotations from the page cited.

8. Suggett, *A History of Magic and Witchcraft in Wales*, fig. 3.

9. Suggett, *op. cit. supra*, 14–18. Clark & Morgan, 'Religion and magic in Elizabethan Wales', 35.

10. Suggett, *op. cit. supra*, 27–41.

11. A photograph of the text is given in Suggett, *op. cit. supra*, fig. 8.

12. A. D. Carr, 'The Mostyns of Mostyn, 1540–1642', *The Flintshire Historical Society Journal* 30 (1981–82), 131.

13. See further I. Mortimer, *The Time Traveller's Guide to Elizabethan England*, London: The Bodley Head 2012, 9–10, 194–198, and the literature cited there.

14. Sharpe, 'Witchcraft in the early modern Isle of Man', 13, 19.

15. *The Lex Scripta of the Isle of Man*, new ed. Douglas 1819, 72.

16. Bellows, *Channel Islands Witchcraft*, 65.

17. Balleine, 'Witch trials in Jersey', quoted in Bellows, *op. cit. supra*, 8 and 9.

18. Bellows, *op. cit. supra*, 20. Ogier, 'Night revels and werewolfery', 53–54.

19. Quoted in Lake, *These Haunted Islands*, 54–55.

20. Cf. the sentence passed on Simon Vauldin in 1591. 'Whereas Symon Vauldin, of the parish of St Brelade, having confessed to have communicated and spoken to the Devil on many occasions, under the form of a cat or crow, and having for long been suspected of the crime of sorcery as well as the said apparitions, and having been subjected to the question of his guilt or innocence, his life or death, to an Enquête du Pays, according to the laws of the country. The said Enquête of 24, having examined their conscience on the action of the said Vauldin, unanimously swore on their soul that they believed that the said Vauldin was a sorcerer who lived a wicked and detestable life. After the Enquête the said Symon Vauldin was condemned to be dressed in a linen surplice, tied to a post and strangled and his body burnt until it be reduced to ashes. All his goods, chattels and property confiscated and forfeited for the Crown and others to whom it should belong.' Quoted in Lake, *op. cit. supra*, 129. Lake reproduces pictures of the Greffier's doodles in the margin of the official record, showing the accused hanging from a gibbet over a fire, *Ibid.*, 57, 58.

21. *Channel Islands Witchcraft*, 14.

22. D. M. Ogier, *Reformation and Society in Guernsey*, Woodbridge: The Boydell Press 1996, 62. Foxe, *Acts and Monuments* (1583), 1969. Linwood Pitts, *Witchcraft and Devil Lore in the Channel Islands*, 7. Ten years later, on 11 April 1566, Gosselin publicly turned Protestant, although how far this may have been genuine and how far political is difficult to say, Ogier, *op. cit.*, 83.

23. Ogier, *op. cit. supra*, 41, 63–69. T. Thornton, *The Channel Islands, 1370–1640: Between England and Normandy*, Woodbridge: The Boydell Press 2012, 97–99.

24. Guillaume de Beauvoir had applied to be relieved of his office by 30 July, when he is described by an official document as 'the late Bailiff', but the Eustace incident is dated 15 May, so it seems to have taken place under his stewardship. See F. B. Tupper, *The History of Guernsey and its Bailiwick*, Guernsey: S. Barbet 1854, 152.

25. Linwood Pitts, *Witchcraft and Devil Lore*, 35. He seems to have missed information about an incident in 1581. Lake, *These Haunted Islands*, 132. A more up-to-date list is given at http://archiver.rootsweb.ancestry.com/th/read/CHANNEL-ISLANDS/2002-12/10405.

26. Ogier, *Reformation and Society in Guernsey*, 157. *Recueil d'ordonnances de la Cour Royale*, ed. R. MacCulloch, Vol. 1, Guernsey: E. Barbet 1852.

27. This account is based on McGuinness, 'The Guernsey witchcraft trials', 623–644.

28. This must surely mean small pieces of the mechanism, since the whole treadle would have been very large and one, not to mention more than one, impossible to fit inside a mattress, let alone pass unnoticed by the occupant of the bed.

29. Gifford, *A Dialogue Concerning Witches and Witchcrafts*, 21. Perkins, *A Discourse of the Damned Art of Witchcraft*, 110. Roberts, *A Treatise of Witchcraft*, 42. See also Almond, *The Witches of Warboys*, 38–43.

30. MacCulloch, *Guernsey Folk Lore*, 306–314.

31. See further Thornton, *The Channel Islands*, 111–131.

32. Figures from W. Monter, 'Toads and eucharists: the male witches of Normandy, 1564–1660', *French Historical Studies* 20 (Autumn 1997), 573. Cf. appeals to the Parlement of Paris against conviction for witchcraft rose very noticeably in the 1580s, dipped in the early 1590s, and then picked up and rose dramatically once more, continuing into the first decade of the seventeenth century. See A. Soman, *Sorcellerie et Justice Criminelle: Le Parlement de Paris, 16e–18e siècles*, Hampshire: Ashgate Publishing 1992, fig. 1.

33. Maxwell-Stuart, *Satan's Conspiracy*, 30–34. Black, *A Calendar of Cases of Witchcraft*, 21.

34. She had been Queen Regnant of Scotland since December 1542 and Queen Consort of France since July 1559.

35. 'The Scottish Witchcraft Act', 42–51. I am indebted to Dr Goodare's seminal article for this summary.

36. *The Acts of the Parliaments of Scotland*, Edinburgh 1844, 2.539. This version is translated from Scots, and divided into paragraphs for greater ease of reference.

37. *Demonology* Book 2, chap. 2. The king's treatise was published in 1597, but was written or at least planned several years earlier, quite possibly in 1591, as a result of his personal experiences of witchcraft. See further Normand & Roberts, *Witchcraft in Early Modern Scotland*, 327–328. The Jesuit Del Rio pointed to something similar. 'Sortilegi' was an ancient name for those who sought to foretell the future by a superstitious casting of lots. But later theologians and lawyers confused this with the impious crime committed by witches', *Disquisitiones Magicae* Book 1, chap. 2.

38. 'Devices and directions', 95.

39. 'The Scottish Witchcraft Act', 55.

40. At one point the Act refers to 'sorceries' instead of 'sorcery'. This may simply be the same as 'witchcrafts', an indication of more than one act, or it may be a clerical or printing error. 'Sorsarie' appears twice and 'sorsareis' once, all three times in combination with 'witchcraftis' (always plural) and 'necromancie' (always singular).

41. Del Rio, *Disquisitiones Magicae* Book 4, chap. 2, question 5. Grillando, *De Sortilegiis*, Frankfurt-am-Main 1592, Question 2, sections 1 and 9.

42. See Goodare, *op. cit. supra*, 42.

43. Maxwell-Stuart, *Satan's Conspiracy*, 42.

44. The countess was not alone. Lord Ruthven, the Earl of Bothwell, and the Countess of Atholl were known to be well versed in magic, and Patrick Adamson, Archbishop of St Andrews, was notorious for consulting witches when he was ill. Maxwell-Stuart, *op. cit. supra*, 47, 49, 100–101.

45. Here I differ slightly from Goodare who takes 'abuser' to mean 'misuser' and 'abusing' to mean 'misleading', 'The Scottish Witchcraft Act', 52–53.

46. There is no such ambiguity in Hamilton's *Catechism* which takes magic and divination with complete seriousness and condemns them as an insult to God and a breaking of the First Commandment.

47. Maxwell-Stuart, *Satan's Conspiracy*, 45–46. *The Acts of the Parliament of Scotland* 3.44 (para. 86). Maxwell-Stuart, *op. cit.*, 53, 57–59, 60–61. *The Acts of the Parliament of Scotland* 3, Appendix, 87b; 3.140. 'Fast and loose' was a cheating game played with a stick and a string or a belt.

48. *Register of the Privy Council of Scotland*, series 1, Vol. 2, 198, 317–318.

49. Pitcairn, *Criminal Trials in Scotland*, Vol. 1, part 2, 70.

50. Quoted in Black, 'Scottish charms and amulets', 511. See also *Ibid.*, 440, 450–451, 454, and 481 where nuts are used instead of stones.

51. Maxwell-Stuart, *Satan's Conspiracy*, 94–95.

52. Henderson, 'Witch-hunting and witch belied in the Gàidhealtachd', 95. Black, *Calendar*, 22 (date 1585), 23 (date 1586). Maxwell-Stuart, *Satan's Conspiracy*, 90–91. Cf. a case of murder by witchcraft from 1588, John Millar and Marjory Blaikie from Aberdeenshire, accused of killing William Robertson by bewitching him, Pitcairn, *op. cit. supra*, Vol. 1, part 2, 167, and the cases of Adam MacAlastair (1577) and William Gilmour (1582), Black, *loc. cit. supra*.

53. See further Hall, 'Getting shot of elves', 23–28.

54. Maxwell-Stuart, *op. cit. supra*, 62–66. Henderson & Cowan, *Scottish Fairy Belief*, 127–129.

55. *The Visions of Isobel Gowdie*, 278–282. Quotations, 281, 282.

56. Cf. Job 38.1, 'Then the Lord answered Job out of the whirlwind.'

57. On fairy whirlwinds, see Wilby, *Cunning Folk and Familiar Spirits*, 88.

58. See Bever, *The Realities of Witchcraft and Popular Magic in Early Modern Europe*, 31, 84–85.

59. Wilby, *The Visions of Isobel Gowdie*, 278–288. Hutton, *Shamans: Siberian Spirituality and the Western Imagination*, London & New York: Hambledon & London 2001, 48–49, 147.

60. Quoted in Wilby, *Cunning Folk and Familiar Spirits*, 171.

61. See further M. Todd, *The Culture of Protestantism in Early Modern Scotland*, New Haven & London: Yale University Press 2002, 393, 377–378.

62. *An Abundance of Witches*, 167–177.

63. Quotation from Todd, *The Culture of Protestantism*, 50. A. G. Debus, *The English Paracelsians*, New York: Franklin Watts Inc. 1965, 51–52.

64. Maxwell-Stuart, *Satan's Conspiracy*, 76–87.

65. If William was a ghost, of course, or a spirit which had assumed his form, this mode of access would not have been necessary.

66. Maxwell-Stuart, *op. cit. supra*, 102–107. Carol Lederman quoted in D. E. Young & J. G. Goulet (eds), *Being Changed by Cross-Cultural Encounters: The Anthropology of Extraordinary Experience*, Ontario: Broadview Press 1994, 101–102.

67. This range, by no means exhaustive, can be found in Mitchell, 'On various superstitions in the north-west Highland and Islands of Scotland' and J. G. Dalyell, *The Darker Superstitions of Scotland*. Martin Martin, *A Description of the Western Islands of Scotland*, ed. D. J. MacLeod, Edinburgh: Birlinn 1994, 30.

68. James VI, *Basilikon Doron*, Edinburgh 1599, 22. Crichton's map is reproduced in M. J. Yellowless, *So Strange a Monster as a Jesuiste: The Society of Jesus in Sixteenth-Century Scotland*, Colonsay: House of Lochar 2003, Plate VIII and 182–183.

69. Pitcairn, *Criminal Trials in Scotland* Vol. 1, part 3, 192–200 and part 4, 201–204.

70. Wilby, *The Visions of Isobel Gowdie*, 196.

71. The dittay suddenly switches from singular to plural in this account, so we must presume there was also an image of Marjory Campbell ready to be subjected to the same treatment.

72. Pitcairn's text puts this in August 1578, but it makes more sense, in the light of one of the following incidents dated to 24 August 1577, to regard this whole section of the dittay as referring to 1577.

73. It is difficult to tell from the dittay, whose items are not in chronological order, exactly when this incident took place, but I have included it here as one of the more likely times for it.

74. This almost certainly refers to the burning of their dead bodies, since condemned witches in Scotland were garrotted before being burned.

75. See further MacKenzie, *History of the Munros*, 43–60.

76. See, for example, Black, 'Scottish charms and amulets', 438, 441, 442.

77. The printed dittay says 'Arteis', but if this refers to Altass, we should be considering a journey of perhaps a hundred miles or so across country with no roads beyond drivers' tracks.

78. MacKenzie, *History of the Munros*, 55.

79. *Register of the Privy Council of Scotland*, Series 1, Vol. 4, ed. D. Masson, Edinburgh: Register House 1881, 255, 392–393. Hector is referred to as Katharine's 'son-in-law' in the text, but this should not be misunderstood. The only 'Hector' to fit this literal description, the second son of Katharine's daughter-in-law, Anne Fraser, would have been born far too late to fit. This 'Hector' cannot be other than Katharine's stepson.

80. MacKenzie, *op. cit. supra*, 66–67.

81. On Craig, see further J. W. Cairns's entry in *Oxford Dictionary of National Biography* 13.956–959 and J. Finlay, 'The early career of Thomas Craig, advocate', *The Edinburgh Law Review* 8 (2004), 298–328.

82. D. M. Walker, *A Legal History of Scotland, Vol. 3: The Sixteenth Century*, Edinburgh: T&T Clark 1995, 431–435.

83. Christina Larner says, 'It was necessary to pass a special act in 1591 in order to allow their testimony in witchcraft cases', *Enemies of God*, 51, but the only sitting of Parliament in 1591 (6 August) did not deal with this at all, and a Privy Council commission issued on 26 October simply gave authority for accused witches – therefore male as well as female – to be tortured if necessary. See Norman & Roberts, *Witchcraft in Early Modern Scotland*, 427–428.

84. On Hector generally, see MacKenzie, *History of the Munros*, 62–73.

7 Prosecution in a Time of Upheaval: 1604–1624

1. Maxwell-Stuart, *Satan's Conspiracy*, 145–147.

2. Bothwell quotation: Maxwell-Stuart, *op. cit. supra*, 153. Larner, *Witchcraft and Religion*, 9. It should be noted that the North Berwick episode, as it is usually called, contains more than

one subplot and is much more complex than the simple outline of some of it given here. The documents have been published in Normand & Roberts, *Witchcraft in Early Modern Scotland*. For further disparate accounts, see G. Watson, *Bothwell and the Witches*, London: Robert Hale 1975; E. J. Cowan, 'The darker vision of the Scottish Renaissance: the Devil and Francis Stewart' in I. B. Cowan & D. Shaw (eds), *The Renaissance and Reformation in Scotland*, Edinburgh: Scottish Academic Press 1983, 125–140; D. Willis, *Malevolent Nurture: Witch-Hunting and Maternal Power in Early Modern England*, Ithaca & London: Cornell University Press 1995, 117–158; B. P. Levack, *Witch-Hunting in Scotland*, 34–42.

3. Normand & Roberts, *Witchcraft in Early Modern Scotland*, 353. I have anglicised James's text.

4. Normand & Roberts, *op. cit. supra*, 371, 386, 389, 401.

5. See J. Goodare, 'The Scottish witchcraft panic of 1597' in Goodare (ed.), *The Scottish Witch-Hunt in Context*, 51–72. Spottiswoode quoted, 59. See also MacDonald, *The Witches of Fife*, 38, 59–62, 73–75. Texts relevant to the trials may be found in *The Miscellany of the Spalding Club*, Vol. 1, Aberdeen 1841.

6. Goodare, *op. cit. supra*, 63. James revised his text quite a lot between writing and publication. See J. Rickard, *Authorship and Authority: The Writings of James VI and I*, Manchester & New York: Manchester University Press 2007, 100–105.

7. C. Holmes, 'Witchcraft and possession at the accession of James I' in Newton & Bath, *Witchcraft and the Act of 1604*, 69–90. Thomas, *Religion and the Decline of Magic*, 575–579. Walker, *Unclean Spirits*, 43–73. M. MacDonald (ed.), *Witchcraft and Hysteria in Elizabethan London*, London & New York: Tavistock/Routledge 1991, ix–xxvi.

8. Text in MacDonald, *op. cit. supra*, page 2 of text.

9. Holmes, *op. cit. supra*, 87.

10. James had expressed clearly enough that he thought Catholic priests could not actually cure demoniacs and that apparent cures were either fraudulent or devices of the Devil 'to obtain the perpetual hurt of the souls of so many that by these false miracles may be induced or confirmed in the profession of that erroneous religion', Book 3, chap. 4.

11. Ewen, *Witchcraft and Demonianism*, 393; *Witch Hunting and Witch Trials*, 194–195. Cockburn (ed.), *Calendar of Assize Records: Kent Indictments: James I*, no. 31; *Calendar, Essex Indictments, James I*, nos 25, 34, 26, 36. C. J. Palmer, *History of Great Yarmouth*, Great Yarmouth & London 1856, 68–70.

12. Cockburn, *Calendar: Kent Indictments*, nos 71,177. In Chester, three men were held on 7 May 1604 for prophesying, and bailed to appear again in November; and in Northumberland, Katherine Thompson and Anne Nevelson were tried as 'common charmers of sick folks and their goods' on 23 July. James, however, is most unlikely to have been aware of either. See Ewen, *Witchcraft and Demonianism*, 414, 451.

13. The text is given in Gibson, *Witchcraft and Society in England and America*, 6–7. I have modernised the English and split the text into separate sections.

14. *Witchcraft and Witch Trials*, 179, 180–181. Francis Bacon's response was measured. The explanation of the law which he gave to a jury was, 'For witchcraft, by the former law it was not death, except it were actual and gross invocation of evil spirits, or making covenant with them, or taking away life by witchcraft. But now, by an Act of his Majesty's times, charms and sorceries in certain cases of procuring unlawful love or bodily hurt, and some others, are made felony the second offence, the first being imprisonment and pillory', *The Judicial Charge upon the Commission of Oyer and Terminer held for the verge of the court* in *The Works of Francis Bacon*, London 1803, Vol. 4, 386. Note, as the anonymous *Laws Against Witches* explained in 1645, that witches were to be indicted for specific acts, such as killing or laming, not for *being* witches, 6.

15. Normand & Roberts, *Witchcraft in Early Modern Scotland*, 147, 364.

16. Stephen Bradwell, *Mary Glover's Late Woeful Case* (1603), 28. Text in MacDonald (ed.), *Witchcraft and Hysteria in Elizabethan London*.

17. This is not to say he was a bigot. He recognised fraud when he saw it, and was willing to accept a not guilty verdict in a witchcraft case when he thought it was the right decision. See

Maxwell-Stuart, 'King James's experience of witches', 44.

18. MacDonald, *op. cit. supra*, xiv. S. Sheppard (ed.), *The Selected Writings and Speeches of Sir Edward Coke*, Indianapolis: Liberty Fund 2003, Vol. 1, chap. 6.

19. Kittredge, *Witchcraft in Old and New England*, 281–314. Ewen, *Witchcraft and Demonianism*, 200–202, 451.

20. Cockburn, *Calendar, Essex*, no. 84. Two others were tried, one in March, the other in July. Both were found not guilty: nos 98, 156. *Hertfordshire*, nos 133, 161, 162. *Sussex*, no. 73. *Surrey*, no. 102. *Kent*, nos 100, 139.

21. Brooks, 'Witchcraft and stage spectacle' in Newton & Bath, *Witchcraft and the Act of 1604*, 148–151. K. Briggs, *Pale Hecate's Team*, London: Routledge & Kegan Paul 1962, chap. 5. Harris, *Night's Black Agents*, 33–46, 65–67.

22. Suggett, *A History of Magic and Witchcraft in Wales*, 64, 34–35, 14–19.

23. Seymour, *Irish Witchcraft and Demonology*, 68–69, 77–78. Lapoint, 'Irish immunity to witch-hunting', 81–82, 87–89, 90–91. R. Gillespie, 'Women and crime in seventeenth-century Ireland' in M. MacCurtain & M. O'Dowd (eds), *Women in Early Modern Ireland*, Edinburgh: Edinburgh University Press 1991, 46–48. W. Kramer, 'English reformation and Irish witches: the effects of confessionalisation in suppressing witchcraft accusation in early modern Ireland', *The Forum: Cal Poly's Journal of History* 1 (2009), 27–28, 29.

24. Larner, Hyde Lee, McLachlan, *Source-Book of Scottish Witchcraft*, 10–11, 61–62, 181–182. Dalyell, *Darker Superstitions of Scotland*, 521.

25. Lake, *These Haunted Islands*, 132–133, 136–137.

26. Thornton, *The Channel Islands, 1370–1640*, 120–134. Lake, *op. cit. supra*, 133.

27. Spenser: Book 3, Canto 7, Stanza 6. Scot: *Discoverie of Witchcraft*, Book 1, chap. 3. 'Another sort', as he adds at the end of the chapter, are merely frauds, knowing and deliberate 'cozeners'.

28. Arnobius, *Libri Septem Adversus Nationes* 1.43; Lactantius, *Institutiones Divinae* 2.16.1; Sozomen, *Historia Ecclesiastica* 6.35.

29. See further E. E. Burriss, 'The terminology of witchcraft', *Classical Philology* 31 (1936), 137–145. *Lamia* might also slip into the word *lania*, 'butcher', as it does in the title of Ulrich Molitor's *De Lamiis et Pythonicis Mulieribus*.

30. S.A. Mitchell, *Witchcraft and Magic in the Nordic Middle Ages*, Philadelphia & Oxford: University of Pennsylvania Press 2011, figs 9, 10, 11. The details of these pictures render them more complex documents than I have indicated here, and on balance Mitchell is in favour of interpreting the figures as witches.

31. Zika, *The Appearance of Witchcraft*, fig. 2.22.

32. Zika, *op. cit. supra*, figs 2.8, 2.9,1.8.

33. Zika, *op. cit. supra*, fig. 5.10 (Dossi); figs 3.7, 3.10, 3.11, 3.12 (Baldung Grien); fig. 3.2 (Paulus Frisius, 1583); old witches, figs 2.25 (1514–16), 3.3 (1582); young witches, figs 4.10 (*c.* 1513), 3.10 (1515), and perhaps 3.12 (1523).

34. Thomas, *Religion and the Decline of Magic*, 244–245, 278–279, 237–238, 296–297. Bever, *The Realities of Witchcraft*, 342–345. J. Gibson, *Hanged for Witchcraft*, 199.

35. L. Martin & J. Miller, 'Some findings from the Survey of Scottish Witchcraft' in Goodare-Martin-Miller (eds), *Witchcraft and Belief in Early Modern Scotland*, 59–60. A. Rowlands, 'Age of accused witches' in Golden (ed.), *Encyclopaedia of Witchcraft* 1.16–20. Cf. Gaskill, 'In most witch-trials, however, misfortunes were not randomly blamed on women who looked like witches, but fitted into specific patterns of social relations involving conflict and fear between neighbours. This explains why young as well as old women were accused, not to mention a significant minority of men', *Witchcraft, A Very Short Introduction*, 52. Edward Bever records two German magical workers who had been practising for fifteen and seventeen years respectively before being brought to a formal accusation, *op. cit. supra*, 345–346. Raisa Maria Toivo notes that older women in Finland frequently appeared as accusers, which is also true elsewhere, *Witchcraft and Gender in Early Modern Society: Finland and the Wider European Experience*, Aldershot: Ashgate 2008, 86. Toivo also notes that Agata Pekantytär was about forty when she was first accused and brought to court, *Ibid.*, 22–23. On the somewhat different

case of witches and old age in Germany, see A. Rowlands, 'Witchcraft and old women in early modern Germany', *Past and Present* 173 (2001), 50–89; *Witchcraft Narratives in Germany: Rothenburg, 1561–1652*, Manchester & New York: Manchester University Press 2003, 135, 170–171. L. Roper, *Witch Craze*, New Haven & London: Yale University Press 2004, 151–178. These observations are interesting and instructive, but do not necessarily apply to other European societies and cultures.

36. Kittredge, *Witchcraft in Old and New England*, 320, 321. Sharpe, *The Bewitching of Anne Gunter*, 179–182.

37. Harington, *Nugae Antiquae*, ed. H. Harington, Vol. 1 (London 1804), 366–371; quotation, 368–369.

38. T. A. Birrell, *English Monarchs and their Books, from Henry VII to Charles II*, London: The British Library 1987, 26. V. Hart, *Art and Magic in the Court of the Stuarts*, London & New York: Routledge 1994, 10. D. Brooks-Davies, *The Mercurian Monarch: Magical Politics from Spenser to Pope*, Manchester: Manchester University Press 1983, 85–88.

39. Kittredge, *Witchcraft in Old and New England*, 314–315.

40. Cockburn (ed.), *Calendar of Assize Records, Essex Indictments, James I*, nos 475, 496, 506, 514, 519, 549, 742. See also no. 814 from July that year.

41. Sharpe, 'Familiars' in Golden (ed.), *Encyclopaedia of Witchcraft* 2.347–349. Gibson, 'Applying the Act of 1604', 119–124.

42. Cockburn, *op. cit. supra*, nos 843, 1039, 1088, 1083, 1084, 1089.

43. Guazzo, *Compendium Maleficarum* Book 2, chap. 2. De Lancre, *Tableau de l'Inconstance des Mauvais Anges et Démons* Book 6, discourse 5, section 5. Potts, *The Wonderfull Discoverie of Witches*, 44. In 1606, searchers in the house of Joan Harrison and her daughter, executed on 4 August that year for witchcraft, found a chest full of human bones, hair, and a coloured anatomical map, Gibson, *Early Modern Witches*, 152–153. It is perhaps worth noting that the skull was used in magical medicine as well as witchcraft. Reginald Scot records that 'pills made of the skull of one that is hanged' are a cure for being bitten by a mad dog, *Discoverie of Witchcraft* Book 12, chap. 14; and Henri Boguet observes disapprovingly that in order to cure epilepsy, witches got their patients to use the powdered skull of a man hanged for robbery, *Discours des Sorciers* chap. 35. This, however, can also be found as a remedy for the same affliction in orthodox medicine, noted by Giovanni Francesco Olmo in 1576. See L. Thorndike, *A History of Magic and Experimental Science* Vol. 6 (New York: Columbia University Press 1941), 233. Such a powder remained in use for a long time. See Thorndike, *op. cit.* Vol. 6 (1958), 89, from the *Pharmacopoeia medico-chymica* (1641) of Johann Schröder, and Vol. 8, 161, from Michael Ettmuller's *Chimia rationalis ac experimentalis curiosa* (1684).

44. Cockburn, *Calendar, Hertfordshire*, nos 345, 383, 497, 524, 525, 627, 669.

45. Gaskill, 'Witchcraft in early modern Kent', 268–275. It is worth bearing in mind that while male witches were in a minority in Britain, this was not so in many places elsewhere in Europe where they formed either a significant minority or a majority of those accused. See W. Monter, 'Male witches' in Golden (ed.), *Encyclopaedia of Witchcraft* 3.711–713.

46. Cockburn, *Essex*, nos 1453 and 1596.

47. *Witches and Neighbours*, 398.

48. Sussex had no prosecutions for witchcraft between 1606 and July 1616 when Margaret Pannell was accused of making two people fall ill and killing a sow and eight pigs, offences of which she was found not guilty, Cockburn, *Sussex*, no. 362. Kent had only two trials, both in February 1611, one defendant being found not guilty, the other trial being voided, Cockburn, *Kent*, nos 552 and 577. Surrey had no witchcraft trials at all during these years.

49. The charge of killing a child by witchcraft was also laid against them, but we get no details about it from the pamphlet which records the trials. For the text of this, see Gibson, *Early Modern Witches*, 159–172. On the sources and composition of the available information, see also Gibson, *Reading Witchcraft*, 66–72. Poole & Stokes, *Witches of Northamptonshire*, 83–85, 86–87, 56–57.

50. Darr, *Marks of an Absolute Witch*, 173–183. Scratching was still being practised in the nineteenth century, Kittredge, *Witchcraft in Old and New England*, 47 and 236. For further

examples, see Ewen, *Witchcraft and Demonianism*, 190–191. See also *The Most Strange and Admirable Discourse of the Three Witches of Warboys*, London 1593, 7 and 10.

51. See further Darr, *op. cit. supra*, 111–138, and H. Pihlajamäki, 'Swimming the witch, pricking for the Devil's mark: ordeals in the early modern witchcraft trials', *Journal of Legal History* 21 (August 2000), 35–58.

52. *Daemonologie* Book 3, chap. 3.

53. Mitchell, *Witchcraft and Magic in the Nordic Middle Ages*, 118–141. Marwick, 'Northern witches', 333–342.

54. Marwick, *op. cit. supra*, 349, 350, 376–379.

55. *Calendar of Cases of Witchcraft in Scotland*, sub 1603, 1604, 1616, 1643, 1644, 1673, *c.* 1675, *c.* 1700. There had been one notorious case, that of Alison Balfour, who was executed after unusually cruel tortures, in Kirkwall on 16 December 1594, having been charged with image magic intended to kill. John Stewart, Master of Orkney, it was said, had consulted her, almost certainly with a view to harming his brother Patrick. P. D. Anderson, *Black Patie: The Life and Times of Patrick Stewart, Earl of Orkney, Lord of Shetland*, Edinburgh: John Donaldson Publishers Ltd 1992, 49–50. Pitcairn, *Criminal Trials* 1.375–377.

56. R. S. Barclay (ed.), *The Court Books of Orkney and Shetland, 1614–1615*, Edinburgh: T. & A. Constable Ltd. 1967, 18–20; quotations, 19.

57. Black, *Witchcraft and Witchcraft Trials in Orkney and Shetland*, 12–16, 26–27. Cf. Katharine Grant (1623) who had people push a sick cow into the sea until it was washed by nine surges, Marwick, 'Northern witches', 358–359.

58. *The Miscellany of the Spalding Club*, Vol. 1, Aberdeen 1841, 180.

59. Purkiss, *Troublesome Things*, 90–96, 103–104. Black, *op. cit. supra*, 62–66, 6. Henderson & Cowan, *Scottish Fairy Belief*, 98.

60. *Miscellany of the Abbotsford Club* Vol. 1, Edinburgh 1837, 135–142. Black, *op. cit. supra*, 6–12.

61. Barclay, *The Court Books of Orkney and Shetland*, 31, 32. The jougs were an iron collar fastened to a wall or a tree. There are surviving examples still attached to a church wall and the wall of a private house.

62. E. Ewen, 'Crime or culture? Women and daily life in late Mediaeval Scotland' in Y. Galloway Brown and R. Ferguson (eds), *Twisted Sisters: Women, Crime and Deviance in Scotland since 1400*, East Lothian: Tuckwell Press 2002, 129–131. M. Graham, *The Uses of Reform: Godly Discipline and Popular Behaviour in Scotland and Beyond, 1560–1610*, Leiden-New York-Köln: Brill 1996, 217–218.

63. *Scottish Fairy Belief*, 79–80.

64. Todd, *The Culture of Protestantism in Early Modern Scotland*, 68–69.

8 Religious Stirs and Civil Wars: 1625–1649

1. Cockburn (ed.), *Calendar of Assizes: Indictments: James I: Essex*, nos 1572, 1573, 1596; *Hertfordshire*, nos 1164, 1185, 1186. It should be noted that there is no particular fall in the number of other crimes committed for trial in this same region during the 1620s.

2. Baddeley, *The Boy of Bilson*, 46.

3. Baddeley, *op. cit. supra*, 60–62, 70.

4. See further Johnstone, *The Devil and Demonism in Early Modern England*, 157–158.

5. S. Pumfrey, 'Potts, plots and politics' in Poole (ed.), *The Lancashire Witches*, 31. Potts, *The Wonderfull Discoverie of Witches*, F3.

6. M. Cahill, *The Diocese of Coventry and Lichfield, 1603–1642*, unpublished PhD thesis, University of Warwick, October 1981, 219–223; quotation, 222–223. In 2009, archaeologists unearthed a mid to late seventeenth-century Bellarmine jug in Stafford. If this was a witch-bottle (although it may simply have been a jug, *pace* the journalists who were eager to shout 'witches'!) it is a small indication of local people's nervousness and their desire for protection, *The Telegraph*, 3 October 2009. Thus, a man whose wife was suffering from 'a languishing condition' and lack of proper sleep was advised to take some of his wife's urine, cork it in a

bottle with nails, pins, and needles, and bury it in the earth. He did so, and although it did not work the first time, it did when he essayed it again, Glanvill, *Saducismus Triumphatus*, Part 2, 109. See also V. Theile & A.D. McCarthy, 'Superstitions, literature, history, and the creative imagination' in V. Theile & A. D. McCarthy (eds), *Staging the Superstitions of Early Modern Europe*, 1–7.

7. *Demonologia*, 32.

8. *Op. cit.*, 38–39, 42–43.

9. *Op. cit.*, 42–46; quotation, 45–46.

10. *Op. cit.*, 51, 52.

11. Cf. an incident from 25 January, when a strange woman claiming to be Helen's aunt from York came to the house and, according to Helen, tried to force her to eat some 'spices' which turned out to be raisins. Helen refused, saying, 'Get thee away! Thou art a witch and not my aunt!' and the woman threw the raisins into the fire, *op. cit.*, 64–65.

12. *Op. cit.*, 54–55, 91–92. *Witch of Edmonton*, Act 3, scene 3, vv. 1–3.

13. *Op. cit.*, 71–73, 78, 79–80.

14. *Saducismus Triumphatus*, 104–105. Cf. Florence Newton, an Irish witch, who was unable to say 'and forgive us our trespasses', *Ibid.*, 97. For further examples, see Darr, *Marks of an Absolute Witch*, 187–188.

15. *Demonologia*, 87–89.

16. *Op. cit. supra*, 98, 125–127.

17. *op. cit.*, 142–143.

18. Suggett, *A History of Magic and Witchcraft in Wales*, 78. Cf. Ann Armstrong's evidence to magistrates in Newcastle in 1673 that she had been told that if she ate a piece of cheese left for her by fairies, she would not be able to keep her experience secret, *infra* 000–000.

19. Ewen, *Witchcraft and Demonianism*, 239–240. Fairfax, too, briefly wondered whether something similar might not be the cause of Helen's infirmities, before he became convinced that these were of spiritual origin, *Demonologia*, 37.

20. On Grace Sowerbutts, see Ewen, *op. cit. supra*, 226–227. Almond, *The Lancashire Witches*, 110–114, 126–128. On Smith: Walker, *Unclean Spirits*, 81–82. There was also the case of Katharine Malpas, a young married woman, schooled and apt in the art of counterfeiting trances which were blamed on the witchcraft of a local woman. She, too, was investigated by King James. See Walker, *op. cit.*, 83, Sharpe, *Instruments of Darkness*, 193, and Haining (ed.), *The Witchcraft Papers*, 130–132.

21. Quoted in Ewen, *op. cit. supra*, 326.

22. Bernard, *A Guide to Grand Jury Men*, 98, 73. Gifford, *A Dialogue Concerning Witches*, 33.

23. Suggett, *A History of Magic and Witchcraft in Wales*, 53.

24. Sir Francis Hubert, *The Historie of Edward II*, quoted in Haining (ed.), *The Witchcraft Papers*, 134–135. See also Harris, *Night's Black Agents*, 95–97.

25. *Op. cit. supra*, 27.

26. Thornton, *The Channel Islands*, 142–143.

27. Linwood Potts, *Witchcraft and Devil Lore in the Channel Islands*, 38–39.

28. Bellows, *Channel Islands Witchcraft*, 66.

29. Craine, *Manannan's Isle*, 14.

30. *Register of the Privy Council of Scotland*, Series 1, Vol. 12, 412, 423, 425, 472, 490, 580; 711, 720, 734, 738, 750. Vol. 13, 49–50, 62–63, 69, 181, 192–193, 230, 352–353, 270, 422, 439–440, 443, 451, 460–461, 464, 484–485, 489–490, 499–500. Series 2, Vol. 8, 355–360.

31. *Privy Council*, Vol. 12, 362, 412, 423.

32. Series 2, Vol. 8, 345–347; quotations, 347.

33. Henderson & Cowan, *Scottish Fairy Belief*, 19, 137–138, 46–47.

34. Wasser, 'The Privy Council and the witches', 32–33, 35.

35. *Privy Council*, Vol. 13, 620.

36. Wasser, *op. cit. supra*, 45, note 145.

37. Whyte, *Scotland before the Industrial Revolution*, 123. C. W. J. Withers, 'Emergent nation:

Scotland's geography, 1314–1707' in I. Brown (ed.), *The Edinburgh History of Scottish Literature: From Columba to the Union*, Edinburgh: Edinburgh University Press 2007, 148. Larner, *Enemies of God*, 82. We may note that in 1623, the Privy Council issued commissions for only two places as opposed to the previous and following years.

38. For details, see the individual entries in *Fasti Ecclesiae Scoticanae*, 9 vols, Edinburgh: Oliver & Boyd 1915–1961.

39. Graham, *The Uses of Reform*, 299.

40. Larner, *Enemies of God*, 146. Levack, *Witch-Hunting in Scotland*, 44–45. MacDonald, *The Witches of Fife*, 195.

41. Wasser, 'The Privy Council and the witches', 45. Johnstone, 'The Protestant Devil', 179–186, 196–201. Calvin himself was more interested in this conflict between God and Satan than in the malefices performed, or allegedly performed, by witches. See P. F. Jensen, 'Calvin and witchcraft', *The Reformed Theological Review* 34 (1975), 76–86.

42. Quoted in Parker, *Global Crisis*, xxi and xxiii.

43. Roberts quoted in Walsham, *Providence in Early Modern England*, 116. See also *Ibid.*, 181–186. J. Crawford, *Marvellous Protestantism*, 114–145. Cf. D. Cressy, *Travesties and Transgressions in Tudor and Stuart England*, Oxford: Oxford University Press 2000, 29–50. C. Durston, 'Signs and wonders and the English civil war', *History Today* 37 (1987), 22–28. Valletta, *Witchcraft, Magic, and Superstition*, 63–75. Hony quoted in Oldridge, 'Light from darkness', 400. This was not a cast of mind peculiar to Britain. An attack upon the settlers of Chesapeake in 1622, for example, was interpreted as a demonstration that 'the hand of God [was] set against us ... for the punishment of our ingratitude in not being thankful .... [and] for our greedy desires of present gain and profit', quoted in K. S. Murphy, 'Portents and prodigies: providentialism in the eighteenth-century Chesapeake', *Maryland Historical Magazine* 97 (2002), 399; and in France, the sight of deep holes appearing suddenly in the ground at Pivry and flames issuing therefrom made one observer think of Sodom and the punishment inflicted by God upon that city for its sins, J. Céard, *La Nature et Les Prodiges*, Genève: Librairie Droz 1996, 478.

44. The popular press did not confine itself to printing stories from Britain. Cf. *A Certain Relation of the Hog-Faced Gentlewoman called Mistress Tannakin Skinker*, London 1640, which tells the story of a German girl born in 1618 with a pig's face, the result of a witch's malice.

45. Quoted in Clark, *Thinking With Demons*, 544.

46. Daston, 'Marvellous facts and miraculous evidence in early modern Europe', *Critical Inquiry* 18 (Autumn 1991), 100–108. P. Béhar, *Les langues occultes de la Renaissance*, Paris: Éditions Desjonquères 1996, 171–180.

47. Stoyle, *The Black Legend of Prince Rupert's Dog*, 169–170, 69–72.

48. See Behringer, *Witches and Witch-Hunts*, English trans., Cambridge: Polity Press 2004, 87–88, 65, 68.

49. Bellows, *Channel Islands Witchcraft*, 63, 66.

50. C. F. Mullett, 'Plague policy in Scotland, 16th–17th centuries', *Osiris* 9 (1950), 445–450. Larner, *Enemies of God*, 61.

51. K. Duncan, 'The possible influence of climate on the bubonic plague in Scotland', *Scottish Geographical Magazine* 108 (1992), 33–34.

52. J. F. D. Shrewsbury, *A History of Bubonic Plague in the British Isles*, Cambridge: Cambridge University Press 1970, 311–334, 337–345, 356–367, 371–399. In times of this kind of crisis, people tended to blame state officials, not witches. Parker, *Global Crisis*, 108.

53. *Enemies of God*, 82.

54. Exceptions can always be found, of course, as in the case of Franconia in 1626 when witches were blamed for the dreadful climatic conditions which destroyed local corn crops and vines, Behringer, *Witches and Witch Hunts*, 113–114. But the point is that these were exceptions, not the general rule. See also G. Jensen, *The Path of the Devil*, Lanham, Maryland: Rowman & Littlefield Publishers Inc. 2007, 61–78.

55. For an example from Franconia, see G. K. Waite, *Heresy, Magic, and Witchcraft in Early*

Modern Europe, Basingstoke: Palgrave Macmillan 2003, 157–158. The connection between bad weather and witchcraft, however, was not universally accepted. Johannes Brenz, indeed, felt obliged to disabuse his parishioners and preach against it in 1539 after a particularly damaging hailstorm in the Duchy of Württemberg, Waite, *op. cit.*, 127.

56. On Scottish prickers, see Maxwell-Stuart, *Witch Hunters*, 98–122. The best account of Hopkins and Stearne is that by Malcolm Gaskill, *Witchfinders: A Seventeenth-Century English Tragedy*, London: John Murray 2005.

57. Ewen, *Witchcraft and Demonianism*, 453, 315.

58. Ewen, *op. cit. supra*, 434. Ewen, *Witch Hunting and Witch Trials*, 220–221.

59. Ewen, *Witchcraft and Demonianism*, 440, 418, 436.

60. Ewen, 394–395.

61. A vivid summary of the effects of descending soldiery is given by Parker, *Global Crisis*, 28–31.

62. Ewen, *op. cit.*, *supra*, 251–253.

63. See further Stoyle, *The Black Legend of Prince Rupert's Dog*, 117–127.

64. Hans Jakob Christoffel Grimmelshausen, *Simplicissimus*, English trans., M. Adair, Lanham, Maryland: University Press of America 1986, 9–10. The novel was first published in 1668.

65. Ewen, *Witchcraft and Demonianism*, 453. More details are supplied by his source, *The Gentleman's Magazine* 151 (1832), 408. In 1653, John Jonson from Yorkshire testified that Elizabeth Lambe and an old man in brown clothes appeared one day at his bedside, whereupon 'his goods fell sick'. So did those of his neighbours, but after they had all given Elizabeth a good beating, everything returned to normal. Ewen, *op. cit.*, 396.

66. Ewen, *op. cit. supra*, 16.

67. Ewen, 395–396. Anne Wagg of Ilkeston, too, was suspected of causing Mrs Fox to fall ill, so Mr Fox fetched her to the bedside and his wife scratched her till she drew blood, *Ibid.*, 319.

68. Ewen, 429, 418, 454, 314–315. Cf. Elizabeth Johnson who, on 21 December 1657, 'exercised invocation and conjuration of evil spirits and bewitched Elizabeth Haigh', aged eight, who died six months later, *Ibid.*, 420–421.

69. Quoted in Ewen, 397.

70. Ewen, 395.

71. Ewen, 453, 307–308.

72. Gaskill, *Witchfinders*, 205–213.

73. Ewen, 312, 417.

74. A. W. Twyford & A. Griffiths, *Records of York Castle: Fortress, Court House, and Prison*, London: Griffith & Farran 1880, 177. A. D. H. Leadman, 'Pocklington parish records, abstracts', *Yorkshire Archaeological Journal* 14 (1898), 85, 115. The practicalities of Isabella's actions raise queries. How did she, even with her husband's help, subdue her mother sufficiently to be able to crucify her? What should we understand by 'crucify' here? How was she able to afford to slaughter and then burn a whole calf? What did she do with her mother's body which must have borne signs of the 'crucifixion', however one interprets that? Cf. the case of Elizabeth Kewin from the Isle of Man in 1666.

75. Anon., *The Lawes Against Witches and Conjuration*, 6–7.

76. Stoyle, *The Black Legend of Prince Rupert's Dog*, 19–20.

77. Amundsen, 'The Duke's devil', 41–52 (Lambe), 52–58 (Anne Bodenham). Gaskill, 'Witchcraft, politics, and memory in seventeenth-century England', *The Historical Journal* 50 (2007), 289–308. Quotations: E. Bowe, *Doctor Lambe Revived*, London 1653, 2, 10. Elizabeth Roberts from Beverley in Yorkshire also turned into a cat (October 1654), and Elizabeth Mallory from the West Riding of Yorkshire claimed she had seen William Wade in the form of a cat sitting on her window sill (July 1656): Ewen, *Witchcraft and Demonianism*, 397, 398. Cunning folk and witches were often distinguished from one another in popular parlance, the former being called 'white witch' and the latter 'black witch', as John Gaule observed. But official religious opinion was that they should not be so separated because 'Satan, being a fiend of darkness, is then worst when he transforms himself into an angel of light, [and] so likewise are his ministers', *Select Cases of Conscience Touching Witches and Witchcrafts*, London 1646,

30, 31.

78. Ewen, *op. cit. supra*, 456–457. Cf. the complaint that in Montgomeryshire Quakers 'bewitched' people into their form of religion, Suggett, *A History of Magic and Witchcraft in Wales*, 83.

79. Quoted in Harley, 'Mental illness, magical medicine, and the Devil', 116.

80. Hopper, 'The Popish army of the north', 23–24, 15. Aveling, *Post-Reformation Catholicism in East Yorkshire*, 31, 35, 47. Aveling, *Northern Catholics*, 257–258.

81. Details of the relevant cases can be found in Ewen, *Witchcraft and Demonianism*, 395–399.

82. H. E. Rollins (ed.), *The Pack of Autolycus*, Cambridge: Harvard University Press 1927, 36–43, quotation, 42.

83. Ewen, *op. cit. supra*, 423, 330–334, 424, 436. The alleged witchcraft is directed almost entirely at making people or animals sick.

84. M. R. Lewis, 'The pilgrimage to St Michael's Mount: Catholic continuity in Wales', *Journal of Welsh Ecclesiastical History* 8 (1991), 51–54.

85. Quoted in Seymour, *Irish Witchcraft and Demonology*, 99.

86. Seymour, *op. cit. supra*, 94–95.

87. Sneddon, *Possessed by the Devil*, 82, 67, 69, 101.

88. Rock, *op. cit. supra*, 30–34.

89. This episode has been studied in detail by Robertson, *Panics and Persecution*. See in particular 8–9, 12–26, 41–64, 103–114, and the list of suspects in Appendix 2. On the Kirk's determination to eradicate witchcraft, see further J. Goodare, 'Men and the witch-hunt in Scotland' in A. Rowlands (ed.), *Witchcraft and Masculinities in Early Modern Europe*, Basingstoke: Palgrave Macmillan 2009, 149–170.

90. Whyte, *Scotland Before the Industrial Revolution*, 214. Levack, *Witch-Hunting in Scotland*, 85.

91. *Records of the Privy Council of Scotland*, series 2, 7.369, 599, 644, 595, 446. Series 2, 8.12, 18–19, 20, 133–134. The Lanarkshire trials are recorded *Ibid.*, 146–154.

92. For examples, see J. Miller, 'Men in black: appearances of the Devil in early modern Scottish witchcraft discourse' in Goodare-Martin-Miller (eds), *Witchcraft and Belief in Early Modern Scotland*, 149–150.

93. It can also be said that they are reminiscent of the witches' meeting place and some of their activities in the North Berwick affair more than fifty years earlier, but although James VI's *Daemonologie* with its memories of and references to that convention could have been available to the authorities for consultation, it is doubtful whether it actually played any part in formulating the evidence against Margaret.

94. Quoted in Larner, *Enemies of God*, 140.

95. The whole episode can be followed in J. Robertson (ed.), *Selections from the Registers of the Presbytery of Lanark, 1623–1709*, Edinburgh: Abbotsford Club 1839, 35–39. See also *Register of the Privy Council*, Series 2, 8.155–157.

96. *Acts of the Parliament of Scotland* 6.ii.152. Commissions, *Ibid.*, 727, 420, 732–733, 453, 463, 479, 735, 484, 490, 497, 498, 506, 570, 516, 518, 538. Quotations, *Ibid.*, 735. J. Balfour, *Historical Works* 4 vols, Edinburgh 1824–5, 3.437.

96. *Registers of the Privy Council, op. cit. supra*, 156, 189, 190, 194, 195, 196.

97. On conversion crises and terrors, see Yeoman, 'The Devil as doctor', 97, 100. On Calvin, see A. Hallett, 'The theology of John Calvin, Part Three: The Christian's conflict with the Devil', *The Churchman* 105 (1991), 293–325; quotation, 301. On physiological explanations of satanic encounters, see Bever, *The Realities of Witchcraft*, 73–92, An example of a physical encounter with the Devil is given in Maxwell-Stuart, *Satan*, 9–12. On Isobel Watson, see Graham, *The Uses of Reform*, 300–301. On the Devil and swearing, see J. MacCallum, *Reforming the Scottish Parish: The Reformation in Fife, 1560–1640*, Aldershot: Ashgate 2010, 205.

98. The tone of the period can be gathered from the title of a document sent to the English Parliament from the General Assembly of the Kirk in February 1649: *A solemn testimony against toleration and the present proceedings of sectaries and their abettors in England, in*

reference to religion and government.

99. A. F. Mitchell & J. Christie (eds), *The Records of the Commissions of the General Assembly of the Church of Scotland, holden in Edinburgh the years 1648 and 1649*, Edinburgh: T. & A. Constable, 240–241.

100. MacDonald, 'The Devil's mark and the witch-prickers of Scotland', 509. Neill, 'The professional pricker and his test for witchcraft', 205–213. Maxwell-Stuart, *Witch-Hunters*, 98–117.

101. R. Gardiner, *England's Grievance Discovered in relation to the Coal Trade*, London & Newcastle 1796, 114–116. A summary is also provided in J. Brand, *The History and Antiquities of the Town and County of the Town of Newcastle*, Vol. 2, London 1789, 477–478.

102. See further Behringer, *Witches and Witch-Hunts*, 49.

103. In 1987, 121 children were referred to Cleveland social services in six months as victims of child abuse, and in eighteen cases medical practitioners relied on anal reflex dilation alone to determine whether abuse had taken place or not. See further D. Jenkins, *Intimate Enemies: Moral Panics in Contemporary Great Britain*, New York: Aldine de Gruyter 1992, 136–149.

104. 'Torture and the Scottish witch-hunt', 106–109.

105. Black, *Witchcraft and Witchcraft Trials in Orkney and Shetland*, 6, 15–22, 35, 37–38, 38, 74–75, 87–88. Katharine Craigie had been tried first in 1640 and found not guilty.

9 Magical Remedies and Witchcraft under Assault: 1650–1668

1. See further, A. Rowlands, 'Age of accused witches' in R. Goolden (ed.), *Encyclopaedia of Witchcraft*, Vol. 1, 16–20. Ewen, *Witchcraft and Demonianism*, 176, 201. Hopkins & Stearne, *The Discovery of Witchcraft*, 20.

2. 'Towards a politics of witchcraft in early modern England', 106.

3. *A Diary of Public Transactions and Other Occurrences, chiefly in Scotland, from January 1650 to June 1667*, Edinburgh: T. Constable 1836, 212, 214, 213.

4. *Institutions*, Book 1, title 3. On Dalrymple's career, see J. D. Ford, *Oxford Dictionary of National Biography* 14.988–995.

5. The treatise *Investigations into Magic* by the Jesuit Martín Del Rio appears to have been used as an authoritative source by some Scottish courts, and of course there were constant comings and goings between Scotland and the rest of Europe which will have provided conduits of information about what was happening and believed in elsewhere.

6. Letter by Roger Sawrey, Lieutenant Colonel of an English regiment stationed in Ayr, dated 26 April 1658. C. H. Firth (ed.), *Scotland and the Protectorate: Letters and Papers relating to the Military Government of Scotland from January 1654 to June 1659*, Edinburgh: T. & A. Constable 1899, 382.

7. Examples from trials held in 1661: Margaret Allen went with a friend to Haddington where she found witches dancing and the Devil as a man in black clothes and a bonnet. He kissed her and gave her his mark. Janet Miller met the Devil in the likeness of a young man at the How beside the standing stone between the new bridge and Ingliston. Janet Ker met him as 'a grievous black man', that is, dark-skinned and ugly, as she was leaving Edinburgh to go home. Helen Cass from Duddingston saw him at the Links as a man in green clothes, and Isobel Ramsay met him twice, once as she was walking to Edinburgh when she and he, 'a pleasant young man', fell into conversation. 'Where do you live, good wife?' he asked, and 'How is the minister?' He gave her sixpence with which she bought meal, and later on a dollar after he had appeared in her own house while she was in bed with her husband. All these examples come from National Archives of Scotland, *JC26/27*. See also Maxwell-Stuart, *An Abundance of Witches*, 111–116.

8. *De praestigiis daemonum*, Basel 1583, preface, p. 8. The 'spirits' referred to here were natural emanations within the body, operating from the liver, the heart, and the brain, and should thus be understood as parts of the human physiology.

9. *A Treatise of Witchcraft*, 43.10

10. The following account is based on National Archives of Scotland, *JC26/27*.

11. See further, Maxwell-Stuart, *An Abundance of Witches*, 179–181.

12. Details are given in *Fasti Ecclesiae Scoticae* s.v. and in the diaries of John Nicoll (*A Diary of Public Transactions*), sub 27 April 1650, 8 August 1654, and 23 August 1660 (9, 166, 298), and John Lamont, sub 23 August 1660 (126).

13. This was not in the least unusual. Cf. 'Mr Steel's mother died, sick but two or three days. Mary Powell [*her name*] thought by some to be bewitched. Her dame (called Katharine of the Pinfold) is said to have kneeled down and cursed her', P. Henry, *Diary and Letters of Philip Henry MA of Broad Oak, Flintshire, AD 1631–1696*, ed. M. H. Lee, London: Kegan Paul, Trench & Co. Ltd 1882, 152 = 1 December 1663. See also Suggett, *A History of Magic and Witchcraft in Wales*, 56–57, and from modern Transylvania, E. Pócs, 'Curse, maleficium, divination: witchcraft at the borderline of religion and magic' in Blecourt & Davies (eds), *Witchcraft Continued*, 177.

14. A. J. S. Gibson & T. C. Smout, *Prices, Food and Wages in Scotland, 1550–1780*, Cambridge: Cambridge University Press 195, 265–267.

15. National Archives of Scotland, *JC26/26*.

16. The fullest account of Isobel's confessions is given by Emma Wilby, *The Visions of Isobel Gowdie*, Eastbourne: Sussex Academic Press 2010.

17. See further R. Sugg, *Mummies, Cannibals, and Vampirism: The History of Corpse Medicine from the Renaissance to the Victorians*, London: Taylor & Francis 2011, 28–66.

18. Wilby, *op. cit. supra*, 39.

19. Text of the four confessions in Wilby, 37–52.

20. *The Diary of Alexander Brodie of Brodie, 1652–1680*, Aberdeen: Spalding Club 1863, 246, 259, 275–276.

21. *Op. cit. supra*, 135, 296.

22. 'English reformation and Irish witches', 31.

23. For what follows, see Summers, *Geography of Witchcraft*, 94–95 and Seymour, *Irish Witchcraft and Demonology*, 105–131. These are based on an account given by Joseph Glanvill in his *Saducismus Triumphatus*, Part Two, 90–101, which Glanvill in his turn attributed to a record contemporary with the events he describes.

24. P. G. Maxwell-Stuart, *Poltergeists: A History of Violent Ghostly Phenomena*, Stroud: Amberley Publications 2011, 53, 54, 146–147. A. Gauld & A. D. Cornell, *Poltergeists*, London-Boston-Henley: Routledge & Kegan Paul 1979, 114–115.

25. Cf. Ewen, *Witchcraft and Demonianism*, 337–338, a case from Somerset in 1663. Interestingly enough, there are slight parallels with Florence's case. A servant girl was bewitched by a woman, Julian Cox, and then began to have convulsions and visions of Julian and a 'black' man. She also produced large pins from swellings in her body, and on one occasion stabbed the Julian-apparition in the leg, after which blood was found on Julian's bed, and a fresh wound in her leg which fitted the knife-blade. Margaret Elmore from Suffolk was also manacled, and when her manacles were removed, Mrs Rudge whom she was alleged to have bewitched felt worse. Her condition improved once Margaret was manacled again, Ewen, 460.

26. Thomas, *Religion and the Decline of Magic*, 219, 649.

27. P. Elmer, *The Miraculous Conformist: Valentine Greatrakes, the Body Politic, and the Politics of Healing in Restoration Britain*, Oxford: Oxford University Press 2013, 39, 57–60. Elmer identifies 'Mr Blackwell' on 128, note 46. Fleming, *The Dark Side of the Enlightenment*, 35–70.

28. The Earl of Orrery, too, would be pleased, for he was notoriously anti-Catholic.

29. W. Borlase, 'Some account of the extraordinary agitation of the waters in Mount's Bay and other places on 31st of March, 1761', *Proceedings of the Royal Society of London: Philosophical Transactions* 52 (1761), 420.

30. Ewen, *Witchcraft and Demonianism*, 361. The date is 1673.

31. Ewen, 362. This is not to deny that witches were sometimes deliberately deprived of sleep – they certainly were – but the two procedures should not be elided, as they frequently are.

32. Maxwell-Stuart, *Poltergeists*, 177, 207.

33. See, for example, Johann Wier, *De praestigiis daemonum* Book 4, chap. 2.

34. For some English examples from the first half of the seventeenth century, see Ewen, *Witchcraft and Demonianism*, 190–193, 195–196, 452, 348–350. For some examples from the second half of the century, see Barry, *Witchcraft and Demonology in South-West England*, 88–90, 118, 122. See also Geis & Bunn, *A Trial of Witches*, 55–72 and Sharpe, *Instruments of Darkness*, 190–210.

35. On Aston, see the entry in F. Elrington Bell, *The Judges in Ireland, 1221–1921*, 2 vols, London: John Murray 1926, 1.346.

36. These points are developed further by Elmer, *The Miraculous Conformist*, 131–132. The Irish situation at the time was complex, of course, with dissident Protestants coming under as much suspicious or hostile scrutiny as Catholics. See T. Bernard, 'Enforcing the Reformation in Ireland, 1660–1704' in E. Boran & C. Gribben (eds), *Enforcing Reformation in Ireland and Scotland, 1550–1700*, Aldershot: Ashgate 2006, 202–205, 208–212.

37. Suggett, *A History of Magic and Witchcraft in Wales*, 52, 53, 57, 59, 60, 77, 74, 83.

38. Sharpe, 'Witchcraft in the early modern Isle of Man', 17, and 26, note 46.

39. Sharpe, *op. cit. supra*, 13–14. According to David Craine, Jane made her renunciation most unwillingly and then cursed her servants for causing the scandal in the first place, *Manannan's Isle*, 17. The text of the Governor's order is given in Moore, *Folklore and Magic of the Isle of Man*, 6.

40. What follows is based on transcripts from the episcopal registry made by David Craine, www.isle-of-man.com/manxnotebook/jmmuseum/d151.htm.

41. Martin Martin, *A Description of the Western Isles of Scotland circa 1695*, ed. D. J. MacLeod, Edinburgh: Birlinn 1994, 30–31.

42. Bellows, *Channel Islands Witchcraft*, 67. In Guernsey, the trials had come to an end in 1634.

43. A. Soman, 'La décriminalisation de la sorcellerie en France' in A. Soman, *Sorcellerie et Justice Criminelle (16e–18e siècles)*, Hampshire: Ashgate Variorum 1992, No. XII.

44. *Advice to a Son*, new ed. London 1896, 125–126. Cf. the hesitations of a clergyman when faced by odd behaviour from someone reputed to be a witch, recorded by Richard Josselin in his diary for 19 July, 1657: 'Mr Clarke, the minister of Gaines Colne, told us that he saw one Ann Crow, counted a witch, take something out of a pot and lay by a grave. He considered what was to do. When he drew near, he espied some baked pears; and a little thing in shape like a rat, only reddish and without a tail, run from them and vanished away, [so] that he could not tell what became of it. The party said she laid them there to cool. She was under the window when we exercised. I pressed her what I could. She protests her innocency.'

45. See, for example, the diagram showing indictments in England's Home Circuit assizes, 1560–1709, in Sharpe, *Instruments of Darkness*, 109.

46. Cf. Aubrey Ginset from Dunwich, tried in 1665, who had been enticed into witchcraft by the Devil who appeared first as a handsome young man and then as a cat or kitten which sucked blood from a 'teat', Ewen, *Witchcraft and Demonianism*, 354.

47. Sugg, *Mummies, Cannibals, and Vampires*, 7–8, 18–19, 110.

48. Ewen, *op. cit. supra*, 337–338, 339–341, 341–345.

49. *Witchcraft and Demonology in South-West England*, 45. This, of course, as Barry observes (p. 51), does not preclude the possibility that other people were driving the whole process in Somerset and thus introducing certain expectations into the minds of officials involved. Anne Baites from Morpeth in Northumberland also met the Devil several times in various places, describing him as a little black man in black clothes. Raine, *Depositions from the Castle of York*, 191–201; the Devil's description, 197.

50. Ewen, *op. cit. supra*, 437 (1663 & 1664), 438 (1666, 1667, 1668, & 1669). This last took place in Wales.

51. Ewen, 422. Casting the evil eye was not, of itself, an offence which inclined juries to convict, because two other cases, one in 1664, the other in 1666, ended in acquittal. Ewen, 437, 438.

52. Ewen, 347–352; quotation, 350–351. Sharpe, *Instruments of Darkness*, 224–226. Darr, *Marks of an Absolute Witch*, 274–275. The most complete examination of the trial is that of Geis & Bunn, *A Trial of Witches*.

53. Victoria Silver has analysed Browne's thinking on the validity or otherwise of witchcraft and concludes that, in the Lowestoft case, 'he does not identify Cullender and Duny as the human agents of the children's afflictions: he only expounds their symptoms' medical aetiology within the providential scheme of God's permissive will and the Devil's preternatural orchestration of human suffering and delusion', 'Wonders of the invisible world', 140. See also R. Barbour, *Sir Thomas Browne, A Life*, Oxford: Oxford University Press 2013, 367–372.

54. Anon., *A Tryal of Witches*, 20.

55. Geis & Bunn, *A Trial of Witches*, 14–17, 191. Geis, 'Lord Hale, witches, and rape', 33–34. Silver, 'Wonders of the invisible world', 118–145.

56. Anon., *A Tryal of Witches*, 17–18.

57. 'Judicially elbowed' is a phrase used by Geis & Bunn, *A Trial of Witches*, 156. On other opinions, see *Ibid.*, 102. It is worth comparing a case from *c.* 1680. A thirteen-year-old girl started having fits and vomiting pins, which resulted in a man being put on trial. The fact that she vomited straight rather than crooked pins, however, made the judge suspicious and the jury must have thought so, too, for it acquitted the accused. His mother then called out her gratitude, saying (in one version of her words), 'God bless your Lordship, they would have made me a witch twenty years ago!' Barry, *Witchcraft and Demonology in South-West England*, 72–73.

58. Raine, *Depositions from the Castle of York*, 125. People often slept more than one to a bed, so there is nothing unusual in Anne's being next to Dorothy. She was almost certainly sleeping with her so that she could act as a reassurance and a nurse in case of a reoccurrence of Dorothy's fitting.

59. See Darr, *Marks of an Absolute Witch*, 50.

60. Ewen, *Witchcraft and Demonianism*, 375–376, 445.

61. Ewen, *op. cit. supra*, 458. The murderers were arrested, tried, and executed.

62. *The Gentleman's Magazine* 102 (1832), Part 1, 410.

63. Ewen, 458–459, 364–365. More elaborate variations upon this kind of ritual include drawing images upon parchment at dawn on a Saturday, and pricking them with a bodkin or nail two or three times a day until 'she' (the text is specific) comes to ask the offended person's pardon, Klaassen, 'Three early modern magic rituals', 8–10.

64. *Daimonomageia*, 32–41; quotations, 40, 41. On Drage, see further Thorndike, *History of Magic and Experimental Science* 8.529–531. Culpeper did not say that mistletoe was useful against witchcraft, but did recommend it in cases of convulsive fits, palsy, and vertigo. He did, however, note that bittersweet was 'good to remove witchcraft in both men and beast, as all sudden diseases whatsoever', *Complete Herbal*, London: W. Foulsham & Co. Ltd n.d., 237, 54.

65. *The Astrological Practice of Physick*, London 1671, 159–166; quotation, 166.

66. Raine (ed.), *Depositions from the Castle of York*, 127.

67. Quoted in Gasser, *Manhood, Witchcraft, and Possession*, 200. Pro-Catholic narratives were not lacking, but tended to come from earlier decades, as in the case of William Perry in 1622. See French, 'Possession, Puritanism, and prophecy', 152–154.

68. Ewen, *Witchcraft and Demonianism*, 459.

69. Ewen, *op. cit. supra*, 401, 412, 478; 458, 441. These cases span 1664 to 1678.

70. Ewen, 405 (1674), 406 (1680).

71. *Marks of an Absolute Witch*, 278. See also Sharpe, *Instruments of Darkness*, 213–234, 111–113.

72. Ewen, 445, 378–380. Ewen, *Witch Hunting and Witch Trials*, 68. Low, *The Weem Witch*, London: Steve Savage Publishers 2006, 67–76. Rock, *Wicked Practice and Sorcerye*, 47–51.

73. K. Wiltshire, *Wiltshire Folklore*, Compton Chamberlye: Compton Press 1975, 3–4. Cf. other stories about local witches' being injured while in animal shape, W. S. Weeks, 'Witch stones and charms in Clitheroe and district', *Transactions of the Lancashire and Cheshire Antiquarian Society* 27 (1909), 104–110.

74. Waldron, *The History and Description of the Isle of Man*, 2nd ed. London 1744, 31, 34, 52, 53–74, 129–130, 42–46. On the language, note the remark of Thomas Wilson, Bishop of Sodor and Man. 'English is not understood by two-thirds at least of the island, though there is

an English school in every parish', Craine, *Manannan's Isle*, 115.

75. 'The Royal Society and the decline of magic', 104. 'Individual Fellows might dabble in alchemy or astrology, or promote miraculous cures, or compile accounts of witchcraft: but they left such pursuits behind when they attended meetings of the Society', *Ibid.*, 110. Further on some of these pursuits, see Monod, *Solomon's Secret Arts*, 100–105.

76. As, for example, in the case of Robert Hunt and witches in Somerset in 1665 and 1668. See Barry, *Witchcraft and Demonology in South-West England*, 14–57.

77. *Leviathan*, London 1651, Part 1, chap. 2.

78. Glanvill, *Saducismus Triumphatus*, 1–2. More, quoted in Hall, *Henry More*, 138.

79. *The Virtuoso*, London 1676, 27, 33. For a study of Shadwell's deeper purposes in his satire, see H. Maddux, 'The Virtuoso and Puritanism in 1676', Tennessee State University 2007, http://e-research.tnstate.edu/llp_wp/1. John Shanahan argues that Shadwell's point was that the Royal Society's science was, in effect, another form of theatre, 'Theatrical space and scientific space in Thomas Shadwell's Virtuoso', *Studies in English Literature, 1500–1900*, 49 (Summer 2009), 549–571.

80. *A Candle in the Dark*, 50, 63.

81. Jobe, 'The Devil in Restoration science', 346. Butler, *Hudibras*, Part 2, canto 3, vv. 125–148. The 'ledger' refers to a supposed Parliamentary warrant giving Matthew Hopkins authority to search out witches in East Anglia. This may have been an invention of Butler himself. Whatever commission Hopkins and Stearne had would have been much more local. See Gaskill, *Witchfinders*, 78–79.

82. *A Blow at Modern Sadducism*, 141, repeated in slightly different terms in *Saducismus Triumphatus* Part 2, 61. A full analysis of the episode is given by M. Hunter, 'New light on the Drummer of Tedworth', 311–337.

83. *An Antidote Against Atheisme*, 2nd ed. London 1662, Preface, para. 2.

84. *Saducismus Triumphatus*, 9 and preface, 5.

85. See further, Monod, *Solomon's Secret Arts*, 134–144, 122–134.

86. A clear reference to a famous incident from March 1661 when John Mompesson and his family from Tedworth were plagued by an invisible drummer banging his drum and behaving generally in a poltergeist manner.

87. N. Curnock (ed.), *The Journal of John Wesley, AM*, 8 vols. London 1909–1916, Vol. 6, 109. Wesley was in Scotland at the time, in Aberdeen in fact, when he wrote that affirmation. He noted he had just been reading Thomas Pennant's *Tour in Scotland, 1769*, and it may be significant that Pennant remarked of the area round Rannoch Moor in the Highlands 'In this part of the country the notion of witchcraft is quite lost. It was observed to cease almost immediately on the repeal of the Witch Act', although one should also note that Pennant said belief in ghosts still existed there. 2nd ed. London 1772, 94, 93.

10 The Fight for Witchcraft, a Northumberland Visionary, and Fears for National Security: 1669–1684

1. *A True and Faithful Relation of what passed for Many Years between Dr John Dee and Some Spirits*, London 1659, last page of preface.

2. Cameron, *Enchanted Europe*, 273. Casaubon, *Of Credulity and Incredulity*, 173. *A Letter of Meric Casaubon, D.D. etc., to Peter du Moulin, D.D. and Prebendary of the same church, concerning Natural Experimental Philosophy, and some books lately set out about it*, Cambridge 1669, 30.

3. *The Question of Witchcraft Debated*, 12–47, 63–78; quotations, 124, 127–128.

4. *Ibid.*, 121, 130.

5. Wagstaffe certainly did not help his case by providing potential opponents with ammunition in the form of phrases or clauses which could easily be taken out of context. For example: 'The vanity and falseness of their opinion who believe there are witches appears from nothing more than from this, that it ascribes unto the Devil an omnipotent power, in as much that no rational man by the light of reason shall be able to tell from the history of the Gospel whether Christ

were a witch or no. For let some men think what they please, the holiness of His doctrine is not the thousandth part such a proof of His acting by a divine power, as the miraculousness of His works. But alas! What were His miracles, or how were they to be valued, if malicious creatures, without a divine commission enabling them thereto, can make frogs and serpents, raise the dead, give law unto the winds and seas – to mention no more of those prodigious works ascribed unto devils upon account of witchcraft?' *Op. cit. supra*, 94–95.

6. *The Opinion of Witchcraft Vindicated*, 6, 15, 61. See further Hunter, *Science and the Shape of Orthodoxy*, 292–304.

7. *A Magical Vision*, 4–5.

8. *Ibid.*, 21–22.

9. 1672: Sneddon, *Possessed by the Devil*, 32–33. 1673: Sharpe, 'Witchcraft in the early modern Isle of Man', 18, 21. 1674: Suggett, *A History of Magic and Witchcraft in Wales*, 60.

10. This is a reminder of the way the night was divided in earlier times into two periods of sleep with a wakeful hour or two between them, during which various tasks might be done both within and outwith the house.

11. Raine, *Depositions from the Castle of York*, 202–203.

12. 'Spinster' refers to the way she earned a living, not necessarily to her marital status. The following account is based on Raine, *op. cit. supra*, 191–201.

13. The following is based on Raine, *Depositions*, 191–201. A brief summary of the case is given in Bath, *Dancing with the Devil*, 32–35. See also Rushton, 'Crazes and quarrels', 13–17.

14. K. Briggs, *The Fairies in Tradition and Literature*, London & New York: Routledge Classics 2002, 13. C.G. Silver, 'Tabu: Eating and Drinking. Motifs C200-C299' in J. Garry & H. El-Shamy (eds), *Archetypes and Motifs in Folklore and Literature: A Handbook*, New York & London: M. E. Sharpe 2005, 105–106.

15. Dipton Burn was described in 1825 as a fairly hazardous mountain stream which was difficult to cross until a good bridge was built in 1822. Other structures had existed, of course, before.

16. Murray, *The God of the Witches*, reissued Oxford: Oxford University Press 1952, 68–69.

17. On 'shamanic' trance, see Wilby, *The Visions of Isobel Gowdie*, 253–254. I am reluctant to use the word *shaman* because, as Ronald Hutton has pointed out, actual shamanic experiences and practices stem from cultures other than Western European, and so while aspects of those experiences may seem similar to those of people such as Isobel Gowdie and Ann Armstrong, in many respects they are different, *Shamans: Siberian Spirituality and the Western Imagination*, London & New York: Hambledon & London 2001, 47–51, 140–149.

18. *Op. cit.*, 347–348.

19. *The Mediaeval Vision: Essays in History and Perception*, Oxford: Oxford University Press 1976, 29. Ann's mention of a golden throne is reminiscent of a manuscript image from 1570, 'A Genevan wagon-driver and his devil come upon a witches' Sabbat in the woods near the city', Zentralbibliothek, Zurich, *Wickiana* F19, fol. 147v, in which the central figure is a horned and cloven-footed demon seated upon a golden throne.

20. Guazzo, *Compendium Maleficarum*, Book 1, chap. 12. He adds, 'Often again they are fast asleep at home, and yet think that they are at the Sabbat. For the Devil deceives their senses, and through his illusionings many imaginings may enter the minds of sleepers, leaving them with a conviction of their reality when they awake, as if it were not a dream but an actual experience and an undoubted physical action.' Goodwin, *The Mystery of Dreames, Historically Discoursed*, London 1658, 11–12. 'We see, then, dreams are the thought-works of the waking mind in the sleeping man', *Ibid.*, 13.

21. Cf. Briggs, 'In many of the witch-trials – in Dorset, in the north of England, in Scotland, and the Isle of Man – fairies and witches were believed to work together', *The Fairies in Tradition and Literature*, 168. G. Henningsen, 'The Ladies from Outside: an archaic pattern of the witches' Sabbath' in B. Ankarloo & G. Henningsen (eds), *Early Modern European Witchcraft: Centres and Peripheries*, Oxford: Clarendon Press 1993, 191–215.

22. J. Thirsk, *The Rural Economy of England*, London: Hambledon Press 1984, 395–398.

23. Quoted in Thomas, *Religion and the Decline of Magic*, 591.

24. On bed sharing, see Ekirch, *At Day's Close*, 279–282. Richard Johnson, too, mentions in evidence that in August 1672 he was 'lying in bed at Riding mill betwixt two of his fellow servants' (198).

25. One version of the pamphlet gives her name as 'Mary'. It is clear, however, from the contents of all the versions that they are talking about the same woman.

26. See further B. Capp, 'Arson, threats of arson, and incivility in early modern England' in P. Burke, B. Harrison, P. Slack (eds), *Civil Histories: Essays Presented to Sir Keith Thomas*, Oxford: Oxford University Press 2000, 197–199, 207–210.

27. The last heretic had been Edward Wightman, burned in Lichfield on 20 March 1612 for a variety of highly unorthodox religious opinions. An associate of his, Bartholomew Legate, had been burned for similar reasons three weeks earlier. I. Atherton & D. Como, 'The burning of Edward Wightman: 'Puritanism, prelacy, and the politics of heresy in early modern England', *English Historical Review* 120 (2005), 1215–1250. On 'Mother' Lakeland, see Darr, *Marks of an Absolute Witch*, 72–73.

28. *Displaying*, 277.

29. A. Clericuzio, 'John Webster (1611–1682)', *Oxford Dictionary of National Biography* 57.891–893.

30. See further Jobe, 'The Devil in Restoration science', 350–352.

31. *Witchcraft and its Transformations*, 73.

32. Raine, *Depositions from the Castle of York*, 208–210.

33. Suggett, *A History of Magic and Witchcraft in Wales*, 60. Craine, *Manannan's Isle*, 21. Sharpe, 'Witchcraft in the early modern Isle of Man', 21. Suggett, *op. cit.*, 76.

34. *Register of the Privy Council of Scotland*, Third series, Vol. 6, 629.

35. A. J. S. Gibson & T. C. Smout, *Prices, Food and Wages in Scotland, 1550–1780*, Cambridge: Cambridge University Press 1995, 321.

36. *A Hind Let Loose: An Historical Representation of the Church in Scotland*, n.p. 1687, 191.

37. It is interesting that some of these points had been made twenty-five years earlier by Sir Robert Filmer in his rebuttal of William Perkins in his *An Advertisement to the Jury-Men of England*, London 1653.

38. Montaigne had made a similar point in 1588 in his essay 'Concerning Cripples', when he remarked of witches that 'it is putting a very high price on one's conjectures to have a man roasted alive because of them'. But before we let ourselves run away with MacKenzie's references to 'innocents' and 'martyrdom', let us remember that these sentences represent his plea to the court on behalf of his client and that he is clearly playing on his hearers' emotions, and of course 'multitudes' does not square with his earlier statement that he does not believe there are many witches.

39. Levack, *Witch-Hunting in Scotland*, 137, 139. *Register of the Privy Council of Scotland*, Series Three, Vol. 1, 188–189, 233–234, 48.

40. Quoted in Larner, *Enemies of God*, 117.

41. *Witchcraft and Demonology in South-West England*, 59–62.

42. Barry, *op. cit.*, 66, 68, 69.

43. *Op. cit.*, 92.

44. In addition to Barry's account, see also Timmons, 'Witchcraft and rebellion in late seventeenth-century Devon', 297–330, which focusses on the political aspects of the case.

45. *A Full and True Account of the Proceedings at the Sessions of Oyer and Terminer holden for the City of London*, London 1682, 3–4.

46. *An Account of the Tryal and Examination of Joan Buts*, London 1682, 1–2.

47. *Strange News from Shadwell*, London 1684, no pagination.

48. *Great News from the West of England*, London 1689, 5.

49. Brinley's apparent linking of astrology with witchcraft becomes less odd if we remember that astrologers seem sometimes to have used techniques more reminiscent of magic than predictive calculation as, for example, when John Partridge denounced one astrologer ('a little, ruddy-faced conjuror') for using finger- or toenail clippings to help him predict the future.

Monod, *Solomon's Secret Arts*, 136.

50. This is probably a reference to the Sami peoples of the Arctic regions of Norway and Finland. See further, Rune Hagen, 'Sami shamanism, the Arctic dimension', *Magic, Ritual, and Witchcraft* 1 (Winter 2006), 227–233.

51. Winkler, *O Let Us Howle Some Heavy Note*, 13, 19–28.

52. See further Barry, *Witchcraft and Demonology in South-West England*, 103–123. (This also appears in J. Newton & J. Bath (eds), *Witchcraft and the Act of 1604*, 181–206). Bostridge, *Witchcraft and its Transformations*, 190–191.

53. The prevalent anti-Catholicism is continued here as well with Thomas D'Urfey's epilogue pointing out, 'Rome may allow strange tricks to please her sons,/But we are Protestants and English nuns.' See Winkler, *op. cit. supra*, 27–61; quotations, 31, and 57.

11 Witchcraft and Wonder Still on the Rise: 1685–1697

1. Burns, An Age of Wonders, 70–80; quotation, 74. J.

2. *Astrologia*, 122. *Hagiastrologia*, 41, 46; quotations, 44, 45–46; preface xxiv; 117–120. Butler was rector of Litchborough in Northamptonshire and in 1671 had published a horoscope of Christ. G. Baker, *The History and Antiquities of the County of Northampton*, 2 vols. London: Nicholls & Rodwell 1822–30, 1.409–410.

3. *Deadly Words: Witchcraft in the Bocage*, English trans. Cambridge: Cambridge University Press 1980, 35. The date of *Le Monde's* article was 1973.

4. *A Compleat History of the Most Remarkable Providences, Book of Judgement and Mercy, which have happened in this Present Age*, London 1697, 7.

5. J. Crawford, *Marvellous Protestantism: Monstrous Births in Post-Reformation England*, Baltimore & London: The John Hopkins University Press 2005, 178–185. Monod, *Solomon's Secret Arts*, 58–61, 134–141. Thomas, *Religion and the Decline of Magic*, 111–112.

6. Quoted in Burns, *op. cit. supra*, 106.

7. Ewen, *Witchcraft and Demonianism*, 375, 444–445. Deane's case bears some similarity to that of John Tonken in as much as a lad and a girl, both aged eighteen, suffered fits, saw visions, and the boy expelled several pins and a nail. But this was fairly standard behaviour in cases of demonic possession.

8. Seymour, *Irish Witchcraft and Demonology*, 171–172.

9. *A Discovery of the Impostures of Witches and Astrologers*, preface.

10. On Crouch, see J. McElligott, *Oxford Dictionary of National Biography* 14.465–466.

11. These occur on pp. 37–45.

12. The professor in question, David Dickson, died in 1663 and so was in no position to object. Dickson had had experience of witchcraft when he was minister in Irvine, for he had attended Margaret Barclay, John Stewart, and Isobel Crawford during their savage treatment before and after their trial in 1618. There is a somewhat sketchy entry on Sinclair by J. Anderson in the *Oxford Dictionary of National Biography* 50.748.

13. Sharpe, 'Witch-hunting and witch historiography: some Anglo-Scottish comparisons' in J. Goodare (ed.), *The Scottish Witch-Hunt in Context*, 195.

14. There was actually a relative lull in Scottish persecution of Quakers between 1679 and 1688, but it picked up again after the change of monarch in 1689. G. B. Burnet, *The Story of Quakerism in Scotland*, London: James Clarke & Co. Ltd 1952, 109. The Conventicle Act had been ruthlessly applied to Quakers between 1673 and 1679, *Ibid.*, 70–78. Sinclair's remark indicates that in spite of the lull, hatred still burned below the surface of some Scottish society.

15. See further Wasser, 'The mechanical world-view', 210–212.

16. It is possible he may simply have been unwilling to waste any material he had discovered, or which had come his way, because he does something similar at the end of chapter 17 where he throws in a few anti-Catholic sentences anent charms and the use of holy water, along with one or two other scarcely relevant bits and pieces. Anti-Catholicism, of course, always helped sell a book at this time, so his motives may merely have been mercenary.

17. Summers, *The Geography of Witchcraft*, 244–245. Black, *A Calendar of Cases of Witchcraft*

in Scotland, 78–79. Ross, *Aberdour and Inchcolme*, 332–334.

18. Sharpe, *A Historical Account of the Belief in Witchcraft in Scotland*, 151–158; quotations, 152–153, 155, 157.

19. Sharpe, *op. cit. supra*, 160–168; quotations, 162, 165–166, 168.

20. Suggett, *A History of Magic and Witchcraft in Wales*, 44, 46, 41.

21. Sharpe, 'Witchcraft in the early modern Isle of Man', 15, 16, 20. Craine, *Manannan's Isle*, 18–19.

22. Ewen, *Witchcraft and Demonianism*, 376–377, 460, 445–446, 378–380.

23. *A Relation of the Diabolical Practices of above Twenty Wizards and Witches*, 23–24.

24. Adam, *Witch Hunt*, 170.

25. Adam, *op. cit. supra*, 187–188.

26. *Sadducismus Debellatus*, page unnumbered, but 59 in the sequence.

27. 'The bewitchment of Christian Shaw', 61–77. This documentation can be found in H. V. McLachlan (ed.), *The Kirk, Satan, and Salem*, 152–219.

28. McLachlan & Swales, *op. cit. supra*, 65–67. Wasser, 'The western witch-hunt of 1697–1700', 148.

29. Quality of evidence also troubled the author of *Witchcraft Proven*, Glasgow 1697, as Christina Larner points out, 'Two late Scottish witchcraft tracts', 234.

30. For a detailed discussion, see Westaway & Harrison, 'The Surey Demoniack', 264–277. This was by no means the only example of fraud, if fraud it was, at this time. Francis Hutchinson recorded that in 1698, Sarah Fowles from Hammersmith was tried at the Old Bailey and pilloried for pretending to be possessed, when she was not, *An Historical Essay concerning Witchcraft*, 46, and an Irish pamphlet, *The Detection of a Popish Cheat* (1696), purported to tell the story of James Day, an eighteen year-old apprentice, who had sold his soul to the Devil and was encouraged to turn Catholic in order to free himself of this covenant. Later on, however, according to the pamphlet, James confessed it was all a lie and that he had been put up to it by his Catholic uncle and some priests.

31. See Porter, 'Witchcraft and magic in Enlightenment, Romantic, and Liberal thought', 201–205.

32. Similarly, the excuse for reissuing a pamphlet about a murder, a robbery, and a ghost in Shrewsbury in March 1694 is contained in a paragraph inserted between general reflections and the details of the story itself. 'I know there are some men in the world so hardy and bold as not only to deny apparitions, demons, and spectres, but the very being of spirits. These I look upon as men possessed with such an incurable madness as no hellebore is sufficient to quit them of. Others who believe they [do exist], yet think them so confined to their own apartments that they may not intermeddle with human affairs, at least, not show themselves to men. There is, no doubt, variety of imposture in the stories of them, but to reject all such appearances as fabulous is too severe a reflection upon the credit of the best historians, both ancient and modern', *An Account of a Most Horrid and Barbarous Murther and Robbery committed on the Body of Captain Brown, a Gentleman*, Edinburgh 1694, 1.

33. It is a moot point whether we are here dealing only with an operative lodge, or whether it may have been speculative. An Edinburgh House Register House manuscript dated 1696 contains 'Questions anent the Mason word', divided into two points: (i) 'Some questions that masons use to put to those who have the word, before they will acknowledge them', and (ii) 'The form of giving the mason word'. See further T. Churton, *Freemasonry: The Reality*, Hersham: Lewis Masonic pbk 2009, 289–294.

34. For the doubts, see Larner, 'Two late Scottish witchcraft tracts', 227, 230–231.

35. Even in a public sermon, delivered very soon after the Bargarran episode to people, many of whom, if not all, will have known the details of the case, a preacher felt the need to explain to the congregation what a witch was and the meaning of the biblical terms for workers of magic. See the transcript of this sermon in B. P. Levack (ed.), *Articles on Witchcraft, Magic, and Demonology*: Vol. 7, *Witchcraft in Scotland*, New York & London: Garland Publishing Inc. 1992, 379–381. On Margaret Atkin, see P. G. Maxwell-Stuart, *Witch Hunters*, Stroud: Tempus Publishing Ltd. 2003, 98.

36. Henri Boguet, *Discours des sorciers*, Lyons 1608, 131. Normand & Roberts (eds), *Witchcraft in Early Modern Scotland*, 226–227.

37. Bodin, *La démonomanie des sorciers*, Book 3, chap. 3. Cf. C. M. Woolgar, *The Senses in Late Mediaeval England*, New Haven & London: Yale University Press 2006, 121–124, 127, 130–131. M. Summers, *The History of Witchcraft*, 44. H. Pleij, *Colours Demonic and Divine: Shades of Meaning in the Middle Ages and After*, English trans. New York: Columbia University Press 2004, 86–87. On Greatrakes, see Fleming, *The Dark Side of the Enlightenment*, 60–61. G. P. Largey & D. R. Watson, 'The sociology of odours', *American Journal of Sociology* 77 (1972), 1021–1023. A particularly useful survey is given in C. Classen, *Worlds of Sense: Exploring the Senses in History and Across Cultures*, London & New York: Routledge 1993, 79–105.

38. Henderson, 'The survival of witchcraft-prosecutions', 53–56.

39. Black, *Calendar of Cases of Witchcraft*, 81. Adam, *Witch Hunt*, 218–219. A. J. S. Gibson & T. C. Smout, *Prices, Food, and Wages in Scotland, 1550–1780*, Cambridge: Cambridge University Press 1995, 334.

40. National Archives of Scotland, CH2/122/69/10, and CH2/122/69/3.

41. Quoted in Thomas, *Religion and the Decline of Magic*, 547.

42. We hear of a Manx charmer boasting in 1694 of the effects of her herbal potion, and the ecclesiastical punishment of Thomas Gell the same year for using sorcery four times to protect his property. But these are glimpses only and offer no evidence for constant or even frequent official monitoring of magical activity on the island, Craine, *Manannan's Isle*, 13, 19. There would be a burst in the early 1700s, but that was because of the deliberate efforts of one bishop to stamp out 'superstition'. On Caithness, see Robertson, *An Orkney Anthology* 1.369.

12 People *Versus* the Law: 1704–1730

1. Sutherland, *The Brahan Seer*, 82–85. Dalyell, *The Darker Superstitions of Scotland*, 336–337. Pugh, *The Deil's Ain*, 158. This was not the only case there in 1699. Donald MacConchie Roy complained to the kirk session that ever since 1691 his small flock of sheep had been dying off year by year because Anna MacCullie, with whom he had quarrelled, had cast a spell on them. K. J. Cullen, *Famine in Scotland: The Ill Years of the 1690s*, Edinburgh: Edinburgh University Press 2012, 48–49.

2. Chambers, *Domestic Annals of Scotland* 3.94–95.

3. Henderson, 'The survival of witchcraft prosecutions', 64–65. Cf. Elspeth Goldie who was only rebuked in open kirk in 1699 for scolding her brother-in-law and consulting a witch with a view to killing her brother-in-law's new wife by magic. Janet Harestanes, too, who allegedly caused the minister's house to collapse in 1700, and himself nearly to drown, was merely banished, a punishment which lasted a bare three weeks before she came back into the parish again, Henderson, *op. cit.*, 63, 66.

4. Wood, *Witchcraft and Superstitious Record in South-West Scotland*, 82–87.

5. H. M. B. Reid, *A Cameronian Apostle*, London 1896, 51.

6. Reid, *op. cit. supra*, 99–101.

7. L. Abrams, 'From demon to victim: the infanticidal mother in Shetland, 1699–1899' in Y. Galloway Brown & R. Ferguson (eds), *Twisted Sisters*, q.v. 180–203. S-M. Kilday, 'Maternal monsters: murdering mothers in south-west Scotland, 1750–1815', *Ibid.*, 156–179. B. P. Levack, 'The prosecution of sexual crimes in early eighteenth-century Scotland', *Scottish Historical Review* 89 (2010), 173–180. C. Kennedy, 'Criminal law and religion in post-Reformation Scotland', *Edinburgh Law Review* 16 (2012), 178–197. L. Leneman & R. Mitchison, *Sin in the City: Sexuality and Social Control in Urban Scotland, 1660–1780*, Edinburgh: Scottish Cultural Press 1998, 50–66; quotation, 54. See also *Ibid.*, 116–117. P. G. Maxwell-Stuart, 'Wild, filthie, execrabil, detestabil, and unnatural sin: bestiality in early modern Scotland' in T. Betteridge (ed.), *Sodomy in Early Modern Europe*, Manchester & New York: Manchester University Press 2002, 82–93. Leneman & Mitchison, *op. cit. supra*, 40–49.

8. A. Fletcher, *Two Discourses concerning the Affairs of Scotland*, Edinburgh 1698, second discourse, 24–25.

9. M. F. Graham, *The Blasphemies of Thomas Aikenhead: Boundaries of Belief on the Eve of the Enlightenment*, Edinburgh: Edinburgh University Press 2008, 102–103, 130–132. Cf. the case of Thomas Woolston who, in 1727–1730, poured doubt on Jesus's miracles, describing them as metaphors or allegories rather than facts, Midelfort, 'The Gadarene demoniac', 51–53.

10. *A Good Expedient for Innocence and Peace*, Edinburgh 1704, 3.

11. Anon., *The Trial of Richard Hathaway*, 5.

12. Ewen, *Witchcraft and Demonianism*, 446.

13. *A Full and True Account of the Discovering, Apprehending, and Taking of a Notorious Witch*, London 1704.

14. Webster, *A Collection of Rare and Curious Tracts*, 129–146.

15. Suggesting the Devil may have been a real person brings with it all kinds of implications, and I do not intend these to be pursued either with respect to Lillias's case in particular or other appearances of the Devil in general. We lack any firm information which might allow us to build upon such a suggestion and therefore, while it should be noted as one rational possibility among others, it should not and cannot be taken as the starting point for any fanciful theory.

16. Maxwell-Stuart, *An Abundance of Witches*, 98, 101, 145. F. Gunn, *The Artificial Face*, London: Trinity Press 1973, 110.

17. Webster, *op. cit. supra*, 144. Black, *Calendar of Cases of Witchcraft*, 82. *New Statistical Account of Scotland*: Vol. 9, *Fife and Kinross*, Edinburgh & London: William Blackwood and Sons 1845, 731, 732. Chambers, *Domestic Annals of Scotland* 3.298–299.

18. Couper's career is set out in *Fasti Ecclesiae Scoticanae* 5.227–228. Details of the charges against Beatrix and the others, and subsequent events, are given in Cook, *Annals of Pittenweem*, 109–129.

19. Webster, *Collection of Rare and Curious Tracts*, 69–94; quotations, 74, 85.

20. Cook, *op. cit. supra*, 117 has a note to the effect that by an Act of Parliament three years previously, magistrates and judges were forbidden to grant bail in capital cases. But if this is a reference to the 'Act for preventing wrongful imprisonment and against undue delays in trials' of 1701, otherwise known as the Criminal Procedure Act, it does not apply, since the relevant chapter of the Act (6) discusses the actual granting of bail under various circumstances, not its non-granting. There seems to be no other Act of this period dealing with this subject.

21. Cook, *op. cit. supra*, 118–119.

22. Webster, *op. cit. supra*, 76, 87–89.

23. Cook, 119–124.

24. Cook, 125–126.

25. Cook, 125.

26. *Domestic Annals of Scotland*, 299.

27. Wood, *Witchcraft and Superstitious Record*, 131. Clergymen at this time were not always hostile to magic. Robert Forbes, vicar of Rougham in Norfolk, died in November 1709 and was found to have been wearing round his neck a charm against ague in a small blue silk bag. O. Davies, 'Healing charms in use in England and Wales, 1700–1950', *Folklore* 107 (1996), 23.

28. Davies, 'Decriminalising the witch', 211, 212. For the 1717 case, see Ewen, *Witchcraft and Demonianism*, 390 and *Witch Hunting and Witch Trials*, 314–316.

29. G. Lamoine (ed.), *Charges to the Grand Jury, 1689–1803*, London: Royal Historical Society 1992, 98.

30. *Crime and Mentalities in Early Modern England*, 89.

31. M. Hunter (ed.), *The Occult Laboratory: Magic, Science, and Second Sight in Late 17th-Century Scotland*, Woodbridge: The Boydell Press 2001, 2–12. K. Hutchison, 'Supernaturalism and the mechanical philosophy', *History of Science* 21 (1983), 298–301; 'What happened to occult qualities in the scientific revolution?' *Isis* 73 (1982), 250–253. M. G. Cook, 'Divine artifice and natural mechanism: Robert Boyle's mechanical philosophy of Nature', *Osiris*, 2nd series 16 (2001), 133–150.

32. 'A constant prodigy?' 282.

33. *Historical, Physiological, and Theological Treatise of Spirits*, 394–396.

34. The whole phenomenon of dreaming is complex. Edward Bever usefully summarises some of the recent thinking on the subject in *The Realities of Witchcraft and Popular Magic in Early Modern Europe*, Basingstoke: Palgrave Macmillan 2008, 106–115.

35. Beaumont, *op. cit. supra*, 63–69, 293–295.

36. On Beaumont, see further Barry, *Witchcraft and Demonology in South-West England*, 124–164. Beaumont's 'astral man' may be connected with ideas derived from Paracelsus and transmitted via Van Helmont whose *Paradoxical Discourses* Beaumont translated in 1685.

37. S. Pain, '1709: the year that Europe froze', *New Scientist*, 7 February 2009, 46–47. Once again, however, it should be noted that there is no correlation in the British Isles between these events and a rise in the number of prosecutions for witchcraft. Such a rise did not take place.

38. For the trial, see Sneddon, *Possessed by the Devil*, 139–171. On the judges, see further F. E. Ball, *The Judges in Ireland*, 2 vols. New York: E. P. Dutton & Co. 1927, 2.35, 37, 65–67.

39. Guskin, 'The context of witchcraft', 55. Hutchinson, *An Historical Essay Concerning Witchcraft*, 130.

40. *Op. cit. supra*, 56–57. John Fleming draws attention to the networks of means of communication which burgeoned in the eighteenth century. His immediate topic is Freemasonry, but his remarks hold good for the way in which ideas, gossip, scandal, and sensation could speed from town to country in a very short space of time, *The Dark Side of the Enlightenment*, 161–164.

41. Bostridge, *Witchcraft and its Transformations*, 132–136. Monod, *Solomon's Secret Arts*, 152–154.

42. Interestingly enough, what Addison fails to mention is that Otway's witch spoke the truth to the man who met her.

43. Quoted in Bostridge, *op. cit. supra*, 127.

44. Davies, 'Decriminalising the witch', 214–218. Bond, *The Supernatural Philosopher*, 282. Sutherland, *The Brahan Seer*, 104–105. Boiling urine to identify the source, including witchcraft, of an illness, was still being done in Wales in the 1760s. See Suggett, *A History of Magic and Witchcraft in Wales*, 105. Addison's partner in the journal, Richard Steele, also joined in with a pseudo-letter from 'Dulcibella Thankley', giving an account of a supposed visit to Campbell, Wednesday 3 September 1712. It is reproduced in Bond, *op. cit.*, 245–246. A lengthy puff for Campbell, written by Eliza Haywood and entitled *A Spy upon the Conjuror*, appeared in 1724. See further, K. R. King, 'Spying upon the conjuror: Haywood, curiosity, and the novel in the 1720s', *Studies in the Novel* 30 (Summer 1998), 183–187.

45. See also Bostridge, *Witchcraft and its Transformations*, 95–96. Sneddon, *Witchcraft and Whigs*, 114–116.

46. *Op. cit.*, viii. The *Essay* is dedicated to the Lord Chief Justice of England, the Lord Chief Justice of Common Pleas, and the Lord Chief Baron of Exchequer.

47. Sneddon, *op. cit. supra*, 101–109.

48. See Bostridge, *op. cit. supra*, 34–35, 143–144.

49. M. E. Novak, *Daniel Defoe: Master of Fictions*, Oxford: Oxford University Press 2001, 350–359.

50. Quoted in Novak, *op. cit. supra*, 660.

51. J. Richetti, *The Life of Daniel Defoe*, Oxford: Blackwell Publishing 2005, 170–171. Quotation; Novak, *op. cit. supra*, 661.

52. *A System of Magick*, preface ii–iii.

53. *Op. cit. supra*, 333–334.

54. Suggett, *A History of Magic and Witchcraft in Wales*, 142.

55. Sharpe, *An Historical Account*, 181–194; quotations, 192, 193.

56. Sharpe, *op. cit. supra*, 187, 192, 193, 190. Burt, *Letters from the North of Scotland*, 149–151. C. MacKay, *Extraordinary Popular Delusions and the Madness of Crowds*, Ware: Wordsworth Editions Ltd. 1995, 525–526.

57. Sir Walter Scott likewise dismisses the episode as a prank, 'under instructions, it is said, from a knavish governor', *Letters on Demonology and Witchcraft*, 198.

58. *A Brief and True Discourse* in P. C. Almond, *Demonic Possession and Exorcism in Early*

Modern England, Cambridge: Cambridge University Press 2004, 209.

59. *Satan's Invisible World Discovered*, 172–174; quotations, 172, 173.

60. Black, *Calendar of Cases of Witchcraft in Scotland*, 83.

61. *Letters from the North of Scotland*, 245, 125. Sharpe, *An Historical Account*, 199–200. The episode is sometimes dated to 1722, as in W. N. Neill's article on the subject, but it seems clear from other evidence that 1727 is the correct year.

62. *Witchcraft and its Transformations*, 170–179.

63. *The Freeholder*, ed. J. Leheny, Oxford: Clarendon Press 1979, 141.

13 The Act Repealed, and Witchcraft's Afterlife: 1735–

1. M. Ellis, *The History of Gothic Fiction*, Edinburgh: Edinburgh University Press 2000, 162–164.

2. Sugg, *Mummies, Cannibals, and Vampires*, 228–230.

3. Samuel Clarke, quoted in Gaskill, *Crime and Mentalities*, 114. The date is 1730.

4. Quoted in Davies, *Witchcraft, Magic, and Culture*, 161.

5. *Witchcraft and its Transformations*, 182. I am indebted to Bostridge's chapter 8 for this brief description of how the Act was repealed.

6. As Bob Bushaway observes, '[David Vincent] writes, "If the oral tradition largely defined the pre-industrial popular culture, the significance of its decline revolved around the question of superstition. The world of those whose horizons were limited by the oral tradition was suffused with the supernatural." In eighteenth- and nineteenth-century England, as in earlier periods, rural popular culture was the subject for humour or condemnation by elite culture or was treated as the object of crusade by reformers and radicals in the name of reason', 'Things said or sung a thousand times: customary society and oral culture in rural England, 1700–1900' in A. Fox & D. Woolf (eds), *The Spoken Word: Oral Culture in Britain, 1500–1850*, Manchester & New York: Manchester University Press 2002, 256.

7. *Journal of the House of Lords*, Vol. 24.

8. This text is given in Newton & Bath, *Witchcraft and the Act of 1604*, 243–244.

9. 'Decriminalising the witch', 221–222.

10. Quoted in Gaskill, *Crime and Mentalities*, 117.

11. Craine, *Manannan's Isle*, 21, 22. 24, 28. Sharpe, 'Witchcraft in the early modern Isle of Man', 15, 16, 18.

12. Suggett, *A History of Magic and Witchcraft in Wales*, 88, 89, 102, 103, 109–110, 109.

13. Seymour, *Irish Witchcraft and Demonology*, 226–227.

14. 'The Ballad of Mary Butters' in P. F. Byrne, *Witchcraft in Ireland*, Cork: The Mercier Press 1967, 52–55.

15. Midelfort, 'The Gadarene demoniac in the English enlightenment', 53–57.

16. Journal quoted in Davies, 'Decriminalising the witch', 222–223. Gypsies, *Ibid.*, 222. Davies, *Witchcraft, Magic, and Culture*, 188.

17. *Witchcraft in Old and New England*, 236.

18. Quoted in Carnochan, 'Witch-hunting and belief in 1751', 392. My account of this incident is based on Carnochan's article.

19. Carnochan, *op. cit. supra*, 394, 395. For another example of a similarly violent episode which took place in 1737, see Davies, *Witchcraft, Magic, and Culture*, 94–95. Spitting and voiding pins was still taking place in 1762 when the *Gentleman's Magazine* recorded a case form Kent, as Davies records, *op. cit.*, 198.

20. *A Narrative of Some Extraordinary Things that happened to Mr Richard Giles's Children at the Lamb without Lawford's Gate*, Bristol: R. Edwards 1800, 54.

21. See O. Davies, *A People Bewitched: Witchcraft and Magic in Nineteenth-Century Somerset*, Trowbridge: Redwood Books Ltd 1999, 65–91, 151–152.

22. Davies, *Witchcraft, Magic, and Culture*, 164.

23. S. Hoyle, 'The witch and the detective: mid-Victorian stories and beliefs' in W. de Blecourt & O. Davies (eds), *Witchcraft Continued: Popular Magic in Modern Europe*, Manchester &

New York: Manchester University Press 2004, 51–54.
24. M. Gaskill, *Hellish Nell, Last of Britain's Witches*, London: Fourth Estate 2001, 363.

SELECT BIBLIOGRAPHY

Details of other sources used are given in full in the endnotes.

Primary Sources

Ady T, *A Candle in the Dark*, London 1656.

Anonymous, *Fasciculus Morum: A Fourteenth-Century Preacher's Handbook*, ed. & trans. S. Wenzel, University Park & London: The Pennsylvania State University Press 1989.

Anonymous, *Witchcrafts Strange and Wonderfull: Discovering the Damnable Practices of Seven Witches against the Lives of Certain Noble Personages and Other of this Kingdom*, London 1635.

Anonymous, *Signs and Wonders from Heaven*, London 1644.

Anonymous, *The Lawes Against Witches and Conjuration*, London 1645.

Anonymous, *A Magical Vision, or, a perfect discovery of the fallacies of witchcraft as it was lately represented in a pleasant sweet dream to a holy sweet sister, a faithful and precious asserter of the Family of Stand-Ups, for preservation of the Saints from being tainted with the heresies of the Congregations of the Do-Littles*, London 1673.

Anonymous, *A Pleasant Treatise of Witches, their imps and meetings, persons bewitched, necromancies, incubus and succubuses, familiar spirits, goblins, fairies, spectres, phantasms, places haunted, and devilish impostures, with the differences between good and bad angels, and a true relation of a good genius*, London 1673.

Anonymous, *Relation of the Most Remarkable Proceedings at the Late Assizes at Northampton*, London 1674.

Anonymous, *Strange and Wonderful News from Yowel in Surrey*, London 1681.

Anonymous, *A Tryal of Witches at the Assizes of Bury St Edmonds for the County of Suffolk ... before Sir Matthew Hale*, London 1838.

Anonymous, *The Gentleman's Magazine* 102 (1832), Part 1, 406–410, 489–492.

Anonymous, *The Impossibility of Witchcraft*, London 1712.

Anonymous, *The Trial of Richard Hathaway at Surrey Assizes*, London 1754.

Anonymous, *Anti-Canidia: or, Superstition Detected and Exposed*, London 1762.

Baddeley R, *The Boy of Bilson: or, a true discovery of the late notorious impostures of certain Romish priests, etc.*, London 1622.

Ballantyne J. H. & Smith B (eds), *Shetland Documents, 1580–1611*, Lerwick: Shetland Island Council, Shetland Times 1999.

Barrow J, *The Lord's Arm Outstretched in an Answer of Prayer*, London 1664.

Baxter R, *The Certainty of the World of Spirits Fully Evinced* (1691), London 1854.

Beaumont J, *An Historical, Physiological, and Theological Treatise of Spirits, Apparitions, Witchcrafts, and other Magical Practices*, London 1705.

Bell J (attributed), *Witchcraft Proven, Arraigned, and Condemned in its Professors, Professions, and Marks*, Glasgow 1697.

Bernard R, *A Guide to Grand Jury Men*, 2nd ed. London 1619.

Bond W, *The Supernatural Philosopher: or, The Mysteries of Magick in all its Branches clearly unfolded*, London 1728.

Boulton R, *A Compleat History of Magick, Sorcery, and Witchcraft*, 2 vols, London 1715–16.

Boulton R, *The Possibility and Reality of Magick, Sorcery, and Witchcraft Demonstrated*, London 1722.

Bovet R, *Pandaemonium: or, The Devil's Cloyster*, London 1684.

Blagrave J, *Astrological Practice of Physick*, London 1671.

Bragge F, *A Full and Impartial Account of the Discovery of Sorcery and Witchcraft practised by Jane Wenham*, London 1712.

Bragge F, *Witchcraft Farther Displayed*, London 1712.

Brinley J, *A Discovery of the Impostures of Witches and Astrologers*, London 1680.

Brinley J, *A Discourse proving by Scripture and Reason and the best authors that there are witches*, London 1686.

Burt E, *Letters from the North of Scotland*, ed., A. Simmons, Edinburgh: Birlinn 1998.

Butler J, *Hagiastrologia: or, Astrology, a Sacred Science*, London 1680.

Butler J, *Astrologia: or, The Most Sacred and Divine Science of Astrology Vindicated*, London 1680.

Camfield B, *An Appendix containing some reflections upon Mr Webster's Displaying of Supposed Witchcraft*, London 1678.

Casaubon M, *Of Credulity and Incredulity in Things Divine and Spiritual*, London 1670.

Chambers R, *Domestic Annals of Scotland*, Vol. 3, Edinburgh & London: W. & R. Chambers 1861.

Cockburn J. S (ed.), *Calendar of Assize Records: Home Circuit Indictments: Elizabeth and James I: Introduction*, London Stationery Office 1985; *Essex Indictments: Elizabeth I*, 1978; *Hertfordshire Indictments: Elizabeth I*, 1975; *Sussex Indictments: Elizabeth I*, 1975.

Cockburn J. S (ed.), *Calendar of Assize Records: Home Circuit Indictments: James I: Sussex Indictments*, London: Stationery Office 1975; *Essex Indictments*, 1982; *Hertfordshire Indictments*, 1975; *Kent Indictments*, 1980; *Surrey Indictments*, 1982.

Cook D, *Annals of Pittenweem*, Anstruther: Lewis Russell 1867.

Cooper T, *Sathan Transformed into an Angel of Light: expressing his dangerous impostures under glorious shewes*, London 1622.

Coxe F, *A Short Treatise declaring the detestable wickednesse of magicall sciences, as necromancy, conjuration of spirits, curious astrology, and such like*, London 1561.

Crouch N, *The Kingdom of Darkness: or, The History of Daemons, Spectres, Witches, Apparitions, Possessions, Disturbances, and other Wonderful and Supernatural Delusions, Mischievous Feats, and Malicious Impostures of the Devil*, London 1688.

Cullen F. G, *Sadducismus Debellatus: or, A True Narrative of the Sorceries and Witchcrafts Exercised by the Devil and his Instruments upon Mrs Christian Shaw*, London 1698.

Defoe D, *A System of Magick: or, A History of the Black Art*, London 1728.

Depositions and Other Ecclesiastical Proceedings from the Courts of Durham, extending from 1311 to the reign of Elizabeth, London & Edinburgh 1845.

Drage W, *Daimonomageia: A Small Treatise of Sicknesses and Diseases from Witchcraft and Supernaural Causes*, London 1665.

Ewen C. L'Estrange (ed.), *Witch Hunting and Witch Trials*, London: Kegan Paul, Trench, Trubner & Co. Ltd 1929.

Ewen C. L'Estrange (ed.), *Witchcraft and Demonianism*, London: Heath Cranton Ltd. 1933.

Gifford G, *A Dialogue Concerning Witches and Witchcrafts* (1593), Brighton: Puckrel Publishing 2007.

Glanvill J, *A Blow at Modern Sadducism in some philosophical considerations about witchcraft*, London 1668.

Greenwel T, *A Full and True Account of the Discovering, Apprehending, and Taking of a Notorious Witch*, London 1704.

Grainge W, *Demonologia: A Discourse on Witchcraft as it was acted in the family of Mr*

Edward Fairfax, Harrogate: R. Ackrill 1882.

G.R.A.M, *The Belief of Witchcraft Vindicated*, London 1712.

Grant F, *Sadducismus Debellatus: or, A True Narrative of the Sorceries and Witchcrafts exercised by the Devil and his Instruments upon Mistress Christian Shaw*, London 1698.

Hale J, *A Modest Enquiry into the Nature of Witchcraft*, London 1702.

Hale M, *A Collection of Modern Relations of Matter of Fact Concerning Witches and Witchcraft*, London 1693.

Hallywell H, *Melampronoea: or, A Discourse of the Polity and Kingdom of Darkness*, London 1681.

Higgs D, *The Wonderful and True Relation of the Bewitching of a Young Girl in Ireland*, London 1699.

Hopkins M & Stearne J, *The Discovery of Witches and Witchcraft*, Brighton: Puckrel Publishing 2007.

Hutchinson F, *A Historical Essay Concerning Witchcraft*, London 1718.

Jollie T, *A Vindication of the Surey Demoniack as no Imposter*, London 1698.

Law R, *Memorialls: or, The Memorable Things that Fell Out within this Island of Britain from 1638–1684*, Edinburgh: Archibald Constable & Co. 1818.

McLachlan H. V (ed.), *The Kirk, Satan and Salem: A History of the Witches of Renfrewshire*, Glasgow: The Grimsay Press 2006.

Muggleton L, *A True Interpretation of the Witch of Endor*, London 1669.

'M. Y', *The Hartford-shire Wonder: or, Strange News from Ware*, London 1669.

Petto S, *A Faithful Narrative of the Wonderful and Extraordinary Fits which Mr Thomas Spatchet (late of Dunwich and Cookly) was under by Witchcraft*, London 1693.

Price L, *The Witch of the Woodlands: or, The Cobbler's New Translation*, London 1655.

Raine J (ed.), *Depositions from the Castle of York, relating to offences committed in the northern counties in the seventeenth century*, London: Surtees Society 1860.

Robertson D. M (ed.), *Goodnight, My Servants All: The Sourcebook of East Lothian Witchcraft*, Glasgow: The Grimsay Press 2008.

'R. P', *A True Account of a Strange and Wonderful Relation of one John Tonken of Pensans in Cornwall*, London 1686.

'R. T', *The Opinion of Witchcraft Vindicated*, London 1670.

Shadwell T, *The Lancashire Witches and Tegue O'Dively, the Irish Priest*, London 1682.

Sinclair G, *Satan's Invisible World Discovered*, Edinburgh 1685.

Spencer J, *A Discourse concerning Prodigies, wherein the Vanity of Presages by them is reprehended and their true and proper ends asserted and vindicated*, Cambridge 1663.

Telfair A, *A True Relation of an Apparition, Expressions, and Actings of a Spirit*, Edinburgh 1696.

'T. P', *A Relation of the Diabolical Practices of above Twenty Wizards and Witches of the Sheriffdom of Renfrew in the Kingdom of Scotland*, London 1697.

Wagstaffe J, *The Question of Witchcraft Debated*, London 1671.

Walton R, *The Genuine Life and Confession of Richard Walton, a Reputed Conjuror*, Birmingham: T. Warren 1733.

Secondary Sources

Adam I, *Witch Hunt: The Great Scottish Witchcraft Trials of 1697*, London: Macmillan 1978.

Amundsen K, 'The Duke's devil and Doctor Lambe's darling: a case study of the male witch in early modern England', *Psi Sigma Siren* 2 (2012), Issue 1, 29–60.

Ankarloo B. & Clark S (eds), *The Athlone History of Witchcraft and Magic in Europe*: Vol. 5, *The Eighteenth and Nineteenth Centuries*, London: Athlone Press 1999.

Aveling J. C. H, *Post Reformation Catholicism in East Yorkshire, 1558–1790*, East Yorkshire Local History Society 1960.

Aveling, J. C. H, *The Catholics of the West Riding of Yorkshire, 1558–1790*, Leeds:

Proceedings of the Leeds Philosophical and Literary Society 1963.

Aveling J. C. H, *Northern Catholics: The Catholic Recusants of the North Riding Yorkshire, 1558–1790*, London: Geoffrey Chapman 1966.

Bailey M. D, 'The disenchantment of magic: spells, charms, and superstition in early modern European witchcraft literature', *American History Review* 111 (April 2006), 383–404.

Bailey M. D, 'Concern over superstition in late Mediaeval Europe' in S. A. Smith & A. Knight (eds), *The Religion of Fools? Superstition Past and Present*, Oxford: Oxford University Press 2008, 115–133.

Bailey M. D, *Fearful Spirits, Reasoned Follies: The Boundaries of Superstition in Late Mediaeval Europe*, Ithaca & London: Cornell University Press 2013.

Balleine G. P, 'Witch trials in Jersey', *Bulletin of the Société Jersiaise* 13 (1939), 379–398.

Barry J, Hester M, Roberts G (eds), *Witchcraft in Early Modern Europe: Studies in Culture and Belief, Cambridge*: Cambridge University Press 1996.

Bates B, *The Real Middle Earth: Magic and Mystery in the Dark Ages*, London: Sidgwick & Jackson 2002.

Bath J, *Dancing with the Devil and Other True Tales of Northern Witchcraft*, Newcastle: Tyne Bridge Publishing 2000.

Bath J, 'The treatment of potential witches in north-east England' in Newton & Bath (eds), *Witchcraft and the Act of 1604*, q.v. 129–145.

Bellows T, *Channel Islands Witchcraft: A Critical Survey*, ePub: Adobe Digital Editions 2011.

Bennett G, 'Ghost and witch in the sixteenth and seventeenth centuries', *Folklore* 97 (1986), 3–14.

Bildhauer B & Mills R (eds), *The Monstrous Middle Ages*, Cardiff: University of Wales Press 2003.

Billingsley J, *The Mixenden Treasure*, Hebden Bridge: Northern Earth 2009.

Black G. F, 'Scottish charms and amulets', *Proceedings of the Society of Antiquaries of Scotland* 27 (1892–3), 433–526.

Black G. F, *Witchcraft and Witchcraft Trials in Orkney and Shetland*, London 1903, reprinted 1974.

Black G. F, *A Calendar of Cases of Witchcraft in Scotland, 1570–1727*, New York: New York Public Library 1938.

Blakiston H. D, 'Two more Mediaeval ghost stories', *English Historical Review* 38 (1923), 85–87.

Blécourt W. de, 'The making of the female witch', *Gender & History* 12 (July 2000), 287–309.

Borman T, *Witches: A Tale of Sorcery, Scandal and Seduction*, London: Jonathan Cape 2013.

Bostridge I, *Witchcraft and its Transformations, c.1650–c.1750*, Oxford: Clarendon Press 1997.

Briggs K, *The Fairies in Tradition and Literature*, New York & London: Routledge, reprint 2002.

Briggs R, *Witches and Neighbours*, London: HarperCollins 1996.

Burns W. E, *An Age of Wonders: Prodigies, Politics, and Providence in England, 1657–1727*, Manchester & New York: Manchester University Press 2002.

Caciola N, 'Wraiths, revenants, and ritual in Mediaeval culture', *Past & Present* 152 (1996), 3–45.

Cambers A, 'Demonic possession, literacy, and "superstition" in early modern England', *Past and Present* 202 (February 2009), 3–35.

Cameron E, *Enchanted Europe: Superstition, Reason, and Religion, 1250–1750*, Oxford: Oxford University Press 2010.

Cardini F, *Demoni e Meraviglie: Magia e Stregoneria nella Società Medievale*, Bitonto: Rafaello 1995.

Carlson E, "Witchcraft is a rife and common sinne in these our daies": the powers of witches in English demonologies, 1580–1620', *Western Illinois Historical Review* 3 (2011), 22–57.

Carnochan W. B, 'Witch-hunting and belief in 1751: the case of Thomas Colley and Ruth Osborne', *Journal of Social History* 4 (1971), 389–403.

Carter C, 'A constant prodigy? Empirical views of an unordinary Nature', *The Seventeenth Century* 23 (Spring 2008), 265–289.

Carver M, Sanmark A, Semple S (eds), *Signals of Belief in Early England: Anglo-Saxon Paganism Revisited*, Oxford: Oxbow Books 2012.

Chardonnens L. S, *Anglo-Saxon Prognostics, 900–1100*: Study and Texts, Leiden-Boston: Brill 2007.

Cheny A. D, 'The holy maid of Kent', *Transactions of the Royal Historical Society* n.s. 18 (1904), 107–129.

Clark S (ed.), *Languages of Witchcraft: Narrative, Ideology, and Meaning in Early Modern Culture*, Basingstoke: Macmillan 2001.

Clark S & Morgan P. T. J, 'Religion and magic in Elizabethan Wales', *Journal of Ecclesiastical History* 27 (1976), 31–46.

Cohn N, *Europe's Inner Demons*, London: Book Club Associates 1975.

Cope J, 'The Irish stroker and the King: Valentine Greatrakes, Protestant faith healing, and the Restoration in Ireland', *Eire-Ireland* 46 (Autumn 2011), 170–200.

Coudert A, 'Henry More and witchcraft' in S. Hutton (ed.), *Henry More (1614–1687): Tercentenary Studies*, Dordrecht-Boston-London: Kluwer Academic Publishers 1989, 115–136.

Cowan E. J & Henderson L, 'The last of the witches? The survival of Scottish witch belief' in Goodare (ed.), *The Scottish Witch-Hunt in Context* q.v. 198–217.

Craine D, *Manannan's Isle: A Collection of Manx Historical Essays*, Man: Manx Museum and National Trust 1955.

Crawford J, 'Evidences for witchcraft in Anglo-Saxon England', *Medium Aevum* 32 (1963), 99–116.

Crawford J, *Marvellous Protestantism: Monstrous Births in Post-Reformation England*, Baltimore & London: The John Hopkins University Press 2005.

Curran R, *A Bewitched Land: Ireland's Witches*, Dublin: The O'Brien Press 2005.

Dalyell J. G, *The Darker Superstitions of Scotland: Illustrated from History and Practice*, Edinburgh: Waugh & Innes 1834.

Davies O, *Witchcraft, Magic, and Culture, 1736–1951*, Manchester & New York: Manchester University Press 1999.

Davies O, 'The nightmare experience, sleep paralysis, and witchcraft accusations', *Folklore* 114 (2003), 181–203.

Davies O, 'Decriminalising the witch: the origin of and response to the 1736 Witchcraft Act', in Newton & Bath (eds), *Witchcraft and the Act of 1604* q.v. 207–232.

Davies O, *Grimoires: A History of Magic Books*, Oxford: Oxford University Press 2009.

Davies R. T. *Four Centuries of Witch Beliefs, with special reference to the Great Rebellion*, London: Methuen 1947.

Davies S. F, 'The reception of Reginald Scot's Discovery of Witchcraft: witchcraft, magic, and radical religion', *Journal of the History of Ideas* 74 (2013), 381–401.

Decker R, *Witchcraft and the Papacy*, English trans. Charlottesville & London: University of Virginia Press 2008.

DeWindt A. R, 'Witchcraft and conflicting visions of the ideal village community', *Journal of British Studies* 34 (October 1995), 427–463.

Dewar S, *Witchcraft and the Evil Eye in Guernsey*, 2nd ed. Guernsey: The Toucan Press 1970.

Duffy E, *The Stripping of the Altars: Traditional Religion in England, 1400–1580*, Newhaven & London: Yale University Press 1992.

Dye S, 'To converse with the Devil? Speech, sexuality, and witchcraft in early modern Scotland', *International Review of Scottish Studies* 37 (2012), 9–40.

Easlea B, *Witch-Hunting, Magic, and the New Philosophy: An Introduction to Debates of the Scientific Revolution, 1450–1750*, Brighton: Harvester Press 1980.

Ekirch A. R, *At Day's Close: A History of Night Time*, London: Weidenfeld & Nicolson 2005.

Elmer P, 'Towards a politics of witchcraft in early modern England' in S. Clark (ed.), *Languages of Witchcraft*, q.v. 101–118.

Elmer P, *The Miraculous Conformist: Valentine Greatrakes, the Body Politic, and the Politics of Healing in Restoration Britain*, Oxford: Oxford University Press 2013.

Ewen L'Estrange C, *Robert Ratcliffe, 5th Earl of Sussex: The Witchcraft Allegations in his Family*, London 1938.

Fleming J. V, *The Dark Side of the Enlightenment: Wizards, Alchemists, and Spiritual Seekers in the Age of Reason*, New York & London: W. W. Norton and Company 2013.

Flint V. I. J, 'Magic in English thirteenth-century miracle collections' in J. N. Bremmer & J. R. Veenstra (eds), *The Metamorphosis of Magic from Late Antiquity to the Early Modern Period*, Leuven: Peeters Publishers 2003, 117–131.

Forbes T. R, 'Verbal charms in British folk medicine', *Proceedings of the American Philological Society* 115 (1971), 293–316.

Freeman E, 'Wonders, prodigies and marvels: unusual bodies and the fear of heresy in Ralph of Coggeshall's Chronicon', *Journal of Mediaeval History* 26 (2000), 127–143.

Freeman J, 'Sorcery at Court and manor: Margery Jourdemayne, the witch of Eye next Westminster', *Journal of Mediaeval History* 30 (2004), 343–357.

French A, 'Possession, Puritanism, and prophecy: child demoniacs and English reformed culture', *Reformation* 13 (2008), 133–161.

Friedman J. B, *The Monstrous Races in Mediaeval Art and Thought*, Syracuse, New York: Syracuse University Press 2000.

Gaskill M, 'Witchcraft and power in early modern England: the case of Margaret Moore' in J. Kermode & G. Walker (eds), *Women, Crime, and the Courts in Early Modern England*, London: UCL Press 1994, 125–145.

Gaskill M, 'Witchcraft in early modern Kent: stereotypes and the background to accusations' in Barry-Hester-Roberts (eds), *Witchcraft in Early Modern Europe*, q.v. 257–287.

Gaskill M, *Crime and Mentalities in Early Modern England*, Cambridge: Cambridge University Press 2000.

Gaskill M, 'Witchcraft, politics, and memory in seventeenth-century England', *The Historical Journal* 50 (2007), 289–308.

Gaskill M, *Witchcraft: A Very Short Introduction*, Oxford: Oxford University Press 2012.

Gasser E. A, *Manhood, Witchcraft, and Possession in Old and New England*, unpublished PhD thesis, University of Michigan 2007.

Geis G, 'Lord Hale, witches, and rape', *British Journal of Law and Society* 5 (Summer 1978), 26–44.

Geis G & Bunn I, *A Trial of Witches: A Seventeenth-Century Witchcraft Prosecution*, London & New York: Routledge 1997.

Gerulaitis L. V, 'The rise and persistence of a myth: witch transvection', *Fifteenth-Century Studies* 33 (2008), 106–113.

Gibson J, *Hanged for Witchcraft: Elizabeth Lowys and her Successors*, Canberra: Tudor Press 1988.

Gibson M, *Reading Witchcraft: Stories of Early English Witchcraft*, London & New York: Routledge 1999.

Gibson M (ed.), *Early Modern Witches: Witchcraft Cases in Contemporary Writing*, London & New York: Routledge 2000.

Gibson M (ed.), *Witchcraft and Society in England and America, 1550–1750*, Ithaca, New York: Cornell University Press 2003.

Gibson M, 'Applying the Act of 1604: witches in Essex, Northamptonshire, and Lancashire before and after 1604' in Newton & Bath: *Witchcraft and the Act of 1604* q.v. 115–128.

Golden R. M (ed.), *Encyclopaedia of Witchcraft: The Western Tradition*, 4 vols. Santa Barbara: ABC-CLIO, Inc. 2006.

Goodare J (ed.), *The Scottish Witch-Hunt in Context*, Manchester & New York: Manchester University Press 2002.

Goodare J, 'The Scottish Witchcraft Act', *Church History* 74 (2004), 39–67.

Goodare J, Martin L, Miller J (eds), *Witchcraft and Belief in Early Modern Scotland*, Basingstoke: Palgrave Macmillan 2008.

Goodman B. A, 'The female spellcaster in Middle English romances: heretical outsider or political insider?' *Essays in Mediaeval Studies* 15 (1998), 45–56.

Gourley B, 'Feminised idolatry and the subversion of religious orthodoxy in John Bale's Three Laws', *eSharp* 9 (2007).

Greenslet F, *Joseph Glavill: A Study in English Thought and Letters of the Seventeenth Century*, New York: Columbia University Press 1900.

Griffiths R. A, 'The trial of Eleanor Cobham: an episode in the fall of Duke Humphrey of Gloucester', *Bulletin of the John Rylands Library* 51 (1968–9), 381–399.

Griffiths W, *Aspects of Anglo-Saxon Magic*, Hockwold-cum-Wilton: Anglo-Saxon Books 1996.

Grigg E, 'Mole rain and other natural phenomena in the Welsh annals: can *mirabilia* unravel the textual history of the *Annales Cambriae*?' *The Welsh History Review* 24 (2009), 1–40.

Guskin P. J, 'The context of witchcraft: the case of Jane Wenham (1712)', *Eighteenth-Century Studies* 15 (1981), 48–71.

Hall A, 'Getting shot of elves: healing, witchcraft and fairies in the Scottish witchcraft trials', *Folklore* 116 (2005), 19–37.

Hall A, *Elves in Anglo-Saxon England*, Woodbridge: The Boydell Press 2007.

Hall A. R, *Henry More: Magic, Religion and Experiment*, Oxford: Blackwell 1990.

Hand W. D, *Magical Medicine: The Folkloric Component of Medicine in Folk Belief, Custom, and Rituals of the Peoples of Europe and America*, Berkeley: University of California Press 1980.

Harley D, 'Mental illness, magical medicine, and the Devil in northern England, 1650–1700' in R. French & A. War (eds), *The Medical Revolution of the Seventeenth Century*, Cambridge: Cambridge University Press 1989, 114–144.

Harris A, *Night's Black Agents: Witchcraft and Magic in Seventeenth-Century English Drama*, Manchester: Manchester University Press 1980.

Hart W. H, 'Observations on some documents relating magic in the reign of Queen Elizabeth', *Archaeologia* 40 (1867), 389–397.

Henderson L, 'Witch-hunting and witch belief in the Gàidhealtachd' in Goodare-Martin-Miller, *Witchcraft and Belief in Early Modern Scotland*, q.v. 95–118.

Henderson L, 'The survival of witchcraft prosecutions and witch belief in south-west Scotland', *The Scottish Historical Review* 85 (2006), 52–74.

Henderson L, 'The witches of Bute' in A. Ritchie (ed.), *Historic Bute: Land and People*, Edinburgh: University of Edinburgh Press 2012, 151–161.

Henderson L & Cowan E. J, *Scottish Fairy Belief*, East Linton: Tuckwell Press 2001.

Hester M, *Lewd Women and Wicked Witches: A Study of the Dynamics of Male Domination*, London & New York: Routledge 1992.

Holmes C, 'Popular culture? Witches, magistrates, and divines in early modern England' in S. L. Kaplan (ed.), *Understanding Popular Culture: Europe from the Middle Ages to the Nineteenth Century*, Berlin-New York: Mouton *c.* 1884, 85–111.

Holzmann V, 'Ich beswer dich wurm und wyrmin: die magische Kunst des Besprechens', *Die Zeitschrift für Literaturwissenschaft und Linguistik*: Lili 33 (2003), 25–47.

Hopper A, '"The Popish army of the north": anti-Catholicism and Parliamentary allegiance in Yorkshire, 1642–6', *Recusant History* 25 (May 2000), 12–28.

Hunter M, *Science and the Shape of Orthodoxy: Intellectual Change in Late Seventeenth-Century Britain*, Woodbridge: Boydell Press 1995.

Hunter M, 'New light on the Drummer of Tedworth: conflicting narratives of witchcraft in Restoration England', *Historical Research* 78 (2005), 311–353.

Hunter M, 'The Royal Society and the decline of magic', *Notes and Records of the Royal*

Society 20 (June 2011), 103–119.

Hutton R, 'The changing faces of Manx witchcraft', *Cultural and Social History* 7 (2010), 153–169.

Hutton R, 'Witch-hunting in Celtic societies', *Past and Present* 212 (August 2011), 43–71.

Ireland R. W, 'Medicine, necromancy, and the law: aspects of Mediaeval poisoning', *The Cambrian Law Review* 18 (1987), 52–61.

Jackson L, 'Witches, wives, and mothers: witchcraft persecution and women's confessions in seventeenth-century England', *Women's History Review* 4 (1995), 63–83.

Jolly K. L, 'Magic, miracle, and popular practice in the early Mediaeval West: Anglo-Saxon England' in J. Neusner, E. S. Frerichs, P. V. McCracken Flesher (eds), *Religion, Science, and Magic in Concert and Conflict*, Oxford: Oxford University Press 1989, 166–182.

Johnstone N, 'The Protestant Devil: the experience of temptation in early modern England', *Journal of British Studies* 43 (April 2004), 173–205.

Johnstone N, *The Devil and Demonism in Early Modern England*, Cambridge: Cambridge University Press 2006.

Jolly K. L, *Popular Religion in Late Saxon England: Elf Charms in Context*, Chapel Hill, NC: University of North Caroline Press 1996.

Jones N, 'Defining superstitions: treasonous Catholics and the Act against Witchcraft of 1563' in C. Carlton, R. L. Woods, M. L. Robertson, J. S. Block (eds), *State, Sovereigns, and Society in Early Modern England*, New York: St Martins Press 1998, 187–203.

Jones W. R, 'Political uses of sorcery in Mediaeval Europe', *The Historian* 34 (1972), 670–687.

Joynes A (ed.), *Mediaeval Ghost Stories*, Woodbridge: The Boydell Press 2001.

Kelly H. S, 'English kings and fear of sorcery', *Mediaeval Studies* 39 (1977), 207–238.

Kennedy A, '"A heavy yock uppon their necks": Covenanting government in the northern Highlands, 1638–1651', *Journal of Scottish Historical Studies* 30 (2010), 93–122.

Kirby D (ed.), *Marvels, Magic and Witchcraft in the North Riding of Yorkshire: David Naitby's Bedale Treasury*, North Yorkshire: Summerfield Press 2005.

Kittredge G. L, *Notes on Witchcraft*, Worcester, Mass: The Davis Press 1907.

Kittredge G. L, *Witchcraft in Old and New England*, Cambridge, Mass.: Harvard University Press 1929.

Klaassen F, 'Three early modern magic rituals to spoil witches', *Opuscula* 1 (2011), 1–10.

Kramer W, 'English reformation and Irish witches: the effects of confessionalisation in suppressing witchcraft accusations in early modern Ireland', *The Forum: Cal Poly's Journal of History* 1 (2009), article 6 *http://digitalcommons.calpoly.edu/forum/vol1/iss1/6*

Kramer W. E, *Filid, Fairies, and Faith. The Effects of Gaelic Culture, Religious Conflict, and the Dynamics of Dual Confessionalisation on the Suppression of Witchcraft Accusations and Witch-Hunts in Early Modern Ireland, 1533–1670*, M.A. thesis. Faculty of California Polytechnic State University, May 2010.

Lambert M, *Mediaeval Heresy*, 2nd ed. Oxford: Blackwell 1992.

Larner C, 'Two late Scottish witchcraft tracts: Witch-Craft Proven and The Tryal of Witchcraft' in S. Anglo (ed.), *The Damned Art: Essays in the Literature of Witchcraft*, London-Henley-Boston: Routledge & Kegan Paul 1977, 227–245.

Larner C, *Enemies of God*, Oxford: Basil Blackwell 1983.

Larner C, *Witchcraft and Religion: The Politics of Popular Belief*, Oxford: Basil Blackwell 1984.

Larner C, Hyde Lee C, McLachlan H. V (eds), *A Source-Book of Scottish Witchcraft*, reprinted Glasgow: The Grimsay Press 2005.

Larson H. R, 'Keening, crooning, and casting spells: women, sleep, and folk genres in Mediaeval Irish poetry', *Proceedings of the Harvard Celtic Colloquium* 18 (1998), 134–149.

Lea D, 'The supernatural on the stage: an analysis of early modern literary and theatrical representations of Lancashire witches and demons' in V. Theile & A. D. McCarthy (eds), *Staging the Superstitions of Early Modern Europe*, q.v. 85–105.

Leland J, 'Witchcraft and the Woodvilles: a standard Mediaeval smear?' in D. L. Biggs, S. D.

Michalove, A. Compton Reeves (eds), _Reputation and Representation in Fifteenth-Century Europe_, Leiden-Boston: Brill 2004, 267–288.

Le Roy Ladurie E, _Montaillou_, English trans. London: Penguin Books 1978.

Levack B. P, 'Possession, witchcraft, and the law in Jacobean England', 52 _Washington and Lee Law Review_ (1995), 1613–1640.

Lewis J. E, 'Spectral currencies in the air of reality: A Journal of the Plague Year and the history of apparitions', _Representations_ 87 (Summer 2004), 82–101.

Lewis M. C. G, _Dreaming of Dwarves: Nightmares and Shamanism in Anglo-Saxon Poetics and the Wid Dweorh Charm_, unpublished MA thesis, University of Georgia 2009.

Licence T, 'The gift of seeing demons in early Cistercian spirituality', _Cistercian Quarterly Studies_ 39 (2004), 49–65.

Linwood Pitts J, _Witchcraft and Devil Lore in the Channel Islands_, Guernsey 1885.

MacCulloch E, _Guernsey Folk Lore_, London: Elliot Stock 1903.

MacCulloch J. A, 'The mingling of fairy and witch beliefs in sixteenth and seventeenth century Scotland', _Folklore_ 32 (December 1921), 227–244.

MacDonald M (ed.), _Witchcraft and Hysteria in Elizabethan London_, London & New York: Tavistock/Routledge 1991.

MacDonald S, 'Torture and the Scottish witch-hunt: a re-examination', _Scottish Tradition_ 27 (2002), 95–114.

MacDonald S, 'Enemies of God revisited: recent publications on Scottish witch-hunting', _Journal of Scottish Historical Studies_ 23 (2003), 65–84.

McDonald S. W, 'The witch doctors of Scotland', _Scottish Medical Journal_ 43 (August 1998), 119–122.

MacFarlane A, _Witchcraft in Tudor and Stuart England: A Regional and Comparative Study_, 2nd ed. London: Routledge 1999.

McLachlan H & Swales K, 'The bewitchment of Christian Shaw: a reassessment of the famous Paisley witchcraft case of 1697' in Y. Galloway Brown & R. Ferguson (eds), _Twisted Sisters: Women, Crime and Deviance in Scotland since 1400_, East Linton: Tuckwell Press 2002, 54–83.

Mack E, 'The Malleus Maleficarum and King James: drafting witchcraft', _Voces Novae: Chapman University Historical Review_ 1 (2009), 181–203.

MacKenzie A, _History of the Munros of Fowlis (sic)_, Inverness: A. & W. MacKenzie 1898.

MacLeod M & Mees B, _Runic Amulets and Magic Objects_, Woodbridge: The Boydell Press 2006.

L. Martin, 'Witchcraft and family: what can witchcraft documents tell us about early modern Scottish family life?' _Scottish Tradition_ 27 (2002), 7–22.

Marwick E. M, 'Northern witches' in J. Robertson (ed.), _An Orkney Anthology: The Selected Works of Ernest Walker Marwick_, Vol. 1, Edinburgh: Scottish Academic Press _c._ 1991, 333–383.

Maxwell-Stuart P. G, _Satan's Conspiracy: Magic and Witchcraft in Sixteenth-Century Scotland_, East Linton: Tuckwell Press 2001.

Maxwell-Stuart P. G, _Witch Hunters_, Stroud: Tempus Publishing 2003.

Maxwell-Stuart P. G, 'Witchcraft and magic in eighteenth-century Scotland' in O. Davies & W. de Blécourt (eds), _Beyond the Witch Trials: Witchcraft and Magic in Enlightenment Europe_, Manchester & New York: Manchester University Press 2004, 81–99.

Maxwell-Stuart P. G, _An Abundance of Witches: The Great Scottish Witch-Hunt_, Stroud: Tempus Publishing 2005.

Maxwell-Stuart P. G, _Satan: A Biography_, Stroud: Amberley Publishing 2008.

Maxwell-Stuart P. G, _Witch Beliefs and Witch Trials in the Middle Ages_, London: Continuum 2011.

McDonald S. W, 'The Devil's mark and the witch-prickers of Scotland', _Journal of the Royal Society of Medicine_ 90 (1997), 507–511.

McGuiness M, 'The Guernsey witchcraft trials of 1617: the case of Collete Becquet', _Law and Literature: Current Legal Issues_ 2 (1999), 623–644.

Midelfort H. C. E, 'The Gadarene demoniac in the English enlightenment' in E. Michelson, S. K. Taylor, M. N. Venables (eds), *A Linking of Heaven and Earth*, Aldershot: Ashgate 2012 49–66.

Miller J, 'Devices and directions: folk healing aspects of witchcraft practice in seventeenth-century Scotland' in J. Goodare (ed.), *Scottish Witch-Hunt in Context*, q.v. 90–105.

Mitchell A, 'On various superstitions in the north-west Highlands and Islands of Scotland', *Proceedings of the Society of Antiquaries of Scotland* 4 (1860–2), 251–288.

Moir S, 'The crucible: witchcraft and the experience of the family in early modern Scotland' in E. Ewan & J. Nugent (eds), *Finding the Family in Mediaeval and Early Modern Scotland*, London: Ashgate 2008, 49–59.

Moore A. W, *Folklore and Witchcraft of the Isle of Man*, Douglas & London: Brown & Son, Nutt 1891.

Myers A. R, 'The captivity of a royal witch: the household accounts of Queen Joan of Navarre, 1419–21', *Bulletin of the John Rylands Library* 24 (1940), 263–284.

Napier J, *Western Scottish Folklore and Superstitions* (first published as *Folklore: or, Superstitious Beliefs in the West of Scotland within this Century*, 1879), Maple Shade, NJ: Lethere Press 2008.

Narváez P (ed.), *The Good People*, Lexington, Kentucky: University Press of Kentucky 1991.

Neame A, *The Holy Maid of Kent: The Life of Elizabeth Barton, 1506–1534*, London: Hodder & Stoughton 1971.

Neary A, 'The origins and character of the Kilkenny witchcraft case of 1324', *Proceedings of the Royal Irish Academy. Section C: Archaeology, Celtic Studies, History, Linguistics, Literature*, Vol. 83C (1983), 333–350.

Neill W. N, 'The professional pricker and his test for witchcraft', *Scottish Historical Review* 19 (1922), 205–213.

Neill W. N, 'The last execution for witchcraft in Scotland, 1722', *Scottish Historical Review* 20 (1923), 218–221.

Newall V (ed.), *The Witch Figure: Folklore Essays by a Group of Scholars honouring the 75th Birthday of Katharine M. Briggs*, Boston: Routledge & Kegan Paul 1973.

Newton J & Bath J (eds), *Witchcraft and the Act of 1604*, Leiden-Boston: Brill 2008.

Ogier D, 'Night revels and werewolfery in Calvinist Guernsey', *Folklore* 109 (1998), 53–62.

Ogier D, 'Glimpses of the obscure: the witch trials of the Channel Islands' in A. McShane & G. Walker (eds), *The Extraordinary and the Everyday in Early Modern England*, Basingstoke: Palgrave Macmillan 2010, 177–191.

Oldridge D, 'Light from darkness: the problem of evil in early modern England', *The Seventeenth Century* 27 (2012), 389–409.

Osler M. J (ed.), *Rethinking the Scientific Revolution*, Cambridge: Cambridge University Press 2000.

Otto B-C & Stausberg M, *Defining Magic*, Sheffield: Equinox Publishing Ltd. 2013.

Owst G, 'Sortilegium in English homiletic literature of the fourteenth century' in J. C. Davies (ed.), *Studies Presented to Sir Hilary Jenkinson*, Oxford: Oxford University Press 1957, 272–303.

Parker G, *Global Crisis: War, Climate Change, and Catastrophe in the Seventeenth Century*, New Haven & London: Yale University Press 2013.

Parkin S, 'Witchcraft, women's honour, and customary law in early modern Wales', *Social History* 31 (August 2006), 295–318.

Parson C. E, 'Notes on Cambridgeshire witchcraft', *Proceedings of the Cambridge Antiquarian Society* 19 (1915), 31–45.

Pearson M. F, 'Vision on trial in "The Late Lancashire Witches"' in V. Theile & A. D. McCarthy (eds), *Staging the Superstitions of Early Modern Europe*, q.v. 107–127.

Peters E, *The Magician, the Witch, and the Law*, Philadelphia: University of Pennsylvania Press 1978.

Peters E, 'The Mediaeval Church and state on superstition, magic, and witchcraft' in B.

Ankarloo & S. Clark (eds), *The Athlone History of Witchcraft and Magic in Europe, vol. 3: The Middle Ages*, 176–245.

Petzoldt R & Neubauer P (eds), *Demons: Mediators between This World and the Other*, Frankfurt am Main: Peter Lang 1998.

Pitts J. L, *Witchcraft and Devil Lore in the Channel Islands*, Guernsey 1886.

Polito M, 'Governing bodies, tempering tongues: Elizabeth Barton and Tudor treason', *Law and Literature: Current Legal Issues* 2 (1999), 603–621.

Pollington S, *Leechcraft: Early English Charms, Plant-lore, and Healing*, Ely: Anglo-Saxon Books 2008.

Poole G & Stokes K, *Witches of Northamptonshire*, Stroud: The History Press 2006.

Poter R, 'Witchcraft and Magic in Enlightenment, Romantic, and liberal thought' in B. Ankarloo & S. Clark (eds), *The Athlone History of Witchcraft and Magic*, Vol. 5, q.v. 193–274.

Purkiss D, *Troublesome Things: A History of Fairies and Fairy Stories*, London: Allen Lane 2000.

Raymond J, *Pamphlets and Pamphleteering in Early Modern Britain*, Cambridge: Cambridge University Press 2003.

Riddell W. R, 'The first execution for witchcraft in Ireland', *Journal of the American Institute of Criminal Law and Criminology* 7 (1917), 828–837.

Riddell W. R, 'Sir Matthew Hale and witchcraft', *Journal of the American Institute of Criminal Law and Criminology* 17 (1926), 5–12.

Rider C, *Magic and Impotence in the Middle Ages*, Oxford: Oxford University Press 2006.

Robertson D. J, 'Orkney Folklore', *Proceedings of the Orkney Antiquarian Society* 2 (1923–4), 37–46.

Robertson E. J, *Panic and Persecution: Witch-Hunting in East Lothian, 1628–1631*, unpublished Master's thesis, University of Edinburgh 2003.

Rock R. S, *'Wicked Practice and Sorcerye': Witchcraft, Magic, and Politics in Early Modern Ireland*, unpublished Master's dissertation, University of Ulster 2012.

Ross W, *Aberdour and Inchcolm, being Historical Notices of the Parish and Monastery*, Edinburgh 1885.

Rushton P, 'Women, witchcraft, and slander in early modern England: cases from the Church courts of Durham, 1560–1675', *Northern History* 18 (1982), 116–132.

Rushton P, 'Crazes and quarrels: the character of witchcraft in the north-east of England, 1649–80', *Bulletin of the Durham County Local History Society* 31 (1983), 2–40.

Rushton P, 'Texts of authority: witchcraft accusations and the demonstration of truth in early modern England' in S. Clark (ed.), *Languages of Witchcraft*, q.v. 21–39.

Russell J. B, *Witchcraft in the Middle Ages*, Ithaca & London: Cornell University Press 1972.

Ryrie A, *The Sorcerer's Tale*, Oxford: Oxford University Press 2008.

St John Seymour J. D, *Irish Witchcraft and Demonology*, New York: Dorset Press 1992.

Schulz M, *Beschwörungen in Mittelalter*, Heidelberg: C. Winter 2003.

Scott W, *Letters on Demonology and Witchcraft*, Ware: Wordsworth Editions Ltd. 2001.

Sharpe C. K, *A Historical Account of the Belief in Witchcraft in Scotland*, London & Glasgow 1884.

Sharpe J, 'The Devil in East Anglia: the Matthew Hopkins trials reconsidered' in Barry, Hester, Roberts (eds), *Witchcraft in Early Modern Europe*, q.v. 237–254.

Sharpe J, *The Bewitching of Anne Gunter*, London: Profile Books 1999.

Sharpe J, 'Witchcraft in the early modern Isle of Man', *Cultural and Social History* 4 (2007), 11–28.

Silver V, '"Wonders of the invisible world": the trial of the Lowestoft witches' in R. Barbour & C. Preston (eds), *Sir Thomas Browne: The World Proposed*, Oxford: Oxford University Press 2008, 118–145.

Simpson J, 'Repentant soul or walking corpse? Debatable apparitions in Mediaeval England', *Folklore* 114 (2003), 389–402.

Skemer D. C, *Binding Words: Textual Amulets in the Middle Ages*, Pennsylvania: Pennsylvania State University Press 2006.

Sneddon A, *Witchcraft and Whigs: The Life of Bishop Francis Hutchinson, 1660–1739*, Manchester & New York: Manchester University Press 2008.

Sneddon A, *Possessed by the Devil: The Real History of the Islandmagee Witches and Ireland's Only Mass Witchcraft Trial*, Dublin: The History Press, Ireland, 2013.

Snobelen S. D, 'Lust, pride, and ambition: Isaac Newton and the Devil' in J. E. Force & S. Hutton (eds), *Newton and Newtonianism*, Dordrecht-Boston-London: Kluwer Academic Publishers 2004, 155–181.

Stokes L, 'Experiments in pain: reason and the development of judicial torture' in M. E. Plummer & R. Barnes (eds), *Ideas and Cultural Margins in Early Modern Germany*, Farnham: Ashgate 2009, 239–254.

Stone L. G, *Terrible Crimes and Wicked Pleasures: Witches in the Art of the Sixteenth and Seventeenth Centuries*, unpublished PhD thesis, University of Toronto 2012.

Stoyle M, *The Black Legend of Prince Rupert's Dog: Witchcraft and Propaganda during the English Civil War*, Exeter: University of Exeter Press 2011.

Summers M, *The Geography of Witchcraft*, reprint 1927 ed. Evanston & New York: University Books 1958.

Sutherland A, *The Brahan Seer: The Making of a Legend*, Bern: Peter Lang 2009.

Tangherlini T, 'How do you know she's a witch? Witches, cunning folk, and competition in Denmark', *Western Folklore* 59 (2000), 279–303.

Tatlock J. S. P, 'Some Mediaeval cases of blood-rain', *Classical Philology* 9 (1914), 442–447.

Tenno S, *Religious Deviance in the Elizabethan Diocese of Durham*, MA thesis, Department of Theology and Religion, Durham University, September 2009.

Theile V & McCarthy A. D (eds), *Staging the Superstitions of Early Modern Europe*, Farnham: Ashgate 2013.

Thomas K, *Religion and the Decline of Magic*, London: Penguin Books 1973.

Timmons S, 'Witchcraft and rebellion in late seventeenth-century Devon', *Journal of Early Modern History* 10 (2006), 297–330.

Tomlinson S, *Demons, Druids, and Brigands on Irish High Crosses: Rethinking the Images Identified as the Temptation of Saint Anthony*, unpublished PhD thesis, University of North Carolina at Chapel Hill 2007.

Tyler P, 'Church courts at York and witchcraft prosecutions, 1567–1640', *Northern History* 4 (1969), 83–109.

Unsworth C. R, 'Witchcraft beliefs and criminal procedure in early modern England' in T. G. Watkin (ed.), *Legal Record and Historical Reality*, London: Hambledon 1989, 71–98.

Valletta F, *Witchcraft, Magic, and Superstition in England, 1640–70*, Aldershot: Ashgate 2000.

Voss P. J, 'Print culture, ephemera, and the Elizabethan news pamphlet', *Literature Compass* (2006), 1053–1064.

Walker S, *The Witches of Hertfordshire*, Stroud: Tempus Publishing Ltd. 2004.

Walsham A, 'Recording superstition in early modern Britain: the origins of folklore' in Smith & Knight (eds), *Religion of Fools?* q.v. 178–206.

Wasser M, 'The Privy Council and the witches: the curtailment of witchcraft prosecutions in Scotland, 1597–1628', *The Scottish Historical Review* 52 (April 2003), 20–46.

Wasser M, 'The western witch-hunt of 1697–1700: the last major witch-hunt in Scotland' in J. Goodare (ed.), *The Scottish Witch-Hunt in Context* q.v. 146–165.

Wasser M, 'The mechanical world-view and the decline of witch beliefs in Scotland' in Goodare-Martin-Miller, *Witchcraft and Belief in Early Modern Scotland* q.v. 206–226.

Watkins C. S, *History and the Supernatural in Mediaeval England*, Cambridge: Cambridge University Press 2007.

Westaway J & Harrison R, 'The Surey Demoniack: defining Protestantism in 1690s Lancashire', *Studies in Church History* 32 (1996), 263–282.

Whyte I. D, *Scotland before the Industrial Revolution: An Economic and Social History, c.1050–c.1750*, London & New York: Longman 1995.

Williams B, 'She was usually placed with the great men and leaders of the land in the public assemblies: Alice Kyteler, a woman of considerable power' in C. Meek (ed.), *Women in Renaissance and Early Modern Europe*, Dublin: Four Courts 2000, 67–83.

Williams J. G, 'Witchcraft in seventeenth-century Flintshire', *Journal of the Flintshire Historical Society* 26 (1973–74), 16–33; 27 (1975–76), 5–35.

Williams M, *Fiery Shapes: Celestial Portents and Astrology in Ireland and Wales, 700–1700*, Oxford: Oxford University Press 2010.

Willumsen L. H, 'Seventeenth-century witch trials in Scotland and northern Norway: comparative aspects', *History Research* 1 (December 2011), 61–74.

Wilson S, *The Magical Universe: Everyday Ritual and Magic in Pre-Modern Europe*, London & New York: Hambledon & London 2000.

Winkler A. E, *O Let Us Howle Some Heavy Note: Music for Witches, the Melancholics, and the Mad on the Seventeenth-Century English Stage*, Bloomington & Indianapolis: Indiana University Press 2006.

Wood J. M, *Witchcraft and Superstitious Record in Southwest Scotland*, Dumfries: J. Maxwell & Son 1911.

Yeoman L. A, 'The Devil as doctor: witchcraft, Wodrow, and the wider world', *Scottish Archives* 1 (1995), 93–105.

Yeoman L. A (ed.), 'Witchcraft cases from the Register of Commissions of the Privy Council of Scotland, 1630–1642', *Scottish History Society, Miscellany XIII*, Edinburgh: Lothian Print 2004, 223–265.

Young A. R, 'Elizabeth Lowys: witch and social victim, 1564', *History Today* 22 (1972), 879–885.

Zika C, *The Appearance of Witchcraft: Print and Visual Culture in Sixteenth-Century Europe*, London & New York: Routledge 2007.

LIST OF ILLUSTRATIONS

1. Witches' activities included making a wax or clay image of someone they wished to hurt, and either sticking pins in it or putting it near a fire so that it would melt or become red hot.

2. Witches were said to carry out their magic by the aid of the Devil, who appeared to them in both human and animal form. This composite picture illustrates those two possibilities in one.

3. The intermediary acting on behalf of Satan in helping the witch was an evil spirit referred to as her familiar. 'Familiar' is derived from a Latin word meaning 'close friend'. The familiar could take the shape of any living creature and imprisoned witches were often watched to see if their familiar would visit them in gaol with a view to helping them escape.

4. Among the nefarious activities attributed to witches was interfering with the weather, causing storms at sea to wreck ships or summoning hail to destroy other people's crops or vineyards.

5. Body parts taken from corpses were said to be used in witches' magic. Fingers and toes from the bodies of hanged men and women were readily available because executed criminals were often left on the gibbet where they died as a warning to onlookers and passers-by.

6. Witches were said to fly to meetings with demons and the Devil, sometimes on brooms, sometimes on people or demons in the shape of horses. These meetings were called 'synagogues' in the Middle Ages and 'Sabbats' later on. There witches worshipped the Devil, danced, ate, and received instructions for further deeds of evil.

7. At the Sabbat, the witches danced, often facing outwards from their circle, the opposite of what would happen at normal gatherings such as weddings. They moved in a distorted fashion to discordant music, but dancing for pleasure, not as part of a magical ritual.

8. In 1589–90, James VI of Scotland suffered three magical plots against his life from a large number of witches in East Lothian. They whipped up a storm to wreck his ship as he returned from Denmark with his new queen, Anna; they manufactured a poison from a toad and other material, which was meant to drip upon him as he passed through a doorway in one of his palaces; and they made a wax image to represent him and placed it near a fire so that it would melt, and the king with it.

9. Anne Bodenham was executed as a witch in 1653. She had been a servant to a 'Dr' Lambe who told fortunes, used counter-magic against witches, practised astrology, and found lost or stolen articles with the help of a crystal ball. Anne had learned her craft from him and was alleged to have worked the same range of occult practices.

10. In the mid-seventeenth century in East Anglia, Matthew Hopkins and John Stearne operated as self-appointed witch finders, identifying large numbers of people as witches and causing many to be put to death in what was England's worst incident of witch persecution.

11. Matthew Hopkins produced a pamphlet in 1647, outlining a number of his witch detection methods, partly for other people's benefit, partly to justify himself in the face of a growing tide of criticism.

12. In Scotland, witches and other malefactors might be chained to a wall to prevent their escaping. This device was meant to go round the neck and was known as the 'jougs'. This

example comes from Duddingston church in Midlothian.

13. Sir Matthew Hale was an important and influential English judge who presided over the trial of Amy Duny and Rose Cullender in Bury St Edmunds in 1664. Despite disagreement among learned counsel about the quality of evidence presented to the court, both women were convicted and hanged.

14. The regular capital punishment for witches in England and Wales was hanging. In Scotland they were garrotted and their dead bodies burned. In the Channel Islands they were sometimes burned alive, but were usually strangled first. Burning alive was most unusual. Witches in Britain were not drowned.

15. Isobel Gowdie was a witch from Auldearn in Moray. She was arrested in 1662 and made a series of detailed confessions involving fairies, shooting people with elf-arrows, changing shape, and ploughing the land with a plough held by the Devil and pulled by toads. This nineteenth-century engraving gives an idea of the extraordinary material contained in her accounts to the local ministers.

16. A battle for acceptance or dismissal of belief in witches, magic, spirits, and apparitions arose in the mid-seventeenth century and was still in full flood a century later. Joseph Glanvill (1636–1680) collected material for the Royal Society in the form of anecdotes and reminiscences so that they could form the basis of a new study of these phenomena.

17. In 1697, Christian Shaw, daughter of the laird of Bargarran near Paisley, accused seven people of being witches and tormenting her into prolonged fits. Five of the seven were tried, found guilty, and executed. One died in prison, the other committed suicide. It is still disputed whether Christian was a fraud or not.

18. Richard Dugdale from Whalley in Lancashire suddenly began to fall into a series of violent fits which were taken to be caused by witchcraft. Several ministers took them as genuine, but Lord Chief Justice Holt dismissed them as fraudulent, and soon afterwards they stopped.

INDEX

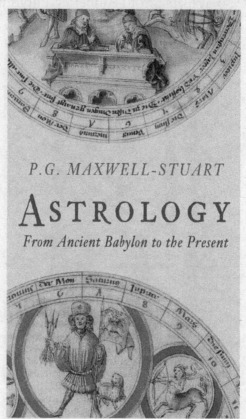

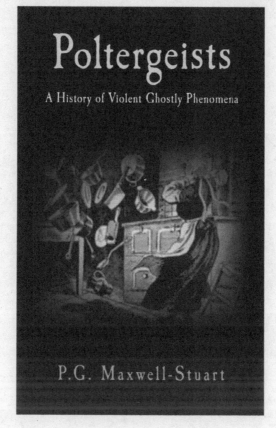